"Exhaustive yet vigorous." —*The New York Times*

"The ultimate hip-hop blueprint." —*The Source*

"Charnas' epic account of the music's rise from Bronx parks to Wall Street is gripping, stylish, impossible to put down." —*Flavorpill*

"A must-have for any rap fan." —*XXL*

"Charnas' 'American success story' unfolds vividly and briskly, and no hustle goes unturned." —*Rolling Stone* (4 stars)

"[Charnas] brings to life the story of the dollars behind the ballers in this absorbing account of hip-hop's transformation from South Bronx cottage industry to multibillion-dollar global business." —*Spin*

"The rap tome you have to read. . . . Dan Charnas' chronicle of the genre's rise to multibillion-dollar industry is essential. Wisely, *The Big Payback* focuses not on the beefs you know but on the back-room battles you don't." —*Details*

continued . . .

"*The Big Payback* stands out as a must read for any fan—or detractor—of the genre." —*Forbes*

"The riveting dialogue culled from more than three hundred interviews makes it seem as if Charnas was in the room for every detail that ever went down in hip-hop, and sometimes he was." —*The Austin Chronicle*

"Hands-down, *one of the best books ever written about hip-hop* . . . Absolutely *essential* . . . this isn't just the most important book on hip-hop that's come out in years; it's one of the most important books on pop music, period." —Oliver Wang, Soul-Sides.com

"Charnas has the shrewdness and experience as a journalist to pull it off extremely well. . . . [He] is a highly skilled chronicler of the forty years that have paved the way to hip-hop's present. . . . The staggering anecdotes knock your mind around, but the excellence of the storytelling will have you surrendering them out loud to your fellow fans." —KEXP.com

"Charnas captures an epic story full of joy and pain, triumph and failure, grace and greed with the skills of a journalist, the wisdom of an insider and the passion of a microphone fiend."
—Jeff Chang, author of *Can't Stop Won't Stop:
A History of the Hip-Hop Generation* and *Total Chaos:
The Art and Aesthetics of Hip-Hop*

"His cast of characters—producers, agents, label executives, talent scouts—is every bit as compelling and dramatic as the musicians themselves. . . . It's an unforgettable odyssey."
—Samuel G. Freedman, *New York Times* columnist and author of
Upon This Rock, Who She Was, and *Jew vs. Jew*

"[A] stunning achievement. Not only does it manage to pack in countless unprecedented anecdotes about hip-hop that you can't find anywhere else—the read is effortlessly smooth."
—Cheo H. Coker, coscreenwriter of *Notorious* and author of
Unbelievable: The Life, Death, and Afterlife of the Notorious B.I.G.

THE
BIG
PAYBACK

The History of the
Business of Hip-Hop

DAN CHARNAS

NEW AMERICAN LIBRARY

NEW AMERICAN LIBRARY
Published by New American Library, a division of
Penguin Group (USA) Inc., 375 Hudson Street,
New York, New York 10014, USA
Penguin Group (Canada), 90 Eglinton Avenue East, Suite 700, Toronto,
Ontario M4P 2Y3, Canada (a division of Pearson Penguin Canada Inc.)
Penguin Books Ltd., 80 Strand, London WC2R 0RL, England
Penguin Ireland, 25 St. Stephen's Green, Dublin 2,
Ireland (a division of Penguin Books Ltd.)
Penguin Group (Australia), 250 Camberwell Road, Camberwell, Victoria 3124,
Australia (a division of Pearson Australia Group Pty. Ltd.)
Penguin Books India Pvt. Ltd., 11 Community Centre, Panchsheel Park,
New Delhi - 110 017, India
Penguin Group (NZ), 67 Apollo Drive, Rosedale, Auckland 0632,
New Zealand (a division of Pearson New Zealand Ltd.)
Penguin Books (South Africa) (Pty.) Ltd., 24 Sturdee Avenue,
Rosebank, Johannesburg 2196, South Africa

Penguin Books Ltd., Registered Offices:
80 Strand, London WC2R 0RL, England

Published by New American Library, a division of Penguin Group (USA) Inc. Previously published in a New
American Library hardcover edition.

First New American Trade Paperback Library Printing, November 2011
10   9   8   7   6   5   4   3   2   1

New American Library Trade Paperback ISBN: 978-0-451-23478-0

THE LIBRARY OF CONGRESS HAS CATALOGED THE HARDCOVER EDITION OF THIS TITLE AS FOLLOWS:

Charnas, Dan.
The big payback: the history of the business of hip-hop/Dan Charnas.
p. cm.
Includes index.
ISBN 978-0-451-22929-8
1. Rap (Music)—Social aspects. 2. Hip-hop. 3. Hip-hop—Social aspects.
4. Sound recording industry. 5. Music trade. I. Title.
ML3918.R37C52   2010
304.4'84249—dc22   2010016062

Set in Aldus
Designed by Ginger Legato

Printed in the United States of America

For Wendy and Isaac

CONTENTS

NOTE FROM THE AUTHOR

This is a book about an American success story.

In 1977 hip-hop was a marginal urban subculture, largely confined to two of the most notorious ghettos in the United States, Harlem and the South Bronx. Over three decades later, hip-hop has become global culture itself, spanning music, language, film, television, books, fashion, sports, and politics. Hip-hop supplanted rock and roll as the signature creative expression for a new generation. It became a multibillion-dollar industry, transcending entertainment and moving into consumer products and services.

The Big Payback tells the tale of how hip-hop made this improbable leap. It is the story of executives and artists, entrepreneurs and hustlers who together surmounted incredible odds and opposition out of a belief that hip-hop would one day be as powerful as any American pop culture that preceded it.

Hip-hop changed our society. The commodification of hip-hop fostered a multiracial generation of young Americans brought up on a culture forged largely by Black youth, and transformed the racial dynamic in the United States. The hip-hop generation helped to elect our country's first Black president. Our society also changed hip-hop. Some would argue the culture lost much of its diversity and its virtue as it became mainstreamed. *The Big Payback* is about all of these changes as well.

The phenomenon of hip-hop can't be understood by examining the lives of the artists alone, because the culture could not have survived and thrived without the people who funded, promoted, and sold it. Therefore, *The Big Payback* is a book about the *business* of hip-hop, and about the relationship between artist and merchant—who, in hip-hop, are often one and the same.

If hip-hop has four elements (DJing, MCing, graffiti, and breaking), and perhaps a fifth (style), then I argue for the recognition of a sixth: marketing. The flyers promoting hip-hop's earliest parties were integral to the culture. One man in particular began his career passing out these things; look at Russell Simmons now.

The Big Payback follows the evolution of famous businesspeople like Simmons and dozens of unsung others who, wittingly or unwittingly, furthered the cause of hip-hop. Some did it for profit, some for fame, some for fun, some for the art's sake, and many for a combination of motives. Without these people, few would have heard of the artists they introduced to the world, legends like Tupac Shakur and Eminem, Jay-Z, and Run-DMC. These impresarios, promoters, programmers, and managers put their jobs, fortunes, and lives on the line for hip-hop. Now you will know their names, too.

Some notes about the creation of this book:

The Big Payback is a work of journalism, culled from personal interviews with over three hundred people, as well as court documents, correspondence, contracts, memoranda, memorabilia, newspaper and magazine articles, radio and television archives, photographs, films, Web pages, and the research and reporting of colleagues both published and unpublished.

The Big Payback focuses on the lives of a select group of characters chosen for a combination of criteria: their contributions, the compelling nature of their personal stories, and my access to them.

Whether the narrative describes events, silent thoughts and feelings of characters, or things those characters said aloud, that material is the result of reporting, not invention. For dialogue I use quotation marks to denote exact replication and italics to signify approximation. Often a particular story will be told from two or more viewpoints, a result of reporting from two or more sources. On rare occasions multiple sources have described one incident with irreconcilably different descriptions. Where that kind of conflict occurs in the narrative, I have either addressed this directly in the text, or chosen what I believe to be the most plausible story and then footnoted the conflicting description.

This book employs several linguistic conventions: I often use the words "hip-hop" and "rap" and "rap music" interchangeably—even though they are not technically the same—to denote only the musical and lyrical portion of hip-hop culture; in other words, the stuff you hear. I have used the term "Black" interchangeably with "African-American," though I know that those terms are not always synonymous. I have capitalized the words

"Black" and "White" where they refer to a group of people. When I use the term "racism," I really mean "systematic White supremacy." For characters who are more commonly known by their stage names or nicknames, I generally refer to them by those sobriquets *after* first establishing their given name and reaching the point in the narrative where they take their alias. For characters whose identities shift back and forth, I try to move with them; one notable exception being Sean Combs, who has adopted one too many professional aliases over the years. In my book he's "Combs." Lastly, hip-hop fans and followers know well that there are two figures named "Dr. Dre": Andre "Doctor Dre" Brown from the East Coast who hosted *Yo! MTV Raps* and DJed on Hot 97 in New York; and Andre "Dr. Dre" Young from the West Coast, member of NWA, founder of record labels Death Row and Aftermath, and producer of Eminem. Luckily for me, they never meet in this book.

Finally *The Big Payback* is a book about the hip-hop industry written by someone who was once a part of that industry. The few things I accomplished during my time in the business don't merit my own entry into the book; thus, this is not a memoir. Nonetheless I personally witnessed several of the events and scenes depicted herein; in some of them, I played an active role, which I have detailed in the footnotes. As noted in the acknowledgments, I worked for several of the prominent characters in this book. Others have been my friends or colleagues. A few were competitors or adversaries. Many I met only in passing and some not until I interviewed them for this book. In journalism this kind of intimacy with the subject and sources can be both beneficial and problematic. I have endeavored to be fair to all the characters in this book without regard for my relationship to them.

My motto for the writing of this book was "everyone gets to be human." That credo is unusual, because even some of the journalists, writers, and lyricists I respect vilify businesspeople without question, research, or reporting as rapacious exploiters of innocent, unsuspecting artists and their audiences. I abhor that cliché. In my years as a record executive, I saw plenty of exploitation. But I also saw plenty of businesspeople who were honest and sincere, moved by a love of hip-hop culture; and artists, producers, and DJs who cared nothing for culture and permitted themselves to live without ethics. My goal for this book was to toss the platitudes and show how hip-hop was cocreated by the artists and by the people who pushed them out into the world.

My approach may not appeal to hip-hop fans who believe that the culture existed in some pristine state before it was sold, nor to those who believe that corporate executives assembled in a room and decided to promote violent, misogynist hip-hop for profit and the degradation of Black people. My experience and research uncover a more nuanced reality. I invite hip-hop's devotees to witness the true story of hip-hop's commercial evolution in the pages that follow.

Despite the dramatic ascent of the culture, some critics and fans alike argue that hip-hop is *not* a success story; that its failure to sustain itself as political, "positive," and uplifting art makes it superfluous and anachronistic; that its continued fascination with all things crude and violent make it dangerous; that its commercial prosperity is yet another cultural sellout or co-optation.

I think those conclusions are unfair. Materialism, vulgarity, and violence are not hip-hop's ills. They are America's ills. Hip-hop is a child of America.

Hip-hop resulted from unfettered young urban Black expression finding its own way to the masses after being denied access to mainstream and Black marketplaces. Thus, the cultural squeeze that created gangster rap also caused a precipitous rise in Black entrepreneurship. The ostracism of Black youth from traditional modes of commerce and communication created a self-sufficient and self-confident generation. That's why hip-hop has done as much for the economic, political, and social advancement of Black America as any cultural movement in history. Who desegregated radio stations and video channels across the country? Hip-hop blasted through that wall. Who climbed into the upper echelons of Hollywood? The rappers did. Who truly made good on the Black Nationalist dream of economic independence? The hip-hop entrepreneurs of the late 1990s led a 45 percent growth in Black-owned businesses. Who fulfilled the civil rights–era vision of the "table of brotherhood"? The hip-hop generation, which intermarries four times as much as their parents did. In so doing, hip-hop set all of America free.

Hip-hop is nothing less than a triumph. Even in its blatantly commercial forms, the culture has given a tremendous gift to this country and the world. *The Big Payback* is thus a work of passion for hip-hop in all its messy glory.

With that, here's a little story that must be told.

—Dan Charnas, New York City, 2010

ALBUM ONE

NUMBER RUNNERS

Hip-hop's earliest entrepreneurs

(1968—1981)

Uptown

The man who invented American money lived and died in Harlem.
He arrived from the Caribbean at the age of seventeen, an orphan
subsisting on a modest scholarship. But when he retired in 1800 after
founding the first national bank, launching the U.S. Mint, and serving as the
first secretary of the treasury, Alexander Hamilton purchased an estate in
upper Manhattan. Hamilton Grange sat on the high cliffs overlooking the
former Dutch village of Nieuw Haarlem, a pastoral getaway for wealthy residents of the growing city of New York, then still confined to the lower part of
the narrow island. On that same rocky ridge, almost twenty-five years earlier,
Hamilton fought the British at the Battle of Harlem Heights. Later he became
General George Washington's chief of staff.

After the Revolutionary War, Hamilton fought a different kind of battle,
one that would decide what kind of nation America would become. The battle
pitted Hamilton against another founding father, Thomas Jefferson. Hamilton wanted to keep New York as the national capital. Jefferson, who detested
cities, wanted to move it to the banks of the Potomac across from his native
Virginia. Hamilton saw the future of America in business and manufacturing. Jefferson advocated agriculture. Hamilton was an immigrant. Jefferson
was born into a wealthy plantation family. Hamilton was an abolitionist.
Jefferson owned slaves.

This debate—between city and country, between North and South, between abolitionist and slaveholder, between liberal and conservative—would
dominate America's history long after Hamilton died, shot down in a gun
duel with a political enemy. It would ultimately lead to the Civil War. By

then, the land Hamilton owned was split into parcels for the growing city, and renamed Hamilton Heights. After Abraham Lincoln signed the Emancipation Proclamation, after the surrender of the Confederacy, the argument continued. *What is to become of the sons and daughters of African slaves? Will they become fully American, enfranchised with the rights America's founders accorded to themselves? Or will Negroes in America be remanded to a kind of limbo, neither chattel nor citizen?*

For many years the answer was clearly the latter. By 1920, Hamilton Heights looked down on the biggest Black ghetto in the country. Harlem had become the catchall neighborhood for New York's Black population, and for the Negro migrants who streamed in from the South and the Caribbean, fleeing poverty and oppression, in search of work. For those escaping Jim Crow's clutches, New York may well have been paradise. But it was a bleak existence. Black women found work as domestics in middle-class White homes. If factory jobs weren't available, Black men took custodial work, if they found employ at all.

Still Harlem buzzed with new life. Southern migrants brought their music with them—blues and its refined, citified cousin, jazz. Nightspots opened along Harlem's main drag, 125th Street, attracting White revelers from downtown. In those audiences were the founders of the modern entertainment industry—White radio broadcasters, film producers, sheet music distributors, and phonograph record manufacturers. Soon, boisterous Black jazz was being beamed, performed, and published across the United States, becoming the favorite music of young White people across America. Even though segregation put Black performers at a significant disadvantage, and swindlers often robbed Black composers of their rights, entertainment proved to be one of the few ways that Black folks could make a buck in America.

Harlem also gave rise to an aspirational class who held forth the Hamiltonian dream of an equal society where one's position was decided on merit, not on lineage or the color of one's skin; where ingenuity and hard work trumped race. Some of these Harlemites were Black entrepreneurs and professionals: doctors, lawyers, shopkeepers. Others were authors, artists, musicians, poets, philosophers, professors, politicians, and activists. Harlem bore the first institutions of the civil rights movement, the NAACP and the National Urban League, and the first organization to champion Black power, Marcus Garvey's Universal Negro Improvement Association. By the 1920s, Harlem had become the virtual capital of Black America, and the artistic, social, and political ambitions of Harlemites comprised a movement known as the Harlem Renaissance.

The wealthiest among these strivers lived in Harlem's most expensive homes, up on the ridge overlooking the flatlands, on acreage once owned by Alexander Hamilton, who in his time personified American ambition. It was a place where even Black folks could live "the sweet life" that inspired its nickname.

The locals called it Sugar Hill.

Ira Jack Allen had come to Harlem all the way from Tuscaloosa, Alabama, to live with his uncle, Levert Burrell, who worked as a bouncer at the Savoy Ballroom, one of Harlem's integrated nightclubs. Jack Allen was still a teenager when he arrived in the late 1940s, but he already had streaks of gray running through his curly black hair. Allen sacrificed vials of blood to doctors who tried to help him figure out why his hair was constantly changing color—from black to gray and back again. In the end, they couldn't tell him much. Maybe it was hereditary, they said. Maybe it was stress.

Allen turned his gray hair to his advantage, for even at sixteen years old, he could get into any nightclub. Broad shouldered and standing well over six feet tall, he soon found work as a road manager for blues artists like Big Joe Turner. Allen could get even notoriously unscrupulous show promoters to pay up at the end of the night, doing more with his soft, deep voice and imposing presence than most men could do with their fists. In 1951, while performing at Harlem's Apollo Theater, Joe Turner was approached by two young Turkish-American entrepreneurs who wanted him to record for their new recording company, Atlantic. Soon both Turner and Allen were in the record business.

By then, music was changing. After World War II, the blues literally sped up, assuming a more danceable form that younger fans loved. They called it by many names: "jump blues," "rhythm blues," "rhythm and blues," or simply "R&B." A local variant of R&B was especially popular in New York—called "doo-wop," a name that mimicked the scatty harmonies of the Black vocal groups who performed it. Allen managed a popular doo-wop group called the Moonglows, and became a partner in a small record label called Spectrum, often conducting business out of a phone booth downtown on Broadway outside the Brill Building, the epicenter of the 1950s record industry. The talent may have been uptown, but the business was downtown.

As the music changed, Harlem changed. In the 1950s, the influx of Black Southerners became a deluge. The refugees from Dixie were joined by Spanish-speaking immigrants from Puerto Rico. These newcomers arrived at precisely the moment that manufacturing jobs began leaving New York City. The poorest of them crowded into tenements and apartments, overwhelmed the city's social services and schools. Crime rose. White-collar Black Harlemites—doctors, lawyers, and artists who lived on Sugar Hill— began leaving for safer, newer suburban homes in Queens, Long Island, Westchester, and New Jersey. The sweet life vanished from uptown. Shops closed. Hundreds of blocks of older buildings were razed to erect housing projects that compounded the problems they were built to solve. Soon Harlem and huge swaths of other New York neighborhoods in the South Bronx and Brooklyn became vast slums. Harlem's buildings fell into disrepair as banks refused to finance businesses and real estate. Despite new successes in the long African-American battle for equality—namely the rise of the civil rights movement—Harlem, Black America's capital, was becoming a desolate place.

Born of aspiration, the only enterprise that Harlem had left was "the hustle": like the illicit rackets selling women or drugs. The most common hustle, however, was the numbers.

Before the first legal state lottery was established—New Hampshire in 1964—the numbers game was the main gambling enterprise in the country, a favorite in poor, ethnic neighborhoods like Harlem. The game was simple. Every day, players could pick a three-digit number. If that number was selected in a drawing, or determined by the last three digits of the local racetrack's daily pari-mutuel handle, the player won, usually 500 to 600 times the money he or she had waged. The odds of winning the numbers game were 1 in 1000, but anecdotes of victory and the occasional lucky draw by a neighbor or friend kept people playing religiously. For many poor people, those long odds seemed equal to the possibility of attaining a lucrative profession in a segregated America anyhow. In Harlem, "hitting the number" was a very common life goal, a palpable hope. If you won, you could buy a house. You could send your kid to school. You could pay off your debts.

The numbers game was run by "policy banks," cellular, neighborhood-based organizations where the bosses tallied bets and ran drawings. Of course, all of these so-called banks were illegal, so they needed insulation from the law in order to operate, usually in the form of payment to local police called a "pad." The numbers racket in Harlem was run for a time by a Black woman,

Madame Stephanie St. Clair. But the business proved too lucrative to leave in Black hands, and White gangsters like Dutch Schultz forced their way in during the 1930s. Despite their illegality, Harlem's policy bankers in many cases provided the only capital to build a building or start a business. By the 1950s, the numbers represented more than half of the Harlem economy.

The numbers offered Harlemites something even more tangible: an entry-level job from which one could earn a decent wage. Almost anyone could be a "runner." The runner's job was to collect bets and distribute winnings within a certain area, usually a few city blocks, making a commission on all the bets collected. It was a dangerous business. You had to keep a lot of numbers in your head: dates, handles, bet amounts, payoffs. As with all hustles, if you got in trouble—came up short with the money, ran afoul of your bosses, your customers, or the law—you had to talk fast and talk slick, or else speak with your fists.

That's what happened one day in the late 1950s on top of Sugar Hill. Jack Allen was playing handball against the side of a sports bar on Amsterdam Avenue. Out of the corner of his eye, he spotted one of the local number runners—a tall, thin guy with a pockmarked face—surrounded by a group of angry men. One of them was saying that his number had "hit," and the young runner, for whatever reason, didn't have the money to pay him. Allen immediately sensed that the runner was in serious trouble. In his fashion, the levelheaded, soft-spoken, gray-haired young man walked over to cool things down. The entertainment hustle wasn't so different from the numbers hustle. Jack talked fast, Jack talked slick. And the young number runner, Joe Robinson, was able to walk away intact.

Allen knew that Robinson wouldn't last much longer in the numbers game. If he wanted to survive, Robinson would have to find a safer, better hustle. The guy couldn't rap to save his own life.

A decade later, thirteen-year-old Anthony Holloway seemed headed toward the same line of work.

It was a summer evening in 1968, and Anthony was rolling as usual with Charles, the number runner, watching the brownstones of Sugar Hill flow past him from the passenger seat of Charles's car. Anthony was in the streets now. He wasn't going back home, that was for sure, now that he was on the outs with his mother.

Dorothy Holloway had come home from work one day to find her son and a bunch of his friends in her living room, skipping school, playing cards, and listening to her records. Anthony was a good kid, pudgy and smiley, who could sing and dance like nobody's business. It was only recently that he had started acting up. So she didn't ground him. She didn't beat him. Instead Dorothy did something to scare the hell out of Anthony. She had the police arrest him for truancy. The court sent Anthony for a time to Spofford, a juvenile detention center in the South Bronx, and then a youth camp.

Now that he was out, Anthony drifted. And who better to glide with than Charles, the number runner, who rolled a purple Ford Thunderbird made of pure steel. Charles got a lot of attention from pretty girls with that car, and Anthony loved riding around with him as Charles made his stops, pockets filled with cash, collecting bets and paying on wins.

One of Charles's regular collection spots was Lou's Place on Sugar Hill. Lou's was a small bar, but they had a lively clientele. In the corner, an old-timer named W.T. spun records on a BSR McDonald turntable, speaking to the crowd over a microphone as he changed the records to keep the party going. Every time he came to Lou's, Anthony couldn't take his eyes off of the spinning records and the microphone.

Anthony learned the power of the disc jockey at his mother's house parties. While he was still in grade school, she would put him in charge of the stack of 45 rpm singles that comprised her record collection. If he ruined the "vibe" with a bad record, his mother scowled.

"Why would you play *that*?" Dorothy Holloway barked. "Put on the *hits*!"

Anthony learned which records made people dance and which didn't. In junior high, Anthony was captivated by the between-song spiel of New York's most popular Black DJ, Frankie Crocker, on the AM soul station, Harlem's WWRL. Frankie talked fast, Frankie talked slick.

"I'll put a dip in your hip, more cut in your strut, and more glide in your stride," he said. "If you don't dig it, you know you've got a hole in your soul. / Don't eat chicken on Sundays. / Other cats be laughin' and jokin'. / Frankie Crocker steady taking care of business, / Cookin' and smokin'. / For there is no other like this soul brother."

I could do that, Anthony thought. So Anthony practiced his own rhymes over the intros of records, trying to time them so that they ended right when the vocal came in, just like Frankie Crocker did on the radio.

W.T. must have noticed the hunger in Anthony's eyes, because tonight the DJ approached the thirteen-year-old with a proposition.

"Listen," W.T said. "I gotta go and do something. I will be *right back*. All I need you to do is, when a record goes off, put another record on."

W.T. left. As Charles, the number runner, held court with his customers and admirers, Anthony stepped behind the turntable and did what W.T. told him to do. He spun "Tighten Up" by Archie Bell and the Drells into "Cool Jerk" by the Capitols, dancing as the music played. But Anthony couldn't resist the microphone. So he said some rhymes in between the songs, just like Frankie Crocker did, to keep the party going while he changed the record.

"Hey, y'all!" Anthony began. "If I was snow I would be cold. /If I was a jug of wine I would be old. /But since none of this is true / And I'm right here with you, / Passing the time / With the baddest jams I could find, / Without further time wasted / Or another drink tasted, / Let's go!"

It went on like this for a while—Anthony dropping in at Lou's and covering for W.T. whenever the older DJ had to step away. It was a great deal for W.T., this kid who loved to DJ and didn't cost him any money. Soon, W.T. asked Anthony to come with him to his after-hours gig at Lovey's on 148th Street and 7th Avenue. By 1971, Anthony was working the club all by himself, playing records for a roomful of hustlers.

This was the year that Anthony Holloway finally hit his number. It was a two-digit number—to be exact: 15, the amount, in dollars, that Anthony made for a night's work at Lovey's. One Hamilton and one Lincoln.

It wasn't a lot of money, but there was sniff and smoke and women, and the gig kept him busy enough that he had to stop rolling with Charles, the number runner.

Holloway—who now called himself DJ Hollywood—had found a hustle of his own.

It may have been mere coincidence, but "Hollywood" was also one of the many nicknames that Frankie Crocker took for himself. Crocker had others: "Fast Frankie," "the Chief Rocker," and so on. Years later, after the two men had become the most popular DJs in New York—Crocker on the radio and Holloway in the nightclubs and discotheques—the shared sobriquet became a point of contention. But it would take quite some time before Holloway would make it onto Crocker's radar. Crocker, after all, was a superstar well before Holloway made his first $15 as a DJ.

In the early 1960s, Frankie Crocker came from his hometown of Buffalo, New York, to work at Harlem's WWRL, the premier radio station serving

New York's Black community. Crocker was one of a roster of Black DJs, like Hank Spann and Gary Byrd, serving up R&B with a side of hip patter. The on-air shtick of WWRL's personality jocks was as important as the music they played. WWRL's Jocko Henderson was legendary for his slick talk: "Eee tiddly ock, / This is the Jock / And I'm back on the scene with the record machine. /Correct time now, 10:17."

If Henderson was going to tell you the time, he'd work it into the rhyme.

Black DJs talking fast and talking slick was nothing unusual. One heard that kind of talk on every street corner, playground, and in every church in Harlem. The ability to "talk shit" had always been prime currency in Black communities. It was especially vital for hustlers, whether they were preachers trying to hustle their flock to Jesus, or young men trying to hustle up a Friday-night date with a pretty girl. The better your rap, the better your rep.

For African-Americans, the slang word "rap" was the measure of the way a person talked. To talk was merely to converse. To rap was to get a particular point across with style, perhaps make someone smile or laugh, or get a rise out of them. It was no wonder, then, that the men who spoke to the Black masses through the radio perfected this skill. One of them, "Jockey Jack" Gibson, who got his start in 1948 on the first Black-owned station in the country, Atlanta's WERD, called himself "Jack the Rapper."

Dozens of these new Black-oriented radio stations began popping up across the United States after World War II. Disc jockeys like Henderson and Gibson said their crazy rhymes and played rhythm and blues records. Suddenly, slang and music by and intended for Black folks was now accessible to anyone with a radio. Many White kids who had never met a person of color in their lives found their way to these stations with a simple twist of the dial. The music was furious, funny, and often filthy, with rampant references to sex, about "rocking" and "rolling" all night long.

Soon Black radio stations amassed a huge underground White following.

In 1951, a Jewish disc jockey who played classical music on WJW in Cleveland discovered that White kids were buying Black rhythm-and-blues records by the hundreds at a local record store. The jock, Alan Freed, asked his station manager for permission to play the records on his show.

This was tricky. Rhythm and blues was well-known as Negro music, and one couldn't just start playing Negro songs on a respectable station. The solution required a bit of subterfuge. So Freed changed his handle to "Moondog," and changed the name of the music from "rhythm and blues" to a phrase unknown to Whites, "rock and roll"—which, when one considered the meaning of the term, was even more suggestive.

Freed's "Moondog Rock and Roll House Party" became a sensation for both White and Black teenagers across the Midwest. By the time Freed was hired by the biggest pop station in the country, New York's WINS, Freed had riled parents and civic authorities by throwing regular, sold-out integrated concerts featuring Black rhythm-and-blues acts that were attended equally by Black and White youth. Soon, Freed was joined by other White "rock and roll" jocks playing rhythm-and-blues records and talking fast and slick like Black DJs—including Wolfman Jack, whose show on huge 250,000-watt XERF-AM just across the Mexican border with Texas could be heard from coast to coast in the United States.

This was how radio DJs, Black and White, sparked the cultural desegregation of young America. The rhythm-and-blues/rock-and-roll revolution formed the soundtrack to the civil rights era, and many of the White children who grew up loving Black music in the 1950s became supporters of the Black liberation movement in the 1960s.

Ironically, while America desegregated, the music business itself remained one of the most segregated industries in the country. The big record companies of the 1950s—RCA, Columbia, Capitol—traditionally relegated "race music" to smaller imprints, if they dealt with Black music and Black artists at all. These companies simply ignored the new Black youth music, raunchy rhythm and blues, and barely flirted with R&B's White doppelgänger, rock and roll. Thus, the windfall of R&B and rock and roll largely fell to smaller, independent labels like Chess, Kent, and Atlantic. Many of these labels were owned by entrepreneurs whose ethnicity put them outside the American capitalist mainstream—Jewish Americans in particular and some Black Americans as well. Black-owned Vee-Jay Records was the first American label to take a chance on a British R&B group called the Beatles.

Race and class blinded corporate America to the opportunities with the new music, so Black entrepreneurs like Berry Gordy enjoyed a virtual monopoly on local music scenes like Detroit's. Gordy's Motown Records not only became an industry powerhouse to rival the corporate record labels; Motown was, until it was sold in the 1980s, the largest Black-owned business in America.

The segregation of radio eased in the 1960s, mainly because radio stations played the records that sold and were requested the most. As the popularity of Black music increased among White kids, "Top 40" played more of it. The opening of radio created opportunity for a few Black DJs, too. In 1969, Frankie Crocker was hired away from WWRL to become one of "the Good Guys," the lily-white roster of Top 40 DJs at New York's WMCA.

The success of the Black music business eventually attracted the corporate attention that nearly killed it. Clive Davis—the new, young chief of Columbia Records who signed Sly and the Family Stone to Columbia—saw untapped potential in Black music and needed some ammunition to make his point. Davis commissioned an analysis of the Black music market from the Harvard Business School. "A Study of the Soul Music Environment Prepared for Columbia Records Group" was delivered to Davis on May 11, 1972. The Harvard Report, as it came to be called, advocated that Columbia buy its way into the Black music market.

Columbia soon purchased two independent labels, Stax and Philadelphia International. Other majors followed suit, Warner Bros. purchasing Atlantic. By the mid-1970s most of the Black independents had been either bought up or edged out, their artists and executive talent lured away to the growing "Black departments" at the six big record companies—CBS, Warner, RCA, MCA, EMI, and Polygram. These companies were called "majors" because they owned their own national distribution networks.

Meanwhile the brief years of integrated pop radio were drawing to a close. AM radio was losing listeners to high-fidelity FM stations that played only certain kinds of music—"rock" or "soul" or "country," for example. "Narrowcasting" was an attempt to deliver specific audiences to advertisers. Because many advertisers and programmers assumed that White listeners preferred music by White artists, many FM stations began dumping Black artists.

By the mid-1970s, the lucrative business of Black music was largely out of Black hands. Motown remained the only viable Black-owned label. Most of the new Black-oriented FMs were not Black-owned. But in 1971, a Harlem lawyer and politician named Percy Sutton led a group of Black investors, including David Dinkins, to buy two New York stations, WLIB-AM and FM. Sutton changed the FM station's call letters to WBLS, and hired Frankie Crocker as his star air personality and first program director.

The call letters "BLS" were said to stand for "Black Liberation Station." Indeed, WBLS gave Frankie Crocker freedom during a time of corporate captivity for Black music and Black artists. In turn, Crocker's WBLS freed the minds of a generation of New Yorkers. Under Crocker, WBLS redefined and expanded the concept of the "Black" radio station. To the traditional soul and R&B fare of James Brown, Aretha Franklin, and Stevie Wonder, Crocker added an eclectic mix of rock, jazz, and pop standards—everything from the Rolling Stones to Frank Sinatra. Crocker's tastes were broad and cosmopolitan, and he expected no less from his listeners. He gave New Yorkers their first taste of a Jamaican rock-and-roller named Bob Marley. Crocker was among the first on radio to play the beat-heavy, dance-oriented soul that was becoming so popular in the new DJ-driven nightclubs called "discotheques," records like Manu Dibango's "Soul Makossa" and MFSB's "Love Is the Message." Crocker presented a show that was sophisticated and grown-up. If WWRL was Harlem, WBLS was Sugar Hill—a cut above, a station that gave its listeners a taste of upward mobility. WBLS was more than just a so-called Black station, just as so-called Black music included more than music played by Black artists.

In a time when Black music was being pushed from the airwaves across the country, and record and radio executives subscribed increasingly to the notion that there were records that were simply "too Black" for White listeners, Frankie Crocker turned WBLS into the number one–rated music station among all listeners in the largest city in the country.

More profoundly, Crocker created a generation of young music aficionados in New York, kids from the inner city and from the suburbs, to whom he gave the gift of an open mind and the notion that a DJ could change the world.

The nightclubs where bands played live music were vanishing from Harlem, replaced by spots like Lou's and Lovey's, where disc jockeys spun records over a loud sound system for a crowd that came to dance. All over the city, "discos" were on the rise. In this new world order, the DJs were the stars—like Pete DJ Jones, who spun for Black folks uptown and mixed crowds downtown. This new breed of disco DJ developed techniques and technology to keep the party going nonstop.

In 1972, DJ Hollywood heard his first "mix." He was still spinning records for short money at Lovey's when he decided to pay a visit to a new disco on 125th Street called Charles Gallery, where the men wore suits and ties and the women pretty dresses. He couldn't see behind the smoked glass of the DJ booth, but Hollywood got chills as he heard a Booker T. & the MG's song,

"Melting Pot," blended seamlessly into "Power" by Earth, Wind & Fire. The music never stopped. The disc jockey—a Puerto Rican kid named Angelo—didn't even talk between songs. Hollywood had been thinking of himself as a DJ at the top of his game, but now he realized he had a lot more to learn.

Hollywood befriended Bo Huggins, another DJ and the brother of the Gallery's owner, Charles Huggins. The next Sunday, Bo invited Hollywood back to the booth for a closer look. Hollywood almost fainted when he saw the secret weapon that the Charles Gallery DJs used to blend beats. They had two record players and, between them, a small box with separate volume knobs for each turntable. Bo called it a "mixer." Best of all, it had a headphone jack that allowed him to listen to one record while the other one was playing.

Charles Gallery literally became DJ Hollywood's Sunday school. How did Bo get two different records to "lock" together, their drumbeats falling at exactly the same time? First, Bo selected two records of roughly the same tempo. He then matched their speeds by moving a "pitch adjustment" lever on one of the turntables. While the first record played, he muted the second turntable so the crowd couldn't hear it. Listening to the second record in his headphones, he found the spot where its beat started by rubbing it back and forth with his fingers to position the needle. Bo held the second record steady with his thumb until the precise moment where it would match the beat of the first, and then released it into the rotation of the spinning platter below. Slowly, Bo would bring the volume of the second turntable up and—voilà—the beats were matched.

DJ Hollywood practiced these techniques with devotion, coming back to Charles Gallery week after week until, inevitably, Bo turned to Hollywood one evening and said, "I'll be *right back*. Take over for me." Soon, Hollywood was DJing his own set of nonstop music at Charles Gallery, the big time in Harlem. But with his new nonstop mixing techniques, there wasn't any silence in between songs. This was a problem. For Hollywood, talking to the crowd was the best part of being a DJ. So Hollywood began using any part of the record that didn't have singing on it to talk over—sometimes the intro, and sometimes the breakdown, which was the part of the song where the musicians literally "broke it down" to just drums, or drums and bass. Hollywood not only matched the beat of one record to another; he started matching his rhymes to the beat, as well:

"Can you feel the groove? Everybody, let's make a move. . . ."

Hollywood always had routines where he would involve the crowd. He called them "conversations":

"Party time is anytime / And anytime is party time. / Say what?"

And the crowd would answer: "Say we-oooo, baby!"

Not everyone in Charles Gallery understood. "Bo! What's up with your man yapping?" one hustler shouted. "Tell him to stop talkin' and let the music play!"

Hollywood was offered another regular gig, at a new disco farther east on 125th Street called A Bunch of Grapes. The place was perfect. It had new Technics SL-1200 "vari-speed" turntables. The DJ booth was encased in glass, sitting in the middle of the dance floor, so everyone could see him. At Charles Gallery, Hollywood had been a junior DJ. But at A Bunch of Grapes, he was the star attraction. Hollywood developed set lists of music and a repertoire of call-and-response rhymes that regular clubgoers recognized and repeated with glee. After his shows, he sold eight-track tapes of his mixes for $15 a pop.

As word spread about the rhyming DJ, Hollywood was lured up to the Bronx to play at a new disco called Club 371. The owners, who called themselves the "Ten Good Guys," were a bit stiff. One of them, Bob Knight, was the regular DJ. Much to Hollywood's frustration, Knight wouldn't let his guest DJ even touch his turntables.

"You can talk on the microphone," Knight said.

So Hollywood asked Knight to play MFSB's "Love Is the Message"—Frankie Crocker's favorite disco anthem—because it had a long instrumental breakdown. Hollywood talked fast, talked slick, and by the time the song ended, the audience was yelling and screaming for more.

Hollywood left in frustration, vowing never to return. Knight didn't even know how to mix. Hollywood couldn't do his act the way he wanted to under those conditions. But Knight did him a favor that night. For the first time, DJ Hollywood was liberated from the turntables. He had danced and performed his rhymed routines with only a microphone in his hand.

Eventually, DJ Hollywood did return to Club 371, and Bob Knight let Hollywood touch anything he wanted. At the end of the night, Hollywood collected $50 from the Ten Good Guys. As his following grew, his act expanded. Hollywood got some girls to dance onstage with him, and he found a young apprentice DJ who called himself Junebug. Now Hollywood was free to spin records, or roam the stage at will. The crowds grew. Between his various disco gigs, he was pulling down $500 a week.

In 1973, that wasn't a bad living.

———

If you wanted to see DJ Hollywood play in a nightclub or disco, you needed a few things. You needed to be eighteen years old or look it. You needed money to get inside. You needed clothes: nice shoes, good slacks, a dress shirt. Discos, in short, were for grown-ups. If you were older and had money, you could go out and party. If you were young and didn't have money, you made your own party.

That's what Cindy Campbell did in August of 1973. Cindy lived in the West Bronx with her Jamaican-born parents and older brother, Clive, in a tall apartment building on 1520 Sedgwick Avenue, at the foot of the Alexander Hamilton Bridge, just across the Harlem River from upper Manhattan. With fall approaching, Cindy Campbell needed money for school clothes. Her father had a huge sound system, and Clive—whom everyone called Hercules or "Herc" on account of his size—was a good DJ. Cindy suggested they rent the rec room in the basement, throw a party, and charge their friends admission. If they got enough people, she would have the money to buy her gear on Delancey Street in Manhattan, rather than on the even more downscale Fordham Road in the Bronx. Cindy and Herc created handwritten flyers on ruled index cards: A DJ KOOL HERC PARTY, BACK TO SCHOOL JAM, they read; $.25 LADIES, $.50 FELLAS.

On August 11, 1973, Herc assembled his father's system in the basement. As dozens of kids descended to the rec room, Herc began to spin the songs he knew would drive them crazy. They didn't want to hear the smooth songs that Frankie Crocker played on WBLS and Hollywood played in the discos, records like "Love Is the Message." They liked *funk*, music that sounded raw and angry like James Brown. They preferred songs with long breakdown sections, or "breaks," like "Get Ready" by Rare Earth, which had a drum break that lasted two full minutes. The "get-down part," as Herc called it, was the moment that the kids let loose with their best dances, spinning footwork that often recalled Brown's manic performances and the Bronx's own crazy history of mambo and swing.

Cindy turned a profit that night, and she and Herc started throwing monthly parties in the rec room. When those got too crowded, Herc hauled his sound system to nearby Cedar Park. His reputation grew for several reasons. First, he had the loudest system that most people had ever heard. Second, his parties were generally safe; no one wanted to piss off Hercules. And third, he focused on the records with good breaks: "It's Just Begun," by Jimmy Castor; "Apache" and "Bongo Rock" by the Incredible Bongo Band.

In fact, Herc had taken to playing *only* the break sections of his records—just the parts where the song stripped down to a bare beat. But it was frustrating, because the breakdowns were usually only seconds long. It meant that Herc had to go through a lot of records in quick succession, or else pick up the needle and drop it back to the start of the break, which he could often discern by looking at the texture of the grooves in the vinyl. But that meant that the music had to stop, which was jarring for the "b-boys," Herc's nickname for the kids who came to dance to the breaks.

What if, Herc thought, *I could extend the break without stopping the beat?* The solution came to him. He needed two copies of the same record. Placing one copy on each turntable, as soon as the break section ended on the first, he'd start the second. Back and forth he'd go, turning a fifteen- or thirty-second breakdown into a three-, five-, or ten-minute beat-down, before moving onto the next break, and the next.

Herc called it the "merry-go-round." It was a small innovation, but in that moment of inspiration, something huge happened: The DJ transformed from a person who merely presented music into a person who altered it.

In short, the DJ became a musician himself.

Herc, too, had grown up with the slick talk on the street corners and the radio, as well as the reggae chatting of sound system DJs back in his native Jamaica. So it was only natural—as it was for DJ Hollywood—for Herc to call out to the crowd over a microphone as he played. Soon, Herc's chatter became more elaborate: "You never heard it like this before, / And you're back for more and more and more."

Herc's "merry-go-round" required constant attention, and so—as it was with DJ Hollywood—the labor got divided. Herc's friend, who called himself Coke La Rock, had become the master of ceremonies: "There's no story that can't be told. / There's no horse that can't be rode, /No bull that can't be stopped, / And ain't a disco that we can't rock."

Herc and Coke assembled a small band of MCs, the Herculords, who found their way into some small venues like the Webster Avenue Police Athletic League and nightclubs like Hevalo. Herc could make $150 for a night's work, and Coke would make ten times that amount by hustling weed on the side.

Herc's true audience was the kids who couldn't get into the discos, children still in middle school and high school. From all over the Bronx, they were coming to see this new mix of DJing, MCing, and b-boying or breakdancing. Kool Herc made people want to be b-boys themselves, made them want to MC and DJ.

Joseph Saddler was another teenager from the Caribbean, raised in the Bronx, who shared Herc's obsession with music and electronics. But unlike the muscled Herc, the dimunitive Saddler was a perfectionist. Saddler spent hours watching Herc in Cedar Park run his "merry-go-round," and saw that Herc was visually locating the starting point of the breaks, dropping the needle and hoping for the best. When he switched back and forth between the turntables, Herc never really stayed on beat.

Saddler went home and worked at getting it right. Living in the South Bronx, he didn't know about the downtown DJ innovations that Hollywood had discovered, like "beat matching" (aligning the tempos of records) and "slip-cueing" (using headphones to audition and cue a record before releasing it into play). Saddler had to invent them himself. He came up with his own names for the techniques: the "peek-a-boo system," and "clock theory." In the laboratory of his bedroom, Saddler took the science of DJing further than anyone had. Before long, he could "cut" between duplicate copies of a record seamlessly, without dropping a beat. Since most breaks were agonizingly brief, the quicker he cut, the shorter breaks he could use. Saddler got really fast. His friends called him "Flash," like the comic-book hero who possessed superhuman speed.

Flash came up with more homegrown innovations that Harlem DJs like Hollywood or the downtown disco jocks had never imagined. The "punch phase"—throwing in a momentary guitar lick or vocal from one record while another one played. The "rub"—invented as he accidentally opened the volume on a turntable too early, revealing his method of moving a record back and forth to find its precise release spot just before he let it slip. Practicing in his partner Gene Livingston's apartment, Flash's skills caught the fancy of Gene's kid brother, Theodore, who added a new technique to Flash's repertoire when he took Flash's "rub" and kept rubbing. In so doing, he invented the "scratch."

DJ Flash used all these techniques for percussive effect, treating turntables like drums. Flash put his hands all over his records, marking them with grease pencils and smearing them with fingerprints. By the time he began playing the playground at Intermediate School 63 on Boston Road in the South Bronx, Flash made Kool Herc look sloppy.

To keep the party going at "63 Park," Flash assembled his own crew, just like Herc did. Flash's MCs were as innovative with their rhyme routines as Flash was on the turntables: Keith "Cowboy" Wiggins and the Glover brothers, Mel and Nathaniel, who called themselves "Melle Mel" and "Kid Creole," respectively. The three MCs took turns rhyming, and divided the lines into short bursts, trading them back and forth as fast as Flash could cut.

"Eeenie meenie," Cowboy would say.

"Miny," Creole would continue.

"Moe," Mel would finish.

Their routines and rhymes became more elaborate. "One, two, this is for you, you and you. / Three, four, cuts galore is what we have in store."

One winter day, as Flash and his "3 MCs" were rocking in 63 Park, Flash was approached by an older guy from the neighborhood, an ex-cop named Ray Chandler. Chandler asked Flash why he and his crew were performing outside. *Because*, Flash replied, *we have no place else to go.* Chandler was opening a social club nearby, and he invited Flash and his MCs to come in from the cold.

The Black Door on Prospect Avenue was a tiny venue to hold a disco. Chandler charged a dollar a head and always packed the place. But the problem with having a successful business in the Bronx was that it inevitably became a target for stickup kids and street gangs. Ray Chandler was an imposing man, but he wasn't bigger than the Casanova Crew, who demanded free admittance. Instead of fighting the Casanovas, Chandler enfranchised them. He gave them bulk discounts on tickets. He hired them as security. On some nights, Chandler even gave them the entire take from the door if they covered his expenses, which included paying Flash. But even with the Casanovas on his side, Chandler always faced the threat of robbery and violence.

The Casanovas were an offshoot of the Black Spades, one of several street gangs that alternately secured and terrorized neighborhoods in the Bronx throughout the 1970s. The Bronx River Projects were once Black Spades territory, until a burly young Spade formed an alternative for kids looking for something safer and more fun to do. The Bronx River Organization centered around DJing and party promoting. But with a healthy dose of Black Nationalism and pan-Africanism, it eventually became known as the Zulu Nation, and its creator as Afrika Bambaataa. The flyers for Zulu parties always read, "Come in Peace."

Bam's parties weren't always peaceful, and the Zulus, many of them ex-Spades, too, could be as menacing as any gang. But Bambaataa himself was known for crossing the Byzantine boundaries of the Bronx with respect, and for respecting outsiders in turn. Bambaataa's ecumenical spirit translated into an openness in music, too. As a DJ, Bam became known for being able to find a danceable break in any kind of record: rock, jazz, even music from television show and cartoon themes, like *The Monkees* and *The Pink Panther*.

Tales of Bambaataa's skills and taste lured many kids to make the risky cross-borough pilgrimage to Bronx River. Slowly Bam's mystical vision of peaceful warriors rising to supplant the gangs of New York became a self-fulfilling prophecy. As more Bronx kids became DJs and MCs, and b-boys and b-girls, their creative pursuits began to soak up the poisonous pool of competitive energy from which the gangs drew. Where the map of the Bronx was once parceled into fiefdoms by the Savage Skulls, Savage Nomads, and Black Spades, by the mid-seventies it was carved into spheres of influence for DJ, MC, breaking, and graffiti crews: Kool Herc in the West Bronx. Flash in the South Bronx. Bambaataa in the East Bronx. DJ Baron in the North Bronx. Gang colors were replaced by shiny jackets with the names of sound crews. Battles were fought less with guns and knives and more with styles. Breaking crews battled for neighborhood pride, and to gain an edge, their routines became more elaborate. Dancers now dropped to the floor, whirled their legs and feet, spun on their backs and heads. Graffiti artists, among the first to escape the gangs' clutches, created elaborate flyers to advertise local dances. Promoters like Ray Chandler could take in hundreds of dollars a night and, occasionally, thousands. DJing and MCing for a bunch of kids wasn't as lucrative as the stuff that DJ Hollywood and Pete DJ Jones were doing for the adult crowd in the discos. But money wasn't the point for the Bronx DJs like Bam, Flash, and Herc. Recognition was. Intrepid partygoers from other boroughs carried bootleg cassette tapes of park jams in the Bronx back home with them. They made copies for their friends and cousins, who blasted them on "boom box" radios for their entire block to hear. Graffiti writers and taggers sent their names and murals on subway trains streaking like rainbows through all parts of the gray city.

Most New Yorkers saw it as blight.

Some saw it for what it truly was: a bona fide culture.

And then there were those who saw what it could be: a business.

———

They called him "Sal the Nigger Lover."

He drove around Pelham Parkway in a purple Eldorado. He wore apple-jack hats and alligator shoes. He dressed like them. He talked like them. He hung out with them. The Italians of Pelham Parkway had left the South Bronx to get away from them, but Sal Abbatiello and his whole family still consorted with the *mulignane*.

Teenage Sal tended bar for his father, Allie, who coowned a nightspot in the old neighborhood with a Black partner. They called it Pepper-n-Salt, a jazz joint serving an upwardly mobile Black clientele. Sal had grown up in and around his father's club. He learned to dance, learned to play basketball, learned to talk shit in South Bronx. Half of his life was spent in the old neighborhood, where his grandmother still cooked Christmas dinners for the families who couldn't afford their own. The other half was in Pelham, where he worked his father's goomba hangout, the Golden Hour. The wise guys didn't like Sal, but Sal didn't take any shit from them. One night, while breaking up a fight, Sal punched a connected guy from Arthur Avenue. A few days later, at a sit-down meant to squash the beef, Sal was struck in the head and dragged, unconscious, into an alley. Sal woke as he was being shot— *bam! bam!*—in the shoulder and hip. Sal ran as the Arthur Avenue crew gave chase. He lost them in the Bronx Zoo and took a cab to a hospital.

While he healed, Sal decided to stay where it was safe: the South Bronx. In 1977 he helped his father open a new club just down the block from Pepper-n-Salt on 167th and Jerome. Sal's mother suggested they call it The Disco Fever. Sal, now twenty-four, tended bar and helped with the books while he figured out his next move.

One night in the wee hours while he was fixing a cigarette machine, Sal heard a commotion on the dance floor. He rushed out to see what all the yelling was about. George Godfrey, the night manager who called himself "Sweet G," was spinning records for the remaining party stalwarts. But he was talking over the microphone, calling out to the crowd, and the crowd was shouting back. It was four in the morning, but the party was *jumping*. To Sal, Sweet G's rapport with the crowd was like some secret language, something that everyone seemed to be in on but him.

"What the fuck are you doing?" Sal asked.

Instead of explaining, Sweet G took Sal to Club 371 to see DJ Hollywood.

"This is the best guy at talking on the microphone," Sweet G said.

Sal discovered that Hollywood wasn't merely a DJ. He rhymed. He sang.

He danced. He had girls onstage called "Holly's Angels," and another DJ named Junebug. When Hollywood entered the club, his entourage shouted, "Holly," and the crowd would chant, "Wood," as they cleared a path for the big man through the adoring throng. The crowd seemed to know every word to his routines. DJ Hollywood was a genuine entertainer, a ghetto celebrity.

What would it take to hire Hollywood at the Disco Fever? Too much, Sal discovered, as Hollywood was making $1,500 a night opening for live acts at the Apollo Theater. The guy could hit four small spots all over the city in one night, do one or two songs, and collect $500 at each joint. Sal couldn't afford any of these new talking DJs who played Club 371, people like Reggie Wells, or Hollywood's friend, Eddie Cheba.

Sweet G suggested an alternative approach to securing talent. "There are plenty of DJs in the parks," he said.

So Sweet G took Sal to see Flash in the park. Sal couldn't believe it. Flash mixed records behind his back. He mixed with his feet, with his *teeth*, even. His "3 MCs" put on a hell of a show. Sal Abbatiello decided that these street kids were even better than the disco DJs.

First, Sal convinced his father to let him experiment with a Flash show on Tuesday nights. Getting Flash to say yes was harder. Sal offered him $50 to play every Tuesday night. Flash balked. When Pete DJ Jones hired him as a backup DJ, Flash made hundreds.

"But how often is that?" Sal countered. "Every two months? I'm offering a steady gig. If you come to the Fever, you're gonna be a star, because you're going to have a place every week where people could come to see you. As it gets busier, you get more money."

Flash agreed to try it.

Sal devised a promotion—$1 to get in and $1 to drink—and spent the week before Flash's first show at the Fever papering the Bronx with flyers: the high schools, Bronx Community College, Grand Concourse, Fordham Road, 149th Street. He had no idea what what to expect the night of the show. The club held 350 people. On a good night, they were lucky to get 200. Sal hoped he could just break even. On Tuesday night, "Grandmaster" Flash showed up with his 3 MCs, and demanded more money on their behalf. Sal kicked in an additional $25.

Sal opened the doors to find a long line had formed out front. The kids poured in and kept coming. When Sal realized he was going to pack the club, he called his father, Allie, in a panic. How the hell was he going to handle all these kids? Allie sent a bunch of guys from Pepper-n-Salt to help Sal keep the club under control.

The Disco Fever made $1,000 that first Tuesday night. Even so, Allie Abbatiello and Sal's "uncles"—his father's Black friends—took the crowd of youngsters as a bad omen. Street kids showing up in sneakers and jeans would destroy the club's reputation as a nice place for a respectable clientele, they said. So Sal started charging $5 for anyone wearing sneakers. On the next Tuesday, the kids dressed better, and the Fever made even more money. While Club 371 and DJ Hollywood went after the fickle hustler crowd, Sal and the Disco Fever went for the steady customer, the teenager with $2 in his pocket. Suddenly the Disco Fever became the one reliable spot in the Bronx where the younger crowd could come in off the street and hear the "jams," the world's first true indoor residence for b-boys and b-beats.

The success of Grandmaster Flash's Tuesday-night residency at the Disco Fever forced Allie to expand the club, building the back room into another bar. Then Allie put Sal in charge of the club's best nights, Friday and Saturday. Sal hired DJ Junebug away from Hollywood, making him Sweet G's DJ. Sal finally had money to hire some disco-style DJs, too. He gave Sundays to Eddie Cheba, and Mondays to Lovebug Starski, who was so good that Sal put him on weekends, too. Now the Disco Fever had the older, DJ Hollywood–type crowd on the weekends, and the street-and-park-jam kids during the week.

The Disco Fever became an oasis of sorts, a community center. On one hand, the place wasn't exactly wholesome. Cocaine was consumed openly at the bar, and it was easy for underage kids to get into the club and drink. On the other hand, Sal let homeless kids stay in the club rather than ride the trains all night. If the children were in school, Sal would make them sit in his office and do their homework. At the end of the quarter, they had to show Sal their report cards. It was a poor neighborhood, and if customers or employees needed money, Sal would loan it to them, interest free. Sal kept a big red ledger of all the transactions—$20 for rent, $5 for food, $1 for the train—sometimes holding on to a pair of earrings or a watch as collateral. Sal's biggest loans could rarely be paid back: abortions and funerals. Sal's mother made Italian feasts for the staff and customers on holidays, just like his grandmother had. And the club was, for the most part, a safe haven from violence, protected by Sal's six-foot-five ex-con bouncer, Mandingo; a feared Black Spade called "Bam-Bam"; and the universally accepted but false notion that Allie and Sal were part of the Mafia. The Disco Fever became the after-hours spot to which New York's party people would come after their after-hours spots closed. Sal would joke that that there were only two reasons that people risked their lives to come to the Bronx: Yankee Stadium or the Disco Fever.

On July 13, 1977, bolts of lightning struck several nodes on the Consolidated Edison grid providing electricity to New York. Within an hour, the biggest city in North America was without power.

Minutes after the Blackout of 1977 began, the people of New York City began one of the biggest looting sprees in history.

For most poor people, the blackout was an opportunity to stock up on simple household necessities like food and diapers.

But for the young fans of the new DJ and MC culture, the blackout was an unprecedented opportunity to get into a game that had a rather high cost of entry.

The price of two turntables and a mixer.

Audio electronics stores across the five boroughs were emptied of their wares. Nightclubs weren't spared either, but the Disco Fever got lucky.

Sweet G was on his way to meet Sal and the manager, Horace, to open the club, when the lights went out on the Grand Concourse. On Third Avenue, Sweet G saw kids riding bicycles down the escalators of Alexander's department store and out the front door. By the time he, Sal, and Horace arrived at the Fever, all seemed quiet. Then Horace heard something.

"Somebody's on the roof!" he hissed, pulling his gun. Horace was always strapped.

Horace shot into the ceiling, and then came the sounds of shouting and scrambling. Sal, Sweet G, and Horace climbed up the stairs to the roof. There they saw the club's two turntables and Numark mixer next to a hole in the roof that the would-be thieves had cut.

In the days after the blackout, new DJ crews popped up all over the city. A formerly exclusive scene was suddenly democratic. And the explosion in the DJ population of New York led to a surge in demand for the one commodity that kept all DJs in business.

When Nick deKrechewo opened up his record store in 1970, he set his sights low. So low, in fact, that his shop was literally underground, in a cramped six-foot-by-twelve-foot stall located in the subway station at 42nd Street and Sixth Avenue in Manhattan. He called it Downstairs Records.

DeKrechewo's business plan was twofold. He could make a lot of money selling the new disco "12-inches," which were wider and held longer songs than the old 7-inch 45 rpm singles from the 1950s and 1960s. But he also felt there was a market for those older 45s too. DeKrechewo had an affinity for old doo-wop and soul music, and he loaded up his van with crate after crate of out-of-print records that distributors and wholesalers across the city had left to rot in their back rooms, basements, and warehouses.

Downstairs Records caught a lot of Midtown foot traffic on lunch breaks and after work. Soon, deKrechewo had to knock down a wall, and then another, expanding his store five times over. In a back room, deKrechewo set up a turntable where customers could listen to dusty 45 rpm singles before they purchased them.

But sometime in 1977, deKrechewo noticed a bizarre trend among his young Black and Latino customers. They were buying a ton of his old 45s—and not just one copy of each, but two. *Why two?* deKrechewo wondered. A lot of them were inquiring about the same records too: "Take Me to the Mardi Gras," by Bob James. "Amen, Brother," by the Winstons. "Bra" by Cymande. Weirdest of all, Black kids were coming in asking for records by White rock groups like AC/DC and Led Zeppelin. They wanted "Mary, Mary" by the Monkees and "Honky Tonk Woman" by the Rolling Stones. Listening to the emanations from the back room, deKrechewo eventually figured it out. The kids were looking for records with instrumental breaks, drumbeats that they could talk over. DeKrechewo started to make mental notes of these "break" records for his customers. His friend and nearest competitor—Stanley Platzer over at the Music Factory in Times Square—did him one better. Platzer made an actual list of "breaks," compiling them into a thick reference book.

Platzer and deKrechewo became key resources for uptown DJs like Afrika Bambaataa, and for an enterprising, itinerant record purveyor that Bambaataa nicknamed "Record Lenny," or sometimes "Breakbeat Lenny." By trade, Lenny Roberts was actually a livery driver, but Roberts spent more and more of his off hours scouring the record stores of New York for the particular records that DJs wanted, then reselling them at a higher price. Roberts became a familiar face at deKrechewo's Downstairs Records, buying dozens of records at a time. When he couldn't find singles for a particular song he wanted, he would buy the entire album. When Downstairs didn't have an album, deKrechewo would order more from the record company. And if records were out of print, Roberts pressed up his own bootleg copies, and sold them back to deKrechewo, Platzer, and other record buyers around town.

Then, one day in early 1979, a man named Paul Winley walked into Downstairs Records. Winley was a former doo-wop producer who ran a small record label out of an office on 125th Street. On occasion, deKrechewo visited Winley in Harlem, buying up a lot of his older stock. But when Winley came to visit Downstairs and the Music Factory, and saw what deKrechewo and Platzer were charging for these old records—$10, $20, $30, sometimes more—Winley welled with a mixture of righteous anger and jealousy.

They're robbing these kids blind, Winley thought. *I'll fix all these mother-fuckers.*

If anyone was going to do the robbing, it would be him. Winley quickly bootlegged eight of the most popular breakbeats onto one record album, called *Super Disco Brakes—Volume One*, and like Lenny Roberts, Winley sold his "break" compilations to record stores around town. Some merchants, like deKrechewo, kept them behind the counter, lest the copyright owners waltz in.

Winley was perhaps the first record producer to notice the DJ-and-MC culture pervading the streets of Harlem and the Bronx. First there were the boom boxes and street-corner rapping sessions that formed a subtle, sonic backdrop to life on 125th Street. Next he had his revelation at Downstairs Records, and success with *Super Disco Brakes*. Then there was his daughter, Tanya, who seemed to always have her head in a spiral notebook, pen in hand.

"How much homework you got?" Winley joked. "You must really love school!"

She didn't, at least not as much as it seemed. Tanya was writing rhymes.

A few of his clients, record buyers for local stores, shared their amazement at the street phenomenon. One suggested that he record some of these "raps." The kids, he said, would probably go crazy for it. At first, Winley dismissed the idea. With a kid on every block rapping, he said, why the hell would anyone want to buy it on a record?

But thinking about his success with *Super Disco Brakes*, Winley reconsidered. At the end of a recording session for another group, Winley had the band stay on to play a loose funky groove with a tinny piano and heavy bass, while his teenage daughters Tanya and Paulette traded rhymes of the style they heard in the streets, the school cafeterias, and the playgrounds. Tanya went on and on, bragging about how she had so much to say that the rhymes were literally coming out of her ears and eyes. "MC Sweet T is my DJ name," she said. "I'm in the history books, and the hall of fame."

To Tanya Winley the line about the history books was a mere boast. She could not possibly have known it would come true.

Side B
Downtown

"Rhymin' and Rappin'," by Paulette and Tanya Winley, released on Paul Winley Records in 1979, was one of the first rap records.

So, too, was the Fatback Band's "King Tim III (Personality Jock)," released around the same time. The popular R&B group's leader, Bill Curtis, called his music "country funk." The dirtier and grittier, the better. Curtis and his partner, Gerry Thomas, had heard the rhymes of New York's rapping DJs in the parks where Fatback often played outdoor concerts, on cassette tapes played by friends, and at the Apollo, where DJ Hollywood performed. The partners were in a Manhattan studio finishing "Catch the Beat," a song for Fatback's next album, when the idea struck them to find one of these rappers to add a wild element to the track. Their roadie, Anthony Bee, knew "someone," who turned out to be a cocky young MC from the Bronx named Timothy Washington, a rapper with little reputation, and a style akin to that of Hollywood.

It was Washington's first time in the studio, but he was convinced he was about to become a star. He laid down his vocals over the completed song, and "Catch the Beat" was transformed into "King Tim III (Personality Jock)," so named because Curtis understood the connection between the rappers of New York and the traditional rap of Black radio DJs.

The Fatback Band's record label, Spring, wasn't enthusiastic about the song. Spring's owners, two Jewish brothers named Roy and Jules Rifkind, were afraid that some guy doing a radio DJ's shtick on a record would alienate the very DJs who were supposed to play it. Curtis was worried, too, but he was convinced that the song would be a hit and argued passionately for it to be a single.

We'll put it on the B-side, the Rifkinds said.

The song that Spring Records planned to promote was "You're My Candy Sweet." But some radio DJs found their way to the flip side. Frankie Crocker was an old friend of "Julie" Rifkind, and a fan of Fatback, so he played "King Tim III." It seemed like Curtis was right after all.

But then, just a few weeks later, another "rap" record started getting airplay, easily pushing "King Tim III" out of the way. It succeeded largely because it was an exact replica of the biggest song of the summer of 1979—"Good Times," by Chic, only with rapping instead of singing. The record was perfectly timed and shrewdly produced. Once it began its swift ascent, "Rapper's Delight" by the Sugar Hill Gang rendered forever academic any argument about which rap release came first. How could you possibly compare anything to the record that became, in its day, the biggest-selling single of all time?

"You curse a lot, Mr. Rifkind," James Brown once remarked to the man who had arranged for Brown's first major label deal, with Polygram.

"You know why I curse, James?" Jules Rifkind responded. "Because I don't have a big vocabulary."

Rifkind knew fucking well the people who had knocked his Fatback record out of contention. Sugar Hill Records was the latest incarnation of a small label called All Platinum Records, and All Platinum was run by a guy who everyone around town thought was a gangster, Joe Robinson.

Rifkind knew that Joe Robinson was no gangster. He was a number runner from Harlem, a street guy who had gotten himself into the music business by marrying teenage singing star "Little" Sylvia Vanderpool. Julie Rifkind met Sylvia back when she was part of the singing duo Mickey & Sylvia, who had a huge hit in 1957 called "Love Is Strange." Sylvia was petite, copper skinned, and gorgeous, and she jokingly flirted with Rifkind when he booked Mickey & Sylvia for Tommy Smalls's live revues. After Sylvia married Joe Robinson, she made a point of introducing the two men.

"Julie was my first love," she said, ribbing Joe.

Rifkind became friendly with Joe Robinson, perhaps because Rifkind and Robinson both knew, like the Abbatiellos did, that there was some value to people thinking that you were a connected guy, especially in the music business. Rifkind got Barbra Streisand and Elvis Presley some of their first shows in Las Vegas. Everyone knew that the mob controlled Las Vegas, so everyone thought Rifkind was a mobster. Rifkind never disabused anyone of that notion. His reputation brought him a lot of respect, especially from Black artists.

Rifkind wasn't really connected, not like Morris Levy, the notorious owner of Roulette Records who had ties to the Genovese crime family. But Rifkind did manage to navigate the perils of the music business by mentoring the right people. He gave a former army sergeant named Nate McCalla his start in the record business. Now that McCalla was the de facto "boss" of Harlem, his friendship was a kind of insurance policy. Rifkind had also taken another young Black kid under his wing, a sixteen-year-old prodigy preacher from Brooklyn named Al Sharpton. The young Sharpton worked out of Spring's offices and collected money for Rifkind, until he left to be James Brown's tour manager. But Sharpton was an influential community organizer, and kept militants like the Black Muslims from harassing Rifkind. Because of his friendships and reputation, Rifkind never felt he had to muscle or scare anyone.

Joe Robinson, on the other hand, carried a gun and tried to scare all the record executives as if *he* were the boss of Harlem. But Rifkind knew the truth: All Platinum was bust, and Joe was broke. The only way he could fund his new company was by going to Morris Levy for money. Now his new company would receive all the promotion and distribution muscle that Levy could muster. Most important, distributors who might otherwise stiff a small, Black-owned company would pay, for fear of angering Levy. Joe Robinson was a play gangster, now playing with real gangsters. He might one day regret doing so.

The real genius behind All Platinum was Sylvia. She took a song that was already a hit, had some kids talk over it, and now her record was bigger than "King Tim III," maybe even bigger than "Good Times." She and Joe took all the publishing, and didn't give any label credit to the real songwriters, Chic's Nile Rodgers and Bernard Edwards. And why bother? Who thought the song would get that big?

No one would ever know just how many copies Joe and Sylvia Robinson's Sugar Hill Records would sell of "Rapper's Delight," because Joe Robinson was selling just as many out the back door as he was the front. He was so afraid of people looking at his books that he wouldn't pay the Recording Industry Association of America to certify the record. Rifkind heard the orders were in the millions, from all over the country, all over the world.

Shit like this didn't happen more than once in a record man's lifetime. It wasn't just a result of Levy's muscle, Joe's hustle, or Sylvia's genius.

It was, Rifkind swore, a goddamned miracle.

Dear Lord, help us through this terrible time. Watch over me. Watch over Joe. Please keep us safe from the people who want to destroy us.

Sylvia Vanderpool Robinson lowered her head in prayer, shutting her eyes tight amid dozens of other shouting, singing congregants at Pastor Wright's revival in the mountains of northern New Jersey. It was a sort of religious picnic, really, on a sunny Sunday in late June of 1979. She had come here with her sister Audrey, and nieces Donna and Ahwanetta, as a kind of last-ditch attempt to stave off the darkness enveloping her during the most difficult period in her forty-three-year life.

The last few years had not been good. Her singing career was over, and her run as a successful rhythm-and-blues songwriter and producer seemed to have ended. Sylvia had always been able to write her way out of a financial predicament. Not this time. The record business that she founded with her husband, Joe, was insolvent. They had been forced to file for bankruptcy. As far as Sylvia was concerned, she and Joe were driven there by people who wanted them out of the business. First, the feds came for Joe. They tried him on payola charges, but got him on tax evasion. For the last few years their distributor, Polygram, had been trying to take their company along with all the masters she had produced, even their prized asset—the Chess/Checkers/Cadet back catalog, which included the works of Muddy Waters and Etta James. She and Joe were two independent Black businesspeople who had taken back just a fraction of the art Black folks had created in this country. The White establishment, she thought, wouldn't let them have even that.

Sylvia had gotten sick from it all. Burning ulcers. Painful fibroids. She felt depressed, drained of her usual creativity. Joe was working himself to death—in Europe right now—looking for a financial lifeline that would allow them to stay in business.

Audrey and her nieces had been coming lately to Sylvia's house to pray with her. They even baptized Sylvia in her backyard pool. Once, Sylvia thought she heard the voice of the God speaking from her rhododendrons, telling her everything was going to be all right. The revival was one more way to get closer to Him.

Dear Lord, please show us a way through.

As the music played, Sylvia Robinson thought she heard angels. She lifted her head and was suddenly gripped by an ecstatic vision.

Yes! God would destroy their enemies, and she and Joe would be on top again!

And Sylvia Robinson wept, danced, and praised the Lord.

"Amen!" she cried.

When she returned home to her house in Englewood, New Jersey, Sylvia was exhausted. Her feet hurt from standing in her heels all day. But then her nineteen-year-old son, Joey Junior, reminded Sylvia that her niece Deborah was throwing a birthday party for her that night at the club Deborah managed, Harlem World.

Sylvia really didn't want to go, but she had to put in an appearance at her own party, for Deborah's sake. So she and Joey got back in the car, picked up her younger sister Diane, drove across the George Washington Bridge and down the West Side Highway. They exited at 125th Street, back home in Harlem, the old neighborhood.

The Harlem World disco was located on both floors of a squat storefront building on the corner of 116th and Lenox Avenue. Sylvia put on a happy face and walked to the door, but the smile vanished when she found out that the club was charging people to get in.

"How are you going to invite people to a birthday party and then charge them money?!" Sylvia protested as she, Joey, and Diane worked their way into the club. Up in the risers, they reunited with Deborah and Sylvia's big brother Daschel. It was only then that Sylvia noticed that discos had changed a bit since she had last been on the scene.

Deborah managed the club for a local hustler named Jack Taylor, whom everyone called "Fatjack." Over the past few years, Taylor had transformed Harlem World into the uptown version of the Disco Fever, the Harlem home of rapping DJs and MCs. Onstage tonight was Lovebug Starski, a protégé of DJ Hollywood and an alumnus of the Disco Fever, controlling the crowd with the call-and-response power of a preacher: "Say, 'Hey, money money, hey, money money money'!"

The crowd answered: "Hey, money money, hey, money money money!"

And then Starski rapped: "A hip, hop / A hibbit a hop da hop da hop hibby dibby hibby dibby hop."

The kids were going crazy, and Sylvia was transfixed. She had never in her life seen anything like this.

Just then, Sylvia realized that God had answered her prayers. She turned to her little sister.

"Can you imagine what this would be like if they were rapping for the Lord, Diane?" Sylvia said.

"Sylvia!" Diane replied with feisty impatience. "This is what I was trying to tell you about!" Sister Diane had a similar epiphany weeks earlier when she first saw DJ Hollywood perform at another party thrown by another niece, Donna Jones.

Sylvia had ignored her testimony. But now she was waxing rhapsodic about her new vision, one that she claimed would save the company. God, she said, had told her so.

"Little Sylvia" was only thirteen when she recorded her first single for Savoy Records in 1951. Her song, "Little Boy," brought Sylvia celebrity in the neighborhood, and jealousy, too. Some kids on the block thought Sylvia needed to be taken down a peg or two. One day a gaggle of them congregated outside the Vanderpools' apartment bulding on 138th between Lenox and Fifth. The children shouted toward the family's window, challenging Sylvia to a fight. Sylvia ran upstairs, braided her hair, and spread Vaseline over her face.

"I'll help you fight them," six-year-old Diane said as her sister readied for battle.

Their mother, Idalia, stopped them both before they reached the front door.

Idalia and Herbert Vanderpool were both immigrants from Saint Thomas in the Virgin Islands. Herbert had a good job at a General Motors plant in New Jersey, and the family made it through the Depression better than most in Harlem. Herbert played the saxophone, and he made sure that all of his seven children learned an instrument. His oldest daughter, Audrey, sang in the USO during World War II, and danced on Broadway. She had, for a time, been married to a handsome Black talent agent named Foch Pershing Allen. But Allen was a philanderer, and Audrey soon got wise. Their marriage ended when Audrey stormed into Foch's apartment with a photographer, catching her husband and another woman, Margaret Brown, in a state of undress. Allen explained that he was sick, and that Miss Brown was only bringing him some soup.

One good thing did come out of their doomed union: Allen had facilitated a music business connection for Audrey's little sister. "Little" Sylvia recorded at least a half dozen sides for Jubilee Records in the early 1950s. Her father enlisted one of the best session players in the city, McHouston "Mickey" Baker, to instruct his daughter in rhythm-and-blues guitar. But by the time Sylvia Vanderpool entered her twenties, she found that a recording artist—especially one Black and female—could not make a decent living. While she recorded, Sylvia held a job as a typist at Metropolitan Life. She wore white gloves to work, like the other secretaries, and thought perhaps of enrolling in nursing school.

One evening she and a few friends took a dinner cruise up the Hudson River to Bear Mountain, a lovely, wooded spot near West Point, about forty miles north of the city. On the ride back, she met Joe Robinson. Tall, gravel voiced, and ruggedly handsome—his face pockmarked by adolescent acne—Robinson was a former navy man, like her father had been. Unlike Herbert Vanderpool, the workingman, Robinson was a hustler, and a prosperous one at that. His success in the numbers racket won him enough capital to purchase some legitimate investments: two apartment buildings and a few bars. Joe was a friend of her older brother Delano, so Sylvia felt safe enough to let Joe court her.

Robinson would pull up in front of the Vanderpools' home in his Oldsmobile convertible with a big red wheel in the back. He would take Sylvia for meals in fancy establishments like Patricia Murphy's Candelight Restaurant in Westchester, where they would dine on roast beef and popovers. Joe Robinson had very good taste. Which isn't to say he had class. He wouldn't necessarily think to hold the door open for a lady. But to Little Sylvia, Joe Robinson was a star.

Robinson also had a keen business sense, and within a year's time, he became Sylvia Vanderpool's manager. Once he did, Sylvia's career took off. Joe suggested that Sylvia team up with her guitar teacher, Mickey Baker, for a couple of recordings. As a solo artist, Sylvia had served up meager teenage confections. But as the female half of the new guitar act Mickey & Sylvia, she became sassier, sexier, and, even more than that, sovereign. Joe urged

Sylvia to form a publishing company with him, to assure that she—and he—didn't miss out on an oft-overlooked income stream for neophyte artists.

In 1956, Sylvia's idea to rework a Bo Diddley tune and add some new lyrics led to her first uncontestable hit: "Love Is Strange," which topped the Billboard R&B charts for two weeks and peaked on pop radio at number eleven. The song itself included a little "rap," in the classic sense of the term—a spoken interchange between the two partners, Sylvia calling her "lover boy," Mickey calling back.

The naughty repartee transformed Mickey & Sylvia into a showbiz act, and they toured the country for years on the strength of that one record. Sylvia danced sinuously in dresses designed by Felix DeMasi, and held her own onstage with the talented Mickey Baker, eleven years her senior. They were so convincing as a duo, many people thought they were lovers. In reality, Sylvia and Mickey couldn't stand each other. In any case, there was only one man for Sylvia, the handsome numbers man Joe Robinson.

Sylvia found, in time, that her true calling wasn't performing, but writing and producing. She helmed a hit song for Joe Jones called "You Talk Too Much," on the label owned by Morris Levy, Roulette Records. She arranged, played, and produced the first huge hit for Ike & Tina Turner, "It's Gonna Work Out Fine." But in the early 1960s, women simply didn't work behind the mixing consoles of recording studios, and Sylvia Vanderpool received no credit for what she may very well have been: American pop music's first female record producer.

The Mickey & Sylvia duo was finished in 1962, when Mickey Baker and his White wife, Barbara, left the increasingly turbulent racial landscape of America for a discreet expatriate life in Paris. Meanwhile, Joe and Sylvia married and left the increasingly treacherous streets of Harlem for Englewood, New Jersey—one of the few truly integrated American suburbs of the era and home to a growing Black middle class including Wilson Pickett, Dizzy Gillespie, Sarah Vaughan, and Marvin Gaye. Even Harlem heroin kingpin Nicky Barnes chose to rest his head in Englewood, rather than in the cesspool of drugs and crime he helped create. Englewood was a good place to raise kids, and Sylvia dabbled in recording and performing while she had three of them—Joe Junior, Leland, and Rhondo.

Joe expanded his bar and grill enterprise to include the Blue Morocco in the Bronx, an upscale joint on Boston Road. There, little sister Diane tended bar, and Sylvia conspired with a new crop of musicians that included a group called the Moments. By 1968, Joe and Sylvia were ready to get back into the music business, this time as owners. They called their record company All Platinum Enterprises, so named because experience had taught them that record distributors tend to pay their vendors in alphabetical order.

At All Platinum's studios on Palisade Avenue in Englewood, Sylvia began her production career in earnest, still one of the only female record producers in the industry. Sylvia wrote and produced two huge R&B hits for the Moments, "Not on the Outside" and "Love on a Two-Way Street," as well as "Shame, Shame, Shame" for Shirley & Company. Her style was raw, heavy with reverb and light on precision, just slightly behind the curve. Looking to increase her standing in the industry, she sought production gigs outside her own label. So Sylvia composed and sang a demo for soul singer Al Green. When Green's producer, Willie Mitchell, wanted her publishing rights, Sylvia shelved the song.

One year later Sylvia was digging through a closet when that same heavy tape box fell and smashed onto her foot.

"Motherfucker!" she cried.

It was exactly that, Sylvia determined after listening again. *A mother-fucking smash.*

She and Joe drove the tape over to WBLS to see their friend Frankie Crocker.

"Hey, movie star," Frankie greeted Sylvia, as was his custom with her.

Frankie played the song on WBLS as they drove back to New Jersey. They knew they had a hit.

"Pillow Talk" by Sylvia ended up going to number one on Billboard's soul singles chart and number three on the pop chart in 1973. At the dawn of the disco era her moaning, groaning, whispering come-on became her biggest hit ever, and All Platinum's as well.

It had been over a decade since Sylvia's last performance with Mickey Baker. Removed from her studio cocoon and suddenly thrust onstage alone at age thirty-six, Sylvia seemed uncomfortable. On *Soul Train*, she was still beautiful and stylish—bell bottoms, a long braid, and a yellow muffy cap—but she was nearly tongue-tied as Don Cornelius asked her about her praise-worthy production career.

Cornelius began Sylvia's interview only after asking an important first question: "How is your handsome husband, Joe Robinson?" It was a measure of the reputation and regard that Robinson had built for himself in the music business. In a time when many Black music companies were selling out to the major corporate labels, All Platinum remained independent. It was a family enterprise, too, with Vanderpool sisters Diane and Audrey working in the office on occasion. But a Black-owned company like All Platinum could be just as ruthless with its artists as the Man himself. Joe and Sylvia snatched up publishing rights, were slow to pay royalties when they paid at all, and switched out personnel from groups like the Moments when one of their artists complained too loudly.

Hit records can cover a multitude of sins that surface when the hits dry up. By the end of the 1970s—after his conviction, legal battles with his European distributor, Polygram, and now bankruptcy—Joe Robinson was looking at a dead end. He couldn't even afford to pay his lawyers. So on a Saturday afternoon in the spring of 1979, Robinson drove to Morris Levy's Sunnyview horse farm in upstate New York. Levy was hosting a wedding—not for his daughter, but like Puzo's Godfather, Levy wasn't one to turn down the request of a friend on a special day. Levy dug into his pocket and came out with $5,000 cash.

"Take care of your obligations," Levy said. "When you're done, come see me. We'll start a new label together."

Sylvia Robinson needed to find a suitable rapper to fulfill her vision. First, she dispatched her neice Deborah to get Lovebug Starski, the MC she witnessed at Harlem World. Starski wasn't interested. Next, she turned to her son for help. Joey, being a suburban kid, didn't know too much about the DJ and MC scene in the city. Instead, Joey played Sylvia a tape of his friend Casper, who had circulated a cassette among friends and rap fanatics in New Jersey.

"Go get him!" Sylvia said. Joey called Casper, who seemed keen on the project.

In the meantime, Sylvia scheduled a session to record a backing track with one of All Platinum's funk groups, Positive Force. In the studio, Sylvia coaxed from them an uncanny replica of the breakdown of Chic's "Good Times"—the record that she heard Starski rapping to at Harlem World.

But when the track was done, Joey couldn't track down Casper. After a few days, Casper surfaced, confessing to Joey that his father, a radio DJ, had warned him not to go into business with the Robinsons. Casper's father had heard about the lawsuits, the bankruptcy, the mistreatment of artists, and didn't want his son caught up in all of that.

Sylvia was crestfallen. Joey's school buddy Warren Moore took pity on her. "Mrs. Rob," Moore said, "we know some other people that rap. Don't you worry about that. Get in the car and we'll take you to hear somebody."

The three of them drove a short distance along Palisade Avenue, Englewood's main drag, to Crispy Crust Pizza.

"I know this guy who works here," Moore said, "who's always rapping."

Inside, Henry "Hank" Jackson was working, in part to pay off the $2,000 loan he took to purchase the equipment for the Cold Crush Brothers, a respected rap crew from the Bronx that he helped manage.

Moore burst into the pizzeria as Hank twirled dough behind the counter.

"Mrs. Rob is auditioning for a rapper!" Moore said. "She's outside in the car right now!"

Moore emerged with Hank, and walked across Palisade Avenue to the car, where Joey and Sylvia were waiting. The car groaned as Hank, a former football player, lowered his huge body and dough-soiled apron into the backseat of Joey's turquoise Oldsmobile.

"Watch the springs!" Joey said.

Sylvia cued the cassette of her backing track, and Hank dug into his storehouse of memorized Cold Crush routines. Hank's voice was husky from his weight, but he rapped exuberantly, pizza flour flying everywhere as he gesticulated.

The commotion in the car started to attract attention from passersby, friends of Joey's, who also wanted to audition. Soon, another kid, Guy O'Brien, joined Hank in the backseat. They traded rhymes with each other, vying for the slot. Then another hopeful rapper showed up, a tall, handsome, light-skinned kid named Mike Wright. Now there were too many people around, so Joey invited Mike to come along with them to the Robinsons' home.

At the house, Sylvia listened to Hank and Guy rap together. *Why not two?* she thought. Then she heard Mike, who had a smooth, deep voice that was a nice contrast to the other two.

"Okay," she said. "The three of you are married."

Sylvia informed the three New Jersey rappers that the name of their new group would be the Sugar Hill Gang. And then she went off to take a nap.

The name of Sylvia and Joe Robinson's new label, Sugar Hill Records, Ltd., served a triple purpose. In one sense, it was meant to impart a bit of street credibility to a suburban company and its artists by conjuring visions of the old neighborhood. In another, the phrase rang of success and aspiration. But the main function of the new name was more practical: to create a separate business entity from the doomed All Platinum Records.

To finance the first record, Joe Robinson and Morris Levy each kicked in $300. Sylvia wasn't happy about being in business with Levy, and she and Joe fought about it. "He's the devil," Sylvia insisted.

But the Robinsons had little financial recourse. Their studio was in need of repair, and everything had to be done on the fly. On a Monday in August of 1979, after contracts were presented to and signed by the newly christened Sugar Hill Gang, the three rappers gathered to record their vocals.

Sylvia bobbed behind the recording console as the track played, looking through the plate glass into the vocal booth at Hank, Guy, and Mike, cueing each rapper in turn with a point of her finger. They were a bizarre trio, a study in contrasts: the fat and boisterous "Big Bank" Hank; the short, slightly lisping "Master Gee"; and the towering, mellow "Wonder" Mike. Hank mostly blasted away with his memorized Bronx and uptown routines, including a line he may well have copped from DJ Hollywood: "Ho-tel, mo-tel, Holiday Inn, / If your girl starts acting up, then you take her friend."

Mike came up with a funny, rhymed tale that began: "Have you ever been over a friend's house to eat and the food just ain't no good?"

But he also came up with a subtle stroke of marketing genius. The song needed, he felt, *an explanation*. Something that would describe what they were about to do to people across the country who hadn't heard the strange sounds of rapping DJs and MCs: "Now what you hear is not a test. / I'm rappin' to the beat. / And me, the crew, and my friends are gonna try to move your feet."

It was a conscious invitation and an unconscious prediction. The implication hit young Joey, too, in the moment near the end of the session when Mike scatted: "Skippidy-be-bop, a we rock, a Scooby Doo. / Guess what? / America, we love you!"

Joey, with the musical ear of a Vanderpool and the business nose of a Robinson, knew a magic conjunction of art and commerce when he heard and smelled one.

The session was interrupted once, when the manager of Crispy Crust Pizza called to fire Hank. Joe Robinson smoothed things over so Hank could keep his job, and the trio finished the song in one take. When they were done, the song Sylvia called "Rapper's Delight" was fifteen minutes long.

Joe told his wife that she had to edit the song to a more radio-friendly length. The idea of a "rapped" song was weird enough. But Sylvia resisted.

"We're going to keep every word," Sylvia said. "This is the way the Lord gave me the idea."

"Hey, movie star!" said Frankie Crocker.

But this time, neither Sylvia's star power nor Joe's influence could get Crocker to play "Rapper's Delight" on WBLS. Crocker was not a fan of the "rapping DJs" who now rivaled him in the eyes of young New Yorkers. One of them, DJ "Hollywood," had even taken his nickname.

Rebuffed, the Robinsons approached New York's AM pop behemoth, WABC, where they got similar resistance.

One radio show, on a low-power community station in Manhattan, played the record. "Disco Showcase" was the brainchild of John Rivas, a DJ from Brooklyn who performed as "Lucky the Magician." Lucky, too, dreamed of being Frankie Crocker, while he built custom speakers at S&H, an electronics shop in downtown Manhattan. He enrolled himself in a radio course at the New York School of Announcing and Speech, where fellow students told Lucky about a small FM station on the Upper West Side called WHBI that sold airtime for $75 an hour. If he could get S&H to give him $150 for four commercials, he would be in business. With the fish shop across the street kicking in for a few more spots, he would be making money. In the spring of 1979, Lucky the Magician shortened his handle to "Mr. Magic," and launched his "Disco Showcase" from two to four a.m. every Sunday morning. Even before the first rap record had been released, Magic brought break beats to the airwaves and rappers into the studio for live routines. Soon, Sal Abbatiello signed the Disco Fever on as a regular sponsor. With the release of "Rapper's Delight," "Mr. Magic's Disco Showcase" became the world's first rap radio show, helped now by regular checks from Joe Robinson. This wasn't payola. This was "sponsorship."

Save for "Mr. Magic's" two-hour show, "Rapper's Delight" made it to New York's record stores without airplay. But airplay didn't matter. As soon as the store played "Rapper's Delight," the record was sold. As soon as the record was sold, it was in the clubs, and in the streets, and on cassette tapes, and into the tens of thousands of handheld boom boxes that now broadcast louder and with more authority than Frankie Crocker ever could. Everyone in New York remembered where they were when they first heard *that record.* Especially the people who could have, and probably should have, made it.

Grandmaster Flash was sitting with Cowboy in the VIP room at the Disco Fever when the familiar sounds of Chic's "Good Times" came from downstairs. DJs and MCs loved "Good Times" because of its long, perfect break. In the late summer of 1979, it was all you heard in New York—some DJ cutting "Good TIMES! . . ." and an MC rapping over the beat.

That was what someone downstairs was doing right now, rapping over the "Good Times" beat: "I said a hip-hop / A hibbit, a hibby-dibby / Hip-hip-hop and you don't stop."

That "hip-hop" rhyme was Cowboy's. It had started as a joke, Cowboy making fun of the sound that a drill sergeant makes while marching his troops—*"Heeeyip-hoppp-heeeyip-hoppp."* Lots of MCs borrowed Cowboy's rhymes, especially his "hip-hop-you-don't-stop" rhyme, which was like standard-issue MC filler now.

So if Cowboy is sitting right here, who is that downstairs, rapping . . . ?

". . . to the beat. / And me, the crew, and my friends are gonna try and move your feet."

Flash and Cowboy raced down the stairs to see who was on the mic. They saw no one. No MC. Just the DJ, in the booth, playing a record.

Flash walked to the booth, expecting to see the familiar Atlantic Records green-and-red label of the "Good Times" single. But the record wasn't "Good Times" at all. It had a solid red label. It read "Sugar Hill."

It was then that Flash realized that the rap was *on* the record.

"I heard your record! I heard you on the radio!"

DJ Casanova Fly, or Caz for short, was one of the most popular and imitated MCs in New York. Caz was part of the Cold Crush Brothers. All the b-boys had tapes of their legendary routines. Caz himself sold hundreds of them.

Caz, however, had never made a record. Yet people were coming up to him on the street, congratulating him. Caz said, "It's not me." They replied: "How could it not be you? You say your *name* on it!"

"I'm the C-A-S-A-N-O-V-A and the rest is F-L-Y. / You see I go by the code of the doctor of the mix, / And these reasons I'll tell you why."

Even before Caz heard the record, he knew who did it. It was Hank.

Hank worked the door at the club Sparkle, in the Bronx, where the Cold Crush Brothers performed. Hank was a nice guy, a hanger-on, who had worked his way into the Cold Crush inner circle by volunteering to buy the crew a louder sound system for their gigs.

One day, Hank dropped by Caz's place, and breathlessly told Caz that someone in Jersey wanted to record him rapping.

"You ain't no MC!" Caz laughed.

Hank asked Caz if he could use some of his rhymes. Thinking that the whole fantasy of making a record would amount to nothing, Caz threw one of his rhyme books at Hank.

"Use whichever one you want."

Apparently, Hank did. And didn't even bother to change the part where Caz spelled out his name.

Caz hadn't even thought to ask Hank for money. The idea of rapping on a record was just that ridiculous.

One night in October of 1979, DJ Hollywood rolled into the Jamaica Armory in a white limousine. The crowd parted around the vehicle; Hollywood jumped out and then bolted onstage to cheers.

Hollywood had refused the gig at first. Only when the promoter nearly doubled his offer from $500 to $900 did he reconsider. Hollywood had just finished his set, leaving the stage to Eddie Cheba, Lovebug Starksi, and others, when "Rapper's Delight" came on.

Hollywood had heard the record before. Some kids called the Sugar Hill Gang who weren't even from Sugar Hill. They had no reputation. No following. Who cared?

But Lovebug Starski had already begun to think he had missed out on an opportunity, especially since he had been Sylvia Robinson's first choice to MC her record.

Starski got onstage after the record played, and called out to the crowd:

"Y'all know we started this shit. Don't worry. We're still gonna go to the moon."

DJ Hollywood, getting high and on top of the world, got back in his limousine and rolled away.

Radio came around.

A few spins of "Rapper's Delight" by Jim Gates, a disc jockey at a Black station, WESL in East St. Louis, provoked an order of 5,000 copies from a local distributor.

Back in New York, Sal Abbatiello prodded Crocker's competitor, Carlos De Jesus, the program director at FM disco station WKTU. De Jesus was more amused than impressed by the record, and played it as a joke. When the station was inundated with calls, De Jesus stopped laughing and added "Rapper's Delight" to the station's playlist.

"Big Bank" Hank was working his shift at Crispy Crust Pizza in Englewood, spinning dough and ladling sauce, listening to WKTU, when he heard his voice coming from the speakers. They were not only playing the record; they were playing the *entire* record, all fifteen minutes of it. Paco, the DJ, asked listeners to stop calling for the song. To keep the phones clear, WKTU announced that the song would be played at designated times, every other hour.

The initial trickle of orders became an avalanche. Suddenly, Joe Robinson had to scramble to keep pace with the demand, dividing the work among several major and minor pressing plants, manufacturing up to 50,000 copies a day. Demand was so great that bootleggers began pressing counterfeit records and selling them directly to stores. Joe's distributors were shipping tens of thousands of copies a day. Nobody in the industry seemed to have ever experienced a single that moved this fast. Staff writers at *Billboard* magazine, estimating sales at over two million records and counting, were already sure that "Rapper's Delight" had become the biggest-selling 12-inch single ever.

The sales of "Rapper's Delight" forced radio stations nationwide to consider or, in some cases, reconsider the bizarre talking record. First came the traditionally Black stations, whose programmers held their noses as they gave the younger listeners what they wanted. Then came the pop stations, who treated the song as a novelty record. "Rapper's Delight," the first release from a tiny independent label, rose to #4 on the Black singles charts and #36 on the pop charts. But the impact of "Rapper's Delight" reached over borders and oceans. It went to #1 in Canada and Holland, #3 in the U.K., #4 in West Germany, and charted in South Africa and Israel as well. Sugar Hill claimed that "Rapper's Delight" sold two million copies domestically and eight million worldwide.

Back home, even Frankie Crocker at WBLS came around when he realized that the Sugar Hill Gang mentioned his name in the song. Crocker reedited the track so it repeated the line:

"Frankie Crocker in stereo . . . Frankie Crocker in stereo . . ."

It wasn't just the DJs like Flash and MCs like Starski and Caz who felt left behind by the success of "Rapper's Delight."

Bobby Robinson—no relation to Joe and Sylvia Robinson—was the most famous record man in Harlem. Back in 1946, after returning from wartime deployment in Hawaii, where he made money loan-sharking to other servicemen, Robinson had become the first "colored" man to open up a music shop on 125th Street, Bobby's Happy House. In the 1950s and 1960s, he had produced doo-wop records, discovered Gladys Knight & the Pips, and produced the first hits by King Curtis on his label, Enjoy.

Bobby Robinson had a reputation for being Harlem's greatest "ear." But despite hearing the street-corner rappers for years; despite DJ Hollywood's visits to his record shop; despite his own nephew, Spoonie, whom he raised as a son, reciting rhymes constantly under Bobby's roof, it never occurred to Bobby that he could record and sell this stuff.

It took the torrent of Sugar Hill Gang vinyl moving through his store and another small-time producer making a record with Spoonie to finally provoke Bobby to action. Unlike his old friends Joe and Sylvia, Bobby went to the source of the culture. *Who's the best at this stuff?* Bobby asked his young acquaintances. His scouts came back from the Bronx with two prospects: a group named the Funky Four Plus One More, and a DJ who called himself Grandmaster Flash, who had added two more to his crew of three MCs to comprise his "Furious Five."

The two singles that came out of Bobby Robinson's initial foray into rap in late 1979—"Rappin' and Rockin' the House" by the Funky Four Plus One More and "Superrappin'" by Grandmaster Flash & the Furious Five—made Bobby Robinson's Enjoy Records the first label to record reputable DJs and MCs. And while neither record approached the gargantuan success of "Rapper's Delight," each sold copies in the hundreds of thousands—a huge windfall for a small operation like Enjoy.

In the months after "Rapper's Delight," other tiny labels and small entrepreneurs followed. Paul Winley released two records with Afrika Bambaataa. The "Ten Good Guys" of Club 371 put out a record with Eddie Cheba. The most successful "rapper" in New York, DJ Hollywood, however, was earning too much money on the local disco circuit to be bothered with making records.

This sudden flurry of rap singles merited an article in *Billboard*.

"At least six rapping deejay records have appeared in New York record stores in the past month," wrote Nelson George, a twenty-one-year-old stringer for the magazine, in an article buried deep within the December 22, 1979, issue. "Most are on small independent labels," George continued, "created just to capitalize on the popularity of rapping."

George's article included one curious exception to that rule: a Christmas rap record coming out on a major label. What George failed to disclose was that this record had been produced by his friend, roommate, and mentor at *Billboard*, twenty-nine-year-old Robert "Rocky" Ford Jr.

If you worked at *Billboard* magazine, the leading trade publication of the music industry, you had lots of opportunities to go to live shows. So many, in fact, that it was hard to find a date for them all if you were a single man. Girls didn't want to see shows in the middle of the week. Robert "Rocky" Ford Jr. and J. B. Moore III, two colleagues at *Billboard*, usually went together.

Rocky Ford was Black, the son of a corrections officer from Jamaica, Queens, a working-class kid who worked his way up the ladder to the post of production manager for *Forbes* magazine, and then *Billboard*, by the age of twenty-four. Ten years older, James Biggs Moore III was a White prep-school graduate; a descendant of Col. James Biggs Moore, an aide to General George Washington and Alexander Hamilton; and the son of a commodore of a Long Island yacht club; he had worked his way down the ladder by enlisting with the army in Vietnam, knocking around as a rock musician after the war, and landing a position in *Billboard*'s sales department. Yet Ford and Moore startled each other with their similar tastes in music; their jazz record collections nearly replicated each other's.

In addition to his production duties, Ford wrote reviews and articles for *Billboard*. One day in 1978, Moore came to Ford's desk with a story tip for his friend.

Moore had just come back from his lunch break. He had walked one long city block from *Billboard*'s Times Square offices to Nick deKrechewo's Downstairs Records, as he often did, just to check out what was selling. DeKrechewo's partner, John Kulish, was working behind the counter.

"What's happening, John?" Moore inquired.

"B-boys and b-beats," Kulish answered, explaining the phenomenon of break beats, rapping DJs, and MCs to the intrigued Moore. *There's something going on in the streets of New York*, Moore told Ford, likening the phenomenon to the early stirrings of doo-wop.

After some investigation, Ford found his way to the founding father of the "b-beats" movement, Kool Herc, on the asphalt schoolyard of William Taft High in the Bronx. Accompanied by his roommate, Nelson George, Ford viewed a tidy synopsis of the culture played out before him in microcosm: Kool Herc arriving with his Herculords, setting up their turntables, jacking power for the equipment by tapping into the nearest lamppost, playing the breaks and rapping their routines for a crowd of Black and Latino b-boys, some who danced, others who scrutinized Herc's techniques with the absorption of disciples.

The experience was immortalized in two articles in 1978—Rocky Ford's piece for *Billboard* and Nelson George's for the *Amsterdam News*—the first ever written about the culture. If anyone noticed, no one cared.

From there on, Rocky Ford continued to keep an eye on the scene, mainly by paying attention to the creative promotional flyers for DJ parties posted all around town. One day, as Ford rode the Q2 bus, escorting his pregnant girlfriend to a doctor's appointment, he spied a rangy Black teenager plastering stickers on the walls. He had seen this kid's stickers everywhere—at the Seventh Avenue station at 53rd Street, and all along the E train line to Queens. RUSH—THE FORCE IN COLLEGE PARTIES, they read, promoting gigs at uptown clubs like the Renaissance, and downtown spots like the Hotel Diplomat in Times Square. Ford walked over and introduced himself, telling the kid he was from *Billboard* and was interested in writing about him for an article about local party promoters.

"These are my brother's stickers," the kid said. Ford gave the kid his card and told him to have his brother call him at the office.

The next day, Rocky Ford got a phone call from the promoter, twenty-one-year-old Russell Simmons. Ford understood why the guy's nickname was "Rush." Simmons talked fast and talked slick, rarely stopped to take a breath, and asked lots of questions. Halfway through their phone call, Rocky realized that Simmons was interviewing *him*, and not the other way around.

Between fielding Simmons's excited queries about *Billboard* and the music business, Ford found out that Simmons was from southeast Queens, too. They even had some mutual friends. Simmons had gone to City College for a time, but dropped out to do party promotions. His kid brother, Joey, helped him distribute flyers, and DJed too. Over the next few months, Simmons became Rocky Ford's hyperactive tour guide through the world of "rapping DJ" parties that Simmons referred to, in hustler's terminology, as "the track": City College, Charles Gallery, and the Renaissance in Harlem; Club 371, Sparkle, and the Fever in the Bronx; and Hunter College, Broadway International, and the Hotel Diplomat downtown.

At *Billboard*, Ford had interviewed some of the greatest musicians of his time, seen groundbreaking bands like Steely Dan perform in their infancy. But when he first witnessed DJ Hollywood, Ford decided that he had never seen any human being with more natural talent. These rapping DJs were treated like rock stars in New York. They opened for R&B acts, yet the kids actually came to see the DJs perform, not the musicians. The DJs made thousands of dollars in one night, and they carried themselves like royalty. Eddie Cheba was another favorite of Ford's, but when Ford approached the DJ for a *Billboard* interview, Cheba could barely be bothered.

Sometime in the summer of 1979, around the same time that Sylvia Robinson had her epiphany, it dawned on Rocky Ford to try to make a record with one of these guys, maybe Cheba. Simmons had a better idea. On the last day of August, he invited Ford down to the Diplomat to see his own rapper, his friend from City College. Curtis Walker, who had already made a name for himself opening for Grandmaster Flash as Kurtis Blow, was explosive, every bit the star that Cheba and Hollywood were.

Now that "Rapper's Delight" had hit the airwaves, the idea of making a record became more urgent than ever, and making it with Kurtis Blow seemed the right decision. Both Rocky Ford and J. B. Moore were about to leave their full-time positions at *Billboard*—Moore to write a book and Rocky to freelance. With a baby on the way, Ford needed money. Ford decided to make a record, not the safest bet.

But Ford's experience at *Billboard* gave him one good idea. He knew that an ad salesman named Mickey Addy had once written a few Christmas songs for Perry Como. Years later, Addy still received a nice annual check from the record company, and took a yearly cruise with his royalties. Christmas songs, Addy had told him, were music business gold.

Ford told Moore that he had decided to produce a Christmas rap. The next evening, Moore surprised Ford by calling him at home with the completed lyrics to a rapping parody of "The Night Before Christmas." They were surprisingly good, Ford thought, coming from a thirty-seven-year-old White guy with a name like James Biggs Moore III.

Ford brought Moore in as his coproducer, and a musician friend from Queens named Larry Smith to assemble a studio band. With the money Moore had been saving to write his novel, they recorded and mixed the song into two versions. Part one, called "Christmas Rappin'," would go on the A-side of the record; part two, with some of Kurt's standard routines and rhymes, would go on the B-side, in the hope that the record would have some legs after the holidays were over.

It was mid-October, and the partners had a Christmas record that needed to be in stores within a month to be relevant. Ford called his entire list of record company contacts. Despite the huge success of "Rapper's Delight," Ford was surprised by the chilly reception he received, especially from Black executives at the major labels like Columbia and Atlantic. Ford tried everything. He even gave the tape to a friend of his who worked in royalty disbursement at Mercury Records. Dottie Psalitas didn't sign acts, but she told Ford that she would carry his tape around and try to drum up some interest.

Over twenty record companies had turned him down when he finally got a call from Cory Robbins, a twenty-two-year-old kid who ran a tiny label called Panorama. Somehow, Robbins had heard that Ford and Moore were shopping their Christmas rap song around town, and he tracked them down. Robbins offered $10,000 for the single, just enough to reimburse Moore's investment. For that fee, he wanted to claim half of their publishing royalties as well, which was a standard attempt by smaller companies to squeeze a little more cash out of their records. With no other offers in hand, Ford and Moore reluctantly agreed to the deal.

With Christmas around the corner, Cory Robbins needed to move fast to make sure that the single would be in stores in time for the holiday. He couldn't wait until the paperwork was finished. So Moore sent Robbins a copy of the master tape, and Robbins began the manufacturing process.

A few days later, Ford got a call from a fellow with a heavy English accent. He introduced himself as John Stainze—Mercury's Artists and Repertoire (or A&R) representative from London. Apparently, the copy of "Christmas Rappin'" that Dottie Psalitas promised to pass around made its way to Stainze during his current swing though the U.S. offices. "I told New York to sign you guys up," Stainze said. "I can recoup it out of England." Mercury immediately sent over a contract that, while low like Robbins's offer, would at least allow Ford and Moore to keep all their publishing.

Ford had to call Cory Robbins at Panorama and cancel their deal. But Robbins had already mastered the record. Panicked, Robbins suddenly offered better terms—giving their publishing back, a bigger royalty percentage. But there was no way that Ford and Moore were going to turn down a deal with a major label. Robbins was stuck for his investment.

Days before the release of "Christmas Rappin'," Ford and Moore made the rounds at Mercury. No one really believed that their "rap" record would sell, especially Bill Haywood, Mercury's head A&R executive for Black music.

Rocky Ford's personal life was in upheaval as Christmas approached. His brother-in-law's mother had died, his son had just been born, and he was still living with his mother in St. Albans, Queens. When he first heard "Christmas Rappin'" on WKTU, he jumped ten feet into the air and hit his head on his mother's seven-foot ceiling. Later, while driving in the funeral procession on Christmas Eve, his radio tuned to WBLS, Ford wept as Frankie Croker segued from Nat King Cole's "Christmas Song" into Kurtis Blow's "Christmas Rappin'," symbolically passing the torch from one musical generation to the next.

As the new decade dawned, Rocky Ford and J. B. Moore's sales gambit proved prescient. "Christmas Rappin'" sold 100,000 copies before the holiday, and the B-side pushed it to more than 300,000 afterward.

Ford and Moore quickly arranged for Kurtis to go out on tour to support his single, and sent Simmons with him as his road manager. The problem was that Russell couldn't seem to come home with the money. After one gig in Newark, New Jersey, Simmons and Blow met two girls, went to a hotel room with them, and spent the night. When they woke up, the girls and the cash were gone. Or so they said.

That's how Rocky Ford became Kurtis Blow's *new* road manager.

Blow's smile and physique made him an instant favorite with girls on the road. But most people outside of New York didn't understand the performance value of a guy who came onstage and talked over records. "I didn't pay to hear you play a record!" one audience member at a concert down South jeered.

In the Spring of 1980, Mercury Records exercised their option to have Kurtis Blow record a second single for them. The new record was built around another lyrical premise from J. B. Moore—a triple entendre on the phrase "that's the breaks," as in breaks that you rhyme over, brakes on a car, and bad breaks in life. "The Breaks" did even better than "Christmas Rappin'," and would become, in the summer, the first rap record to be certified gold (more than 500,000 copies sold) by the Recording Industry Association of America.

It was a distinction that should have gone to "Rapper's Delight," which sold millions more than "The Breaks." But Joe Robinson refused to pony up for membership in the RIAA. *Why should I pay them two percent of my gross profits just to send an accountant to look at my books?* he told people. Instead, Robinson made his own gold plaques, and gave those to his artists.

When Joe Robinson saw that Bobby Robinson's little Enjoy Records was having some success, he and Sylvia swooped down to take his artists. He dispatched Sylvia to the Disco Fever on a Tuesday night, to lure Grandmaster Flash and his group out to their studio. Joe, flush with cash from "Rapper's Delight," waved a check in front of Flash and his five MCs, who had been hounding Bobby Robinson for money for months, to no avail. Then Joe dangled another $10,000 in front of Bobby Robinson. Very soon, all three rap acts on Enjoy Records—Grandmaster Flash & the Furious Five, the Funky Four Plus One More, even Robinson's nephew, Spoonie Gee—would all leave Bobby Robinson's Harlem-based business for the greener pastures of Englewood, New Jersey.

Grandmaster Flash and rapper Melle Mel argued over whether to sign with Sugar Hill, as they argued over everything else. Flash was reluctant and suspicious of the Robinsons. The rest of the group sided with Mel, and Flash went along. For their first Sugar Hill record, they decided to record the routine they performed to the opening bars of "Get Up and Dance," by Freedom, an eight-piece funk band from Jackson, Mississippi. In the clubs, Flash had provided the music by spinning the breaks. In the studio, the musicians did his job. Sylvia had her house band replicate the song, down to the kazoos that played over the intro. It was a bizarre sensation for Flash, always the musical core of the group, now relegated to watching as Mel and the other four MCs rapped. There was, after all, nothing for him to do.

Flash was compensated for his demotion with fame when he heard his first Sugar Hill song, "Freedom," on the radio. Sylvia even got the Furious Five up to WBLS, where Frankie Crocker himself interviewed the crew during his drive-time show.

The Enjoy acts paid off for Sugar Hill quickly, lending a new air of credibility to the label on the streets of New York. Sugar Hill's first 12-inch with
the Funky Four, "That's the Joint," was an even bigger record, and the Sugar
Hill Gang scored a second hit with "8th Wonder," both bolstered by the
tireless promotion efforts of Joe Robinson.

Like All Platinum had been, Sugar Hill Records was a family affair. Joe
ran the business. Sylvia produced the music. Joey Junior helped in Sylvia's
new studio on 96 West Street in Englewood and formed his own group, the
West Street Mob. The group was named by Sylvia's sister Diane, whom
Sylvia brought back into the fold as head of the promotion department. Joe
taught Diane how to call record stores, and how to send them "cleans"—a
box of free records without the "For Promotional Use Only" stamp—when
the stores needed an added incentive to report Sugar Hill's records as hot
sellers for *Billboard*'s weekly charts. To record stores, these "cleans" were as
good as cash. When it came to Diane herself, Sugar Hill wasn't so generous.
Diane had to supplement her salary by running numbers back in Harlem.

Diane and Sylvia brought their sister Audrey's daughters in. Deborah
Jones, who had thrown the party for Sylvia at Harlem World, designed outlandish outfits for Sugar Hill artists now touring the country—opening
shows for R&B groups, baffling and very often upstaging them. Donna Jones,
who introduced Diane to DJ Hollywood, was hired to call Black radio stations.

Donna, in her early twenties, was Joe Robinson's secret weapon. She was
pretty, with a smile and sweet voice like her aunt Sylvia. Joe handed her a
list of stations in secondary markets. When Donna called to ask programmers for airplay, the programmers had requests of their own for her. *What
do you look like?* they inquired. *When are you coming to town? Can you
send me a picture?* Donna flirted back, and dug into her albums and scrap-
books for photographs, sending them off to Saginaw and Cleveland and
Charlotte. When Donna ran out of photographs, Joe showed her the rest of
the promotion game. He took her to record conventions, like Jack "the Rapper" Gibson's annual "Family Affair," where she, Joe, and Sylvia threw lavish parties in Sugar Hill's hotel suites. When radio programmers came to
town, Donna put them up at the nicest hotels in Manhattan, took them out
for dinners at Tavern on the Green, and got them tickets to Broadway shows.
For his part, Joe provided his programmers and DJs with anything they
wanted: money, marijuana, cocaine, and sometimes women. One radio programmer in Philadelphia had a special request for Donna.

"Bring me a White girl," he said.

Donna convinced one of her girlfriends to come with her to Philly, promising an extravagant night on the town. Unfortunately, the radio executive didn't get what he expected.

"She acts too Black," he complained.

That phrase, "too Black," was something that Joe heard a lot these days from Black radio programmers. Some of them didn't even call their stations "Black" anymore, for fear of losing advertisers. They had adopted a euphemism, "Urban Contemporary." To broaden their appeal, programmers were falling all over themselves to play records by White groups like Hall & Oates, who recorded for White-owned labels. Yet they resisted and often refused to play good records made by Black kids, released on a Black-owned label that employed dozens of Black people, that supported hundreds of Black-owned record stores across the country.

Joe didn't want to be beholden to Black radio. So he sold most of his records through in-store play at mom-and-pop shops. Joe didn't want to be at the mercy of White-owned major labels for international distribution, so he pieced together his own web of licensees across the globe. He noted with irony and pique that White foreigners seemed less resistant to rap than some Black Americans.

The Robinsons retained some of their bad habits from the All Platinum days. Money was doled out to artists sparingly, only upon request. Demands for an accounting of funds were often met with cold stares. Flash found himself increasingly ostracized for asking such questions, both at the label and within the group. And the Robinsons paid nothing to the actual authors of the songs they replayed in the studio as backing tracks for their rappers. Sylvia Robinson listed herself as the composer of "Rapper's Delight." Nile Rodgers and Bernard Edwards of Chic had to come in with lawyers to get their due credit and cash.

Joe and Sylvia had money to spare. With the only full roster of rap acts in the world and the quiet but powerful backing of Morris Levy—who made sure that the distributors paid on time—Sugar Hill Records provided a miraculous reversal of fortune for the Robinsons.

It was now one of the largest independently owned and distributed record companies in the United States.

In the Sugar Hill of her own making, Sylvia Robinson was indeed living the sweet life. She sank $500,000 into her new studio. In the parking lot outside, Mercedes sedans sat alongside her new Rolls-Royce Silver Shadow. Sylvia bought new furs, and when coats weren't warm enough, she would take her sister Diane on a Caribbean vacation. Sweetest of all, after five years of showbiz exile and financial scandal, she now had the hottest new company in the business. After decades of being a "runner-up" to the pop powerhouse of Motown and the disco empire of Philly International, she could now rightfully lay claim to the sound of young America. She called herself the "Queen of Rap."

Of course, Sugar Hill was in a precarious position, because rap had all the makings of a fad. Disco had turned out to be just that, and most of the major labels wouldn't touch rap for that very reason. It was said: *You can smell the end when the parody records start.* Disco had its "Disco Duck," and now rap had its many sundry spoofs, not the least of which was comedian Mel Brooks's "It's Good to Be the King," a record and music video based on a one-liner from his 1981 comedy film *History of the World, Part One.*

Sylvia Robinson, not to be outdone, made her first appearance as a solo artist since the early 1970s with her answer record, "It's Good to Be the Queen," rapping about her money, her furs, her cars.

Sylvia Robinson may well have sensed that this was an opportune time to resume her career as an artist. But she might have smelled the end. Perhaps that was why Sylvia and Joe Robinson took pains to diversify their roster. Who knew how long their rap ride would last?

While the "Queen of Rap" made her vanity record in New Jersey, other artists and entrepreneurs back in New York took rap very seriously.

To them, what was happening wasn't a fad. It was the flowering of a true culture that had both a deep history and a manifest destiny.

To Fred Theopholis Brathwaite, Marcus Garvey's Harlem street-corner rap was compelling. *Everywhere around the world,* the Jamaican-born Garvey said, *the Black man is exploited and oppressed. What the Black man needs is global racial unity.*

And when in the 1920s Garvey needed someone to head the Brooklyn chapter of his Universal Negro Improvement Association, he called on Brathwaite, a fellow West Indian with a similarly sophisticated perspective.

Brathwaite passed his political outlook to his son, Fred Delacey Brathwaite, who sat in Harlem's Audubon Ballroom in 1965 as assassins cut down another champion of Black Nationalism, Malcolm X.

The second Fred bequeathed that viewpoint to his own son, Fred Leroy Brathwaite, who listened as his father hosted an ongoing salon in the Brathwaites' Brooklyn brownstone. The impromptu gatherings often included the greats of the jazz world: Miles Davis, Dizzy Gillespie, Thelonious Monk, and Fred's godfather, Max Roach.

As the 1960s gave way to the 1970s, little Fred had one advantage over his friends who ran the streets of Brooklyn's declining Bedford-Stuyvesant neighborhood: a history. Fred, the third in his line, knew the world was bigger than the block. He ran wild during the day, but his activities were bounded by his father's example, his mother's nightly curfew, and a sense that he was part of something bigger than himself.

Within that frame, Fred developed a picture of the street culture around him. He was barely out of grade school when the sound systems, rapping DJs, breakers, and graffiti writers came to the streets and subways of Brooklyn. He cut classes at Dewey High School on Coney Island to "bomb" trains in the rail yard, tagging his alias, BULL 99, between the morning and evening rush.

While studying art history at Medgar Evers College in Brooklyn, Fred Brathwaite discovered how pop artists like Warhol took the everyday objects of mass media and consumer culture and turned them into daring and worthy works. For Fred, the parallels to the graffiti world were clear. Even the element of vandalism had its precedent in the art world, like Futurism and Dadaism. Brathwaite mused: *If the pop artists can appropriate an image of Mickey Mouse on a canvas and be taken as serious artists, why can't we be respected for our murals on trains, or on the side of a building?* Brathwaite's question became a quest to create legitimacy for the reviled graffiti culture of New York.

First, Brathwaite would have to create legitimacy for himself. He had little reputation in the graffiti community. But he did have a strong rap. Brathwaite talked fast and talked slick, befriending the legendary Lee Quiñones, who wrote as part of a crew called the Fabulous Five—so named because they virtually "owned" the number 5 train line that snaked its way through the Bronx. Brathwaite pitched Lee on his idea: He wanted to take the Fabulous Five to bomb an even better train line, the art world. For Fred, who never touted himself as a great artist, the partnership was a chance to align himself with the best crew in the city. Brathwaite ditched his former tag of BULL 99 for a new one, FRED FAB 5. For Lee, it was an opportunity to see his work on a bigger canvas than he had ever imagined. Quiñones was the genius for painting. Brathwaite was the guy with the gift for framing things.

Just to make his argument plain, Brathwaite "bombed" a car on the 5 train, covering it with spray-painted Campbell's soup cans, an homage to Warhol. It was a deliberate attempt to show graffiti's critics that the young artists of New York were more than vandals. The "Soup Can Train" became Brathwaite's calling card.

His next target was a lieutenant of Warhol himself. Glenn O'Brien edited Warhol's *Interview* magazine, and was intrigued enough by Brathwaite's graffiti manifesto that he made an introduction to Howard Smith of the *Village Voice*. But Smith was a bit more cynical than O'Brien when Brathwaite announced his intention to sell the Fab Five's graffiti services for $5 per square foot. "You name it, pay us, we'll paint it," Brathwaite boasted.

"Are you *kidding*?" Smith responded. "Most people I know in the city are trying to get rid of you spray-can freaks!"

Smith reported Brathwaite's indignant reaction in his February 12, 1979, *Village Voice* article: "He puffed himself up in his spiffy suit and tie, and pounced back: 'It's that kind of attitude I have to fight. I think it's time everyone realized graffiti is the purest form of New York art.'" Despite their disagreement, Smith was impressed enough by the Fab Five's sketches that he printed Brathwaite's phone number in the article.

Brathwaite got calls. Italian art dealer Claudio Bruni invited the Fab Five to submit five canvases for a show at the Galleria La Medusa in Rome. The opening would be Brathwaite's first trip to Europe and an auspicious entry into the art world. The five pieces sold for $1,000 each.

Upon his return to New York, Brathwaite became a fixture on the downtown art scene. A promoter named Michael Holman, who found Fred through the *Voice* article, introduced him to another young Black artist from Brooklyn who tagged esoteric sayings around town under the sobriquet SAMO. FRED FAB 5 and SAMO—real name, Jean-Michel Basquiat—already knew of each other's work. Brathwaite and Basquiat became good friends.

The center of Brathwaite's new world was Glenn O'Brien's cable access show, *Glenn O'Brien's TV Party*, where Fred became a regular behind and in front of the camera, and made friends with the Clash and the Talking Heads. Brathwaite was tightest with O'Brien's cohost, Chris Stein, and his girlfriend, Deborah Harry, who led the new-wave group Blondie.

For most of the late 1970s, Blondie had been a respected underground new-wave band in New York. But a hit record in 1979 called "Heart of Glass" had made Blondie world-famous, and Debbie Harry an international star. Brathwaite could scarcely believe that the cool chick he hung out and smoked with was now on the cover of *Rolling Stone*, a glamorous pinup girl. But Harry still doted on Fred, pushing food on the lanky teenager when he visited the West Side apartment she shared with Stein. Brathwaite couldn't resist the opportunity that came with being this close to stardom.

"I plan to be very big. I want you to make a song about me," Brathwaite said, lobbying for the ultimate "tag."

"Freddie," Harry replied. "You're so crazy. You want a sandwich?"

Fred's downtown friends became more curious about the uptown culture he peddled. So Brathwaite organized a field trip. The whole O'Brien *TV Party* crew came up to Harlem and the Bronx. Harry, Stein, O'Brien, and friends took in a show at the Webster Avenue Police Athletic League, experiencing breaking, DJing, and MCing firsthand. Brathwaite, true to form, framed everything for them. This was a true culture, he said, because it incorporated all the necessary elements—music, dance, and a visual art. He described the parallels he saw between the uptown scene and the punk movement—two underground cultures, one White, one Black, but both rebellions against the status quo. Fred described the players: the Cold Crush Brothers, he said, were one of the best rapping crews around. The Mercedes Ladies were fly. And the man on the turntables was Flash, who got his name because he was the fastest of all the DJs.

What Brathwaite hoped to get out of the excursion was a cultural event— to get Blondie and Chic to do a show together, and put Grandmaster Flash & the Furious Five on the bill. Brathwaite's big gig never happened. But Brathwaite did get his cultural event. Just not in the way he thought.

"We just finished a new record," Stein and Harry told Brathwaite over the phone. "We have some new things that we can't wait to play for you."

Brathwaite dropped by the couple's apartment on 58th Street, and Stein played a song for him on cassette. It was a funky groove, with a bare-bones bass riff, and church bells accompanying Debbie Harry's sweetly sung melody: "Toe to toe, dancing very close, / Barely breathing, almost comatose, / Wall to wall, people hypnotized, / And they're stepping lightly, hang each night in rrrrrapture. . . ."

Then, to Brathwaite's surprise, Harry started to rap: "Fab 5 Freddy told me everybody's fly, / DJ's spinnin', I said, 'My, my.' / Flash is fast, Flash is cool."

Brathwaite smiled. Debbie had taken their Bronx trip and turned it into a song. How sweet that she even remembered his request to mention his name—although Harry had reversed the words in Brathwaite's tag, FRED FAB 5. *Still*, Brathwaite thought, *Fab 5 Freddy is cool. I could work with that.*

At first, Brathwaite assumed that Chris and Debbie had made the record as a goof. But Stein intended to make it part of a "visual album" issued on a new technology called laser disc. When the time came to shoot, Stein and Harry asked Brathwaite to fill the set with the characters and color of the uptown culture. Maybe get Flash himself to appear, as he was the only other person mentioned in the song besides Fred.

But Brathwaite could not get a commitment from Flash. So on the day of the shoot Brathwaite grabbed his friend Jean-Michel Basquiat and told him to stand behind the turntables.

"Act like you're the DJ," Brathwaite told him.

Basquiat just looked at him. *Whatever.*

As the music played and cameras rolled, Debbie Harry strolled around the set, stepping from Basquiat to Brathwaite, who painted a mural with Lee Quiñones in the background.

In the winter of 1981 Brathwaite made his second trip to Europe, trying to raise money for a scheme he had launched with filmmaker Charlie Ahearn—to shoot a movie that takes place in and around the Bronx b-boy culture. Brathwaite met with the investors in Germany then went to Italy for an art show. In Milan he ran into his friends from *TV Party*, the B-52s and the Talking Heads, who invited Brathwaite to Paris.

Fred Leroy, grandson of Fred Theopholis, watched the City of Light sparkle as he rode in a car with Talking Heads members Tina Weymouth and Chris Frantz. *This is the life*, he thought. The radio played, and Brathwaite slowly realized what he was hearing.

"Fab Five Freddie told me everybody's fly, /DJ's spinnin', I said, 'My, my.' / Flash is fast, Flash is cool."

This is Chris and Debbie's new song, right? Weymouth and Frantz asked. Brathwaite was numb. He could barely get the words out of his mouth.

"They played it for me," he said, dumbly. "I thought it was a joke."

It wasn't. "Rapture" was not only a huge hit for Blondie in the spring of 1981, selling over 500,000 copies as the second single from *Autoamerican*. The song that Brathwaite inspired was also the first record containing rap to reach number one on the U.S. pop charts, though that rap was written and performed by a tourist. Later on that summer, Stein's "Rapture" video aired on the very first day of broadcast for a new cable venture, one devoted entirely to playing promotional clips of rock songs, called Music Television. It was rap's stealth debut on the channel, and Fab 5 Freddy's first appearance on MTV. It would not be his last.

Blondie and Fred Brathwaite actually helped bring rap to television more than once. In February of 1981 Debbie Harry was invited to host NBC-TV's *Saturday Night Live*, and on Brathwaite's recommendation, she pulled in as her musical guests the Funky Four Plus One More, a crew that mirrored Blondie in that both groups boasted a central female member. In the case of the Funky Four, MC Sha-Rock was the "Plus One."

At ten minutes to one in the morning, the group performed their Sugar Hill record "That's the Joint" live for a national audience.

A few months later, in the wake of "Rapture," Debbie Harry and Fred Brathwaite were approached by a TV producer who had just started working for the ABC newsmagazine show *20/20*. He introduced himself as Danny Schechter and said he wanted to shoot a segment on rap, break dancing, and graffiti.

The uptown culture reminded Schechter of his childhood in the Bronx, when doo-wop groups sang on every corner, when he used to listen to Jocko Henderson rap on WWRL. A friend and coconspirator of Abbie Hoffman, Schechter had long been an activist and a subversive—in the 1960s, he had helped plan the March on Washington and conspired with the NAACP to integrate Baltimore's weekly "bandstand" TV dance party, *The Buddy Deane Show*, on which White teens danced on certain days and Black teens on others. Now rap culture provided Schechter with yet another opportunity to sneak some Black people in through mass media's back door.

Fred Brathwaite in particular helped Schechter understand the history of the culture and introduced him to important figures. Finally, Schechter went to sell his idea to *20/20*'s executive producer, Av Westin. The prominence of "Rapture" on the charts helped convince Westin to give Schechter the green light, with one caveat: In order to sell this Black street stuff to his overwhelmingly White audience, their guide through this strange world had to be the most whitebread anchor on the *20/20* roster, the blond-haired, blue-eyed Steve Fox.

When "Rapping to the Beat" finally aired in the spring of 1981, the first nationally televised piece of journalism on the rap and b-boy phenomenon, it was a concise and respectful guide to the culture, covering every major step in rap's evolution—from the oral poetry of the Black South, to the call and response of Black preachers and congregations, to Black street games of "double Dutch," to Cab Calloway's jazz scatting, to reggae toasts, to Muhammad Ali's boasts. At the end of the piece, Fox read Schechter's audacious prediction.

"Rap is likely to influence popular music for years to come," Fox said. "It has tremendous staying power, because it lets ordinary people express ideas they care about, in language they can relate to, set to music they can dance to."

The music quieted, and the picture dissolved to host Hugh Downs and Steve Fox, sitting together behind the anchor desk.

"That's marvelous," Downs said. "And it *is* infectious, too, isn't it? Thank you, Steve."

The first rap records were released into an environment that was arguably the most hostile to Black music in American history. Whipped into a fury by the "death to disco" movement, many Americans—mostly young, White males who became alienated from Black music when their favorite rock stations stopped playing Black artists in the mid-1970s—declared "rap" to be disco's insipid offspring in need of ridicule and, if possible, a lynching. Disco's White opponents took great advantage of the fact that rap rhymed with "crap."

Of course, many of the founders of the b-boy movement rejected disco, too, and with it the upscale, older rapping disco DJs like Hollywood. The enmity toward the glitzy disco scene was the reason why they had become b-boys and b-girls in the first place. To people like Fred Brathwaite and Afrika Bambaataa their culture was more than "rap," as rapping had been a part of Black culture since the first slaves arrived in America, and went all the way back to Africa. *What we're doing in the streets of New York*, they claimed, *is something new.* Soon, figures like Bambaataa and Brathwaite began using the term "hip-hop" to distinguish themselves from disco and to name an entire street culture that had, until then, been nameless. To them, hip-hop comprised four disparate but related activities—MCing, DJing, breaking (or break dancing), and graffiti writing.

"Hip-hop" was purist terminology. It was partly a backlash against the commercial sensibilities of the Sugar Hill Gang; and also against the bourgeois, mercenary attitudes of Sugar Hill Records' proprietors, whom Afrika Bambaataa dubbed Sylvia and Joe "Rob-a-Nigger." It may even have reflected a bit of rivalry between the decidedly downtrodden Bronx and the more flashy, ambitious Harlem. The term "hip-hop" was also an endeavor to claim a real musical and cultural distinction between disco and the park jams, between processed music and raw funk, between grown folk and kids, between conformists and rebels, between people who saw themselves as the lubricant for partygoers and others who saw themselves as serious artists.

The flyers for Charlie Ahearn's and Fred Brathwaite's film *Wild Style* announced that "the hip-hop movie has arrived." The film showcased the talents of the originators of the Bronx street culture: MCs like Caz and the Cold Crush Brothers, DJs like Grandmaster Flash, breakers like the Rock Steady Crew, and graffiti writers like Lee Quiñones and Lady Pink. The movie captured rap in its street milieu, from Cold Crush battling the Fantastic Five on the basketball court to the duo Double Trouble on a front stoop. "Here's a little story that must be told," they rapped, "about two young brothers who were put on hold."

Even Brathwaite brought his slick talk to the screen as a promoter named "Phade." There was room for everyone. Everyone, except the *other* originators, the rapping DJs of the discotheques, like DJ Hollywood, Eddie Cheba, and Lovebug Starski.

The eclipse of the great rapping DJs of the discos was accelerated because the artists didn't make records fast enough or good enough. Grammy-winning producer Ralph MacDonald was the first to tap the talents of the legendary DJ Hollywood on a single called "Shock, Shock the House." MacDonald had enough clout to walk the record into Epic, the major label that was home to Michael Jackson. But he couldn't capture the energy of Hollywood's live shows.

Meanwhile, cocaine had turned Hollywood's already superhuman work ethic and enthusiasm into something toxic, and transformed his confidence into egomania and denial. The chubby entertainer didn't sleep. He would run from party to after-party, spending the daylight hours indoors, sniffing lines, and then return wired to the next night's round of gigs on the club circuit. Hollywood had started out getting high. Now the high was getting Hollywood.

As a result, Anthony "DJ Hollywood" Holloway—the first person to rhyme to the beat over instrumental sections of records, the first DJ to head-line the Apollo Theater, the first successful entrepreneur of the rap era—faded into obscurity. Kool Herc, the gentle Bronx giant who married rhymes with the breaks, became viewed as hip-hop's sole originator. The two DJs had disparaged each other in the past, and the real-life antipathy between the two figures mirrored the tension between the polar impulses of rap and of Black America as a whole—upscale versus downscale, aspirational versus proletarian, commercial versus street, profit versus principle.

However, the "hip-hop" notion—that all this stuff was a real culture, a true art form—opened up the possibility that the rapping, the breaking, the DJing, the art, and the fashion could be more than an ephemeral craze. As rock and roll had proven decades earlier, it could be good business. But rock's staying power as a music was assured by the development of recording artists, who made not only hit singles, but held their audience's interest over the course of entire albums and entire careers; whose success could also support the growth of not just one record company but an industry.

Rock and roll had long had its kings. Now hip-hop would need kings of its own, and, with them, kingmakers.

ALBUM TWO

GENIUS OF RAP

Creating hip-hop's first superstars

(1980—1984)

Side A
Disco Inferno

T he New York Yankees needed to win this one. They had dropped the first two games of the 1980 American League Championship Series to the Royals in Kansas City, but on a Friday in early October, the Bronx Bombers returned home for their last shot at the pennant.

Cory Robbins, the twenty-three-year-old head of Panorama Records, wasn't much of a baseball fan. For Robbins, the best part of a game was the beer and conversation. He had been invited to the play-offs by his friend Tom Silverman, who ran an industry "tip sheet" called "Dance Music Report." Tom—a half-Italian, half-Jewish kid in his twenties—was always quick with a witty comment or clever observation. The two talked through a rain delay and most of the game.

A lot can happen when you take your eye off the ball. By the seventh inning Reggie Jackson helped the Yankees to a 2–1 lead. But when the Yanks sent in their ace closer "Goose" Gossage, he gave up a three-run home run to George Brett that landed in the upper decks. With just two innings left to play, the Yankees never recovered. The team that took the World Series just two years earlier was swept clean by the Royals. Robbins and Silverman walked down the ramps with thousands of dejected fans.

Robbins felt a bit like the Yanks himself. He had come so close to success with the label he ran, Panorama, which had a promising start with disco singles from groups like the Fantastic Aleems. But after two years with no breakthrough hit, Panorama was likely going to be shut down.

In the past year the fortunes of both Robbins and Silverman had taken a turn for the worse, in part because of what had happened at another baseball game halfway across the country. On July 12, 1979, in between the games of a White Sox–Tigers doubleheader at Chicago's Comiskey Park, a local rock radio station, WLUP-FM, sponsored "Disco Demolition Night." The event was the brainchild of disc jockey Steve Dahl, who told his listeners on "The Loop" that anybody who brought a disco record to the stadium would be admitted for 98 cents. So many people brought disco records to destroy that Dahl's people couldn't collect them all. Between the two games—to the jeering of fans chanting and holding banners that read, DISCO SUCKS—twenty thousand records were placed in a wooden crate at center field and blown up. Then things got out of hand. Thousands of antidisco fanatics—most of them young White men—swarmed the field, ripping up the sod and overturning the batting cage. The uncollected disco records whistled down from the stands like Frisbees, cracking and crashing onto the field and into the crowd. In the end, four people were injured, forty arrested, and the White Sox were forced to cancel the second game.

The Comiskey Park riot marked the symbolic end of the disco era. "Disco Sucks" became the rallying cry of millions of young Americans. At the time of the "Disco Demolition Night," six out of the top ten Billboard pop singles were disco records—including Chic's "Good Times," the musical template for "Rapper's Delight." On the same date one year later, the number had been reduced to just one out of ten. Disco-oriented record companies and their artists, like RSO Records and the Bee Gees, tanked. Few in the industry saw it coming, but a lot can happen when you take your eye off the ball.

For Tom Silverman this was a huge problem. He had ditched his graduate studies in environmental geology to start "Disco News," a newsletter intended to create communication between record companies and the DJs who played their records, and to make some money for Silverman. He had heard that the leading rock tip sheet, "Friday Morning Quarterback," billed up to $50,000 a week in record company advertising, and he had hope "Disco News" would do the same. But now that record companies were dropping disco artists, and "disco" itself had become a dirty word, Silverman hastily changed his publication's name to "Dance Music Report." As a result of disco's fall, Silverman was looking at a much less lucrative business than he had imagined. But Silverman, a DJ himself, understood that disco hadn't really died. It had just returned home to the Black and gay underground.

For Cory Robbins, disco had been his entrée into the music business. As a "song plugger" for MCA Music Publishing, he had signed the disco hit "(Push Push) In the Bush." Panorama, MCA Music's boutique label, was

Robbins's reward for his success. He had often said that Panorama was the perfect job, and if he ever lost it, the only thing left to do would be to start his own company. Robbins hadn't quite figured out that part yet.

Robbins's last shot at a hit record slipped right through his fingers when Rocky Ford and J. B. Moore welshed on their agreement with him for Kurtis Blow's "Christmas Rappin'." Instead, they gave the record to Mercury. *Those gold records for "Christmas Rappin'" and "The Breaks" would have been mine*, thought Robbins. Who knew if there would ever be another "rapping" hit, especially with disco on the wane?

By the time that Robbins and Silverman filed out of Yankee Stadium and onto River Street, the rain had broken, and it wasn't too cold. Silverman made a suggestion: Instead of taking the train back to Manhattan, why not stay in the Bronx and go to a disco to check out this really fantastic DJ named Afrika Bambaataa? Robbins had never heard of the guy before, and the prospect of staying in the crime-racked Bronx until the wee hours of the morning wasn't exactly appealing.

Silverman knew that Robbins was a creature of habit. Robbins liked to eat at the same restaurants and go to the same clubs in an almost unvarying daily routine. So Silverman offered a challenge: "'Peculiar travel suggestions are dancing lessons from God,'" he said, quoting Kurt Vonnegut. The words surprised and delighted Robbins, who thought perhaps that they came from Silverman himself.

"Okay," Robbins said.

The two travelers pushed deeper into the Bronx. They took a car to the corner of White Plains and Gun Hill roads, where they could see a late-night crowd milling in front of a four-story brick building. Above a record shop, on the second floor, a bright yellow sign fringed in flashing electric bulbs read, T Connection Discoteque. As far as Robbins could see, they were the only White people in the entire neighborhood. He had certainly never been to an all-Black club.

Silverman and Robbins entered and walked up a steep flight of steps, the beats growing louder as they climbed to a door that opened up onto the dance floor. They made their way through the packed disco to the DJ booth. Robbins saw Bambaataa for the first time—huge, dark skinned, and imposing. When Bambaataa greeted Silverman and his guest with a warm smile, Robbins loosened up, enjoying his behind-the-scenes view of the DJ as he worked through his set.

Something was different about this disco. First, Robbins noticed that

Bambaataa wasn't spinning the 12-inch records that most downtown DJs favored, but reaching into stacks of old, dusty 45s instead. He wasn't playing disco at all, rather a bunch of old rock songs like "Dizzy" by Tommy Roe. Bambaataa didn't even play the whole song, just the drum intro. The kids were dancing like crazy. Over on the stage, some guys were rapping to the beat into a really crappy microphone. The tinny vocals along with the scratchy records created a racket. In the chaos, a new world slowly opened up for Cory Robbins. *This*, he realized, *is where rap comes from.*

This meant that there might be more rap records coming, too. Maybe he would have another shot after all. This, it seemed, was a whole new ball game.

Cory Robbins was a born hit man.

Warren and Paula Robbins claimed that their son's first word as a baby was "radio." As a toddler, little Cory would issue the word as a command when he walked into the homes of friends and relatives. The adults would oblige with the flick of a switch and turn of the dial, and Cory would sit for hours, listening, remembering every song.

His grandfather owned a bar in Queens called the Red Velvet Lounge. Every few weeks, a man would come to change the records in the jukebox, pulling out fifteen to twenty 7-inch records, pushing in replacements. Grandpa saved the old records for Cory, who took dozens of 45s back home to Warren and Paula's house in the modest, middle-class neighborhood of Hollis. Cory amassed a collection of hundreds before he reached grade school, songs like "He's So Fine," by the Chiffons, and "Sherry," by the Four Seasons.

As Hollis declined, the Robbins family moved to suburban Rockland County. Cory's father owned a chain of discount clothing stores in suburban New York called the Sample Nook, and Cory inherited his entrepreneurial spirit. He shoveled snow, got a paper route, performed magic shows, and started a mail-order company to sell magic tricks. Cory spent all the money he made on two things: records, and books about records—especially the expensive hardback volumes of historical Billboard charts compiled by Joel Whitburn. They were expensive, almost $40 apiece. Cory bought as many as he could afford, and he prided himself on knowing release dates, discographies, and chart positions of records. To Cory, the science of hits was even more compelling than the art of music.

As a teenager, Cory played guitar in a band called the Centrifugal Force, and started writing "hits" of his own. Usually, the songs were throwbacks to the 1950s, with titles like "When Oldies Weren't Old," and "We're out of Love." Dion might have recorded the songs, Cory thought, if it weren't 1972.

If Cory Robbins's compositions were behind the times, so were his aspirations. During an era when most bands created their own material, Robbins wanted to be a songwriter.

At the turn of the twentieth century, before the advent of records and recording artists, composers were the kings of the music business: Irving Berlin, George M. Cohan, Scott Joplin. Songwriters were signed by music publishers, who distributed the songs as sheet music, paying the composers a royalty for every copy sold. When phonograph record companies and radio stations emerged, songwriters and their publishers received a couple of pennies for each disc sold, and more every time a radio station played one of their songs. After World War II the pennies from records and radio added up to millions. But the rise of rock and roll changed the balance of power in the music industry. Performers became their *own* composers, eclipsing freelance songwriters and the "song pluggers" who pitched their work to artists. Music publishers became more like bankers, collecting tens of millions of pennies and nickels, while record company executives became the new moguls, accumulating the largest cut of the music consumer's dollar.

But in the 1970s, the geography of the music business still echoed the old order of things. Many record companies were still huddled in the two buildings where the greatest songwriters and music publishers were once headquartered: in the Brill Building on 1619 Broadway at 49th Street, and at 1650 Broadway two blocks to the north.

In 1974 sixteen-year-old Cory Robbins made regular trips to both buildings to pitch his songs to publishers. One day, he stood in the lobby of 1650 Broadway with a reel-to-reel demo tape in his hand, gazing up at the directory of hundreds of small companies.

"Are you trying to audition material?"

Cory Robbins turned around to see an older man standing behind him.

"Yes, I am," Robbins replied.

"Come on up."

The man was Bob Reno, the head of Midland International Records. Reno listened to the songs while Robbins sat in his office. When he told Robbins he wasn't impressed, Reno went out of his way to be nice about it. Robbins kept coming back to play Reno more mediocre songs, all the while meeting people in Midland's offices, like Reno's partner Eddie O'Loughlin. Eventually Robbins decided that he liked what the publishers were doing more than he liked songwriting. Still in high school, Robbins asked Reno for a job.

Bob Reno had developed a soft spot for the cute, unflappable kid, so he let Robbins listen to Midland's incoming demo tapes. After Robbins's high school graduation, Reno gave him a summer gig. Robbins was so helpful that, while he was still a freshman at the State University of New York at New Paltz, Reno coaxed him to quit school to run Midland's nascent publishing division. Working for Midland full time, Robbins found songs for Midland recording artists to perform and pitched Midland-owned songs to other labels.

When Robbins took the job in 1976, Midland International was already a successful disco label, with hits like Silver Convention's "Fly, Robin, Fly," Carol Douglas's "Doctor's Orders"—both signed by O'Loughlin—and most recently, "Let Her In," a top-ten pop record sung by a sitcom heartthrob named John Travolta, who had just signed on to play the lead role in a small film about the disco scene in Brooklyn. Robbins had come to love disco and even worked as a club DJ on weekends. One day, Reno decided that he didn't want his young employee moonlighting, and he ordered him to stop. Robbins thought it was unfair, and puzzling, too: How could Reno not understand how DJing kept him at the center of the disco scene, kept him knowing what was hot? After only seven months at Midland, Robbins decided that he would rather keep DJing than stay.

The next year, the nineteen-year-old Robbins coproduced his first record with a friend named Joe Tucci. They recorded the song "Keep It Up" for $1,600. They sold it a few days later to RCA Records for $4,000. Soon Eddie O'Loughlin recommended Robbins for a job picking and plugging songs for MCA Music Publishing. By the time Robbins was twenty-one, he was running Panorama Records.

At Panorama, during disco's heyday, Cory Robbins met Steve Plotnicki, another Jewish guy in his early twenties, who worked at a local record distributor while pursuing his dream of being a rock songwriter. But no one wanted to buy rock songs. Irwin Schuster, a VP at Chappell Music Publishing, told Plotnicki flat out that if he wanted to sell his music, he had better start writing disco. Plotnicki did it grudgingly. He was a Grateful Dead fan. When it came to Black music, he liked old jazz and blues. He didn't know anything about disco. But good songwriting, like any other discipline, has a structure that transcends specific styles: interesting lyrics, a compelling refrain, and a catchy melody. These qualities Plotnicki kept in mind as he wrote, guitar in hand. These qualities a good music executive could hear even through the worst recording.

When Robbins found Plotnicki's demo tape for a song called "Love Insurance," he paired the song with a singer named Sharon Redd. "Love Insurance" by Front Page became a top-five disco hit. Plotnicki's daily calls to Robbins to track the progress of the song evolved into a friendship.

By the time that Panorama's distribution deal had expired in early 1981, Robbins and Plotnicki were kicking around an idea that they might start a record company together. Plotnicki would write the songs and Robbins would produce the records. The only problem was that, in the last two years, disco had crashed and taken the record business with it.

To survive, Robbins and Plotnicki chose to mine what was left of the 12-inch-singles market, which still supported small labels in New York like Prelude and West End. Dance songs were getting slower, funkier, and Blacker, like the song "Heartbeat" by Taana Gardner, proof that you could still make some money with the right song.

Robbins never forgot his missed opportunity with Kurtis Blow. Sugar Hill was a huge company now, and uptown labels like Enjoy were selling records, too. Plotnicki regaled Robbins with tales of the "street guys" who would come into the distributor where he worked, unloading boxes of rap 12-inches out of the trunk of their cars and leaving with thousands of dollars in cash. He would often sell the entire trunkload to his own customers in less than an hour.

"Clearly," Plotnicki told Robbins, "if those guys can do it, we can do it."

When Cory Robbins and Steve Plotnicki decided to open Profile Records in May of 1981, they each borrowed $17,000 from their parents. With the $34,000 in start-up cash, they rented a room for $700 a month in a building on the corner of Broadway and 57th Street, just blocks from the Brill Building and 1650 Broadway on one end, and the offices of Sugar Hill partner Morris Levy on the other. West End Records, their soon-to-be competition, was upstairs.

Running a record company wasn't like they thought it would be. Plotnicki never got around to writing songs, and Robbins didn't end up producing. Instead, Robbins handled talent scouting and promotion. Plotnicki, with his experience at the distributor, took care of sales and manufacturing.

For its first single, Profile Records paid $3,000 to license a disco record from England called "I'm Starting Again." It seemed like a good idea: The singer, Grace Kennedy, was a TV star in the U.K. But in America, her record flopped, selling only a few thousand copies.

Profile's second record was the label's first rap release. Robbins made a deal with his former Panorama artists, the Fantastic Aleems, who had already put out a 12-inch single on their own Nia label with a young Harlem rapper, Lonnie Love. The reissue, called "Young Ladies," cost Robbins and Plotnicki a very uncomfortable $5,500. The track was a replay of Cheryl Lynn's "Got to Be Real"—a dance hit which, like "Good Times," was ripe for a rap sendup in the tradition of "Rapper's Delight." Another good idea, and it flopped, too.

Robbins then licensed a second record from England, a dance-infused medley of the Four Seasons' greatest hits recorded by Gidea Park called "Seasons of Gold." The song seemed to be another safe bet. But by the time he had closed the deal on "Seasons" in October 1981, Profile was in peril.

Profile Records' founders hadn't drawn salaries from their fledgling company. To survive, they were still collecting unemployment checks, illegally. But between the costs of licensing and commissioning the records, pressing and shipping them, along with their overhead—rent, electricity, phones— they were down to their last $2,000.

For a moment, Robbins and Plotnicki considered asking their parents for more money. Instead, they decided to gamble the rest on one more record. Plotnicki suggested a rap version of "Genius of Love," the new record by the Tom Tom Club.

One of the dominant club tracks of 1981, "Genius of Love" was a successor to Blondie's "Rapture," a product of the collision of uptown and downtown cultures happening in New York. A funk record conceived by Fab 5 Freddy's friends Tina Weymouth and Chris Frantz, "Genius of Love" was embraced enthusiastically by young Black kids who had never heard of Weymouth and Frantz's other group—the new-wave band Talking Heads.

"Genius of Love" was an inspired candidate for a rap remake. But Plotnicki and Robbins had to move fast. Another label, like Sugar Hill, was sure to come out with their own version. And Profile's rent was due.

First, Robbins called his old friend Joe Tucci, who had recorded a huge disco hit called "Keep on Dancin'," right out of his own sixteen-track home studio.

"Joe," Robbins asked, "can you record an exact replay of 'Genius of Love'?"

No problem, Tucci answered. Robbins offered him $750 for the entire project.

Next, Robbins called Island Music Publishing to secure the rights to re-record "Genius of Love." They would pay Island ten cents per record sold, a rate mandated by U.S. law.

After that, Robbins called the only rapper he knew: Lonnie Love.

Before he met Cory Robbins and Steve Plotnicki, Alonzo Brown had never had a real conversation with a White person.

Brown had grown up in the DeWitt Clinton housing project in East Harlem with his mother, Margaret, and older brother, James. Their father, Baxter, had died of heart failure when Brown was only fourteen. An older Puerto Rican girl who lived in the building, Miriam, took pity on the Brown brothers—both quiet boys who mostly stayed inside and played records. She took them to the ice-skating rink at the Harlem Meer, just a few blocks away in the northeast corner of Central Park.

The rink became an obsession for Alonzo and James, who kept sneaking in until they got caught. The foreman of the rink, Mr. Johnson, cut them a deal. "People are complaining about the music here," he said. If the Brown brothers came in and played records for the crowd of kids, he would let them in for free.

Alonzo and James formed the Lasker Skate Crew, hauling records to the rink every Saturday. They even got a grant from the city to purchase speakers, which they did on Canal Street from none other than Mr. Magic, who still worked at S&H Electronics while broadcasting his rap radio show on WHBI.

On the night Brown went to Harlem's Renaissance Theatre and saw his first rapper—Lovebug Starski telling the crowd to scream, "Oh, yeah!" and seven hundred people responding in unison—he knew he wanted that kind of power. Brown began writing rhymes and practicing them in the hallways of Charles Evans Hughes High School with his classmate, Andre Harrell. Soon Brown and Harrell were writing routines together. While Brown focused on the substance of the lyrics, Harrell was concerned with style—clothes, hair, presentation. Harrell was also good with marketing—hustling for gigs, getting into the mix—and he insisted they needed a gimmick.

At first Harrell and Brown billed themselves as "the Lone Ranger" and "Tonto," but by the time they finally started to perform at clubs and community centers around East and Central Harlem, they were calling themselves "Dr. Jeckyll" and "Mr. Hyde," respectively. They sported mustaches, wore pants from A. J. Lester's men's shop on 125th Street, Cortefiel coats, and sneakers called Playboys. Alonzo was the taller of the two, standing a lean six feet even, not including his Afro. His girlfriend, Wanda Majors, had even made herself a sweatshirt that read, "Mrs. Hyde."

By the time they made it to the rapping contests at Harlem World on 116th and Lenox, Dr. Jeckyll & Mr. Hyde were the neighborhood favorite. They even recorded a few routines that ended up on 12-inch records for two small uptown imprints, Rojac and Tayster, run by Harlem World's owner, "Fat" Jack Taylor. At Harlem World, Alonzo Brown's lyrical abilities caught the attention of two huge, muscled twin brothers, Taharqa and Tunde Ra Aleem. The Aleems were accomplished musicians who had shared an apartment with Jimi Hendrix in the 1960s and collaborated with him on a few projects, even contributing backup vocals to his song "Dolly Dagger." By 1980 the Aleems were already accomplished recording artists and had an R&B hit on their label, Nia Records, called "Hooked on Your Love," reissued by Panorama Records after being signed by its young general manger, Cory Robbins.

Alonzo Brown adopted a solo moniker—Lonnie Love—and cut "Young Ladies" for Nia, giving his partner, Andre Harrell, label credit for helping with the lyrics. Meanwhile, Robbins had told the Aleems that he had started a new record company and was looking for music. The Aleems took Brown to meet Robbins and his new partner at Profile. This new label with the downtown office seemed like the big time, and Brown was nervous. He was surprised to see that Robbins and Plotnicki were, too. The two White guys tried to project confidence, but he suspected that they didn't know what they were doing.

"Young Ladies" sold a few records—in Florida, for some reason—and then quickly went away. Brown grew restless. He didn't want to spend the rest of his life in East Harlem. By the time he got a call from Robbins in October of 1981 asking him to rap on another record, "Lonnie Love" had already enlisted in the air force.

But Alonzo Brown agreed to make the record anyway, and asked if he could record the song with his partner, Andre Harrell.

"Genius Rap" came together quickly. Plotnicki had gotten the idea on a Monday. On Tuesday, Joe Tucci recorded the backing track, playing all the instruments himself: bass, guitar, synthesizer, and the Linn drum machine. On Wednesday, Brown and Harrell piled into a car with Plotnicki and Robbins and headed out to Tucci's row house in Richmond Hill, Queens.

Tucci had retrofitted his one-car garage into a recording studio, building an addition for a control booth, and suspending a wooden floor six inches above the concrete for sound insulation. In the live room, on a floor covered in red indoor-outdoor carpet with black musical notes and staves, Harrell and Brown recited their rhymes culled from old, well-rehearsed routines as Dr. Jeckyll & Mr. Hyde. In the singsong, showman style of DJ Hollywood and Eddie Cheba, Mr. Hyde rhymed about the life for which his alter ego, Alonzo—still living with his mother in the Clinton projects—longed: a real stereo system and a Sony TV in a penthouse with a view of Central Park; women, money, and the microphone.

Brown watched the young record execs in the booth, Plotnicki smiling and bobbing his head to the music, Robbins more intense and focused. Recording was harder than Brown expected. It wasn't like rocking in a club. Tucci had to keep reminding them: *Keep your heads still. Don't face each other; face the microphone. Stop touching and knocking the mic; all that extra sound ends up on tape.*

Robbins, Plotnicki, and their girlfriends entered the booth and recorded all the "party people" sounds: clapping, screaming on cue, adding their responses to the rappers' calls.

By Thursday Tucci had mixed the song. On Friday, Robbins took a reel-to-reel tape and dropped it by WHBI in time for Mr. Magic's show that night.

On Saturday, less than twenty-four hours after Mr. Magic had played "Genius Rap" for the first time, Robbins stopped by a record store called the Music Factory, tucked into a storefront on the southeast corner of Times Square. Behind the counter sat, as always, Stanley Platzer. An obese, balding Jewish man, Platzer had compiled "the book"—a handwritten catalog of every vital "break" record he had ever heard mentioned or requested by the DJs who visited him. Because of his obsessive dedication to his clientele,

Platzer had become the improbable, indispensable authority on rap records and breaks for New York's best hip-hop DJs.

Robbins—with his baby face, dimpled chin, and curly hair—could still pass for a college kid. So he chose not to reveal his identity as a label owner when he asked Platzer if he had any copies of the new rap song that sounded like "Genius of Love" that he had heard on Mr. Magic's show. He knew that Platzer didn't have any. Robbins had, in fact, just put the tapes on a bus headed to the pressing plant in Pennsylvania.

"Twenty-five people have already asked me that question today," Platzer responded. "If one more person asks me for that record, I'm gonna kill myself."

Andre Harrell was driving down Bruckner Boulevard in the Bronx when the sounds of "Genius Rap" came from his car stereo, tuned to dance station WKTU. Overcome, he had to pull to the shoulder, listening to himself beneath the drone of a thousand cars on the expressway above him.

Alonzo Brown was stacking boxes and testing equipment at a medical supply store on York Avenue when he heard his song on the radio for the first time.

If Harrell was elated, Brown was dubious. Although he was happy to hear his voice on the radio, he assumed that they would play it once, and that would be it.

"Genius Rap" ended up being played enough times—in New York and across the United States—to sell almost 150,000 12-inch singles for Profile Records, this despite the efforts of Sugar Hill Records to promote its own, inevitable remake of "Genius of Love," called "It's Nasty" by Grandmaster Flash & the Furious Five.

Cory Robbins and Steve Plotnicki counted their winnings. At $2.25 per record wholesale minus 75 cents a record for manufacturing and some more for artist and publishing royalties, they would net about a dollar per record sold, or $150,000 total. Although they didn't see all that money right away, they were both able to do two things within a few weeks: pay off their parents and start taking a salary.

Dr. Jeckyll & Mr. Hyde were now Profile's first real artists. Robbins and Plotnicki called Brown and Harrell into their office and offered them a deal: $2,000 for the right to publish all the songs they would record for Profile. It was, in truth, an awful deal. Profile's new publishing entity, Protoons, Inc., wasn't designed to pitch Brown and Harrell's songs to other artists or for television and movie soundtracks. Instead it was a simple grab for another source of income, a common practice among smaller labels of the day. Profile was offering to pay the rappers a small amount of cash up front so the company wouldn't have to pay them more on the back end.

Without the benefit of experience or the help of legal counsel, Brown and Harrell agreed. Plotnicki insisted that the two rappers complete their next song before they could have the money. They wrote the song right there in Profile's offices. Then the rappers signed their publishing over to Profile and walked off with the first cash they had ever made from the record business.

Alonzo Brown's mother first thought he was dealing drugs when he handed her a wad of bills. With the money he kept for himself, Alonzo bought some sneakers, and took his girlfriend out to dinner at Beefsteak Charlie's.

Around the same time that "Genius Rap" was released, Profile Records' Four Seasons medley had finally broken onto New York radio, selling a respectable and profitable 40,000 copies. But the two partners could see that the return on investment for rap records far surpassed anything they could expect from pop and dance singles.

Cory Robbins and Steve Plotnicki now had a new plan for Profile Records. With the emerging break-beat DJ culture in New York—wherein kids would collect their paychecks every Friday and head to stores like the Music Factory to buy one and often two copies of any new rap 12-inch—Robbins and Plotnicki expected to sell at least 20,000 copies of each rap single they issued. They vowed to release one per month. Steve did the math in his head: $2.25 wholesale times 20,000 equaled $45,000. Over twelve months that was about a half million gross. Plotnicki realized that they could make a nice living at this.

Tom Silverman persevered in the years after the disco crash with his "Dance Music Report," making the rounds of the nightclubs and small, independent labels who served the newly truncated world of dance music. For his efforts, Silverman's tip sheet became influential enough that he started to receive demo tapes at his offices on the Upper East Side from hopeful artists and producers, like a DJ from Boston named Arthur Baker.

Silverman wasn't making much money, though, and he felt he now had enough knowledge and connections to sell some 12-inch dance singles of his own. He could take those demo tapes, the stuff that other labels didn't want or understand, and put them out himself.

In 1981, the same year that Profile released "Genius Rap," Tom Silverman founded Tommy Boy Records. He approached DJ Afrika Bambaataa—who had a horrible first recording experience with Paul Winley—about doing some music together. First, Bambaataa brought Silverman a demo by another producer, a song called "Havin' Fun." Released on Tommy Boy under the artist name Cotton Candy, the single didn't fare much better than Bambaataa's records with Winley. The next record would be Bambaataa's own, an interpolation of Gwen McRae's R&B hit "Funky Sensation," for which Silverman called on the production talents of Arthur Baker. "Jazzy Sensation" by Afrika Bambaataa & the Jazzy Five sold 35,000 copies, and got Silverman out of the debt from the first record.

Silverman had three businesses running out of his Upper East Side apartment now—"Dance Music Report," Tommy Boy Music, and the New Music Seminar, a small convention that aimed to pull together young artists and industry people to discuss the evolution of the music business in the wake of the disco crash. Silverman decided that he needed help juggling all these responsibilities.

Silverman placed an advertisement in the back of the *Village Voice* for a "guy/girl Friday." The person who called on him was a twenty-five-year-old woman named Monica Catherine Lynch—a tall, Midwestern girl with a shock of red hair and a wry smile. Lynch had a lot of experience, though none of it in the music industry. Back in Chicago she had been a bartender, a performer in a lip-synching troupe at a gay disco, an actress in an experimental theater company, an assistant to a fashion designer, and a member of a punk rock band in which she characterized her function as "lead hairdo."

Lynch had come to New York City a few years earlier to be a model. When her money ran out, a friend and mentor, Anya Phillips, suggested another line of work. Among Phillips's other occupations—managing a punk rock group called the Contortions and a venue called the Mudd Club—she was a dominatrix, and made custom G-strings for her friends, girls who go-go danced on the side to pay rent or support their drug habits. Phillips offered to make one for Lynch.

Go-go dancing was a very punk rock way to make money, and Lynch hired herself out as a topless dancer across the five boroughs, including a residence at the massive porn palace on 42nd Street and Eighth Avenue,

Show World. After a few years, when the job started to sour her view of men, Lynch quit.

By the time she saw Tommy Boy's ad in the *Voice*, she had already met Silverman once at the first New Music Seminar—a small gathering in an East Side music rehearsal space. There, Lynch heard the keynote speaker, Bob Pittman, talk about his new venture, Music Television. After a few interviews, she drove with Silverman to a pressing plant in Queens, and helped him lug heavy boxes of records into his car. Lynch won Silverman's approval by showing him she wasn't afraid to get her hands dirty.

No sooner did Lynch show up for work at Silverman's apartment than Tom left for a two-week vacation with his girlfriend. Lynch panicked. Then, one day, Cory Robbins stopped by.

"If you need anything, if anything goes wrong, just give me a call," Robbins said.

Lynch thought it was incredibly sweet—and interesting, too, how these young entrepreneurs who were also competitors looked out for one another. While Silverman was gone, Lynch learned by doing: calling stores and distributors, taking care of shipping, even writing a column for "Dance Music Report." After Silverman returned from vacation, it was time to record Afrika Bambaataa's follow-up to "Jazzy Sensation."

Happy as he was to have his first successful record, Afrika Bambaataa didn't want to keep remaking R&B hits, like most rap records of the day. Among all the Bronx hip-hop DJs, his tastes had always been the most versatile. Bambaataa was legendary for finding funky breaks in places that other DJs couldn't fathom: the first four bars of the reprise of "Sgt. Pepper's Lonely Hearts Club Band" by the Beatles; the first two bars of "Honky Tonk Woman" by the Rolling Stones. He would play these rock records, and Black kids would dance harder, not realizing they were partying to music made by, as Bambaataa said, "a bunch of White boys." Bambaataa was especially enamored of the electronic music coming out of Europe in the 1970s, like Gary Numan and Kraftwerk. For his next single, Bambaataa decided to pull the same sonic sleight-of-hand he had been doing for years in the clubs: *Watch*, Bam would think, *what I can get these kids to dance to.*

Kraftwerk's "Trans Europe Express," a German synth-dance track that was almost a rap record itself, formed the basis of Afrika Bambaataa's "Planet Rock," produced by Arthur Baker with ticking drums, bleeping synths, and huge orchestral chords played from a Fairlight keyboard, each key triggering an actual digital recording, or sample, of real-life instruments. Bambaataa and his Zulu MCs traded rhymes back and forth in a variety of unconventional patterns, exhorting the "party people" to "love, life, live." Musically and lyrically, "Planet Rock" broke with the Sugar Hill Records paradigm. To Lynch, "Planet Rock" embodied the ethos of the New Music Seminar: out of the ashes of disco, all the genres of underground music coming together in one song—hip-hop, punk, and new wave.

Silverman and Lynch drove the test pressing over to WHBI's studios on Riverside Drive, and rode away as Mr. Magic played the strange new record on air for the first time. Lynch had never experienced the thrill of hearing a record make its way out into the world. She felt that rush anew every day, as the sounds of "Planet Rock" began wafting out of windows and spilling out of passing cars on the streets of New York. The song electrified the dance clubs. It exploded on local radio stations like WKTU, WBLS, and a new competitor that had started playing the occasional rap record, WRKS, or "98.7 Kiss FM." From there, radio stations across the country, as far south as Miami and as far west as Los Angeles, began spinning Bambaataa's experimental track. Not that folks cared that "Planet Rock" was radical. They danced because the record was fun.

"Planet Rock" sold 650,000 12-inch singles for Tommy Boy—a company not much more than a year old—and was certified gold on September 16, 1982.

Now the number one record in Silverman's "Dance Music Report" was his very own.

For a decade, Frankie Crocker had been the tastemaker of young New York on WBLS. As the years went by, and Percy Sutton's "Black Liberation Station" changed its motto to the "Best-Looking Sound," the station became less political and Crocker became an even bigger personality. He posed naked on a leather couch for a WBLS bus billboard campaign. He once entered Studio 54 mounted on a white stallion. He often took an on-air "bath" with a different lucky lady guest during his show. When there wasn't a celebrity around, Crocker literally interviewed himself on the radio—asking questions, then pausing to give thoughtful answers.

Frankie "Hollywood" Crocker, the "Chief Rocker," was still the king, often trailed by his improbable sidekick, Juggy Gayles—born George Resnick, a Jewish record promoter in his sixties who was widely recognized as

Crocker's "bagman." WBLS enjoyed the spoils of Crocker's reign: the fawn-ing attentions of record executives, exclusive access to top artists, the patron-age of major corporate advertisers, and a perch atop the quarterly radio ratings. Nobody in New York radio had been able to knock WBLS down, at least not for long. During the height of the disco era "Disco 92," WKTU, had taken a chunk of his White and Latino audience. But WBLS roared back to first place as the disco craze waned in the early 1980s. No one could beat Frankie Crocker. And to cross Crocker was to do so at your own peril.

Barry Mayo learned that the hard way. The Bronx native had grown up idolizing Crocker, who inspired Mayo's career in radio. After taking Chi-cago's Black FM station, WGCI, from "worst to first," Mayo returned to New York at the age of twenty-eight. Cocky and ready for a new challenge, he pitched himself for a job programming WXLO, "FM 99 From The Streets," a low-rated New York station that had just switched formats from rock, then to "Adult Contemporary," then to a mishmash of pop, disco, and R&B.

Frankie Crocker was beatable, Mayo proclaimed in his presentation to the station's general manager, Lee Simonson. "His station plays records that nobody knows," Mayo said, referring to Crocker's penchant for program-ming anything he damn well pleased, from Dinah Shore to Frank Sinatra.

Simonson offered Mayo a job as assistant PD, under current programmer Don Kelly—who, in Mayo's estimation, looked to be the squarest of square White men.

"We don't need him," Mayo said brashly, in Kelly's presence. *Why talk behind the man's back?* Mayo thought. "I should be program director."

Simonson eventually convinced Mayo to take the APD job, with the promise that Kelly would exit within a year if Mayo were successful. The general manager also revealed his plans to change the station's call letters and branding to shed its rock-and-roll past. Soon after Mayo's arrival, WXLO would become WRKS, or "98.7 Kiss FM."

In May 1981, during his first week on the job, Mayo met the man with whom he was poised to do battle. Backstage at the Beacon Theatre—during a concert sponsored, of course, by WBLS—Mayo spotted the great Crocker himself, holding court amongst a throng of record executives and hangers-on. *It looks like a press conference*, Mayo thought. After a few minutes, Mayo got his nerve up, walked across the room to his hero, and extended his hand.

"I'm Barry Mayo. I'm the new APD over at WXLO. I'd love to have lunch with you sometime and talk about the market."

The suave DJ with the impeccable clothes and chiseled features looked down at the diminutive Mayo, his attire, and excitable demeanor transmitting all the cool of a freshly certified public accountant. Crocker took a pull of the slim, long brown cigarette in his hand, and then blew a lungful of smoke in Mayo's face.

"You want to talk to me?" Crocker asked.

Then Crocker laughed and turned away.

Mayo, blood rising to his face, withdrew and walked back across the room.

That night, Mayo didn't sleep. The next morning, he got to work, programming a tighter, slicker, and more hit-oriented station than Crocker's personality- and whim-driven playlist at WBLS. Within a year of Mayo's arrival, 98.7 Kiss FM rose to number three in the market, Don Kelly left to start a consulting business, and Mayo became program director.

Mayo distinguished himself from Frankie Crocker in two important ways. First, Mayo had quickly developed a reputation that he couldn't be bought or paid. Second, Mayo's addiction to numbers and statistics put him on the forefront of a new trend in radio: research. In the coming years, radio stations would be programmed less by gut instinct, like Crocker did, and more by polls and surveys. Mayo saw success when he balanced his feelings with facts.

But Mayo was never going to catch Crocker when WBLS had all the big artists on lockdown for exclusives and promotions. No one, not the people at the record companies, not the concert promoters, not the artists themselves, wanted to get on Crocker's bad side.

Then, one day, fate smiled upon Barry Mayo. A concert promoter named Jesse Boseman had a show booked at Madison Square Garden with a couple of R&B artists. Not just any couple, but the hottest in the business—Rick James and Teena Marie, in the midst of their smash duet "Fire & Desire." At the time, Boseman was livid with Mayo's nemesis.

"Fuck Frankie Crocker," Boseman said. "I'm sick of paying him, and him not doing what he's supposed to do."

Boseman told Mayo that he wanted to do the show with Kiss FM.

"But I need you to blow it out," Boseman warned. "Because I will never be able to go back to 'BLS."

Mayo threw all of his station's resources behind the concert, and Boseman sold out Madison Square Garden. The evening of the big show was like a debutante ball for Barry Mayo and Kiss FM, whose "lips" logo adorned banners throughout the stadium. Mayo was jubilant.

Then, about halfway through Teena Marie's opening set, Mayo noticed a green Mercedes-Benz on the backstage runway. *Crocker's* green Mercedes. How Crocker got his car into the Garden was beyond Mayo's comprehension, but there Crocker was, talking to another group of ass kissers, acting like it was *his* show. Mayo took small comfort in knowing that it wasn't.

As intermission drew to a close, Mayo waited for his morning announcer, Chuck Leonard, to bring on Rick James. Instead, he saw another person stroll to the microphone. Mayo couldn't believe his eyes. It was Ricky Ricardo, a DJ from WBLS and one of Crocker's protégés.

"Ladies and gentlemen," Ricardo announced, "Mr. Frankie Crocker!"

Mayo stood in the wings, apoplectic, helpless as his archrival strode to the middle of the stage—*his stage!*—to thunderous applause. And amid the Kiss FM banners, Crocker calmly introduced the headliner of the show, his personal friend—they had both grown up in Buffalo, you see—*the incredible Rick James!*

Frankie Crocker had literally stolen the show. He had ripped Mayo off in front of 19,500 people. Mayo was worlds beyond embarrassed, worlds beyond livid. Crocker stood backstage, thronged by more record people. Mayo caught Crocker's eye, and slowly mouthed the words:

I ... am ... going ... to ... get ... you ... mother ... fucker!

Mayo ran from the Garden, from his own show, down West 34th Street with tears of rage streaming down his face. As he cried, he made a vow. He would not rest, would not cease, would not be happy until he had vanquished Frankie Crocker, and not just in the ratings. Crocker had to leave. He had to be fired. The fucker had to go.

But tonight, Mayo had been defeated and the conventional wisdom had prevailed:

You really *couldn't* beat Frankie Crocker. And you crossed Crocker at your own peril.

Unbeknownst to Mayo and his rival, somebody else *was* beating Frankie Crocker already, at least in the hearts and minds of the youngest New Yorkers.

Crocker's music director, Mae James, found out as much when she caught her teenage daughter Crystal in her bedroom late one Saturday, past midnight, listening to the radio under the covers.

"What are you doing?" James asked.

"Listening to Mr. Magic," her daughter replied.

Like tens of thousands of other kids, Crystal waited all week, stayed up late, and defied her parents just to hear her favorite DJ. Every Saturday night (or Sunday morning, depending on your perspective), Mr. Magic and his WHBI crew, which included Jalil Hutchins and John "Ecstasy" Fletcher, served up the latest rap records, broadcasting live routines from MCs and sets from guest DJs, and playing other hot dance music. Kids taped the show, and during the intervening week, the streets of the five boroughs and beyond would resonate with the sounds of the show blasting from thousands of boom boxes. If Mr. Magic played a new record, shops like Downstairs Records, the Music Factory, and Disc-o-Mat would be flooded with requests, and distributors would receive a deluge of orders. For Sugar Hill and the upstart record companies like Profile and Tommy Boy, the good graces of Mr. Magic mattered a lot more than those of Frankie Crocker. Each company "sponsored" Mr. Magic's airtime with weekly checks, ensuring the airplay of their records.

As for Mr. Magic's loyal following, most of them weren't old enough to go to grown-up discos, or simply couldn't afford the clothes and the price of admission required for the adult nightlife that Crocker represented. Hip-hop had freed them of all that.

WBLS was no longer about liberation, but about looking good. The new kids didn't care about Frankie Crocker's upscale world. Their hero was Mr. Magic.

Luckily for WBLS, Mae James had a daughter who knew Mr. Magic personally. Luckily for Magic, Crystal James's mom worked for Frankie Crocker.

Sal Abbatiello's Disco Fever nightclub was like a family. But the inner circle—Sal, Sweet G, Junebug, Magic, Flash, Melle, Mandingo, Bam-Bam—the guys who hung out until dawn, breaking balls, playing cards, drinking, and sniffing—had a special designation. They called themselves the "Juice Crew." Sal even made them special "Juice rings" to commemorate their degenerate bond.

One morning, after the Disco Fever closed, Sal Abbatiello and Mr. Magic found themselves up at an Irish bar downtown, tossing back beers until ten a.m.

"Oh, man, I never went home," Magic slurred. "I'd better call my mother."

Sal watched Magic as he walked to the bar's pay phone, dialed, and connected.

After a brief exchange with his mother, Magic's eyes went really wide.

"Oh, shit, Sal!" Magic said. "Frankie Crocker called!"

"Called for what?" Sal replied.

Magic hung up the phone, fumbled for some more change, and dialed WBLS. Magic got Mae James, who wanted him to come in to meet with Crocker himself.

Magic already had a sense of how important he was—why else would Crocker be on his dick, and not the other way around? So Magic didn't say much in the meeting at WBLS's Second Avenue offices, where Crocker offered him $750 a week to host shows on Friday and Saturday nights at WBLS. But in truth, it was the break of a lifetime: better time slots on the best station in the city. When Magic accepted Crocker's offer on the spot, neither man realized that they had just made history again. In May of 1982, Mr. Magic's "Rap Attack" became the first-ever rap show to be broadcast on a commercial radio station anywhere in the world.

For Magic, it was an opportunity to dramatically increase his audience and influence. For Frankie Crocker, it was a way to keep himself, and his station, relevant. But for Crocker, it was also a way to *confine* rap, to give it boundaries, to keep it from seeping into the regular programming. *Friday and Saturday nights were the time for this rap stuff. The weekdays were still for real music.*

Magic suffered two disappointments, however, in his transition to WBLS. First, he could no longer openly take sponsorship checks from record companies. Second, while the DJ was still at WHBI, a young executive who headed the American office of a small British label had approached Magic about making a record. But with Magic headed for commercial radio, the DJ couldn't be a recording artist as well—a double duty that might be viewed as a form of payola.

So Magic passed his recording opportunity to the guys in his crew, Jalil and Ecstasy. The record executive, Barry Weiss, instead found himself recording a tribute to Mr. Magic called "Magic's Wand," conjured by the duo who now called themselves Whodini, the first rap artists released by Weiss's label, Jive Records.

By 1982, New York sustained a healthy crop of independently owned and distributed labels plying their trade in the post-disco market. Prelude had segued from disco to R&B with the success of its group, D Train. West End had Taana Gardner's "Heartbeat." Sound of New York scored a huge hit by Indeep called "Last Night a DJ Saved My Life," a rap-funk hybrid that seemed to signal a bright future for a post-disco world.

"There's not a problem that I can't fix," rhymed the DJ, "'cause I can do it in the mix."

But of all these labels, Profile, Tommy Boy, and Jive were the only ones presenting a formidable challenge to the rap dominance of Sugar Hill Records, who still had two of the biggest rap acts in the business: the Sugar Hill Gang and Grandmaster Flash & the Furious Five.

Flash and his crew had been beaten two times. First, they were outrun by the Sugar Hill Gang in the race to become the first hip-hop act on vinyl. And now that Grandmaster Flash & the Furious Five were on Sugar Hill Records, they had been bested again—not just commercially, but creatively—by Afrika Bambaataa's "Planet Rock."

Sylvia Robinson played a key role in the two records that evened the score.

From the time that Flash and his five MCs first entered a recording studio to tape "Superrappin'" for Enjoy, the legendary DJ had literally been benched while the in-studio band provided the backing for the rappers. So much was lost in hip-hop's translation to wax that most consumers of rap records outside of New York didn't know that Grandmaster Flash's virtuoso performances had once been the main attraction.

"In the real world," Sylvia once told Flash, "no one knows you from a can of paint."

At some point in 1981, Sylvia and Flash agreed that he should get his shot in the studio—no MCs, no band—just him, two turntables, and a bunch of records. The result was "The Adventures of Grandmaster Flash on the Wheels of Steel," a seven-minute set of live cutting and scratching that marked the debut of DJ-as-musician on vinyl.

The next record would do for the MC what "Adventures" did for the DJ.

"The Jungle" was the title of the demo submitted to Sylvia by Ed Fletcher, the percussionist of her house band. The track moved along at a slow, sinister pace, and Fletcher's rhymes almost sounded like Gil Scott-Heron's political beat poetry, not rap: "It's like a jungle sometimes, / It makes me wonder how I keep from going under." Sylvia heard something in "The Jungle," and called her keyboard expert Reggie Griffin and arranger "Jiggs" Chase to flesh out the track. Griffin contributed the song's melodic hook—a freehand synthesizer lick that evoked the sound of echoes between stark project buildings. All the while, Sylvia tweaked and fussed over the details. Griffin marveled at Sylvia's musical intuition. She could walk into a session and, in a few seconds, make an observation or a slight change that would elevate a song.

"Don't use that bass drum," she might say. "Use the Willie kick." She said "Willie," but she meant the Oberheim DMX drum machine. In Sugar Hill's studios, they gave their electronic equipment human names, just for fun.

Sylvia played "The Jungle," complete with Fletcher's scratch vocals, for Grandmaster Flash, hoping he would embrace the idea. But in Sylvia's mind, Flash was being as difficult as ever. He balked at the idea of his MCs rhyming over the dirgelike track. You couldn't dance to it. And who could party to depressing talk about people getting pushed in front of trains and stabbed in the heart? No way, Flash said. *The fans will boo me off the stage with that shit.*

Adamant, Sylvia did an end run around Flash and convinced one of his Furious Five, Melle Mel, to try it. Mel was of a different mind from Flash anyway, both about the song and about his relationship with Sylvia. He had already written some "reality rhymes" for their first record, "Superrappin'." So, at Sylvia's urging, Mel incorporated them into a greater story that could have been about him, or Joe Robinson, or DJ Hollywood—or anyone from Harlem, the Bronx, or forlorn neighborhoods around America: Kids growing up admiring the "number book takers, thugs, pimps, pushers, and the big moneymakers."

Unfurling a relentless litany of urban decay, Melle Mel and Fletcher traded verses, rhyme after rhyme, climaxing each time with the following line, choking off each word one at a time, for emphasis: "Don't. Push. Me. Cause. I'm. Close. To. The. Edge. / I'm. Trying. Not. To. Lose. My. Head."

By the time the song was done, and Sylvia had renamed it "The Message," she decided to market the song under the aegis of the label's most popular group, Grandmaster Flash & the Furious Five. After the track was complete, she coaxed Flash and the other MCs to contribute an ad-libbed street scene reminiscent of Stevie Wonder's "Livin' for the City": While planning their evening's festivities ("We can go to down to the Fever . . . check out Junebug"), the guys get harassed by police and arrested. During this recording session, Flash tried to have his MCs replace the lines rapped by the song's composer, Ed Fletcher. But by that time, Sylvia wasn't having it. The song went out as it was, with an added credit to "Duke Bootee," Fletcher's performing name.

"The Message" climbed to the same spot on the R&B charts that "Planet Rock" occupied: number four. It sold fewer records than "Planet Rock," but in one sense, "The Message" accomplished more. "Planet Rock," like the few successful rap records before it, reinforced the idea that rap could be viable pop music. But "The Message" showed that rap could be serious, too, even meaningful. Across the world, people took notice. Britain's *New Musical Express* called "The Message" the "first really big political record since James Brown's 1970 'Say It Loud.'"

The message for Grandmaster Flash was that his own name had become just a brand to be used at the Queen's will. That only Melle Mel performed on his group's most successful record to date became a wedge that would soon break the crew in two. Only after a lawsuit and a court ruling would Grandmaster Flash win his freedom from Sugar Hill and the right to use his name. By then, Melle Mel was calling himself a "Grandmaster," and had supplanted his former DJ as Sugar Hill's hot property.

Before Melle Mel, only one rapper had national name recognition, Kurtis Blow. And Blow owed his rap career to the unremitting chatter and relentless promotion of one man: Russell "Rush" Simmons, the hyperactive twenty-two-year-old party promoter from Hollis, Queens, who had convinced Robert Ford and J. B. Moore to choose Kurtis Blow as their MC for "Christmas Rappin'."

Since "Christmas Rappin'," Russell Simmons had begun producing his own rap and R&B records. They were small but noteworthy singles by Jimmy Spicer, Lovebug Starski, and Orange Krush—put out either through the Rifkind brothers' Spring Records, or Blow's label, Mercury. All of these records were made possible by Simmons's salesmanship, and his continuing partnership with Larry Smith, Rocky Ford's multi-instrumentalist friend from Queens.

While Smith supplied the musical know-how for Kurtis Blow's records,

Simmons tried to limit the musicality of Smith's arrangements. Simmons hated the dominant Sugar Hill sound—the antiseptic remakes of popular dance tracks that had no relation to the raw sound of hip-hop in the parks and the clubs. He also hated the electro-funk sound of "Planet Rock." One night, just before the song broke wide, he spotted Monica Lynch at a club.

"That record's nervous," Simmons sputtered. "That shit's never going to be a hit."

Simmons might have been a tad envious when it did hit. But for Simmons, hip-hop had always been about *beats*, not music. *Rap shouldn't sound like disco*, he thought. *And it shouldn't sound like new-wave synth pop, either. Rap should sound like itself.* So Simmons kept goading Smith into creating increasingly sparse arrangements. Less melody, Simmons said. More drums.

Simmons also hated the uptown and Bronx crews' fanciful aesthetic— Flash's magical costumes, Cowboy's fringes, Melle Mel's go-go boots, and Bambaataa's tribal chieftain getup. Not only should rap sound like where it came from, Simmons thought, it should look like where it came from.

Russell Simmons's sentiments were shared by his younger brother, Joey, a high schooler who helped Russell spread the word about his shows, and, for a time, had even served as Kurtis Blow's DJ. Even after Joey Simmons broke his arm, he could cut incredibly fast between the two turntables. Kurtis dubbed him "DJ Run." The nickname stuck, even though Joey was as good an MC as he was a DJ.

Joey had been pestering his older brother to let him record a rap with his friend Darryl McDaniels, a tall, quiet fellow with thick-framed glasses. Russell didn't think much of "D," but Joey was an even bigger pain in the ass than Russell, and he eventually won the argument. Russell and Larry Smith composed a track in the Simmonses' attic in Hollis: a simple rhythm generated by a drum machine, with occasional stabs from a synthesizer. *This was how hip-hop was supposed to sound*, Russell thought. Joey loved it: *a real "b-boy" record*, he thought, not that corny Sugar Hill stuff. Joey had, ironically, been influenced by one Sugar Hill record, "The Message," as he began his own reality rap: "Unemployment at a record high, / People coming, people going, people born to die."

Joey and Darryl traded verses, punctuating each with the brief refrain, "It's like that. And that's the way it is."

Hollis, Queens was once a suburb. With tree-lined streets and good schools, it was a great place to raise a family. But not long after Daniel Simmons moved his pregnant wife and two boys—eleven-year-old Danny Junior and seven-year-old Russell—into their new house, Hollis's White residents like Cory Robbins's parents started moving out. Shops closed, trash collection slowed, and road repair crews stopped coming. The blight that swallowed Harlem and the South Bronx began gobbling up this neighborhood out on the far edge of the city, too. By the time Daniel Simmons's third son, Joey, was in grade school, Hollis was slouching towards slum status.

For the Simmons boys, the influence of the hustlers on nearby 205th Street was too powerful. Russell's older brother, Danny, got addicted to heroin and was sent to live with his grandmother. Russell followed, not as a user, but as a small-time dealer, selling nickel and dime bags of marijuana along with his friends in the "Hollis Crew." Eventually, the teenage Russell Simmons was recruited into the 17th Division of a city-wide gang called the Seven Immortals.

Russell was given the rank of "warlord" in the Junior Immortals. But Russell wasn't very warlike. The only time he had ever fired a gun at someone, he couldn't muster the depravity to aim. On another occasion, during one sunny outing at Coney Island, he and his crew scattered at the sight of a gang of bigger, older Black Spades. In fact, Russell's gang career was successful by only one measure—he talked and talked until he had recruited hundreds of new members. But when a fellow Immortal was killed by a member of a rival gang from the south side of Jamaica, Queens, Russell set aside his gang colors for good, and finished high school.

At City College in Harlem, Simmons pursued interests closer to his heart. He got high—mostly on weed but sometimes on angel dust. He went to discos. He bought clothes from AJ Lester's men's shop so he could look fly like the kids from Harlem, and not like a yokel from Queens. Simmons prided himself on sporting pristine sneakers, and spent days in pursuit of fresh pairs of discontinued footwear, like the three-stripe PRO-Keds that Simmons and his friends called "69ers." His sartorial quests knew no bounds. Simmons even found a legal way to finance his rather desultory lifestyle: He sold fake drugs, namely sticks of coco-leaf incense that provided a buzz when crushed and snorted, but contained no cocaine.

Simmons's college friend Rudy Toppin had a different kind of hustle: He distributed flyers for shows at the Harlem club Charles Gallery, which meant Rudy could get in for free. The night that twenty-year-old Russell Simmons tagged along with Toppin was the first time Simmons saw a rapper. It was Eddie Cheba, rocking the crowd. The clubgoers even finished Cheba's rhymes for him, which meant they were coming back week after week. That night, sometime in 1977, Simmons found himself a new high—rap—and a new hustle—promoting parties.

Simmons and Toppin threw some cash together, and began negotiating with venues and acts. Sometimes they made money. Sometimes, they lost it. After one particularly bad show in Harlem, Simmons was broke, and went back to his parents in Hollis for help. Daniel Simmons never thought much of his son's lifestyle, which he immortalized in a rhyme of his own about Russell:

Eat, sleep
Don't shovel no snow
Get up, get dressed, go disco!

Daniel Simmons refused to help, ordering Russell back to college. Russell's mother, Evelyn, dug into her own stash and came out with a stack of one-hundred-dollar bills, amounting to $2,000 of her personal savings. Simmons's requests for capital eventually exhausted the goodwill of his entire family. His older brother, Danny, who had conquered his heroin addiction and just come back from prison, helped extract some money that Russell was owed by a local club owner. When Danny asked for some of that cash as repayment for a $1,000 loan, Russell refused to give the money back.

"I gotta reinvest this!" Russell said.

Livid, Danny punched his little brother in the face. They brawled until Russell finally kicked him in the head. Danny went to the hospital to get three stitches in his ear. Russell kept the money.

Simmons put everything he had into more parties, most of which now featured the talents of a friend from City College named Curtis Walker, who performed as Kool DJ Kurt. Walker served for Simmons as a sort of discount Eddie Cheba, but he quickly proved to have his own distinct allure. Girls, in particular, loved Kurt. He was tall, brown skinned, and muscular, and he rhymed in a buttery, low voice. Simmons redubbed him Kurtis Blow—partly as an emulation of the drug-laced sobriquet of Eddie Cheba, and partly because Kurt, too, was known for selling coco-leaf incense.

The world of "rapping DJ" parties was still very small and insular, based mostly in Manhattan and the Bronx. In this world, Russell Simmons was a nobody from Queens. But he was tenacious. With his big eyes, wide smile, and slight lisp, Simmons was hard to hate, and even harder to shake. He would let the occasional disrespect (or "dis," for short) pass, and keep talking. He would introduce himself and Kurt to anyone important. Simmons even found a way to turn his Queens pedigree to his advantage. When booking a show in Harlem or the Bronx, he billed the Harlem-bred Kurtis Blow as "Queens's number one MC," marketing Kurt as a must-see oddity. When hiring Bronx DJs like Flash at venues in Queens, Simmons used the occasional lateness or absence of the Furious Five MCs to insert Kurtis Blow into Flash's mix.

Gradually, Simmons became a powerful promoter. After making Kurtis Blow rap's first marquee name and sex symbol, Simmons applied that same relentlessness to producing records and managing the careers of other rappers. That went double for the hip-hop aspirations of his little brother, Joey.

Side B
Kings from Queens

Every time Russell Simmons came out of the studio with a new demo tape, he made the rounds of the major labels. And every time, the labels' talent executives turned him down, particularly the Black ones— like Bill Haywood at Mercury Records, who hated rap.

The only labels that signed rap were the smaller, independent companies, but the problem with those outfits was that most of them didn't pay. You could get a small advance, but forget about royalties. Spring was like that. And Sugar Hill? Simmons did not want to be in business with Joe and Sylvia Robinson.

One new label had a decent reputation. Profile Records offered the same stingy contracts as other small labels, but at least they honored their contracts and paid their royalties. So Simmons found Profile to be an oasis of sorts. He dropped by occasionally, playing tapes for Cory Robbins, who never liked any of Simmons's records enough to sign one of them. But Robbins, at least, would listen.

Since their success with "Genius Rap," Profile had moved to bigger offices in their building, next to West End Records. In 1982, Robbins inked Profile's first R&B hit, Sharon Brown's "I Specialize in Love," produced by his old Midland colleague, Eddie O'Loughlin. It sold over 100,000 copies. Profile did another single with Dr. Jeckyll & Mr. Hyde, and a couple of moderately successful rap singles with the Disco Four.

In the fall of 1982, Simmons came by again, this time with his brother Joey's demo.

Robbins respected Russell Simmons. He never held Simmons responsible for the broken deal with Kurtis Blow at Panorama, blaming Rocky Ford and J. B. Moore instead. But Robbins wasn't sure about this new tape. Unlike most other rap records at the time, it wasn't a replay of a popular song. This was just Russell's brother and a friend shouting over a beat, monotonous and metallic. Driving home, Robbins listened to the cassette in his car.

The next morning, Robbins decided that he loved the chorus: "It's like that! What? And that's the way it is." He told Plotnicki that he thought they should sign Simmons's strange little record as one of their monthly rap singles. Simmons asked for $4,000 to rerecord it in a proper studio. Robbins offered $2,000. Simmons went to Steve Loeb, the owner of Greene Street, the SoHo recording studio where Kurtis Blow had cut all of his records, and talked until Loeb let him defer payment on the remainder of the $3,700 bill.

Russell, Joey, Darryl McDaniels, and Larry Smith were joined in the studio by Kurtis Blow, who was proving himself to be as handy behind the boards as he was on the microphone. Simmons returned to Profile with not one, but two songs: "It's Like That"—the one that Robbins had heard on the demo—and "Krush-Groove 1," which had no instrumentation, save a beat box. Robbins didn't like the title, which had nothing to do with the lyrics.

"They keep talking about 'sucker MCs' in the song," Robbins told Simmons. "Call it that." Simmons shrugged. *Fine by me.*

Then there was the matter of the group's strange name, as it was written on the cassette Russell had given him: "Runde-MC." Robbins didn't understand it. Simmons explained: Two rappers, Joey "Run" Simmons and Darryl "DMC" McDaniels. "Well," Robbins said, "shouldn't you spell it 'Run-DMC'?" Simmons shrugged again. *Fine by me.*

Robbins never knew that Joey and Darryl detested the name that Russell had given their duo.

"Don't call us that," they begged. "*Please* don't call us that."

Who would like a group with a retarded name like "Run-DMC"?

Just before Profile released Run-DMC's single in March of 1983, they hired their first employee.

Manny Bella was a wise-cracking, skinny Filipino kid from Queens who worked in the Disc-o-Mat on Lexington Avenue, right across from Bloomingdale's department store. When he worked at Panorama, Cory Robbins was a frequent visitor to the record shop. He wanted to know what was selling. Bella, for his part, wanted another job.

"You've gotta get me out of here," Bella would plead every time he saw Robbins.

Robbins came to see in Bella the makings of a persistent promotion man. He hired Bella as an intern at Panorama, where Bella made tape duplications and called college stations. After Panorama folded, Bella went to work for West End Records.

Over the phone Manny Bella did not sound like he was born in Manila, nor did he come off like the son of a research biochemist and an accountant from the Philippines. By voice alone, he sounded just like the Italian- and Irish-American kids in his neighborhood, Jackson Heights. A soft, lazy "Whaddyadoin?" was how Bella would begin many of his phone calls to radio programmers. If they didn't take his call, Bella would call back, and call again. The legendary White program director for Black station WDAS in Philadelphia, Joseph "Butterball" Tamburro, snubbed Bella's first call and got a phone call almost every working day for the next six months until he finally picked up the phone. Once he did, it didn't take long for Butterball and Bella to become good friends. Persuasive, not abrasive, was how Bella described his technique. And it worked. At West End, Bella had fought nine long, hard months to get Black stations to play Taana Gardner's "Heartbeat." For his effort, he scored his first hit on American Black radio.

Cory Robbins eventually lured Bella away from West End for the salary of $25,000 a year. For Bella, it wasn't a comfortable transition. Profile and West End shared the same floor, and Bella had to see his fuming former employers every day.

Bella worked together with Profile's owners in their cramped space. He didn't care too much for Steve Plotnicki, the moneyman. Bella didn't like the way Plotnicki talked to him. The guy could make "good morning" sound condescending. Bella liked Cory Robbins better, although he was a little quirky. Robbins came in late—usually after noon—and worked until he headed out to the clubs around midnight. Robbins wore the same outfit nearly every day: tight jeans and a Lacoste shirt. Each afternoon, Robbins would send Manny to the deli to get his afternoon refreshment: a can of Tab, a cup of ice, and a straw. "Don't let them pour the soda," Robbins would say, saving that fizzy pleasure for himself. Robbins was similarly obsessive with the way he promoted records.

To get his songs onto the radio, Robbins devised a system. Week by week, visiting club after club, Robbins had deduced the names of all of the DJs who reported their favorites to New York's dance station, WKTU—supposedly a secret list. By servicing these DJs, Robbins was able to get almost all of his records added to WKTU. After Robbins's vaunted system for getting music added to WKTU was discovered by the station's management, Bella devised something simpler. He called his best friend—Carlos De Jesus, the program director for WKTU—and simply asked him to play the record. *Why call twenty guys*, Bella thought, *when you could just call one?*

De Jesus would usually spin the records that Manny gave him. When Bella gave De Jesus "It's Like That" by Run-DMC, he played it, too, making WKTU the first station to air the song. But De Jesus hated it.

"I don't play this rap shit!" De Jesus complained. "We're a dance station!"

"This is the future, Carlos," Manny deadpanned, not really believing his own bullshit. Manny realized he wasn't going to get anything else out of KTU. Nor would he find a sympathetic ear in Frankie Crocker at New York's top-rated black station, WBLS. Crocker detested rap.

Only one option remained. A guy who was getting killed in the ratings race: Barry Mayo at WRKS, 98.7 Kiss FM.

Barry Mayo hated rap music as much as his nemesis Frankie Crocker did. Maybe more so. Not long after Mayo arrived, he started playing his own favorites—smooth jazz fusion artists like Al Jarreau, Bob James, and Eumir Deodato.

Mayo's changes didn't sit well with one person at the station. Tony Quartarone was just twenty-two years old, and only recently promoted from unpaid programming intern to research director at $10,000 a year. Quartarone knew he would probably make more money pumping gas. But Tony "Q" loved the station. For an Italian kid from the Bronx, he was completely dedicated to helping Kiss FM become a "Black Top 40" station, vanquishing WBLS through professional presentation and rigorous market research—eliciting listener feedback through "call-out" phone campaigns and biweekly focus groups. This was supposed to be Mayo's mission, too. But Quartarone thought that Mayo was committing the cardinal sin of broadcasting: turning a radio station into your own personal jukebox. Quartarone's mistake was telling Mayo so.

"I know you've got this big name," Quartarone told his new boss one day. "But my understanding is that I do the research for this station. I thought we were supposed to be a Top 40 Black station, and you're making it something that it's not."

When Mayo heard this candid critique coming from the mouth of a low-level employee, he did what he felt any reasonable supervisor should do: Mayo picked up a baseball bat and chased Tony "Q" around the station.

Mayo and Quartarone's volatile relationship continued because Tony "Q" repeatedly pushed rap music on the unwilling Mayo. But Quartarone was a vigilant researcher, and, to his credit, his picks became hits—songs like "Planet Rock" and "The Message." He also learned a curious thing about researching rap music. If you asked people in WRKS's target audience of twenty-five-to-forty-four-year-olds whether they liked rap, they'd say no. But if you asked them about an individual song title—say the new Sugar Hill single "White Lines" by Grandmaster Melle Mel & the Furious Five—they'd respond with enthusiasm. Quartarone understood that rap music's biggest problem was not the music, which was universal in its appeal, but the *image* of rap held by so many people. To older, upscale Black listeners, rap was ghetto music. To some White people, rap was disco. But when it came down to the songs themselves, everybody danced.

Mayo cared less about the music and more about doing anything that would beat Frankie Crocker. He would play a record if only for the reason that Crocker *wasn't* playing it. Manny Bella understood Mayo's quest, and in the interest of both of their careers, made Mayo an ally.

So Bella sat in the on-air studio at WRKS as Mayo tested "It's Like That" during afternoon "drive time." Bella watched the multiline phones light up. Then Mayo flipped the record over, playing "Sucker MCs." The record was everything that Mayo couldn't understand: no music, just drums and talking. And in the middle of the song, the beat cut out and it sounded like somebody was on air—*his air!*—scratching the record, while a kid talked about being light skinned and living in Queens, eating chicken and collard greens, some shit like that. It was embarrassing.

In the three minutes that it took the song to finish, Manny Bella and Barry Mayo watched the phones. It seemed that all of New York was trying to call Kiss FM.

Mayo "tested" the record over the next few weeks, playing it once a day. Requests intensified. Mayo swallowed his personal feelings and put Run-DMC's strange record in "heavy" rotation, meaning that listeners could be certain to hear one of the two songs within any given hour.

Kiss 98.7 FM surged in the ratings in the summer of 1983, based largely on Run-DMC's record. Mayo told Bella that it saved his career. It also saved Tony Quartarone's. After that, Bella had little trouble getting other Profile records played.

WRKS became even friendlier to rap after Bella introduced Mayo to Afrika Bambaataa. Mayo offered him a weekend "mix show" on the station—akin to Frankie Crocker's gambit with Mr. Magic's "Rap Attack." Bambaataa, in the flower of his recording career with Tommy Boy, couldn't maintain that kind of regular schedule. So Bam assigned the show to Afrika Islam, who already hosted his own "time-lease" slot on WHBI called "Zulu Beats." When Islam proved unreliable, Bam passed the show to his first Zulu lieutenant, Jazzy Jay. But the radio station wouldn't pay Jay for his mixes. He quit, and in October of 1983, handed the show off to his cousin—a red-haired, back-bench Zulu DJ named Frederick Crute, whom everyone called "Red Alert."

Unlike Jay, Red understood the true compensation of an unpaid radio show: exposure. With exposure, however, came ridicule. Mr. Magic, like his boss Frankie Crocker, didn't take kindly to competition from the crosstown station. When Jazzy Jay had the on-air shift, Magic called him "Jazzy Wack." And now that Red Alert had taken his place, Magic came up with a new nickname: "Red Dirt."

Red—normally a quiet, friendly guy—was furious. He went to Barry Mayo to complain.

"He's dissing me, man!" Red said.

Mayo laughed.

"No," Mayo replied. "He's advertising you."

Red thought about it and agreed.

Now Mayo had a new ally in his quixotic quest to best Frankie Crocker, Mr. Magic, and WBLS.

Manny Bella spent eight hours a day on the phones, searching for Black stations outside New York that would play "It's Like That." Equally relentless, Russell Simmons called Bella every day for the latest update. Together, they made a good promotion team. Russell sent Run-DMC down South—Maryland, the Carolinas, Georgia, Louisiana—to do free shows for radio stations called "track dates." In return, the stations added the record for Bella. From there, "It's Like That" spread to the Midwest, and then to KACE and KDAY in Los Angeles and KSOL in San Francisco.

"It's Like That" peaked in the summer of 1983 on Black radio stations across the U.S., and at number fifteen on the Billboard Black singles chart. By then, the name "Run-DMC" had become a curse to Sugar Hill Records and its roster of rap acts, whose disco-rooted recording style would soon fall beneath the beat-box rhythms of the two b-boys from Hollis, Queens. Run and DMC had a dismissive term for these Sugar Hill acts, the Furious Fives and the Funky Fours and the Treacherous Threes:

"Old-school," they called them.

With the success of "It's Like That"/"Sucker MCs," Profile's single-a-month strategy paid off in an unexpected way. Run-DMC's first 12-inch sold 250,000 copies, grossing Plotnicki and Robbins their year's goal of a half million dollars with just one single.

Charlie Stettler, a thirty-two-year-old Swiss émigré, had also sold 250,000 copies of his own unconventional debut recording.

Run-DMC had done it by performing all over New York dressed in b-boy fashion—sneakers, jeans, and fedora hats, an image painstakingly crafted by Russell Simmons.

Stettler had done it by walking all over New York in a gorilla suit.

His record was called *Tin Pan Apple*. Stettler's inspiration had come from a trip to the Bahamas, where he found he couldn't sleep without the soothing clatter of the New York City streets. Upon his return to the Big Apple, Stettler roamed the city with a tape deck and a microphone, recording hawkers, winos, garbage trucks, and ambulances. His partner and girlfriend, Lynda West, designed the album and cassette artwork—complete with a King Kong–on–Empire State Building motif, and the tagline, "Take the City with You!" West gave Stettler thousands of flyers to distribute. The King Kong outfit was Stettler's addition.

First, Stettler walked up the middle of Fifth Avenue, against traffic, handing the leaflets to bemused motorists. Then he ran into Republican gubernatorial candidate Lewis Lehrman on the street. The picture of Lehrman being hugged by a gorilla holding the *Tin Pan Apple* cassette ended up in the *Village Voice*, with the caption, "If Lehrman Is So Smart, Why Is He So Dumb?" Next, Stettler hung out in front of Macy's department store. Then he went to the newspapers and TV stations. Stettler told the folks at CBS News that he was a "Gorilla-gram" for anchor Dan Rather. He got as far as the broadcast studio before being thrown out. When he came home, West told him that Bloomindale's had just put in a huge order, in time for the 1982 holiday season. They even sold it in the gift shop on top of the Empire State Building. King Kong would have been proud.

Next, in 1983, came Stettler's rap version, *Tin Pan Apple After Dark*.

The record tanked. So Stettler came up with a new promotion: hold a break dance and rap contest at a local nightclub and require that all the entrants perform their routines to his record. First, Stettler approached WBLS executive Charles Warfield, who said he would donate airtime if Stettler could enlist a corporate sponsor. Warfield suggested a fellow named James Patton at Coca-Cola's bottler in Purchase, New York. Warfield cautioned Stettler: Patton, he said, didn't always deliver on his promises.

So Stettler and West went up to Coca-Cola—with an easel and presentation, rather than a gorilla suit. After listening Patton told them that Coca-Cola was in, and he suggested that they move the show to a grander venue. To make sure Patton made good on his word, Stettler immediately issued a press release thanking Coca-Cola for allowing thousands of "underprivileged ghetto kids" the opportunity to attend a free rap talent show at Radio City Music Hall—a place much grander than even Patton had in mind. Stuck, Coca-Cola eventually kicked in $150,000 for the event, and hung promotional cards on tens of thousands of bottles of Coke.

Charlie Stettler had not only booked the first rap show at Rockefeller Center's venerated venue. He had also secured the very first corporate sponsorship deal in hip-hop history.

Stettler had been hustling since he arrived in New York thirteen years earlier, on March 4, 1970, in search of sex, drugs, and R&B. He had been a teenage soccer star in his native Switzerland, but he was kicked off his team, Xamax Neuchatel, for using drugs and refusing to cut his long blond hair. On his first night in New York, he was robbed of all his possessions. Penniless, and knowing only a few English words, he found work in a 42nd Street theater that produced live sex shows. His fluent Italian helped him land a job managing a mob-controlled massage parlor, Aphrodite Studio on 51st Street. In October 1971, he appeared naked in a *Playboy* spread with some of the Aphrodite girls. Then he took a role in his first porn movie. Billed as Charles Delon, he would eventually appear in a handful of adult films. Stettler fell in love with an older woman, a thirty-one-year-old niece of a Mafia captain in one of New York's Five Families. It was around the time of the Joe Colombo murder, and war between the Mafia organizations. Stettler was slowly drawn into the life. He witnessed his first murder. One day, his girlfriend begged him not to go to work at the Middle Earth, another Midtown massage parlor where he came to collect money. Stettler stayed home. Later that day, two people were killed at the massage parlor in what Stettler would call a "rubout" by the Colombo family. Stettler got an ulcer.

His hair fell out in clumps. He disappeared for a few years until things quieted down.

Charlie Stettler knew he didn't have the heart of a gangster. He did have, however, the soul of a huckster. Like Russell Simmons, Stettler made a living doing party promotions. During the disco era, when the Roxy roller-skating rink wouldn't admit Black and Puerto Rican kids, Stettler and Lynda West opened a rink that did, Busby's. When he visited the Disco Fever, he got his first up-close view of the rap scene. He fell in with Sal Abbatiello. Later, when it came time to assemble a roster for the Tin Pan Apple After Dark Dance & Rap Contest Finals, Abbatiello helped bring in established talent like the Fearless Four and the Rock Steady Crew, Kurtis Blow and Whodini. Along with the radio spots and promotional T-shirts emblazoned with the Coca-Cola and WBLS logos, Stettler's street marketing had created an amazing buzz for the event, scheduled for May 23, 1983.

But there were problems. Lynda West sat in the balcony with some of the genteel ladies from the Radio City back office, all dressed in smart suits and shirts with pussycat bows. West told them how she planned to stage a show that including rapping and break dancing.

"Break dancing?!" one of the ladies said. "Breaking *what*?!" West realized this woman actually thought that people were going to literally break things onstage.

It got worse. Four days before the show, Stettler, Abbatiello, and West were summoned to Radio City by some union officials from the International Brotherhood of Electrical Workers, Local 3. The officials gave Stettler an ultimatum: Cancel his show, or none of them would show up for work. "We don't want any niggers at Radio City Music Hall," one union representative told him. "Those kinds of niggers don't belong in here." Stettler managed to persuade them to relent, in part by soliciting their pity.

"I will be a dead man in New York City if this show doesn't happen," he said.

After that, Stettler still had to pay for a certain amount of union-mandated musicians for the evening, musicians he didn't need. Radio City's union guys didn't understand that rappers performed with only a DJ.

The day of the show, Sal Abbatiello brought as many security guys down from the Disco Fever as he could—Mandingo, Bam-Bam, and a few others. As soon as the lights went down in the auditorium packed with five thousand kids, there was a fight in front. The lights went back on, and the host, Mr. Magic, begged the crowd to behave.

"Don't you understand?" he pleaded. "That's what these people want us to do!"

The show continued without incident. Many from the nascent hip-hop business were there: Sylvia Robinson came down to judge the rap contest, as did Tommy Boy's Tom Silverman and Monica Lynch. In the audience as well were Barry Mayo and Russell Simmons, who passed by Stettler without knowing that this tall, balding White man with the goofy smile was responsible for the entire night.

The winners of the rap contest were the Disco 3, three oversize kids from East New York. The shortest, fattest kid, Darren Robinson, brought the house down by mimicking the sounds of a drum machine with his mouth. They called him Buffy, the Human Beat Box.

Stettler had promised a record deal to the winner of the contest, none of which, of course, was in place. Disregarding the warning of his friend from Busby's, record producer Nile Rodgers of Chic, Stettler sought out Art Kass of Sutra Records—a partner of Morris Levy—using his success with "Tin Pan Apple" as his calling card. Kass took Stettler to meet Levy, who was still in business with Joe Robinson and Sugar Hill, but in a five-year process of cashing out to the tune of $1.5 million. Stettler, who knew little of Levy's background, calmly insisted on a fifty/fifty deal, the kind of arrangement that Levy, to say the least, did not normally make. Levy looked at Stettler, chuckled, and said, "Okay." Over the next few weeks, Stettler and West set up shop in the Roulette/Sutra offices on 1790 Broadway.

When Stettler told Rodgers about his arrangement with Levy, Rodgers was dubious. "He gave me fifty percent," Stettler said.

"Well," Rodgers responded, "he may have signed a contract that says fifty percent. Good luck getting paid."

Stettler wasn't scared of Levy. He had been around gangsters before.

One by one, artists got tired of Joe and Sylvia Robinson's bullshit.

Flash went to court and sued successfully for the right to use his name. Spoonie Gee was granted a release from the label in exchange for relinquishing all claim to the material he recorded for them. Everyone involved with Sugar Hill made a choice: Stay and get money doled out piecemeal. Or you could leave, knowing that all the money you were owed was staying.

For Keith LeBlanc, a White session drummer in the Sugar Hill house band, his entreaties about payment were received with the same cold stares that Flash had endured. His reward was even colder: His buddies in the band, Doug Wimbish and Skip McDonald, were paid salaries, while Sugar Hill continued to pay LeBlanc by the session. His poor treatment at the hands of his Black employers would be avenged, ironically, by an icon of Black Nationalism.

LeBlanc had been moved by Alex Haley's *The Autobiography of Malcolm X*. Knowing that Sugar Hill's Chess catalog contained recordings of some of Malcolm's speeches, LeBlanc put together a five-minute-forty-four-second collage of the Black leader's words over an electronic funk beat.

LeBlanc sought the approval of Malcolm X's widow, Betty Shabazz, who was working in the administration of Medgar Evers College in Brooklyn. Shabazz listened as the young drummer nervously chattered about his song.

"Stop talking," she said. Shabazz felt burned before by artists using her husband's words, not the least of whom was Alex Haley. "This is my life. I'll listen to the tape and call you after I've heard it." LeBlanc left his mother's telephone number, thanked her, and walked out.

A few days later, LeBlanc heard from his mother.

"Malcolm X's wife called. She says you're a wonderful musician." Shabazz's only request was that LeBlanc remove the sound of a gunshot at the end of the song.

LeBlanc had the blessing of Betty Shabazz and soon secured the same from the son of Chess cofounder Leonard Chess. Joe Robinson had hired Marshall Chess as a consultant to help him with the catalog. Together, Chess and LeBlanc brought the record to Sylvia Robinson, who listened to the track and told them that she would get back to them with some "changes." When no changes were forthcoming, both Chess and LeBlanc knew they were getting the queen's royal rebuff. Furthermore, LeBlanc knew that even if the record did come out on Sugar Hill, both he and Betty Shabazz probably wouldn't get paid. Chess and LeBlanc decided to shop the record elsewhere.

The producers found a willing partner in Tom Silverman, who quickly made a deal for the record and released it on Tommy Boy Music. When Joe and Sylvia heard the record on Mr. Magic's show, they were furious. The Robinsons pressed up their own record of the song from the Tommy Boy version and released it under the artist name "Sugar Hill All Stars." Both labels filed copyright infringement suits against each other on November 17, 1983. The U.S. District Court in New Jersey issued an injunction against distribution by both labels until a judge could sort the mess out.

During the wait before the trial, Tom Silverman got a call from Joe Robinson.

"We should settle this," Robinson said. "Why don't you come out here to Englewood and we can talk?"

Silverman demurred. There was no way he was going out to some rendezvous with Joe Robinson. *No way.*

Instead, a few days later, Silverman got a surprise visit from an emissary of Robinson's at Tommy Boy's Upper East Side office. It was a mutual acquaintance, the Reverend Al Sharpton—whom Silverman knew from a recording session that James Brown had done with Afrika Bambaataa. Sharpton was friendly as he sat down with Silverman and tried to encourage him to settle. Silverman explained his side of the story, all the while nervously eyeing the gun poking out of the suit jacket of the burly friend who accompanied the reverend. Sharpton was courteous, but Silverman didn't budge. LeBlanc refused Sharpton's mediation, too. He knew he had Betty Shabazz on his side.

The day in court finally arrived, with Silverman, LeBlanc, and Shabazz on one side, and the Robinsons on the other, Sharpton in the benches behind them. Sylvia Robinson strode over to Betty Shabazz, and the two queens stood face-to-face.

"I am honored to meet you," Sylvia said.

"Get out of my face!" Shabazz shouted. "You are a pirate and a liar."

Her royalty challenged, Sylvia slunk back to her chair.

Shabazz turned to LeBlanc and whispered, "That was just for effect."

The Robinsons were about to get another surprise, as the presiding judge, Herbert Stern, took the bench.

"Mrs. Shabazz, do you remember me?" Stern said.

"No," she replied.

"We met when I was the assistant DA in the grand jury investigation of your husband's murder," Stern said.

Silverman suspected that they were going to have a very good day in court.

Ten days of discovery followed, with Silverman, LeBlanc, Chess, and Joe Robinson offering testimony. Tommy Boy's argument was that Betty Shabazz was the exclusive owner of all rights to the speeches of Malcolm X, not Chess. Sugar Hill's claim was that the song was made in their studios by their employee and, thus, their property. But the Robinsons quickly realized that things weren't going their way. One day, while waiting for the Robinsons and their lawyers to arrive, Judge Stern actually asked, "Where are the gangsters?"

By mid-December, the Robinsons and Silverman agreed to a court-approved settlement. Tommy Boy had exclusive rights to the record, and would pay Sugar Hill an escalating royalty based on sales.

The legal victory was bittersweet for LeBlanc. Joe Robinson still had a lot of friends in Black radio, and many of them refused to play the record after the trial, including Jim Gates at WESL, who had been the first programmer to play "Rapper's Delight." Gates had played the record before the controversy, but now he told *Billboard* magazine that he had a change of heart, claiming it "gave me time to think that Malcolm would have never approved of putting himself in a dance music context."

Even where the record *was* played, Silverman observed, it wasn't a hit. Making matters worse for LeBlanc, Silverman said that all the funds made by the sales of the record had been eaten up by his legal fees. He would not, therefore, be paying any royalties to him and Betty Shabazz.

Same bullshit, LeBlanc thought. *Different record company.*

Two decades earlier, during the grand jury testimony that followed the assassination of Malcolm X, Betty Shabazz told then-assistant district attorney Herbert Stern that she never saw the men who killed her husband. The assailants ran out of the Audubon Ballroom and onto the street. The police got to Talmadge Hayer before the crowd outside could tear him apart. Hayer was later sentenced to twenty years to life in prison.

Even as a teenager in upstate New York, Claudia Ann Carli knew who Talmadge Hayer was—one of her father's students at the Attica Correctional Facility. He was always complaining to her father about being framed by the FBI and the CIA. Her father, an English professor, lived to be helpful and was trusting to a fault. When one of his students was released, Professor John Carli would take him home, feed him, and let him stay overnight until he could find transportation home, usually to New York City. Ann grew up with a parade of ex-cons coming through the house. But John Carli believed that literacy was liberation, and he used any means at his disposal to teach people how to read. He had even taught Ann to diagram sentences before she reached kindergarten. Ann learned English, but John Carli's parents were adamant that his Japanese wife not teach her native language to her own children. By the time Ann Carli was in her twenties, she rectified that, living in Japan with her grandparents, and speaking fluent Japanese.

Carli planned to stay in Japan. She was making a lot of money with her new language skills, translating for touring rock artists like David Bowie. But she reconsidered after a South African expatriate entrepreneur named Clive Calder—one of the few in the world to take a chance on rap music—offered her a job.

She had met Calder in New York, back when he was still an artist manager for rock bands and she worked as an assistant to his friend and fellow expat, a concert promoter named Cedric Kushner. Calder dropped by one day. Carli made small talk, asking him what group he represented.

"You wouldn't have heard of them," Calder replied. "They played at NYU last night."

"Was it Dwight Twilley or City Boy?"

Calder was dumbfounded. "City Boy. How did you know that?" he asked.

"Because I was at the show last night," Carli answered. "I just bought City Boy's record."

By 1983, Calder had his own record company, Jive, and a new distribution deal with Clive Davis's Arista Records. He wanted the capable, quick-witted Ann Carli on his team. Calder wrote Carli that he would hold a position for her if she promised to come by the end of the year. Floored by Calder's gesture, Carli accepted.

She showed up for work on January 8, 1984, at Jive's American headquarters, a barely furnished brownstone on the Upper East Side—with an apartment on the top floor reserved for visits from Calder or out-of-town artists. Carli met her new colleagues: Barry Weiss, Jive's manager of sales and promotion; and Rachelle Greenblatt, who handled publishing. Upon her arrival, Greenblatt took Carli aside to remind her that even though she wasn't as senior as they were, they were all equals at Jive.

"You don't work for Barry," Greenblatt whispered. "He's gonna try to get you to do his typing. You don't have to do it."

"I can't type," Carli replied.

Carli was hired as manager of creative services, but she wasn't yet sure what that meant. Most of the acts on Jive were recorded and packaged in Britain—the most successful being the MTV new-wave sensation A Flock of Seagulls. Even Jive's rap group, Whodini, was produced at Calder's studios in London by Thomas Dolby. There wasn't much for her to do. After a few days at the company, Carli met her first Jive artist—a soul singer from Trinidad, by way of England, who was staying in the upstairs apartment while he recorded with some American producers.

He introduced himself as Billy, and then joined Carli in vacuuming and picking up her new office. Afterward, he played her some of his material, including a song called "European Queen." Billy asked Carli what she thought. Carli said that she liked everything except the song's name.

"'European Queen' sounds too cold," she said. "It makes me think of Queen Elizabeth."

Carli didn't know it yet, but she was already doing her job. Later that year, Billy Ocean's "Caribbean Queen" became a number one pop single in America, a huge crossover hit for Jive Records.

Carli hated how the British office of Jive handled the imaging of their artists. For Whodini's first album cover, they posed the group in front of a wall of graffiti; to Carli, even with little knowledge of hip-hop, the picture seemed passé. So she took control of packaging and artist development for the American market.

Whodini were now working with Run-DMC producer Larry Smith, and Russell Simmons had picked them up for management. Simmons fought to restrain Smith's more melodic tendencies on Run-DMC's records; but Smith's musical approach worked perfectly with Whodini, two MCs who were very serious about matching their vocal tone to the key of the music, a process they called "rhyming to the scale." When Carli heard the rough mixes of the group's R&B–inflected songs—"Five Minutes of Funk," "Friends," and "Freaks Come Out at Night"—it was clear that Smith and Whodini were an inspired pairing.

After meeting Whodini's new product manager, Simmons had decided that he and Carli were an inspired pairing as well, and it wasn't long before he made a proposal of his own.

"When are you coming to work for me?" he said.

But Carli could tell that Russell Simmons was proposing just a bit more than that.

Four and a half years after the first rap record, hip-hop was still a singles business. No one had ever had commercial success with a rap album, not even Kurtis Blow. As for artistic merit, most rap albums, like those on Sugar Hill Records, were merely rushed collections of throwaway filler songs to justify selling a hit single at a higher price. Steve Plotnicki at Profile Records didn't think there was a market for rap albums.

Cory Robbins saw things differently. After "It's Like That" and "Sucker MCs," Run-DMC had another huge single. "Hard Times"—backed with another song, "Jam Master Jay," a paean to their DJ, Jason Mizell—climbed four spots higher than their first single, to number eleven. With four Run-DMC songs in the can, Cory Robbins became convinced that Profile could release its first album.

Plotnicki told his partner that he was crazy.

"You're only gonna sell 20,000 copies," Plotnicki yelled. It would be a disaster for the company.

"No," Robbins said calmly, "you're wrong." Robbins never raised his voice. The angrier Plotnicki became, the calmer Robbins would get. Plotnicki eventually relented.

Unfortunately for Robbins, Russell Simmons agreed with Plotnicki—at least with the part about rap albums being pieces of shit. Simmons wanted to do a Run-DMC album, but to do it right, he needed a real budget, more than the amount specified in the contract. Robbins countered that the group needed only four or five more songs to make up a good album.

The label owner and artist manager waged battle via phone for the better part of a week until Robbins informed Simmons that he and the group had no choice in the matter. Run-DMC had agreed in their contract that Profile could release a Run-DMC album if the record company so opted, and Robbins sent a formal letter to Simmons indicating that Profile was exercising that option.

For Robbins, the group's feelings and fears were unimportant. A deal was a deal, just like it should have been with "Christmas Rappin'." Going forward, Robbins and Plotnicki would wield Profile's rights—to approve or to block songs, to sequence albums, to dictate album art—by the book and without hesitation. It was an old-fashioned way of doing business in an increasingly artist-driven industry.

Run-DMC, Russell, and Larry Smith headed back to Greene Street. One night, the musical tensions between the group and producer Smith boiled over. Run and DMC were laying down a hard beat from a drum machine, a big, round kick drum and a mean metal snare. Smith added a warm, synthesized bass line that, to the rappers' ear, seemed more appropriate for an R&B song. To Simmons and the group, hard was important, and loud was vital.

"You're ruining everything with that soft-ass, wack-ass bass line!" they screamed.

"That bass line is not soft," Smith said. To prove his point, he changed the sound setting on the synthesizer. Suddenly, the room filled with a jagged, loud crunch of electric guitar. The two MCs were convinced.

Later, Larry arranged for a guitarist, Eddie Martinez, to join them in the studio to replay the programmed pattern. Run-DMC emerged from their sessions with a new single, "Rock Box," one of the first mergers of rap and rock on record.

In the spring of 1984, Profile Records released a nine-song album, *Run-DMC*, along with "Rock Box" as a 12-inch single. "Rock Box" wasn't a favorite of Black programmers, as it clashed with the smooth R&B sounds of their playlists. But Black radio's younger listeners requested it, and "Rock Box" rose to number twenty-two on the Billboard R&B singles chart.

Profile had also issued "Rock Box" as one of their first 7-inch singles, signaling Robbins and Plotnicki's hopes of a crossover onto pop airwaves. But despite a wall of wailing guitars, "Rock Box" was still a rap single, and as such, simply "too Black" for mainstream, Top 40 radio stations.

Cory Robbins at heart was still the kid who compulsively listened to the radio and tabulated hits. But when he tuned in to WRKS's "Top Eight at Eight" during the summer of 1984, Robbins experienced a life-fulfilling vindication: four of those eight songs were his records. And all four were from Run-DMC's first album.

The summer of Run-DMC was also the summer that Barry Mayo's dreams became reality. Not only had he become the first Black general manager of an RKO General radio station, but his successor as program director, Tony Quartarone, had made 98.7 Kiss FM the number one music station in the market, for the first time ever. Tony "Q," the former intern, had finally beaten WBLS and Frankie Crocker.

For Mayo, it was time for champagne and payback. Mayo had Crocker's in-studio hotline number, and every afternoon, in the seconds before Crocker would start his shift, Mayo would call his archrival:

"Frankie, this is Barry," Mayo hissed. "I'm kicking your *fucking* ass. I'm enjoying beating the *shit* out of you."

By the time Crocker opened his microphone, he was completely provoked, ruffled and sputtering.

"I just spoke to that short, ugly program director at that station with the lips," Crocker would say. "Don't listen to that station with the lips. You'll get mononucleosis."

Mayo sat back, listened, and laughed. *More advertising for me*, he thought.

Cedric Walker arrived for his meeting with Sugar Hill Records on foot. He had to take the train to Englewood because he didn't have money to rent a car. Walker didn't have cash for a hotel either, so he stayed with family across the river in New York. Even his plane ticket from Atlanta had been purchased with borrowed funds. But Walker had a scheme to make some money, and this appointment with Sylvia Robinson was the key.

Cedric—everyone called him "Ricky"—was thirty years old, and looked twenty. Yet Ricky Walker had an expertise that belied his youthful appearance: He had been promoting and producing live shows for almost half his life. He started as a teenager, working the door and backstage in his uncle's nightclub every summer in Tuskegee, Alabama. The Black Forest had a regular "house band," some students from nearby Tuskegee Institute who called themselves the Commodores. When the band—and their lead singer, Lionel Richie—landed a recording contract with Motown in 1972, they took Ricky Walker on tour with them as their production director.

After years on the road handling the logistics of lights, sound, and transportation for the Commodores and other groups, Walker became a booking agent, then a promoter, and finally started his own marketing business—going into cities across the country, setting up advertising and promotions in advance of national tours. By 1980, he had worked closely with many of the most important Black acts in the country, including the Jacksons.

Walker succeeded largely because he knew how to make a plan, and how to work it. So when he saw rap records starting to get some play in clubs across the country, he went to record stores and studied artists and labels. He holed up in the library and read as much as he could find in newspapers and magazines about the nascent culture—not just the music, but the dances as well. Walker was intrigued by the notion that "rapping" was part of an oral tradition that went all the way back to Africa, where "griots" would tell long stories in rhyme. He connected break dancing to other African-derived forms of dance, like Brazilian capoeira. When he finished his investigation, Walker concocted a master plan to bring all of this stuff, the best rap groups and the best dance crews, together in one place. It would be a national stadium tour with multiple stages to keep the show going—almost like P. T. Barnum's three-ring circus.

To make his "Fresh Festival" happen, he would need to partner with the most successful rap label, Sugar Hill. So Walker secured an audience with Sylvia Robinson.

Their meeting in the Queen's sumptuous study was brief. Sylvia took one look at Walker and started blasting him.

"I don't know what you're coming here for, motherfucker! I can promote my acts my damn self! Why the fuck do I need you?! I can do my own damn tour! I was the *first* one to do a rap tour!"

Robinson continued cursing, calling Walker some names that he'd never even heard before. "Get the hell out of my office!" she concluded.

"Thank you," Walker replied. Then he left.

Walker couldn't figure out what went wrong. Was she expecting somebody older? Was she having a bad day? Was it the unconventional stuff, the break dancing, that turned her off? He never got the chance to ask.

Luckily, when Ricky Walker made a plan, he always added a plan B. He had already set up an appointment with an artist manager who had some less established acts. Walker rode the bus back to the city and walked to 1133 Broadway, the offices of Rush Productions.

Russell Simmons rented office space from Rocky Ford and J. B. Moore, and had inherited their receptionist, Heidi Smith. Rush represented a handful of rap clients spread out among several record labels: Kurtis Blow, Simmons's first artist, on Mercury; Jimmy Spicer on Spring; Whodini on Jive; and two groups on Profile—Run-DMC, and Dr. Jeckyll & Mr. Hyde.

Simmons now employed a publicist, too: a tall, redheaded Jewish guy from Michigan named Bill Adler—a music journalist who had helped Danny Schechter research the first *20/20* segment on rap. Adler met Simmons while he was doing an article on the Disco Fever for *People* magazine, and they bonded over their mutual belief that rap was best understood and best marketed as teen music, rock and roll for a new generation. Adler was taken in by Simmons's blazing charisma. Simmons, in turn, flattered the freelancer into a full-time gig.

"I can't believe a guy as smart as you doesn't have a job," Simmons said. "Why don't you come work for me?"

Adler worked for free for the first six months. He began talking Rush

acts up to the mainstream press, while Simmons dreamed of bigger things—
tours, movies—without quite knowing how to get there. So when Ricky
Walker came in to pitch his proposal for a "Fresh Festival," he found a much
more receptive audience than he had at Sugar Hill. Simmons, who normally
had a lot to say, remained silent until Walker finished.

"I've been sitting here trying to figure out how I can make a thousand
dollars a week with each of my guys," Simmons said. "And now you're sitting here telling me I can make a thousand dollars a night? Let's *go*!"

Together, they plotted a lineup starring Kurtis Blow and the other up-
and-coming Rush acts, including Run-DMC and Whodini. Walker mentioned
another rap group he wanted to get, a group he really liked.

Simmons replied that he didn't manage them. But he knew who did.

Charlie Stettler was livid. After the Disco 3's first single on Sutra Records bombed, he spent his own money to take the rappers to his homeland
of Switzerland. The Disco 3—who had never been in a hotel, much less an
airplane—appeared on television shows and attended a yodeling convention.
But when they ran up a $350 room service bill, Stettler lost it.

"You're nothing but a bunch of fat boys!" he cursed them in his stilted
English.

After they returned to the States, the Disco 3—Darren "The Human
Beat Box" Robinson, Mark "Prince Markie Dee" Morales, and Damon "Kool
Rock Ski" Wimbley—didn't speak to Stettler for six weeks. But Stettler now
had suddenly found an angle for the foundering group. With Sal Abbatiello's
help, Stettler reached out to Kurtis Blow to produce a new single. Driven by
Morris Levy's connections at Black radio, "Fat Boys," the Disco 3's second
release, did so well that Stettler decided to rechristen the group in a midnight ceremony at Roseland Ballroom, raising $10,000 in cash for the United
Negro College Fund in the process.

Stettler hatched more stunts: He got Pepsi to sponsor a "Guess the Fat
Boys' Weight" promotion. The Fat Boys donned yellow satin jackets—
adorned with their new logo, designed by Lynda West—and stood on a scale
in the window of Tower Records on the corner of 4th and Broadway. The
winner was awarded $898 and 898 cans of Diet Pepsi (one for each of the Fat
Boys' collective pounds). Charlie Stettler had proven that he had as much
hustle as Russell.

Both Stettler and his Fat Boys made Russell Simmons cringe. Stettler was corny, and his Fat Boys skirted the border of buffoonery. But with Kurtis Blow as their producer, Simmons now had a stake in their success. With Walker by his side, Simmons picked up the phone and dialed Stettler.

"There's a guy over here who's trying to put together a national tour," Simmons told Stettler. "I'm down. He wants you to be down. Can you be a part of it?"

"I might not be able to do it." Stettler sighed when Walker visited him at Tin Pan Apple's offices. Stettler told him that the Fat Boys might be opening for Michael Jackson's "Victory" reunion tour with his brothers, scheduled for the summer of 1984.

It was complete bullshit. Stettler and Lynda West sent out a bogus press release, and Walter Yetnikoff, the head of Jackson's label, CBS Records, called Morris Levy, screaming. Levy had Yetnikoff on the speakerphone, and Stettler could see Levy shaking his head and laughing as the CBS exec sputtered and swore. After the call, Levy turned to Stettler:

"You're dangerous," Levy said.

But Stettler had his reasons. He wanted to get Polygram excited about picking up the Fat Boys' contract from Sutra, which—along with Levy's whole empire—was looking increasingly like a sinking ship. And he wanted Walker to sweat a little bit.

But days later, Stettler returned to Walker, not only with the Fat Boys, but with the thing he needed most: a corporate sponsor. Stettler had called a friend from back home in Switzerland, who introduced him to Max Imgruth, the head of a new Swiss watch company attempting to reclaim the downscale sector from Japanese competitors like Seiko and Casio. Stettler bragged to Imgruth about how much this American rap tour was going to make, and schooled him on how Black youth historically set the fashion trends for mainstream America. When Imgruth made an offer, Stettler called Walker.

"I've got this guy at a new company called Swatch. He wants to give us $350,000," Stettler said.

Walker started hyperventilating. *$350,000!*

But first, Stettler had to show Walker the virtue of lying as a negotiation tactic.

"Listen, when you get on the phone with him, tell him you might not be able to do it. Tell him Coca-Cola might have the sponsorship."

On the phone with Imgruth, Walker did as Stettler bade him. Within a few weeks, he was signing a deal with Swatch while sitting on crates in the company's as yet unpacked New York offices.

Suddenly Walker saw Stettler for who he really was: a modern-day P. T. Barnum.

Imgruth may have seen the resemblence, too. Perhaps that was why he made one thing very clear: If Stettler fucked this tour up, he would kill him.

Run-DMC's album sold more every week—5,000, then 7,500, then 10,000. The total was now close to 250,000 copies.

Selling a quarter of a million units of a single could net a record company about the same amount in dollars. But selling 250,000 albums could bring in two to three times that much, a huge windfall for a company with only four employees, like Profile Records. Cory Robbins and Steve Plotnicki could afford to put some of it into marketing and promotion. With Bill Adler engendering some newfound acclaim for Run-DMC from White rock critics at the *Village Voice*, *Rolling Stone*, and *Creem*—Robbins initiated another Profile and Run-DMC first. They would shoot a video for "Rock Box."

In the three years since the debut of Music Television, the music video had gone from an artistic frivolity to the greatest influence on record sales. But even in 1984, the market for videos by Black artists remained dismal, mainly because MTV, with few exceptions, refused to play their videos. As for rap videos, the channel hadn't played one since "Rapture."

The reason for this bald-faced segregation was simple: The network was founded by men who came out of 1970s radio, when Black artists had been casually jettisoned from FM stations with the rationale that the broadcasters' White male target audience didn't like soul and funk music. But Black rock artists were shut out of these stations, too. On MTV, soul and funk were allowed as long as the artists who played it were White.

When Motown Records rock-funk artist Rick James went public with his criticism of the channel, a huge internal debate began at MTV. Some employees in the nascent news division subverted the programming department by covering groups like Chic. The channel's only Black VJ, J. J. Jackson, debated leaving the channel. Finally MTV succumbed to internal and external pressure. On March 2, 1983, Bob Pittman, MTV's chief executive, approved Michael Jackson's "Billie Jean" for rotation on the young network's playlist. The megastar's MTV breakthrough resulted in the bestselling album of all time, *Thriller*.

MTV enjoyed a Michael Jackson boost, but they remained inhospitable to other Black artists. Local shows like *Video Music Box* and syndicated programs like *New York Hot Tracks* were the only outlets for most R&B and dance music. But doing a video was still a risky proposition for any Black artist, especially for a small independent label.

Profile budgeted $25,000 for the video—more than they had advanced Run-DMC for their entire album. The video itself was shot in and around the club Danceteria, where Steve Plotnicki decided that the group would perform onstage with a band. Director Steve Kahn captured Run-DMC on grainy black-and-white film, with some color shots of White girls dancing in rainbow tights. The video featured comic relief from a character named Professor Irwin Corey, and Eddie Martinez playing and making guitar faces. Most tellingly, Jam Master Jay exchanges winks with a cute White kid, who pushes the adults aside to get a peek at his new favorite band. All the visual and sonic cues for crossover were in place.

Run-DMC gave an energetic performance, solidifying their iconic image—black hats, black leather, white sneakers, DMC's glasses. Coming from two black rappers, it was pure rock showmanship. Yet at the heart of the video, Run and DMC silenced the cacophony of the guitars, and yielded the floor to a turntable solo from Jam Master Jay, proclaiming, "Our DJ is better than all these bands." Run-DMC, in the midst of crossing over, hadn't sold out. It was the fulfillment of Russell Simmons's vision, and Profile's persistence.

In the summer of 1984, "Rock Box" by Run-DMC became the first video by a rap group to air on Music Television. Robbins and Simmons argued to get it in rotation, and the video wasn't played as often as the channel's rock clips. But "Rock Box" did last through the summer, and Run-DMC joined Michael Jackson and Prince among the rare Black artists on MTV. It was good company.

The sudden appearance of rap polarized MTV's audience. Rocker Lou Reed saw in rap music something kindred to rock. When he hosted a show on an MTV series called *Rock Influences*—in which established artists chose their favorite bands to perform—Reed invited Run-DMC. The crowd, bred during an era of segregation on radio and MTV, was not so open-minded. At the show's taping on September 25, 1984, some young White men in the audience ran up and down the aisles jeering Run-DMC as they performed. Indeed, with Run-DMC's ascendance, rap faced a resurgent White backlash not unlike the antidisco rebellion five years before.

But there were also signs of a growing crossover to White audiences and more firsts. In the fall of 1984, Run-DMC headlined the first national rap tour, the Swatch Watch New York City Fresh Fest.

Ricky Walker's brainchild sold out ten- to twenty-thousand-seat arenas from Atlanta to Philadelphia, bringing rap to diverse audiences as far west as Hawaii. In Providence, well over half of the tickets sold were bought by White kids. And the show they saw was diverse, too—rappers, DJs, and breakers, bringing the complexity of hip-hop culture to mainstream American audiences. In four months, the Fresh Fest grossed $3.5 million over twenty-seven performances.

Walker was proud of something else: He took a bunch of young kids out of the inner city, put them on the road, and not one act of violence blemished the tour. Again, Walker's planning was the key. He hired a hotel coordinator to handle the load-ins and load-outs in each city. Every night, he stationed security guards on the floors where his artists roomed. And he brought along some added insurance: six feet, four inches, and three hundred pounds of bad news from Macon, Georgia. "Big Charles," as everyone called him, was a professional fighter. The tour rule was, if anybody fought each other, then they had to fight Big Charles, too.

Nobody wanted to fight Big Charles.

Big Charlie Stettler was on the tour as well, doing advance promotion for the Fat Boys that garnered them a national audience. The Fresh Fest was not only a landmark for Run-DMC and the Fat Boys; it was a sort of coming-out party for Whodini, too. Ann Carli secured a budget to shoot live footage of the group performing their single "Freaks Come Out at Night," but she couldn't get money for the song she thought would be a huge hit, "Friends." So Carli took the camera crew backstage and, in front of the tour bus, had Whodini lead an a cappella rendition of "Friends," with shots of Run-DMC, and a crew of breakers that included a young dancer from Atlanta named Jermaine Dupri. Carli made "Friends" the opener for her video, and got two videos for the price of one.

In the fall of 1984, based largely on those two songs and one video, Whodini achieved a rarity for a rap group: a welcome reception on daytime Black radio, and hundreds of thousands in sales.

On December 17, *Run-DMC* became the first rap album—and the first album on Profile Records—to be certified gold by the Recording Industry Association of America, having sold over 500,000 copies.

Run-DMC were not only rap stars now. They were rock stars.

———

Barry Mayo's final wish came true. In late 1984, Frankie Crocker was fired.

The departure of Crocker from WBLS rocked the once-stable station. Charles Warfield, now the general manager of WBLS, decided to take the playlist in a more adult direction, ditching rap entirely. Warfield offered Mr. Magic a new air shift playing "Quiet Storm" music—soft R&B and jazz. On the one hand, it was a compliment: Mr. Magic was seen as an asset regardless of the music he played. On the other, Warfield misread reality. Hip-hop was not just a genre of music. It was a lifestyle. Mr. Magic and hip-hop were inseparable, both for his audience and for the DJ himself. Faced with Warfield's ultimatum, Mr. Magic departed WBLS, resumed his show on WHBI, and took an additional weekly gig on a Black station in Philadelphia, WDAS.

Alonzo Brown had grown bitter. None of Dr. Jeckyll & Mr. Hyde's new singles—not "The Challenge," not "Fast Life"—had come close to matching the success of "Genius Rap." Profile didn't give them any money to make an album, so they dug into their own pockets to record one, looking out of town for a cheaper recording studio. They recorded their album *The Champagne of Rap* in Cleveland.

Brown and his partner, Andre Harrell, had toured the East Coast a bit, but that was all they were going to get from Russell Simmons and Profile, who were now fully devoted to developing Run-DMC. The always upwardly mobile Harrell, who arranged for himself and Alonzo to wear suits and ties on their album cover, had bailed out of the group to work at, of all places, Rush Productions, Simmons's management company.

Brown scrambled and got a job as a runner at the American Stock Exchange. Dr. Jeckyll had transformed. Mr. Hyde, on the other hand, was dead.

Once more, the hits dried up for Sylvia Robinson. By 1984, Sugar Hill Records—the Black-owned company that dominated the early years of rap on record—had been eclipsed by other, smaller companies run mostly by young, Jewish entrepreneurs and executives like Cory Robbins, Steve Plotnicki, Tom Silverman, and Barry Weiss.

Other labels were bound to cash in as rap records started to make money. But Sugar Hill Records' swift decline was largely of their own making. Part of it was hubris: Sylvia Robinson turned away potential partners like Ricky Walker, ignored changes in the music to her own disadvantage, and even rejected a free video for "White Lines" made by a young student filmmaker at New York University named Spike Lee, which featured the acting talents of his friend, Laurence Fishburne. Part of it was greed: The Robinsons' tight-fisted ways with their artists, combined with their profligate personal spending, scarred their already shaky reputation in the business and scared away many good artists and managers. Part of it was ignorance: The Robinsons didn't understand the growing value of artist development, as Russell Simmons, Charlie Stettler, and Ann Carli did. Part of it was recklessness: Joe Robinson chose the mob as his partner. Whereas Charlie Stettler got out as business got better, Robinson got in deeper as business got worse.

Again, the hit records covered a multitude of sins—sins revealed when the hits dried up. Sugar Hill spent too much and made too little. Now it needed money. Joe and Sylvia Robinson faced financial ruin the last time they tangled with a major label, but a new major distribution arrangement—with an advance to cover their debts—seemed to be the only hope of avoiding a second bankruptcy. CBS Records wouldn't give Joe Robinson a deal: An internal memo called Sugar Hill "the Black Mafia," and valued their Chess catalog at $500,000, not the $5 million held forth by the Robinsons. Capitol Records turned them down, too. Desperate, Robinson turned to friends of Morris Levy.

Like Levy, Salvatore Pisello had ties to organized crime. Pisello told Robinson he could broker a deal between Sugar Hill and MCA. And Pisello did broker one, albeit not the deal that Robinson wanted. MCA offered distribution, but no advance. Losses would be recouped against the value of the Chess catalog.

If Sugar Hill Records had produced more good records, this might have been a profitable arrangement. But they didn't, and it wasn't. Sugar Hill had MCA manufacture records that didn't sell, and they ran up a tab of $1.7 million. MCA settled the tab by taking the Chess catalog and covered Sugar Hill's final payment to Morris Levy as part of Levy's cash-out deal. When the FBI began probing Pisello, Levy, and MCA regarding a side deal for out-of-print ("cutout") records a few years later, Robinson again became the subject of a federal investigation. Even Al Sharpton volunteered his services to the FBI to inform on his old friend Joe.

This time, Robinson was left with next to nothing. He was broke and broken; at one point, in the offices of MCA, he shook and cried as he waited for an audience with label head Irving Azoff to plead for a better deal. Robinson later sued MCA, claiming that the major label and Pisello had conspired to swindle him.

Joe and Sylvia Robinson were back to where they started with All Platinum. Sylvia couldn't write or produce herself out of financial trouble. Joe was entangled with another major label, as he once was with Polygram in the 1970s. Furthermore Joe mortgaged his dream of a strong, independent, Black-owned company by dealing with people who clearly thought they owned *him*. A federal witness revealed that the Mafia wiseguys referred to Joe Robinson as "Morris's nigger." Once, a reputed mobster named Sonny Brocco came to Sugar Hill Records and called Robinson a "nigger" to his face.

Joe Robinson—the proud number runner from Harlem, the Black entrepreneur who gave young Black Americans a new platform for their voices—didn't say a word.

ALBUM THREE

THE BEAT BOX

Def Jam fosters a revolution in hip-hop
art and commerce
(1984–1988)

Side A
High

If you heard a rap record on the radio in 1984, Russell Simmons had something to do with it. Run-DMC, Kurtis Blow, Fat Boys, Whodini—Simmons got paid off of them all as either a producer, manager, or promoter.

Then Simmons caught a record that wasn't his. The song had no music. No Sugar Hill house band, no cheesy melody, no keyboards, no bass line. The record took Simmons's stripped-down, beat-box sound and amplified it. The drums were bigger, the scratches louder, the rhymes harder. The rap was nothing like he had ever heard, the MC talking in polysyllables, calling out to the "analyzing, summarizing, musical myth-seeking people of the universe, this is *yours!*"

It was as if the MC were speaking directly to him. Here was the rap music Simmons envisioned when he made "Sucker MCs." It was street; it was uncompromising. And it wasn't his record.

Whose record is it? thought Russell Simmons.

Simmons eventually tracked it down—"It's Yours," by T La Rock & Jazzy Jay. He knew Jazzy Jay very well: Afrika Bambaataa's DJ, Red Alert's cousin. Jay spun regularly at the hottest club in town, the Roxy.

But Simmons didn't know anything about the label that released Jay's record, Def Jam, nor the person listed as the song's producer, Rick Rubin.

Whoever this nigger is, Simmons thought, *he just made the Blackest record ever.*

———

A White, Jewish college junior hailing from suburban Long Island, Frederick Jay Rubin operated "Def Jam Recordings" out of his dorm room at New York University. As for the song that electrified Russell Simmons and the streets of New York during the summer of 1984, Rubin recorded it with a drum machine and $300 from his parents, who had been funding his dreams for years.

"Ricky," his mother exclaimed, "can do anything!"

Linda Rubin—a big, bleached-blond, boisterous woman—often regaled family, friends, and visitors with tales like this: One year when Ricky was in grade school, she and her husband, Mickey, took him to one of the Jewish resorts in the Catskills. These hotels, like Grossinger's and the Concord, packed their daily schedules with activities, classes, and games for children. When the Rubins arrived, there was already a science competition in full swing.

"All those other kids had been working for days on their projects when Ricky entered it," Linda later bragged. "And would you *believe* it, he FUCK-ING WON?!"

When Ricky wanted to learn magic tricks, Linda and Mickey drove him into the city to mix with real magicians at their friend's Irv Tannen's legendary magic shop. He conversed well with adults as he plied them for tips and tricks. Soon he was performing professional-level magic shows for kids and grown folks alike, pocketing hundreds of dollars for his efforts.

Mickey Rubin—a tall, heavyset man with a deep voice and a sensible manner—owned a discount furniture store, and he and Linda supported their son's projects with plenty of cash and praise in equal measure. When Ricky wanted to take up photography and design, they bought him a camera and enrolled him in a summer course at Harvard. When Ricky wanted to learn guitar, they bought him a used Gibson SG. When Ricky took to punk rock, and wanted to see bands like the Cramps and the Contortions play at Manhattan clubs like Max's Kansas City or CBGB, they drove him—letting Ricky go inside alone, waiting patiently in their Cadillac for him to emerge. When Ricky formed a band called the Pricks, Linda designed the logo. When Ricky started bringing girls home, they gave him an entire room in the basement for his privacy. And when Ricky turned sixteen and desired even more independence, Mickey and Linda got him a brand-new Fiat—which he drove to Long Beach High every day even though the school was right across the street from their house.

Long Beach High served three distinct groups of students, from three different parts of the same, narrow island between the Atlantic Ocean and the Middle Bay. The upper-middle-class Italian and Jewish kids like Rick lived on the east end, in Lido Beach. The less wealthy Italian and Irish kids lived on the west end, in Atlantic Beach. And the Black kids lived in between them, in run-down Long Beach. During Rick's years there, Long Beach High closed a few times because of pitched battles between groups of Black and White kids. Rick called them "race riots."

But Rick—a big, stocky kid with long hair—stayed above the fray. He quietly disdained many of his White classmates for their pedestrian tastes. While he was in the city listening to the latest cutting-edge music, his peers on Long Island remained stuck on the old stalwarts of rock radio: Led Zeppelin, Yes, and Pink Floyd. The only people at school who listened to new music, in fact, were the Black kids. And all the Black kids were listening to rap.

Where many White kids hated rap, Rick was curious. Every week, it seemed the Black kids at Long Beach High were all about some new group. One week, it was the Crash Crew. The next, it was the Funky Four. Whoever had the new record out, that was the new favorite. In this way, Rick grasped that rap and punk were a lot alike. Punk and rap groups made songs for the moment and tossed them away a minute later, because there was always something newer, better, and fresher. Both were created by near amateurs, for the sheer fun of it. Both were rejections of the puffed-up, dressed-up pretention of 1970s music—whether art rock or disco. In both punk and rap, if it sounded raw, it was authentic. The "worse" it was, the better.

Rick tore into hip-hop the same way he did his other childhood fixations, trading magic for Mr. Magic. Rick recorded the DJ's WHBI show every Saturday night and listened to it all week with the rest of the Black kids in school. He bought every 12-inch single he could lay his hands on. He purchased a mixer from a local DJ and practiced turntable techniques. By the time he graduated in the spring of 1981, rap had become Rubin's second all-consuming musical passion. The school's yearbook printed a parting proverb from Ricky: "I wanna play loud. I wanna be heard. I want all to know. I'm not one of the herd."

In the fall Mickey Rubin moved his son into NYU's Weinstein Hall dormitory at 5 University Place in Greenwich Village. When Ricky moved out of the house, Linda Rubin left everything in both of Ricky's rooms exactly the way it was. Yellowing stacks of old rock magazines and newspapers. Curling posters of Devo and the Dead Kennedys. Dusty records and car repair manuals on the shelves. On a cabinet in the living room was Ricky's school portrait. Linda always liked looking at his smiling baby face in that photo. She might never see that face again.

Ricky was growing a beard.

For Rick, Weinstein Hall was the perfect new home, just blocks away from a number of fantastic downtown punk rock clubs. But two months after Rubin moved into the city, a small reggae club nearby began hosting a weekly hip-hop party. The "Wheels of Steel" nights at Negril were Rick's first opportunity to see his favorite rap groups live.

Rubin was shocked by how much better hip-hop was in person than on record. The cutting by DJs like Jazzy Jay and performances by MC crews like the Treacherous Three exploded from the stage like any Ramones or Dead Kennedys show. Their gigs sounded nothing like their records, which by comparison seemed like canned disco music with a bit of rap thrown on top. Live hip-hop, to Rick's surprise, rocked. Negril immediately became an every-Thursday-night thing for Rick Rubin.

The "Wheels of Steel" night at Negril was a convergence of uptown artists and downtown audiences, hip-hop and punk, Black and White; one of the unpredictable consequences of the chance meeting four years earlier between Fab 5 Freddy Brathwaite and Michael Holman.

At the time, Fab 5 Freddy was a graffiti writer looking to break into the art world, and Holman a junior credit analyst on Wall Street by day, an art promoter by night. Holman, a lanky, light-skinned army brat from San Francisco who once danced onstage with the new wave group the Tubes, introduced Freddy to Jean-Michel Basquiat. Freddy, in turn, acquainted Holman with hip-hop.

Holman adopted Fab 5 Freddy's quest to unite the uptown and downtown scenes. Just as Fred led Blondie to the Bronx, Holman brought Malcolm McLaren, the British impresario behind the Sex Pistols, to witness Afrika Bambaataa and the Zulu Nation DJs in their milieu, the Bronx River Projects. McLaren was both terrified and transfixed by the field trip, and asked Holman to bring the Zulus to safer environs—opening up for his new punk-pop act, Bow Wow Wow, at the Ritz downtown. Holman assembled an unprecedented roster of DJs, MCs, breakers, and graffiti artists, and in September of 1981, all four elements of hip-hop played out before a stunned, enthusiastic White audience.

In the crowd was Ruza Blue, a British expatriate who ran McClaren's SoHo boutique. Blue asked Holman if he could book that kind of show every Thursday night at her friend's venue, a club called Negril. Holman drew in the Zulus to DJ, and Fab 5 Freddy to MC—in the classic sense of the term, since Freddy didn't consider himself much of a rapper. The parties attracted an adventurous mix of b-boys and punks, clubgoers and college students— including Rick Rubin, the stocky kid with tousled brown hair and a scruffy beard.

By early 1982, the club was filled to capacity, and the fire department shut the Thursday parties down. Ruza Blue looked for a bigger place. Holman decided not to go with her. Instead, he embarked on a grander mission: to create a TV show that would be the hip-hop version of *American Bandstand*.

Fab 5 Freddy hipped Blue to a possible new venue: a cavernous, empty former roller-disco in Manhattan's Chelsea district called the Roxy.

"I can't see you packing that joint, though." Fab 5 Freddy told her. Blue's solution to the problem of the extra space was simple: Make the room look smaller by bringing in some huge canvas curtains to section off the rest of the rink from the party.

Rick Rubin was among the hundred and fifty or so regulars who came to Blue's first party at the Roxy. He knew Blue and Fred, and became chummy with Bambaataa's DJ, Jazzy Jay. The NYU student watched and learned as Jay spun records with other Zulus like Afrika Islam upon a platform in the middle of the dance floor. It was the middle of 1982, when their "Planet Rock" ruled the clubs and airwaves.

Week by week, as the hip-hop night began to catch on, and hundreds became thousands, Rick Rubin saw Blue move the curtains back, farther and farther, until they were no longer needed. Graffiti artists created murals onstage. MC crews descended from the Bronx in a cascade of numbers: the Treacherous Three, the Fearless Four, the Furious Five. The Rock Steady Crew danced before incredulous, infatuated downtown scenesters, including Fred's friends like Basquiat and Keith Haring, Glenn O'Brien and Andy Warhol, the Talking Heads and the B-52s, the Clash and David Bowie.

Artist managers used the club as a launching pad for new, unknown music artists, like Madonna and New Edition. Established pop record producers took the sounds of the Roxy hip-hop scene onto the radio and MTV.

Malcolm McLaren told Blue he wanted to make a rap record. Blue suggested Fab 5 Freddy as the MC, but Fred demurred; he had heard bad things about McLaren being an exploiter of artists and a "culture vulture." Fred passed McLaren off to the Supreme Team, two MC/DJs who had bought the time slot on WHBI just after Mr. Magic. Malcolm McLaren's "Buffalo Gals" became an international hit.

Fab 5 Freddy made his own record when Jean Karakos, the owner of a French record label called Celluloid, saw a photo spread of the Roxy scene, and enlisted the help of French journalist and Roxy regular Bernard Zekri to produce a French hip-hop song. Zekri's French-speaking American girl-friend, Ann Boyle, taught Fab 5 Freddy the lyrics, and they both took passes, Fred's on the A-side, Boyle's on the B-side. "Change the Beat," by Beside & Fab 5 Freddy, became one of the first French-language hip-hop hits. Zekri eventually transported the entire Roxy crew to Europe—with Fab 5 Freddy as ringleader—for his New York City Rap Tour, which lit up the continent.

Freddy's record rippled, too. The woman who designed the record sleeve was a French photojournalist and graphic artist named Sophie Bramly. Bramly, a sultry, dark-haired Tunisian Jew, had been coming to New York since she was eleven years old and was a familiar face on the downtown scene. Bramly returned to Paris in the wake of "Change the Beat" and helped to produce the very first hip-hop TV show outside America. The show, called *Hip-Hop*, featured live performances and music videos, and became a huge hit in France while Michael Holman was still trying to get his own show, *Graffiti Rock*, off the ground in the States.

Freddy's exclamation at the end of "Change the Beat" ("This stuff is reeee-ally freshhhhh!") became the scratched backbone to another big record, the brainchild of Celluloid house producer Bill Laswell. A collaboration between jazz pianist Herbie Hancock and Roxy DJ DST, "Rockit," scored another huge European pop hit. The song had a narrower impact in America—it went to number one on Billboard's club play chart—but it garnered five trophies at the first annual MTV Video Music Awards in 1984.

Songs like "Buffalo Gals," "Change the Beat," and "Rockit" all rippled out from the Roxy parties, but they were one-hit wonders, musical step-stones in hip-hop's journey into the American mainstream and global consciousness.

Rick Rubin, however, was about to take his Roxy experiences and turn them into something with lasting impact.

———

It was long past midnight when Rick Rubin and his friends returned to his dorm room from one of their nightly club crawls. Rubin threw a rap record on his turntable, and the guys joked and hollered over the music blasting through Rubin's huge Cerwin-Vega speakers.

Suddenly Nancy Heller—the girl that Rick Rubin referred to as "that Hell-bitch"—burst into the room, shrieking over the pounding music.

"You fucking idiots! I can't stand you anymore!"

Rubin and his friends stopped laughing. Heller looked crazy, standing in the middle of the room in a T-shirt and shorts, her face beet red, her hair wild. Rubin and his friends—most of them big, beefy guys—froze for a moment of real fear.

"You motherfuckers!"

Rubin, whom Heller called "Rick the Prick," was the first to bolt from the room, his heavy steps followed by those of Sean Travis, Warren Bell, and the rest of the guys. They left Rubin's younger roommate, Adam Dubin, to face the enraged woman's wrath alone.

Nancy Heller was mad only because she had been driven to madness by Rubin over the course of one torturous semester.

Rick Rubin lived in the B wing of Weinstein dorm, room 712. Heller lived in 812. Like Rubin, Heller had enrolled at NYU in part to be closer to the music scene, albeit one of a different sort. She regularly sang and played guitar at folk clubs like Speakeasy and Gerde's Folk City. But Heller's sleep and study times seemed to directly coincide with Rick's nocturnal, three-digit-decibel sonic booms of rap and punk. Heller found that she lived atop a virtual beat box.

Over the weeks, Heller tried phoning Rubin. She tried knocking on his door. After that, Heller complained to the resident assistants and the front desk. Nobody, it seemed, would help her. Nobody would do *anything* about Rick Rubin.

Finally, Heller resorted to banging on her floor.

Rubin returned the gesture by turning up the volume.

Heller banged some more.

Rubin turned on his old upright vacuum cleaner and began rolling it along the ceiling, to howls from Dubin and friends.

Moments later, Heller exploded through the door, livid, sending the big boys scrambling into the hallway.

The administration couldn't ignore this incident: One student had invaded another's room. The dorm committee announced that they would be convening a rare "student court" to get both sides' stories and determine a course of action. The potential repercussions were serious for both Heller and Rubin: They might be kicked out of the residence hall. But for Rubin and his confederates, the whole episode was occasion for farce. Before the trial, Rubin, Dubin, and friends replayed the incident until they had spun their story to ridiculous new heights.

"Did you see her come in?"
"She had something silver in her hand."
"It could have been keys."
"I thought it was a knife*!"*
"It probably was *a knife!"*

On the day the student court assembled in the basement recreation room of Weinstein Hall, Nancy Heller, the political science student on her way toward law school, seemed to have a distinct advantage over Rubin, who studied film. But Rubin's parents always thought he would make a great lawyer, and during the trial, he would prove them right.

Rubin told the court that he thought Nancy Heller was brandishing a weapon, and that he and his friends feared for their lives. To address Heller's complaint about the excessive noise, Rubin drafted an equally audacious defense.

"Punk rock and hip-hop are my art form," Rubin said. "They necessitate volume. There is no such thing as acoustic punk rock, or acoustic hip-hop."

Rubin contended that his DJing at high volumes was directly relevant to his course of collegiate study and burgeoning music career, and thereby as legitimate a need as, say, a political science student's need for quiet.

Rubin's friends corroborated his story. Even the nighttime desk clerk—a rotund, balding graduate film student named Ric Menello—testified on his behalf.

"She has been persecuting him for no reason I can understand," Menello said of Heller. "He plays his stereo quite low. Someone would have to have extrasensitive hearing like a dog, *like Superman*, to think it was too loud." Menello's affidavit added his belief that Nancy Heller was "unstable."

Menello's allegiance had been long since been secured by Rubin through countless late-night food orders and conversations at Menello's desk. For cold cash, Menello regularly ghostwrote the term papers that kept Rubin in good academic standing, even though the sophomore rarely attended classes. Menello routinely ignored or deflected complaints about the noise from 712-B, once writing a report that stated, "Rick Rubin is the kindest, sweetest, quietest student in the dorm . . . the most cooperative young man."

Rubin had Weinstein Hall locked up. He was their party planner, their caterer, their DJ. If you were close enough to Rubin, you got to roll with him to CBGB and the Roxy. You got to be a part of the in crowd wherever Rubin roamed. Then he treated you to late-night grub at Cozy Soup 'n' Burger on Broadway, on his ample allowance. Rubin and his "7B Mafia" threw parties in the rec room and hung around the front desk until the wee hours as Menello spouted film theory for the rapt undergrads.

Against Rubin's hegemony, Nancy Heller never had a chance. At the conclusion of the trial, the committee decided that Rubin could stay—provided that he keep the volume under a certain threshold. Heller moved out shortly thereafter.[1]

Rick Rubin was accustomed to complete freedom, the kind that Mickey and Linda Rubin afforded him—the kind that didn't work so well in a crowded dormitory. He slept when he felt like sleeping and stayed up until he tired, usually the crack of dawn. Rubin's younger roommate, Adam Dubin, had a nine a.m. class on Friday mornings, and Rubin took it almost as a personal offense.

"Ohhhh!" Rubin exhaled, like a balloon deflating. "How could you *do* that?!"

Rubin soon freed his young friends, too, and they began staying up with him to watch reruns of *The Abbott and Costello Show* at four thirty in the morning.

Rubin adored this program, and his whole college life seemed to be one extended routine inspired by the show. To most people, Abbott and Costello represented unsophisticated slapstick. But Rubin's hearty laughter in the

---

[1]Nancy Heller claims that the student court actually ordered both her and Rubin to move simultaneously, but Adam Dubin and Ric Menello insist that Rubin remained in the room for some time. If the court ruled as Heller claims, and Rubin wasn't forced to move, then it is another example of the double standard that Heller now claims was a life lesson that guides her current law practice: "Life isn't always fair," she said. "Just because you're right doesn't mean you win."

wee hours was provoked more so by the surreal, absurdist cruelty of "Bud" Abbott toward his dim-witted partner: *Abbott slaps Costello. Costello tries to defend himself. Abbott replies, "How dare you raise a hand to me!"*

Abbott always put his partner in situations where Costello was bound to fail, or left him quite literally holding the bag: *Costello buys a sack of tomatoes. Abbott picks the rotten ones out and throws them over his shoulder. Tomato hits landlord. Abbott slips away, leaving Costello with the tomatoes and a very angry landlord.*

"Abbott's gone," Rubin would deadpan, delighted.

Rick played the Abbott role with his own friends. He persuaded the lead singer of his high school band, the Pricks, to jump into the audience, pick a random person, stare him down, and then slap him for no reason at all. When Rubin's new band with his Weinstein friends, Hose, played City Garden in Trenton, Rubin goaded a friend to set off the sprinkler system with a lighter during their set. Like Abbott, Rubin loved to instigate chaos and then walk away—claiming ignorance, or indignance, or innocence. And, like Abbott, Rubin lived to feign indifference to suffering.

One evening, Ric Menello informed Rubin that a fellow student had been shot.

"That's horrible," Rubin replied. "What are we eating?"

During their late-night sessions at Weinstein's front desk, Ric Menello helped Rubin parse his sense of humor—why Rubin liked comedians like Abbott and Costello and Jerry Lewis, the bluster of pro wrestlers like Rick Flair, the braggadocio of rappers and the insolence of punk rockers. It wasn't the vulgarity alone, Menello suggested. It was the *combination* of extreme vulgarity *with* extremely sophisticated visual and verbal form. It's art that appears aimed at the cheap seats but also has appeal for the few people who truly see its complexity. Menello knew this to be true, because he had seen another side of Rick Rubin: the young man who revered the beauty of a perfectly executed work of art, the young man who cried at the simple woe of a Roy Orbison song.

"It's a highbrow-lowbrow game," Menello said, paraphrasing film critic Andrew Sarris. "Middlebrows beware."

This theory of "high-low"—paired with a disdain for the "middle," anything tame or tepid—guided Rick Rubin's artistic endeavors through college and beyond. Rubin aimed to create, in his words, "the worst shit." But he did it with the intention and all-consuming focus of an artist.

———

Rick Rubin learned to make records the same way he learned magic: He sought the counsel of people who knew the tricks.

Ed Bahlman was a magician of sorts. He ran a small record store and custom label out of his girlfriend's clothing boutique on 99 MacDougal Street, not far from Weinstein. He put out interesting, experimental music—some of which, like ESG's song "UFO," had become part of the growing hip-hop canon of breaks.

To Rubin, Bahlman was a hero: a guy with great taste who made only records that he really loved. So when Rubin decided to make a record with his punk band, Hose, he turned to Bahlman, who was generous with his advice. He recommended a cheap recording studio for Rubin to mix his record, Power Play in Queens; a place to get his "master discs" cut; a record plant in Canada that would manufacture vinyl from those masters at a low price; and a press in Brooklyn where he could get labels printed. Finally, Bahlman agreed to wholesale the records through 99's already established network of small record stores and distributors.

Rubin recorded Hose's satirical, dirge punk on the cheap, playing the guitar and, on occasion, the vacuum cleaner from his altercation with Nancy Heller. But as ugly as Hose's music was, Rubin paid painstaking attention to the band's packaging and aesthetic. For Hose's first record, Rubin designed a cover inspired by the Dutch artist Piet Mondrian. For the second, Rick ditched traditional packaging altogether, opting for a plain brown paper sleeve, etching the song titles right into the vinyl where the paper label would have been. And even though Hose was a punk band, Rubin's growing fascination with hip-hop was evident, with phrases like "Smurf it up, y'all," referencing a new dance called "The Smurf," embedded in the grooves.

Another indication of hip-hop's influence was the name Rick chose for his record label, based on another bit of slang Rubin had picked up at clubs. When hip-hop fans liked a record, or a "jam," they might call it "fresh." If they really liked it, they might say that it was "death."

Rick Rubin, however, spelled the word "death" as it was pronounced.

Def Jam Recordings, operating out of room 712 of 5 University Place, was funded with Rubin's parents' money. His business plan was about art, not profit: sell just enough records so that he could afford to put out another. But Rubin was dogged in pursuing his affairs. He dragged Adam Dubin along when he made his rounds to record stores to check on his inventory. He booked Hose in local clubs and on a brief jaunt to California. Hose developed a reputation on the New York hard-core punk scene, alongside groups like

Murphy's Law, Reagan Youth, and the Beastie Boys—a quartet of middle-class city kids. Guitarist Adam Horovitz's father was a playwright. Vocalist Michael Diamond attended St. Ann's Prep School in Brooklyn. Bassist Adam Yauch attended Bard College. Drummer Kate Schellenbach, the sole girl among the "Boys," had been a child actor on Broadway.

Like Rubin, the Beastie Boys hung out at the Roxy, and dabbled in hip-hop. On a small punk label called Rat Cage, they had even done a quasi-rap song wherein Diamond repeatedly calls Carvel ice cream, home of the famous "Cookie Puss" cake, refusing to believe that "Cookie Puss" is not a real person.

Rubin loved the resulting track "Cooky Puss" so much that he made everyone in 7B request it repeatedly on the campus radio station, WNYU. Rubin befriended the boy Beasties, especially Adam Horovitz, who was entertained by Rubin's bluster, play-bravado, and penchant for saying cruel things for maximum comedic effect. Horovitz called Rubin a "dick," meaning it as a compliment. When the Beasties needed a DJ to help them play "Cooky Puss" live, they turned to Rubin, who had both the right equipment and, vitally, a bubble machine.

As Horovitz, Diamond, and Yauch shifted their creative focus to hip-hop, their need for their drummer lessened. Schellenbach was simply ignored out of the group and Rick Rubin became "DJ Double R," the fourth member of the Beastie Boys.

Rubin got the notion to make a rap record from "Sucker MCs," the first song Rick ever heard that captured the energy of live hip-hop. No band, just a drum machine, two MCs, and a DJ, scratching.

"This is the real shit," he enthused to his roommate, Adam Dubin.

Then he added: "I could do this better."

Rubin borrowed a Roland TR-808 drum machine from Horovitz and began programming beats. He wanted to make a record with the Treacherous Three—Kool Moe Dee (the MC name for Mohandas Dewese), Kevin "Special K" Keaton, and Lamar "LA Sunshine" Hill. Rubin had become friendly with Kool Moe Dee and Special K at Negril, and he invited them over to the dorm to hang out.

Rick Rubin still had a lot to learn about the record business. Special K informed him that the Treacherous Three were signed exclusively to Sugar Hill, and therefore couldn't appear on Def Jam. Rubin had a lot to learn about

Black people, too. He was baffled by Kool Moe Dee's request for some "lotion." *Lotion?* Rick puzzled. *What did he need lotion for?*—unfamiliar as Rubin was with the grooming needs of a dark-skinned guy trying not to look "ashy."

At Weinstein, Special K suggested an alternative. His older brother, Terry Keaton, worked at a pharmacy. But back in the day, Terry used to rap under the MC name of "T La Rock." A few weeks later, Special K brought his brother to Weinstein, and the older MC hit it off with Rubin right away. Together they recorded a cassette demo for the song that would become "It's Yours." Rubin booked some time at Power Play, inviting Jazzy Jay to DJ, and Beastie Boy Adam Horovitz to hang out.

Rubin had little experience in the recording studio. But he knew what he wanted to hear. Everything had to sound huge—the bass lower, the vocals sharper, the drums louder, the scratches explosive. He and the studio engineer experimented with recording each drum sound on multiple tracks, mustering as much magnetic real estate for them as possible. With Horovitz's Roland TR-808 drum machine plugged into the patch bay, Rubin turned a knob to detune the kick drum sound all the way down so that every time it triggered, it made a prolonged, hollow boom that shook the room.

Most important, Rubin wanted to conjure something that he hadn't yet heard in a rap record—parity between DJ and MC, in the same way that rock records might feature the singer and lead guitarist equally. So Rubin arranged breaks in T La Rock's lyrics, and in the spaces had Jazzy Jay cut not one, but two turntable parts—playing off each other almost as a rock band might have rhythm and lead guitar. Last, Rick Rubin gave equal billing to T La Rock and DJ Jazzy Jay.

Rubin intended to release "It's Yours" through 99 Records, but Special K informed him that Arthur Baker, the producer of "Planet Rock," was looking for music for the soundtrack to a new movie about hip-hop called *Beat Street*—a kind of Hollywoodized version of *Wild Style.*

Rick Rubin went to Baker's Shakedown Studios and got an audience with the producer, who nodded his head as the beat played.

"I like it," Baker said.

Instead of the soundtrack, Baker proposed releasing "It's Yours" as a single on his indie label, Streetwise, which recently launched New Edition as huge teen stars. Baker offered $2,000 for the record, which would barely cover the recording costs. But Rubin didn't care too much about the money. Instead, he negotiated for branding: his Def Jam logo would be featured prominently on the label and cover.

Rubin designed the logo himself at the offices of Estée Lauder, where his aunt Carol worked. Installed at a workstation with plenty of tools and type, he spelled the words "Def Jam" in Helvetica, enlarging the "D" and "J" to make a hip-hop double-entendre. For the sleeve, Rubin had a friend trace a rendering of the tonearm for a Technics SL-1200, the turntable of choice for professional DJs. When finished, the artwork made an implicit statement. Other record companies made rap records for money. But Def Jam's name and packaging made a novel promise: it would be a label by and for hip-hop fans.

When Streetwise shipped the first 12-inches in late 1983, Rubin's promotional efforts consisted of taking the record to the Roxy every night and asking the DJs to play it. T La Rock had forgotten about the record altogether and went back to work at the pharmacy. After several months the record caught on, and even garnered some play on the mix shows of WRKS and WBLS. By then Rubin realized that he didn't know the first thing about promoting a rap record. Again, he sought the advice of someone who knew the tricks.

Aaron Fuchs was a former music journalist who covered rap almost as early as Nelson George and Rocky Ford had. His record label, Tuff City, achieved a first for a rap label: a production deal under the auspices of a major company, CBS. Fuchs put out a few singles by Spoonie Gee, the Cold Crush Brothers, and Davy DMX before he ended the deal over Epic's lack of effort and support. Fuchs was independent again, but had returned with a lot of experience.

"It's very difficult to promote rap records," Fuchs told Rubin. "The only person who has ever had any success is Russell Simmons."

Rubin immediately recognized Simmons's name from his Run-DMC and Kurtis Blow records.

"Even though he manages a lot of people," Fuchs continued, "the only person he has ever actually really *worked* for is his brother, Run. If you could get Russell to focus on your record, he'd be the best person to do it."

After years of work, Michael Holman's hip-hop *American Bandstand* had arrived. Holman found a Wall Street partner, Steve Memishian, who put together a group of investors to fund a pilot for *Graffiti Rock*. Holman enlisted Kool Moe Dee and Special K to cohost the show with him; hired Afrika Bambaataa as his music consultant; and, through the good graces of Russell Simmons, booked Run-DMC as his musical guests. Holman had to make some creative compromises with his producers, who had secured syndication for the pilot in eighty-eight markets across the country.

"You can't make it look too scary," they said.

So Holman made sure there were lots of White faces among the dancers, including two as yet unknown teens from the downtown scene, Debi Mazar and Vincent "Prince Vince" Gallo. In the spring of 1984, Holman taped *Graffiti Rock* at Metropolis, an East Harlem TV studio on the corner of 106th and Park.

In June, on the eve of their debut, Holman and Memishian threw a party at a club in Chelsea to celebrate the debut of America's first hip-hop TV show. The affair marked another milestone, too. It was at the *Graffiti Rock* party that Rick Rubin and Russell Simmons finally crossed paths.

Jazzy Jay facilitated the introduction, bringing Simmons over to meet the NYU student.

"This is Rick, who produced 'It's Yours,'" Jay told Simmons.

Russell stared in disbelief at the chubby, long-haired kid with the scruffy beard. After a moment, Simmons spoke:

"That's my favorite record. That's the best record in the world," Simmons said. "You didn't make that."

"Yeah," Rubin replied. "I did."

And then Simmons said, "I can't believe you're White."

Rubin was twenty-one, Simmons twenty-six. Rubin was a Jew from Long Island, Simmons Black and from Queens. Rubin dressed like a college student and Simmons like a professor—argyle sweaters and sports coats with elbow patches. Rubin didn't drink or do drugs and Simmons did both to excess. But they liked the same kinds of records. Simmons's name was on almost all of Rubin's favorite hip-hop songs—from Jimmy Spicer's "Dollar Bill" to Run-DMC's "Sucker MCs." Both men shared a similar distaste for disco or any music that was "soft." It didn't take long for Rubin and Simmons to find that they were, much to their own surprise, very much alike.

In the wake of the *Graffiti Rock* party, two things happened.

First, despite encouraging ratings, Michael Holman and his producers couldn't sell their TV show. The various station managers from around the country gathered at the yearly convention of the National Association of Television Program Executives told Memishian that they already had *Soul Train* on their schedules. They didn't understand why they needed *Graffiti Rock*, nor did they comprehend the vast difference between the two shows.

Second, Rick Rubin pursued a friendship with Russell Simmons. He hung out at Rush's Broadway offices, and went with Simmons to Danceteria and Disco Fever. Soon enough, Rubin had Simmons promoting his artist T La Rock, whom Rush Management picked up as a client.

Despite the success of "It's Yours," Rubin hadn't seen a dime from Arthur Baker and Streetwise after the initial advance. To Rubin's surprise, Simmons's story was almost as bad. He had signed Run-DMC to Profile because Robbins and Plotnicki had a reputation for paying more than other independent labels like Sugar Hill did. But after selling hundreds of thousands of records for Profile, neither Simmons nor his artists were wealthy.

Simmons knew that Run-DMC's fortunes would have been different if he had signed them to a major label like Mercury. Mercury flew him and Kurtis Blow all over the world, and everywhere they went, the label's huge staff was there to greet them. Profile, on the other hand, could never support a staff of "regionals." And even with the stuff they could afford, Profile was stingy. It was a struggle to get Steve Plotnicki to pay for a taxicab ride or a hamburger.

Rubin suggested that labels like Profile weren't record companies at all. They were banks: They loaned you money to make a record, and then you had to pay them back with your sales. They didn't care about music.

"It's Yours" did bring Rubin one fateful windfall: His dorm room—now on the eighth floor—was flooded with demo tapes. In the summer before Rick Rubin's senior year, Adam Horovitz bunked with Rubin and listened to them. One stood out: a kid rapping with the macho, muscular energy of Melle Mel and the vocabulary of T La Rock. It made Rubin and Horovitz laugh, the juxtaposition of the huge ego with the pipsqueak voice. When the demo became as much a part of their regular rotation as their favorite records, Rick decided to phone the kid, who called himself LL Cool J. When the sixteen-year-old James Todd Smith came to Weinstein Hall, he didn't know what to expect. But he wasn't expecting what he saw.

"I thought you were Black," Smith blurted when Rubin met him at the front desk.

"Cool," Rubin replied.

Rubin played some beats for Smith on his drum machine—programmed by Horovitz—and within a few hours, they had recorded a cassette demo of a new song, "I Need a Beat." Days after that, Rubin plunked down some money to record the song at a nearby studio called Secret Society.

Rubin intended the song to be Def Jam's next release. But this time, he wanted a partner.

Rick Rubin took "I Need a Beat" to Rush's offices and played it for Russell Simmons, who loved it.

"What would you do with this?" Rubin asked.

Simmons shrugged. "I could give it to Profile."

"Why would you give it to them?!" Rubin said. "All you do is complain about how they don't do anything for Run-DMC. Why don't we just do it ourselves?" Simmons, after all, had made a dozen fantastic records for other companies and had little to show for it.

But Simmons didn't want to put out records himself. He didn't want to be Cory Robbins. He wanted a production deal with a major, like Rocky Ford and J. B. Moore had with Mercury, where they turned in records and collected a check, leaving the promotion and sales to others. Simmons was hoping an A&R man named Steve Ralbovsky would secure him a deal at EMI for a label he wanted to call Rush Records. Doing another label now would get in the way of that, Simmons said.

"It won't get in the way," Rubin insisted. "I'll do all the work. I'll do everything. You just be my partner."

Rubin was betting that if the records did well, Simmons would indeed put in work. He had seen Simmons talk people into submission on behalf of his acts. When Simmons promoted something, he was charming and funny, tireless and shameless. People liked him, and wanted to help him.

Rubin's words echoed in Simmons's ears after the college kid left. He talked it over with his lieutenants in the office, Heidi Smith and Tony Rome. Rubin was an incredible, beat-making motherfucker. The kid was coming to him, hit in hand. Maybe, if the records did well, their little company could leverage the major label deal he wanted.

Simmons asked his lawyer, Paul Schindler, to draft a partnership agreement. Simmons came in for half of Rick Rubin's label, Def Jam Recordings. Rubin's parents kicked in $5,000, with the caveat that—if the company didn't work out—Rick would go to law school. Simmons contributed another $1,000, and agreed to manage the acts—booking performances, getting publicity, and shaping their image.

Simmons had his work cut out for him with LL Cool J, who showed up in the typical Sugar Hill–era "showbiz" getup—white lace-up boots and leather pants with leg straps.

"Where you from?" Simmons asked the young James Todd Smith.

"St. Albans," Smith replied, referencing a neighborhood close to Simmons's stomping grounds in Hollis.

"Where the fuck did you get those pants? Is that how they dress in St. Albans?"

Simmons had already begun crucial work for Def Jam. While Rubin concentrated on stripping the music bare—"reducing," as he called it, rather than "producing"—Simmons stripped their artists of artifice. Like Run-DMC, Def Jam's rappers would be marketed as a stylized version of who they actually were: regular kids in regular clothes.

Rubin now ran a record company out of his increasingly filthy, cluttered dorm room. He called on Tom Silverman, who guided the young producer to the right distributors for his records. Simmons introduced Rubin to Manny Bella at Profile, who gave Rubin lists of radio programmers and did a little promotion for Def Jam on the side. Rubin corralled Adam Dubin and another friend, George Drakoulias, to work for Def Jam as unpaid interns. Dubin and Drakoulias dropped boxes of vinyl at local distributors and picked up cash payments. They made the rounds to record stores. They called radio stations from Rubin's dorm room by day and handed 12-inches to club DJs at night.

With Rubin's focus and the addition of Simmons's influence with radio jocks like Red Alert, the success of LL Cool J's "I Need a Beat" came much sooner than it had with "It's Yours." In a few months they had sold 100,000 copies—a huge amount for a homegrown rap record.

But Rubin saw Russell's point: It wasn't easy doing it yourself, and it was very hard to collect from some big distributors. Rubin realized the truth in what folks like Silverman told him: A hit record could be the worst thing that happened to a small company. You could manufacture all those records and go broke before you ever got paid a dime.

Over the next eight months, Rubin and Simmons came with six more singles, each enveloped in a maroon sleeve with the huge Def Jam logo.

The second single came from the Beastie Boys, who—at Rubin's suggestion—rapped their song "Rock Hard" over AC/DC's rock classic, "Back in Black." The Beastie Boys were a tricky proposition for Simmons.

Aside from the tourist rap of Debbie Harry, there had been no successful White MCs in hip-hop. Marketing the Beasties to a real hip-hop audience, a Black audience, would take dexterity and guts. They got jeered at the first gig that Simmons booked for them at a club deep in the Queens ghetto. Simmons policed their style as he had with LL Cool J. Rubin had dressed the Beastie Boys in identical red tracksuits. Simmons knew that the Beasties looked as if they were mocking Black kids.

Dress like you really dress, Simmons insisted. The Beasties ditched the matching costumes, and donned their jeans and T-shirts.

The Beastie Boys record sold well, and the Def Jam singles kept coming: another track from LL Cool J; a record from Simmons's client Jimmy Spicer; and one from Run-DMC's new protégés, Hollis Crew. Quickly, Def Jam became known to radio and club DJs as a label that lived up to its name.

With T La Rock angry that Streetwise hadn't paid him any money, Jazzy Jay became a solo artist, composing a new track, itself called "Def Jam." But the real ode to the label appeared on the B-side: "Cold Chillin' in the Spot" captured the chemistry between the company's two founders.

Russell Simmons was high when he and Andre "Dr. Jeckyll" Harrell dropped by the studio where Rubin and Jay were recording. Summoning his inner Bud Abbott, Rubin told Simmons that it would be a *really good idea* for him to get on the microphone. Rubin watched his partner through the soundproof glass as Simmons began—not rhyming, but rapping nonetheless: "Now, I ain't never sung before, I'm a manager. I like to manage a lot of groups that talk on records," Simmons said. "We gonna save a lot of money because we ain't gotta hire nobody to say nothin'. And we keep all the money."

Rubin doubled over behind the mixing console. In the months since their first meeting, the college kid from Long Island and the hustler from Queens had formed a bond that would ultimately prove stronger than their musical connection: They made each other laugh.

Simmons continued, calling out to "the Doctor" in the house—Dr. Jeckyll, that is—who had become his friend and business partner. Simmons joked that he couldn't ask Harrell to join him on the microphone for fear of being sued by Profile Records.

"So I'm just gonna rap myself and keep all the money. Me and Rick—look at Rick laughing!—we gon' keep all the money!"

Back at NYU, Rubin was four credits short of the minimum required for his diploma. He won an exception to the rules in the same way he had obtained many others from the institution: a long letter, ghostwritten by Ric Menello. In this final appeal, Rubin argued that he had gained much experience from the university, and had during his years there already become a successful record producer. Furthermore, Rubin pledged, he would always remember to mention New York University as the place where he learned everything.

Rick Rubin graduated in May of 1985.

That was not the final concession Rubin wrested from the institution. He also got to stay at Weinstein for the entire summer after graduation, rent-free. Rubin reminded the administration that they never repaid his expenses for a controversial wet T-shirt contest he promoted as the head of the dorm's party planning committee, when female students protested the flyers that he had made for the occasion.

The leaflets read, "Bodies for Sale."

Rick Rubin wasn't the only college student in New York for whom hip-hop aspirations superseded academic achievement.

In a classroom at Adelphi University, only a few miles from Rubin's childhood home on Long Island, an undergraduate student named Andre Brown nodded off to sleep.

"Mr. Brown!" Professor Andrei Strobert boomed.

"Yes!" Brown said, snorting awake.

"We all appreciate the fact that you have to work for an education," Strobert said. "But could you please refrain from snoring so loudly so I can get the lesson to the people who want to listen?"

Brown's friends laughed. Bill Stephney, Carlton Ridenhour and Harold Allen McGregor all came to Strobert's class every Monday morning exhausted.

Stephney was the program director of Adelphi's student radio station, WBAU-FM, hosted a weekly rap and dance music show as "Mr. Bill," and interned during the week at a commercial rock station, WLIR.

Brown threw parties all over Long Island as one half of the Concept, performing as "Doctor Dre" alongside his former high school football teammate Tyrone "T-Money" Kelsie.

Ridenhour worked with the most successful DJ crew on Long Island,

Spectrum City, run by the Boxley brothers, Hank and Keith. A graphic design student, Ridenhour started drafting Spectrum's flyers, but had become Spectrum's main MC, Chuckie D.

McGregor, a budding photographer and writer, hung out with the crew, but couldn't make it to the Friday-night parties because he was an observant Seventh Day Adventist.

The four students comprised an informal hip-hop fraternity. At WBAU, they stayed long after Stephney's shift on the Mr. Bill Show to debate hip-hop, rock, and R&B. In Professor Strobert's class, Black Music and Musicians, they gained perspective on the music they loved. Strobert was one of the few older folks who took hip-hop seriously, who saw the genre as a natural and worthy step in the evolution of Black American music. The four young Black men had gotten into hip-hop because it was fun. But they were beginning to sense that it was important, too.

The intellectual approach to hip-hop came naturally to Bill Stephney, who arrived at Adelphi with a scholarship from the National Urban League. A former Long Island spelling bee finalist, Stephney had been dubbed "DJ Brainiac" by his high school friends. Stephney inherited much from his father, Ted, whose intellect and refinement allowed him to climb from the mailroom of Time, Inc., into a position as a photo editor for *Sports Illustrated*—a nearly impossible ascent for a Black man in 1950s corporate America. Ted Stephney passed his skills for navigating the wider, Whiter world to his son. Bill's childhood in suburban Hempstead was spent partly with his Black friends in the neighborhood—becoming Blacker by the year as White families fled—and partly with White kids in the Police Boys Club bowling league.

Black kids on Long Island grew up with racial duality: proximity to White people and estrangement from them. Suburbia was supposed to be the place where they could be just like other American kids. Even a trip to White Castle was different for Stephney and friends than it was for local White teens like Rick Rubin. One night, as the WBAU crew munched on hamburgers and loudly debated music in the parking lot of the fast-food franchise near Adelphi, police swarmed in with cruisers and a helicopter because they had received reports of a "riot" in progress. Stephney, Brown, Ridenhour, and McGregor didn't grow up in the hardscrabble ghetto that Melle Mel described in "The Message," but their awareness of White supremacy was just as acute. That racial consciousness seeped into their approach to hip-hop.

Bill Stephney's Monday-night WBAU broadcast, "The Mr. Bill Show," became the suburban equivalent of Mr. Magic's show on WHBI. As WBAU's program director, Stephney gave a slot to Chuck Ridenhour and his DJ partners from outside of Adelphi, the Boxley brothers; one play of a record on their "Super Spectrum Mixx Show" could provoke a run on local stores. WBAU became a favorite stopover for established rap artists like Run-DMC, who befriended the collegiate crew of hip-hop mad scientists. The most popular songs on WBAU weren't even records but demo tapes of local crews and on-air promos made by the DJs to advertise their own shows. The Townhouse Three's "Straight from the Back of the N-41," a reference to a local bus route, was a favorite. One of Hank Boxley's childhood friends, Rico Drayton, recorded a manic hip-hop demo called "Claustrophobia Attack." Drayton billed himself as "MC-DJ Flavor," and Stephney gave him his own show, too. Together, Chuckie D and Flavor cowrote their own, widely requested promo called "Public Enemy #1."

When he graduated Bill Stephney wanted to be a radio DJ or a program director like Frankie Crocker. But at the rock station where Stephney interned, WLIR, the owners—two Jewish men named Elton Spitzer and Zim Barstein—had other ideas for their protégé.

"You're going to learn sales," they declared. "That's where the money is."

Spitzer and Barstein taught Stephney about traffic and commercial spot loads. They took him to meetings with advertising clients. They brought him on a pilgrimage to Laurel, Maryland, the home of Arbitron, the company that compiled radio ratings all over the country.

At first Stephney likened the training to being force-fed spinach. But slowly, the years at WLIR set Bill Stephney on a different path from his crew at WBAU: He would be a businessman first and an artist second. While Andre "Doctor Dre" Brown and Carlton "Chuckie D" Ridenhour planned recording careers, Stephney decided he would work from within the industry to further the cause of hip-hop. Just three credits shy of graduation, Stephney left Adelphi, bequeathed his radio shift to "Doctor Dre," and took a job at the *College Music Journal*.

At CMJ, Stephney founded the very first national chart to track rap airplay in the entire music business. He assembled his weekly chart by polling a panel he had created of DJs from commercial stations—like Red Alert of WRKS—and from college and community stations across the country. Stephney's column and chart, called "Beatbox," became a helpful gauge for the performance of rap records for the folks at Profile and Tommy Boy.

Stephney held a special affection for one record company, a new outfit that had released seven fantastic singles on maroon-colored labels. When Stephney took the train into the city to visit the company's offices, located in a dorm room at NYU, Rick Rubin and George Drakoulias felt familiar to him, just like the White guys Stephney grew up with in the bowling league, except that Rubin and Drakoulias liked rap in the same way Stephney had come to appreciate rock.

Rubin saw in Stephney a kindred spirit. Most of the people Rubin met in the business seemed sleazy. Stephney was bright and pure—a student and a fan, just like he and George were. Rubin had big things planned for Def Jam, and he made a mental note to include Stephney in them when the time came.

Meanwhile, a demo tape produced by Stephney's friend Andre "Doctor Dre" Brown had made its way to Rubin via the guys in Run-DMC. Rubin invited Brown to the dorm, and signed him and Tyrone "T-Money" Kelsie to Def Jam as "Original Concept."

It would be almost a year before Def Jam would release that demo as a single called "Can U Feel It." By that time, the signature maroon label had turned black, and Def Jam had become a much bigger enterprise than even Rubin had envisioned.

It seems absurd that a tiny record company with just a handful of singles in its catalog would, within one year, inspire the story line of a major motion picture and land a multimillion-dollar production deal with the most prestigious record conglomerate in the world.

But that is exactly what happened to Def Jam in 1985.

It began with an article in the *Wall Street Journal*. Meg Cox, a reporter hired to cover new trends in the arts, received a tip from Rocky Ford about some incredible developments in the rap world: the first corporate-sponsored national stadium tour, the Fresh Fest; the first group to achieve a gold album, Run-DMC; and the rise of the twenty-seven-year-old artist manager with the seventeen-client roster at the center of it all, Russell Simmons.

Cox joined Simmons on one of his nightly expeditions to the Disco Fever in the South Bronx where she had her first experience of being frisked for weapons before entering a nightclub. Simmons rather enjoyed guiding the reporter through this strange world.

"You are the Whitest person I have ever met," Simmons told Cox, whom he affectionately dubbed "the Ivory Snow Queen." In her seventeen-hundred-word front-page article about the emerging rap scene for the *Wall Street*

Journal on December 4, 1984, Cox came up with a nickname for Simmons, too. She called him "the mogul of rap."

Menahem Golan, the fifty-five-year-old Israeli-born head of Cannon Films, read the article on a flight from New York to London. When he landed, he called his New York office and ordered them to track down this "mogul of rap," Russell Simmons.

Golan made his reputation producing Charles Bronson and Chuck Norris movies, but he had also been the first person in Hollywood to latch onto the break dancing "craze," with his films *Breakin'* and *Breakin' 2*. These low-budget exploitation flicks were derided in the hip-hop world. When Russell Simmons agreed to meet with Golan, Simmons expected the worst.

Golan did not disappoint. He came across to Simmons as every bit the stereotype of the cigar-chomping, vulgar movie producer. Golan wanted Simmons to procure the talent for the film—to be called, of course, *Rappin'*—and he wanted a rushed script and shoot to get the film out in time for the spring of 1985.

Simmons had turned down better ideas than this, like the previous year, when Harry Belafonte and Stan Lathan approached him with the idea for their movie, *Beat Street*. While *Beat Street* wasn't exactly Russ's idea of a real hip-hop film, it was infinitely more respectful than Golan's proposed quickie flick, designed to cash in on rap before the fad inevitably died.

"If I make the wrong movie with you," Simmons said, "I'm going to destroy everything I spent years building." Simmons passed, and Golan moved on.

Simmons's principled stand against Golan got a little easier when another Hollywood producer who read the *Wall Street Journal* story took a run at Simmons, literally, in the lobby of the building where he was meeting with Golan.

The producer, George Jackson, was more to Simmons's liking. He was Black, energetic, and in his twenties. Better still, Jackson was originally from Harlem and had made films for comedian Richard Pryor. Jackson introduced Simmons to his production partners—another young Black producer named Doug McHenry; and Michael Shultz, the director of two Pryor films, *Car Wash* and *Which Way Is Up*, and another Simmons favorite, *Cooley High*. The three producers had seen the Fresh Fest when it came to Los Angeles, and they pitched Simmons on a documentary about it called *Rap Attack*.

Simmons instead proposed a fictional feature about the New York rap scene starring Run-DMC. After they came to an agreement with Simmons, the producers set up funding and distribution through Warner Bros. Pictures, and hired a young Black TV writer named Ralph Farquhar to craft a script. Simmons suggested a story loosely based on Junebug, the former lieutenant to DJ Hollywood and star jock for Sal Abbatiello's Disco Fever, who had become a drug dealer and subsequently been murdered. Farquhar returned, however, with a tale of a young White girl trying to break into the music business. Simmons hated this blatant surrender to sensibilities that his partner Rick Rubin might have called "middlebrow."

Starting over, the producers settled for the story unfolding right in front of them. Hadn't they been hanging out for months with Simmons and Rubin as they built their cool, independent label, Def Jam? In the revised script, the name of the company was changed to Krush Groove, but the main characters' names, Rick and Russell, remained—a saga about two hip-hop entrepreneurs who, after an unsuccessful search for legitimate financing, eventually turn to ruthless gangsters for money.

Except for the part about the gangsters, it wasn't far from the truth. Simmons and Rubin both were now actively seeking a distribution arrangement for Def Jam with a major label. The movie deal with Warner Bros. opened up an opportunity for Simmons and Rubin to take a meeting at the company's sister record label in California. Warner Bros. Records' affable chairman, Mo Ostin, seemed interested. But as the music played, the blank White faces of Ostin's vice presidents and A&R staff showed that these people understood nothing about rap music.

Upon his return to New York, Simmons got a surprise call from Steve Ralbovsky, his friend from EMI Records. Ralbovsky explained that he had taken a new job at Columbia Records, the flagship label of Warner's rival, CBS. He wanted to know if Simmons would come in for a meeting.

By the mid-1980s, the record business had consolidated into six "major" record companies. Warner Music comprised three labels: Warner, Elektra, and Atlantic. CBS had two: Columbia and Epic. Polygram ran Mercury. EMI ran Capitol. RCA distributed Arista, and MCA had a subsidiary called Uni, short for Universal, the movie studio owned by MCA Records' parent company.

But in the five years since Mercury became the first major-run label to release a rap record—Kurtis Blow's "Christmas Rappin'"—all of these companies treated rap much as Menahem Golan did: a passing fad.

In the majors' absence, strong independent labels like Sugar Hill, Tommy Boy, Profile, and Jive thrived, selling millions of records.

Finally one executive sniffed opportunity.

"I can't walk twenty feet in Manhattan without seeing a kid with a boom box playing rap music," Columbia Records' general manager Al Teller told his A&R chief, Mickey Eichner. "What's the story here?"

Eichner shrugged. Teller turned to the A&R executives in Columbia's Black music department, who derided rap as "a ghetto thing," not dignified enough for a serious label like Columbia.

But Al Teller persevered, eventually asking Eichner the right question, a question that no executive before him ever had:

"Find whoever's really good at this and bring them in."

Eichner landed on Tom Silverman and Tommy Boy Records. Eichner hadn't noticed that Silverman didn't currently have a breakthrough rap act; since "Planet Rock," Silverman had ventured further into electro-funk and dance music. And Eichner couldn't have known that Tommy Boy was, in fact, struggling for its life—Silverman was $500,000 in debt to his manufacturers after the closing of a few distributors who owed him money.

Nevertheless, Eichner sold Teller on the idea of Tommy Boy. They called in their new A&R man Steve Ralbovsky to hear a record from Tommy Boy's latest act, the Jonzun Crew. When Ralbovsky finally understood what his bosses were getting at, he told them straight out:

"I've got another idea for you."

Ralbovsky told Russell Simmons to prepare a presentation for the CBS executives. The meeting was the exact opposite of the Warner Bros. Records debacle. Simmons, loquacious and animated, didn't just present Def Jam as a label. He laid out, in passionate detail, the entire scene of which he had become the undisputed master—from Run-DMC to Whodini, from the Fresh Fest to *Krush Groove*. Simmons insisted that rap music couldn't be understood simply as Black music. It was *teen* music.

If this was rap, then Teller, Eichner, and Ralbovsky were rapt—sold on the idea before Simmons even finished talking.

Rick Rubin hadn't made the Columbia meeting. He was preparing to play himself in *Krush Groove*, now in preproduction at Silvercup Studios in Queens. As for Simmons, the producers wanted more of a leading-man type to play the role of "Russell." Simmons and Rubin suggested the dark, suave Fab 5 Freddy for the role, but Jackson, McHenry, and Shultz selected a clean-cut, brown-skinned twenty-one-year-old named Blair Underwood for the part.

Rubin and Simmons began to see *Krush Groove* as a parade of concessions to commercialism. Another was the casting of Sheila E.—a talented and beautiful protégée of Prince, whose *Purple Rain* movie and soundtrack had been huge for Warner Bros. the previous year. But as a leading lady, she was the antithesis of the stripped-down, unpretentious street aesthetic of the rappers with whom she shared the screen. Even worse, Simmons felt that the producers were slowly pushing Run-DMC's story line to the side in favor of comic relief from the Fat Boys, due in part to the persistence of Charlie Stettler. Simmons later discovered that Stettler had cut a deal with Jackson to helm an upcoming Fat Boys movie, and suspected that Jackson's stake in that new venture was reason enough to make the Fat Boys more prominent in *Krush Groove*.

On the set, Rubin could scarcely contain his frustration. As Michael Shultz coached Underwood and Run on some dialogue, Rubin stepped in front of the director.

"No! That's *not* how it goes," Rubin shouted. "*This* is how it goes!"

Shultz put his arm around the young record producer and walked him away from the others. I'm *the director*, Shultz lectured the recent graduate.

"I'm really sorry," Rubin said, shifting back into his calm voice. "But it was making me really mad. Because once you put it on film, that's the way it's gonna be. And it's gonna be wrong."

The two men walked back over to the two actors and waiting crew.

"Do what Rick said," Shultz ordered.

Ultimately, the movie was out of Rubin's control. So, too, was the soundtrack, which was set to conclude with an "all-star" rap song featuring Run-DMC, the Fat Boys, Kurtis Blow, and Sheila E. Rubin hated the track that Kurtis Blow put together; he thought it was goofy. Instead, he produced a separate section of the song for Run and DMC—with whom he had grown close—to protect the group's credibility. To protect his own, Rubin insisted that the credits show he had produced *only* Run-DMC's portion.

Still the *Krush Groove* soundtrack featured two new songs by LL Cool J and the Beastie Boys. Ironically the first major-label appearance by Def Jam artists would be with the company that rejected them, Warner Bros. Records. In another irony, the *Krush Groove* soundtrack proved a boon to the label that lost out to Def Jam at Columbia, the struggling Tommy Boy Records.

Monica Lynch, Tommy Boy's newly annointed president, began dating Doug McHenry during the production of the film, and kept ribbing her new boyfriend to include Tommy Boy's new doo-wop-hip-hop hybrid group, the Force MDs, on the soundtrack. Their moment came when Warner failed to strike a deal for New Edition to record a "love theme" for the movie. Lynch hurried the Force MDs off to Minneapolis to record the song with two hot new producers, Terry Lewis and Jimmy Jam, also former protégés of Prince. "Tender Love" became the first Top 10 pop single for Jam and Lewis, and the first for Tommy Boy as well, which retained the singles rights—skillfully negotiated by Tom Silverman with Warner chairman Mo Ostin.

The success bought Silverman time and the esteem of Ostin as well.

While Paul Schindler hammered out the fine points of the Def Jam–Columbia agreement, Russell Simmons regularly shared his progress with a person he knew he could trust.

Ann Carli knew that a distribution deal with a major label wasn't necessarily a ticket to paradise. Carli fought constantly to keep Jive's acts a priority for Arista's promotion staff. Arista's head, Clive Davis, had even tried to stop the release of Billy Ocean's album because he thought the record wasn't good enough, and because his staff thought Ocean "ugly." Billy Ocean's album went on to sell over two million copies, and Davis reaped the benefits in spite of himself. The political and business aspects of the Jive-Arista deal required a deft hand, and Carli credited Jive's success to the genius of Clive Calder.

Carli worried for Simmons, and she asked Calder for advice. After all, smaller labels could do many kinds of deals with the majors. On one end of the spectrum, a "production deal" would give Def Jam less responsibility and a quick infusion of cash, but only a fraction of the profits. On the other, a "pressing and distribution deal" would give Def Jam the larger share of back-end profits and ownership of the "masters" (meaning that if the deal ended, Def Jam could take its records with it); but then Def Jam would have to risk its own cash and promote its own records. Carli knew that Calder liked Simmons and would probably tell him to go for less money up front in return for more of the back end.

"Tell Russell I'd be happy to spend a day with him," Calder said, offering to impart the benefit of his experience to the young artist manager.

To Carli's surprise, Simmons wasn't interested.

"That's okay," Simmons said.

Carli suspected that Simmons didn't want to look like he needed advice, especially now that she and Simmons had transformed their professional partnership into a personal one; a relationship that Carli tried to keep discreet, though without much help from Simmons.

In September of 1985, as *Krush* *Groove* was edited and prepared for release, Columbia and Def Jam closed their $2 million production deal with a signature from Russell Simmons.

In the first year, Simmons promised to deliver four albums to Columbia—each needing approval by Ralbovsky and the Columbia brass. For each album, Def Jam received an advance and 14 royalty points, from which they had to pay their artists. All of the royalties were "cross-collateralized," meaning that profits from one artist's album could be used by Columbia to cover losses from another. And Columbia retained the all-important rights to the "masters," meaning that when the deal ended, Columbia owned the albums, not Def Jam.

It wasn't a generous arrangement by major-label standards. It wasn't even the first major-label production deal ever for a rap label—that place in history went to the small label owned by Aaron Fuchs, Tuff City. But it was the first deal of a magnitude that made a rap label a clear priority for a major company.

"I will be your project manager," Al Teller promised Rubin and Simmons, an indication of Teller's sincerity and Columbia's commitment. Notably, the Def Jam deal had come through the pop department, not the Black music department, which had been so negative about "ghetto" rap music from the start.

The two partners received a large advance in the form of a check for $600,000. Rubin promptly photocopied the check and sent it to his parents, an ancient Jewish message that meant, translated roughly, "I'm not going to law school."

Def Jam and Columbia celebrated their marriage with a reception on the rooftop of Danceteria, catered by Rubin's favorite burger joint, White Castle. Rubin sent George Drakoulias out to Queens with an order for a thousand hamburgers, and Drakoulias returned in a cab with White Castle boxes stuffed in the trunk and tied to the roof. Many of the burgers ended up on the guests after Rubin encouraged the Beastie Boys to start a food fight. While their new clip for "She's on It" was looped and projected onto the side of a building across the street, one of the cheeseburgers hit CBS Records chairman Walter Yetnikoff in the head. As Al Teller circulated through his party—an awkward mix of b-boys, scenesters, and buttoned-down CBS execs, he overheard a remark from one of his own people:

"Teller has lost his mind."

Columbia's chief competitor made a rap deal of its own shortly thereafter. The chairman of Warner Bros. Records, Mo Ostin, didn't just admire smart people; he liked to collect them. So Ostin bought half of Tommy Boy at a bargain price, saving the struggling venture, and he added Tom Silverman and Monica Lynch to his ever-growing list of vice presidents.

In 1985, two rap-oriented labels made the big time. No longer would Rubin and Silverman have to hound distributors around the country for the money to pay their bills. Instead, they would have to pester their new corporate benefactors to make their records a priority.

Krush Groove **debuted in 515 theaters** across America on October 25, 1985.

Russell Simmons brought Ann Carli as his date to the New York premiere in Times Square. Carli showed up wearing a severely boxy blue corduroy suit. She was petite and pretty, but the outfit seemed to swallow her hundred-pound frame whole.

"Are you really wearing that?" Simmons asked.

"Yeah," Carli replied. "I made it last night." Carli liked to sew her own clothes, just for kicks.

"You *made* it?!" Simmons exclaimed. He didn't know anyone who made their own clothes, least of all in the record business.

"You know, I really love you," he told her.

Carli's outfit, however, may have confused Simmons's father, Daniel Senior, who somehow got the impression that Carli was his son's cleaning woman.[2]

---

[2]Perhaps because Simmons had recorded another rant on an LL Cool J song called "That's a Lie," about a Japanese girl who "cleans up behind me."

Russell was mortified. "Daddy, she's my date," he said.

Inside the theater, the movie's fictional characters were portrayed by many people in the real world of Rush and Def Jam. Rubin starred as himself, while Simmons was relegated to playing the bit part of a club owner. Charlie Stettler provided comic relief as a sleazy record executive named Beiker. Heidi Smith, Rush's receptionist, reprised her real-life role for the make-believe "Krush Groove Records." Andre Harrell and Alonzo Brown donned their Jeckyll and Hyde suits to participate in an on-screen audition, in which LL Cool J's appearance became one of the few unbridled moments in a relatively tepid movie.

Sal Abbatiello and the Disco Fever played a role in *Krush Groove* as well, with the Fever serving as the venue for the film's grand finale. In reality, the Disco Fever wasn't open for regular business anymore: The club had just been shut down by the city of New York for operating without a cabaret license. It was part of a crackdown on Abbatiello himself, recently arrested for gun possession and awaiting trial. Abbatiello's legal problems were the least of his worries. As it was almost a decade earlier, another wise guy was gunning for Sal after a perceived slight. Abbatiello wasn't taking any chances. He came to the *Krush Groove* set at the Disco Fever wearing a bulletproof vest.

Krush Groove grossed $3 million in its first weekend.

Janet Maslin, critic for *The New York Times*, hated it, arguing that "rap music is infinitely more original" than the boring fare produced by Warner Bros. In the days and weeks that followed the film's release, newspapers and magazines linked the rap movie to a number of violent incidents—kids rushing the locked doors of one suburban theater, and a bloody brawl in which one young man pushed another through a plate-glass window.

"Movie Sparks New Teen Riot," read the headline in the *New York Post*.

It was one of the first instances of media coverage linking hip-hop and violence.

Not everyone in American media bought the connection. *Time* magazine even wrote their own rap about the movie's bum rap: "Now there've been fights at the Plexes, kids've got out of hand / But they must've spiked the sodas at the popcorn stand. Because this movie has the innocence of bygone years / Like the films of Fred (*Rock Around the Clock*) F. Sears."

But innocence is not what Rubin, Simmons, and Run-DMC really wanted. They despised Hollywood. They wanted "Holliswood," something truer to their aesthetic. Rubin and Simmons vowed to do another Run-DMC movie, one that they would fund and control completely.

LL Cool J's first album, *Radio*, hit record stores in late 1985. Despite the album's title, the vaunted radio promotion department of Columbia didn't need to do much for it. The three singles that Def Jam issued in advance of the album, along with LL's appearance in *Krush Groove*, created anticipation for the teenage rapper among hip-hop fans, both urban and suburban. Ladies— girls, especially—loved Cool J, who became the first "heartthrob" rapper since Kurtis Blow. The record began selling copies in the tens of thousands, then hundreds of thousands. By the end of the year, Columbia Records had made back all the money they spent on Def Jam's initial advance. Within months of signing, Al Teller and Steve Ralbovsky's groundbreaking deal was profitable for Columbia.

Everything about Def Jam's first full-length release was meticulous— from the artwork, to the liner notes written by Nelson George, to the music itself. *Radio* was not the first successful rap album, but it was perhaps the first album conceived as one, integral long-playing listening experience.

Success meant that Rubin and Simmons needed a staff. First, they tried to hire the best rap promotions man in the business, Manny Bella. But Bella was under a solid contract to Profile Records. Bella wanted to be loyal to Cory Robbins—and Profile didn't let people break contracts in any case. With Bella refusing to bite, Rubin remembered Bill Stephney of CMJ, and offered him the job. Rubin wasn't, however, offering any money.

Stephney told Rubin that he could easily make $40,000 a year elsewhere. He was interviewing with Barry Mayo to be the music director at WRKS. Aaron Fuchs had already offered him a job at Tuff City. Why would he work for Def Jam for free? Besides, the label's situation was chaotic. They didn't even have an office. And every time he went to go meet Simmons at Rush, Simmons wasn't there.

Secretly, Stephney was dying to work for Def Jam, because he believed that Rick Rubin was making the most important music in the world: Black records with a rock aesthetic. Rap albums that stood up against the greatest albums of any other genre. All he needed was some sort of signal that Rubin was serious.

When Rubin finally offered him $16,000 a year, Stephney took it. He wasn't in it for the money, but for the thing that Professor Strobert always championed: making an impact.

Next, Simmons and Rubin asked Ann Carli to be Def Jam's president. Carli was flattered, but demurred. She could never leave Clive Calder. And frankly, she was too close to Simmons.

"I can't work for Russell," Carli told Rush publicist Bill Adler. Adler understood. If she did, Russ would be chasing her around the desk all day.

Ann Carli was at Arista Records when someone informed her about a strange visitor: a guy at the front desk claiming he was from Rush Productions, trying to pick up a box of Whodini records. Carli went downstairs to investigate, and saw a tall, lumbering young man, who seemed to have a heavy speech impediment.

"I'm sorry," Carli replied patiently. "I don't know who you are." Carli got Simmons on the phone, who told her that the young man was indeed his employee.

Carli gave him the box of records. Later, she called Heidi Smith at Rush to talk about Simmons's new errand boy.

"I can't believe Russell hired a handicapped person!" Carli exclaimed. "That's really nice!"

But the young man who called on Ann Carli was of able mind indeed. Twenty-five-year-old Lyor Cohen talked the way he did because he was shuttled between America and Israel as a young child, his accent never quite settling on either English or Hebrew. And Cohen carried packages for Simmons because he had vowed to carry any load, great or small, to win the respect of his new boss.

The year prior, Cohen was a business-school graduate working an entry-level job at a minor outpost of Israel's national bank in Beverly Hills. He was bored. In his spare time, he promoted punk parties in Los Angeles at a run-down theater in Hollywood called the Stardust Ballroom. Cohen understood the crossover appeal of Run-DMC for his audience, and he rang Russell Simmons repeatedly to book the crew for a gig.

Cohen had placed Run-DMC on a punk-meets-rap bill at the Stardust that included the Red Hot Chili Peppers and Fishbone. On a $700 loan from his mother, Lyor Cohen made $35,000 for one night's work, more than his current annual salary. He quit his job at the bank. He moved to a nicer apartment. He bought dinners for his friends. Cohen brimmed with confidence. *The shit was easy.* For his next show, Cohen booked another Rush artist, Whodini, as headliners. But Whodini wasn't a rock act like Run-DMC, and had no cachet with White hard-core fans.

As he stood on the sidewalk outside the Stardust, barely any tickets sold, Cohen's chest burned with an unbearable pain, somewhere below his heart and above his stomach. He lost everything he had that night.

Broke, Cohen grasped for a lifeline: his cursory relationship with Russell Simmons, and a feeling that Rush was on the cusp of something big. In one of their transcontinental phone calls, Cohen heard Simmons intimate that if Cohen came to work for him, he could take a piece of the company.

Cohen talked the proposition over with his mother and stepfather.

His psychiatrist stepfather, Dr. Phillip Shulman, said: "If you are going to uproot your life in such a tremendous way, there's a thing called a contract."

But his mother, a lawyer named Ziva Naumann, cut in: "You're young. Contract or no contract, what's the worst thing that can happen? If it doesn't work out, you'll come home."

When Cohen showed up at Rush's offices on 1133 Broadway, he was immediately disappointed. He had envisioned a marching-band welcome, some excitement about the arrival of a new partner straight off a plane from the West Coast. But nobody expected Cohen nor knew who he was. Simmons was nowhere to be found.

Simmons never recalled making an offer of equity to the stranger from Los Angeles. Even so, Cohen began interning for Andre Harrell. He proved himself useful almost right away: Run-DMC needed to catch a flight to Europe, and their road manager was on a drug binge and couldn't be found. Nobody responsible at Rush had a passport.

"I have one," Cohen said.

By the time Cohen finally called to tell his parents that he had made the journey to New York safely, he was already in Britain.

Run, DMC, and Jam Master Jay didn't quite know what to make of this clumsy-looking, awkward-talking fellow, whom they had previously met only in passing. "Girallama" is what DMC dubbed Lyor: a cross between a giraffe and a llama.

Cohen was an alien indeed. He was born in New York City to two Israeli immigrants. The marriage between his parents crumbled because of his father Elisha Cohen's increasingly abusive behavior. To get a divorce, Lyor's mother, Ziva, gave custody of her infant son to her husband, who promptly dumped Lyor with a foster family in Israel. At the age of three Lyor was returned to his mother, who had resettled and remarried in Los Angeles. The young Lyor had to get used to a new country, a new language, a new father, new stepsiblings, and a new last name: Shulman. Years later, as a teenager at John Marshall High, Lyor was still an outsider—driving his mother's two-stroke Citroën around a city filled with muscle cars and convertibles, the only White kid hanging out at rap parties thrown by a mobile DJ crew called Uncle Jamm's Army. And when his mother divorced anew, Lyor lost a second father and the means to pay for college. His biological father, Elisha, would pay for Lyor's tuition only if his son separated from his mother yet again and reverted to his given family name. Lyor Shulman became Lyor Cohen again.

Lyor Cohen was used to being perpetually out of place. Now he was on the road in Europe with three hip-hoppers and their homeboy, a slow-moving roadie they called Runny Ray.

On a sweltering summer day in London, Run-DMC arrived to play their biggest gig in Britain, a matinee at the Electric Ballroom. The venue had no air-conditioning, and condensation dripped off of the walls and the ceiling. Even worse, by the time the crew got backstage, Runny Ray discovered that he had forgotten to bring the records that Jay used to supply the beats for Run and DMC. Cohen and Ray raced back to the hotel. No records. *The Schmuck left them at the last gig*, Cohen realized. And it was a Sunday. All the record stores were closed.

Riding back to the ballroom, Lyor Cohen felt that old pain returning, burning in his chest, somewhere below his heart and above his stomach. *This was a short career*, Cohen thought. He had failed Run-DMC, and he had betrayed Russell Simmons.

As Cohen walked inside the venue and looked over the crowd, he noticed something he hadn't seen before: *The crowd had brought their own Run-DMC records for the crew to autograph*. Quickly, Cohen made an announcement, and dozens of records were suddenly passed forward toward the stage. The show was saved.

From then on Lyor Cohen belonged in a way he never had before. Run and DMC trusted him. Jay taught him how to settle shows and collect money. Out on the road, Lyor was Run-DMC's tour manager; back at the office, Cohen found a way to make money for Simmons, and himself: He negotiated a huge deal for all of Rush's artists with Winterland, the largest manufacturer of tour merchandise in the world.

Rush was another family for Cohen, made all the more familiar by its dysfunction. And if Simmons was the father of this family, then Cohen was going to do anything to make sure he was the favorite son.

Simmons and Rubin ran their disjointed partnership in disparate places, with Simmons at Rush's Broadway headquarters, Rubin renting a loft apartment more than twenty blocks downtown, and Def Jam with no offices at all.

Rubin proposed they use a portion of the $600,000 advance to purchase a building to house the two entities of Rush and Def Jam. They found an inexpensive brownstone on a run-down block in the East Village. The building at 298 Elizabeth Street had five floors, enough for offices, a recording studio, and—of prime importance for Rubin—on-premise residences for both him and Simmons, to keep them in sync.

Rubin envisioned 298 Elizabeth Street as a re-creation of the chaos, camaraderie, and close quarters of Weinstein. But the building was a mess and would take months to renovate. Rubin had lots of aesthetic requirements, too—walls of glass brick and polished hardwood floors. Neither Rush nor Def Jam could wait that long for office space, and neither Rubin nor Simmons had the patience to deal with the problem.

Instead, Lyor Cohen took action, renting a former dance studio on 40 East 19th Street. Half of the space was walled off as a residence, and since both Simmons and Cohen were looking for a place to live, Simmons ended up living with Cohen, not Rubin.

On his first day of work, Bill Stephney took his place at the new Rush/Def Jam offices along with Heidi Smith, Bill Adler, Lyor Cohen, and Andre Harrell, who would soon leave to start his own label, Uptown Records.

Cohen pounced on Stephney as soon as the young promotion man had settled in.

"Don't forget you're not only on the Def Jam team, you're on the Rush team, too," Cohen declared. "In fact, Whodini now needs a road manager. If you're not doing anything, you are going to go out with Whodini for the next two months. And then I want you to go out with Captain Rock," who was another Rush client.

An incredulous Stephney called Rubin, who hardly visited the Rush offices.

"I just want to figure out something here," Stephney said. "Who do I work for? Because Lyor wants me to road manage Rush acts."

"Fuck that!" Rubin bellowed, livid at Cohen's ham-handed attempt to hijack his new hire. "You work for Def Jam. You've got records to promote!"

Between Rush and Def Jam, management company and record company, the lines were always blurred.

What the two companies had in common was Russell Simmons.

What separated them were the differing agendas of Lyor Cohen and Rick Rubin.

Krush Groove had not only been a boon to Def Jam and Tommy Boy, but to Profile Records as well, which was promoting *King of Rock*, the second album from the movie's main musical act, Run-DMC.

Simmons and Larry Smith again employed the "Rock Box" formula— rock guitars over hip-hop beats. For the "King of Rock" video, Cory Robbins and Steve Plotnicki invested in a smart-looking, well-produced video, and hired another well-known TV personality, Larry "Bud" Melman, to add comic relief.

"You guys can't come in here; this is a rock-and-roll museum!" Melman laughed, before Run and DMC burst through the doors.

MTV played the video, and gave the group their own live concert special. Weeks later, Run-DMC became the first rap act on *American Bandstand*. They headlined Ricky Walker's second annual Fresh Fest tour, this time sponsored by Sprite. Run-DMC's album quickly went gold, selling more than 500,000 copies. *King of Rock* grossed more than $2 million for Profile, still a small business with only eight employees.

Robbins and Plotnicki moved Profile to bigger offices across the street, and expanded their roster to include an instrumental synth-funk artist named Paul Hardcastle ("Rain Forest") and a new-wave rock group called Boys Don't Cry ("I Wanna Be a Cowboy"). Hip-hop had made Profile's fortune, and Run-DMC was undoubtedly the company's anchor artist. But Cory Robbins never conceived his company as a rap label, and he wanted Profile to be as diverse as any major.

One day, Cory Robbins got a call from his hero, Joel Whitburn, whose books of Billboard charts Robbins had been collecting since he was a boy. Whitburn had a question for *him*, about one of *his* artists! It was a thrill, and Robbins called his friends as soon as he and Whitburn got off the phone. Robbins was tickled again when a young executive called from K-tel Records. K-tel, of course, was a famous company that compiled the hottest hit records from other record companies, and then sold the compilations on TV, with titles like *20 Original Hits! 20 Original Stars!* The K-tel representative, Bryan Turner, was a young guy in his twenties, just like Robbins, trying to drag K-tel into the new age of rap music. Turner wanted to license Run-DMC's "It's Like That." But when Turner offered a mere five cents per track for every album sold, Robbins balked.

"Why would I do that?" Robbins asked. "I'm selling these records for two dollars a copy and making a dollar profit on each of them."

"Five cents is what we pay everybody," Turner replied.

They went back and forth for the better part of an hour, until Turner relented.

"I'll give you six cents."

Robbins had made an extra penny, and Turner had made a friend. The next time Turner came to New York, the two met up. Robbins took Turner to a local club, Pizza-A-Go-Go, and introduced him to Will Socolov, one of Robbins's close-knit group of indie label buddies. Socolov owned a tiny, avant-garde dance label called Sleeping Bag Records, which just had its own first rap hit, "Fresh Is the Word," by Mantronix.

Similar salvation befell another friend of Robbins. Fred Munao, whose ex-wife managed disco queen Donna Summer, founded Select Records to release cool rock 12-inch singles. Munao put out a rap record on a whim. It did nothing. Nothing, that is, until a DJ at WOWI-FM in Virginia Beach played the single's B-side, a song in which the group's three rappers vie for the affections of a girl named Roxanne. The group, UTFO, were still Whodini's dancers on the Fresh Fest tour, but now their record, "Roxanne, Roxanne," had gone Top 10 on the Billboard R&B chart, selling nearly a half million copies.

Even Eddie O'Loughlin, Cory Robbins's friend from Midland International Records, had found success with rap music. O'Loughlin had formed a label called Next Plateau, signing two young female MCs who called themselves Salt-N-Pepa.

Cory Robbins, Steve Plotnicki, Bryan Turner, Tom Silverman, Will Socolov, Fred Munao, and Eddie O'Loughlin all started their careers in the disco era, but hip-hop had made them successful. These young, Jewish-, Italian- and Irish-American entrepreneurs formed a brotherhood of sorts. All of them were fighting to promote and sell rap records. Their shared experience as industry underdogs created camaraderie and a willingness to help one another and share information, an impulse that didn't exist for executives in the major-label world. Robbins and his friends formed a kind of "Rap Pack": They talked constantly. They hung out nightly. They ate together. They even vacationed together.

In December of 1985, Robbins, Turner, Socolov, and Munao all flew to the Club Med resort on Turks and Caicos. On the beach, under warm sunshine that glinted off of the turquoise Caribbean waters, they debated which of the two biggest rap acts in the business would end up being bigger: Run-DMC or the Fat Boys. Both acts had gold albums. Both had music and videos with great pop crossover appeal. Who would end up having the longer career? The vote was split evenly, with Cory Robbins coming down, of course, on the side of his own group.

In the end, it was no contest. Upon Robbins's return to New York, Run-DMC went back into the studio to record their third album. This time, they would be working with a new producer. Now that Rick Rubin was involved, Run-DMC was about to make some records, and break some, too.

Together, Russell Simmons and Larry Smith created Run-DMC's signature sound. But their partnership was always a struggle, with Simmons wanting less music and Smith desiring more. Therefore Rick Rubin was a more fitting partner for Simmons when it came time to create Run-DMC's third album, *Raising Hell*.

The album was recorded for Profile, but it had the big-beat Def Jam sound: fewer instruments and less melody, more cuts and scratching. In a new studio process, Rubin, Run, DMC, and Jam Master Jay took long pieces of real break records—like Bob James's "Take Me to the Mardi Gras" or "My Sharona" by the Knack—and ran them right in from the turntables and onto the tape. It was the closest that recorded hip-hop had come to the sound of the old park jams even if its legality remained questionable.

One of Run-DMC's favorite breaks happened to be the first two bars of Aerosmith's classic rock hit "Walk This Way." Rubin suggested that instead of rhyming their own lyrics over the original break, that they do a complete remake of the entire song with help from the rock band itself. Aerosmith, who had been hitless for many years, were game. Run and DMC, however, had to be convinced. Even in the studio, they resisted reciting Aerosmith's lyrics, which they barely understood. At the urging of Rubin and Jam Master Jay, the MCs came around, and the song became the culmination of Run-DMC's continuing creative and commercial quest to equate rock with rap. Rubin knew instinctively that "Walk This Way" would make that point clear, even for the hardest of hearing.

Profile's video completed that campaign in visual form: Run-DMC and Aerosmith performing on opposite sides of a wall, each distracted by the other's "noise," until they break down the flimsy barrier between them and find that they are, in fact, singing and rapping the same tune. MTV added the clip immediately, as it spoke directly to the channel's own rock radio origins.

Cory Robbins and Manny Bella worked together to conquer pop and Black radio respectively, with Bill Stephney providing an assist at college stations. "Walk This Way" was the first rap song that many Top 40 and rock stations ever played, and it rose to number four on the pop charts—six notches higher than Aerosmith's original had in 1977. But not everybody liked the concept. Back in Aerosmith's hometown of Boston, disc jockeys at local rock station WBCN were bombarded with calls about the "niggers" ruining the rock group's greatest song.

The walls between rock and rap, Black and White, were coming down regardless. At Profile, Run-DMC's *Raising Hell* garnered the group new White fans, and quickly hit a milestone—the first platinum rap album in history, with sales of over one million units and showing no signs of stopping. Back at Def Jam, Rubin and Simmons had created a rarity in the music business—and in America: an interracial company, in terms of the people who owned it, who worked there, and the artists who called the label home. In addition to Black rap acts like LL Cool J, and Simmons's first R&B singer, Oran "Juice" Jones, Rubin had signed Def Jam's first nonrap act, the heavy-metal band Slayer. And now that his work with Run-DMC was done, he could turn his attention to finishing the first album from Def Jam's White rappers, the Beastie Boys.

Before the first sessions for the Beastie Boys album, Rick Rubin and his group obsessed over a new rap record out of Philadelphia. The record, pressed up by the artist, looked cheap. Even the text on the yellow label was handwritten, just like Rubin had done for his Hose single back in college. The beats were raw and big, and the audacity of the lyrics made them laugh, about an MC who walks into a bar: "Got to the place, and who did I see? A sucker-ass nigga tryin' to sound like me. Put my pistol up against his head, I said, 'Sucker-ass nigga, I should shoot you dead.'"

The rhymes in "P.S.K." by Schoolly D weren't entirely new. More than twenty years earlier, in 1963, a folklorist named Roger Abrahams collected similar street poems in Philadelphia: "I walked in and asked the bartender, 'Dig, chief, can I get something to eat?' / He threw me a stale glass of water and flung me a fucked-up piece of meat. /I said, 'Raise, motherfucker, do you know who I am?' / He said, 'Frankly, motherfucker, I just don't give a damn.' / I knowed right then that chickenshit was dead. / I throwed a thirty-eight shell through his motherfucking head."

These grisly rhymes were the sidewalk versions of the slick radio raps by Philadelphia DJ Jocko Henderson or New York's Frankie Crocker. Black men recited these tales of braggadocio and violence on street corners and bars— any place where females weren't present or decorum wasn't required.

Schoolly D's record marked the first time that these tough street raps made it to vinyl. Both extremely crude and wonderfully creative, Schoolly D's rhymes appealed directly to Rubin's love of the "highbrow-lowbrow" union he had discussed with Ric Menello back in college, and they inspired Rubin's work with Adam Horovitz, Adam Yauch, and Michael Diamond.

Since the summer that Rubin and Horovitz roomed together at Weinstein, ordering pea soup from Cozy Soup 'n' Burger and sifting through demo tapes, they had been writing rhymes designed to make each other laugh, each one more outlandish than the one before. The writing continued with Yauch and Diamond until the lyrics became a mixture of b-boy routines and boyish bombast. That these lyrics about "hip-hop body rockin'" and "busting caps" came out of the mouths of White boys made them sound all the more ridiculous.

The tracks that Rubin and the Beasties created matched that insanity. Songs began with one beat pattern; then a sudden break thrown in from a turntable would change everything. Rubin played with song structure— bridges, turnarounds, false endings—to maximize the element of surprise, something that had been a big part of rock production, but had never been done in recorded hip-hop.

Singles trickled out from the sessions for a full year prior to the album's release, building the crew's reputation with a skeptical audience. "Hold It Now, Hit It" floored Black fans who could scarcely believe that three White boys had made the record. By the time the Beastie Boys recorded what would become the leadoff single, "The New Style," the lyrics had gone ridiculously over the top: "I've got money and juice, twin sisters in my bed. Their father had envy so I shot him in the head."

In the early morning hours after each Beasties session, Rick Rubin returned to his alma mater, the Weinstein dorm to sit with Ric Menello at the front desk. They were writing the script for the "real" Run-DMC movie that Rubin and Simmons envisioned in the wake of *Krush Groove*, based on a story called "Who Shot Runny Ray?" concocted by Bill Adler and Lyor Cohen: Run-DMC's roadie is murdered; the cops don't give a shit because he's Black; Run-DMC have to find the killer.

Night after night, Rubin and Menello crafted a dark comedy that invoked their "high-low" ethos: lots of excessive violence and racial epithets but executed as a sort of "urban spaghetti Western" in which the revenge fantasies of disempowered Black men could play out through the film's heroes, Run-DMC.

At least, that was how it was written.

The movie, however, would be helmed by a completely inexperienced director who hadn't been the most attentive student in film school: Rick Rubin.

Columbia president Al Teller found his self-inflicted role as Def Jam's unofficial product manager more headache than he imagined. Simmons and Rubin complained about everything, and his own people complained about Simmons and Rubin. The entrepreneurs didn't care for Columbia's process and didn't respect Columbia's priorities. Simmons was a screamer, and the artists' manager, Lyor Cohen, even more so.

Teller finally lost his cool in one tense meeting with the Def Jam partners. Simmons was yelling again. Teller climbed up on the conference room table, stood and screamed louder. Simmons then leaped onto the table himself to draw even with the executive. Bill Stephney and Rubin looked up in amused disbelief at the two men arguing near the ceiling.

But success seemed to calm everyone down.

By April of 1986 Def Jam's debut album, LL Cool J's *Radio*, had gone gold. By the summer Simmons scored his first number one R&B hit with a song from Def Jam's Oran "Juice" Jones called "The Rain."

And on the Rush side—now redubbed "Rush Artist Management"—

Run-DMC's *Raising Hell* reached double-platinum status and was heading ultimately for an unprecedented three million in sales. Run-DMC had the biggest-selling album in rap music history once again.

Simmons leveraged the popularity of Profile Records' star group for Def Jam's benefit when he sent the Beasties to open up for Run-DMC on their *Raising Hell* summer tour. Rubin stayed behind to mix the Beastie Boys album. Unable to fufill his role on the road as "DJ Double R," he sent Original Concept's Andre "Doctor Dre" Brown in his stead. The Beasties were now an interracial group on an interracial bill, performing for multiracial audiences on a national tour. From the road, The Beasties called Rubin repeatedly to ask when their album would be completed.

"It will be finished," the perfectionist Rubin replied, "when it's good."

By fall the record was complete: fifteen tracks ranging from rap, to metal, to puerile punk pop. Rubin and the Beasties tossed around one proposed album title, *Don't Be a Faggot*, like a Weinstein-era joke, letting the threat dangle for a while before thinking the better of it. They finally settled on *Licensed to Ill*. Rubin wrangled with Columbia Records over two songs: "Scenario," a Schoolly D knockoff that got canned for the lyrics, "shot homeboy in the motherfucking face"; and a rapped remake of the Beatles song "I'm Down." The rejection of "I'm Down" was a bitter disappointment to Rubin, especially because the person who wouldn't give them the right to remake the song was another CBS artist, Michael Jackson. Despite the loss of the two songs Rubin was confident enough to give the Columbia executives a bit of quiet assurance: *This record will live up to anything you do for it.*

In November of 1986, *Licensed to Ill* fell into the hands of fans who had been collecting the Beastie Boys' singles since "Cooky Puss," and people who'd first seen them on *Krush Groove*; White kids who'd seen them open for an ill-fated early tour with Madonna and Black kids who'd caught them on tour with Run-DMC. The Beastie Boys' slow build made their first album one of the fastest-selling debuts in Columbia Records history.

Columbia rushed out a video for the song they believed had the most potential at radio and MTV, "Fight for Your Right to Party," a teenage rebellion song rapped over three power chords and a beat box. Rubin would have directed the video himself, but he was in the midst of preproduction for Run-DMC's movie, *Tougher Than Leather*. Rubin offered the job to his old friends from Weinstein, Adam Dubin and Ric Menello. With only days to prepare for a shoot over the Thanksgiving weekend, Dubin and Menello concocted a story loosely based on the "wild" house party from the movie *Breakfast at Tiffany's*, another bit of "high-low" art. By early December, the clip debuted on MTV, just in time for the Christmas buying season. The channel booked the Beastie Boys for their New Year's Ball.

The cover of *Licensed to Ill* depicted a plane crash. But by February of 1987, the Beastie Boys album had flown where no other rap artist had—to the number one spot on the Billboard album charts—and landed Def Jam's its first platinum album.

During the ascent of *Licensed to Ill*, Al Teller's phone rang. Not his regular phone, either, but the *executive* line, which ran solely between the offices of the top executives of CBS, bypassing their secretaries. The protocol for the executive line was strict. When it lit up, you answered simply by saying your name.

"Al Teller."

"Al, Larry Tisch," said the voice on the phone. The chairman of the entire CBS empire was calling.

"Yes, Larry, what can I do for you?" Teller responded.

"I just got off the phone with Bob Crandall, who is chairman of American Airlines, and he is livid," Tisch said. "He says that we just put out a record that shows an American Airlines airplane crashing into the side of a mountain."

The plane on the cover of *Licensed to Ill* had markings resembling an American Airlines plane. But not quite.

"Do you know that American Airlines is one of the biggest advertisers on CBS Television?" Tisch continued. "You have to take all these albums back from the stores and you have to change the cover immediately."

Teller paused. "Larry, I can't do that."

Now Tisch was yelling at him. "What do you mean, you can't do that?"

"Larry, if I call these guys up and said that they have to change our cover because American Airlines is unhappy with it, we will become the laughingstock of the music business. We will lose credibility, and it will cost us serious business. Artists will be reluctant to sign with us because of this interference by advertisers on a television network. I cannot do that. I will not do that."

Tisch called Teller "crazy" and hung up on him. Teller expected to be fired. He wasn't.

Still, there were some executive decisions that Teller wouldn't fight.

During a break in the recording of the Beastie Boys album, Rubin had traveled to Los Angeles to produce his first album with Slayer, *Reign in Blood*. Slayer incorporated occult imagery into their lyrics and packaging. In one song, "Angel of Death," lead singer Tom Araya took on the persona of the Nazi scientist and torturer Dr. Josef Mengele. Afraid of potential controversy, Teller's boss, Walter Yetnikoff, informed Rubin that Columbia would not be distributing Def Jam's Slayer album. He would be free, however, to shop it elsewhere.

Steve Ralbovsky took pity on Rubin, and introduced him to John Kalodner, an A&R man at David Geffen's boutique label with Warner Bros. Within weeks Rubin arranged for *Reign in Blood* to come out through Geffen Records. Now Def Jam effectively had two distributors, and Rubin had vindication. Critics were already counting *Reign in Blood* among the best metal albums of all time.

"Go around the block again," Rick Rubin ordered his driver.

Rubin was doing anything to postpone the inevitable. At some point, he would have to go to the set and direct the movie.

Shooting *Tougher Than Leather* was the most uncomfortable experience of Rubin's life. Directing a movie required him to wake at the hour when he usually went to sleep. When he got to the location, it was cold, with dozens of people standing around waiting for him to tell them what to do.

Half the time, Rubin didn't know what to say. After twelve hours on the set, he was too fried to plan the next day and didn't have enough time to sleep before some production assistant was knocking on his door again to take him back to hell. One morning Rubin told the PA to call Ric Menello to set up the first shot, closed the door, and went back to sleep.

"Fuck Rick!" Menello said when his cousin, the film's producer, Vincent Giordano, called. "I'm not directing this movie for him."

Menello, of course, didn't want the blame if the movie got fucked-up. And it was already fucked-up. When Giordano shot things without the reluctant director, Rubin would inevitably change them after he showed up. The production was behind schedule and bleeding tens of thousands of dollars daily. Since *Tougher Than Leather* was a completely independent affair for Simmons and Rubin, all the money was coming out of their pockets.

Menello noticed that Rubin wasn't directing the movie in the tone of the script, either. The original concept was a comedy, but Rubin's direction was more dramatic, losing the irony and subtlety. Still Menello saw some good points. Rick Rubin and his dad, Mickey, portrayed racist father-and-son Italian gangsters, and Mickey was, in Menello's estimation, a pretty good actor. The whole racial revenge-fantasy thing was still there, too. In the last scene, Rubin's character, Vic Ferrante, prepared to kill Jam Master Jay. Then Run and DMC came in, guns drawn.

"I ain't walkin' outta here," Rubin said.

"Then you leave in a motherfucking casket," Run replied.

Rubin's character then sneered his final words before being shot, a line written by Menello:

"Never thought I'd die on account of a *nigger.*"

The production limped along and wrapped up before the New Year. The footage sat unedited for months while Rubin went off to produce an album for the Cult—a rock band that wasn't even on Def Jam. Meanwhile, the brownstone at 298 Elizabeth Street was finally opened for the combined staff of Rush and Def Jam. Rubin moved into the loft above it, alone.

With rap airplay still a scarce commodity, Ann Carli and Barry Weiss of Jive Records decided to rent time on WHBI—starting a radio show called "Jive 105" to showcase their own records. Carli gave herself the sobriquet "Tokyo Rose" to host an on-air gossip segment.

The code name didn't matter; everyone knew who she was. Pretty soon, people were shouting "Tokyoski!" in clubs and asking for her autograph. LL Cool J grabbed Carli once as he made his way through a crowd.

"She's my fiancée, ladies," he said. "Back off!"

Carli started writing a rap gossip column for a small newsletter called the "Hip-Hop Hitlist." Published by three young men from New Jersey, Jae Burnett and brothers Vincent and Charles Carroll, the "Hitlist" laid claim to being the very first rap magazine, its publication supported by plentiful ads from record companies like Tommy Boy, Def Jam, Select, and, of course, Jive.

In 1986, Carli covered the proceedings at Tom Silverman's ever-growing New Music Seminar for the "Hip-Hop Hitlist." The seminar now included a Battle for World Supremacy, in which hip-hop DJs competed against one another in dexterous displays of turntable tricks. Most of the contestants hailed from New York, except for one underdog DJ from Philadelphia. He looked strange to Carli, this geeky guy with horn-rimmed eyeglasses and a big head. Unfortunately, Carli had the misfortune to be seated next to the DJ's rowdy Philadelphia posse, which included a gangly, obnoxious kid who wouldn't stop yelling his DJ's name: "Jeff! Jeff!"

By the end of "Jazzy" Jeff Townes's winning set, Carli was screaming the DJ's name, too. She wrote about Jazzy Jeff's victory in the "Hip-Hop Hitlist" without knowing that the obnoxious kid next to her was Jeff's MC, "the Fresh Prince," nor that her partner Barry Weiss was currently tracking the sales of the pair's independently released single, "Girls Ain't Nothing but Trouble." Weiss was increasingly using this strategy to expand Jive's rap roster: Find singles on tiny labels already moving units, and buy them. In this way, Weiss picked up three Philadelphia acts—Schoolly D, Steady B, and DJ Jazzy Jeff & the Fresh Prince.

At the duo's first meeting at Jive Records, Ann Carli introduced herself, but they already knew her as "Tokyo Rose." They recited, word for word, her column about Jeff's victory in the "Hip-Hop Hitlist."

"That was our first press!" Jeff's MC said.

"Tokyo Rose" had written about a rapper called "the Fresh Prince."

But in reality, Ann Carli had just launched the media career of Will Smith.

Rick Rubin, too, loved DJ Jazzy Jeff & the Fresh Prince. "Girls Ain't Nothing but Trouble" was a perfect comic mix of virtuosity and violence. In the song, the Fresh Prince rejected the affections of a young lady. When she yelled "rape!" to avenge her hurt feelings, the rapper hit her with a trash can and "ran like hell."

Rubin, excited, called Simmons, wanting to sign them. Simmons told Rubin that the act wasn't "hip-hop" because the Fresh Prince was dissing himself instead of bragging.

"But that's what's so *great* about them!" Rubin explained.

Simmons insisted that the group would be an embarrassment, and Rubin lost the duo to Jive Records.

Rubin soon fell in love with another rapper brought to him via cassette on separate occasions by a few enthusiastic Def Jam/Rush artists.[3] "Public

---

[3] Rick Rubin says that either DMC or Andre "Doctor Dre" Brown brought him the demo. Chuck D believes it was Jam Master Jay who carried it to Rubin.

Enemy #1" by MC Chuckie D was an old, much-loved promo on WBAU, rapped over an old James Brown break and recorded in low fidelity. It was, in Rick's superlative saying, "the worst shit." The song began with an insane, rambling guy introducing Chuck D with an almost stream-of-consciousness rant. Then Chuck D's booming voice—thundering like a Norse god descending from the heavens—answered: "WHAT GOES ON? WEEEEELLLLLLLLLL . . ."

After hearing "Public Enemy #1," Rubin got Chuck's home number, wrote it on a Post-it note, and called to tell the rapper that he wanted to make records with him. Chuck told Rubin that he had phoned a few years too late.

"I'm too old to rap," the twenty-six-year-old Chuck responded. "LL Cool J is sixteen."

The now twenty-three-year-old Rubin said he hoped that Chuck would reconsider, and that he would call him again sometime.

Rubin phoned him the very next day, and Chuck D declined again. So Rubin tacked the Post-it to the wall by his phone at 594 Broadway, and called Chuck D almost every day for the next six months.

Chuck D ducked Rubin's calls, instructing his mother to tell Rubin that he wasn't home. Chuck had his reasons. The slow death of his first single, an independent record called "Check out the Radio," coproduced by Spectrum City's Hank Boxley, left a bad taste in Chuck's mouth. You just couldn't make money making records. He was working for a photo service and thinking about a career in radio.

What rankled Rubin the most about not being able to sign Chuck D was that Rubin's own head of promotion, Bill Stephney, was the rapper's college buddy. Rubin decided to enlist Stephney's help.

"Get Chuck D to sign, or you're fired," Rubin said.

Luckily, Stephney understood Rubin's Bud Abbott routine.

"Rick," Stephney replied, "you want Chuck so bad? The guy put out a song called 'Check out the Radio,' and no one checked it out!"

Stephney pressed Def Jam's case with Chuck D. Rubin's persistence matched with Stephney's pledge to shepherd Chuck's project—to be his man on the inside—finally convinced Chuck to make Def Jam a proposition of his own.

First, Chuck wanted to be a part of a group that included Hank Boxley—now calling himself Hank "Shocklee"—as his silent studio coconspirator, and Rico Drayton, "MC DJ Flavor," as his vocal sidekick.

Second, Chuck wanted the music to have meaning. Stephney agreed; in his final column for *College Music Journal,* Stephney envisioned a group that combined the beats of Run-DMC and the revolutionary politics of the English punk band the Clash. Now, with Chuck and Hank, Stephney found himself conspiring to do just that. Chuck, the former graphic design student, created a logo for the group: the silhouette of a b-boy in the crosshairs of a rifle. Beside the logo, in military-style stencil type, were the words "Public Enemy."

Stephney thought it was a real mistake to include Flavor. If Public Enemy was supposed to be this serious, political group what the hell were they going to do with a clown? Rubin wasn't sure about Flavor either, but he was willing to do almost anything to get Chuck D to sign. Russell Simmons, on the other hand, was no more impressed with Public Enemy than he had been with the Fresh Prince.

"That shit's nervous," Simmons said.

For all their shared tastes in rap, Simmons and Rubin were discovering that they had many dissimilarities. Simmons had embarked on a quest to re-create the "blue light R&B" that he grew up with in Queens, groups like Blue Magic and the Dramatics. But Rubin yawned at Simmons's pet R&B projects: Alyson Williams, Tashan, the Black Flames, and Oran "Juice" Jones. Likewise, Simmons didn't care for metal groups like Slayer. And he couldn't understand Rubin's enthusiasm for Chuck D.

But Simmons and Rubin found a way to pursue their divergent interests. They simply talked to each other less.

Side B
Low

ales of the Beastie Boys album soared, and accolades accumulated for the group and their producer. *Rolling Stone*, the premier rock magazine, hadn't supported hip-hop in the seven years since "Rapper's Delight." But upon the release of *Licensed to Ill*, they published a review entitled "Three Idiots Make a Masterpiece." *Spin* magazine, a sort of *Rolling Stone* for a new generation, put the Beastie Boys on their cover, the first time since *Spin*'s inception in 1985 that a rap group's faces had graced the front of the publication.

It just so happened that those faces were White.

When the Beastie Boys broke all of Run-DMC's previous sales records, selling four million copies of their debut album, they also became the latest in a long history of White musicians and recording artists who found easier access to mainstream media than their Black counterparts. Now, in the wake of the Beasties' success, some rap fans warned that the group was a harbinger of hip-hop's inevitable hijacking by a collusion of White artists and industry interests, with Black artists like Run-DMC fated to be pushed to the sidelines.

After the *Spin* magazine cover, one concerned reader wrote a letter to the editor.

> Your decision to put a White crew on the cover of your magazine as *Spin*'s front-page presentation of hip-hop betrays: 1) the inherent phoniness of your "alternative" stance; 2) your lack of facility with nascent Black musical

forms; and 3) your own racism. One just hopes that those of us who watched this music . . . grow off the sidewalk will remember that, despite thousands of recordings, concerts, and park jams by individuals who were and are far more innovative, creative, and black than the Beastie Boys, the first rap crew on *Spin*'s cover was not only White but white-faced.

The letter's author was Harold Allen McGregor—the friend of Chuck D, Bill Stephney, and "Doctor Dre" Brown from Professor Strobert's class at Adelphi—now writing under the pen name of "Harry Allen."

Indeed, many critics who claimed to be the champions of "alternative" music had ignored Black rap artists—who were perhaps not the kind of alternative they preferred. But when the Beastie Boys arrived, suddenly these critics saw innovation and creativity where before they had heard only noise.

But Allen's rebuke was ironic given that the Beastie Boys had been introduced to the world by a Black rap act, Run-DMC. And now the Beastie Boys were paying that favor forward by making Allen's friends in Public Enemy the opening act on their *Licensed to Ill* tour, exposing them to millions of White, suburban fans.

This was typical Def Jam, where the usual American tropes about race were turned upside down. The Beastie Boys were a White group with a Black DJ, managed by a Black man and his White Israeli-American lieutenant. Their Black-sounding hip-hop records were produced by a White man and promoted to White radio programmers by a Black man. They owed their careers to the endorsement of a Black rap supergroup; and the White MCs now crusaded for a new pro-Black political rap crew whose Black friend had just dissed the White rappers in print. The pro-Black crew, Public Enemy, had been pursued doggedly by a White Jewish record entrepreneur over mild objections and indifference from his Black partner. And Public Enemy was modeled by their Black producer in part after a White punk band.

Bill Stephney read Harry Allen's letter in *Spin* magazine with surprise. The Beasties were Stephney and his crew's favorite group on Def Jam. He recalled Allen liking the Beasties back at Adelphi, when the Beasties' first singles arrived on those maroon Def Jam labels.

If Allen's critique of the Beastie Boys struck Stephney as hypocritical, then Public Enemy's overall situation was ironic for a crew that espoused the politics of Black power. As much as Rick Rubin wanted Chuck D on the label, he refused to negotiate the terms of Def Jam's parsimonious boilerplate contract. Def Jam offered only five percent of the retail price as a recording royalty. That was half the amount of the typical new artist deal from Profile Records, the label that Rubin vilified for being nothing more than a "bank." Rubin also demanded the group's entire publishing share. It was the kind of record deal Bud Abbott might have given to Lou Costello.

Chuck D took the deal. After Rubin had broken down his resistance, Chuck decided he wanted a way into the business, seeing his recording career as only a beachhead. What he and Public Enemy producer Hank Shocklee wanted most was a company of their own, a home for an entire stable of artists. For that, they would need partners who knew how to make deals.

Shocklee and Chuck D formed Rhythm Method Enterprises as a four-way split with their lawyer Ron Skoler, and Skoler's main client Ed Chalpin, a music business veteran who once signed Jimi Hendrix. They signed rap groups True Mathematics and Kings of Pressure to production deals, and picked up DJ Red Alert and his group the Jungle Brothers for management. Rhythm Method's standard take was steep, but not uncommon: Their production deals kept 50 percent of their artist's record royalties, and their management contracts took 30 percent of their artists' total income. But the terms of the relationship between Rhythm Method and its main act, Public Enemy, were unusual. Rhythm Method took a whopping 75 percent of Public Enemy's recording income, and 30 percent of all other revenue. Hank Shocklee and Chuck D devised the split as a way to give Shocklee a decent return for his work on Public Enemy. But the deal also meant that Skoler and Chalpin would be on equal footing with Shocklee, each entitled to nearly 19 percent of Public Enemy's record royalties. With the combined Def Jam and Rhythm Method deals, Chuck D's prophecy of not making money in the record business would soon become self-fulfilling.[4]

---

[4] Ron Skoler claims that he counseled Hank Shocklee against the excessive royalty, but that Shocklee was adamant about keeping it. In later years, after Public Enemy became successful, Shocklee and Chuck D tried to renegotiate the splits in their favor. Skoler says he was willing to compromise, but that Ed Chalpin refused. Skoler and Chalpin sued them for breach of contract, and Shocklee and Chuck D countersued to dissolve the corporation, precipitating a legal battle with their former partners.

Shocklee and Chuck D didn't know much about Ed Chalpin when they first met him. Chalpin made money in the 1960s recording "cover records," quick knockoffs of current hits, selling the sound-alikes in foreign markets where the imitations were less likely to be noticed. His contract with Jimi Hendrix reportedly gave the young guitarist a one dollar advance against a one percent

Public Enemy wasn't generating much income anyway. The group proved
to be a difficult sell for Def Jam, which had until then made records *by* teenagers, *for* teenagers. Public Enemy were adults, making music for other
adults. The tracks and lyrics on *Yo! Bum Rush the Show* were dense and
dark as was the accompanying imagery. The *Licensed to Ill* tour did win
Public Enemy some fans, though the album sold at a much lower rate
than the previous Def Jam releases. In another irony, Bill Stephney found
that Public Enemy's records received a much warmer reception from White
college DJs than they did from Black hip-hop mix jocks on commercial Black
radio stations. Stephney concluded that a key component was missing from
the album he produced. In the group's crusade to make a hard-line musical
and lyrical statement, they had forgotten to make people dance.

Public Enemy's struggle to connect with a larger, Black audience became
conspicuous when Mr. Magic—back on WBLS after another regime change—
finally played their single, "Public Enemy #1."

"I guarantee you," Mr. Magic said as the song played, "no more music
by the suckers."

Then he scraped the needle across the record and yanked it off the air.

A "dis"—short for "disrespect"—was a transgression as severe in hip-
hop as it was in the Mafia.

In the world of organized crime, not showing proper respect could get
you killed. But in mid-1980s hip-hop, a "dis," whether real or perceived,
rarely proved fatal. More often, it set off a wave of spiteful creativity.

Mr. Magic left WBLS in 1985 with a new partner, the station's former

---

royalty. Chalpin later sued Hendrix and gained a percentage of the guitarist's recordings for Warner Bros. Chalpin was often amenable to negotiation, but he zealously guarded what he felt were
his rights and was unafraid of a legal battle to protect them.

Public Enemy would endure several years of litigation to extricate themselves from the production deal. As the suit dragged on, Skoler tired of fighting and sold Chalpin his shares in Rhythm
Method. Chalpin eventually secured a settlement from the group.

Shocklee and Chuck D's lawyers and Def Jam executives condemned the Public Enemy–Rhythm
Method deal as one of the most egregious rip-offs in music business history. It was, however, not
much worse than Def Jam's initial deal with Public Enemy. The real difference between the two
arrangements was was that Def Jam's benefit to Public Enemy's career is indisputable, while
Rhythm Method's remains dubious. In the coming years, other former Rhythm Method artists
would contend with the company's seemingly ineradicable hold over their contracts and careers.

sportscaster, Tyrone "Fly Ty" Williams, who had replaced Russell Simmons as Magic's manager. Williams commuted with Magic to Philadelphia for his show on WDAS, and booked shows and special appearances for the DJ. After one of these shows—at which the rap group U.T.F.O. was scheduled to appear but cancelled at the last minute—Mr. Magic decided that he had been dissed. Magic and "Fly Ty" responded by commissioning an "answer record" to "Roxanne, Roxanne," produced by their lieutenant DJ, Marlon "Marley Marl" Williams, and rapped by a fourteen-year-old girl named Lolita Shanté Gooden. They released "Roxanne's Revenge" on a small Philadelphia label called Pop Art. As "Roxanne Shanté," Gooden in return dissed the four members of UTFO on wax, provoking a flurry of recorded responses, including one from a UTFO prodigy named Adelaida Martinez who called herself "the *Real* Roxanne."

The "Roxanne Wars," as they came to be called, were good for business. They sold hundreds of thousands of records, launched the careers of three viable artists, and laid the groundwork for Tyrone's, Magic's, and Marley's entry into the record industry. The business strategy for the trio was the same as with Shanté: Dis somebody, draw them into a fight, and make money.

Tyrone and Magic used their relationship with Pop Art records to release a new record by another rapper from Marley Marl's neighborhood in Queensbridge. As "MC Shan," Shawn Moltke already had one unsuccessful single on MCA Records and rapped on Marley's debut record, "Marley Scratch," released by the Aleems on their Nia label. For his first single on Tyrone and Magic's new Bridge Records imprint, MC Shan targeted another kid from Queens whom he believed stole, or "bit," the beat from "Marley Scratch" for his own record, "Rock the Bells": "Beat Biter" was Shan's attempt to dethrone the new prince of rap, with Shan telling LL Cool J that he was getting paid "before you ever thought of makin' rap your trade."

In the years after the demise of the Disco Fever, Mr. Magic reconstituted Sal Abbatiello's "Juice Crew": Magic, Tyrone "Fly Ty" Williams, DJ Marley Marl the beat maker, and Shan and Shante the MCs. When Mr. Magic and his Juice Crew were invited back to WBLS after another change in station management, they resumed their competition with WRKS DJ Red Alert, and Red Alert's Saturday night couterpart at Kiss FM, DJ Chuck Chillout. Magic and Tyrone Williams made some new enemies, too. With "Beat Biter," they had started a battle with Def Jam's flagship artist. But the B-side of "Beat Biter" created an even bigger, unintended war.

MC Shan wrote "The Bridge" as a simple tribute to the beginnings of hip-hop in his home of Queensbridge. To others, Shan seemed to be saying that hip-hop *started* in Queensbridge. And if you lived in the Bronx, you might take that as the ultimate disrespect.

Larry Parker lived in an unused, walk-in meat freezer in a garage under the offices of Rock Candy Records in the South Bronx. He had been a nomad since running away from home at the age of thirteen, spending time in group homes and shelters. Parker was thoughtful, literate, and mercurial. At the Franklin Avenue Armory Shelter, he once screamed at a young Black social worker who wouldn't give him his daily allotment of subway tokens, on the rather accurate suspicion that Parker was selling them for alcohol and drugs.

"You're one of those handkerchief-head house Negroes," Parker said. "You ain't got nothing to do with us Black folks. You're a sellout."

The social worker stood up and faced Parker.

"You don't know who I am," he responded.

In fact, Scott Sterling was a talented hip-hop DJ. Parker was a rapper. Eventually, the two men made this discovery, settled their beef, and became friends. Sterling and Parker formed the Boogie Down Crew, in reference to the oft-used hip-hop moniker for the Bronx.

Parker and Sterling hoped their demo would earn them a place on the roster of one of the prominent rap labels—Profile, Jive, Tommy Boy, Def Jam. At each company, Parker and Sterling were dissed. They ended up on Will Socolov's Sleeping Bag Records, part of a second tier of smaller companies that included labels like Fred Munao's Select, the home of UTFO. When their Sleeping Bag release, "Success Is the Word," didn't live up to its name, Parker and Sterling took refuge in the bottom tier, at a small South Bronx record company on 132nd and Cypress called Rock Candy Records and Film-works.

Rock Candy was owned by none other than Joe Robinson's old friend from Harlem, Jack Allen. Since the day he saved the young Robinson from a beating, Allen made his living both in and out of the music business; he also ran a construction company.

Allen made Sterling and Parker a deal. If they recorded a "say no to crack" record for him on Rock Candy, he would let them put another record out on their own imprint, called B-Boy Records. Allen didn't advance the pair any money. Instead, in lieu of payment, Allen let Parker sleep in the downstairs garage. Allen built a small bathroom, and Parker made his bed in an abandoned meat freezer, fashioning a mattress out of milk crates, old newspapers, and clothes, and kept a big brick by the door so the freezer wouldn't slam shut and suffocate him.

The Boogie Down Crew became Boogie Down Productions, or BDP for short. With Parker performing as "KRS-One," Sterling as "Scott La Rock," they rerecorded their demo at Power Play Studios in Queens, the same place where Rick Rubin created "It's Yours." In a stroke of luck, the most powerful, influential DJ in all of rap happened to be in Power Play's other studio at the same time. Excited, Sterling and Parker walked in to introduce themselves to Mr. Magic.

"Get outta here!" Magic barked at them, his work interrupted.

When they returned to the studio the next day, Parker and Sterling's engineer informed them that he had taken the liberty of playing some of their songs for Mr. Magic. Unfortunately, the DJ had dissed them again.

"He said it was wack," the engineer reported.

"I'm wack?" Parker fumed. "*Shan* is wack!" MC Shan's song "The Bridge" had rankled Parker for a while. *Hip-hop started in Queensbridge? Are you kidding?* Now came Parker's retribution, a hurriedly composed answer record called "South Bronx." "So you think that hip-hop had its start out in Queensbridge?" the rapper asked. "If you popped that junk up in the Bronx you might not live."

After dissing MC Shan, Parker then followed Shan's example by picking a fight with another member of the Rush/Def Jam empire, saying that he was a "teacher," not a "king," a sly dig at the "Kings of Rock," Run-DMC. Next, Parker led a lesson on the Bronx origins of hip-hop, starting with the holy trinity of Herc, Flash, and Bambaataa, careful also to acknowledge the presence at the old Bronx jams of both of Mr. Magic's rivals, on "98.7 Kiss FM," Kool DJ Red Alert and Chuck Chillout.

"South Bronx" was not only a salvo against Queensbridge, but against Hollis too: a volley from sons of the "old school" against Simmons, Run-DMC, and Def Jam—the successor to Sugar Hill in the commodification of hip-hop culture.

In the wake of "South Bronx" Scott Sterling sought to orchestrate a war for fame and profit. He approached Marley Marl, thinking that the Juice Crew would understand the value of setting off another fusillade of battle records.

"We don't need you," Marley told Sterling.

Thwarted, Sterling took comfort in the fact that "South Bronx" had mentioned WRKS's rap DJs, so the record had a good shot at airplay. Kool DJ Red Alert didn't need to be convinced. He had been locked in a battle with Mr. Magic since the DJ returned to WBLS, which had launched a new campaign called "Kissbusters." It was Red's pleasure to play a record dissing Magic and Marley's prodigal son, Shan. But even more than that, he had seen the reaction when his friend DJ Raoul played "South Bronx" for the first time at the Times Square hip-hop club Latin Quarter. Everybody stopped dancing and just looked at the DJ booth, listening. After the crowds got familiar with it, the kids from the Bronx would "wild out" whenever the song came on: chain snatching, sucker punching time.

"South Bronx" by Boogie Down Productions set off an even bigger battle than the "Roxanne Wars." MC Shan recorded a quick response on tape, a song called "Kill That Noise," and Magic played it immediately on WBLS. KRS-One returned fire with "The Bridge Is Over," and Red Alert spun it the following week on WRKS. While the rest of the country flocked to Run-DMC and the Beastie Boys concerts, New York hip-hop fans were riveted by entirely new artists that few outside the tristate area knew existed.

All parties reaped the rewards of battle. Boogie Down Productions released a full album, *Criminal Minded*, on B-Boy Records. The album's lyrics and artwork reflected both the war of words with the Juice Crew, and the growing war in the streets of New York, as crack cocaine exploded the drug trade and drug-related violence. Both Sterling and Parker appeared on the cover with guns, draped in ammunition. To Jack Allen's delight, the record began selling copies in the hundreds of thousands. Meanwhile, Tyrone Williams had partnered with Len Fichtelberg, the Jewish owner of a small dance music label called Prism, to create a new label. Cold Chillin' Records would be the permanent home for Juice Crew artists like Roxanne Shanté; Shan; Shan's protégé, Biz Markie—a heavyset, clownish rapper with a slurry but sly delivery; and a suave lyricist from Brooklyn who called himself Big Daddy Kane.

Russell Simmons and Andre Harrell dissed Tyrone Williams about his seemingly uncommercial roster of artists, most of whom came not from suburban neighborhoods, like Def Jam's artists, but from inner-city projects. They dubbed Tyrone the leader of the "red brick brigade."

Red Alert was more merciful than his rivals at WBLS. Mr. Magic wouldn't spin records by Red's friends in Boogie Down Productions. But Red Alert didn't hesitate to play Biz Markie's hits "Make the Music with Your Mouth," and "Nobody Beats the Biz." Biz Markie was a member of the Juice Crew, but Biz Markie had never dissed Red. *Why drag Biz into a fight merely by association?* Red thought. If a record was good, he gave it respect.

So when a duo called Eric B & Rakim put out their first single, Red Alert played it, even though it was produced by his archrival's lieutenant, Marley Marl. How could Red *not* play the two incredible songs on the record—"Eric B Is President" and "My Melody"? Hip-hop fans were mesmerized by the intricate lyrics and low-key delivery of the MC, William "Rakim" Griffin, because they were the antithesis of the Def Jam aesthetic, where beats boomed and mouths roared.

The beats under Rakim's incantations were different, too. Instead of using turntables to manually loop breaks, as Rick Rubin had, Marley Marl employed new technologies to do the same thing—a digital recorder called a "sampler," coupled with a digital clock called a "sequencer" to trigger the samples—making it possible to perfectly time the breaks like a DJ would, or to cut up the individual drum sounds into pieces to play in new rhythms. In the records of the "Bridge Wars," both Marley and Scott "La Rock" Sterling used sampling as their chief weapon, too; their records were a departure from the crisp and clean Def Jam sound.

The culmination of this new technique came in the late spring of 1987 with the release of Eric B & Rakim's "I Know You Got Soul." The premise was simple: Two well-known breaks—one from James Brown and the other from Funkadelic—were layered on top of each other, running at the same time; no drum machine at all, save for a triggered, booming 808 kick drum. The impact was revolutionary. In using computers to sample and layer long pieces of real drum breaks, hip-hop had freed itself from the rigid grid of drum machines. Suddenly, the music behind Rakim was as loose and syncopated as his rhymes. The versatility of the digital sampler allowed an infinite range of musical expression. The beat-box era was over.

No one understood this more suddenly and viscerally than Chuck D. He was home now from the tour with the Beastie Boys, listening to Mr. Magic's show when he heard "I Know You Got Soul" for the first time. Here was a song that rendered his current album obsolete. Alarmed and inspired, Chuck raced to the studio he shared with Hank Shocklee on Franklin Avenue in

Hempstead, and began rifling through their huge collection of breaks. Within minutes, Shocklee burst through the door.

"I just heard the most amazing song on Mr. Magic," Shocklee said, breathless.

The partners knew they wanted to make a song with this new production concept. But they had to do it their way. *If "I Know You Got Soul" had an evil twin,* Shocklee wondered, *what would it sound like?* If Rakim was smooth, Public Enemy would have to be rough. So Shocklee picked the nastiest, ugliest break he could find—the opening bar of another James Brown–produced record, "The Grunt," which began with the atonal, ascending screech of a saxophone. Sampled in their equipment and repeated ad infinitum, the break looped endlessly like a sinister siren. They made a quick tape for Chuck to write his lyrics to, and went home. The next morning, Chuck called Shocklee.

"It's done," the rapper said.

"Done?" Shocklee responded. "We haven't even arranged it!"

"No, it's perfect," Chuck D said. "It's called 'Rebel Without a Pause.'"

The partners booked studio time in Manhattan to finish the song, which contained poetic references to their treatment at the hands of Mr. Magic, to Rakim, their new object of musical inspiration and jealousy, and toward the man they saw as their real enemy in 1987, Ronald Reagan. It was the perfect union of beats and politics. It sounded, as Rick Rubin might have gushed, like "the worst shit ever."

Bill Stephney rushed the song onto the B-side of Public Enemy's second single from *Yo! Bum Rush the Show.* A few weeks later, in June of 1987, Shocklee and Chuck D dropped off two test pressings to Chuck Chillout at 98.7 Kiss FM. By the time they returned to their car, the DJ was playing the song. By the Fourth of July, "Rebel" was blaring out of cars across the Northeast, from Philadelphia to Boston, the teakettle screech echoing off of buildings and drifting off into the night. When Stephney went to clubs, the opening of the song electrified the b-boys in the house in the same way that "Sucker MCs" once had, only the effect was much darker. One day, Larry Smith came into the Def Jam/Rush offices and spotted Stephney, telling him that he heard Public Enemy's record at a Bronx club the previous night.

"They put 'Rebel' on and a fight started," Smith reported. "That song will make you want to punch your wife."

"Rebel" was indeed the evil twin, a song so ubiquitous on the streets that even Mr. Magic had to play it. Before "Rebel," few cared about Public Enemy or Chuck D's political rhymes. Now that people were bobbing their heads, they were listening, too.

The Beastie Boys and Run-DMC were still the biggest acts on MTV. LL Cool J's second album had even spawned a teenybopper rap ballad called "I Need Love." But while these artists reached the apex of their success, something shifted beneath them.

On the streets, Public Enemy, Eric B & Rakim, and Boogie Down Productions now ruled. And the three MCs who fronted these crews—Chuck D, Rakim, and KRS-One—presented themselves as something different in hip-hop. They weren't just out to rock the crowd. They were serious Black men with something important to say.

In 1987, the world outside Def Jam's offices on 298 Elizabeth reflected the worsening situation on the streets of New York. At the nearest subway stop on Bleecker, across from the only restaurant in the neighborhood, the NoHo Star, crackheads mugged people in broad daylight. The asphalt on Elizabeth Street glittered with shattered glass from broken car windows. Addicts lit up in the basketball court across the street and in the abandoned church that faced Def Jam's offices. Rick Rubin insisted that the architects install a glass front door, and every so often, Def Jam employees would arrive in the morning to find the door cracked and shattered.

In the offices, too, cracks appeared.

The fissures first went public on the eve of the release of the Beastie Boys' album. Barry Walters of the *Village Voice* wrote a feature on the white-hot, twenty-three-year-old record producer Rick Rubin, called "The King of Rap." It was far from a fawning portrayal: Walters dug into Rubin's pampered childhood. He interviewed Rubin's guitar teacher from high school, who had less than flattering things to say about his former student's manipulative ways. Walters even asked Rubin why he deleted his best friend Adam Horovitz's publishing credit for "I Need a Beat" when the song appeared on LL Cool J's first album.

The piece mentioned Rubin's partner, Russell Simmons, only once. If Simmons was hurt, his publicist, Bill Adler, was offended. Adler helped Run draft a letter to the editor.

"If anybody's the King of Rap, it's Run-DMC," Run wrote. "And if it's not us, it's my brother Russell Simmons. . . . Rick Rubin is not just a very close friend of mine, he's a great multitalent deserving of acclaim. But it fucks me up that anybody thinks that he made my album."

But few in the Rush/Def Jam camp were more upset by the article than the Beastie Boys, who felt the writer depicted them as bystanders in the creation of their own album, while elevating Rubin to the status of a Svengali.

Rubin had more plans for his group: an MTV show based loosely on the cruel humor of the old Abbott and Costello shows with episodes like "The Beastie Boys Get Stupid" and "The Beastie Boys Get Ill" written by Ric Menello and Adam Dubin. The Beastie Boys loved the scripts. But on the eve of their *Licensed to Ill* tour, when Horovitz, Yauch, and Diamond met with Rubin to ask for a financial interest in the proposed show, Rubin turned them down flat. Over the past couple of years, Rubin had quietly slipped over the line from friend and band member into producer and employer, and their former DJ suddenly wielded veto power over their creative and professional lives. The group left for their tour with the blood still boiling in their veins, and the development of the TV show languished.

Rubin and Menello planned another project—a Beasties movie called *Scared Shitless*. But that project, too, got hung up in the power struggle between Rubin and the group. When the *Licensed to Ill* tour hit Los Angeles, Lyor Cohen set up a meeting for the Beasties with Hollywood producer Scott Rudin at Universal Studios, who offered $4 million for the Beasties' movie. Then Rick Rubin found out about the deal. Even though his own directorial debut had been a debacle, Rubin refused to share creative control with Hollywood executives who were already talking about turning *Scared Shitless* into more middlebrow fare, renaming it *Scared Stupid*. Rubin told the Beastie Boys that if they did the movie, they couldn't perform music in it, as Def Jam held exclusive rights to distribute their recordings. Universal Studios reconsidered the value of a Beastie Boys movie without music, and pulled the offer. Rubin believed that he was saving the group from their own bad ideas, from being manipulated by people who didn't care about their image or their art—chief among them, the architect of the movie deal, Lyor Cohen.

To Rick Rubin, who built the house of Def Jam with his records and aesthetic direction, Cohen was the antithesis of the artistic purity he was trying to achieve—motivated it seemed by money and, even worse, a desire for his own artists' approval.

Rubin and Cohen dined at the NoHo Star with Adam Yauch one day when the Beastie announced one of his personal fantasies: He wanted to go to L.A., rent a Ferrari, and drive two hundred miles an hour.

"How cool would that be?" Yauch asked.

"I don't think that would be cool at all," Rubin replied, for once relinquishing his Bud Abbott role.

But Cohen leaped forward: "That sounds great." Cohen said he knew some rich Africans in Los Angeles with a garage full of luxury cars. "We'll go to L.A. and we'll all rent them."

This guy is their manager, Rubin thought. *Isn't he supposed to discourage this kind of stuff?* Between the Ferrari and the film, Rubin saw Cohen trying to wedge himself next to the Beastie Boys, one bad idea at a time. *I'm the enemy now, and Lyor their good new friend.*

To Lyor Cohen, who built the house of Rush with his deals and vigilance, Rubin wasted time and spent money on bullshit.

Like the time Cohen went to a recording studio to pick up some cocaine from the studio's owner and sneaked a peek at Rubin, hunched over a high hat in a sound room cooled to near freezing. When Cohen returned hours later to pick up some more blow, there was Rubin, in that same meat locker, killing himself over that same high hat. *What a schmuck*, Cohen thought.

To Cohen, Rubin was the one with the bad ideas. Spending your own money to make a movie when you've never made one before? *Bad idea*. Turning down somebody else's money to make one just because you want *all* the control? *Bad idea*. Worst of all, Rubin was proposing unconscionable splits on the movie deals with Run-DMC and the Beastie Boys: one-third for him, one-third for Russell, and one-third for the group. What made it worse was that these kids were, quite literally, their friends and family.

This is unfair to your brother, Cohen chided Simmons.

To Russell Simmons, who built the houses of Rush and Def Jam with his vision and persistence, the struggles between Rubin and Cohen, and between Rubin and the Beasties, were battles he didn't much care to referee. One day, as Bill Adler sat with Simmons at a recording session for one of his R&B acts, the entrepreneur confided in him.

"Bill," Simmons said, "my Jews are fighting."

Simmons struggled for good reason. Although Rick Rubin produced the records that made Def Jam into a cultural powerhouse, record royalties paled in comparison to the deals that Lyor Cohen was doing. Three years earlier, when Cohen showed up in New York, he was an afterthought. Now he had become indispensable.

The Adidas deal was Cohen's breakthrough achievement. "My Adidas," Run-DMC's first single from *Raising Hell*, was the crew's paean to their favorite hip-hop fashion statement. To Run-DMC, the song and the sneakers were art, nothing more. But "My Adidas" was a virtual three-minute radio commercial for the German sneaker company. Yet the group had no ulterior motive, no intent to capitalize on the song. Cohen set about to change that.

First, Cohen found his way to Angelo Anastasio, who ran Adidas's one-man American marketing operation from a lonely outpost in Los Angeles. A native of Turin, Italy, who once played soccer with Pelé on the New York Cosmos, Anastasio had already realized that musical artists often had more influence than sports figures in selling sportswear, because artists weren't tied to localities like players were. He had already noticed a spike in sales of the style that Run-DMC wore, the black-and-white shell-toed Superstar shoe. The mirthful Anastasio flew out to New York to meet with Cohen, Simmons, and the group, who rapped the song for him in person. In return, Anastasio opened up his supply closets to the group, sending them tracksuits and shoes.

Cohen wanted more than free clothes. So he arranged for Anastasio to visit New York on the evening that the *Raising Hell* tour hit Madison Square Garden. The marketing executive watched from the stage as Run asked thirty thousand fans to thrust their Adidas into the air. Anastasio looked at the ocean of Adidas and found himself crying. He he had never witnessed anything quite as powerful, not even scoring a soccer goal in front of a stadium full of people. When Run-DMC came to Europe, Anastasio brought them to Munich to perform for his boss, Horst Dassler, the son of Adidas's founder and namesake, Adi Dassler. The CEO gave Anastasio what he was asking for, something Run-DMC had already earned: a $1 million endorsement deal—the first of its kind for a rap group—that would eventually grow to include their own branded line of Adidas.

Cohen negotiated tenaciously on behalf of the artists he managed. When he won, he was happy. When he won by the largest possible margin, he was ecstatic. When he felt himself losing, and that old burning sensation returned—below his heart and above his stomach—Cohen could turn bitter and vicious.

Cohen began disposing of many of Simmons's old partners, whom he thought superfluous. When the time came to negotiate the third Fresh Fest tour in the summer of 1986, Lyor Cohen had other ideas.

"You have become too expensive," Cohen told Ricky Walker. Suddenly, Walker was out, and Rush ran its own tours.

Simmons had hired his first mentor, Rocky Ford, to work at Rush. One day, Cohen turned to Ford and told him it was time to go. Cohen even wanted to fire Heidi Smith, Russell Simmons's longest-serving assistant. He didn't for fear of angering Simmons.

Cohen's zeal and combative style ended up destroying several deals, like the proposed partnership between the Beastie Boys and the skateboard company, Action. But the relationship that both Cohen and Simmons eventually killed was the one between their most important client, Run-DMC, and their label, Profile Records.

Run-DMC sold millions of records for Profile, netting the label tens of millions of dollars. Profile moved to lavish new offices, taking up an entire floor of a building on Broadway and Astor Place. Cory Robbins and Steve Plotnicki had both become rich men, and more than doubled the number of employees on their payroll.

But even with all of Profile's success, Simmons hadn't been able to renegotiate the original contract that he had signed when Run-DMC were rookies. The terms were almost medieval. Profile offered a 10 percent royalty rate, which meant that Run-DMC earned a mere 71 cents for each album sold. Profile had the right to request two albums a year, and those albums had to be delivered within sixty days of the label's request. If Run-DMC failed to fulfill those terms, Profile had the right to suspend the contract until the group did. Which meant that Profile could hold back royalties just by requesting an album they knew Run-DMC couldn't deliver.

During the summer of 1986, in the middle of the group's *Raising Hell* tour, Profile requested a new Run-DMC album, due contractually by October 1. A month later, Simmons received Run-DMC's latest biannual royalty statement, along with a check for $486,944, which included money for 250,000 units of *Raising Hell*. But Profile had already certified sales of over *one million* units, and actual sales were approaching *three* million. Profile was holding back payment on millions of records because, like many record companies, their contracts gave them the right to reserve half of all payable royalties for up to two years, in case their distributors took too long in paying. But if Simmons didn't deliver the next album by October 1—which was impossible because Run-DMC would be touring until January—Profile could suspend all payment until the group delivered. To Simmons, the group's situation was ridiculous.

Simmons had suspicions that Profile Records was selling records "out the back door" in order to not pay royalties on those units. He hired a private investigator, Al Zaretz, to dig up evidence. Zaretz found none, but did find a high-level industry executive who claimed—off the record—that Run-DMC's sales were 25 percent higher than Profile was reporting. Simmons and Cohen had long believed that Profile had two sets of books—one for the artists, and one for themselves.

Run-DMC was now one of the hottest acts in all of pop music, but stuck on a tiny label. If the group were free, they could snare a multimillion-dollar major-label deal in a heartbeat. If Rush were ever going to try to put Run-DMC in a better position, now was the time. So Simmons decided to engage in brinkmanship with Profile. He simply requested the money he believed he was owed—$6.8 million—and refused to deliver any new music until he got it. On August 3, 1987, over a year after the release of *Raising Hell*, Rush Productions filed suit in New York Supreme Court to break Run-DMC's contract with Profile, accusing them of nonpayment of royalties and "fraudulent accounting practices." Simmons and Cohen were betting that a small company like Profile would blink at the prospect of extended litigation and investigation of their business practices, and let the group go for a price.

They bet wrong. Robbins and Plotnicki had long ago made a solemn vow to never sell off Profile's assets. Independent labels went out of business all the time because of this: As soon as an indie gets a hit record, it sells the act to a bigger label. And then that label was back where it started, with nothing. Profile never sold off a hot artist. Furthermore, Plotnicki wasn't intimidated by the money or legal muscle of a major label. He would fight on principle, if he had to. The more Cohen and Simmons yelled, the more Plotnicki wanted to do battle.

Profile filed a countersuit claiming their contract was sound and that Rush was making a bald-faced play to get Run-DMC to a larger label, perhaps onto Russell's own venture with CBS. After all, a lot of people mistakenly thought that Run-DMC was on Def Jam anyway.

Robbins and Plotnicki didn't apologize for being a small company, nor for the terms of the contract that Run-DMC signed. That was the trade-off that Simmons made when he signed his group with Profile Records, Plotnicki thought. That was what Profile got for taking the chance, and that was what Simmons got when nobody else would sign his group. And hadn't Profile had done an incredible, unprecedented job for an independent label?

"I find talent when it's cheap, and I make it worth a lot," Plotnicki said. "Once artists are worth a lot, they feel they don't need you anymore."

Plotnicki thought that Simmons wasn't acting in his brother's best interests. What sane artist manager would tell his group to walk away from $2 million in unpaid royalties to get a deal with another major that might yield them only 10 percent more in sales? What manager who truly wanted to protect his artist's career would have them go "on strike," holding back an album, not to mention the release of their long-planned movie, while their lawyers pursued a case against a record company without any evidence? What happens to your artist's career while the case drags on? Simmons and Cohen had other artists; they could walk away.

Run-DMC couldn't.

While Simmons and Cohen brawled with Profile, Rick Rubin was in Los Angeles working on Def Jam's first soundtrack album for the movie *Less Than Zero*.

Despite his stance on the proposed Beastie Boys movie, Rubin had indeed found a benefit to working with Hollywood. He was now a hot producer of music in the fringe genres of rap and heavy metal, but with the money of a major movie production behind him, Rubin could suddenly make any record he wished with anyone he wanted. Rubin chose to make rock.

With George Drakoulias, Rubin moved into the Mondrian Hotel on the Sunset Strip. He remade classic rock 'n' roll songs with Def Jam's Slayer; with Columbia Records' girl rockers the Bangles; and with his new friends in Aerosmith—whose career he and Run-DMC had so dramatically revived.

Rubin didn't always attain creative bliss. He recorded the movie's title track with Glenn Danzig of the legendary punk band the Misfits; but Danzig's bass player didn't like Rubin telling him how to play his part, so Drakoulias played bass instead. Rubin hated the mix that the Bangles had done for their remake of "Hazy Shade of Winter." But Rubin produced a beautiful, melancholy song for his personal hero, the aging rocker Roy Orbison, called "Life Fades Away."

Rubin had visited Los Angeles several times before and never liked it. But something shifted for him on this trip. He liked driving everywhere, like he had growing up on Long Island. He loved listening to music in the car. And the recording studios were fantastic, much better than in New York, as were the musicians. A new band called Guns N' Roses was leading a revival of the local rock scene. Rubin liked that the town seemed set up for making music.

L.A. was also the center of the porn universe—another obsession for Rubin. During his sojourn, Rubin started dating an adult film star named Melissa Melendez, who starred in movies like *The Return of Johnny Wadd* and *Eaten Alive*. By the time Rubin was scheduled to return to New York in the late summer of 1987, nine months had passed. He wasn't sure he wanted to stay in L.A., but he wasn't sure he wanted to go back to New York either. In the end, he brought Melendez with him back to his loft apartment at 298 Elizabeth Street.

Rubin avoided the Def Jam/Rush offices as much as he could. A lot had happened in his absence, including the recording and release of the second album from Def Jam's first star, LL Cool J. The teenage rapper was upset that Rubin hadn't been around for him. Ironically, while Rubin was in California two producers from Los Angeles came east to record LL's sophomore release, *Bigger and Deffer*, which spawned LL's first pop radio record, "I Need Love." At two million copies sold, LL's second album dwarfed the sales of his first.

"I Need Love" was the kind of rap record that Rubin would never have made—too soft, too conventional—and LL's reputation was already suffering for it in the streets. But Rubin wanted to make sure his rap artists were represented on the *Less Than Zero* soundtrack, so he booked some studio time for himself and LL Cool J.

The track that Rubin played for LL was *completely* unconventional, even by hip-hop standards, influenced by his time in L.A. The song began with the sounds of a muted trumpet, the musician dueling with a DJ who slowly rubbed a record, and then threw a huge rock chord into the open space between them.

Rubin was never shy about producing his artists' lyrics, so he shared with LL his idea for the chorus of the song.

It's about a guy, Rubin said, *who can't decide whether or not he wants to go back to California.*

Success had made LL Cool J a target. MC Shan had launched his career by dissing him. Then a man named Lawrence Humphrey filed suit against Def Jam, claiming that he was the "real" LL Cool J.

Now Kool Moe Dee was aiming for the young rapper produced by his old friend Rick Rubin.

After the Treacherous Three won their release from the ailing Sugar Hill Records, Kool Moe Dee signed to Jive Records, where Ann Carli helped develop him as a solo artist. Russell Simmons ridiculed Carli about her involvement with Kool Moe Dee, whom Simmons thought was an "old-school" artist who would never make a good record, especially when compared to his own artist, the young crown prince of rap, LL Cool J.

LL Cool J had an even higher opinion of himself. "The greatest rapper in the history of rap itself," he rhymed on his second album, *Bigger and Deffer*. Kool Moe Dee took that boast very personally.

The title track for Kool Moe Dee's new Jive album, "How Ya Like Me Now," brimmed with teasing references to the younger rapper. Carli, seeking playful payback of her own against Simmons, helped Moe Dee make his point graphically. She crafted a "Kool Moe Dee Rates the Rappers" chart for the album's inner sleeve, in which Moe Dee gave LL a predictably low score. And she provided a subliminal, final touch to the album cover by placing LL's signature headgear—a red Kangol—underneath the tire of Kool Moe Dee's Jeep.

It worked. Kool Moe Dee put out a good record, made even hotter by the buzz about his battle with LL Cool J. Suddenly, the old-school rapper was a new artist again, especially to many younger rap fans who had never heard of the Treacherous Three. Carli knew she had won when she suggested that they engineer a pay-per-view cable TV battle between the two MCs, and Simmons refused.

While Carli worked with Kool Moe Dee, Barry Weiss prepared to bring another act to Jive who already had a hugely successful record on a tiny indie label. Weiss offered Jack Allen a percentage of future profits for Boogie Down Productions for signing the contract over to Jive. Soon, Carli had become friends with rapper KRS-One, his seventeen-year-old sidekick Derrick "D-Nice" Jones, and producer Scott "La Rock" Sterling, who was particularly excited about making his next album.

Sterling, however, never got the chance.

In late August of 1987, he went to the South Bronx with a few friends to calm a local drug dealer who had threatened to kill his partner D-Nice over a perceived offense. Sterling—still a social worker and counselor at heart—couldn't find the dealer, so he returned to his friend's Jeep, jumping into the backseat. Suddenly, bullets started clinking down on them as they raced away. They seemed to be in the clear when Sterling spoke up.

"Turn the radio down, man!" Sterling said.

His friends told him that the radio wasn't on. Sterling was hallucinating because he had been shot in the head and neck.

Carli got a frantic call from DJ Red Alert, who rushed to meet Sterling's friends at Lincoln Hospital in the Bronx.

"Please, Annie, please," he cried. "He could live. But they're not treating him right because he's Black. They don't know who he is."

Carli frantically tried to reach the right people at Lincoln by phone, while Scott "La Rock" Sterling died in the operating room.

Back in New York, Rick Rubin finished editing the Run-DMC movie nearly a year after he shot the film.

But now that *Tougher Than Leather* was complete, it was useless. Run-DMC was still on strike, embroiled in a lawsuit with their label. Profile wouldn't license any of the crew's music for the film, and the group had no album to promote. Run was particularly distraught. Folks around Rush worried that the rapper was having a nervous breakdown—smoking weed heavily, cursing, walking around shirtless, talking about Jesus.

The Beastie Boys were experiencing a breakdown of their own. They came home from a gargantuan, successful tour exhausted and depressed. Horovitz had been jailed during their tour of England, accused of throwing a can at a girl in the audience of their Liverpool show when he was actually fending off a hail of bottles, cans, and spit. Simmons wanted them back in the studio as soon as possible for their second album. The Beasties balked. Now Simmons got a taste of what he had been feeding Cory Robbins and Steve Plotnicki. The group had stopped talking to Rubin altogether, demanding to renegotiate their contract. Their attorney, Ken Anderson, inquired about unpaid royalties. But Def Jam wasn't paying because they couldn't.

Jimmy Castor, the composer of many songs like "It's Just Begun" that had become great b-boy breaks had sued Def Jam and CBS for their unlicensed use of a piece of another of his songs, "Hey Leroy," in the Beastie Boys' track, "Hold It Now, Hit It." Columbia immediately froze Def Jam's royalties until the resolution of the case. Def Jam couldn't pay the Beastie Boys, nor could they deliver an album to Columbia. Ken Anderson argued that the situation put Def Jam in breach of their contract, and that it meant the Beastie Boys, Def Jam's top-selling act, might be able to walk.

Rubin was disgusted with Columbia over the situation. His frustrations with the major label—and its chief executive, Al Teller—had begun years before, when he discovered how shoddily Def Jam acts were being promoted by CBS Records in Britain. Hugh Atwell, ostensibly his international product manager at CBS, was frank. *The American operation is an albatross*, Atwell told him. "We give America great records; they give us shit. We have nothing against you. But if you're coming from them, we're just not interested."

Alarmed, Rubin reported his findings to Teller when he returned to New York.

"Why not let us take this music to someone else abroad who really wants it?" Rubin suggested.

Rubin was even more shocked by Teller's response.

The standing corporate policy at CBS, Teller said, was to keep the international rights to their acts rather than risk one of their rivals having great success with one of their artists, and having CBS look bad for letting them go.

To Rubin, everything that Columbia Records did seemed insane. What was even crazier was that his partner, Simmons, didn't seem to care. They were approaching their own renegotiation with Columbia, and Rubin and Simmons couldn't agree on what to do.

Rubin wanted a pressing and distribution deal, which would give them little in the way of advances, but much more control. Columbia wouldn't be able to tell Def Jam which records to release or dictate their spending. Best of all, Def Jam would have the majority of the back-end profits, and control of its own masters.

Simmons, on the other hand, wanted to continue with a larger version of Def Jam's production deal, yielding a much lower profit in return for more cash up front.

Simmons, of course, had handled the negotiations with Columbia back when their relationship with the major began. He was the one who knew Steve Ralbovsky. It had been his deal, and Rubin wasn't thinking about the fine points. But now that Rubin was involved, he believed that Def Jam had been ripped off from the start. Def Jam's lawyers, Allen Grubman and Paul Schindler, ran a law firm with strong ties to CBS Records. Grubman was proposing a softer line of negotiation with Columbia. That didn't surprise Rubin. Once, in a meeting at CBS, he had seen Walter Yetnikoff haul off and slap Grubman. It was horrifying. The last person Rubin wanted for a lawyer was Lou Costello, Esq.

Rubin decided to take matters into his own hands, and arranged a meeting with Teller.

Teller's assistant ushered the twenty-four-year-old producer into the executive's office, where Teller sat behind his desk, impassive. Rubin unfolded a long list of issues he had made in preparation for the meeting, problems that needed to be resolved so the Def Jam–Columbia partnership could move forward. He wasn't asking for money, as Simmons was. He was asking Columbia to do what was right, so that Def Jam could live up to its true potential.

As Rubin began talking, Teller seemed uninterested. But Rubin was completely unnerved when Teller picked up a baseball bat lying near his desk and began slapping it against his palm.

Rubin spoke again of Def Jam's horrible situation abroad. *Thwak!*

Rubin brought up Columbia's refusal to distribute artists like Slayer. *Thwak!*

Rubin complained about Def Jam artists being lesser priorities for Columbia's promotion department. *Thwak!*

Rubin talked about the Jimmy Castor suit—*thwak!*—and how Columbia was frustrating Def Jam's attempts to fulfill its own contract to the Beastie Boys—*thwak!*—and how they were going to lose the group if Columbia didn't release the Beasties' royalties.

As Teller continued to slap and twirl the baseball bat, Rubin felt a tightness in his throat. Def Jam was his whole life, and here he was, in front of the one person who had the potential to make his life better. But Al Teller was no Mickey Rubin. He didn't care about Rick's betterment. Hot tears welled in Rubin's eyes, and he began to cry as he choked his words out.

Thwak!

"You know, I'm not signed here," Rubin said. "Only Russell signed. So if we can't work things out, I'm gone."

The baseball bat stopped moving.

"Wait. What was the last thing that you just said?" Teller asked, speaking for the first time.

"I said I'm not signed here, and I'll leave."

"How did that happen?!" Teller demanded.

"I never signed the contract," Rubin answered. "Russell signed. You were pursuing Russell, and I came with Russell, but I was never part of the CBS deal. I never signed with Columbia. My lawyer says I can leave." Rubin had retained his own outside counsel.

Teller called to his assistant. "Get Allen Grubman on the phone!"

And then he turned back to Rubin.

"Well," Teller said. "If you're not signed, and you can leave, you're gonna have to start at the beginning. Because I wasn't listening to anything you were saying."

Not long after Rubin's disastrous meeting with Teller, the Columbia head sent Def Jam a check for $300,000, by way of amends.

Simmons was happy. Rubin was not. Teller was throwing money at them without promising to make any changes.

Aside from their business disagreements, the partners' musical differences came into stark relief upon the release of the *Less Than Zero* soundtrack in late 1987. Rubin contributed rock and rap songs—the appropriate music for a film about rich White kids in Beverly Hills. But he had to share the soundtrack with Simmons's R&B acts, like Alyson Williams and the Black Flames. Rubin held his nose over these acts, as Simmons did with Rick's metal records. And Simmons still didn't understand what Rubin saw in Public Enemy, who contributed a new song to the soundtrack called "Bring the Noise."

"Why are you wasting your time with a Black punk rock group that's never going to sell any records," Simmons asked, "when you're making hit records with the Bangles?"

Simmons was right on one account. The Bangles' "Hazy Shade of Winter" shot up the Billboard Hot 100 to number two, Rubin's biggest pop hit yet—although Rubin hated the band's mix-down so much he insisted his name be taken off of the record. But when Def Jam released a single for Black radio—with Simmons's R&B group the Black Flames on the A-side and Public Enemy on the B-side—DJs ignored Simmons's record and "Bring the Noise" became an even bigger street anthem than "Rebel Without a Pause" had been, again with barely any radio play. Chuck D dared Black stations to play his record. "They call themselves Black," he rapped, "but well see if they'll play this."

At a time when the future of Def Jam was in doubt, "Bring the Noise" was Chuck D's argument not only for the Def Jam ethos of rap-is-rock

("Run-DMC first said a DJ could be a band"), but for the Def Jam crew's growing confidence that hip-hop was actually bigger and more meaningful than anything else in music. Public Enemy was now the hottest group on Def Jam, even without a new album in stores. Robert Christgau, the dean of American rock criticism, ranked "Bring the Noise" as his best song of the year, calling it "the greatest piece of rock and roll released in 1987."

The *Less Than Zero* soundtrack also began Rick Rubin's reputation as a resuscitator of careers. For the B-side of the "Going Back to Cali" single—for which Ric Menello directed an artful black-and-white video—Rubin rushed LL Cool J into the studio to record a response to Kool Moe Dee's attacks, a blistering comeback called "Jack the Ripper": "How you like me now?!" LL said. "I'm gettin' busier. I'm double platinum, I'm watchin' you get dizzier!" Rubin's record with Roy Orbison began a revival of the rocker's career that would make the last year of Orbison's life a bit sweeter.

"In some ways," wrote a reviewer for the *Los Angeles Times*, "it is helpful to think of *Less Than Zero* as the first Rick Rubin album."

The movie tanked. The soundtrack went gold.

With Rubin off making records in studios on both coasts, or hiding in his loft apartment; with Simmons out drinking and getting high, holding court in nightclubs or on tour with his artists; someone had to be the adult. Increasingly, the responsibilities of running the day-to-day operations at Def Jam fell to the levelheaded, sardonic twenty-four-year-old head of promotion and Public Enemy producer, Bill Stephney.

Rubin didn't believe in titles, but Stephney became the general manager of Def Jam by caring about the things that Rubin and Simmons didn't. Foremost of these were the atrocious working conditions for the staff. The Elizabeth Street brownstone had no air-conditioning in the summer, and no heat in the winter. One cold day, Stephney complained to Rubin. "What do you think I got you your Def Jam jacket for?" Rubin replied.

But the Bud Abbott routine wasn't funny anymore. Nor was the lack of job descriptions, health insurance, benefits, and incentives for a passionate, underpaid staff. On the Def Jam side, Stephney was assisted with Black radio by Lindsey Williams, while a young Black kid from East Harlem named David Gossett called college stations. Two enthusiastic, devoted White hip-hop fans filled gaps and lapses at the label: Rubin hired Faith Newman to clean up A&R administration and publishing; and Dave Klein—whom everyone called "Funken-Klein"—helped with tours and merchandising. Scott Koenig handled Rubin's heavy-metal projects.

On the Rush Artist Management side, Lyor Cohen was in charge, where the staff cringed under his volatile temperament. Lisa Cortes had graduated from being Cohen's assistant to running her own offshoot, Rush Producers Management, while bequeathing her chair to Rush's messenger, a pugnacious White kid from the Lower East Side named Dante Ross. Bill Adler led Rush's increasingly successful media mission, and Rush's first employee, Heidi Smith, continued to mind the details that no one else cared to do.

Stephney dealt with the tasks that Rubin and Simmons neglected, handling corporate communications, signing purchase orders and checks, and poring over the books with Def Jam's accountant, Dawn Greco. Stephney was appalled. The company had spent $100,000 recording an album by one of Simmons's R&B signings, Tashan, that sold only 15,000 copies. Simmons and Rubin regularly doled out advance money and studio funds to artists without the promise of any funding from Columbia: $18,000 given to Simmons's friends from Queens Davy D and Larry Green; $40,000 for Andre "Doctor Dre" Brown's Original Concept; $51,000 to Danzig; $13,000 to an artist named Blossom; $85,000 to another named Breeze. For the projects that Columbia had funded, Def Jam's spending regularly exceeded its approved allocations. Alyson Williams's album was already overbudget by $30,000.

Stephney blamed Simmons for most of the financial mess. After all, none of Simmons's signings had been successful. Rick Rubin brought in every one of Def Jam's big artists: LL Cool J, the Beastie Boys, Public Enemy, Slayer. But Stephney's sympathies always lay with Rubin—in whom he saw the vision for the Def Jam aesthetic and at least some amount of focus. Simmons, on the contrary, was all over the place. A funny guy, a bright guy, a visionary, for sure, but you could never find him. When you finally did, he'd be having seven different conversations, with seven different people, all at the same time; unless you tailed him on one of his regular trips to the Russian baths— Simmons facetiously called it "getting my dick washed." Simmons was starting other businesses, too, like a modeling agency. *What the hell did hip-hop have to do with fashion?* Stephney thought. *What the hell was Russell doing?*

Stephney lamented Simmons's lack of focus. But there was plenty of blame to go around. It was Rubin's idea to buy the shitty brownstone, sink cash into a half-assed remodeling, build a recording studio, and independently fund a movie, all at the same time. And both of his bosses had gotten into the annoying habit of communicating and, often, arguing through Stephney. *Tell Russell I said . . . Tell Rick I said . . .*

In the new year, Stephney resolved to do something about Def Jam's mess—detailing his concerns in a two-and-a-half-page memo that he sent to Rubin and Simmons in late January of 1988.

"The company is like a body with no head," Stephney wrote. "Al Teller does not make records: He runs a record company. Cory Robbins and Steve Plotnicki (think of them what you will) don't make movies or records, or manage artists: They run a record label. It is a full-time job!"

Stephney scorned Rubin's high-minded drive for a "pressing and distribution-only" type of deal with Columbia. Without active participation from either Rubin or Simmons, without adequate staffing or a habitable workplace, Stephney wrote, the company would immediately starve to death.

Stephney concluded: "We can no longer operate as two labels with the same bank account: Def Records, the rap/hard-rock side run by Rick; and Jam Records, the quasi-R&B side, which is Russell's baby."

Neither Rubin nor Simmons responded.

Ignored, Stephney channeled his frustrations into a sarcastic comic strip that he circulated around the office called "Deftoons," lampooning the foibles of both his bosses, who, he joked, had "the combined work experience of ten days at an Orange Julius"—a reference to Simmons's only job, since Rubin had never had one.

Then Stephney went back to work. Despite Def Jam's problems, he couldn't quite stomach leaving. His group Public Enemy was recording their follow-up album. From what he heard, they were achieving the Holy Grail of pop music: provoking thought while making people dance—or, as Chuck phrased it in one of their new songs, "Reach the bourgeois / And rock the boulevard." The new album, tentatively titled *It Takes a Nation of Millions to Hold Us Back*, was one of the best albums he had ever heard, in any genre.

Of course. It was on Def Jam.

The NoHo Star, on the corner of Lafayette and Bleecker, was still the only decent restaurant within walking distance of 298 Elizabeth Street. And it was there that Rick Rubin finally leveled with Russell Simmons.

"I don't think that we should do this together anymore," Rubin said.

When Simmons immediately agreed, Rubin was surprised. No words of reconciliation, like, *Come on, everything is doing so good*, or, *Let's figure out how to do this.* Simmons didn't want to work with him anymore, either. The mood at the table was weird and tense, especially for two guys who didn't have the inclination to deal with anything weird and tense.

"Do you want to leave the company?" Rubin asked.

"No," Simmons answered.

Rubin was surprised yet again. He always assumed that Russell Simmons had thought of Def Jam as *Rubin's* company. After all, Rubin founded Def Jam by himself. He came up with the name. He designed the logo. He signed the artists. The reluctant Russell Simmons came on board only after Rubin made his pitch: *I'll do all the work. I'll run the company. I'll do everything. Just be my partner.* Rubin saw Simmons basically pursuing his own, separate dream of an R&B company for the past few years. He didn't think that Simmons even cared. Apparently he did.

Rubin was unwilling to fight with a person whom he wanted to keep as a friend.

"Then I'll leave," Rubin said.

"Okay," Simmons replied.

They broke the news to Bill Stephney during a late-night meeting at the Empire Diner across town. Rubin would be moving out to California and taking the artists that Simmons didn't care to keep: Danzig, Slayer, Masters of Reality, and the up-and-coming comedian Andrew "Dice" Clay. Everything else would remain on Def Jam. Rubin would keep his share of the company until Simmons found a way to buy him out.

Stephney despaired for Def Jam and for himself. He imagined that this was what it felt like to watch your parents divorce. It didn't matter that Simmons would, in Rubin's absence, promote Stephney to president of the label. Now that the man who hired and inspired Stephney was moving on, Stephney was forced to think about the inevitability of his own departure. And then what would become of Def Jam when the only owner left was out partying every night, dating models, and smoking dust?

In one of their late-night bookkeeping sessions, Dawn Greco shared her prediction—a notion that Stephney thought preposterous, even sacrilegious.

"One day," she said, "Lyor's gonna run everything."

The case of *Rush Productions v.* Profile Records, Inc. dragged into early 1988. Nearly two years had passed since the release of Run-DMC's last album.

Each party accused the other of using the court proceedings as a "fishing expedition" for evidence. When Rush claimed that Profile's "suspension clause" was unconscionable, Profile produced copies of Def Jam's Beastie Boys and Original Concept contracts that featured that very same clause. Rush's lawyers asked the judge to subpoena Profile's books and prepared to depose a cross-section of executives and accountants from distributors, manufacturers, and record stores, as well as the owners and staff of Profile itself, including Cory Robbins, Steve Plotnicki, Manny Bella, and Profile's comptroller, Jesse Maidbrey.

Before he split with Simmons, Rubin filed an affidavit with the court on behalf of his estranged partner. In it, Rubin claimed that Maidbrey had once "admitted . . . that he and Profile have been ripping off Rush and Run-DMC for years," and that Maidbrey bragged to Rubin that Profile would never be caught because Maidbrey "had learned from the best."

Maidbrey denied Rubin's allegations. In fact, years earlier, Maidbrey had relayed to Robbins and Plotnicki quite a different story about that exchange with Rubin. Back when Profile's offices were still in Midtown, around the time of Def Jam's founding, Rubin had accompanied Simmons to Profile's offices. While Simmons talked to Plotnicki, Rubin detoured to Maidbrey's office and sat down.

"I *know* you know what they're doing," Rubin allegedly said.

"Rick," Maidbrey reportedly replied, "these guys have paid Run-DMC every dime that's due them."

"You tell me what they're doing, and I'll pay you!"

Maidbrey alleged that Rubin then offered him a "significant bribe" to disclose what Rubin believed were Profile's unscrupulous accounting practices, probably in an attempt to swipe Run-DMC for his new record company with Simmons.

The competing allegations never made it to court. With both parties shuddering at the prospect of beginning the next lengthy and expensive phase of their litigation—and Simmons worried about his brother's physical and mental well-being—Rush Productions accepted a settlement offer from Profile Records. Run-DMC would remain on Profile for ten more albums, for better terms, including a 40 percent increase in royalties. Simmons accepted. If Profile had won, the victory was pyrrhic.

It was March of 1988. The songs for Run-DMC's new album had been sitting on the shelf for almost a year. It was May before Profile shipped the *Tougher Than Leather* LP, which was supposed to be released in tandem with Bill Adler's *Tougher Than Leather* book (which went on sale a year earlier) and Def Pictures' *Tougher Than Leather* movie (which wouldn't hit theaters until September).

Run-DMC's video for their first single, "Run's House," was received politely by hip-hop fans, in the way a person might greet an old lover after having been swept off one's feet by another. Both Rush and Profile paid dearly for their excessive sales expectations, printing and distributing far more albums than they sold. *Tougher Than Leather* became an industry joke: *It shipped platinum. It returned double platinum.*

Finally, upon the release of the movie *Tougher Than Leather*, one reviewer called Rick Rubin and Ric Menello's exploitation flick "vile, vicious, despicable, stupid, sexist, racist and horrendously made." Nobody could see the "high" for all the "low." Even Rubin himself called it "embarrassing."

But he wasn't around to face the consequences, nor did he have to look in the eyes of Run, DMC, and Jam Master Jay as their reputation and career prospects evaporated.

Like Abbott, he was gone.

The summer of 1988 was fantastic for music at Def Jam. Public Enemy's *It Takes a Nation of Millions to Hold Us Back* became the group's first gold album. Public Enemy also assisted in the production of the first album from Slick Rick, another Rubin signing.

But financially the label was still in trouble. Def Jam renegotiated its production deal with Columbia Records' new owner, Sony. Al Teller was fired shortly after the changeover by his boss, Walter Yetnikoff. But in the fall of 1988, Def Jam lost their bestselling act when the Beastie Boys signed with Capitol Records. Def Jam filed suit but ended up releasing the group after the Beasties relinquished their claim to *Licensed to Ill* and the millions in royalties due them.

Meanwhile, Lyor Cohen found new ways for Rush make money. He and Simmons brokered a distribution deal for Tyrone Williams and Lenny Fichtelberg's Cold Chillin' Records at Warner Bros. It was unusual, facilitating a marriage between an indie and a major who were already active rivals with Def Jam. But Simmons and Cohen had a simple strategy in the growing world of hip-hop: *Try to get a piece of everything.*

Cohen continued to enlarge the roster of Rush Artist Management by strong-arming rather than suasion. Rush now ran the top-grossing rap tours in the country, and you had to be managed by Rush to roll with Rush. In this manner, Cohen signed Eric B & Rakim, Tommy Boy's Stetsasonic, Sleeping Bag's EPMD, and Jive's DJ Jazzy Jeff & the Fresh Prince.

Even though Simmons had initially rejected the Fresh Prince at Def Jam, he now found himself collaborating with Ann Carli on the rapper's career. As a couple Carli and Simmons were through, despite Simmons's talk of marriage. Still, after the end of their liaison, Carli remained one record executive whom Simmons completely trusted, and her creative instincts made her more vital than Simmons in the career of the group he managed.

DJ Jazzy Jeff & the Fresh Prince were preparing to release a double album—a first in hip-hop—with a song that Carli was sure could be another rap pop hit like "I Need Love."

Carli hired Scott Calvert to shoot the video for the song "Parents Just Don't Understand" on a colorful, cartoonish set on which the Fresh Prince conveyed his comedic tale. When Carli saw the footage in the transfer session, she was stunned by the rapper's performance. She called Jive's owner, Clive Calder, with her revelation.

"Will Smith is going to be a movie star," Carli said. "We've got to do something with him."

But Calder wasn't anxious to get into the film business.

Then she called Simmons, Smith's manager, to prod him into action.

"I think Will Smith can be as big as Eddie Murphy," Carli enthused, comparing Smith to the biggest movie star of the moment. Simmons shrugged.

"He might be as big as Malcolm Jamal Warner," Simmons opined. "But he's no Eddie Murphy."

When Rick Rubin left New York for good, he took nothing with him. He simply closed the door to his loft at 298 Elizabeth Street, locking inside his books, records, furniture, files, even his clothes. He left his phone and answering machine on. "This is Rick," he deadpanned. "Leave a message. Don't call back."

Before Rubin departed, he and Ric Menello used the loft to shoot a short promotional film introducing Rubin's new record company, Def American.

"I shall read from a prepared statement," Menello said to the camera, Rubin standing behind him, mute. Menello then began an intentionally rambling, insane speech on behalf of the silent record executive about how Def American Recordings was going to "take back rock and roll" from the

British. All the while, Rubin nodded as if what Menello was saying made perfect sense.

Rubin laid the groundwork for Def American when his first Slayer album got picked up by Geffen Records. He created a relationship with David Geffen, and the older music mogul offered the young record producer a distribution deal that included ownership of his masters with a clause that let Rubin release any kind of record he wanted. Rubin's new label roster was completely comprised of rock bands.

Rubin had lost interest in hip-hop. When people asked him why he left rap, Rubin responded that he felt rap left *him. Hip-hop isn't about art anymore,* he said. *It is about getting paid.*

In reality, hip-hop was now about both, largely because of Rick Rubin and his former partner, Russell Simmons.

Before Def Jam, there were no truly great, cohesive rap albums. Def Jam was the first record label to prove to fans, critics, and the artists themselves that they were capable of creating not just one-off singles, but a true body of work; and that they could do so with artistic freedom and in defiance of low expectations. Def Jam was the first business entity to envision hip-hop with the same importance, creativity, and possibility that rock had enjoyed since its own artistic maturation in the mid-sixties. Only Def Jam could have produced Public Enemy's new album, *It Takes a Nation of Millions to Hold Us Back.* The *Village Voice*'s national poll of mainstream music critics called it the best album of the year; not the best *hip-hop* album, but the best album *period.* As such, *Nation of Millions* was the culmination of Def Jam's artistic legacy. Ironically, Rubin didn't like Public Enemy's second album as much as he had their first, even though *Nation of Millions* disproved his contention that rap was just about "getting paid."

Yet the commercial success of hip-hop was also largely due to the work of Rubin and Simmons. With their first records, "It's Yours" and "Sucker MCs," Rubin and Simmons turned rap records from nine-minute "toasts" to three-minute songs with classic pop structure—verse, bridge, and chorus. In so doing, the Def Jam partners made it possible for rappers to express themselves as pop artists. Def Jam's records and tours opened hip-hop to a vast global audience.

Def Jam, in a real sense, became the first suburban rap label. Simmons's family wasn't as wealthy as Rubin's, but both were children of privilege whose parents helped finance their entrepreneurial dreams. Def Jam's artists, too, were suburban, well educated, hailing not from the ghettos of Harlem and the Bronx, but from better neighborhoods in the outlying parts of the city and beyond. And even though these suburbs weren't necessarily racially integrated, the world created at Def Jam/Rush by Rubin, Simmons, their staff, and all of their artists was at once both color-blind and colorful. White and Black people at Def Jam and Rush didn't question one another's legitimacy.

Hip-hop was bringing Black and White kids together to listen to Black music. So had jazz and R&B; the phenomenon was nothing new. But, as Bill Stephney surveyed crowds of White fans wearing T-shirts with the Public Enemy crosshairs logo, chanting along to lyrics like, "The follower of Farrakhan / Don't tell me that you understand / Until you hear the man," he felt that this time something was different—and America might be the better for it.

As for Rubin, he had lived his professional and personal life alongside Black people, somehow without ever having a serious discussion about race. In one way, it was a testament to the unifying power of hip-hop and the beginning of a new, hopeful episode in America's long, tortured racial history. But Rubin's lack of interest in questions of race—and his quick estrangement from hip-hop just as it was becoming political and race-conscious in the turbulent late 1980s—signaled that even the most credible and creative White participants in hip-hop could remain both unfamiliar and uncomfortable with the realities that their Black counterparts faced. In the end, it was Simmons who guided Rubin's act Public Enemy to cultural prominence; Simmons who reconsidered his early indifference to the group; and Simmons who ultimately understood Chuck D's political mission.

As Rubin installed himself in Los Angeles—going to shows, looking for a home and new offices, spending time with David Geffen—the new, rock-centric world that Rubin built for himself was largely White. The only break in his new routine came when he received the occasional friendly visit from his erstwhile partner, Russell Simmons.

One evening, Rubin brought Simmons—along with Bill Stephney and Nelson George—back to his new, Mediterranean-style, three-story stucco house, perched on a steep hill above Sunset Boulevard, where Rubin made sure to keep his stereo volume low after complaints from neighbors. As Rubin led them into his foyer, his guests were greeted by the sight of a ten-foot-tall, stuffed white polar bear.

Simmons screwed his face into a look somewhere between fascinated and repulsed. "Rick," he lisped, "what's this for?"

"To scare niggers," Rubin replied with the slightest of smiles.

ALBUM FOUR

HIP-HOP NATION

Rap traverses the continent

(1988–1991)

Side A
West Side

Rick Rubin's new life in Los Angeles let him revisit two lost loves of his Long Island youth: rock and roll, and cars. He bought a Rolls-Royce, a Corvette, and a rumbling, fuel-guzzling, black Dodge Charger that reeked of gasoline and Armor All.

In Los Angeles the auto was essential. By the time Rubin moved to Southern California in 1988, the region had developed its own variant of hip-hop, heavily influenced by the local car culture in ways that most train- and bus-riding New Yorkers could scarcely comprehend.

For kids on Long Island, cars symbolized freedom. But in the ghettos of South Central Los Angeles, cars could actually save young men from the lure of gangs. Having a car was more than a means to simply drive away; it gave teenagers another, safer way to belong.

Back in 1976 a nineteen-year-old kid from the mostly Black suburb of Compton named Alonzo Williams Jr. joined fifty other guys in the "Vega Club." The Chevrolet Vega was a cool car, Williams discovered, because you could make it look almost like a Camaro if you added rims, a fender flare kit, and dropped the suspension. Williams and his Vega friends met the members of the Volkswagen Club in the park on Sundays—not to rumble, but for a picnic and a football match. Afterward they would snake through the city streets in convoy.

The members of the Vega Club wanted matching satin jackets, so they planned a fund-raising dance at the Chester Washington Golf Course. Williams's cohorts asked him to DJ because they knew he was studying to be a broadcaster in L.A.'s Regional Occupation Program. He had already been told he would never make it in radio, on account of his lisp. But Williams could work the turntables, so the guy whom friends affectionately called "Daffy Duck" borrowed a record player and some speakers to play the disco favorites of the day. They raised $1,500. After deducting the $400 for the jackets, Williams and a partner split the remainder. Five hundred and fifty dollars was equal to a month's salary. *Five hundred fifty dollars for four hours' work? This*, Williams thought, *is the job for me.*

Alonzo Senior, a Mississippi migrant who had come to Southern California to work in the factories of military contractors, saw that his son was serious about DJing. He loaned Alonzo Junior a few hundred dollars to buy turntables, and set up an account for him to rent equipment from Hogan's House of Music in neighboring Lawndale.

Alonzo Junior bought some metal shelves and particleboard. He fashioned the shelves into a turntable stand, welding wheels to the bottom so it converted into a rolling dolly that could carry his speakers, too. To the particleboard he glued tufts of "angel hair," the fluffy pink material that local low-riders put on their dashboards, so it looked like he was DJing on a fuchsia cloud. His friend at a Plexiglas shop made him a sign that read, DISCO LONZO, SUPERSTAR DJ, above a logo of a muscle-bound star with a turntable in the center. Atop Williams's head sat the finishing touch: a construction hat with a rotating siren light.

"Disco Lonzo" cleared $150 a week DJing at schools, house parties, nightclubs, and dances at bigger venues, and he attracted a following. One night, during a gig at the Long Beach Convention Center, two guys whom Lonzo had seen watching him at other shows came into his makeshift DJ booth to talk to him. The big, light-skinned kid introduced himself as Rodger Clayton and claimed he was a DJ, too. As Clayton rifled through Lonzo's records, the tall, skinny one, Andre Manuel, fiddled with Lonzo's rented smoke machine. After Lonzo determined that the pair wasn't going to rob him, he put Clayton and Manuel to work for him. As their friendship developed, Lonzo taught Manuel to DJ and made him part of his "Disco Construction and Wreckin' Cru." Clayton got Lonzo a daytime job in the warehouse of a record distributor, and hired Lonzo to DJ at parties he threw under the aegis of his nascent promotion company, Unique Dreams.

One day in 1979, Lonzo's father walked in on him counting several hundreds of dollars in cash. He accused his son of dealing drugs. He was already upset that his son had rejected a real job with Caltrans, working on one of their sweeper crews that cleaned the region's freeways. It was dangerous, deadly work—Lonzo knew some guys who had gotten killed by speeding cars. Even worse, it was *dirty*; Lonzo had a thing for keeping clean. Still, his father didn't understand. *How does a kid decline an offer like that, especially now that he's got a baby daughter of his own?*

Lonzo's father never imagined that his son's DJ hobby could bring in much money. But Alonzo Senior was chastened when he finally made it out to see "Disco Lonzo" in action, playing a packed room at a German-style dance hall in nearby Torrance called Alpine Village.

"How much does it cost to rent this room?" his father asked.

"A thousand dollars," Lonzo responded.

"That's too much," his father declared. The elder Williams reached out to a friend in their hometown of Compton who owned a social club called Eve's After Dark. It was smaller than Alpine Village, but half the rent, and a more dependable source of income. Before long, Lonzo was pulling down nearly $10,000 a month at Eve's, and his crew expanded from Andre Manuel, who called himself "DJ Unknown," to include Antoine Carraby, whom Manuel dubbed "DJ Yella." As the first Sugar Hill records hit Los Angeles, Lonzo jettisoned the words "Disco Construction" from his collective's name.

While Lonzo Williams and the "Wreckin' Cru" built a following by staying put, Rodger Clayton made his name by moving around. Clayton became the most successful of a new breed of mobile DJs who rolled their parties from one end of the Los Angeles basin to the other. Soon, Clayton's "Uncle Jamm's Army" was filling venues like the Veterans' Auditorium and the Sports Arena with thousands of people lured by word of mouth and Clayton's ubiquitous flyers. But after the Uncle Jamm gigs, the party continued at Eve's for the folks who weren't afraid to go to Compton. Burgeoning gangs made the area risky for outsiders.

Owing to good security and a strict dress code, Eve's was mostly tranquil. Guys wore the retro "zoot suit" style of the early 1980s: silk shirts with skinny ties, baggy pants, and Stacy Adams shoes. If you weren't "clean," you couldn't get inside.

That was the reason Lonzo wouldn't let seventeen-year-old Andre Young into the club—even though Young knew Lonzo's family, and even though Lonzo had been told that Young was a DJ prodigy. Young was wearing his street clothes—jeans, T-shirt, and sneakers—so Lonzo left him outside along with his short little running buddy, a Jheri-curled drug dealer named Eric Wright.

"Fuck you, man," the pipsqueak Wright said from the sidewalk.

"Yeah?" Lonzo replied with a smirk. "Fuck you, too."

One night Young came to Eve's dressed correctly. Lonzo let him in, and Young worked his way to the turntables. At first, Lonzo didn't quite understand what he was hearing: the Marvelettes singing "Please Mr. Postman," mixed in perfect time with a song that ran twice as fast, "Planet Rock" by Afrika Bambaataa. The whole club stopped dancing just to listen to what the kid was doing. After that, Lonzo made him a part of the "Wreckin' Cru." Andre Young morphed the moniker of his favorite basketball player, "Dr. J," into his own stage name, "Dr. Dre"—right around the same time that *another* "Doctor Dre," Andre *Brown*, attended Adelphi University and DJed parties three thousand miles away on Long Island.

The record that Young played that night was significant. Bambaataa's "Planet Rock" resonated with the practitioners of local dance styles called "locking," "popping," and "boogaloo." Before "Planet Rock," Los Angeles produced only a handful of rap singles. After hearing Bambaataa's brand of electro-funk, Angelenos created their own unique hip-hop sound—influenced as much by the synthesizer-driven music of Kraftwerk, George Clinton, and Prince as it was New York beat-box and break-beat records. DJ Unknown called the new genre "techno-hop."

Unknown made some of the first of these records. So did the Wreckin' Cru—which now featured Lonzo, Yella, and "Dr. Dre" Young. So, too, did Rodger Clayton and his DJ partner, the Egyptian Lover—who wasn't Egyptian at all, but a fair-skinned kid from South Central named Greg Broussard.

Most remarkably, none of these new West Coast releases were issued by a record company. If Los Angeles hip-hop was different, so was the way it hopped onto wax.

The East Coast hip-hop scene yielded several strong, independent rap labels—Profile, Tommy Boy, Def Jam, Select and Jive.

But the records of almost *every* West Coast hip-hop artist came through the doors of just *one* business.

Macola Records wasn't a record company at all, but a pressing plant, run by a mild-mannered, silver-templed Canadian named Don Macmillan.

Back in Vancouver, Macmillan's father had been a "rack jobber"—someone who maintains "racks" of records in all kinds of retail stores. When Macmillan, still in his twenties, moved down to Southern California during the

1960s, his father got him a job working at Cadet, the largest vinyl manufacturing plant on the West Coast.

Every day, Macmillan would put on old clothes and walk among the dozens of record presses. The machines heated mounds of raw vinyl, flattened them between two stampers, cooled and trimmed them. Each press could churn out over a hundred records an hour. They were manually operated, and required constant maintenance. Stampers needed to be changed, and there were all kinds of leaks: steam, water, hydraulic. The plant also included printing presses and a photo lab. After six years, Macmillan became the plant superintendent. By the 1970s, he was Cadet's general manager.

Cadet pressed up vinyl for its parent company, Kent Records, owned by Jules Bihari and his brothers—Jewish entrepreneurs who had made a fortune in the 1950s by providing a home to Black artists whom the major labels of the era wouldn't touch: B. B. King, John Lee Hooker, and Ike & Tina Turner. But the most interesting part of Cadet's business to Macmillan was how they made small-time artists' dreams come true with their custom pressing deals.

Cadet's plant was located in the heart of L.A.'s Black community, on Normandie and Slauson. Aspiring musicians could pay Cadet a few hundred dollars to manufacture a thousand records, which the artist could sell to stores across Los Angeles. After Jules Bihari succumbed to lupus in the early 1980s, Kent folded. Macmillan found some financing and, for $10,000, bought a small plant on Santa Monica Boulevard with twelve manual vinyl presses that was being unloaded in a bankruptcy sale.

Macola—a name derived by conjoining "Macmillan" with "Olaug," the name of his Norwegian-born bride—launched its custom pressing business just as the Los Angeles rap scene began to explode. Rodger Clayton's partner, Greg "Egyptian Lover" Broussard, was Macmillan's first client. In early 1984, Broussard paid Macola close to $1,000 to press up 500 records of his song "Egypt, Egypt," and even got Macmillan to print custom labels that read, "Egyptian Empire Records." The next week, Broussard returned for 500 more. The week after that, Broussard came for another 500.

"What the hell are you doing with all this stuff?" Macmillan asked Broussard.

Broussard replied that he was selling it out of the trunk of his car on street corners, at gigs, and to record stores and swap meets—makeshift superdiscount malls for Southern California's bargain hunters and lower-income clientele.

Macmillan liked Broussard, so he offered to help the DJ sell his records. Macola would print up more copies, free of charge. Then he would send the records out to his friends at independent distributors across the country— outfits like California Record Distributors, Select-O-Hits in Memphis, Schwartz Brothers in Baltimore, Big State in Texas—the same distributors who sold for labels like Profile and Tommy Boy. If the records didn't sell, Macmillan would eat the cost. If they did, they'd split the profits.

Broussard took the deal, and Macmillan started spreading the word about "Egypt, Egypt." To Macmillan's surprise, orders poured in. When another rap-and-DJ crew from Riverside, California, called 2 Live Crew became his second client, Macmillan made them the same distribution offer.[5] Macmillan found that both of these up-tempo, electronic, bass-heavy rap records sold especially well in *Miami*, of all places. Broussard and the members of 2 Live Crew flew to Florida to take advantage of their success. Broussard returned; the 2 Live Crew, their fortunes boosted by a local promoter named Luther Campbell, decided to move there for good. Campbell would become their manager, and eventually, the lead member the group.

Lonzo found his way to Macola Records, starting his Kru-Cut custom label for the Wreckin' Cru, songs featuring the production of Andre "Dr. Dre" Young. DJ Unknown started his own imprint, Techno Hop Records. Other acts flocked to Macola—with names like the L.A. Dream Team, and Bobby Jimmy & the Critters—making records that sold across the West and the South with little promotion and marketing.

Macmillan had no idea what had hit him. He didn't even know what this music was, exactly. But by 1985, Macmillan's small custom record plant was starting to act more and more like a record company. Macmillan called record stores and radio stations. He took his client-artists to sales and radio conventions. He even had a lawyer draft a small boilerplate agreement that he used with some artists, securing Macola the option to release one or more of their future records. But it was more work than Macmillan alone could handle or understand. So he phoned Morey Alexander, the cigar-chomping, Chicago native who ran Kent Records for the Bihari brothers and managed blues artists like Charlie Musselwhite.

"There's some weird stuff happening here," Macmillan began. "These guys are making this music and they keep coming in and ordering more and

---

[5]Macmillan's typical deal would be fifteen percent of net profit for Macola, eighty-five percent for the artist.

more records. And none of them know anything about the business. They need management."

Alexander visited Macola and met Rufus Perison, a friendly kid who, in addition to performing as "Rudy Pardee," one half of the L.A. Dream Team, called record stores and radio stations to promote records for Macola in the tiny upstairs office of the plant. Alexander signed Pardee as his client.

Alexander knew he could handle Pardee's recording career. To make real cash, the L.A. Dream Team needed to get out and do shows. Alexander wasn't a booking agent, but he knew someone who used to be.

Jerry Heller was a comrade of Alexander's from the 1970s, when Heller worked for Associated Booking and Chartwell Artists, representing artists like Elton John, Pink Floyd, Marvin Gaye, and Van Morrison. But Heller had hit a rough patch: cocaine and alcohol abuse and a bad divorce. When Alexander finally tracked him down, the forty-five-year-old Heller looked more like he was fifty-five, his thick beard gone and his mop of black hair turned a shocking white. He was living with his parents, sleeping on their couch, and nursing a hangover.

Alexander's pitch was similar to Macmillan's. Within days, Heller paid a visit to Macola and sized up the situation immediately: Don Macmillan was the simplest of simple White men; a *gimmel goy*, as Heller's mother might say. The guy *looked* confused. Macmillan wasn't a long-range thinker. Heller found that he and Morey could cherry-pick the best artists, get them deals at real labels, and pay Macmillan a pittance for the pleasure. Morey Alexander and Jerry Heller formed a loose confederation—two companies, one Artists Alexander and the other Artists Heller. When either of them made money, they exchanged checks in a byzantine series of transactions. Alexander called an old protégé, a Black kid named Jheryl Busby who had made a good career for himself and now headed Black music for MCA Records. Busby signed the L.A. Dream Team and gave Alexander a check for $62,000 as an advance on the act's first album. Alexander passed half the commission to Heller, and paid a small tribute to Macmillan in return for relinquishing the right to release future records by the artist. Alexander and Heller picked up more Macola clients: Egyptian Lover, Russ Parr, and Lonzo Williams, who soon had landed a major-label deal for the "World Class Wreckin' Cru" at Epic/CBS. When the group's Epic album tanked, Lonzo Williams and "Dr. Dre" Young came back to Macola. Ironically, they would have their first national hit upon their return.

Don Macmillan's little pressing plant had become a place where anybody

who was nobody could become somebody. But the explosion of the Los Angeles rap scene in the mid-1980s owed a debt not just to one man named
Macmillan, but two.

Greggory Macmillan began spelling his name "Macmillion" as a
teenager when he discovered that the midwife who delivered him in Emory,
Texas, spelled it that way on his birth certificate. He liked the name "Macmillion" because it sounded like money. Yet Greggory didn't meet his fortune
until he changed his name again, shortening it to "Greg Mack" when he
became a radio DJ.

Mack started as a high school intern answering the request lines at
KTSA and KTFM in San Antonio. He wasn't much of a music fan. But
Mack—a brown-skinned fifteen-year-old with a quiet demeanor and a be-
guiling smile—found that his job was a great way to meet girls. He worked
hard, too, impressing the program director, Lee Randall, who hired Mack
part-time while he was in school and full-time after he graduated in 1977.

When Randall left for a job in Corpus Christi. Mack's mentor was replaced by a new program director: a skinny White guy with lamb-chop
sideburns who summoned Mack into his office straightaway.

"I know that they liked you," the new programmer told Mack. "But I'm
gonna do everything I can to get your nigger ass out of here."

When Mack called Randall to tell him what had happened, Randall of-
fered him a job down in Corpus as a weekend DJ at his AM station, KEYS.
One of Mack's first assignments was to select the music for KEYS' "Top 1000
Hits of all Time." His knowledge of music went from nil to encyclopedic.
Shortly, Mack found that he had an uncanny ability to program records that
became hits.

Mack's tenure in Corpus was cut short when his fiancée, Cynthia, left
him and moved to Houston. Bereft, Mack decided he needed to follow her
there to salvage his engagement. Luckily, Randall's consultant, Jerry Clif-
ton, knew of an open position at a station in Houston. Mack took the job and
married Cynthia.

Working the six-to-ten-p.m. shift at KMJQ, "Magic 102," Mack's career
as an air personality exploded. He attracted guests like Charlie Wilson from
the Gap Band and Roger Troutman from Zapp, who met each other for the
first time on Mack's show and vowed to record together as a result. Their

collaboration, "Computer Love," would become a Top 10 R&B hit. Much to Cynthia's consternation, Mack was an incorrigible flirt, maintaining a strictly on-air affair with the sixteen-year-old younger sister of Michael Jackson, Janet, who was just starting her own career as a recording artist. He developed a reputation for saying just about anything over the radio.

"How are you doing, Greg?" callers would ask.

"I don't know. Let me check," Mack would answer, leaving listeners little doubt about what part of himself he was actually checking.

Mack's antics made him the number one DJ in his time slot. The program director of the rival station in Houston, KYOK, was so vexed that he began taping Mack's show and sending the "air checks" to programmers in bigger markets, hoping that a faraway station might lure Mack out of town. One did.

KDAY was a legendary R&B station in Los Angeles that hosted many star DJs over the years: Wolfman Jack, Art Laboe, Alan Freed. But as an AM broadcaster—with a fickle fifty-thousand-watt clear-channel signal that skipped across the Pacific to Hawaii at night, but couldn't reach many parts of L.A. by day—KDAY was long past its prime.

Mack didn't care. He was being offered a music director job in the second-biggest market in the country, just over the hill from Hollywood and the entire entertainment industry. In July of 1983, Mack, Cynthia, and their daughter, Nicole, rode together in a pickup truck through the desert to California and moved in with Mack's mother, who lived in South Central L.A.

KDAY claimed to serve Los Angeles's Black community. Many people assumed their studios were in South Central, owing to a prominent KDAY sign outside a Crenshaw Boulevard storefront. In reality, KDAY occupied a windowless red brick bunker built into a steep hillside miles to the north, near Hollywood. Outside, on the grassy hilltop, six tall antennae presided over a vista that stretched from the San Gabriel Mountains to the sea. Inside, however, the White general manager, Ed Kirby, and Black program director, Jack Patterson, maintained a bunker mentality and nearsighted vision. In a time when listeners were flocking to FM stations like KJLH, Kirby and Patterson told Mack his number one objective was to beat another low-rated Black AM station, KGFJ.

Kirby and Patterson laughed at Mack's country boots and cowboy hat. But the newcomer from Texas, living in the heart of South Central, quickly discovered that KDAY wasn't playing anything that young Black and Latino

Angelenos were listening to. The sounds coming from car stereos and boom boxes in his neighborhood, the records selling in shops and swap meets, were the sounds of rap, which Mack began adding to the station's playlist.

Mack discovered that the epicenter of the rap scene in Los Angeles wasn't a place, but a moving target: the roving series of parties thrown by Uncle Jamm's Army. When Mack finally attended one, he was astounded by what he saw: nearly ten thousand kids crowding the Sports Arena to see not live acts, but a group of DJs performing—Egyptian Lover, Bobcat, and the ringleader, "Uncle Jamm" himself, Rodger Clayton. Mack realized that Uncle Jamm's Army and KDAY could be a symbiotic combination. KDAY needed credible DJs who had mixing techniques and knew the records the kids liked. And Clayton's DJs needed promotion, the kind of publicity only radio could bring. Mack worked his way to the stage, introduced himself to Clayton, and made his pitch.

"Fuck radio," Clayton said. Uncle Jamm's Army had amassed a following of tens of thousands solely by word of mouth and photocopied flyers. What did he need KDAY for?

Rebuffed by Clayton, Mack vowed to start his own rival "army," the "Mack Attack Marines," and lure Clayton's DJs out from under him. That strategy didn't work either. Mack approached Bobcat, who urged Mack to develop his own identity, rather than copying Clayton's military motif. Bobcat suggested a name: the "Mack Attack Mix Masters." Still, Bobcat balked when he discovered that KDAY wouldn't pay him a cent for creating on-air mixes—which, Mack argued, amounted to free advertising.

Mack needed DJs who would work solely for the value of exposure. He found them when he paid a visit to Dotto's—a new club run by Alonzo Williams after the county sheriff's department had started harassing him at Eve's. Lonzo, who regularly paid to advertise on KDAY, offered Mack his Wreckin' Cru DJs, Dr. Dre and Yella, in return for free on-air plugs. Dre and Yella became KDAY's first mixers, taping daily blends of R&B and rap music called "Traffic Jams" at Lonzo's home studio for Greg Mack's nightly show.

Bobcat led Mack to another hot DJ: a young, New York–born Cuban-American named Antonio Gonzalez. Mack found Gonzalez's ethnicity just as compelling as his turntable antics, especially in a metropolis with millions of young Latino potential listeners. He hired the DJ, who called himself "Tony T," but made him use his real name, Tony Gonzalez, on-air. Gonzalez thought a Latino surname might ruin his credibility in hip-hop. Mack knew better.

Mack's innovations paid off quickly for KDAY. One night, while he listened to music in his office, Mack heard shouts from upstairs. He tracked the sounds to program director Jack Patterson's office, where Patterson, Kirby, and a few other station executives were drinking champagne and laughing. The new ratings had come out. KDAY had beat KGFJ on Mack's first "book" as music director. Mack was hurt that Patterson hadn't thought to invite him to his little party. To add insult to injury, Patterson added: "I wouldn't get too excited. It's probably a fluke." It wasn't.

KDAY, the old R&B mainstay, began to enjoy a second life as the only rap-friendly station in town and, frankly, in the entire country. While Black stations had been the first in commercial radio to play rap records, most Black radio programmers had remained hostile to the music: quarantining rap to specialty "mix shows" on the weekends and "day parting" the records for evening-only play. Programmers usually reserved daytime rotation only for the heavily requested rap records that were impossible to deny their younger listeners. Not all Black programmers were hostile to rap: Lynn Tolliver at WZAK in Cleveland and Steve Crumbley at WOWI in Virginia Beach played more rap in the daytime than most of their contemporaries. But Greg Mack's KDAY was the first station to commit most of its playlist to the new American youth music. By 1986, three years after Greg Mack's arrival, at least 60 percent of the songs in KDAY's rotation were rap records.

At first, the bulk of Mack's rap programming came from the East Coast. Mack's arrival at KDAY was perfectly timed with the rise of Rush/Def Jam acts like Run-DMC, Whodini and LL Cool J; and Mack formed a useful alliance with Russell Simmons. As Don Macmillan's Macola Records pressed up more local rap vinyl, KDAY's playlist filled with homegrown rap artists from Southern California: the L.A. Dream Team, the World Class Wreckin' Cru, Egyptian Lover, and a Mexican-American rapper and breakdancer from East L.A. named Kid Frost, whom Tony Gonzalez introduced to the Wreckin' Cru at Lonzo's studio. With production help from Yella and Dr. Dre, Kid Frost became the first Mexican-American hip-hop recording artist.

The confluence of mobile DJ crews like Uncle Jamm's Army and KDAY's airplay created a rich hip-hop scene throughout Southern California. But simultaneous events in the streets provided equally fertile ground for the growth of something sinister. The ranks of Black and Latino street gangs swelled with rising unemployment and the slashing of job training courses like the Regional Occupation Program that once trained Alonzo Williams to be a DJ. Gangs began selling crack. Suddenly competition over territory wasn't just about neighborhood pride; it was about profit. Those territorial wars began seeping into the live hip-hop scene.

When Run-DMC brought their triumphant *Raising Hell* tour to the Long Beach Arena on August 17, 1986, they never made it to the stage. As Greg Mack walked to the microphone to introduce Whodini, a body fell from the seats—*wham!*—right onto the stage. Within moments, hundreds of gang members began fighting one another and terrorizing fans. Run-DMC, Whodini, and the Beastie Boys barricaded themselves backstage. Greg Mack plowed through the crowd to rescue some friends while innocent young men and women were beaten, stabbed, and shot by thugs who came to settle scores with one another and prey on civilians. Security guards ran, tearing off their shirts so gang members wouldn't target them. The police, who were summoned at eight p.m., didn't arrive until thirty minutes later. By the end of the night, one person had been killed and forty-one injured. Ricky Walker and Russell Simmons, in Atlanta for a record convention, watched cable news coverage from their hotel room with horror.

In the concert's aftermath, KDAY fielded hundreds of calls from listeners, many of them offering apologies to Run-DMC for their less than hospitable welcome in Los Angeles. Meanwhile police, city officials, and major media outlets blamed Run-DMC and rap music itself for the gang riot. Ed Kirby, KDAY's general manager, suggested to Mack that the station promote a "Day of Peace," to take place on October 9, 1986, and invited Run-DMC to join him and a host of local guests on the air.

Until October 9, the yearly tally of murders in Los Angeles stood at 136; of those, twelve occurred on the weekend just before the broadcast. But on the "Day of Peace" there were no murders. Not a single incident of gang violence was reported. Two weeks later, the two large L.A. gang affiliations, the Bloods and Crips, signed a peace treaty.

The "Day of Peace" was a real measure of how important both hip-hop and KDAY had become in the daily lives of young Angelenos. But it was also an indication that the gang culture and violence had reached a similar point of saturation. In the coming years, KDAY would not be able to protect its listeners from gangs and violence, nor would hip-hop itself be able to stave off the gang culture's influence.

When Lonzo Williams cashed the $10,000 check for the World Class Wreckin' Cru's first and only CBS album, he bought a BMW. He sold his old car, a Mazda RX7, to his lieutenant, Andre "Dr. Dre" Young, who began accumulating speeding tickets. Each time, Dre would miss his court date, and each time, the court would issue a warrant for the young producer's arrest. Inevitably Dre would get stopped by the cops, who would drag him to jail, and then Dre would call Lonzo to bail him out.

Lonzo spent thousands of dollars over the next year covering Dre's tickets and bail. But what else could he do? The Wreckin' Cru couldn't very well record or perform with their DJ in the slammer. After the CBS deal ended and gigs got scarce, Lonzo was stuck paying Dre's car note, too. *Dre is becoming one expensive cat*, Lonzo thought.

"You gotta get me out of here," Dre called again from jail one evening, crying.

This time, Lonzo was through.

"We're not gigging this week; I can't get you out. I don't need to get you out. Maybe you should sit in jail for a couple of days so you'll start paying these fucking tickets. I pay mine; you need to pay yours."

With that, Dre paged the one guy he knew would have the money.

Eric Wright—the short drug dealer who, years ago, had exchanged blithe fuck-yous with Lonzo outside Eve's—had been asking Dre to produce a track for a nascent label he wanted to call Ruthless Records. Ever since Dre had become a successful radio jock and producer, he always seemed to be too busy. But once Wright had sprung the DJ from jail, Dre owed him a favor.

Wright arranged to record an unknown rap duo out of New York called HBO. But when the group arrived and heard Dre's music, they balked. It was a typical reaction: To New Yorkers' ears, Los Angeles rap music sounded years behind the times. Dre and DJ Yella convinced Wright that he himself should rap the lyrics, written by another artist in Lonzo's Kru-Cut Records stable, O'Shea Jackson. Still in high school, Jackson was a rap junkie and a prolific poet, one-third of a Beastie-inspired crew called CIA (for Criminals in Action). Performing under the name "Ice Cube," Jackson wrote similar tales of street crime and delinquency for the song that Eric Wright rapped that night in the studio.

Ice Cube modeled the track and lyrics for "Boyz-N-the Hood" after another song called "6 'N the Mornin'"—released the previous year through Macola, on DJ Unknown's Techno Hop Records, by a rapper who called himself "Ice-T."

The tales in "6 'N the Mornin'" struck a nerve for many local kids: "Six in the mornin', police at my door, fresh Adidas squeak across the bathroom floor. / Out the back window I make an escape, don't even get a chance to grab my old school tape."

Ice-T's song, in turn, drew direct inspiration from the rough street raps of Philadelphia's Schoolly D, and from Ice-T's own life as a hustler in L.A.

Ice-T was born in New Jersey as Tracy Marrow. After both of his parents died, Marrow was sent to live with his aunt in Los Angeles in the tony Black neighborhood of Baldwin Hills. Initially, Marrow was bused to a junior high school in a middle-class area across town, but by the time he was a teenager, he didn't want to ride the bus every day. He set his sights instead on Crenshaw High, just down the hill from his aunt's house. Crenshaw put Marrow in rougher surroundings, and soon the young, light-skinned kid from Baldwin Hills was rolling with gangbangers and drug dealers from the ghettos of South Central. After he graduated in 1976, Marrow spent four years in the army, stationed in Hawaii.

Marrow returned to Southern California just as rap music started to break, with dreams of earning a living as a DJ. But Marrow's friends were all criminals, making a lot more money than Marrow could hope to gain through legal means. DJing and rapping became Marrow's creative outlet as he amassed a hoard of cash through a string of robberies and jewelry heists, pimping and drugs. He was now living the life he once read about in books by hustler-author Iceberg Slim, his hip-hop namesake. Tracy Marrow's recordings as "Ice-T," like Iceberg Slim's books, translated that life to wax. Soon his lyrical talents landed him a breakthrough role in *Rappin'*—the Menahem Golan exploitation flick that Russell Simmons had turned down to make *Krush Groove*.

Compared to Ice-T, Eric Wright was small-time as both hustler and rapper. Wright's lyrical timing was off, and his high-pitched voice cracked as he rhymed. But hearing tiny "Eazy-E" talk shit was enough to make the toughest gangster smile: "Cruisin' down the street in my six-fo', / Jockin the bitches, slappin the hoes."

Wright paid to press the vinyl at one of Macola's few competitors, Bill Smith Custom Records, and Dre helped Wright take it to the two main outlets for rap in Los Angeles. First, Dre approached Greg Mack at KDAY, who agreed to play it if Dre edited the curses. Then Wright and Dre carried boxes of records to a record stall at the Roadium swap meet in Torrance. The spot was run by a second-generation Japanese-American named Steve Yano, who hired Dre and other DJs to spin rap records for the passing throngs, selling hundreds of copies in the process. "Boyz-N-the Hood" became a bona fide

Los Angeles street anthem, for real gangsters, wannabes, and civilian rap fans.

Wright knew he couldn't handle the business end on his own. To go legit, he'd need help. So Wright turned to Lonzo—who had already extended Eric $650 worth of studio time on credit. Wright offered an extra $100 if Lonzo would introduce him to his manager, Jerry Heller, and the crew at Macola Records.

In 1987, Don Macmillan picked up "Boyz-N-the Hood" by Eazy-E for national distribution, and Jerry Heller and Morey Alexander picked up Eric Wright for management for their usual 20 percent fee. The record was selling well, and both Dre and Wright felt they had found a formula. They recorded a few more tracks with Ice Cube, Yella and other friends, and Macola issued an album credited to a loose confederation of rappers and DJs called "NWA"—Niggaz With Attitudes.

The release of *NWA and the Posse* propelled Macola Records' best sales year yet. Artists from Northern California now used the pressing plant's custom service. A song called "Rumors" by the Timex Social Club, an R&B group from Berkeley, had become Macmillan's biggest hit ever. A rapper from nearby Oakland named MC Hammer was selling lots of copies of his first album, *Feel My Power*. Another rapper from that same city, Too Short, came to Macola to press his own 12-inch singles. Lonzo's World Class Wreckin' Cru had finally scored a bona fide national smash, with a slow R&B song called "Turn Off the Lights," sung by Dr. Dre's girlfriend, Michel'le Toussaint. Macmillan was acting more than ever like a record executive now, hiring expensive independent promoters to "work" his R&B records at Black and pop radio stations. Best of all, rap records like NWA's sold hundreds of thousands of copies with almost no radio play (excepting, of course, KDAY).

Dre had long chafed under Lonzo Williams's leadership, and the success of NWA gave him the opportunity he needed to leave the Wreckin' Cru. Yella left with him. Even with the success of "Turn Off the Lights," Dre was more excited by the music he was doing with Eazy-E, Ice Cube, and Yella: hard, uncompromising, and rebellious. Jerry Heller's rock-and-roll heart was electrified by NWA; he understood the mainstream potential of Black rebellion. And he was especially fond of Eric Wright for whom he developed a kind of paternal affection. Eazy-E, NWA, and Ruthless Records became Heller's first priority.

Heller's other clients—Lonzo Williams, Rudy Pardee, and Greg "Egyptian Lover" Broussard—revolted. It wasn't just a matter of loyalty and attention, they told Heller and Alexander at a hastily called meeting at Martoni's, an Italian restaurant in Hollywood. It was also the "gangster" image promoted by NWA. Heller told them that if they didn't like his relationship with Eazy, they were free to stay on with Alexander or find other management.

The situation was particularly galling for Lonzo Williams, as Heller had facilitated the rise of NWA, precipitating Dre's and Yella's exit from the Wreckin' Cru just as the group garnered its first hit. Now Heller was coming at him to reconstitute the Wreckin' Cru with replacement members, in order to join the NWA–Ice-T national tour.

"Money will cure *all* this shit," Heller told him.

But the money didn't. It was the most awkward experience of Lonzo's life, standing on the sidelines to watch *his* guys perform with Eazy-E, and then have Dre and Yella watch as he performed the hit *they had* recorded together with completely new band members. The Wreckin' Cru was the only nongangster artist on the tour, and much of the audience was there to see NWA and Ice-T, not to hear his slow jam. Knuckleheads started fights in the audience almost every night. The police fucked with them everywhere they went. Before he left L.A. for the last date on the tour, Lonzo went to the Carson Mall to buy some fresh underwear. There, he found Dre and Eric at the sporting goods store, HQ, buying shotguns, pistol grip Streetsweepers.[6]

"Where y'all going with those?!" Lonzo asked, incredulous.

"On tour," Dre and Eric responded.

"Tour what? Motherfucking Beirut?!"

Lonzo knew Dre's family and Ice Cube's as well. The Youngs and the Jacksons were solidly middle-class people. They had all grown up around gangs and guns—in South Central, that was reality. But Dre, Eazy, and Cube were turning that reality into theater, and now that theater was becoming real, too. *Of course* they were buying guns. Everywhere they went now, *real* gangsters were trying to test them.

After the gig Eric and Dre set to work on their first full-length NWA album, with a lineup that now included Eazy, Dre, Cube, Yella, and Eazy's friend Lorenzo "MC Ren" Patterson. If "Boyz-N-the Hood" drew from the

---

[6]Heller claims he deducted the cost of the guns from the label's taxes, writing them off as "stage props."

bare beats of Schoolly D, Dre's new material echoed the sampled cacophony of Public Enemy's summer of 1988 opus, *It Takes a Nation of Millions.* NWA's new approach grafted the political anger of Public Enemy onto gangster nihilism.

The result was a song called "Fuck the Police." Even before the album's release, tapes of the song circulated around Southern California. The song even made it, with curses "bleeped," into KDAY's mixes. "Fuck the Police" perfectly captured the zeitgeist of young Blacks and Latinos suffering under the twin oppressions of gangs and police, not just in L.A., but across the country. The song was harder and more urgent than anything New York hip-hop had yet produced. Thus, for perhaps the first time, some hip-hop fans on the normally skeptical East Coast became avid fans of a West Coast rap group.

Like Don Macmillan, another Canadian had come to Los Angeles seeking his fortune in the music business. Even though Bryan Turner had never produced a song in his life, the compilation albums of rap singles that he had assembled for K-tel Records made decent money. After the company went bankrupt in 1984, Turner decided to continue doing compilations, this time for his own company.

Turner relocated to Los Angeles in 1985 and founded Priority Records with Mark Cerami, the son of K-tel's head of sales. Turner's buddies in the rap business—Cory Robbins, Fred Munao, Barry Weiss—gave him an instant edge: They all agreed to license their latest hits to him for no money up front.

Some friends at Capitol-EMI's distribution arm, CEMA, gave Turner and Cerami a pressing and distribution deal—unusual for an untested, independent company like Priority. The CEMA deal enabled Turner to do a few things that would make business a lot easier. CEMA would do all the manufacturing, fulfillment, and billing, so Turner never had to worry about getting paid by distributors, like other indies did. Second, CEMA's clout could get Priority's records into places like Kmart, which didn't buy records from independent distributors. With Priority's very first compilation album, *Kings of Rap*, Turner found himself in the enviable position of being able to get Run-DMC records into stores where Profile Records couldn't. *Kings of Rap* went on to sell 300,000 copies.

Priority's compilations did very well, but Turner longed to *own* some music, rather than simply license it. His first foray into music production was fortuitous. Turner was sitting at home, drinking a beer, when he saw a popular TV commercial featuring some "claymation" raisins singing a cover version of Marvin Gaye's "I Heard It Through the Grapevine." Being that the commercial was such a phenomenon and reissues of songs from the 1960s still did really well on the charts, Turner believed that people might actually buy a whole album of sixties soul ostensibly performed by animated dried fruit. Turner went to the representatives of the California Raisin Advisory Board to license the name and likeness of the "California Raisins." Then he tracked down Buddy Miles, a former Jimi Hendrix bandmate who had voiced the commercials, and put him in the recording studio. Turner bought television spots to piggyback on the existing commercials, and his album, *California Raisins Sing the Hit Songs*, sold two million copies.

Eventually, Bryan Turner started looking for artists who weren't hand-drawn. It just so happened that Jerry Heller had office space in the same building on Sunset Boulevard that Priority did. When Heller failed to find any takers for Niggaz With Attitudes among his old friends at the major labels, Heller turned to Turner, who examined the situation with a solely business-minded judgment: NWA was already selling a lot of records, mostly by word of mouth. That was good, because Priority Records had no radio promotion people. Turner was sold when Heller invited him out to the Sherman Square Roller Rink in Reseda, and saw an entire audience of NWA fans chanting the lyrics to "Fuck the Police," a song that they had memorized even though it had yet to debut on record.

Though Heller may have thought Bryan Turner just another mild-mannered Canadian like Don Macmillan, Turner did something that Macmillan never had: He signed NWA to an airtight artist contract, and had each member sign inducement letters stating that, no matter what happened in their dealings with Ruthless Records or with one another, they had to honor their obligations to Priority Records. Unlike at Macola, no one would be taking NWA's artists away from Priority.

Heller, now completely devoted to building Ruthless Records with Eric Wright, also found a way to similarly divest himself from the past. Since no partnership agreements existed between Jerry Heller and Morey Alexander, the man who introduced him to rap, Heller simply stopped paying him.[7]

---

[7]Heller and Alexander still dispute the facts of their split. Heller maintains that Alexander brought little ongoing value to Ruthless, but continued to pay him for some time out of a sense of obliga-

That is how Ruthless became ruthless, and Priority became heir to Macola's misfortune.

Don Macmillan had asked Morey Alexander to manage a few of Macola's artists, and he and Heller had managed them right off of Macola. Heller and Alexander weren't the only ones. Lonzo Williams observed: *The majors were stripping Macola like a '57 Chevy.* Macola would have a hit and an established label would sweep in and grab the artist. Macmillan—who generated contracts geared toward keeping *records* rather than securing *artists*—would generally take a modest payoff. Tommy Boy and Warner Bros. took the remains of the Timex Social Club, and reconstituted them as Club Nouveau. Sire Records, another Warner venture, signed Ice-T. Capitol Records locked up MC Hammer after a talent scout named Joy Bailey saw one of his performances in the Bay Area. Jive took Too Short. Virgin took Kid Frost. MCA took the L.A. Dream Team. Bryan Turner's Priority had grabbed NWA

Artist-entrepreneurs like Lonzo Williams who remained at Macola had grown wary of Macmillan's lazy way of doing business. Their deals had begun simply enough: Macola offered free pressing and distribution in return for a share of their profits. But things got complicated when millions of records were involved. When Macmillan overpressed and overshipped a particular record—thinking it might sell 100,000 but instead having it sell a fraction of that amount—the artist would end up owing Macmillan the cost of the extra product. This was exactly the thing that helped break up the Wreckin' Cru, Lonzo rued. He could sell a bunch of records but have no money to show for it because he had to cover Macmillan's losses, which had put him in a difficult position with Dre and Yella.

And who could tell how many records were truly shipping anyway? Macmillan, theoretically, could make as many as he wanted under the cover of night, shipping them "out the back door" without their being accounted for. Macmillan wasn't a by-the-book kind of guy, anyway. Lonzo and his lieutenant at Kru-Cut Records—an affable kid from the Bay Area named Atron

---

tion. Heller says Alexander was supposed to be the "muscle" of the operation, but when Alexander failed to deal with harassment from an aspiring record entrepreneur named Marion "Suge" Knight, Heller says he had to give Alexander's shares to a new partner, Mike Klein, "a former Israeli Mossad agent."

Gregory whom Heller hired as road manager for NWA on account of his four degrees (one in business and three on his tae kwon do black belt)—went to Macola on the day specified in their contract to pick up their check. Macmillan told Lonzo that he didn't have the money. Lonzo, rarely provoked, picked up one of Macmillan's golf clubs and smashed it into Macmillan's desk. A few days later Lonzo received the check. To be fair, Macola's lax accounting practices and security worked both ways. Eric Wright would often ask Lonzo to distract Macmillan with conversation while Wright went into the back to steal as many boxes of his own records as he could.

Lonzo and several other Macola artists-entrepreneurs, including Andre "DJ Unknown" Manuel, Greg "Egyptian Lover" Broussard, and Rudy Pardee, decided they didn't trust Macmillan anymore. So they did something that no Black recording artists had ever done in the history of the music business. They decided to form their own distribution company.

Distribution had long been the key factor for success or failure in the record business. The very thing that set major labels apart from independents was that majors owned their own national distribution. But creating a distribution company required a lot of credit, start-up capital, and storage space. Between the group of artists, they were actually able to get it all.

West Coast Record Distributors, however, was short-lived. Lonzo and his partners began to fight among themselves almost immediately. Lonzo, in particular, felt that Broussard was overpressing his own records, running up huge manufacturing bills that Lonzo didn't want to pay out of his share. The partnership and company dissolved shortly thereafter.

When Lonzo's lieutenant, Atron Gregory, decided to start his own label, T-N-T, Gregory returned to Macola, releasing a record by a rap group he had found in the Bay Area called Digital Underground. But there wasn't much of Macola left. Most of Macmillan's established artists were gone, and with so many viable independent and majors picking up rap acts, fewer and fewer came his way. A big independent distributor on the East Coast, Schwartz Bros., had gone belly-up owing Macola close to $5 million. Jerry Heller whispered that Macmillan was taking money from "connected" guys to stay afloat.

"If I catch you stealing," Lonzo heard one of them tell Macmillan in a meeting, "I will take your ass out back, put a funnel up your asshole, and pour vinyl up your ass till it comes out of your eyeballs."

In the early 1990s, Macola filed for bankruptcy. But the artists who launched their careers at the little pressing plant on Santa Monica Boulevard would live on, collectively selling nearly $1 billion worth of records.

A few years after the Roxy in New York City brought uptown to downtown, a club called Power Tools in Los Angeles began bringing the 'hood to Hollywood.

Fab 5 Freddy recognized the parallels immediately when he visited the club at the Park Plaza Hotel on his first visit to California in 1986. He discovered that Power Tools was run by two White guys, a promoter named Jon Sidel and a DJ named Matt Dike.

Dike—a tall, gangly, stringy-haired transplant from upstate New York whose sentences invariably began with the word "dude"—was thrilled to meet the hip-hop legend and star of *Wild Style*. Fred himself found he had a lot in common with the DJ: an encyclopedic knowledge of hip-hop, and a mutual friend, Jean Michel Basquiat, for whom Dike stretched canvases and prepared exhibit space at the Gagosian Gallery in Beverly Hills.

Fred had flown in because a few of his pieces had been selected for an art show at the nearby Ace Gallery. Dike put Fred up on a very important scoop: Basquiat was able to stay in L.A.'s most luxurious hotels simply by bartering art for accommodations. Fred jumped at the chance to spend more time in L.A., and his agent made a similar arrangement with the art-loving Severyn Ashkenazy, the owner of the Mondrian Hotel on Sunset Boulevard.

While in L.A., Fred hung out with Dike a lot. He got to meet Dike's partner, another White DJ named Michael Ross. Ross had attended integrated public schools in Long Beach, where he became immersed in Black music. When he enrolled in UCLA, he began spinning records at frat parties. The two White DJs, Ross and Dike, had met in their late teens, at a club on Melrose Avenue called the Rhythm Lounge. Finding their similar affection for funk, soul, and rap, they plotted to produce music together. They even set up an eight-track studio in Dike's apartment on Santa Monica Boulevard. Dike, in particular, kept pestering Fred to make a record with them. Everybody, *especially* White folks, wanted Fred to rap. But Fred remained focused on earning a place in the art world.

"I'm doing the painting thing now," Fred responded. "What the hell am I going to talk about, anyway?"

"Dude," Dike said. "You've got the best line in that movie!"

Dike wasn't talking about *Wild Style*. He was referring instead to Fab 5 Freddy's brief cameo in *She's Gotta Have It*—a sexy, arty black-and-white film with an all-Black cast, the auspicious directorial debut from a young NYU film student named Spike Lee. Freddy scored big laughs when Lee cast him as one in a parade of men trying to "rap" to the film's heroine, played by Tracy Camilla Johns: "Look, baby. Let's go to my house right now. Let's do the *wild* thing. I mean, let's get loose!"

Dike and Ross wanted to do a song based on Fred's "rap." Fred made a few demos with them, although his heart wasn't completely in it. But Fred stuck around at Dike's place long enough to see the two partners eventually find an MC for their first record: a barrel-chested local kid with a gravelly voice named Anthony Smith.

Dike and Ross discovered soon enough that Smith was two people. On some days, he was Anthony, a nice kid who lived with his mom in a modest house just south of Hollywood: the kid who came into the studio, smoked, and said his rhymes in exchange for bags of weed, provided by Ross. On other days, however, he was "Tone-Loc," short for "loco," a guy who left his mother's home every day to hang out with a notorious street gang called the Rolling 60s Crips. One day, Ross went to pick Anthony up for a session, and Tone-Loc appeared at the door holding a shotgun. On another, Tone-Loc showed up to the studio sweating with a fresh bullet wound in his shoulder. Most days Anthony was the nicest guy on the planet. But some days, Tone could be paranoid and menacing, pretty much scaring the shit out of everyone.

The volatile collaboration yielded a few good tracks—"On Fire" and "Cheeba Cheeba." Ross borrowed $10,000 from his father to press up the first records. The name and logo Dike and Ross took for their nascent label was lifted from the business card for a restaurant called Delicious Sandwiches, which featured a crazed-looking cartoon character biting into a sub. A designer friend replaced the sandwich with a record, and their company, Delicious Vinyl, was born.

"On Fire" became a hit on KDAY in 1987, in large part because Tone-Loc's DJ, Mark "M-Walk" Walker, a protégé of DJ Tony Gonzalez, had become a Mack Attack Mix Master. M-Walk became Delicious Vinyl's de facto in-house DJ, contributing scratches and cuts for two more artists: Young MC, a genial rapper from Queens, New York named Marvin Young, who attended the University of Southern California; and Mellow Man Ace, a Cuban MC from the South Central city of South Gate, who rapped in a mix of English and Spanish.

The first singles on Delicious Vinyl didn't sell much more than several thousand copies each. But the scenes at Rhythm Lounge and Power Tools had put Dike and Ross closer to Hollywood, literally and figuratively, than most of the artists and producers from South Central. Delicious Vinyl had cool records, and even cooler T-shirts, so Dike and Ross's music made its way to the right people quickly. An A&R representative from Capitol Records named Kenny Ortiz heard a kindred spirit in the bilingual Mellow Man Ace and offered to buy the artist's half-finished album from Delicious. In a deal facilitated by Morey Alexander—who picked up Mellow Man Ace as his first non-Macola rap client—Dike and Ross sold the contract to the major label.

A representative of Island Pictures, Marty Schwartz, met Matt Dike at an industry party, and arranged a meeting between Dike, Ross, and his boss. Chris Blackwell—the founder of Island Records and the man who introduced Bob Marley to the world—had only recently discovered hip-hop. But the rapper he signed, Rakim, happened to be Dike and Ross's favorite MC. In fact, the partners had signed Tone-Loc because his smooth style recalled Rakim's.

Blackwell met the two young DJ entrepreneurs at Island's L.A. offices in the summer of 1988. The older record man lounged in jeans and sandals and talked music with Dike and Ross, who spoke of their desire for Delicious Vinyl to do in Los Angeles what Def Jam had accomplished in New York. Island Records soon offered Delicious Vinyl a small production deal—a $50,000 advance and 16 percent of the retail price of each record sold.

By the time Dike and Ross signed the deal, they were ready with their first single: The song inspired by Fab 5 Freddy's line in *She's Gotta Have It*. Instead, they had given it to Tone-Loc.

"Wild Thing" was conceived as a perfect pop song. Matt Dike created an improbably funky track from a rock song, a sample of "Jamie's Cryin'" by Van Halen, assisted with cuts by Grandmixer M-Walk. Young MC wrote three of the four verses, and Tone-Loc delivered the chorus with style, ad-libbing Spike Lee's mantra from *She's Gotta Have It*: *Please-baby-baby-please . . .*

"Wild Thing" took Run-DMC's rap-rock union and updated it for the age of the digital sampler. White radio programmers "got" it. Marty Schwartz ran the record up to Jed the Fish, a disc jockey at local alternative rock radio station KROQ. Within a month of signing the Island deal, Delicious Vinyl's "Wild Thing" was a hit on rock radio. Four hundred miles to the north, in San Francisco, it was the *pop* station, KMEL, that played "Wild Thing" first, rather than KSOL, the ostensibly "Black" station.

On the faith that their rock-rap song might have a long shot at MTV, Dike and Ross commissioned a low-budget video for "Wild Thing." They pulled in lots of favors. A friend named Tamra Davis, who had shot some rock and punk videos, volunteered to direct. A pal of Dike's provided space to shoot. Even Tracy Camilla Johns, the femme fatale from *She's Gotta Have It*, agreed to a cameo. The video concept was as much a collision of pop references as the song: A hip-hop spoof of Robert Palmer's iconic MTV video "Addicted to Love," which featured a dapper, besuited Palmer fronting a band of blasé android models wearing guitars. Ross and Dike enlisted their own bevy of gorgeous women, including Dike's girlfriend, Jade.

"Why these girls all White?" Tone asked when he arrived at the studio, overlooking the petite Filipina down in front, Lisa Ann Cabasa. Then the rapper refused to wear the suit that Davis and her crew had provided for him.

"The suit is the whole *concept*," argued Ross as the crew waited, trying to explain the Robert Palmer reference.

"Fuck, no," the rapper replied. "I'm not wearing that motherfucking suit."

Anthony was swiftly becoming *Tone-Loc*, and Ross was afraid the rapper might not do the video at all if he kept pressing. To make matters worse, M-Walk balked at Ross's idea to have the DJ literally strap on a turntable as if it were a guitar.

Another DJ filled in for M-Walk, and Tone performed in his Delicious Vinyl T-shirt, surprising everyone with his charisma and comic moves. Tone-Loc, to Ross's delight, was *selling it like a motherfucker*. Ross realized that his artist was right. Tone just being himself was much better: suitless, and slightly bemused at being surrounded by a gaggle of sexy, alien-looking chicks.

Matt Dike and Michael Ross spent just $500 to make their grainy, crude video, with no guarantee of airplay. Fortunately, their video would gain a wider audience then they had ever imagined. And, ironically, Fab 5 Freddy—the inspiration for "Wild Thing"—would eventually contribute to the success of the video in a way that none of them, especially Freddy, could have dared dream.

Side B
East Side

Five years after MTV began playing Michael Jackson, you could still count on one hand—and often, no hands at all—the number of videos by Black artists on the music channel at any given time.

Four years after MTV first aired Run-DMC's "Rock Box," the channel had programmed less than ten rap videos total.

MTV's "competition," if one could call them that, hadn't done much better. In 1983 NBC launched *Friday Night Videos*, where viewers were only slightly more likely to see a Black artist than on MTV. The same year another weekly show called *New York Hot Tracks* went into national syndication. Hosted by WKTU's Carlos De Jesus, "Hot Tracks" had a markedly more "urban" sensibility to its video choices.

If you really wanted to see rap videos, only one TV program in the country played them regularly. To watch it, you had to be in New York.

Video Music Box was the brainchild of a Black kid from Southeast Queens, Ralph McDaniels. While in college, McDaniels got an internship as a tape operator at channel 31, WNYC-TV—a city-run station that broadcast public affairs programming and leased time to foreign networks aiming for New York's immigrant population with news shows and soccer matches from back home. After McDaniels graduated, his supervisor, Jim Bowman, gave him a full-time job.

One day, McDaniels opened a box sent from Solar Records, a Black-owned record company in Los Angeles. Inside were videotapes of lip-synched performances from its popular R&B groups, the Whispers and Lakeside.

McDaniels, a DJ, realized that few TV programs played music videos from Black artists. He thought that WNYC should.

McDaniels endured a lot of office politics to get his show on the air; he was just a broadcast engineer, not a producer. But after the station brass let McDaniels execute his idea, *Video Music Box*—clips linked by McDaniels's baritone voice-over—became WNYC's top-rated show by far, airing in the late afternoon on weekdays as kids returned from school.

At first McDaniels played a good amount of mainstream pop, as R&B and rap clips were scarce. But as rap groups like Whodini started making videos, McDaniels shifted the show to a "Blacker" sound. As *Video Music Box* became a guarantor of local sales, it became a reason for rap labels to invest in doing even more videos. Who better to shoot those videos than McDaniels himself, with his partner Lionel "Vid Kid" Martin, who went to City College with Russell Simmons? It was an old music industry practice: Nothing guarantees airplay like hiring the DJ—or, in this case, VJ—as your producer. McDaniels and Martin shot video clips for Profile, Cold Chillin', Def Jam, and others.

The low-key McDaniels became the sole authentic voice of hip-hop on television, conducting extensive on-air interviews with rap artists like Eric B & Rakim, Dana Dane, and Biz Markie. As watching *Video Music Box* became a daily ritual for hundreds of thousands of New York kids, McDaniels won the attention of competitors. One of them was Steve Leeds, the programmer of a new local UHF channel devoted entirely to music videos, U68. Leeds had started a similar show on his own station, *Fresh Rap*.

Leeds and McDaniels became friendly. When Leeds jumped to MTV in 1987 as their head of on-air talent, Ralph McDaniels submitted himself as a VJ candidate. McDaniels wanted to bring *Video Music Box*, one of New York's most successful local shows, to MTV, but Leeds immediately dis- abused McDaniels of any such notion. Leeds had already tried to talk to the channel's head of programming, Lee Masters, about doing a rap show and Masters wasn't biting.

McDaniels went back to his daily show on WNYC, while MTV contin- ued to play its steady diet of White pop—Madonna, Bon Jovi, Poison, and Whitesnake—grudgingly sprinkled with a little Whitney Houston and Lio- nel Richie for "balance."

At the headquarters of the new MTV Europe, things were different.

To run their foreign experiment, the executives at MTV chose Liz

Nealon, an MTV insider from the channel's first days. Nealon disdained MTV's racial iron curtain, and when she helped develop the network's "adult" station, Video Hits One ended up playing more Black music than its sister station. Now thousands of miles away from New York in a fledgling operation with much lower financial stakes, no one could tell her what to do with her blank canvas.

Europe was different, too. With no tradition of racially segregated music, Europeans often proved more open to African-American music than Americans themselves. This was how Sophie Bramly—the raven-haired Franco-Tunisian who designed the cover of Fab 5 Freddy's "Change the Beat"—found a receptive audience for her hip-hop video show on the number one TV station in France while Michael Holman couldn't sell his *Graffiti Rock* to American programmers.

To Liz Nealon, who was assembling a staff for MTV Europe's launch, Bramly fit the perfect profile. Bramly was not only an experienced producer and writer, she was multilingual and attractive enough to throw in front of the camera if need be. Bramly moved to London in the spring of 1987 and dove into round-the-clock preparations for the channel's debut in the fall. Executives from MTV's home office in New York mixed with a staff culled from over a half dozen European countries. Bramly especially felt at home with Jon Klein, the American producer in charge of animation and graphics. Klein was also a hip-hop fan. That summer, while both of them relished Public Enemy's debut album, they developed a daily shtick.

"Yo!" Bramly would yell to Klein.

"Bum rush the show!" he would answer.

Nealon saw Bramly's musical obsession as an opportunity for the new channel.

"If you have such a big background in rap, you should do a rap show," Nealon told her. What was unthinkable in the States was a casual possibility in Europe.

Elated, Bramly quickly developed a framework for the program, which debuted in October 1987—one month after MTV Europe's first broadcast—and ran three times per week. The show had aired for a few months before she finally called her old friend Fab 5 Freddy to give him the news.

"Guess what," Bramly said. "I'm doing a rap show for MTV Europe!"

"You're doing a rap show *on MTV*?!" Fred replied, incredulous. "What's it called?"

"*Yo!*" Bramly said.

"You're saying 'Yo!' . . . on *MTV?!*" Fred said. "So how do you start the show?"

"I say, 'Yo! Whassup?!'"

"You say 'Yo! Whassup?!' . . . *on MTV?!*"

Yo!—Sophie Bramly's little invention on MTV's European experiment—was not only a huge boost to European rap artists like the U.K.'s Derek B and a French group called NTM; it was also an important yet bittersweet stop for many American rap artists, like Public Enemy, who couldn't believe that the same network that rejected them back home was receiving them warmly abroad—with the simple, one-word call that b-boys and MCs had been using for years to get people's attention.

Back in the States, MTV could be a dispiriting place to work, especially for a guy who was still a punk rocker at heart.

Pete Dougherty was a kid from Queens who had come up on the downtown scene with Rick Rubin and the Beastie Boys. Dougherty was known for his massive collection of surreptitiously recorded tapes of live punk shows, and for his collection of hip-hop 12-inches—which his friends in the Clash bought and let him keep after he transferred the songs to cassette for them.

Dougherty partied at night and waited tables by day. But he came from a family of careerists—his father Philip wrote for *The New York Times*, and his older brother Paul was an accomplished video editor. It was only a matter of time before Dougherty had to find a straight gig. With his brother's connections, Dougherty landed a job working in the on-air promotions department of MTV—charged with making all the channel's own commercials and animation.

The music sucked, but Dougherty's job allowed him to be creative. Sometimes he did groundbreaking work. The money was decent. The perquisites, like concert tickets, were plentiful, and Dougherty lavished them on his old downtown buddies Fab 5 Freddy and Rick Rubin. In fact, it had been Dougherty who took Rubin to see his first Slayer show and introduced him to a funky punk band from California called the Red Hot Chili Peppers. Dougherty was one of the key people inside the building who lobbied enthusiastically for the Beastie Boys, making them a true MTV act and securing the fortunes of Rubin and Def Jam.

Pete Dougherty might have continued on his career path at MTV had things remained the same.

Then the kid came.

He was just a PA, a production assistant, a gofer. The kid's movie-director uncle got him the gig. He was a big boy, husky and muscular, like a jock who played football in high school and, after graduation, never stopped eating that way. The kid was always smiling, always joking, but sometimes Dougherty thought he took it too far. He could be loud, overbearing, and—worst of all for a young person breaking into the business—he didn't know his place.

Dougherty remembered the first time he took the kid out on a shoot. They were at the Apollo Theater, taping a promo for an MTV special hosted by Whitney Houston. Houston was only twenty-four years old, but she had already scored the highest chart debut of any female artist ever. Now promoting her second album, Houston was the top priority for Clive Davis's label, Arista Records, and an important artist for MTV. She was a superstar, showbiz royalty.

But Houston was having trouble with her lines. Dougherty thought that MTV was taking the wrong approach with her. It was supposed to be this hyped-up spot—something like "MTV'S GONNA *ROCK* WITH WHITNEY HOUSTON!" But she was a sweet, quiet girl, more tea party than dance party. The whole thing was forced, but now they had to try to make it work, delicately. They resumed shooting, and the artist flubbed her line again.

Then Dougherty heard the kid's booming voice from down in front.

"One more time, Whit."

One more time, Whit? Dougherty cringed. *Did he just call Whitney Houston "Whit"?!*

Houston was nice enough about it, probably not even realizing that the proper decorum of the set had been breached. But Dougherty had to take the kid aside to patiently explain the rules to his new protégé. *You're a production assistant. You're just supposed to hold the cue cards. You're not supposed to open your mouth.*

After the Whitney Houston incident, the kid adopted an overly formal tone that made it hard for anyone to keep a straight face. He held the cue cards at a shoot with a young comedian named Denis Leary. When Leary remarked that he had already memorized his lines, the kid immediately tossed the cards with a flourish.

"Makes my job easier, *sir*!" he bellowed.

Thereafter, Leary and the kid were inseparable.

A gig with MTV was an honor, a rare opportunity to be at the epicenter of American pop culture. But where others might have tiptoed around, the kid acted like he owned the place. He came to work in flip-flops. He talked to everyone the same way, from his fellow PAs, to the talent, to his boss, Peter Dougherty, even to his boss's boss, Judy McGrath. Humans didn't scare him, no matter their accomplishments or station.

Over time, the kid became a great worker. But he never quite got the whole culture of political decorum at MTV.

Like when the kid started asking him about—get this—*how he could get MTV to start a rap video show.*

You can't, Dougherty replied.

Why not? the kid asked.

Dougherty answered with as much patience as he could muster. *Because MTV doesn't like rap music very much. And even if they did, it wouldn't matter. Because we're in the promotions department, which has nothing to do with programming. And even if we were, it wouldn't matter. Because you're a PA.*

The next day, the kid asked him again when they were going to get MTV to do a rap video show.

That was when Dougherty decided he would help the young production assistant. You just couldn't say no to Ted Demme.

When New Yorkers speak of Long Island, they usually refer to the two large suburban counties of Nassau and Suffolk to the east. The western tip of the island, the counties of Queens and Kings, are legally part of New York City—where they are otherwise known as the boroughs of Queens and Brooklyn.

Over the years, the man-made border running from the Long Island Sound to the Atlantic Ocean came to separate not only suburb from city, but rich from poor, and White from Black—with the notable exception of a chain of Black communities running along the southern part of the island, like Hempstead, Freeport, and Wyandanch.

Man's borders mean nothing to God. So when the Episcopal Diocese of Long Island drew its own domain, it encompassed all four counties, and all of their flock within them, without regard to class or color.

Rick Demme, an insurance salesman by trade, raised his family in the mostly White suburb of Rockville Centre. But as an active church organizer,

Demme fellowshipped with Black diocese members like Joan Carrott, of Hollis, Queens. Demme and Carrott sent their sons—Teddy and Curtis, respectively—along with hundreds of other diocese children to the weekend retreats and summer programs at Camp DeWolfe, a wooded spot out on the shores of the Long Island Sound.

"Whiteboyland" is what Curtis Carrott called it. Curtis had convinced his buddy James Ed Roberts to accompany him to Camp DeWolfe, so he would have somebody from back home to hang with. And so, in 1977, the two fourteen-year-olds from Queens who called themselves "Curt Flirt" and "Ed Lover" arrived, convinced they were the coolest guys on the campgrounds.

Until they met Ted Demme. Here was one White boy, the same age as them, who ran even wilder than they did. He played football, he talked shit, he smoked, he went along with them to steal the sacred wine out of the chapel's refrigerator. Even more surprisingly, he knew about the DJs and MCs like Grandmaster Flash and the Furious Five.

Over the next few summers, Ted Demme and Ed Roberts solidified their friendship over sports and hip-hop. During the school year, Ted brought his White friends from Rockville Centre together with Ed's from Hollis for epic games of touch football. It was the early 1980s, when Black and White kids didn't mix much out on Long Island. White kids like Ted weren't supposed to collect rap 12-inches, or know about the legendary MC battle between Kool Moe Dee and Busy Bee at Harlem World; or listen to Frankie Crocker's show on WBLS from beginning to end, drifting off to sleep as Crocker signed off with "Moody's Mood." *There-I-go-there-I-go-there-I-go-theeeeeeere-IIIIII-gooooooooo. . . .*

Even then Ted Demme didn't know his place.

After Ted Demme graduated from Southside High in 1981, he headed to the State University of New York at Cortland to study physical education and play football for the Cortland State Red Dragons. But Demme's plans for a career as a gym teacher and sports coach ended when Ted was blindsided during a play and blew out his right knee. Doctors spent hours stitching his torn ligaments, and Ted ended up in an ankle-to-hip cast for months.

If Ted Demme grieved, he hid it behind his smile. Sidelined, Demme stayed close to the game by giving color commentary and play-by-play for the campus radio station, the fortuitously titled WSUC-FM. The station's logo, predictably, was a pair of open lips, tongue extended.

By the time he healed, Ted Demme determined that he liked broadcasting better than football. He changed his major to communications, studied television directing, and beamed his personal shtick—along with his favorite rock, funk, and rap records—to central New York state in a nightly radio show called "Go to Bed with Ted." Once a year, Demme would feature a segment called "Countdown to the Brothers." Few knew what he meant. But his old friend from Camp DeWolfe, Ed Roberts, did: Demme was counting the days until "Ed Lover" and his boys from Hollis arrived in town for the annual Cortland State Picnic.

During his sophomore year, Ted Demme received another important visitor: His twelve-year-old sister Jennifer. Back home things weren't going so well. The marriage between Ted and Jen's parents, Rick and Gail Demme, was falling apart. Now that her older brother Ted wasn't around, Jen would sometimes sit in Ted's empty room, staring at the walls still covered with an old Farrah Fawcett poster, baseball cards, and Yankee pennants. Like some debauched angel of mercy, Ted sent for Jen one weekend, kept her in his fraternity house, and got her drunk.

If Jen Demme worshiped her older brother, then Ted idolized his uncle Jonathan, who was a screenwriter, movie producer, and director in California. Jonathan Demme worked for Roger Corman, creating low-budget exploitation films with names like *Caged Heat*, *Crazy Mama*, and *Fighting Mad*. In Hollywood, Jonathan Demme was just a B movie director, no big deal. But to Ted, he was the epitome of cool.

It was Uncle Jonathan who exposed his nephew to the movie set and Jonathan who pulled a favor at MTV to get Ted Demme his first gig.

When Ted Demme began lobbying for a rap video show on MTV, he wasn't on some altruistic quest to break racial barriers or propagate hip-hop culture. Ted Demme liked rap music. Ergo, MTV should be playing rap videos.

Peter Dougherty had long ago relinquished the conceit that he could help make MTV more progressive, and resigned himself to the reality that nothing that he liked would ever air there. Instead, Dougherty found covert ways to sneak in subversive music and visuals via the on-air promos he created. The kid Demme had yet to be jaded. He kept pushing. Demme slipped notes under Dougherty's and McGrath's doors.

When are we going to start a rap show?

When word of Sophie Bramly's *Yo!* show came from Europe, Demme sputtered with exasperation.

"What are they waiting for?!" he asked Dougherty.

Alas, the men who programmed the music at MTV were waiting to be disabused of their outdated notions about race and music. These were the same people who founded the channel as a "rock" station, the same people who kept Black artists at bay because they truly believed that they would lose their White, male core audience if they didn't. Many executives at MTV didn't realize that their listeners' tastes had changed—even though they had White kids like Ted Demme in their midst, as well as rap-friendly White executives on their payroll, guys like Dougherty and Doug Herzog, the new head of original programming. Some executives were afraid that rap videos would sully the brand and scare away advertisers. Others, like MTV's programming chief Lee Masters, simply thought there weren't enough rap videos being produced by the labels to sustain a regular show—even though Steve Leeds had shown Masters how he had sustained his show, *Fresh Rap*, on New York's late music-video TV station, U68.

Every year, MTV had been surprised by at least one huge rap hit. In 1984, it was "Rock Box." In 1985, "King of Rock." In 1986, "Walk This Way." In 1987, "Fight for Your Right to Party." Every year, MTV promptly forgot this evidence of rap's currency with mainstream America.

As it turned out, they just needed to be surprised one more time.

In the spring of 1988, the colorful, zany Scott Calvert video that Ann Carli commissioned for DJ Jazzy Jeff & the Fresh Prince's "Parents Just Don't Understand" struck the staff of MTV's programming department as the perfect summer teen record. It was. Suddenly a rap video had become the most popular clip on the channel, and the single vaulted to number twelve on the Billboard Hot 100 chart of pop singles.

Amid the success of "Parents," Pete Dougherty went to Judy McGrath to ask if she might negotiate his politically tricky proposition: to let two guys from the on-air promo department shoot a pilot episode for a rap show. McGrath made sure that Herzog was on board, because he would technically be in charge of the series, not her. Then she secured the blessing of Lee Masters, along with a small budget.

Demme had never produced anything before, and much of the initial work fell to Dougherty. The pair flew down to Austin, Texas, to join the Run-DMC *Tougher Than Leather* tour. The local arena wouldn't book rap acts, so the tour had to stage their show in a hay-filled rodeo shed on the outskirts of town. There, Dougherty and Demme shot energetic "bumpers" from Run-DMC, Public Enemy, and DJ Jazzy Jeff & the Fresh Prince, which, upon the producers' return to New York, were wedged in between videos to comprise an hour-long show. Dougherty hired a graffiti artist named Dr. Revolt to create the show's graphics, and on August 6, 1988, the channel broadcast the pilot episode of *Yo! MTV Raps*.

Demme pestered the research department for word of how the show played with the national audience. Lee Masters, like everyone else, had grown fond of the irrepressible production assistant, and tried to prepare the kid for reality.

"Don't worry about the ratings," Masters told Demme. "It's probably going to do a 0.4 or 0.5"—a very low score. "But don't freak out." Masters reassured him that the show was important, if only for the image of the channel.

When the ratings finally came back, Masters and everyone else at the channel were dumbfounded. *Yo! MTV Raps* had earned above a 2.0 in the Nielsens, a massive figure compared to MTV's baseline numbers, and in so doing became one of the channel's highest-rated shows ever. Masters quickly gave his approval to Dougherty and Demme to turn the pilot into a weekly series.

When the MTV brass finally gave *Yo! MTV Raps* the green light, Dougherty knew whom he wanted to host his show.

Dougherty had heard that the great mayors of old New York used to have an "official greeter"—a person who would go out to meet arriving dignitaries and escort them about the city. Fiorello LaGuardia employed Grover Whelan, who went on to run the 1939 World's Fair. Before Whelan was a fellow named Major William Francis Deegan, who went on to greater, posthumous fame as the namesake for the expressway that shuttled suburbanites safely over the South Bronx, right past the building on Sedgewick Avenue where Kool Herc and his sister threw their first hip-hop party.

Dougherty envisioned the *Yo!* host as the "official greeter" of hip-hop, the Major Deegan of rap—someone knowledgeable enough to take mainstream America on a safe tour through the culture, and charismatic enough to make it a cool experience. One person fit that description perfectly: Fab 5 Freddy, the man with the gift for framing things.

Peter Dougherty and Freddy had remained friends since the early 1980s. Dougherty had taken him to Michael Jackson and Judas Priest shows; and Freddy, in turn, sought Dougherty's advice when he was tapped by Ann Carli to direct his first video, for the debut single from Boogie Down Productions' first Jive Records album, "By All Means Necessary." Rapper KRS-One had turned overtly political since DJ Scott La Rock's murder, and Freddy filmed a clip that reflected the rapper's politics: KRS-One performing onstage at the Apollo Theater, while a slide show of Black political icons flashed on a screen behind him.

Their collaboration was, perhaps, the first rap video made expressly to *not* play on MTV. Thus, no one was more surprised than Freddy when Peter Dougherty chose Boogie Down Productions's "My Philosophy" for the finale of the *Yo! MTV Raps* pilot—the undiluted, complex lyrics of KRS-One and subversive images of Malcolm X and Louis Farrakhan piped to the televisions of mainstream America. After the program aired, Dougherty had another surprise for his old friend.

"We're thinking about doing this as a regular show," Dougherty told him. "I think you should audition."

Dougherty shot some test footage of Freddy on the Williamsburg Bridge. In that shoot, a concept for the show emerged. Unlike the other MTV VJs, who taped their shows in a TV studio, Fab 5 Freddy would always host *Yo!* on location. Every week, he would feature one guest act, meeting the artists in places relevant to *them*. Fred himself, thrust suddenly back into the role of performer, resumed the cool, slang-laden persona of "Phade," his alter-ego from *Wild Style*.

Dougherty and Demme went to a dance studio to tape Fab 5 Freddy's first show with Eddie O'Loughlin's female rap group, Salt-N-Pepa. Since the days of Tanya "Sweet T" Winley, female MCs had played a supporting role in hip-hop. But the emergence of Salt-N-Pepa proved that female rappers could achieve commercial success on a par with the best male MCs. Their first album, *Hot, Cool & Vicious*, had gone platinum—a first for O'Loughlin's Next Plateau Records. The selection of Salt-N-Pepa for the show wasn't random. Ted Demme had helped edit their video, "Push It."

Dougherty and Demme shared an executive production credit on the show, but Dougherty already had a full-time gig running the on-air promotions department. As *Yo!* entered its first season in late 1988, Dougherty gradually ceded the weekly production duties to his younger partner.

Demme had learned to direct by watching Dougherty and, before that, his uncle Jonathan. Demme was also respectful of Fab 5 Freddy's directorial input, and the two men solicited and heeded each other's feedback: Demme asking Freddy to hit the *"Yo!"* harder when he said the name of the show; Freddy suggesting interesting camera moves to get in and out of a particular scene—"Batman angles," he called them. Both Demme and Freddy strove to bring the energy of music video direction into the segments between the videos, making the setting in each show as important as the music. Demme also consulted with Freddy when it came time to program videos and select guests.

"Come here," Demme called from his office. "You've got to see this." It was a video of a rapper whom Freddy had never seen before. MC Hammer's "Pump It Up" was the first clip from the Oakland, California, rapper since being signed to Capitol Records. Ted Demme and Fab 5 Freddy saw in MC Hammer a kid who wasn't so much a rapper as he was a showman, throwing himself into elaborate, breakneck dance routines that trumped almost anything in hip-hop video at the time. In an era when many rappers restricted their physical movements to look cool, MC Hammer was kinetic and irrepressible—a perfect artist for hip-hop's new visual age, and a spiritual match for Ted Demme himself. Demme and Freddy, both visual artists, leaped to book the West Coast rapper for their new show, taped at yet another dance studio. Hammer flew out with his entourage, while Demme cast a few local female dancers to perform with the out-of-town artist. Both Demme and Freddy lavished special attention on the prettiest "extra"—a Puerto Rican girl from the Bronx named Jennifer Lopez.

MC Hammer's first visit to *Yo! MTV Raps* in New York underlined a growing disconnect between the city where hip-hop was born, and the rest of the country—now re-creating hip-hop in its own image.

"We are hitting hard in Oakland!" MC Hammer shouted in the beginning of his next video, "Turn This Mother Out." The rapper reeled off more cities where his records had been selling since his days on Macola: Los Angeles, Atlanta, Miami, Chicago, Cleveland. But someone reminded MC Hammer of the one city that wasn't feeling him.

"You ain't hittin' in New York!"

New York rap fans didn't hear much rap from beyond the Hudson River in the mix shows on WRKS and WBLS, and what they did hear seemed amateurish. The covers of albums from West Coast artists inspired ridicule when on display in East Coast record stores, as they reflected styles that seemed years behind the times—Jheri curls, permed hair, and out-of-fashion clothes.

Ted Demme needed to cultivate a *national* audience for his show to succeed, so he aimed to unite the far-flung expressions of hip-hop under the aegis of *Yo! MTV Raps*. Demme's ecumenical approach perfectly suited Fab 5 Freddy, the grandson of a Garveyite with an internationalist perspective. Demme and Freddy taped shows with the 2 Live Crew in Miami, and in Los Angeles with NWA, the divergent paths of the two former Macola artists demonstrating hip-hop's growing diversity. While 2 Live Crew had absorbed Miami's sun-drenched sexual debauchery, the members of NWA had plunged even deeper into the gangster theatrics, donning bulletproof vests as they rode through Los Angeles, from the beach to the Compton swap meet, on the back of a flatbed truck with the *Yo!* crew.

Demme and Freddy's televised ghetto-to-ghetto travelogue, airing every Saturday morning at ten a.m., gave rap from outside the eastern seaboard its due. It also exposed White kids to the fullest possible range of Black youth culture: political or puerile, Afrocentric or erotic, aggressive or abstract. And *Yo!* helped young Black kids—whether isolated in the inner city or stranded in suburbia—feel connected to one another through hip-hop.

Fab 5 Freddy was especially delighted that *Yo! MTV Raps* played a key role in breaking the video released by his two friends Matt Dike and Mike Ross, "Wild Thing," which MTV quickly added to its regular rotation. Rapper Tone-Loc's album, *Loc'ed After Dark*, became the first multimillion seller for the boutique L.A. label Delicious Vinyl, and the first album by a Black rap artist to reach number one on the Billboard pop albums chart.

Yo! MTV Raps yielded something else, too: the highest-rated show on the prime outlet for pop music in America.

One Saturday evening in early September 1988, Barry Weiss, Ann Carli, and another colleague from Jive Records, Michael Tedesco, drove out to Long Island to see their artists, Boogie Down Productions and Kool Moe Dee, perform on a large bill of rap artists at the Nassau Coliseum—just two miles from Adelphi University and about four miles from the childhood home of Ted Demme.

In the two years since the gang rampage at the Long Beach Arena in California where Run-DMC had been set to perform, rap concerts across the country had become magnets for troublemakers. On the West Coast, the problem was organized gangs. On the East Coast, it was ad hoc groups of young toughs looking to "get paid"—robbing fans for their clothes, cash, or jewelry.

Ann Carli had been to enough rap shows in the past four years to develop a sixth sense for peril. The moment they entered the coliseum's parking lot, Carli knew something was off. She decided that she didn't want to be out on the floor of the arena if anything went down.

"I'm not going to hang with you guys," Carli told her male companions. "Just be really careful. Don't let anybody 'bum rush' you. If you see more than three guys walking together, stay out of their way."

Carli was backstage when Kool Moe Dee's manager, Lavaba Mallison, ran to her.

"Ann, get out of here now," Mallison urged. "They're stabbing people in the audience. I just saw a guy bleed out on a stretcher."

But Carli didn't want to leave her friends behind. She ended up crouching behind a bleacher with rapper Doug E. Fresh's mother and grandmother to wait things out, before KRS-One found her.

"Annie, get out! Go home!" the rapper barked.

Carli, Weiss, and Tedesco eventually got out safely. Over the next few days, local media were ablaze with news of rap-related carnage: A nineteen-year-old kid named Julio Fuentes was held down by several men and stabbed to death after struggling to keep his gold chain. Eight other young people were stabbed, three of them critically wounded. At least a dozen more were beaten or robbed.

Carli got an agitated call from her friend Nelson George.

"Did you hear about this?" George asked.

"I was *there*," Carli replied.

"We've got to do something," George said.

Carli, one of the leading rap record executives, and George, now the Black music editor for *Billboard* magazine, decided to make an all-star rap record and donate the profits to charity. They called their project the "Stop the Violence Movement," after a Boogie Down Productions' song. Carli asked Boogie Down Productions' youngest member, Derrick "D-Nice" Jones, to produce the track. Both she and George enlisted the help of the most popular rappers in the genre: Chuck D and Flavor Flav from Public Enemy, KRS-One and Kool Moe Dee, Heavy D, the members of Stetsasonic. The young prince of rap, LL Cool J, still smarting from his battle with Kool Moe Dee, was the lone holdout; but he helped a female rapper named MC Lyte write her verse. Ann Carli's own artists, DJ Jazzy Jeff & the Fresh Prince, begged to be included, but Carli felt that their image was too "soft" for the project, and might detract from the record's credibility with the "hard rocks" they were trying to reach.

Recruiting the rappers for the project turned out to be easier than securing a record deal, even with the star-studded cast. Russell Simmons's Def Jam and Andre Harrell's Uptown Records passed on the project, because the executives didn't think they could make any money on it. Tom Silverman very much wanted the record for Tommy Boy, but Carli was turned off when Silverman explained to her how they could donate all the *artist royalties* to charity, while keeping the profits from the record's *distribution* for themselves—just like EMI had done with another charity record called "Sun City."

In the end, Carli came home to Barry Weiss and Clive Calder at Jive, who agreed to donate everything but the cost of the project to the National Urban League, for programs combating Black-on-Black violence.

The video for the song, "Self Destruction," was the largest-ever gathering of rappers on one record, uniting the biggest names in hip-hop for the common good. In the video, KRS-One rapped to his colleagues from a podium at Harlem's Schomburg Center for Research in Black Culture, blaming the "one or two suckas, ignorant brothers" for the violence, not the rap audience. While Kool Moe Dee contributed one of the most memorable phrases ("I never ever ran from the Ku Klux Klan, / and I shouldn't have to run from a Black man"), the video featured other extraordinary moments, including the sight of former adversaries Red Alert and Marley Marl standing beside each other in a cemetery, over a plot that few but insiders knew was the final resting place of DJ Scott La Rock.

The video, released in the late winter of 1989, was carried to televisions across the country by *Yo! MTV Raps*, and sold enough records to raise $500,000 for the National Urban League.

The Stop the Violence Movement was largely New York's response to a local incident. Tone-Loc was the only out-of-towner to make a cameo in the video. But Tone-Loc participated in California's answer to "Self Destruction" the following year, when he, Young MC, Ice-T, MC Hammer, Digital Underground, NWA, and others joined forces to create the West Coast All Stars, and their antiviolence song, "We're All in the Same Gang."

Hip-hop was not only national. It was becoming a Nation unto itself, complete with a sense of morality and common cause.

The success of the weekly *Yo!* *MTV Raps* show amazed everyone at the network. In early 1989, Judy McGrath asked Dougherty and Demme to create a daily after-school rap franchise, hoping to extend the Saturday ratings boost throughout the week. The daily *Yo!* show would be taped in studio, ensuring quick and cheap production.

Fab 5 Freddy declined to host the weekday episodes, abhorring the network's stale, static studio productions. So Dougherty had to search for a new master of ceremonies. A show shot in the confines of an indoor set required a host who could be engaging and entertaining without the benefit of being on location. Once again, Dougherty had a candidate in mind.

Three years after Andre "Doctor Dre" Brown had signed to Def Jam, his group's album had finally been released. Original Concept's *Straight from the Basement of Kooley High!* combined thick beats with comic lyrics. But Original Concept hadn't scored a hit since 1986. Brown made the best of the situation, performing shows around the tristate area, including opening for Big Audio Dynamite, an offshoot of the Clash, at Irving Plaza.

Dougherty was in the house that night. He had known Doctor Dre since the portly performer deejayed for the Beastie Boys, but had never seen him perform with his own group. Watching Dre bouncing his three-hundred-plus-pound frame around the stage alongside partner T-Money, Dougherty likened Original Concept to the Three Stooges, only with better beats. Glen Friedman, the de facto house photographer for Def Jam and a friend of Dougherty's, leaned toward the MTV producer.

"You should really get Dre on camera," Friedman said.

Dougherty commissioned a screen test for Original Concept's young master of ceremonies. But this time, Demme had his own idea of the perfect host.

Since their days together at Camp DeWolfe, the lives of Ted Demme and Ed Roberts had diverged. Demme went to college and moved into the world of corporate media. Roberts had been accepted to Florida A&M—with plans to play trumpet in the marching band. Just before he left, his father died, and Roberts stayed in Queens. He still held forth a dream for his R&B band, Funktion Freeks, but in reality, Roberts worked as a security guard at Andrew Jackson High in Queens, the same school once attended by Russell Simmons's associates Rocky Ford and Larry Smith.

After Demme began working MTV, he and Ed didn't speak as often. But when Roberts caught the pilot episode of *Yo!* and spotted Demme's name in the credits, he called his old friend, begging to be involved in the show somehow.

Demme took Roberts's talents seriously. Roberts knew about every record, every mix tape, every DJ and MC in hip-hop. Aside from DJing himself, he was great at "freestyling"—devising impromptu raps to suit any moment—and, in general, he was one of the most naturally funny people that Demme knew. But there had been no place for Ed in the weekly *Yo!* show.

"Let me do a record review," Roberts had asked.

Demme took his old friend to Central Park and taped him, in his old "Ed Lover" persona, but couldn't get Dougherty or Judy McGrath excited about it.

When McGrath floated the idea for the weekday show, Demme pitched Dougherty on Ed Roberts again. But Dougherty was already set on Doctor Dre, as were McGrath and a few other programming executives. After some back-and-forth, Demme and Dougherty agreed to have the two candidates do a screen test together.

Ed Roberts and Andre Brown had never met before. Thrown together, they found comedic common ground, adopting Jamaican accents for a funny improvised skit. Demme saw the chemistry. Roberts and Brown even had that "classic comic duo" look: "Ed Lover" tall and thin, "Doctor Dre" squat and corpulent, like a hip-hop version of Abbott and Costello or Laurel and Hardy.

Now Demme faced a financial problem. The network had budgeted a modest stipend for one host—$1,000 a week. Dougherty told Demme that if he really wanted two hosts, he would have to get them to agree to split the money. Since Doctor Dre was already the corporate favorite, Demme would have to convince him to compromise.

Ted Demme, his voice breaking with emotion, begged Brown to share the bill with Roberts. Brown was philosophical about the request. On the one hand, he could easily insist on keeping the entire check. But on the other hand, Brown acknowledged that there was a palpable energy between him and Roberts, perhaps because they barely knew each other. Rejecting the childhood friend of the show's main producer—whose uncle, in turn, was a Hollywood movie director—wouldn't exactly be a smart opening move. *Be-*

sides, Brown thought, *America was always on this divide-and-conquer shit with Black people.* Together, he and Roberts could achieve what Professor Strobert always talked about: impacting the consciousness of America. Brown agreed to share his check.

For Ed Roberts, the math was simple. He made exactly $723.39 every two weeks on his security job. With the MTV gig, he'd make $1000 over the same time period. Still, Roberts didn't trust that his jump to performing for a living would pan out, or that the new show would last, so he kept his job at Andrew Jackson High. Demme scheduled the weekly taping for late Friday afternoons, after Roberts finished work. In a few hours, Roberts and Brown would tape a week's worth of episodes, and return thereafter to their homes in Queens and Long Island, respectively.

Demme's two-host concept and Brown's decision to go along with it both proved wise. The insanity of Doctor Dre and Ed Lover proved to be a perfect counterbalance to the cool of Fab 5 Freddy. Without a team of writers, the pair devised organic comedy routines that were genuinely funny, like Roberts' unhinged "Ed Lover Dance." Eventually, Doctor Dre's partner, T-Money, came on board to portray a bevy of characters.

Between Fab 5 Freddy's show airing twice on Saturdays and another two times on Sundays, and Dre and Ed's show running twice every weekday, MTV featured fourteen hours of *Yo! MTV Raps* per week by the summer of 1989. And the three Black hosts of *Yo!* became the most recognizable faces on the channel that had recently eschewed undiluted expressions of Blackness altogether.

The impact of *Yo! MTV Raps* reverberated through the entire entertainment business. Sales of rap records rocketed upward during the first year of *Yo!,* and the fortunes of obscure record outfits like Delicious Vinyl were made from airplay on the show. A greater number of rap videos—like "Wild Thing," and a new clip by Delicious Vinyl's Young MC called "Bust a Move"—graduated onto MTV's regular rotation because of their visibility on *Yo!*; and thus pop radio stations felt more pressure to play those songs, too.

Imitators emerged. Denise Barnes—half of Delicious Vinyl's girl group Body & Soul—was tapped to host a nationally syndicated program called *Pump It Up.* The proliferation of hip-hop clips lifted the fortunes of a pay-per-view video channel based in Miami called the Video Music Jukebox, unrelated to Ralph McDaniels's similarly titled New York show. Black Entertainment Television—the only African-American-owned cable channel—came late to the game, launching the show *Rap City* in 1989.

Hip-hop's television triumph extended beyond mere music video. In early 1989, comedian Arsenio Hall parlayed a guest stint on FOX's *The Late Show* into a nationally syndicated late-night talk show of his own—a first for an African-American. Hall regularly featured hip-hop acts as musical guests on his show, and the surging ratings of *The Arsenio Hall Show* began to make the producers of Johnny Carson's *Tonight Show* and David Letterman's *Late Night* nervous.

One year later the FOX network debuted a comedy variety show created by Black comedian Keenen Ivory Wayans, *In Living Color*, which featured a racially mixed cast that included Wayans's brother Damon, Jamie Foxx, and a rubber-limbed funny-man named Jim Carrey. Every episode featured a live performance from a different hip-hop or R&B artist. Hip-hop culture penetrated every part of the show—language, dress, and dance. The "Fly Girls" were a multicultural dance troupe assembled by choreographer-actress Rosie Perez rocking to hip-hop beats in between every sketch, while male viewers across America heatedly debated the relative merits of each dancer. A front-runner for their attentions was Jenny, the pretty Puerto Rican girl from MC Hammer's appearance on *Yo! MTV Raps*. Jennifer Lopez had just jumped to Hollywood.

One more television show rounded out hip-hop's journey into American living rooms. It started when an aspiring White producer named Jeff Pollack got an idea to make a sitcom about intergenerational conflict in a Black family. Pollack grafted that concept onto the life story of his friend Benny Medina—a young Black kid from the ghetto who had been taken in by a rich family in Beverly Hills and later rose to become the head of Black music at Warner Bros. Records.

Pollack and Medina didn't have to look far for the perfect performer to play their protagonist. Ken Hertz, a lawyer at Disney, told Pollack that film director John Landis had been raving about the kid he just filmed for Disneyland's thirty-fifth-anniversary television special, rapping a remake of "Supercalifragilisticexpialidocious."

"He's going to be the next Eddie Murphy," Landis told Hertz.

Ann Carli had uttered those exact words about Will Smith, the "Fresh Prince," two years earlier. But it was that comic image that kept Carli from including DJ Jazzy Jeff & the Fresh Prince in the Stop the Violence Movement. Since the release of "Parents Just Don't Understand," the duo had fallen from favor with the increasingly political, Afrocentric, hard-core hip-hop audience. Though they shared much of the musical and lyrical skill prized by the hard-core crowd, their lighthearted subject matter pushed them, literally, into the wonderful world of Disney.

When Pollack and Medina approached Smith about their sitcom concept, neither of them had any idea that he was in debt to the IRS to the tune of $250,000. Smith attached himself to the project without hesitation. Within a few months, the two producers aligned themselves with a young production executive at Quincy Jones's production company, and gained a spot as a last-minute addendum to a pitch meeting with Brandon Tartikoff, NBC's programming chief.

Tartikoff didn't like any of Jones's pitches. But he liked Pollack and Medina's idea for *The Fresh Prince of Bel-Air*.

Within a year the show was a part of the network's fall lineup, and Will Smith—the rapper from Philadelphia—was a TV star.

Ted Demme started his career at MTV as the plucky intern, then the pushy production assistant. But the *Yo!* show had made him a formidable player in the world of MTV. Now it was Demme's turn to be the mentor. In 1989, the second summer of *Yo!*, the kid came.

He was a White, Jewish Harvard student, a self-declared hip-hop fanatic. He pestered Pete Dougherty for an internship with repeated letters and phone calls. The kid was jumpy, high-strung, always coming with a suggestion or a comment when nobody really gave a shit. He hawked copies of his rap newsletter around the office and pestered artists about it when they visited. Worst of all, the kid thought he was going to be a rap star. He even had his own record out, a wack Beastie Boys rip-off. The new kid talked like he was the ultimate expert on hip-hop. Demme didn't like him. The kid didn't know his place.

"You guys should be interviewing this rapper from Boston, the Guru," the kid said.

The Guru? Some nobody from Boston? Who cared?

"Look," Demme said. "I know you know a lot about hip-hop. But this is TV, and you don't know a lot about TV. So you've got to listen to what *we* tell you to do."

Besides, if there was going to be a White hip-hop expert at MTV, Demme had decided it was going to be him.

But the kid kept on talking, and when Demme's patience reached an end, he stuck the kid in a place where he wouldn't have to hear his mouth.

"Come here for a second," Demme barked. "You see this room?" It was a closet with hundreds upon hundreds of videotape cartridges in unruly piles. "I need you to watch all these tapes and write down everything that's on them."

As Demme walked away, the kid, Jon Shecter, realized that he was screwed.

Shecter had come to MTV because he believed that *Yo!* was the most important force in hip-hop. It was the reason he begged for this unpaid job in the first place, while waiting tables in the evening for rent money. Yet the prospect of spending the rest of the summer in a windowless room logging hundreds of hours of tape wasn't what he had in mind. Neither Dougherty nor Demme seemed to appreciate him or what he had to offer.

One day Shecter walked into Demme's office and saw a bunch of brand-new *Yo! MTV Raps* T-shirts on Demme's desk.

"Oh, man!" Shecter exclaimed. "Can I have one?"

Demme looked at the new kid.

"No," Demme answered.

I'm working for free, and he won't give me a fucking T-shirt? Shecter fumed.

Being sent to the tape room was simply the latest indignity, and Shecter quit a few days later. He walked out of MTV's offices in Times Square toward the summer apartment in Greenwich Village he was sharing his high school friend, Will Braveman, now a student at NYU—and the guy who, by sheer chance, had inherited Rick Rubin's dorm room.

Shecter's MTV gig wasn't the only thing that had gone to hell. His rap career had, too.

The advent of the Beastie Boys convinced Shecter that White kids like him could legitimately participate in hip-hop. Performing as "J the Sultan," Shecter teamed up with another high school buddy, Kevin "Kevvy Kev" Krakower, to form the White Boys. Almost on cue, Braveman called from New York with a proposition. There was an NYU film student named Brett Ratner with lots of connections who wanted to manage a rap group. Ratner sold the idea of the White Boys to Seymour Stein at Sire/Warner Bros. Records, who signed Shecter and Krakower for one single. Unfortunately, the name the

White Boys had been taken by another nascent group diving for the Beasties' coattails. So Shecter changed his group's moniker to BMOC, and Ratner had the pair photographed in Harvard sweatshirts, right on Harvard Yard.

Before the death of Boogie Down Productions producer Scott La Rock in 1987, Ratner had hired him to produce BMOC's record. Shecter was ecstatic to be working with the hottest producer in hip-hop. But in the studio, Ratner said something wrong, and Scott La Rock had bounced.

Scott La Rock's replacement was Chic's producer Nile Rodgers, a man who hadn't enjoyed currency in hip-hop since "Good Times" became the backing track for "Rapper's Delight." Rogers created a predictable musical interpolation of White Cherry's "Play That Funky Music, White Boy." If the track was unimpressive, then Shecter and Krakower's rhymes matched it perfectly.

Still Ratner made a go of promoting his new group, scheduling a showcase for BMOC at Tom Silverman's New Music Seminar, the paramount gathering for the growing rap music industry. The audience jeered at the collegiate shtick of "J the Sultan" and "Kevvy Kev," then howled as "Chill" Will Braveman—one of BMOC's "dancers"—tripped over a cord.

After the disastrous gig, Ratner and his girlfriend, a model named Rebecca Gayheart, met the group upstairs at Sbarro's in Times Square for a postmortem. Ratner screamed at Shecter and Krakower, and ordered Braveman to leave after he made a few sarcastic comments. Braveman tossed his slice of pizza at Ratner and walked away. Ratner ran after Braveman and hit him in the side of his head with a karate chop. Braveman pummeled Ratner until Shecter broke up the fight.

That, pretty much, was the end of BMOC.

Being an MC wasn't Shecter's true motivation. Making a contribution to hip-hop was. Now that the rap career had ended and the MTV gig was over, Shecter would now focus all of his energies on one remaining avenue.

Back at Will Braveman's apartment, Jon Shecter's eyes fell upon a copy of his rap magazine, a scheme concocted by his roommate at Harvard, Dave Mays, to promote their campus radio show. In a year, their one-page newsletter had grown into the new issue before him now: forty pages, with his favorite rapper, KRS-One, on a color cover. At the top, the title read:

THE SOURCE

Three years earlier, as a college freshman, Jon Shecter was playing rap records on the turntable in his dorm, Strauss Hall in Harvard Yard, when he went to answer a knock at the door.

It was the sweatsuit guy. Shecter had seen him around campus, but they had never spoken. Shecter had, in fact, never heard the sweatsuit guy utter a word. He was tall, quiet, with a pencil-thin mustache and always seemed to be wearing Fila or Adidas gear. The sweatsuit guy introduced himself as Dave Mays and asked what Shecter was playing.

"It's DJ Jazzy Jeff," Shecter said. "He's the best DJ in Philly."

"I like it," Mays replied.

Shecter had a fleeting sense that the sweatsuit guy was almost desperate for a friend. He invited Mays inside.

"Are you into go-go?"

"What the hell is 'go-go'?" Shecter asked.

"Man, back in D.C., that's like the biggest music," Mays replied. "Everyone loves go-go."

"Naw," Shecter said. "I'm into hip-hop."

Over the following weeks and months, Shecter taught Mays about Philadelphia rap, and Mays introduced Shecter to Chuck Brown, Rare Essence, Experience Unlimited, and Trouble Funk, the Washington, D.C., groups that comprised the core of the "go-go" scene, where percussion-heavy bands jammed in hours-long sets for sweaty clubgoers. In short order, Shecter and Mays formed a strong friendship upon a simple circumstance: being two White, Jewish guys at Harvard who loved Black music.

Shecter's musical indoctrination began in grade school, at Friends Select, a Quaker institution in center city Philadelphia that he attended with Will Braveman. He had become friendly with a Black classmate, Chris Wilder, in part because they took the same way home from school. Wilder introduced Shecter to hip-hop; local acts like DJ Jazzy Jeff & the Fresh Prince, Steady B, Schoolly D and Cool C; and to the weekly rap show on WHAT-AM hosted since 1979 by "Lady B"—a female rapper named Wendy Clark who was Philly's answer to Mr. Magic. Shecter's obsessiveness about hip-hop soon exceeded Wilder's. With regular trips to the record store, Shecter amassed a library of 12-inch singles, transferring the songs to cassette tape and playing them on a boom box during trips to "Rubber Park"—a playground near the Delaware River, so named for the plastic cushioning installed to protect the knees of toddlers that also served the needs of local break dancers. At Rubber Park, Shecter believed he had found his place in the hip-hop community as a source of information about new records.

Shecter's musical education was, more profoundly, a racial education. As close as he and Wilder had become, as similar as their musical tastes were, Shecter wasn't Black, Wilder wasn't White, and no "integration" was altogether comfortable for either of them. Shecter and Wilder both lived with the discomfort by making fun of it, as kids often do. They shared a running joke about Wilder's proclivity to talk slang with his Black friends and then "translate" for Shecter. And when a new FM radio station—WUSL, or Power 99—emerged during Shecter's freshman year, aiming to bridge the gap between local rock and R&B stations, Shecter and Wilder mercilessly mocked its tactless programming strategy: *Play a bunch of white-bread pop songs. Then play Paul McCartney and Stevie Wonder's "Ebony and Ivory." Transition to a bunch of Black funk and soul songs. Play "Ebony and Ivory" again. And repeat.*

In 1984, Power 99 dumped the pop from its playlist and lifted Lady B's rap show from WHAT. Overnight, Power 99 went from laughingstock to cultural locus. Jon Shecter, only a junior in high school, wanted to be a part of it. Shecter wrote letters and called the station until he got himself in front of Tony Gray, the music director and nighttime jock. Gray started Shecter on simple tasks, like filing music. Eventually, Shecter's enthusiasm made him a nightly presence at the station, where he recorded commercials and on-air promos, and tabulated listener requests for the "Top 9 at 9." Sometimes, Gray would even let Shecter help him announce the countdown. Shecter's friends could scarcely believe he had such a cool job.

But Shecter discovered that Power 99 wasn't as progressive as he had imagined. The guys who ran the station didn't seem to like the music they programmed. Tony Gray, who was Black, preferred Jimi Hendrix, Led Zeppelin, and Foreigner. Gray's boss, a White program director named Jeff Wyatt, seemed to have an aversion to playing rap, except for the undeniable hits like UTFO's "Roxanne, Roxanne." Even Lady B's show, "Street Beat," was tucked away in a Sunday-night slot, where her music could build the station's cachet among young males without offending Power's core audience of older females.

Tony Gray yawned when UTFO actually stopped through to promote their new single, "Leader of the Pack." Instead he handed them off to the appreciative Shecter, instructing the kid to record a few drops and promos with the group. Shecter kept thinking: *I can't believe I am in a room with UTFO*. The group, on the other hand, wondered: *Who is this White boy who knows every word on every track of our album?*

Before UTFO left, Shecter and the group exchanged numbers. Two months later, Shecter got a surprise phone call.

"What's going on, man?" one of the rappers said. "We're in Philly."

Shecter's parents happened to be out of town, so he invited them up to the apartment.

"You know any girls?" one of them asked.

And within a few hours, Jon and a whole bunch of teenage girls were hanging out with UTFO in the Shecters' apartment.

Before they departed, UTFO's Kangol Kid left Jon a souvenir on the out-going message of the Shecter family's answering machine: "Jon went to get a snack, / But if you leave a message, he'll call you right back. / Take it from me, the leader of the pack."

Over the next few weeks, the Shecters received dozens of random calls from rap fans, phoning in just to hear the message.

Shecter wasn't yet through with school, but as far as Jon was concerned, he had just graduated.

When Shecter got to Harvard he gravitated toward the campus radio station, WHRB, where Shecter and Dave Mays launched their own rap show, "Street Beat," named after Lady B's program in Philly. It was a theft of convenience: Shecter needed "bumpers" and promos for his show, so he went back to Power 99 and covertly copied hers.

Commercial radio stations in the Boston area didn't play rap, nor much Black music. Hungry hip-hop fans were forced to surf an audio archipelago of college mix shows: WERS at Emerson, WRBB at Northeastern, and now WHRB at Harvard. Hundreds of listeners lit up the phone lines with requests. Mays reached out to local acts, like the RSO Crew, and played their demo tapes and records. RSO's DJ, Def Jeff, became the show's main jock, because neither Shecter nor Mays were very dextrous on the "wheels of steel."

WHRB was an unusual college station in that it aired commercials. One day the station announced a new fund-raising initiative: If any DJ or staff member sold a spot to advertisers, they would get to keep 10 percent of the fee as a commission. In high school Mays had been a top independent salesperson for Time-Life Books, so he had little trepidation approaching Boston-area record stores. But Mays got a lot of resistance selling ads for WHRB. *Nobody listens to that station*, the proprietors said.

Mays set out to prove them wrong. He began by carefully writing down the name and address of every caller.

"Why are you doing that?" Shecter asked, looking at Mays like he was crazy. *What a waste of time.*

Over the weeks, Mays's list grew into the hundreds. He showed the list to the skeptical shopkeepers, and soon they were buying airtime. After a year, he had accumulated several thousand names, and he had conceived of another way to make money from the list—a newsletter to promote the radio show.

The first, one-page edition of *The Source* contained the "Street Beat" playlist. Mays sold four ads for $65 apiece, one each from the record shops Mattapan Music, Skippy Whites, Spin City, and another from Jive Records. Local shops took reams of the newsletter for their rap-curious customers, and Mays sent *The Source* to record companies around the country, many of whom relied on "Street Beat" to get the word out about their rap acts in Boston.

It was the summer of 1988, just before their junior year, and one year before Shecter took his *Yo! MTV Raps* internship. Jon Shecter was staying at Will Braveman's apartment in New York when he had gotten that first yellow newsletter in the mail. He hadn't taken Dave's idea too seriously until that point. Now he understood. *The Source* was a promotional tool. But it could be something more meaningful.

Jon Shecter had never heard of the "Hip-Hop Hitlist," the small rap magazine from New Jersey featuring the columns of Tokyo Rose that fizzled out the previous year. He had seen a couple of attempts at rap periodicals in Philadelphia, one called "Crush," from a local kid named Mike Elliot, and another from Lady B, but he hadn't been impressed. As a rap fan, Shecter was frustrated that there was so little to read about his favorite artists. Teenybopper magazines like *Black Beat* and *Right On!* were written for little girls, with headlines like "Win LL Cool J's Pinky Ring!" and "Beastie Boys: Naughty Rappers on the Rise!" Most publications that took pop music seriously, like *Rolling Stone* and *The New York Times*, ignored hip-hop. *Spin* was a White alternative-rock magazine, but they made room occasionally for the Beasties, Run-DMC, and

Public Enemy. The *Village Voice* had a similar editorial outlook, and they had just run an incredible collection of articles called "Hip-Hop Nation," which seemed to recognize this pivotal moment in the genre's history.

The "Hip-Hop Nation" special was the first time that Shecter read the writing of Harry Allen, the former classmate of Chuck D and Bill Stephney who penned poetic, political contemplations on hip-hop. Allen called himself "the first person to grow up on hip-hop and write about it." At *Spin*, John Leland was rap-friendly, but the White writer's review of Public Enemy— arguing that rap wasn't best-suited as political music—incurred Chuck D's wrath and inspired the rapper to write "Bring the Noise." *Billboard*'s Nelson George might not have branded himself as a "hip-hop" writer like Harry Allen, but he certainly was writing about it before anyone else. Between these three scribes, Shecter could occasionally read intelligent discourse on hip-hop, but not often enough.

When Mays and Shecter agreed to work together on the second issue of *The Source*, Shecter decided that the publication would be a home to a new, distinctly "hip-hop" journalism. Shecter would do most of the writing, while Mays would publish the newsletter and sell ads.

Shecter and Mays operated on a tiny budget. They began their partnership by pitching in $100 each. Their ad revenue barely covered their printing costs and postage. Shecter enlisted free writing help from high school friends like "Chill" Will Braveman and "Pistol" Pete Goldman. By the third issue, Shecter and Mays started featuring artists on the cover, first Slick Rick, and next, a strange new group from Tommy Boy called De La Soul.

Between Shecter's articles and Mays's distribution tactics, *The Source* quickly gained a readership outside the local area. Retailers and record companies began to see *The Source* as a promotional vehicle even more potent than Mays and Shecter's radio show. Mays sold more half- and full-page slots to record companies like Profile, Tommy Boy, Select, and Def Jam.

In his quest for more record company ad dollars, Mays envisioned *The Source* as the *Billboard* for the rap business. He devoted half of the magazine to charts from record stores and rap radio DJs around the country. *The Source* also published several "regional reports" by knowledgeable people— DJs, retailers, promoters, and writers—from at least ten different markets, reflecting growing rap scenes in places like Houston, Miami, Detroit, and Seattle. Shecter tried to chronicle the regional explosion, devoting one of his first covers to Los Angeles's NWA and Oakland's Too Short, under the headline, "California Rap Hits Nationwide!" By the end of the school year, *The Source* had adopted the slogan, "The Voice of the Rap Music Industry."

During the summer of 1989, while Shecter was interning at *Yo!*, Mays remained in Boston to publish the magazine, manage the RSO Crew, and promote parties. One week, Mays visited Shecter in New York, and Will Braveman's friend brought someone whom he wanted the two *Source* founders to meet, another collegiate hip-hop fanatic from NYU named Matteo Capoluongo. As it turned out, Capoluongo and Mays had known each other from D.C., from the time they were twelve years old, and Capoluongo was a breakdancer. Capoluongo was a lot like Mays, in that his unself-conscious adoption of Black culture, his style of dress and his southern Italian look made him appear racially ambiguous.

The two *Source* partners immediately brought Capoluongo into the fold. He carried stacks of magazines to record shops, checked on inventory, and expanded *The Source*'s national list of DJs and record shops. The latter task, Capoluongo learned, was Mays's master plan: Publish the charts of every important disc jockey and record store across the country and gain their support by giving them publicity in the magazine. Capoluongo soon had a list of contacts just as powerful as those of Def Jam, Tommy Boy, and Profile. As "Matty C," Capoluongo began writing record reviews in the magazine, although Shecter was even more enthused that Matty knew how to do a dance called "the running man." Capoluongo patiently taught the steps to the bespectacled editor.

When the founders returned to Boston at the end of the summer, Capoluongo and his friend Rob Tewlow became *The Source*'s stringers in New York, covering industry parties and rap performances as writer and photographer, respectively. Their credentials granted them free access to any club in the city, and garnered them stacks of promotional vinyl, the sole remuneration for their work. With Capoluongo's help on the publishing and editorial sides, *The Source*'s motto—"The Voice of the Rap Music Industry"—was becoming the truth.

Not everyone agreed. During that long, hot summer of 1989, Shecter listened to a message on his answering machine: *Hello, this is Harry Allen. I believe there are many voices of the rap music industry. I'm a voice of the rap music industry. Chuck D is a voice of the rap music industry.*

Despite Allen's pique, Shecter was excited to hear from his favorite writer.

And Shecter was particularly sensitive to Allen's point. So he invited Allen to contribute an opinion piece about a scandal that had befallen Public Enemy after Chuck D's "Minister of Information," Professor Griff, told reporter David Mills at *The Washington Times* that Jews were responsible for "the majority of the wickedness that goes on across the globe."

It was, perhaps, the first time that most mainstream media paid attention to Public Enemy.

The frenzy over PE was just part of rap's larger public relations problem. That same summer, journalists at local New York newspapers erroneously linked the Central Park Jogger "wilding" incident to Tone-Loc's pop-rap song, "Wild Thing." Shecter began to see *The Source* as an opportune venue to counter the mainstream media's hip-hop disinformation. With regard to Public Enemy, Shecter, as a Jew, didn't take Griff or his words too seriously. He didn't believe that Chuck D felt the same way. And Chuck was the reason why Shecter respected Public Enemy and supported their agenda of Black liberation.

To Harry Allen, that was the very conceit that blinded Shecter. How could Shecter's magazine be an appropriate venue to support Black liberation at all? *The Source* was a White-owned magazine about an African-American culture that was already in White hands. White people owned most of the independent labels and all of the majors to which rap acts were signed. They owned most of the radio stations, even the purportedly "Black" outlets. How could Shecter possibly support Black Nationalism, Allen argued, when he had just insinuated himself as rap's voice—even as a liberal, supposedly well-intentioned one?

Over the past year, Shecter himself had become aware that a few Black students on Harvard's campus shared Allen's skepticism. He and Mays had caused a stir when they escorted their college girlfriends, both of them Black, to a dance sponsored by a Black student organization. Shecter wished he could keep as cool as Mays did under the heated stares they got that night. Mays didn't seem to think that he was doing anything wrong, and didn't give a shit what anybody thought about him. Shecter, on the other hand, cared.

Things at Harvard came to a head when Shecter was approached by KRS-One's publicist, Leyla Turkkan, with a proposition. Turkkan was creating a speaking tour for the political rapper on the college circuit, and she asked Shecter to assist her in bringing KRS-One to Harvard. Shecter, who had been friendly with the rapper since his BMOC days, loved the idea and pledged to help.

Shecter attended a meeting of the Black Students Association, and made a brief presentation. Would they be willing to sponsor KRS-One coming to campus? Shecter asked.

"That's incredible!" said one.

"Let's do it," said another.

In the weeks after the meeting, Shecter busied himself with trying to nail down a date and a venue. Then a friend of his from the Black Students Association called.

"Man, I got some bad news," he said. "We had another meeting and decided that the committee is not going to support KRS-One coming to Harvard."

Shecter couldn't believe what he was hearing. "What? Why!?"

His friend replied that some of the students were concerned about the possibility of violence at a rap-oriented event.

"We wouldn't want to be associated with that."

"You have got to be kidding me," Shecter said. He had already told Turkkan the event was on. He felt like an asshole. Shecter scrambled to find another sponsor. As it turned out, the leaders of the graduate Black student union at the Kennedy School of Government were excited to step in and help.

On the night of the event, thousands of students, faculty, and guests gathered in the Kennedy School to hear KRS-One speak on a panel with a number of Harvard professors. One problem: no KRS-One.

After an hour of waiting, the head of the Kennedy school decided to start the event. A half hour later, the rapper was nowhere to be found. Shecter called Turkkan.

"Where is he?" Shecter demanded.

"He got on the plane," Turkkan replied.

Shecter was jumping out of his skin. He had promised them KRS-One. Now he looked like a fraud. Shecter had to leave the auditorium to gather his thoughts. While pacing outside, Shecter caught a glimpse of a crowd down the block.

It was him. As the crowd drew closer, Shecter saw KRS-One—the rapper well over six feet tall—towering over a bunch of kids, leading them like the pied piper toward the auditorium.

"Yo, Kris, where have you been?" Shecter sputtered. "You're late!"

"What do you mean?" the rapper answered. "I got on the plane. I got off the plane. I'm here."

"You don't understand. There are hundreds of people waiting for you inside!" Shecter said.

"Well," said KRS-One, "what are we waiting for? Let's go."

KRS-One entered to murmurs, and mounted the stage to thunderous applause.

I did it, Shecter thought. *I got KRS-One to Harvard.*

Shecter might have felt a great weight lifted off of his shoulders, if KRS-One hadn't given him his clunky video camera to hold.

"Tape this for me," he requested.

Shecter's upper body was almost numb from holding the camera aloft, as the rapper spoke to a rapt audience. After a while, KRS-One opened the floor to questions, and a young Black woman stood.

"There's two White boys here on the Harvard campus that think they can run a rap magazine," she began. "We don't like it. We don't think this is right. Rap magazines should not be run by White people. What do you think?"

Now the rest of Shecter's body went numb. For what seemed a long, terrifying moment, the rapper said nothing. But what would he say? KRS-One had the power, in that moment, to make or break the reputation of the magazine. *My whole life is on the line here,* Shecter thought. *Dave and I have been working our asses off on* The Source, *day and night. We have no money. We barely do any schoolwork.* Now it all came down to this. The rapper looked at Shecter, then at the student, and began:

"I know who you're talking about," KRS-One said. "You shouldn't point the finger at them and ask why are they doing that. You should point your finger at yourself and say, 'Why aren't *I* doing that?'"

Now even the camera on Shecter's sore shoulder felt light. KRS-One continued:

"If you think you can do better, outdo them. Please outdo them. If you think you can do better, by all means, I *beg* you, outdo them."

Shecter floated through the rest of the night, which passed in a blur until, hours later, he found himself sitting alone at a table with KRS-One in a coffee shop off of Harvard Square.

Shecter thanked him for coming. He thanked him for the perfect answer he gave that very difficult question. But he also needed to ask for something more. It was a question that he and Dave had discussed beforehand, one that was key to the future of the magazine.

"Will you be our spokesperson?" Shecter said. "Will you officially affiliate yourself with *The Source*?"

"Yes," KRS-One responded, without hesitation. "I will." Sitting with the most influential rapper in hip-hop, looking out onto the bustle of Harvard Square, Shecter decided that this was the greatest night of his life. Even better than the night UTFO came to his parents house.

For every skeptic that Shecter encountered, there were thousands of loyal readers and supporters. Shecter got calls from all over the country. A young student from the University of Southern California, a self-described "hip-hop filmmaker," phoned just to say he loved the magazine.

The student, John Singleton, had yet to make his first movie. But he and Shecter shared regular long-distance calls about hip-hop and cinema.

Accolades came from unexpected places. Julian Bond, an ally of Dr. Martin Luther King Jr. and founder of the legendary civil rights organization the Student Nonviolent Coordinating Committee, taught a class at Harvard, which Shecter attended along with dozens of other students.

"I don't know if everyone knows this," Bond began one day. "One of our fellow students is doing a magazine about hip-hop. I got a chance to look through it, and I think it's really something special. You guys should check it out. It's called *The Source*. And the guy's name is Jonathan Shecter. He's sitting over there."

Shecter was stunned. He had never told Bond what he was doing. He approached the professor after class to thank him.

"Hey, I'm just calling it like I see it," Bond replied. "I think it's a great magazine." A few other Black people on campus felt the same way. Two of them would be key to *The Source*'s future success.

James Bernard—the son of a doctor from Nashville, Tennessee—had just finished his first year at Harvard Law School, but he had already soured on the notion that he could create social change though a legal career. He spent more time as a campus activist than he did studying. With his classmate John Bonifaz, Bernard organized a takeover of the dean's office to protest the elimination of the school's public service placement office.

Bernard acquired a taste for direct action in high school, where he led protests against nuclear weapons, and at Brown University, where he and other students were put before a campus tribunal for making a citizen's arrest of a CIA recruiter, then later acquitted. In the year before he arrived at Harvard, he went to work for the Service Employees International Union in San

Francisco. Bernard was only in his early twenties, but he was surrounded by seasoned veterans who knew how to play dirty with their opponents, and with one another. During a hospital strike, one of his colleagues flushed a chemical-filled balloon down a toilet so the pipes would burst. Another time, his organizer was driving in her car and found that her brake lines were cut, most likely by a rival faction in the union.

Bernard understood hip-hop as another powerful form of protest. He saw his first copy of *The Source* in a record store while working a summer job at a law firm in Berkeley, California. He had never read this kind of sophisticated material about hip-hop. A glance at the masthead revealed that the magazine had come from an address near Harvard.

Bernard went back to his firm, dialed the number listed for *The Source*, and left an effusive message, saying he would love to be involved with the magazine in any way. A few days later, he got a call from Shecter. They arranged to meet upon Bernard's return.

If Jon Shecter was surprised that James Bernard was Black when he arrived at *The Source*'s barren offices north of campus in Somerville, Massachusetts, Bernard was even more shocked that Shecter and his partner were White. But Bernard felt at one with the mission of *The Source*—to dignify the coverage of hip-hop—and soon threw himself into the work of writing and editing articles, typesetting on the small Macintosh computers, pasting the layout for publishing, and assembling the bulk mailings of the issues, printed at a nearby Kinko's. Working in close quarters, Bernard observed a world of difference between the two partners, who had, by now, become friends and roommates. Shecter was sloppy, disorganized, a procrastinator. Mays was neat, perfunctory, and rigid. They both loved hip-hop. But Jon was a complete White boy in his baseball cap and round wire-framed glasses. Dave, as Bernard observed, dressed, walked, talked, and even kept his red Volkswagen Jetta like a Black person would: spotless and smelling good.

The trio was soon joined by another eager volunteer. Dave Mays always suspected Ed Young was one of the Black guys on campus who hated him for crossing all kinds of cultural lines without permission. Young disabused Mays of that notion when he showed up one day—fresh from a yearlong internship at the political magazine *The New Republic*—offering to help.

Young heard about *The Source* from a mutual friend, and thought that Dave Mays had already accomplished something special. Mays was the best salesperson Young had ever seen, but Young had publishing experience that

Mays lacked. Gradually, a new division of labor emerged among the four young men. Mays dealt with the record labels. Young joined Mays on the publishing side, assuming the details of printing, production, and budgeting. On the editorial side, Shecter handled the music coverage, but asked Bernard to handle the areas where Shecter felt himself weak: politics and history.

Shecter encouraged Bernard to launch a regular political column. "Doin' the Knowledge" wasn't about hip-hop, but rather the political and socioeconomic events that surrounded and inspired it: the growth of the underclass, police brutality, the crack epidemic, the culture wars in the media and the academy.

"We who are connected to rap culture do more than trade slabs of vinyl," Bernard wrote. "Through our music, young African-Americans inject their previously silenced perspective into the national dialogue. . . . Rap artists remind America that all Black lives have meaning."

These were words, Bernard knew, that even so-called Black magazines like *Ebony* and *Jet* would never print—run, as they were, by the older, establishment-oriented civil rights generation. Nor would those publications do what Shecter was about to: put Malcolm X, the resurgent icon of a new generation of hip-hop fans, on the cover of his magazine.

Shecter and Bernard, Mays and Young worked together over several issues, subsisting on rap and ramen noodles for weeks on end. Each issue made just enough money to cover the costs of the next edition and pay for a celebratory meal at Boston Chicken. Bernard and Young had made themselves indispensable, and Mays and Shecter offered to bring them in as partners. But things were hectic, and with Mays, Shecter, and Young's graduations approaching fast, there would be time, later, to put things on paper.

In the meantime, Young applied some of the lessons he learned at *The New Republic* in mapping out the future of *The Source*. Young knew there were two ways to grow the magazine. One way was to get more subscribers so Dave Mays could charge more for ads. But building a subscriber base was expensive—it involved direct mail campaigns and fulfillment plans that cost lots of money. Young believed that *The Source* should build circulation another way—by getting newsstand distribution. So they set about to find some wholesalers who would take a chance on their rap magazine, and tried to keep cash flow high by collecting money from subscribers up front. No magazines would ever be sent out until money had been collected.

One day, Young presented some unsolicited advice to Shecter and Mays—his theory that musical genres like hip-hop followed the same "S-curve" development cycle that most businesses did. Young announced that hip-hop, unlike disco, had made it out of the crucial "innovation" stage, and was about to embark on the "growth" phase of the curve—with new institutions like record companies, management firms, TV shows, and, *yes*, magazines, rising to fill the growing demand.

"Yeah, Ed," Mays said, shaking his head. "Ed's a goof." He didn't need Young's "S-curve" and talk of "thirteen-year periodicity" to tell him that hip-hop was blowing up.

Young just smiled and restated his conclusion in simpler language.

"Guys," Young said, "if we do this, we're never going to have to work for anybody."

Of course, being "the voice" of the rap music industry meant serving several constituencies simultaneously: the fans who bought the magazine, the artists who created the culture, and the companies who marketed the records and kept *The Source* afloat with advertising dollars. Often giving voice to one of them meant angering another, like the time that KRS-One decried the DJ and MC battles at Tom Silverman's New Music Seminar, ignoring his own philosophy about "outdoing" White-owned businesses:

"By no means should a little wimpy White guy like Tom Silverman— because I think there's a lot more stronger White people than him—come up out of somewhere and have a whole lot of Black rap artists battle each other while he sits back and collects $300 a ticket," Shecter quoted KRS-One as saying.

Silverman's Tommy Boy Records had, up until that point, bought full-page ads in every issue of *The Source* for the past year. In the next issue, Mays and Shecter printed this apology:

"To Tom Silverman and the New Music Seminar, we apologize. We like to think of *The Source* as a unifying force in the rap industry rather than a divisive one. Thus, while we still plan to cover controversial issues, we hope to do so in a more evenhanded manner."

Tommy Boy would continue to be *The Source*'s most important sponsor. KRS-One would continue to grace the pages of magazine. And the owners of *The Source* would continue to balance art and commerce, fanaticism and criticism, realizing that truth was often somewhere in between.

For his first issue of the 1990s, Shecter had something grand in mind to commemorate the end of the 1980s: a sixty-one-page edition, his largest ever, called "The Rap Music Decade."

The issue included the first published time line of hip-hop's history, assembled by Shecter and Bernard; an oral history of "old-school" pioneers including Afrika Bambaataa, Caz, and Kurtis Blow; an overview of the independent labels who funded the hip-hop revolution when major labels wouldn't; and an unprecedented survey of hip-hop producers like Hank Shocklee, Marley Marl, and Andre "Dr. Dre" Young. Funken-Klein, the former Def Jam employee who had formed a management and production company with DJ Red Alert, covered hip-hop's growing scenes in Europe, Asia, and Africa. Harry Allen, John Leland, and even Shecter's old boss, Ted Demme, contributed their memories and favorite records to a copious offering of lists and charts.

When it was put to bed, "The Rap Music Decade" issue was the most comprehensive history of hip-hop to date, from a multiplicity of voices: Black and White, businesspeople and artists. Frank Owen at *Spin* magazine called it "one of the best collections of hip-hop journalism ever." The sheer effort had taken a toll on Jon Shecter's schoolwork, but he considered the issue his senior thesis. He was ready to move on.

Shecter and Mays decided that they would continue their undergraduate experiment after graduation, in New York. But the partners were barely able to cover their expenses in Boston. They wondered how would they be able to afford an office with a Manhattan-size rent, and salaries for themselves and others, much less their already paralyzing printing and shipping costs. Mays suggested that they make their advertising clients a generous offer: a substantially discounted rate if they would pay for a year's worth of advertising up front. The gambit worked. Tommy Boy Records and Sony Music advanced *The Source* a collective $85,000, and in May of 1990, the two founders and Young moved out of their dorms and headed south. Young lived with his parents in Montclair, New Jersey, while Shecter and Mays temporarily bunked with friends.

Meanwhile, Bernard, who still had one more year of law school to finish, finagled a way to complete his studies at Berkeley, back in the Bay Area—because he had a girlfriend there, and because he believed the Bay Area was growing into the hottest hip-hop scene in the country. The Harvard administration allowed him to do it, perhaps relieved that their number one troublemaker would finally be off campus. Shecter approved Bernard's plan to set up the West Coast offices of *The Source*, where he would be responsible for sending back at least a third of each monthly issue. Before he left, Bernard's friends threw him a going-away party, and invited many of his activist coconspirators, like John Bonifaz.

One of the people who came to see Bernard off was a fellow student who had come on a few occasions to see Bernard's speeches and protests, and hung out with Bernard in the student center at Harkness Commons. He was a well-known guy around campus himself, but unlike Bernard, he didn't find his fame from rabble-rousing. He was a stellar student, the first Black editor of the *Harvard Law Review*. And he arrived just in time to see his buddy Bernard being blindfolded and placed in front of a piñata.

The managing editor of *The Source*, stick in hand, took a first swing at his uncharted future—something to do with hip-hop, multiracial partnerships, and social change.

What James Bernard couldn't see was his friend Barack Obama in front of him, smiling.

With a tip from Bill Stephney, *The Source* rented a small one-room office on the tenth floor of 594 Broadway, the building that once housed Rick Rubin and now served as the headquarters for Stephney and Hank Shocklee's new label, Sound of Urban Listeners, or SOUL Records. Mays and Shecter assembled a staff with their meager resources. Shecter hired his old school buddy from Philadelphia, Chris Wilder, as the managing editor. Matty Capoluongo, still a full-time student at NYU, accepted a few hundred dollars a month to edit the monthly charts and compile the "Ear to the Street" industry gossip section. Capoluongo brought Rob Tewlow along as photographer and reviews editor. Mark Weinstein—an older, chain-smoking, gravel-voiced New Yorker who had made a small business for himself promoting rap videos to TV and cable shows across the country—wrote a regular feature as "Captain Video." And Dave "Funken-Klein" penned a gossip column called "Gangsta Limpin'," its title owing to Klein's postoperative gait following surgery for spinal cancer.

In its summer 1990 issue, *The Source* bestowed a rapturous review on the debut rap album from A Tribe Called Quest, part of a new collective of Afrocentric groups that included De La Soul, the Jungle Brothers, and Queen

Latifah. Inspired by Afrika Bambaataa's Zulu Nation and managed by DJ Red Alert and Funken-Klein, they called themselves the "Native Tongues," making a point to spread messages of "positive vibes." *The Source* rhapsodized over the first solo effort from Ice Cube. Freed from NWA and Ruthless Records—but bereft of the stellar production of Ruthless producer Dr. Dre—Ice Cube recorded "AmeriKKKa's Most Wanted" for Priority Records in collaboration with the producers of Public Enemy: Chuck D, Hank and Keith Shocklee, Eric Sadler, and Bill Stephney, who together called themselves "the Bomb Squad."

While Shecter charted new musical movements, Young continued his quest for newsstand distribution. The only places that reliably carried *The Source* were in small record shops or chains that catered to the hip-hop crowd—like the Music Factory in New York and Leopold's in Berkeley, where James Bernard saw his first copy. But Young's attempts to solicit a national distributor were universally dismissed.

"We do not think that your magazine is a viable national title," read a letter from Curtis Circulation Company, one of the biggest distributors. The rejection letters kept coming from more companies—Kable, Hearst, DSI—all of which Young tacked above his desk. He called it the "Wall of Woe."

Without the help of a distributor, Young was forced to approach local wholesalers directly. Young crossed the country by car to convince these outfits to carry *The Source*. Predictably, he met with resistance from the buyers, all of them White, male, and middle-aged. It was around this time that Ed Young began praying for gray hair—something that would make him seem a bit more seasoned.

"I know I'm a young Black guy trying to convince you to sell this magazine," went one of Young's sales spiels. "I know that you just see Black faces here. I know that there's never been any crossover to mainstream audiences with something that looks like this. But let me ask you: Have you bothered to stop and hear what your kids are listening to in their rooms? Or what your wives are dancing to in their aerobics classes?"

Young's evangelism eventually landed *The Source* a relationship with three regional wholesalers in New York, Los Angeles, and Oakland, California. But the economics of these arrangements were tough. To place their magazine on newsstands, *The Source* now had to print hundreds of thousands of copies at their own expense, in an industry where well-established titles sold only one-third of the copies they printed. In *The Source*'s first issue with its New York distributor, Hudson News, the magazine's "sell-through" was 18 percent. If Young was disappointed, Hudson owner Jimmy Cohen was pleasantly surprised. Young worked with Cohen and the other wholesalers to maximize their profits and minimize his printing runs by targeting specific newsstands based on both socioeconomic data and sales figures of rap albums.

For the first time, newsstands in three major cities carried a magazine dedicated strictly to hip-hop.

"The Voice of the Rap Music Industry" now lived on Broadway, at the industry's epicenter, supported in large part by the small, independent companies nearby that produced and promoted most of the hip-hop in America to date: Def Jam, Select, Profile, Wild Pitch, Cold Chillin', and Tommy Boy. Though major corporations like Sony and Warner Bros. bankrolled many of these independents, the major labels themselves had yet to build credible rap rosters of their own. Like the natives who carved Broadway out of the Manhattan wilderness, the independent labels laid down hip-hop's guerrilla paths through the backwaters of the entertainment business. The indies had the maps to this land. The majors, for all their muscle and machinery, did not. For the most part, their early efforts to sign and promote rap failed miserably.

Major labels promoted records directly to radio station program and music directors; but smaller rap labels had direct relationships with the weekend mix jocks who could create a groundswell for new records. Major labels used their huge distribution systems to pump records into large chain stores like Musicland; but independent labels had access to the retail proving ground for hip-hop: the small specialty and "mom and pop" shops, and the independent distributors who sold to them. Major labels had great influence with MTV; but independent labels had long fed the smaller, syndicated and local video shows like *Video Music Box* that still had sizable, loyal audiences. Major labels had publicists with established ties to newspapers and rock music magazines like *Rolling Stone*; but the independent labels cultivated a relationship of mutual respect with *The Source*, viewing one another as partners in the same struggle. So when clueless major label flacks plied *The Source* with advances of some "really great" rap group, Shecter and his staff wrote tepid, often savage reviews. In lieu of acclaim, the majors sank money into full-page advertisements for groups like the UBC, KC Flight, and Movement X—groups that quickly faded from view—proving that marketing budgets couldn't compensate for marketing savvy.

The archetype for independent prowess was increasingly set by Tommy Boy Records. A few years after Tom Silverman sold his company to Warner Bros. in 1985, he and Monica Lynch decided that Warner's vaunted sales machine couldn't do more for them than they could do themselves. So Silverman and Lynch reclaimed their distribution. Their young head of sales, Steve Knutson, helped Tommy Boy something that few independent labels ever had: He cut out the middleman wholesalers who supposedly "owned" the huge chain store accounts—like Musicland/Sam Goody—and sold records to them directly. Tommy Boy's renewed autonomy coincided with its creative renaissance. A rap group called Stetsasonic resonated with hard-core rap fans. Stetsasonic's DJ Prince Paul, in turn, brought Lynch the label's signature signing, a bizarre trio of MCs from Amityville, Long Island, adorned in floral-print shirts, peace medallions, and asymmetrical haircuts. Nothing about this group sounded or looked anything like the popular rap of the day. Even their name spoke of the exotic: De La Soul.

The musically mutinous album that Prince Paul and De La Soul turned over to Tommy Boy was shepherded by the label's first A&R hire, a combative, passionate twenty-one-year-old White kid from the Lower East Side named Dante Ross. Ross had been a friend of the Beastie Boys, and got his start in 1987 as an assistant at Rush, helping assemble tour itineraries for Lyor Cohen. Ross was the perfect match for the band of hip-hop misfits, and his manic enthusiasm was rewarded not only by Lynch with a very visible production credit, but by the crew with an affectionate, ball-busting tribute on the inner sleeve of 3 Feet High and Rising: a comic strip where he was portrayed as frenzied, profusely sweating duck called "Dante the Scrubb."

As De La Soul's debut exceeded the half-million mark—their all-embracing, bohemian outlook making ardent fans out of formerly skeptical White collegians and disinterested rock critics, winning them a slot in MTV's regular rotation—Ross's taste and hustle multiplied the label's fortunes with two key signings. Fab 5 Freddy played Ross a demo tape by a young female MC from New Jersey named Dana Owens. Whether she was rapping or singing in her powerful contralto voice, Ross sensed that Owens could match skills with any man in hip-hop. Ross brought the tape to Lynch, who found common cause with Owens's manifest hip-hop feminism. Lynch gave Ross her blessing to make the signing, and Owens—who dubbed herself "Queen Latifah"—became a Tommy Boy artist.[8] Ross also assisted in acquiring another unconventional rap crew. Atron Gregory's group, Digital Underground, was moving thousands of its Macola-distributed single, "Underwater Rimes," through stores in California. Digital Underground drew heavily on the sound and imagery of George Clinton's funk groups, Parliament and Funkadelic, with leader Shock G mirroring Clinton's penchant for playing several different characters on record and onstage, with an alter ego he called "Humpty Hump."

Tommy Boy's expertise in outlandish talent was matched by its offbeat marketing. De La Soul's album cover was adorned with cartoon daisies, and Monica Lynch created an expensive promotional item to give to DJs, programmers, industry friends, and fans: a leather De La Soul African medallion, fashioned by a vendor in Harlem. Queen Latifah received a comprehensive styling from the label, from the Afrocentric kente cloth sash in her video "Ladies First," to the red-black-and-green "ribbon bar" tchotchkes for tastemakers and ardent fans. To promote the Digital Underground album *Sex Packets*—based on their song about a spurious hallucinogenic drug that felt like "sex in a pill"—Tommy Boy actually mass-produced thousands of jet-black, vacuum-sealed sex packets with a candy wafer inside, the outside featuring photos of different, attractive sex partners.

"Are these real?" one retailer asked Tommy Boy's sales chief, Steve Knutson.

"Yes," Knutson deadpanned. "They're real."

Tommy Boy had its own aesthetic—the groups they signed tended to have fully formed looks, influenced in no small part by Lynch and Knutson's zealotry for the art rock group Roxy Music—one of the first pop bands whose music, lyrics, wardrobe, album art, stagecraft, and advertising comprised a holistic, thematic unity. Tommy Boy assured its artists' visibility by

---

[8]Queen Latifah's mother, Rita Owens, assisted the promotional efforts of Tommy Boy in an unusual way when she appeared in a full-page ad in *Billboard* magazine that promoted De La Soul to skittish bourgeois Black radio programmers. Owens, a middle-aged Black woman dressed in a sweater and pearls, cradles a copy of *3 Feet High and Rising*. "I came in for Patti LaBelle," the caption above Owens read. "I came out with De La Soul." Another ad, pitching De La Soul to recalcitrant rock programmers, featured a suit-and-tie yuppie choosing the rap group's album over another from the Rolling Stones. Rap record companies had been dealing with programmers' bigoted preconceptions for years. Tommy Boy was the first to challenge them in such a creative and forthright fashion.

locking down the back page of *The Source* for its ads. But Tommy Boy had not only created minibrands out of its artists. The label had become a brand unto itself, even selling its coveted Carhartt logo jackets to the general public. Tommy Boy had become what the majors weren't—a machine for making and marketing authentic, innovative hip-hop.

The major labels still had indirect ways into the rap game. They could distribute smaller labels, like Columbia did with Def Jam; or purchase them, as Warner Bros. did with Tommy Boy. The majors could also buy the contracts of established artists themselves if independents were small enough or willing enough to sell. But the artists picked by the "hired ears" at the major labels often reflected more commercial sensibilities in an increasingly creative era. Even good hip-hop albums—like *Paul's Boutique* by the Beastie Boys, issued on Capitol three years after the Beasties' Def Jam debut—could be ruined by the majors' inept, inexperienced promotion.

For the most part, direct-to-major-label signings didn't yield much more than yawns.

But, in 1990, finally, there were two exceptions to the rule of the independents.

Two really big ones.

In fact, the success of these two artists was so colossal that it endangered the vision of diverse, creatively commercial hip-hop cultivated by smaller institutions like Tommy Boy and *The Source*, threatening to replace it with a new order in which sales were the highest aspiration, inoffensiveness was key, and major-label muscle had the edge.

The Oakland Athletics' right fielder Reggie Jackson called the kid "Hammer" because he looked like a miniature "Hammerin'" Hank Aaron, standing outside the Oakland Coliseum in the summer of 1972 with his homeboys on game days. The eleven-year-old Stanley Kirk Burrell negotiated a sweet deal with the players on the baseball team. Before every game, the guys would give him their leftover complimentary tickets. Stanley kept one for himself and sold the rest. Then he'd enter the ballpark and race behind the dugout. Stanley would give them the money, and they'd give him all the broken bats and balls he wanted to sell for his own profit after the game.

For Burrell, his older brothers, and his friends, the A's provided summer jobs and regular diversion from Oakland's increasingly murderous streets.

Stanley's older brother, Louis, was an assistant clubhouse manager. Stanley, meanwhile, hung outside, hawking tickets while he and his friends listened to the radio and danced.

One day, Stanley's quick steps and James Brown–style splits caught the eye of the man who happened to own the Oakland Athletics, Charles Oscar Finley, who struck up a conversation. When Stanley told him about his ticket hustle, "Charlie O" didn't get mad.

"You don't have to be my competition," Finley said. "Why don't you join me. Come on in and be my right-hand man."

Finley brought him into the clubhouse. During Finley's frequent trips back to his hometown of Chicago, Stanley phoned in play-by-play details of the games and other goings-on. The ball players gave "Hammer" a new nickname: "Pipeline." Stanley was serious about his new job. By the time he was fifteen years old, Finley rewarded him with a lofty title—"executive vice president"—and a salary of $7.50 per game. When he wasn't wrangling equipment, Stanley was dancing on the field between innings to entertain the fans.

Stanley Burrell dreamed of being a player, not a performer. But after his graduation from high school, when a professional career wasn't in the offing, Burrell joined the navy to keep himself from being tempted into drug trade. Discipline was the key. Burrell read the Bible daily and went to church every week throughout his tour of duty—from boot camp in San Diego, to bases in Mississippi and Japan. After his discharge several years later, Burrell called on two old friends on the Athletics roster—Dwayne Murphy and Mike Davis—to invest $20,000 in his new business venture: rap music.

"MC Hammer," Burrell's hip-hop alias, was one half of a Christian rap group called Holy Ghost Boys, recording songs like "Son of the King," "Word," and "Sweat." But Burrell's partner, an old friend from grade school named Chris Savoy, wasn't sure the rap thing would lead to success. Savoy saw singing as the route to fame and fortune. Savoy went one way, and MC Hammer the other.

Burrell used his military discipline and religious fervor to teach himself the music business. He recorded music with Felton Pilate, a local producer-performer from the famed R&B band Con Funk Shun. He found out who manufactured and distributed his favorite rap records, and brought his master tapes to Don Macmillan at Macola. With the help of his wife, Stephanie, Burrell made lists of record stores and radio stations, and shipped boxes of his first "MC Hammer" single, "Ring 'Em"—printed on his own custom label, Bustin' Records—out of his garage in the Oakland suburb of Fremont. And he put hundreds of hours into perfecting his stage show. When Hammer visited DJs, programmers, club owners, and shopkeepers, they rarely forgot him. He was irrepressible, but respectful. He was confident, but humble. He made them *want* to help him.

"I'm gonna be the biggest rapper of all time," MC Hammer told Violet Brown, who managed the Wherehouse record store on La Brea and Rodeo in Los Angeles, one of the most important stores in California's biggest record chain. Brown grew to believe him. At Hammer's first in-store appearance, two dozen people came to see him. The next time, at least double that amount packed the store. By the time his self-released album, *Feel My Power*, came out, more than a hundred showed up, and the line snaked out of the store and around the block.

MC Hammer's record sold primarily in the West and across the Sun Belt. But Hammer's one-man campaign took him all the way to New York City, to the New Music Seminar, where he hoped to spread the gospel in the East. Hammer's geniality won him friends—Melle Mel, Grandmaster Flash, the guys in Whodini. His persistence got him a gig at New York's hot club the Latin Quarter. But for all Hammer's hard work, he received scant airplay in the original home of hip-hop.

But America was a big country. Burrell sold an impressive 60,000 units of his album before Capitol Records' A&R representative Joy Bailey walked into the Oak Tree Cabaret in May 1988. Capitol's A&R chief, Wayne Edwards, signed him, and rereleased MC Hammer's Macola album under a new name, *Let's Get It Started*. Capitol put money into a video, Hammer danced, and Ted Demme played it on MTV. The album sold over a half million copies, but the lack of sales in the East Coast was ever a sore spot for Hammer, as evinced in the opening scene for his video for "Turn This Mutha Out."

Thus, Hammer's second Capitol album, *Please Hammer Don't Hurt 'Em*, began its journey modestly. Its first two singles came and went without cracking the Top 10 on the R&B charts. Pop radio paid Hammer no attention at all. The third single, however, fared somewhat better—perhaps because, in a certain sense, it had been a hit already.

"U Can't Touch This" "sampled" its music from a well-known record. As recognizable as it was, Rick James's "Super Freak" wasn't exactly a chart-topper in its day; it actually got the cold shoulder from pop programmers when it was first released in 1981. It didn't even make it to number one on the R&B chart. And Rick James complained loudly that MTV wasn't playing his videos. In fact, nothing about the nine-year-old "Super Freak" suggested that a rap song based on it would match Rick James's original achievement, much less surpass it.

But "Super Freak" wasn't a dangerous song anymore—too salacious, too "Black-sounding" for the White gatekeepers of its day. And the song that sampled it, "U Can't Touch This," wasn't delivered by a druggie, debauched Black rocker. It was performed by a guy with a nice smile who just wanted to entertain. On *The Arsenio Hall Show,* MC Hammer skittered across the stage in a golden metallic jumpsuit, accompanied by a gaggle of female dancers and a live band. Next came an iconic video, spotlighting Hammer's footwork in a pair of loose Druze-like shirwal pants. Despite the song's name, here was a song that traditionally risk-averse pop radio programmers and MTV could easily touch.

The earliest adopters were MC Hammer's hard-won industry friends— radio programmers like Keith Naftaly at San Francisco pop station KMEL, and Ted Demme and Fab 5 Freddy at *Yo! MTV Raps.* The record quickly spread to other pop stations that played a lot of dance music—Power 106 in Los Angeles, Hot 97 in New York. The video was bumped up to heavy rotation on MTV proper. By June 1990, the song reached its peak of number eight on the pop charts, besting "Super Freak," which had peaked at number sixteen.

But the real success story was MC Hammer's album, which shipped several hundreds of thousands per week, became the third number one rap album in history behind the Beasties and Tone-Loc. It went on to break every sales record set by groups like Run-DMC and the Beastie Boys.

To many hip-hop fans back in New York—and especially the writers and editors of *The Source*—MC Hammer's milestone wasn't cause for celebration.

Of the thirty-three albums that *The Source* reviewed for its 1990 "Summer Album Preview," rated on a scale from one ("100% wic-wic wack") to five ("a hip-hop classic"), only one album merited the lowest grade: MC Hammer's *Please Hammer Don't Hurt 'Em.*

"The best thing about Hammer is that he's on top of the business side of rap," began the review. "But this album is about to become the largest-selling rap album of all time (surpassing the Beastie Boys at 4 mil), and we don't know one rap fan who has bought or even listened to it."

Along Broadway, perhaps that statement was true. But beyond the five boroughs, MC Hammer was quickly becoming the face of rap. That fact exasperated the editors and writers at *The Source*, who reveled in the complex music collages of Public Enemy and De La Soul and the lyrical prowess of Rakim and KRS-One. It mattered not that "U Can't Touch This" was, perhaps, the most shrewd commercial move in hip-hop since Run-DMC's remake of Aerosmith's "Walk This Way," both songs being based on well-known, evocative songs. Hammer's detractors drew a distinction between Run-DMC and Hammer. To them, Hammer's one-shot sample of "Super Freak" seemed lazy, not adventurous; pandering, not provocative.

"Duh," *The Source* sneered in their review. "Let's just take the whole thing."

The issue of MC Hammer divided the community of hip-hop artists, too.

A few artists welcomed and defended him. Chuck D of Public Enemy had toured with him. As a person, Hammer was easy to like. Moreover, Chuck D understood that the hip-hop *nation*—the close-knit group of artists, producers, executives, writers who produced and promoted the culture—was swiftly becoming *national*. Unity required understanding the different sounds that appealed to different regions, not mocking or belittling them.

Then there were the purists, like Chuck D's college buddy and label mate Andre "Doctor Dre" Brown, for whom hip-hop connoted commitment to a specific set of aesthetics and ethics, among them: originality, skills, crossing boundaries, and pushing buttons. While Brown's colleagues at *Yo! MTV Raps* catapulted Hammer to stardom, Dre dissented vociferously, calling the Oakland rapper the "John Travolta of rap" at the 1990 New Music Seminar, evoking howls of derisive laughter in agreement. Hammer's years of hard work and his organically grown fan base were accomplishments lost on his critics.

By October 1990, *Please Hammer Don't Hurt 'Em* had rounded six million copies sold. The album showed no signs of slowing down, and neither did the debate, which generally came down to support for MC Hammer as "successful Black entrepreneur," versus scorn for Hammer as "sellout."

"I used to be a die-hard Hammer fan," read a letter to *The Source* from Lisa Ely in Chicago. "But when he decided to go Hollywood, he sold out and no one seems to understand why. . . . Everybody's got to make some money, but the bullshit has got to go. He's to rap what Paula Abdul is to singing . . . WACK!"

For most of the staff at *The Source*, MC Hammer's triumph was their tragedy: hip-hop's new bestselling artist was a singing, dancing minstrel. It was hard to imagine a worse fate for the culture. Except, of course, if that minstrel were White.

A white Chevy Suburban nosed its way through Mississippi. Its driver, forty-one-year-old Tommy Quon, had an appointment to keep with a disc jockey in Jackson. The reason for the meeting was sitting in the passenger seat: the young man with the chiseled Aryan face and slicked blond hair, Quon's client, an aspiring rapper named Robert Van Winkle.

Quon and Van Winkle were in the midst of a thirty-day, two-man tour of the South, stopping at radio stations and nightclubs in markets great and small, promoting Van Winkle's single, "Play That Funky Music," yet another White rapper's take on the 1976 song made famous by the blue-eyed funk group Wild Cherry. Quon had sunk everything he had into this quixotic quest—his life savings and the profits from his nightclubs in Dallas—a fortune amounting to over $200,000.

Quon was familiar with these parts. He had grown up in Greenville, Mississippi, as part of a Chinese community that had roots there since the Civil War, when Chinese laborers were brought in by plantation owners to make up for the loss of Black slave labor. In the back of his grandfather's grocery store, Joe Gow Nue #2, Black blues musicians congregated and improvised as Quon sat for hours, riveted. By the time he was a teenager, his family moved to Memphis, where Quon went to Humes High—the same school attended by Elvis Presley. Quon's English teacher, as a girl, had dated Presley. She told Quon that she didn't think much of the humble truck driver, who would eventually become the great translator of Black R&B for White America.

In Mississippi, Quon had discovered whence Black music came. In Memphis, he realized where it inevitably went.

After college, in the 1970s, Quon opened and closed a series of nightclubs and discos catering to a Black crowd. They would make money, then lose money, then close. After a few years, Quon reunited with his kinfolk in

Dallas to take a straight job running the family restaurant. A few back-breaking weeks in a sweltering kitchen among boxes of withering vegetables and boiling vats of egg rolls was enough to send Quon back to the music world. In Dallas, he got a liquor license and opened two nightclubs, City Lights and Monopoly's. Like his ventures in Memphis, these clubs were successful for a time and then they weren't, forcing Quon to cash out in 1989. But he had come away with two important dividends: a knowledge of hip-hop and how to market it, and his first rap act.

"MC Vanilla," as Van Winkle was known then, caught Quon's attention when he entered a talent contest at City Lights in 1987. Van Winkle rolled up in a pristine white Mustang 5.0 convertible, and asked Quon if he could park it in the back. Quon smiled. The kid carried himself like a star. Van Winkle proved Quon's instincts correct when he won the contest—not so much with his rapping, but with his breakneck dance steps. Quon was doubly impressed that Van Winkle had the balls to come into a Black nightclub and steal the show.

Quon knew whence Black music came and where it inevitably went. He took Van Winkle on as his client, and signed him to his new independent record label, Ultrax.

Quon worked with Van Winkle to transform his act—from a tough-talking, constantly cursing wannabe gangster into a polished pop performer rechristened "Vanilla Ice." Van Winkle, for his part, often toiled six hours a day on his choreography, and soaked up the showmanship of rap acts as they passed through Dallas, including that of MC Hammer. But as Hammer raked in the millions during the summer of 1990, Quon and Vanilla Ice traversed the South on little more than fast food and gasoline fumes, promoting a single that Quon distributed through a small Southern indie called Ichiban.

At Jackson, Mississippi's crossover pop station, WOHT-FM, "Hot 95," a gregarious, chubby-faced, fast-talking twenty-three-year old named Dave Morales ran the music department and DJed nights. He had taken Quon's call and accepted his offer of a dinner meeting; if somebody else was buying the drinks, Morales was always game. Quon's white Suburban pulled up at the radio station in the late afternoon and Morales greeted the unlikely pair—the middle-aged Chinese guy with a slight Southern drawl, and the tall, gangly White kid with the protruding Adam's apple and the worst body odor Morales had ever smelled.

Quon handed Morales a cassette, which the DJ popped into the deck while his two guests stood by. He listened to the A-side, "Play That Funky

Music," nodding his head lightly, not saying much. Quon knew what those silent nods meant: Morales thought that the song was "just okay." To show the manager and rapper symbolic courtesy, Morales flipped the cassette to listen to the single's B-side.

Morales knew what he was hearing instantly. The track was a clever sample of a classic MTV staple, "Under Pressure" by Queen and David Bowie, with a catchy chorus that Morales had no way of knowing was borrowed from a years-old Black fraternity chant: "Ice! Ice! Baby!"

Morales turned to Quon in surprise. "This is the shit!" Morales said.

Over the next few days, Hot 95's listeners proved Morales's instincts correct. Traditionally, he knew he had a hit if he got "phones"—meaning requests that came in at a pace of two to three calls per shift. "Ice Ice Baby" was different. After a few plays, this song got calls, not just in the dozens, but in the hundreds, from both Black *and* White listeners. Another DJ in Columbus, Georgia—Darryl Jay at WAGH—had flipped the record and had the same kind of dramatic reaction. Quon quickly switched promotional gears, ditched his A-side, and, when he returned to Dallas, commissioned an $8,000 video for "Ice Ice Baby." Van Winkle was so broke that he had run out of gas on the way to the shoot. The production assistants had to push Vanilla Ice's lifeless Mustang past the camera. Throughout the shoot Quon made sure to surround Van Winkle with Black dancers . . . for credibility's sake, he thought.

As music director at WOHT, Dave Morales regularly met with the promotion representatives of many record companies. But one of his favorites was a guy named Monte Lipman, an Atlanta-based promotion person for a new start-up label in the EMI family called SBK, which had burst onto the charts in the past year with hits from Technotronic and Wilson Phillips. Morales called Lipman—who, like many regionals, functioned as his label's eyes and ears for hot independent records in his territory—and tipped Lipman off to the little independent record as a possible "pickup" for SBK.

Lipman—too preoccupied with trying to get Morales to add SBK's new boy band, Guys Next Door—didn't pass the word along.

Other labels, however, had seen the Southern explosion of "Ice Ice Baby" and called on Tommy Quon. Cory Robbins at Profile and Bill Stephney at SOUL expressed interest. Before long, Quon had a good offer from Atlantic records for $250,000.

Quon's lawyer, however, happened to be partners with Peter Lopez, who represented Wilson Phillips, the top act on SBK. Lopez thought that Quon might be able to get a better deal from Charles Koppelman, and he called the executive just as the Atlantic deal was being finalized.

Now Koppelman called Lipman to see if his regional knew about this Vanilla Ice record. Lipman, feeling like a complete idiot for not having mentioned the record to his boss, immediately got Morales on the phone. Morales, in turn, played the single for Koppelman, who until that moment hadn't even heard it.

"I'm going to make the deal for this today," Koppelman said. "Dave, I owe you. You've got a chip with me."

Within the next twenty-four hours, SBK made the winning offer for Vanilla Ice at $325,000.

As "Ice Ice Baby" climbed the charts in the fall of 1990, sales of Vanilla Ice's album *To the Extreme*, exploded. Soon enough, Quon secured his client a place on a double bill with MC Hammer, and the two rappers hot-stepped together across the country on tour, battling each other every night—not for the hottest lyrics but for the best stage show. The two rappers were a dynamic duo in more ways than one: With MC Hammer on Capitol Records and Vanilla Ice on SBK/EMI, the distribution arm of the two sister companies, CEMA, at one heady point saw daily orders of 100,000 units per album, equaling over $1,000,000 in revenue per day.

Months later Dave Morales received a package in the mail: a platinum plaque for the sales of Vanilla Ice's album. It was all he received from Koppelman, who would himself be rewarded with the purchase of SBK Records, in a deal valued at up to $400 million, and the chairmanship of EMI Records.

On November 3, 1990, Vanilla Ice made hip-hop history when "Ice Ice Baby" became the first rap song to reach number one on Billboard's pop singles chart.

The song not only beat "U Can't Touch This" (which peaked months earlier at #8), but every other rap record that approached pop's pinnacle: "Walk This Way" (#4), "I Need Love" (#14), "Parents Just Don't Understand" (#12), "Wild Thing" (#2), "Bust a Move" (#7), and even "Fight for Your Right to Party" (#7).

The Beastie Boys, of course, had broken the color barrier in rap in 1987. Given how White recording artists copied and eclipsed Black recording artists for most of the twentieth century, one might well have expected the Beasties' success to unleash a torrent of White rap, drowning popular Black artists like Run-DMC and LL Cool J under a wave of White doppel-gängers.

It didn't happen. Instead, the Beastie Boys promoted the "Blackest" group ever, Public Enemy, to White audiences; while poor Beastie imitators like Jon Shecter's BMOC got no play. In the wake of the Beasties, the level of success engendered by White rap acts seemed commensurate with their skills, not their skin color. Def Jam's 3rd Bass was generally welcomed within the hip-hop community; while Young Black Teenagers, Hank Shocklee and Bill Stephney's provocatively named White rap crew, couldn't live up to Shocklee and Stephney's highbrow quasi-political concept. Hip-hop seemed to be different from previous musical genres, and the White audience for hip-hop was different, too. Perhaps White kids no longer needed White artists to translate or water down Black art for them.

But then came Vanilla Ice, seemingly reconfirming the validity of that age-old process. Indeed, the alacrity with which an older generation of record executives and pop programmers seized on Vanilla Ice echoed Sun Records' proprietor Sam Phillips's fervor at seeing Elvis Presley for the first time. The gatekeepers at pop radio and MTV issued matter-of-fact comparisons between Vanilla Ice and Elvis, as if co-optation were not only inevitable, but welcome.

The success of MC Hammer's and Vanilla Ice's records—eventually topping out at over 10 million and 7 million albums sold, respectively—were so out of proportion to everything that came before them that they drowned out all else, especially in pop radio. In 1990, hip-hop had produced a number of great candidates for pop crossover, especially the sophomoric howl of Biz Markie's "Just a Friend," and the ridiculous farce of Digital Underground's "The Humpty Dance." Both of these records had the requisite novelty element for pop radio. Both of these records came from artists who had built respect among the core hip-hop audience. But both of these records, released in the shadow of "U Can't Touch This," stalled at #9 and #11 on the pop charts, respectively; their sales couldn't touch MC Hammer's.

Not only did "U Can't Touch This" and "Ice Ice Baby" deplete the oxygen for other rap artists in radio's atmosphere, they also obscured the successes of the past. On the September 18 airing of *America's All-Star Tribute to Oprah Winfrey*, seventeen-year-old actor Neil Patrick Harris introduced a performance by MC Hammer, calling him "the man who turned rap into an art form."

Just like that, one *Source* scribe[9] worried, "an entire generation of cultural genius is smothered in an avalanche of mediocrity."

Now that Vanilla Ice had bested MC Hammer on the charts, the hip-hop zealots at *The Source* braced for the inexorable deluge of White rappers and "hip-pop" from major labels. Luckily for them, *The Source* was doing just well enough that Jon Shecter wasn't contemplating a return to his own rap career.

The Source—now calling itself "The Magazine of Hip-Hop Music, Culture & Politics"—was now an influential force in hip-hop, and hip-hop's most influential mogul wanted to be involved. Russell Simmons was impressed enough with the magazine that he made some noises about wanting to buy *The Source* outright. Things turned serious when Simmons came with an actual proposition: He and Quincy Jones would broker a deal between *The Source* and one of the largest magazine publishers in the world, Time, Inc. A recent wave of media coverage of *The Source* garnered by publicist Leyla Turkkan primed the interest in the young magazine.

The owners of *The Source* took this opportunity seriously because they had to. The operation often didn't have enough money to pay their bills. *The Source* had to pay 12 percent printing costs on every issue they manufactured, their print runs numbering higher than five times more than what they sold.

"What are we going to do about this?" Mays cried as he extended a printing bill for Young and Shecter to see. Young, ever the pragmatist, suggested paying half.

"They'll be happier if we pay something rather than nothing."

But Young himself had become too expensive for *The Source*. By early 1991, Young had been offered a job back in Washington, D.C., as associate publisher for *The New Republic*. Young had to take it, and he convinced Mays and Shecter—and *New Republic* editor Marty Peretz—that he could split his time between the two gigs. But his absence slowed the growth of *The Source*.

Initially, Time, Inc., talked about investing in the magazine. Mays entered a period of protracted discussions with Time executives, traveling to San Francisco to create business plans and projection models. Then in July of 1991, the four partners of *The Source* flew to Los Angeles—Shecter, Mays, and Young from New York, Bernard from San Francisco—to attend

---

[9] The author.

a meeting at the Bel-Air home of Quincy Jones. Over a dozen people came, including Simmons; Gil Rogin, one of the top editors at Time, Inc.; and Jane Pratt, the twenty-nine-year-old founder of *Sassy* magazine.

The Source partners sat in Jones's living room for the better part of the day, the latest copies of the magazine spread out on a table before them, discussing the possibility of expanding the scope of the magazine. Jones encouraged the young entrepreneurs to think more holistically—not just about hip-hop, but also R&B; not just music, but also lifestyle: fashion, film, and television. *The Source* partners weren't sure that Jones understood their mission. The multiplicity of opinions at the table was mind-numbing, and the presence of Pratt puzzling. Was this White woman with no relationship to hip-hop whatsoever really going to be put in charge of this magazine?

A few times during the marathon meeting, the attendees wandered off to talk in smaller groups or wander around the famous producer's house. James Bernard chatted off to the side with one Time executive, who hinted at the parameters of a possible deal, different from what Mays initially expected. *The Source* founders would be bought out, and the editors put on salary in the high five figures. That was big money to Bernard—more, at least, than he had ever taken home.

Later, Bernard and Shecter took a walk together around Quincy Jones's pool. Little more than a year ago, they were at Harvard. Now they were in Hollywood. The two friends shared a knowing look: *This is surreal.* As they talked, both acknowledged that the partnership with Time probably wasn't going to work. *The Source* was a young and nimble operation. Time was a clusterfuck of people and opinions.

After Shecter returned to the larger discussion in the living room, he reached into a plate of hard nuts on the table before him, placing one of them into a viselike contraption nearby to crack the tough shell. But no matter how much he leaned on the lever, the nut wouldn't crack. Shecter quietly pocketed the nut, thinking at the very least he would have a souvenir of the bizarre day.

A few weeks later, *The Source* received an offer from Time, Inc.: $50,000 each to Mays and Shecter. It was a lowball figure for a publication that billed hundreds of thousands of dollars per year. And the proposal insulted Bernard because it didn't make a provision for either him or Ed Young. Jon Shecter's father, a corporate attorney, returned a counteroffer to Time with more dignified terms. The counter was followed with a tersely worded fax from Time that rescinded the offer entirely.

The collapse of negotiations with Russell Simmons, Quincy Jones, and Time puzzled and alarmed the four partners of *The Source*. While it was a relief to retain their independence, it also meant a return to their monthly financial grind, not to mention the inevitability of Time starting their own magazine.[10]

The concept of a "hip-hop nation"—the diverse, altruistic, all-for-one, one-for-all community of artists—found its ultimate symbol in the Black Nationalist collective of Public Enemy.

But since Professor Griff's anti-Jewish remarks in the summer of 1989, the crew had been falling apart. To Bill Stephney, the group's producer and theorist, Griff's ramblings made no sense, especially given that so many of Public Enemy's benefactors—Rick Rubin, the Beastie Boys, Lyor Cohen, and Bill Adler—were Jewish themselves. Not that Stephney agreed with those who excoriated his group for bigotry while ignoring the blatant racist lyrics of rock group Guns N' Roses ("Niggers and faggots get out of my way. / Don't want any more of your gold chains today"). Still, Chuck D couldn't make up his mind about expelling Griff—not only for the content of his comments, but for his insubordination within the organization.

Chuck D had originally been a partner with former Def Jam president Bill Stephney and Public Enemy producer Hank Shocklee in SOUL Records. But while Chuck struggled, the rapper realized that his profile as a controversial artist might draw negative attention to his comrades. Chuck D bowed out, and the troika became a duo.

SOUL began as a way for Stephney to start over—to tweak Def Jam's multicultural movement by making it meaningful and political; to progress Public Enemy's Black Nationalism into real ownership; to move beyond the chaos of Def Jam into an entity he could better control. But Bill Stephney couldn't control his new partner.

Hank Shocklee had always been more Chuck's friend than his own, and without Chuck to lend balance and grounding to some of Shocklee's more fanciful ideas—like Young Black Teenagers—Stephney found himself increasingly at odds with SOUL's co-owner. In Stephney's view, Shocklee's

---

[10]Dave Mays and Ed Young, the publishing half of *The Source* in those days, speak of a second, higher buyout offer from Time, Inc., months later, at around $600,000. Mays states he declined that offer, believing that Time, Inc. was simply trying to eliminate *The Source* to make way for the imminent publication of their own hip-hop magazine.

creative output was slow. When Stephney wanted to sign A Tribe Called Quest, he felt Shocklee dragged his feet. When Stephney wanted to hire staff, Shocklee was scarce.

Stephney wasn't the only person who had issues with his partner. Conflicts over credit, money, and workshare prompted Eric Sadler and Shocklee's own brother, Keith, to stop working with him. Stephney, too, had been dismissed from the PE production crew, the Bomb Squad, without so much as a word from his partner. A lawyer from Def Jam informed the producer of Public Enemy's first two albums that he would not be participating in future recordings.

Finally, less than a year after SOUL opened shop, Stephney phoned Shocklee to talk about separating, inviting Shocklee for a private, civil conversation at his Brooklyn town house to hammer out the details. But Shocklee arrived with a third party: Lyor Cohen.

"What is he doing here?" Stephney asked Shocklee, nonplussed, while his black Labrador, Nubie, barked at the uninvited guest. Cohen replied that he was there to represent Shocklee in their negotiations.

"Get the hell out of my house," Stephney replied.

"You can't throw me out so easily, Bill," Cohen said. "I'm your partner."

"Fuck you," Stephney said.

Cohen produced a one-page contract—really a handwritten fax—that seemed to be some sort of agreement between Shocklee and Cohen. "I own twenty-five percent of whatever Hank does," Cohen said triumphantly.

"Hank," Stephney said. "Is this true?"

Shocklee said nothing. Stephney couldn't believe it. It was like the business with Rhythm Method all over again.[11]

Resigned, Stephney took a nominal amount for his half of SOUL— $75,000—just to get away clean and sane. At that, Stephney's long journey from Professor Strobert's class had come to an end, and with it, his dreams of a superempowered group of Afrocentric entrepreneurs conquering the entertainment business. *If the crew that created Public Enemy can't achieve solidarity and build a nation*, Stephney wondered, *who can?*

---

[11]Shocklee has no recollection of this meeting, and claims that the twenty-five percent take for Cohen was really a finder's fee for brokering the original MCA deal. Stephney denies that Lyor Cohen had anything to do with landing SOUL Records' deal at MCA.

Vanilla Ice was missing. He had just won the 1991 American Music Award for favorite new pop/rock artist. But for some reason, he hadn't yet arrived at his victory party. Daniel Glass worried and waited impatiently with other SBK executives and members of the news media. Finally, Glass called the police.

Not long after Glass placed the call, the rapper arrived with his entourage. But he didn't look well. He seemed shaken up. Only later would Glass learn about the events that delayed his artist that evening.

Tommy Quon, Vanilla Ice's producer-manager, was in his hotel suite after the ceremony when the rapper's bodyguards phoned and told Quon that there had "been a breach," and that a few gentlemen had pushed their way into the rapper's room at the Bel Age.

Quon was pissed. Next time he would get army specialists in his security detail, like the ones MC Hammer had. Quon listened as they handed the receiver to the ringleader of the uninvited guests—a six-foot-three-inch, three-hundred-plus pound former football player and bodyguard named Marion "Suge" Knight.

Knight announced that he represented Mario "Chocolate" Johnson—a beat maker/producer who collaborated with Vanilla Ice on "Ice Ice Baby" and other tracks. Knight wanted to talk to Quon about Johnson's getting his fair share of the publishing royalties.

If this guy was Chocolate's manager, Quon thought, he didn't know much about his client's affairs.

"You know what?" Quon told Knight. "I've already handled this. Chocolate already has his share. You can check with your attorney."

And with that, the conversation ended.

In the months after the incident, a story would emerge that Suge Knight muscled his way into Vanilla Ice's room and, after threatening the rapper with bodily harm, emerged victorious with the lion's share of the publishing for "Ice Ice Baby." Vanilla Ice himself may have contributed to this apocrypha—having recently been outed by the *Dallas Morning News* as a liar who told tall tales of a shadowy past involving gangs and guns. But the real story was much less sexy. Knight had indeed come to intimidate Vanilla Ice, but he left with nothing he didn't already have.

Suge Knight's infamy grew after Eazy-E and Jerry Heller accused him of extorting Eazy, forcing him to sign release papers for the recording career of Andre "Dr. Dre" Young and thereby severing his obligations as a performer in NWA and as Ruthless Records' in-house producer.

The ascendance of major-label artists MC Hammer and Vanilla Ice on one hand and the entry of Suge Knight on the other side of the hip-hop stage seemed to signal the end of the dream days for hip-hop nobility. Honest hustle and creative struggle were quaint notions of the past. The future belonged to muscle.

Word trickled out that Quincy Jones and Time were definitely launching a new magazine "for the hip-hop generation," and it would be called *Volume.* The founders of *The Source* realized that love of hip-hop wouldn't insulate them from the merciless world of business. For *The Source* to survive long enough to be competitive, all four of them needed to be working on their company full-time. But if they were going to protect their sweat equity with yet more sweat, Ed Young and James Bernard wanted to formalize their long-standing verbal partnership.

So Young came back from his job at *The New Republic* in D.C., and Bernard from his outpost in San Francisco. At a meeting in Shecter's apartment on Houston Street, the four principals agreed on a split. Dave Mays would give Young 15 of his 55 points. Shecter would give Bernard 15 of his 45, leaving Mays and Shecter with 40 and 30 percent shares of *The Source,* respectively.

Back in his office, Ed Young stared at the rejection letters from national distributors on his Wall of Woe. Young resumed his quest for a firm that could increase the magazine's reach and assume some of the liability for the costs of circulation. But instead of sending letters and cold-calling, this time Young sought an inside connection. A neighbor's friend knew Lew Ullian, a sales executive at Kable Distribution Services. Ullian liked Young, and made a personal introduction for him to the president of Kable. Within weeks, Young finally secured a distribution contract for *The Source.*

The other matter was advertising. While Dave Mays succeeded in selling space to virtually every record company that sold rap records, advertising dollars for other consumer products—all the other obsessions of the hip-hop generation, like sneakers, clothes, and electronics—remained elusive. To date, Mays had sold only one ad to a clothing company, a small line called Van Grack. Mays and Young encouraged Shecter to create new sections in the magazine to cover fashion and film, to help lure potential clients. Shecter ran a half-page article on a new, Afrocentric clothing line favored by hip-hop fans: Cross Colours.

The Source's venture into fashion was assisted by the magazine's new head of marketing, a protégé of Ed Young's from New Jersey named Brett Wright. Since his arrival Wright had turned *The Source* into a potent promotion machine—not only for itself, but for its clients. Wright masterminded the idea of a "Mobile Assault Vehicle," branded with *The Source* name and traveling from 'hood to 'hood blasting the latest hip-hop, giving out magazines and free products from advertisers. At first, the "Source Van" was just a white Ford Econoline with stenciled logos and a rented, makeshift sound system. But within a year, the magazine had commisioned a sleek vehicle with custom loudspeakers.

The Source, however, had walled itself off from two willing sources of advertising income that most other music magazines—including Time, Inc.'s new *Volume* magazine—accepted. The partners decided that alcohol ads wouldn't be defensible, not only because of the young age of their readership, but because alcohol companies had historically targeted Black youth with their advertising. For that same reason, cigarette ads were out, too. Knowing this, one tobacco company tried to give *The Source* an easy way out. At a meeting at the headquarters of a major cigarette company, brand executives pitched the four *Source* partners on a sponsorship deal: They would support a *Source*-branded rap tour, restricting their activities to giving away promotional key chains at the gigs. The budget for the campaign was $300,000, equal to the entire yearly gross of the magazine.

Mays, Young, Shecter, and Bernard left the meeting dejected. Three hundred grand was a lot of money to turn down on principle.

"We can't do it," Mays said. Then he turned to Young, glowering, hoping for some kind of relief. "*Right*, Ed?"

All eyes turned to Young.

"Look," Young said. "I need to be able to look in the mirror and put my head down on my pillow at night. We'll benefit far more in the future if we don't take it. I guarantee you."

It was a quaint notion: a band of hip-hop purists eschewing alcohol and tobacco ads, refusing to put commercial rappers like MC Hammer or Vanilla Ice on their cover. In a time when sponsors like Pepsi and KFC were tripping over themselves to give money to Hammer, *The Source* instead invested their fortune and future in innovative but obscure acts that seemed to have little hope of mainstream appeal: A big-boned female MC named Queen Latifah. Nihilistic, foulmouthed rappers like Ice Cube and Dr. Dre. A trio of Latinos from Los Angeles called Cypress Hill.

In reality, institutions like *The Source* and *Yo! MTV Raps* were idealistic islands in an industry that seemed to be regressing, not progressing. MTV's regular rotation was still the province of rock and innocuous pop. Pop stations eschewed all but the safest, tamest rap songs. Black stations were programming less hip-hop overall.

Hip-hop's vision captured the imagination of a nation, and its self-made prosperity attracted the attention of major corporations. But corporate America was now trumpeting its own vision for hip-hop. Whether it be Vanilla Ice or *Volume*, America would never be able to hear the real thing through all the noise.

ALBUM FIVE

WHERE HIP-HOP LIVES

Rap conquers corporate radio

(1991–1994)

Side A
Color Lines

Despite its weak signal and low-fidelity sound, KDAY—the Los Angeles radio station that Greg Mack transformed into the country's only rap-heavy radio outlet—inspired an almost religious zeal among its young listeners. Hip-hop fans across the city held their limbs at odd angles just to catch better reception. They taped and traded cassettes of the Mack Attack Mix Masters' shows like rare baseball cards.

For Greg Mack, too, KDAY was paramount. He had hung on for as long as he could through the sagging fortunes of the station's sales department, and through the laughable switch to "AM stereo"—which, after much advance hoopla, ended up sounding like *two* tinny AM radios playing side by side. Finally, in 1990, Mack allowed himself to be lured away by crosstown KJLH, an FM station owned by Stevie Wonder. Even then, Mack couldn't quit KDAY in spirit. He had not only made his name there, he had made history. KDAY had been sold to real estate magnate Fred Sands, and the word was that Sands would shut the struggling AM down for a few months, then relaunch it as a talk station. Saving KDAY's legendary "rap-friendly" format now became an obsession for Mack. To rescue KDAY, he'd have to buy it.

Mack spent the rest of the year striving to raise the $6 million it would take to purchase the station. He had breakfast with two of the most powerful Black executives in records and radio, respectively, Clarence Avant and Alfred Liggins. They turned Mack down. Mack then tried to convince the station's new owner, Sands, that the rap-dominated format he had established at KDAY could win in the Los Angeles market.

They had all told him the same thing: AM radio was dead for music. Given its weak signal and anemic ad revenue, KDAY couldn't compete. And anyway, they said, FM radio was already playing rap.

Mack disagreed. The FM stations programmed rap, yes, but the *safe* stuff—MC Hammer and Vanilla Ice, Salt-N-Pepa and the Fresh Prince. Mack knew from experience that audiences were ready for the real thing. Could Eazy-E, NWA, Andre "Dr. Dre" Young, and Ice Cube have sold millions to kids both White and Black, urban and suburban without their start on KDAY?

In the end Mack could only listen in frustration as KDAY made its final broadcast. After his morning shift at KJLH, Mack returned to his home in Valley Village and flicked on the radio in time to hear KDAY's last hour.

J. J. Johnson was taking calls from distressed, emotional listeners.

"I grew up with KDAY," Adrienne Brown told Johnson. "I woke up with KDAY. I went to bed with KDAY. You, Greg Mack, Lisa Canning, you guys were the greatest. I'm crying right now."

"KDAY is like my girlfriend," said a male caller. "What am I gonna do now? My whole life is gone."

"Your life ain't gone, man!" Johnson replied.

"So what's gonna be the station now?" the caller asked, going through a list of L.A.'s Black-oriented radio outlets. "KACE? KJLH? The Beat?"

"The one that gets your attention should be the one who responds to you the best," Johnson said. "Radio stations belong to you; don't you forget that."

"So there's not going to be another rap station, huh?"

"Well," Johnson replied, "certainly not for a while."

At one p.m. Pacific standard time on March 28, 1991, KDAY signed off the air for good. A few weeks later, the fifty-thousand-watt beacons on top of Alvarado Street would begin broadcasting a new radio station, the "all-business KBLA," at 1580 kilohertz on the AM dial.

In the wake of KDAY's collapse, three thousand miles away, a group of hip-hop advocates gathered to brainstorm ways to overcome radio's resistance to rap.

Not long before he left his position as president of SOUL Records, Bill Stephney convened a cabal of coconspirators at his office, including Jon Shecter, the editor in chief of *The Source*; and a DJ who called himself Funkmaster Flex—an assistant to weekend jock Chuck Chillout, who was Marley Marl's replacement at WBLS.

Stephney floated the idea that they all, somehow, might approach Joel Salkowitz—the program director of WQHT, a weakly performing pop FM station in New York nicknamed "Hot 97"—and convince him that hip-hop would give his station an edge in the nation's number one radio market. They would have to approach a *pop* station, and not one of the city's Black stations, like WRKS and WBLS, whose programmers had perennially been hostile to hip-hop, and were even now backing away from the little rap that they played. Hot 97, on the other hand, played what Stephney affectionately called "rice and beans" music—Latin-tinged dance for inner city Latinos and bridge-and-tunnel Italians. And since Stephney and others in attendance felt that hip-hop should be marketed not as Black music, but as *teen* music, a station like Hot 97 was the perfect place to start.

Bill Stephney's idea for Hot 97 never made it out of the meeting. Stephney was in the middle of divorcing his label partner, and didn't have the time or energy to convince radio programmers of the obvious. But he knew the stakes were never higher for hip-hop.

Rap had conquered the record business. With the emergence of Sound-Scan, a new service that tracked sales by bar-code scans instead of manual reports, major labels no longer had the ability to load the charts with their "priority" artists—almost always rock, almost always White. The robust sales of rap albums by artists like NWA were no longer hidden by inaccurate charts.

Hip-hop had launched a successful magazine, Shecter's *Source*. Rap had blown its way into Hollywood with the success of movies like John Singleton's *Boyz n the Hood*. Hip-hop had taken TV, first with *Arsenio* and then *In Living Color*. Hip-hop even had the highest-rated show on America's pop music headquarters, MTV.

Despite this success, hip-hop had failed to penetrate radio, which continued to reject all but the most timid rap. Even in the age of MTV, radio was still the key to breaking new artists. Without it hip-hop would never reach its true potential; it would remain "in a box," as one of Stephney's comrades stated. Stephney concurred: One of the reasons that the sales of L.A. rap had eclipsed those of New York, why the scene was so much more exciting, was that Los Angeles had a vibrant institution like KDAY at its nexus.

Radio's opposition didn't surprise Bill Stephney in the least. The music business was the only industry where racial segregation remained standard practice. Record companies still maintained "Black music" departments, despite the irony that *all* American pop music descended from African-American culture. But radio was even more backward than the record companies. It was hard to imagine another American business where White executives could reject Black suppliers and customers on the basis of race. That was what radio did every day, with programmers regularly and unabashedly declining to play artists because they were "too Black." As far as Stephney was concerned, radio was the last great bastion of sanctioned White supremacy in America.

Stephney discovered the blithe racism of radio when he was a college intern at Long Island FM rock station WLIR. Before Stephney began working there, WLIR was one of the preeminent progressive rock stations in the country. The playlist was diverse. On WLIR, you might have heard a Stevie Wonder song right after a Led Zeppelin record. But over the years, Stephney noticed that the eclectic playlist was changing. Black artists were disappearing from the format. WLIR had no trouble playing rhythmic music, just as long as it was performed by White artists. So Malcolm McLaren's "Buffalo Gals" was cool. But "The Adventures of Grandmaster Flash on the Wheels of Steel" wasn't. When young Stephney mentioned this double standard to a member of the programming staff, Stephney's colleague responded that the changes in the playlist were mandated by their new consultant, Lee Abrams.

Stephney later learned about the special role that Abrams played in radio history. In the sixties and seventies, when FM stations were new, DJs usually played what they wanted. But FM soon became big business, and huge corporations started to buy stations across the country. These corporations hired consultants. To get more advertising dollars, consultants recommended that FM stations narrow their formats to "superserve" specific audiences. One of these consultants—a eighteen-year-old prodigy named Lee Abrams who had only recently moved out of his parents' home in Chicago—convinced his clients to stop playing soul music and only play rock records to get the audience their advertisers wanted most: White males between the ages of twelve and twenty-four. Abrams's "Superstars of Rock and Roll" format turned out to be hugely effective, and over the next decade Abrams and his partner Kent Burkhart spread this philosophy of demographic segmentation via music fragmentation to over 100 client stations across America, most of them rising to first among adults eighteen to thirty-four in their respective markets. White kids who liked both Zeppelin and Stevie could no longer hear them on the same station. Other FM stations adopted a similar "narrowcasting" approach, serving soul and funk records to Black audiences, adopting the "Urban contemporary" moniker as code language for their format, lest the term "Black" discourage potential advertisers. Though Abrams was a technician who worked on both sides of the racial divide—he helped launch New York's disco station WKTU—that didn't stop people from blaming him for the damage his techniques had done. Abrams's innovations had, in effect, led to the resegregation of American radio. Stephney's Def Jam colleague Bill Adler bitterly labeled Lee Abrams "the greatest cultural criminal of the twentieth century."

Things weren't easy for Black artists after the rise of the "Superstars" format in the mid-1970s. As disco declined, all Black artists got lumped in with the genre, even Black *rock* groups like Parliament-Funkadelic. "Disco sucks" was the rallying cry by which an entire generation of artists were marginalized. For years after disco had faded from the charts, most Black artists were still denied entry into rock and pop stations, even if their music was sonically appropriate for the format. Black female singer Cherrelle had a huge Urban contemporary hit with a song called "I Didn't Mean to Turn You On." Pop stations wouldn't play her record. But when Robert Palmer, a White British artist, remade her song, suddenly, it was a pop hit. The Gap Band, a Black funk group from Oklahoma, wrote a brilliant song called "Early in the Morning." A huge Black hit, no pop airplay. Again, Robert Palmer remade it, and topped the pop charts. The early 1980s were like the 1950s, Stephney thought. Reagan and radio were both setting the clock back on equal opportunity.

By 1984 Michael Jackson and Prince had broken some of those barriers, mainly by forcing themselves onto MTV—which originally patterned its programming after "Whites-only" rock radio, but had to relent in the face of public demand. And though *Yo! MTV Raps* was now a huge success among White teens, radio programmers still acted as if hip-hop were music for just Black ghetto kids. White consultants like John Sebastian, who had encouraged his clients to employ the "no disco" slogan in the 1970s, were still in the game, giving *Billboard* quotes like this: "I believe that rap and disco are not very good musically."

Even in 1991, Stephney thought, pop radio was still run by antiques like Sebastian, middle-aged White guys who didn't know the difference between funk and disco, or between disco and rap. They didn't know what their own kids were listening to.

But Stephney reserved special bitterness for the Black programmers of so-called "Urban" stations. To Stephney, these guys should have known better. They were "bubbleheads," Buppies, Black people who ran from their own culture, anything that smacked of the ghetto. Frankie Crocker and the programmers who followed him in Black radio did everything they could to keep rap airplay to a minimum, squeezing it into brief daily mixes and weekend specialty shows.

Now there was a new "no rap" movement afoot at both Black and White stations. The slogans were great: "No rap and no hard rock" (B104 in Baltimore), "No kids, no rap, no crap" (KHMX in Houston). WBMX in Boston aired a TV spot that featured gold chains being pulled out of a radio while the announcer said, "No rap!"

Stephney understood that radio stations on both sides of the racial divide were on a new kick of courting adults. It wasn't because kids weren't a lucrative market. It was just that radio programmers simply didn't have the knowledge or the stomach to play the music that kids wanted to hear. Black stations, Stephney thought, could *slaughter* the pop outlets if they just marketed Black music, including rap, to a young *White* audience. Kind of like selling pizza: It's Italian food, but you don't just sell it to Italians. You sell it to everyone.

One Black radio insider agreed. Gregory Johnson, a young executive at Bailey Broadcasting—which syndicated programming to Urban stations nationwide—had recently written an impassioned open letter to the readers of *The Source*: "Black radio . . . is at the forefront of the anti-rap movement, hiding behind the guise of economics. If the rap listenership is so unmarketable, then why do all the radio trades constantly state that teens have $3 billion in disposable income? Black radio's view is a contradiction. Is rap only for Black youths? . . . 52 percent of all rap bought in the first six months of 1990 was by Whites. Everyone is listening to the music. Economics? I say Black radio does not know how to sell 12–24 or 18–49 [age demographics] and they're playing themselves because they are missing out on valuable advertising dollars."

Stephney believed most programmers in Black radio were too shortsighted to grasp the opportunity before them. They thought themselves so above rap music and rap artists. But the truth was Black radio programmers had the biggest ghetto mentality of all. Stephney tortured these guys every chance he got.

"If Black programmers don't start playing hip-hop," Stephney had said at an industry panel, "they will end up as the janitors at the pop stations that do wind up playing hip-hop."

Stephney predicted that it would be some young White programmer at a pop station, some new Alan Freed, some radio version of Ted Demme who brought rap to the radio masses. All it would take was someone with the knowledge to program hip-hop along like-sounding rock in order to educate listeners—say, the Brand Nubians' song "Slow Down" next to the pop song it sampled, "What I Am" by Edie Brickell and the New Bohemians.

As far as Bill could see, only one guy in American pop radio even came close to doing this. That was why, even though Stephney didn't have the ability to lead the charge, he still held forth a slim hope for progress. That was why, even though rap radio was dying in New York and Los Angeles, there was one place where hip-hop still lived.

Something interesting was happening in San Francisco.

KMEL had once been a "Whites-only" rock station. But since 1987 when the reins of programming passed to a twenty-four-year-old Jewish kid named Keith Naftaly, San Francisco's KMEL had become the only radio station in the country that played hard-core hip-hop as if it were just another kind of pop music.

Naftaly's very first act as program director had been to drop all the rock tracks on the station's playlist and add a rap record: LL Cool J's "I Need Love." Since then, Naftaly had led KMEL though a string of firsts.

KMEL had been first on most of the pop-rap that ended up on Top 40 stations around the country. KMEL was the first pop station in the country to play Delicious Vinyl's groundbreaking hits—"Wild Thing" by Tone-Loc and "Bust a Move" by Young MC—beating MTV to the punch by a month in each case. KMEL was the first radio station in the country to play MC Hammer's "U Can't Touch This" and Vanilla Ice's "Ice Ice Baby."

But while KMEL played the *obvious* rap hits, it also played the hip-hop records that other pop outlets didn't. KMEL was the first and only pop station in the country to add an Eric B & Rakim record to their playlist. They were the first pop station to add Bill Stephney's group Public Enemy, and the only one to add their single "Don't Believe the Hype." They were the first and only to add NWA. The first and only to add Boogie Down Productions, X-Clan, and the DOC. Naftaly recognized early on that hard-core, pro-Black records were popular among kids of all races, and he never flinched when programming them.

KMEL tapped into the vibrant Bay Area hip-hop scene and provided the first pop radio venue for local artists like Too Short and Digital Underground, helping to break both acts nationally. The station created community outreach programs and moved its public affairs programming into prime time. Naftaly coined KMEL's slogan: "The People's Station."

As a result, KMEL had made the Bay Area the only market in the country where the pop station was serving the needs and tastes of Black youth more than the traditional FM Urban station, KSOL. KMEL did it not only by playing more and better hip-hop, but by empowering the young DJs and activists that Urban radio had long shut out. It was Bill Stephney's old warning to Black radio come nearly to fruition. KSOL's music director Bernie Moody hadn't quite been forced to pick up a mop. But Naftaly and KMEL had sent his ratings into the toilet.

Naftaly had made KMEL the top-rated music station in San Francisco for five years straight, while most of his counterparts at pop stations around the country treated hip-hop as if it were beyond the pale. As KMEL thrived, Jeff Wyatt—formerly of Philadelphia's Power 99 and now the program director of Power 106 in Los Angeles—told *Billboard* that playing a lot of rap was "dangerous" for a mass-appeal radio station. Wyatt and others viewed KMEL with skepticism. KMEL was a strange radio station, they said, because San Francisco was a strange place. Even Keith Naftaly explained his programming by telling people that hip-hop was simply pop music for local ears.

The Bay Area *was* different. People of different ethnicities and races mixed with slightly less drama than elsewhere in the country. Huge communities of Asians and Latinos joined Blacks and Whites in the Bay Area's three huge cities—San Francisco, Oakland, and San Jose—and in the suburbs that sprawled between them. True, White racism and bigotry cast a pall across the Bay Area as they did in other cities. But it was also true that, year after year, the Bay Area's magic mix had yielded a crop of kids quite different from, yet very comfortable with, one another.

To live in the Bay Area, then, was to see a glimpse of America's destiny. Naftaly seized on a lyric of Janet Jackson's as another catchphrase for his station: "Pushing toward a world rid of color lines." The world of KMEL's listeners wasn't so much color-*blind* as it was color*ful*. Without giving it too much thought or giving himself too much credit, Keith Naftaly created America's first multicultural pop radio station.

A native son of San Francisco, Naftaly could see a future that other programmers could not because he had grown up in a city where the future
arrived early.

On April 28, 1971, Judge Stanley Weigel of the U.S. District Court for
Northern California ordered the city of San Francisco to integrate its elementary schools by the time they opened in the fall. The school board scrambled to devise a plan that would overcome the ethnic geography of the city.
The solution was massive crosstown busing.

As in other American cities, White parents and politicians protested the
prospect of their young children being sent to substandard schools in Black
neighborhoods. The Chinese community was particularly resistant. Even
many in San Francisco's Jewish community, with its long-standing liberal
tradition, talked of pulling their children out of public school altogether.

Among the latter group, Stanley and Bryna Naftaly's reaction was different. When they discovered that their youngest son, nine-year-old Keith,
would be transfered from their neighborhood school, Miraloma Elementary,
to an all-Black elementary in Hunters Point, they thought it was a good
thing. They believed that racial bigotry could be eradicated only if kids were
commingled at an early age.

The Naftalys paid the price for their idealism. Their Jewish friends from
Temple Sherith Israel mocked Stanley and Bryna's "try it and see what
happens" philosophy. They called Bryna selfish for sacrificing Keith—a budding piano prodigy—for the sake of a dangerous social experiment, for putting political principles over the safety of her own child. At a PTA meeting,
Bryna faced icy stares from the nice ladies of Miraloma Park when she spoke
in defense of the plan. Bryna, normally reserved and polite, returned home
furious.

Keith, mature enough to notice, asked why. Bryna explained that she had
never expected such bigotry from women who she thought, until now, were
just like her. Most of these parents didn't know any Black people, yet they
were so sure that their children would be harassed and hurt. Bryna didn't
tell Keith that she *was* afraid, not of his future classmates, but of his current
ones. Keith could be in danger if any of the mothers' verbal venom trickled
into their children's ears.

For his part, Keith wasn't afraid. In fact, quite the opposite. He told Bryna
that he thought his family was cool for being rebellious. He drew pictures

of buses on every available surface. Bryna made her first trip to the Burnett School in Hunters Point. The school was run-down. Some differences between Burnett and Miraloma were manifest—like padlocked doors—and some subtle—like unpainted curbs where the school buses parked. Still, the principal was excellent, and he assured Bryna and the other Miraloma parents that Burnett would begin a class for "gifted" children in the fall.

On September 13 Keith Naftaly joined the thousands of children crisscrossing San Francisco for the first day of classes. Forty percent of elementary school students didn't show on that day. A boycott—led mostly by the Chinese community—lasted for a few months, and then dwindled. The integration process proceeded without further incident.

Bryna was grateful that Keith seemed to like his new surroundings. When Bryna returned to the school for a meeting with the teachers of Burnett's new gifted class, Miss Heller and Miss Howard gave Keith a very good report. Keith, they told Bryna, had become a quiet leader, and the other kids—a mix of White, Black, and Asian children—seemed to be very influenced by what he did.

As Bryna left the school she noticed that the curbs outside had been given a fresh coat of gleaming white paint.

Onstage in the auditorium of the Burnett School, Keith Naftaly sat on the piano bench with his hands on the keys, launching into Nikolai Rimsky-Korsakov's "Flight of the Bumblebee." Keith's left hand played the accompanying chords as the fingers of his right tore into the blistering chromatic runs up and down the keys, faster and faster.

Upon the final chord, the thunderous applause from the audience sent a shock through Keith's body. He had never performed for so many people before. Afterward, Keith had another surprise, as the Black parents ringed him as if he were a celebrity. Ladies in very important-looking hats, showering him with praise. Men who shook his shoulders and mussed his blond hair.

He liked his new friends at Burnett Elementary. He liked riding the bus, going fast on the freeway, traveling to a new place. But most of all, he liked the radio station that they listened to on the way to and from school: KDIA-AM 1310, "the Boss of the Bay." They played new songs from the Main Ingredient and Stevie Wonder, Rare Earth and Donny Hathaway. He had never heard these records on other radio stations.

Keith began to take bus trips of his own. Sometimes he would stop by Wherehouse Records in the Black neighborhood of Ingleside, the whole store thick with the smell of incense. There, he would buy stacks of 45 rpm records, songs he had heard on KDIA. Occasionally, he would pick up a *Billboard* magazine and pore over the different charts: "The Hot 100," "Country," or "Soul," the kind of music that KDIA played. Keith hadn't realized that there were so many different types of radio stations, nor that somebody chose the music that made each one different from the others.

Keith was already dreaming of what he would play on his radio station, if he had one.

One day, Keith carried his older brother's typewriter into his room and fed some paper into the spool. With the issue of *Billboard* on one side and a stack of 45s to the other, Keith clicked out a playlist of his own. When he was finished, Keith was exhilarated. A radio station he controlled!

The typed playlists became an everyday ritual. Keith launched a multiplicity of imaginary stations, updating their charts regularly, based on a balance between personal taste and national trends. Keith designed logos and created station names—KLUV for the R&B station, KROC for the rock station, KNBN for "Keith Naftaly, Brett Naftaly," the station he programmed with his cousin. Bryna and Stanley joked about how secretive Keith was with his playlists, how his consumption of radio matched his older brother's fascination with baseball statistics. But by the time Keith reached the age of thirteen, his obsession hadn't abated. For his bar mitzvah, Keith asked for a subscription to *Billboard*. His brother Eric obliged.

Bryna and Stanley raised their sons with classical music. Keith listened to soul and funk. The Naftalys thought that Keith might become a concert pianist. Instead, Keith studied radio. He counted how long it took for songs to repeat, some less often, some more. He noticed where commercials were played. By the time he enrolled as a freshman at Lowell—San Francisco's elite high school—Keith knew what he wanted to be when he graduated: the music director at a cool radio station, someplace like KDIA or KFRC, an AM pop station that played a lot of Black music.

Graduation came in 1980. To celebrate, Lowell offered its diverse student body two "boat dances," mainly because the kids at Lowell couldn't agree on the kind of music they wanted to hear. The "rock boat," where the DJ played Led Zeppelin, Rush, and Boston, was for the White jocks and cheerleaders. The "soul boat," where the DJ played Earth, Wind & Fire, Chic, and the

Sugar Hill Gang, was for everybody else—the Black kids, the Chinese kids, the Mexican kids, the Filipino kids, and a few intrepid Whites.

Keith Naftaly rode the soul boat. It felt like home.

Naftaly had about as much patience for his studies at UC Berkeley as he had for their campus FM station, KALX. The station was a mess. The music mix, mostly punk and new wave, was sloppy. The announcers were amateurs. He had no desire to join their ranks. In his own mind Naftaly was on his way to becoming a disciplined programmer, at least for someone who had never worked at a radio station.

So Naftaly hopped the BART train back to downtown San Francisco and hung out in the lobby of KFRC until he got an audience with Sandy Louie, the music director.

"I will do *anything* at this radio station," Naftaly told her. "I will empty the trash cans. I will mop the floors."

Louie, a tiny but tough Asian woman in her late twenties, grimaced at the overeager, tousled-haired nineteen-year-old. *What a freak.* She gave Naftaly a job answering the request lines in the evenings. Naftaly didn't want to leave after his shift. Instead he roamed the offices, thumbing through the music library, reading stray memos left on desks. Then he would tabulate the night's requests and write a detailed analysis of each song's performance.

Sandy Louie looked at Naftaly's unsolicited reports, then at Naftaly. *What a freak.* Everything that Louie hated about her job—prioritizing, cataloging, and researching music—this kid loved. Louie was no fool. She put Naftaly in charge of the drudge work, so she could concentrate on her air shift.

Naftaly couldn't have cared less about being on air. When Louie plopped the official rotation cards in front of him, she gave Naftaly the keys to the station. Naftaly now typed up the official KFRC playlist, called retail outlets to research their sales figures, and talked to record promoters who plied him with free music and tickets to shows. In little more than a year Naftaly taught himself how to run the music department at a radio station.

Despite his eagerness, Naftaly learned to detest some things about his new profession. He was eventually offered a promotion, leaving school to produce the morning show of Dr. Don Rose. But Naftaly hated morning shows—the artificial laughter, sound effects, wacky horns, corny jokes, and parody songs.

At 3:30 every morning, he steeled himself for his daily shift by smoking a joint. Sufficiently buzzed, he donned his trench coat and rode his Vespa though the dark and fog to KFRC. As the AM station began to sink in the ratings against FM Urban contemporary competitor KSOL, KFRC brought on a consultant, Walter Sabo, who sanitized the funky station, taking away much of the newer, edgier, Blacker music and adding White artists like Eddie Money and Huey Lewis, cutting the bountiful library of six hundred songs to a safer, more predictable list of less than a hundred. Naftaly discovered that radio was really run by a bunch of so-called experts who didn't know a thing about music. Soon, the soul boat ride of KFRC was over and Naftaly was out of a job.

At first Naftaly thought he might have to succumb to his father's pressure to return to school. Then he read in *Billboard* that the local rock station "the Camel"—so named for its call letters, KMEL—was switching to a Top 40 format. The owners were bringing in a new program director, Nick Bazoo, who had programmed a pop station in New Orleans that played a lot of Black music. Naftaly seized on this news as a divine sign. He knew he could help Bazoo understand the Bay Area market. He could frame the new KMEL as a true successor to KFRC. Naftaly consolidated his ideas into a impassioned, detailed letter of introduction to Bazoo, asking him to consider him for the position of music director. It wasn't hubris. Naftaly simply felt that he had studied all his life to do that job.

To Naftaly's surprise, Bazoo read his letter, took his call, and hired him. The music director's chair was already filled, Bazoo said, so he made Naftaly "music coordinator," with a yearly salary of $19,500.

"Scooter" was the nickname that the air staff gave young Keith Naftaly. But the kid's music selections had raised KMEL's ratings from a dismal 1.4 percent market share to a respectable 2.4 and earned him the respect of the station's new general manager, Paulette Williams. A former sales executive for the owner, Howard Grafman—and soon Grafman's fiancée—Williams projected an aristocratic air, with her platinum blond hair, dazzling jewelry, hats, and furs. "No one knows the music like Keith," she'd say. When Nick Bazoo left KMEL, Williams made Naftaly the new music director under Bazoo's replacement, the renowned program director Steve Rivers.

At first Naftaly was nervous about working for Rivers, who had a reputation for being a disciplinarian and for building strong stations on supertight playlists. He worried he might lose the freedom to play new music. Instead Steve Rivers bestowed upon Keith Naftaly an advanced degree in radio. Other White programmers might have fretted over the amount of so-called "Black" music that Naftaly played. Rivers didn't care—just so long as it was the music that people in San Francisco wanted to hear. "Bang the hits!" Rivers would say as he wagged his finger at his young music director. New, unfamiliar music was fine with Rivers, too—just so long as it was surrounded by familiar songs. Rivers taught Naftaly "formatics"—not just *what* to play but *when* to play it. From Steve Rivers, Naftaly learned the secret paradox behind the mastery of any craft: Discipline creates freedom. With a tightly formatted station, Naftaly could take risks, be rebellious without being reckless. Under the unlikely partnership between Rivers and Naftaly, KMEL's ratings jumped again.

Rivers eventually left to take a job at KIIS-FM, the big pop station in Los Angeles. Paulette Williams interviewed a Black program director named Lee Michaels whom Naftaly thought would be just the right fit for an Urban-leaning pop station like KMEL. But Naftaly was shocked when Michaels wanted him to play *less* Black music. When Michaels left suddenly in the spring of 1987, Williams began her PD search anew.

By this time Keith Naftaly had become a favorite of record promoters. They didn't have to sell him on funk, dance, and rap records like they did other, older programmers. Naftaly's peers at other stations noticed that he was often among the first in the country to program songs that would eventually become hits. In 1987 a San Francisco–based national radio trade magazine called the *Gavin Report* made Keith Naftaly its "Music Director of the Year" at their annual convention. Naftaly walked to the dais and accepted the award, his voice cracking. Afterward he drove home to Miraloma Park to show the Lucite trophy his parents. Bryna and Stanley brought out the camera and took pictures.

So when Lee Michaels left and the PD job at KMEL became vacant again, a few record reps called Naftaly and told him he should go for the job.

"Do you really want to train another person to be your boss?" asked Kim Hughes, RCA's local promotion woman.

Naftaly replied that he already had his dream job. He liked to focus on music. He wasn't interested in meeting with the sales staff, hiring and firing air personalities—all the duties of a program director.

"Shut up!" Hughes said. "I'm giving you an assignment. Go home and jot down every reason that you should become program director, starting with you don't want anyone questioning your musical decisions."

As Naftaly did his homework he had a change of heart. The next day he walked into Paulette Williams's office, list in hand.

"With all due respect," Naftaly began, his voice trembling, "I'd like to submit myself as a possible candidate for PD of this radio station."

Williams arched her eyebrows and sat back in her big chair. "I'm rather surprised to hear you say that."

Naftaly talked about the station's ratings success under his musical watch. He talked about his strong relationships with the air staff. He talked about ways to increase revenue and solidify KMEL's position in the market.

When he was finished Williams looked at her young music director. "These are some very good ideas. I want you to know that I will give this serious consideration."

Paulette Williams waited for Naftaly to leave her office. Then she picked up the phone to call Howard Grafman.

The appointment of Keith Naftaly as program director of KMEL in June of 1987 was controversial. Some programmers said that putting a twenty-four-year-old in charge of a valuable radio property in a top market was risky. Others derided Naftaly because he was "off-air"—meaning that he hadn't started his career as a disc jockey, as most music and program directors had. But to Paulette Williams and Howard Grafman, Naftaly was a bargain: a kid who could do a better job than most programmers for half the price.

Steve Rivers had given Naftaly a mantra: "Bang the hits." To that, Williams added a new one: "Raise the rates." In other words, Naftaly's programming had to make the station pricier for advertisers. Increasing the market share—the *size* of the audience—was only half of that job. The other half was making sure that audience wasn't too ethnic. KSOL, the Urban FM, got higher ratings than KMEL. But because KSOL was perceived as a "Black" station, its ratings were worth much *less* than KMEL's; therefore the two stations billed about even. Whatever Naftaly did musically it was vital that that KMEL always be perceived as a mainstream radio station with a predominantly White audience.

Naftaly thought he knew exactly what to do. Armed with Rivers's teachings and a visceral understanding of KMEL's audience, he tightened the play-

DJ Hollywood. The first to make a buck rhyming on the disco scene.
COURTESY OF DJ HOLLYWOOD

Sal Abatiello. His **Disco Fever** gave live hip-hop its first real home. With **Kurtis Blow** (left).
COURTESY OF SAL ABATIELLO OF THE LEGENDARY DISCO FEVER NIGHTCLUB

Sylvia & Joe Robinson. The Royal Couple of the rap record business in the 1950s (left), and again in the 1990s (right), after founding **Sugar Hill Records**.
COURTESY OF DIANE HARRIS

Fab Five Freddy. The painter with the gift for framing things brought the uptown scene downtown, and was the inspiration for the first record containing rap to reach #1 on the Billboard charts. Later, he would host *Yo! MTV Raps*.
BOBBY GROSSMAN

The Founders of Profile Records and Run-DMC. Profile founders **Steve Plotnicki** (far left) and **Cory Robbins** (far right) flank the group they made into rap's first superstars, Run-DMC (from left to right: Joseph "Run" Simmons, Darryl "DMC" McDaniels and Jason "Jam Master Jay" Mizell). DAVID SALIDOR

Russell Simmons and Ann Carli. Simmons (right), hip-hop's first great artist manager, and Carli (left), who helped invent hip-hop artist development, made great music together.
RICKY POWELL

Charles Stettler and the Fat Boys. Stettler, the first person in hip-hop to land a corporate sponsorship, seen here with his heavy-weight clients. (From left to right, Stettler's partner Lynda West, Darren "The Human Beat Box" Robinson, Damon "Kool Rock Ski" Wimbley, Mark "Prince Markie Dee" Morales, Charles Stettler).
COURTESY OF CHARLES STETTLER

Frienemies. (left to right) Rivals **Barry Mayo** and **Charles Warfield** ran New York's top radio stations, WRKS and WBLS, respectively; Rivals **Russell Simmons** and **Charles Stettler** managed rap's top two artists, Run-DMC and the Fat Boys.
COURTESY OF CHARLES STETTLER

The Programmers and The Promoter. Profile Records' **Manny Bella** was the first rap promotion soldier to breach Black radio's defenses; Kiss 98.7 FM's program director **Barry Mayo** and music director **Tony Quarterone** were the first to get behind Bella's artists, Run-DMC. Pictured from left to right: (standing) Quarterone; (seated) Run, Mayo, DMC, Kurtis Blow, Bella.   DAVID SALIDOR

ck Rubin. The college student who made the
st art by trying to make "the worst shit,"
oducing hip-hop's first cohesive albums and
unding the most enduring rap record label
d brand name, **Def Jam**.

JENETTE BECKMAN

Bill Stephney. The producer and theorist of Public Enemy who held Def Jam together as Russell Simmons and Rick Rubin split.

COURTESY OF ADLER ARCHIVE

The Future of Music, TV, and Film. From left to right, **Russell Simmons**, **"DJ Jazzy Jeff" Townes**, **"The Fresh Prince" Smith**, **James Lassiter**, and **Lyor Cohen** at Rush Artist Management, circa 1988. The men in this room would years later be among the most powerful in American culture.

RICKY POWELL

West Coast Rulers. The Los Angeles rap scene represented in a trinity:(front row, left to right) **Greg "Egyptian Lover" Broussard** made the music on Egyptian Empire Records, **Roger "Uncle Jamm" Clayton's** Uncle Jamm's Army ruled the stadiums, coliseums and clubs, and **Greg Mack**'s Mixmasters (originally planned as the Mack Attack Marines to compete with Uncle Jamm's Army) controlled the airwaves on KDAY-AM. (Back row, Alonzo Miller and EZ Wiggins, program and music directors of KACE, respectively)

DAVID SALIDOR

Sophie Bramly. The woman who first made MTV say "Yo!"

© BETTINA RHEIMS

Ted Demme and Pete Dougherty. The pushy production assistant Demme (left) pestered his boss Dougherty (right) until MTV allowed them to bring rap videos to the American music channel.

COURTESY OF PETER DOUGHERTY

Matt Dike and Michael Ross. The founders of L.A.'s Delicious Vinyl made some of the first hip-hop records embraced by pop radio, including Tone Loc's "Wild Thing" and Young MC's "Bust A Move."

The Source Mind Squad. Straight outta Harvard and into Manhattan, the young hip-hop zealots tried to keep hip-hop pure but got into a mudfight with each other over issues of integrity. Top row, from left to right: Reginald C. Dennis, James Bernard, Ed Young, Derrick Hawes, Matteo "Matty C" Capoluongo, Jon Shecter, Rob "Reef" Tewlow, Dave Mays, Chris Wilder. Kneeling: Phil Pabon.

The Unlikely Creators of Multicultural Radio. Keith Naftaly (left), **Paulette Williams** (second from left) and **Hosh Gureli** (far right) made San Francisco's KMEL the first pop station to aggressively play hip-hop. **Tom Silverman**, the founder of Tommy Boy Music (second from right), provided much of the soundtrack.

Rick Cummings. Cummings, the first in American pop radio to brand his stations using the term "hip-hop," pushed rap onto the playlists of Emmis Broadcasting's top stations, Power 106 in Los Angeles and Hot 97 in New York. Pictured (left) with **50 Cent**.
COURTESY OF RICK CUMMINGS

Andre Harrell and Sean "Puffy" Combs. Combs (right) began as Harrell's intern at Uptown Records. Years after Harrell (left) fired him, when Combs had become a one-man brand, Combs hired his old boss. CHI MODU/DIVERSEIMAGES

Jorge Hinojosa.
The artist manager who tangled
with Time Warner over Ice-T's
controversial "Cop Killer."
COURTESY OF JORGE HINOJOSA

The Steve Rifkind Company. Steve Rifkind branded hip-hop's underground promotion
methods with his "Street Team" and marketed it to corporate America; while his **Loud
Records** landed an historic deal with the Wu Tang Clan. **Steve Rifkind** (left) pictured
with partners **Jon Rifkind** (middle) and **Rich Isaacson** (right).

list by jettisoning every song that didn't fit his vision for the station. Out went the bland rock records: Huey Lewis, Laura Branigan, and Bananarama. In went rhythmic music: Lisa Lisa, Whitney Houston, and LL Cool J. Henceforth KMEL would have a consistent sound that reflected the lifestyle of its listeners—White, Black, Asian, Latino. The soul boat set sail once more.

Next, Naftaly made changes to his air staff. He thought disc jockeys should sound like real people, rather than the seasoned professionals with the typical "pukey" DJ voice: overdone, artificial, and corny. He shifted sexy-sounding DJs like Evan Luck into prime shifts. He raided KSOL for two "mixers"—Michael Erickson and Cameron Paul—DJs who specialized not in on-air patter, but in blending the hottest dance music in one seamless forty-minute set called a "power mix."

When Naftaly spiked the rotation with mixes, Paulette Williams and the sales staff got nervous. Maybe the station was starting to sound too Black? Maybe Keith had taken things a little too far? Their doubts ceased in early 1988 when the winter Arbitron ratings came in. In his first ratings "book" as program director, Keith Naftaly had lifted the station from a 4.9 to a 6.1 percent share. KMEL was now the top-rated music station in San Francisco. Meanwhile, KSOL had dropped to a 4.5 percent share. KMEL had stolen the Urban station's audience, which also included a good number of White and Asian listeners. KMEL's music had become more "Black," but to Williams's relief, the racial composition of her station's audience remained a reflection of the Bay Area as a whole. While his staff celebrated in the hallway, Naftaly returned to his office and sat behind his desk.

Oh, my God, he thought. *What do I do now?*

Things had happened so quickly, he hadn't even found a replacement for himself as music director. Naftaly's first hire was a brilliant young programmer from Phoenix who had a great ear for hits, Kevin Weatherly. The problem was that their roles were reversed. It was Naftaly the program director who suggested the most unorthodox music—rap records in particular—and Weatherly, his number two, who time and again tried to rein in Naftaly by suggesting safer choices. But Naftaly didn't want to play "Hungry Eyes" by Eric Carmen, no matter how big a hit it was elsewhere, nor any of the other songs on the *Dirty Dancing* soundtrack. Naftaly needed a music director who would push him farther, not contain him.

On cue, Naftaly got a call from a mentor, Sunny Joe White. Naftaly idolized White because he had accomplished the impossible: White was a Black, gay programmer who ran Boston's most successful pop station, Kiss 108, by playing rhythmic music. White urged Naftaly to meet his music assistant at Kiss, a gangly twenty-seven-year-old Turkish-Swedish-American from upstate New York named Hasim "Hosh" Gureli who had made himself the most popular club DJ in Boston.

"He reminds me of you," White told Naftaly.

Naftaly flew to Boston and talked music with Gureli as the young DJ made photocopies in Kiss 108's mailroom. Naftaly realized that he didn't know half the records that Gureli mentioned, much of it the new "house music" coming out of Chicago. For the first time in a long time, Naftaly was being scooped on new music. He discovered that Gureli, too, had grown up on Black music, written fictional playlists just like him, and wasn't afraid to argue a musical point passionately.

"I take pop hits and mix them up with more aggressive records, so the audience learns something," Gureli said. "I push them to the cliff, but never over it."

Weatherly went to work for Steve Rivers at KIIS in Los Angeles. Naftaly hired Gureli and flew him to San Francisco. Gureli, with his East Coast edge, fervent opinions, and encyclopedic knowledge of Black and dance music, might have driven any other program director crazy. For Naftaly he was the perfect match.

Naftaly and Gureli shared a love for edgy music, and rap records were a natural part of that. Immediately after they became partners, they championed two hard-core rap records that even most Black programmers refused to play, "Follow the Leader" by Eric B & Rakim, and "Don't Believe the Hype" by Public Enemy. Naftaly was particularly proud of the Public Enemy record, in which Chuck D castigated radio programmers for not having the guts to play him in prime time. Naftaly and Gureli did. By the end of the year KMEL was playing more rap records than crosstown Urban KSOL.

Naftaly and Gureli kept a lid on the sales department's anxieties through the use of a strategy called "day-parting." The station played female-friendly R&B during the workday. But at two p.m., when schools across the Bay Area let out, KMEL shifted to an hour and a half of the latest rap and dance records. By the afternoon commute, the station slid back into more mainstream hits. Though the beat never stopped, how KMEL *sounded* depended on when you *listened*. In this way, KMEL rendered moot the usual demographic battles between female and male, old and young, becoming almost all things to nearly all people.

One of the reasons that KMEL could program rap so casually is that Bay Area listeners had been prepped for it by the most active hip-hop DJ scene in the country. Mobile jocks had been plying their trade at high school gymnasiums, college frat parties, and parks for almost a decade. Some landed at the many college and community radio stations across the Bay Area. A network of hip-hop shows had been up and running for years, with nearly a hundred hours of rap programming per week. DJs linked together to form several "record pools," which helped spread new music across the area's radio stations and nightclubs.

Keith Naftaly and Hosh Gureli tapped into this matrix by hiring established radio mixers like Erickson and Paul, and club DJs like Dave Moss and Theo Mizuhara. In this way, KMEL's mixers became an early warning system for new music. At other radio stations mix jocks had to fight to get their skeptical program and music directors to place one of their hot songs into the station's regular rotation. At KMEL Naftaly and Gureli welcomed new music from their mixers. Moreover, KMEL's custom mixes could make hits out of otherwise forgettable songs. Cameron Paul's remix of Salt-N-Pepa's "Push It" was the version that Next Plateau Records president Eddie O'Loughlin issued as the official single and video. Because of KMEL, Salt-N-Pepa became stars, and Paul became a sought-after remixer.

For the KMEL mixers who weren't Cameron Paul—with his blue jumpsuit, blue Corvette, and jewel-encrusted sunglasses—life wasn't so easy. KMEL paid its lesser-known mix jocks with exposure, not money. Alex Mejia, a gentle kid from the rough streets of East Oakland, worked for free, earning money on the side by promoting records for a local distributor, City Hall Records. One day, when Gureli discovered that Mejia had carried a record to rival station KSOL, he threatened to fire him.

"But it's my *job!*" Mejia sputtered, tears welling in his eyes. "I haven't gotten paid here for *three whole years*. Do you know what an embarrassment this is to my family that you don't compensate me for my time and effort here?"

Gureli told Naftaly to start paying Mejia.

The KMEL mixers even in competition formed a tight network, with the notable exception of Cameron Paul. Alex Mejia respected Paul's signature tape-editing technique—the "stop and cut," wherein the record was quickly slowed to a complete stop, and then started again, perfectly on beat. One day, Mejia called Paul for advice on how to do his own edits.

"Alex," Paul responded, "I am like a *magician*. I can't tell you the secrets, or there won't be any magic for you guys anymore."

Gureli and Naftaly had organized Saturday nights into a nonstop series of mix hours, one DJ after the other, called Club 106. Mejia and the rest of the gang perfected their mixes in the station's production rooms, then ran their reels into the studio at the last minute. Sometimes, the mixers would band together to "break" a new record, each of them playing it in their own mixes. Paul, not surprisingly, didn't go along with the rabble.

"It won't break," Paul once told Mejia, "until I break it."

Mejia thought otherwise. He took on additional programming duties at the station, calling Bay Area retail outlets to keep tabs on emerging local records. One day, Adrian Santos, a buyer at Star Records in San Jose, told Mejia about a hot record by a local group called Flynamic Force. Mejia hadn't heard of them before. Santos gave him the phone number printed on the record label. Mejia called the number and left a message, requesting a copy of the record for his mix on KMEL and leaving his home address in Alameda.

Later that night Mejia answered a knock on the door of his studio apartment. On his threshold stood two guys in matching black jackets: a Black kid with a high-top fade haircut, and a smaller, muscular kid who looked Latino.

"We're Flynamic Force," they said, looking a bit confused. "Is this KMEL?"

"This is my *house*," Mejia responded, incredulous. "I just needed you to send the record."

They handed the vinyl to Mejia, who thanked them and closed the door. A minute later Mejia could still see them outside, talking, scratching their heads. Mejia went to the door again.

"What's going on, guys?" Mejia asked.

"Well," the smaller guy said, speaking with an accent he couldn't quite place, "you called from KMEL, and we thought you were gonna play the record."

The Black kid spoke up. "My homeboy quit his job!"

"What?!" Mejia said.

"My mom called me at work and said that KMEL needed the record right now," said the smaller guy, "and they wouldn't let me leave, so I quit my job."

"You quit your job to bring me this record?!" Mejia asked.

"Yeah."

Mejia sighed. He understood that kind of dedication. "Come on inside, guys. Let's talk for a second."

Inside, the duo introduced themselves. The black kid called himself "MC Sway." The other one with the funny accent was "King Tech."

Sway, born John Calloway, came from a rough neighborhood in East Oakland a few miles from where Mejia had once lived. Calloway had grown up on welfare, lived in a house without running water and electricity, and seen dead bodies lying in alleys as he walked to school. His mother enrolled him in track and field to keep him out of the streets.

Calloway went to Oakland High, the same high school as Keith Naftaly's mother, Bryna. But by the mid-eighties, Oakland High was all Black. While at Oakland, Calloway traded track for rap music. After graduation, he formed a group with his cousin Chuck and his friend from track, Al. They needed a DJ, and Al said he knew a kid named Rod from Hayward, a well-off suburb between Oakland and San Jose. Rod was rich and had equipment. They arranged a meeting at Al's aunt's house in North Oakland. Calloway saw two Latino-looking guys jump out of an old Porsche. Rod was the guy with the tight jeans, fat laces, and quick step.

The group made plans to meet at Rod's parents' house in Hayward to rehearse. However, on the day of their first practice, Calloway couldn't find Chuck and Al anywhere. So he called Rod himself. "I don't know where everyone else is," Calloway said. "I don't really know you. But I'ma jump on this BART. You pick me up from the station, and we'll just start working from there."

Rod's home was a revelation. He discovered that Rod wasn't Mexican like he thought, but Iranian. He had never been in a Muslim house before. The Sepand family—Rod's parents and sister—treated Calloway like he was a part of theirs. Practice at Rod's house soon became a routine for the two of them.

They took the name of Rod's old dance crew, "Flynamic Force," and Rod dubbed himself the "King of Techniques," or "King Tech" for short. Tech named Calloway "MC Sway," a nod to an Eric B & Rakim song called "Move the Crowd." Now that they were a partnership, they put everything they had into the group. Sway worked to save money to record their music—

cooking hamburgers at a Kwik Way in Oakland that kept getting robbed, stuffing pillows at a furniture factory, running conduits of wire at the Alameda Naval Air Station. Finally in 1988 Sway and Tech had enough to lay down an EP of six songs.

Sway and Tech were hungry, but things were slow going. College airplay hadn't yielded much in the way of sales, perhaps a few thousand copies. KMEL was now the holy grail for local rap acts. That was when Alex Mejia called. At his apartment Mejia listened to their record and promised to play it on the air the following Saturday. He did. At Mejia's behest, so did other KMEL mixers. Mejia then looked for other ways to help the duo get exposure at rap-oriented events that the station was starting to sponsor around the Bay Area.

First he convinced Sway to enter an MC battle at the Southland Mall in Hayward. Sway made quick work of the other rappers and won a thousand dollars' worth of stereo equipment. Broke, Sway would have preferred cash. Next Mejia urged Tech to enter KMEL's upcoming DJ battle at City Nights, a club in downtown San Francisco. This was big, Mejia said. The winner would get to create a forty-minute mix that aired on the station. Tech said he was more interested in the $1,000 cash prize. He practiced for three weeks.

On the night of the battle, DJs from across the Bay Area blended records and brought their best turntable tricks. Mejia and Sway watched Tech take the stage to a chorus of obligatory boos. Tech began his set by triggering a sample of some dialogue from the teen comedy *Fast Times at Ridgemont High*, the scene where Mr. Hand is passing papers back to his slacker students: *C! D! F! F! F!* Tech pointed to each of his rival DJs in succession, as if grading each of them. The crowd began to whoop, realizing the dis. *What are you, people? On dope?!* said Mr. Hand. Tech segued into "Jack the Ripper," LL Cool J's devastating response to Kool Moe Dee's dis record "How Ya Like Me Now."

"How you like *me* now?!" LL Cool J's voice boomed. "I'm gettin' bizzier! I'm double platinum, / I'm watching you get dizzier!"

Tech threw on a second copy of the record and began cutting back and forth between the two until the crowd could hear only:

"Bizzier! *Dizzier!* Bizzier! *Dizzier!*"

As the audience screamed with delight, Tech's arms moved back and forth between the records. Then he added some extra motions to his furious cutting. By the time the clubgoers realized what he was doing, Tech was only a few moves away from taking his shirt off entirely.

When Tech finished his set, his chest bare and heaving, City Nights was a madhouse. Sway and Mejia rushed to the stage, beaming with pride.

"I think you just changed DJing in the Bay Area," Mejia told him.

The members of the panel combined their scores and awarded the top prize of the night to King Tech, in spite of the fact that one of the celebrity judges, Cameron Paul, had given the hot new DJ a score of zero.

When King Tech arrived at KMEL to pick up his check, he had forgotten about his forty-minute mix.

"I heard you killed it the other night," Keith Naftaly told him. "You've gotta come do that on the air."

Tech asked Naftaly if he was serious. "I just need to know what you're gonna play," Naftaly said, adding that Tech would have to throw in some hits for balance—Janet Jackson, Mariah Carey.

Upon hearing that Tech demurred. "I'm cool, man."

Naftaly was surprised. "I'm giving you a big chance here," he said.

Tech replied that as a hip-hop DJ, he had a reputation to uphold. He couldn't play records just because they were safe hits.

"Do me a favor," Naftaly replied. "Just let Hosh see the list. That's all I'm asking."

Tech, the purist, left without committing. Sway, the realist, urged Tech to reconsider. So Tech borrowed a reel-to-reel machine from a producer friend, Dan "the Automator" Nakamura, and went to work. He began his set with an old, obscure R&B record that few other than old Bronx DJs and breakdancers would know. The song was called "I Believe in Miracles" by the Jackson Sisters, treasured for the long drum and clavinet break with which it began. Next Tech threw on one hard-core rap record after another, finally ending with snippets of a Louis Farrakhan speech about Black incarceration over a Public Enemy instrumental.

Hosh Gureli wasn't happy when Tech showed up with the reel only a few hours before his scheduled Tuesday airtime. But Hosh played it, and Tech listened to KMEL with awe as he drove back to his parents' house: "I believe in miracles," the Jackson Sisters sang. "Don't you?"

The next day, Tech got a breathless call from Gureli.

"You played the fucking *Jackson Sisters*? On *KMEL*?! You've got balls!" Tech was stunned that Gureli even knew the record.

In a phone call to Tech later that night, Naftaly was short on compliments. Naftaly had a problem with the Farrakhan speech, simply because the Muslim minister could be a polarizing figure for KMEL's listeners, each one of whom Naftaly wanted to feel comfortable and welcome. Tech hung up the phone feeling that Naftaly had just dissed him.

But on the following day, Naftaly called Tech in for a meeting and invited him to do a weekly mix.

"Honestly, I thought you didn't like it," Tech said.

"The response has been pretty damn good," Naftaly replied. "We had a lot of calls." Despite his reluctant demeanor and his discomfort with the speech, Naftaly actually loved the mix. He needed a crazy guy like this at the station. But he couldn't let a kid like Tech get too comfortable, too soon.

True to form, Tech's Tuesday mixes got wilder. He would play songs like Kool G Rap's "Talk Like Sex," which was nasty enough, even without Tech forgetting to bleep out the curses.

Naftaly, however, didn't mind the *occasional* curse. On the record he had to prohibit them as a matter of FCC regulation and station policy. When he heard them, he might cringe. But Naftaly knew that a listener would have to make a complaint before the station got in trouble, and KMEL was in a market with a progressive audience that wasn't easily offended. Most of the time Naftaly looked the other way. He liked pushing it.

Soon hip-hop heads across the Bay Area were tuning in and taping Tech's mixes religiously. Tech wanted to find a way to involve his partner, so he began a segment called "The Underground Bunker," with Sway and local MCs freestyling over beats. After six months Tech grew restless.

"I really appreciate the opportunity you've given me," Tech told Naftaly. "But I want to *talk* about these records."

"What do you mean?" Naftaly asked.

"I'm on the air for forty minutes and it's over for the rest of the week," Tech said. "Nobody knows what that record was, how I got it, or where it came from." Tech was asking for a specialty program devoted to hip-hop, to raise the political and cultural consciousness of kids in the Bay Area. He wanted to call it "The Wake-Up Show."

Naftaly didn't have to be sold. He knew that Tech was becoming a local celebrity now that Alex Mejia had secured Sway and Tech a deal with Giant/Warner Bros. Records. Their new single, "Follow for Now," was beating Madonna during KMEL's Top Seven at Seven countdown. Naftaly understood that the testosterone and nerdiness of an all-rap show might turn some of his listeners off. But to Naftaly it was worth losing females for a few hours in return for bolstering the reputation of KMEL as the home of cool, underground hip-hop. Plus Tech was slowly learning how to be a more responsible programmer.

On a Friday night in the fall of 1990, "The Wake-Up Show" became the very first rap show on a pop station in the United States.

Sway and Tech were in the house with Alex Mejia and a few of their MC and DJ friends. Keith, as usual, was in his office late, working on the playlist. After Tech's assistant DJ, Joe Quixx, cued up the very first track, Main Source's "Live at the Barbeque," Tech froze. *Joe is playing the unedited version.* The song led off with a verse from an unsigned, unsung rapper named Nasty Nas, who used the "s-word" in the first few lines. Even Tech knew it was too much. A few seconds later Keith poked his head into the studio and shot Tech a look.

"C'mon, Tech. Is this how it's gonna be?"

"Dude, I'm so sorry," Tech replied, meaning it.

The rest of the first show proceeded without incident. But it was chaos, a bunch of kids with no on-air experience all talking at the same time. Naftaly gave them time to get it right. Soon Sway stepped out in front with his booming voice, and the show's regulars and visitors learned to take turns. Gradually a format emerged. Tech would begin each show with a classic break, one that had been sampled in a popular rap song, just to teach a bit of history. Tech and his band of DJs, like Prince Ice, would alternate on the turntables. When artists dropped by, as they did more often, Sway would handle most of the interviews. And it became an implicit rule that artists could not leave the studio without doing a live, impromptu freestyle rhyme. "You'd better catch wreck," they would say, "or feel the wrath of Sway and King Tech."

As 1990 gave way to 1991, and Keith Naftaly and Hosh Gureli placed more rap into their regular rotation, Mejia and Tech became valuable resources for discovering new music. While Mejia *suggested,* Tech *insisted. I'm telling you, Keith, you gotta play the new X-Clan. The new PE. The new EPMD.* Naftaly played more hard-core rap than any pop programmer in the country, and still Tech was coming into his office every two seconds. One day, Naftaly lost his cool.

"Tech!" he said. "You see my desk? This desk represents the entire Bay

Area. You see this *little* area here? That's *your* audience. That's what you have to worry about." Naftaly then spread his arms to embrace the length of his desk. "And *this* is what I have to worry about."

Tech relented. But a few weeks later Tech and Gureli hosted a KMEL event at a local mall, and thousands of KMEL's listeners showed up: White, Black, Asian, Latino. When Gureli threw on "Ice Ice Baby"—a pop rap record and KMEL staple—the crowd started pelting the DJ booth with loose change. Tech returned to Naftaly's office, gloating.

"Isn't it funny," Tech said, "that my entire audience showed up to this one gig?"

Naftaly and Gureli came to realize that their DJs were cultivating an appetite for more authentic hip-hop in KMEL's audience. The mixers came to respect the roles Naftaly and Gureli played at the station. Tech thought of it this way: The DJs were the public faces for KMEL who found and tested new music. Hosh Gureli was the hip guy who filtered that music into regular rotation. And Keith Naftaly's job was to make sure the DJ kids didn't burn the station down.

Outside the world of commercial radio, David Cook had spent the better part of a decade blending hip-hop and community activism in the Bay Area. As "Davey D," he hosted three shows on college and community radio. He wrote a column in the weekly arts magazine *BAM*. He contributed to *The Source*. He led the Bay Area Hip-Hop Coalition that supported struggling hip-hop artists and boycotted others, like NWA, whose nihilism might be a danger to the community. He wrote a regular newsletter, the "Bay Area Beat Report." The *San Francisco Bay Guardian* had honored Davey's work by naming him one of their "Heroes of the Year." But for all his leadership, especially within the Black community, Cook was ignored by the ostensibly "Black" FM station, KSOL. Davey still remembered the uncomfortable feeling of sitting in KSOL's lobby, wearing a suit, steamy sweat on his back and brow, waiting for a meeting with Bernie Moody, the station's MD. Moody never emerged.

Instead, KMEL gave Davey D a home. When Cook showed Naftaly his idea—to reconfigure his newsletter into the "KMEL Beat Report"—Naftaly hired Cook as the station's first public affairs coordinator, and gave him the community affairs program on Sunday mornings at seven a.m. Most music stations hid their public affairs programming. But Cook made "Street Science" a dynamic show, and Naftaly moved Cook into a better slot.

From the moment that Keith Naftaly stepped on the school bus that took him from Miraloma Park to Hunters Point, Naftaly understood that a radio station could be more than just a source of entertainment to a community. It could *be* a community itself. Naftaly thought there was nothing more banal than a pop outlet positioning itself as "the party station." KMEL under Naftaly's reign became "the People's Station." KMEL's first TV spots showed listeners of every ethnicity moving to the beat, culminating in a shot of a mixed-race couple—a Black husband, his Latino wife, and their child. Naftaly's on-air promos pushed education. He started a series called "Knowledge Is Power," forty-five-second, quick-edited, beat-driven spots like "Five things you should know about crack" and "Five things you should know about AIDS," during a time when most commercial music stations wouldn't dare mention the names of those epidemics.

Finally Naftaly solidified KMEL's position in the community with another idea borrowed from Naftaly's hero, Sunny Joe White, who had for years promoted a huge annual benefit show in Boston called "the Kiss Concert." What if KMEL could promote a concert featuring its hottest artists and donate all the proceeds to charity?

Naftaly named his concert idea "Summerjam."

After a lackluster first year, legendary concert promoter Bill Graham took Naftaly under his wing and showed him how to use KMEL's influence with record companies and local artists to leverage a more successful show. The second Summerjam was everything Graham promised. The capacity show featured LL Cool J as the headliner, with twenty thousand fans screaming along to "Rock the Bells." Each year's concert got bigger and more successful. Summerjam began bringing in millions of dollars for charities like the Omega Boys Club, and Naftaly resisted the encroachment of the KMEL sales department, who suggested that they donate only 25 percent of the proceeds. Naftaly refused. By 1990, the concert had become a minifestival, simulcast on KMEL, with huge rosters of rap and R&B artists performing for a peaceful, diverse crowd.

With Summerjam, KMEL not only became the undisputed ruler of the Bay Area but one of the most important radio stations in the country. Now people outside the Bay Area started to take notice.

Keith Naftaly thought the idea was a little ridiculous.

Tom Silverman, head of Tommy Boy Records and the founder of the New Music Seminar, was on the phone, telling the twenty-eight-year-old programmer that he was one of two people who would be receiving the Seminar's *lifetime achievement award* this summer. The other recipient? Ahmet Ertegun, the sixty-eight-year-old founder of Atlantic Records.

"You don't realize what you've done for rap music," Silverman said. "You don't realize what KMEL represents as a radio station, and what this means to indie labels like Tommy Boy."

Naftaly had never positioned KMEL as a rap station. Rap records comprised only one part of KMEL's playlist, which featured mostly rhythmic records by artists like Janet Jackson and Paula Abdul. But with KDAY's demise just months before, Naftaly's KMEL had become by default the best radio station for rap in the country.

In July of 1991 Naftaly, the young Turk, sat in the green room with the old Turk, telling Ertegun how silly he felt being honored alongside such a legend. But even Ertegun knew who Naftaly was. In fact, KMEL had been the only pop station in the country to add Atlantic's rap record "Cha Cha Cha," by MC Lyte. Later, during his acceptance speech, Naftaly made an offhand remark that he couldn't see any reason why a Top 40 station couldn't play a hard-core rap group like Gang Starr along with R&B and pop artists, at *any* time of day.

To Naftaly's astonishment, the audience leaped to its feet and gave him a thunderous ovation. Many of these people, of course, had been working for nearly a decade in service to a truth they held dear: that hip-hop was the new American pop. Now here was the first-ever pop programmer to validate that belief. In that room, in the Times Square Marriott Marquis, Naftaly grasped for the first time the impact of KMEL on the national music scene.

The New Music Seminar had always been rap-friendly territory. But Naftaly's prowess as a programmer was honored in traditional radio circles as well. An annual contest called "AIR" gave away a new Porsche to the programmer who could predict the greatest number of hit singles for that year. Naftaly had won twice. Both Naftaly and Hosh Gureli were lavished with awards from radio trade magazines like *Billboard* and the *Gavin Report*.

Still, KMEL's success exasperated many people in radio and records. Nothing could be more frustrating to a national promotion executive than the biggest pop station in the fourth-largest market consistently refusing to play the Bryan Adamses and the Bon Jovis, the kinds of generic vanilla records that traditionally took precedence over records from Black artists. Some execs accused KMEL of skewing the pop charts and suggested that KMEL's reporting status be changed from Top 40 to Urban. Paulette Williams knew that a format change, even in name only, could be disastrous for the station's ad sales. She fought it by providing the trades with a demographic breakdown of KMEL's audience: 20 percent Black, 20 percent Latino, and 60 percent White, Asian, and other. It was perfectly in line with the Bay Area's ethnic composition and with any other major-market pop station.

KMEL remained a Top 40 reporter. But as more stations began to "lean rhythmic," stations like Power 106 in L.A. and Hot 97 in New York—playing Black artists like Janet Jackson, Latin dance artists like Exposé, and the occasional rap artist like LL Cool J—the industry found a way to distinguish these outlets from their rock-leaning pop counterparts: They created a new subformat called "rhythmic crossover." On one hand, it was a tribute to the growing influence of these stations and the changing tastes of young Americans. On the other, it was another way to preserve the status quo for the established programmers and promoters who got their start in the 1960s and 1970s.

Keith Naftaly called them "rednecks." In many cases they were just that: provincial, White, bred on rock and roll, with attitudes about Black music and Black people that ranged from ambivalent at best to hostile at worst. These were the programmers who had kept radio racially segregated. The rhythmic stations were usually programmed by younger people who came of age in the 1980s: Naftaly and Gureli at KMEL, Michelle Santosuosso at Q 106 in San Diego, Albee Dee at WPGC in D.C., Pam Grund at Q 102 in Philly, Eric Bradley at B96 in Chicago, Kevin McCabe at Hot 97 in New York, Shelly Hart at KUBE in Seattle. The older programmers had their own word for these folks: *brats*. None of these baby programmers was Black, but in most cases they were more urbane than the older guys. Some had grown up on Michael Jackson and Prince, on Run-DMC and LL Cool J, and had much more openness to Black music. None, however, approached the boldness of Naftaly when it came to programming hip-hop.

The generational conflict between the rednecks and the brats came to a head at the 1992 Gavin Convention. Usually the convention was a staid affair, with a mix of seminars and panels—although the record company-sponsored after-parties could get a little wild. Every year the old guard dismissed KMEL's evident success. *Only in San Francisco,* they said, *could a pop station play this much rap.* But this year would be a different kind of convention. A college friend of King Tech's named Brian Samson had started a rap chart in the *Gavin Report.* Samson created a small presence for rap at the previous year's convention. But nothing could have prepared Samson and his bosses for what would happen this year.

The Gavin Convention in February of 1992 was nothing short of a harmonic convergence for hip-hop and pop radio. Indie and major labels came with dozens of new rap artists to promote. Lindsey Williams from Chrysalis arrived with a motley bohemian crew from Atlanta called Arrested Development. A young, unknown producer named Jermaine Dupri came with a kiddie group—two young boys who wore their jeans backward and called themselves Kris Kross. Rick Rubin's Def American Recordings picked up a successful Seattle rapper named Sir Mix-A-Lot, and reps from the label arrived with a thirty-foot-tall balloon in the shape of a voluptuous brown ass, inflating it atop Rough Trade's record shop on Haight Street to support Mix-A-Lot's new single, "Baby Got Back."[12]

Arriving executives and artists landed in a market that had become the most important for rap in the country. Venues like Club Townsend and City Nights welcomed rap acts for showcases. A dozen college radio shows awaited drop-ins from visiting rap acts. And at the center of it all was KMEL, stunning New Yorkers and Angelenos alike by playing credible hip-hop songs like A Tribe Called Quest's "Check the Rhime" in broad daylight. The weekend of the convention, the guests of "The Wake-Up Show" had to line up outside the studio for a turn on the mic.

Back at the Westin St. Francis hotel in Union Square, radio programmers might have wondered if they had returned to the right convention. The lobby was overrun by hip-hop kids. Rappers freestyled in boisterous ciphers by the elevators. Record reps passed out promotional flyers and stickers, and David Paul distributed copies of his local rap magazine, *The Bomb.* White collegians and Filipino DJs mingled with Black street promoters and Latino b-boys. Many older White programmers looked nervous around so many young Black people. But the only confrontations that transpired were between the older and younger programmers at the official discussion sessions, where the issue of rap on radio was more contentious than ever.

---

[12]A group that included the author of this book.

On the penultimate day of the convention, Keith Naftaly, who loathed panels, made a rare appearance. Sitting on the dais, Naftaly listened as Rick Dees—the morning man at L.A.'s KIIS-FM, and the creator of the novelty record "Disco Duck"—declared that his listeners couldn't relate to rap music because they could neither sing along nor understand the words.

"Everyone is so busy, they don't have time to devote to memorize them," said Dees. "With Right Said Fred you know he is too sexy for a dozen things, and in a week I can memorize that."

Naftaly had endured this kind of horseshit for years. Now he had to listen to this moron.

Naftaly leaned into his microphone. "It seems," he said, "like he is referring to freak aliens." Naftaly explained that he had taken the time to educate his audience about hard-core hip-hop, and they had responded by making KMEL the number one station in his market.

The implication was clear. It wasn't just in San Francisco that hip-hop could be programmed as pop. It could happen anywhere.

Everything changed after the convention.

Brian Samson's bosses at *The Gavin Report* considered firing him. They held Samson responsible for the chaos in the lobby and the hallways—which he was, in part. When Samson ran out of official passes to give to artists and their managers, he bought a laminating machine and bootlegged badges in his hotel suite. But Samson's rap section was bringing in too much money for their magazine. CEO David Dalton announced that *Gavin* would curtail rap events at the next convention. The move was blocked by a furious letter-writing campaign by young hip-hop promotion executives, many of them White, who accused Dalton and his organization of racism.

Many of the radio programmers in attendance found they could no longer refuse rap. KIIS-FM eventually forced Rick Dees to play the songs he predicted that no one would understand: "Tennessee" by Arrested Development, "Jump" by Kris Kross, and "Baby Got Back" by Sir Mix-A-Lot. In markets across the country, rhythmic crossover stations were playing more hip-hop.

And in the Bay Area, KMEL finally got some competition.

For years Naftaly's station had ruled in the ratings—with the exception of San Jose, where a dance station called Hot 97.7 had drawn the city's Latin youth away from KMEL. But Naftaly didn't give an inch in the fight. Once, Naftaly visited a live show in San Jose, cosponsored by both stations. Naftaly and Hot 97.7's program director, Steve Smith, quarreled over the placement of their respective banners.

Up in San Francsico, KSOL sat for years with a dismal 2 percent share of the market. But just before the Gavin Convention, the Urban station finally rose from its stupor, hired a consultant, and flipped formats. They were now calling themselves WILD 107, their playlist a carbon copy of KMEL's with a slight Latin lean. They even gave some of their air personalities fake Hispanic names to court the young Latino audience.

Naftaly despised what he saw as a fraudulent, soulless station taking up space in *his* market, programmed by people who didn't know the music. Their staff was all up in his mix, parking their van at KMEL concerts, toilet papering his events. One of their new DJs who actually was Latino, Dave Morales—the same DJ from Mississippi who alerted SBK Records about Vanilla Ice—even copped to digging through KMEL's trash for secrets. KSOL had begun to cut into KMEL's ratings, and Naftaly thought the competition brought out the worst in people. KMEL was about peace, and here they were in a street fight.

For years Naftaly lived to work. Now he dreaded it. Paulette Williams and her new husband, Howard Grafman, were talking about selling the station. Moreover, Cameron Paul—whom Naftaly had fired in 1990 after Paul's ratings and research plummeted—had filed a $50 million wrongful termination suit against KMEL. In the suit, Paul claimed that Naftaly took regular kickbacks of $100 a week in return for keeping him on the air. When Paul stopped paying, the suit alleged, Naftaly fired him. Paul also accused Williams of failing to supervise Naftaly, who, Paul alleged, "was neither qualified nor able to act as program director." To bolster his case, Paul provided the court with copies of $7,600 in cleared checks, each endorsed by Naftaly.

Naftaly, mortified, drove to Miraloma Park to alert his parents to the coming deluge of press. As the news broke in the *San Francisco Chronicle* and *Billboard*, KMEL issued a statement backing Naftaly's version of the story, explaining that the checks were part of an extortion scheme by Paul "to have a continuing hold over Naftaly." As the depositions dragged on, Naftaly received dozens of supportive letters and phone calls from his industry friends. Indeed, Cameron Paul's accusations didn't make much sense to the legions of people who dealt with the young program director. DJs like Alex Mejia and

King Tech had never been approached by Naftaly in the manner that Paul described. Record promoters knew Naftaly as the kid who refused to make deals with the big indie promoters. Why would he then badger one of his DJs for small-time money?

Few would ever know. Williams and Howard Grafman elected to settle the case, reportedly giving Cameron Paul money in return for withdrawing the charges, and all parties signed a confidentiality agreement.[13]

On May 19, 1992 the Grafmans sold KMEL to Evergreen Media for $44 million. Paulette urged Naftaly to come along to their next radio venture, although she offered Naftaly no share of the windfall from the station he helped build. The new owners convinced Naftaly to stay by making him VP of programming for their entire chain. Now they wanted Naftaly to move to Los Angeles to fix one of their stations.

Maybe, Keith thought, it was time to move on. Gureli had done so, taking an A&R job with Clive Davis's Arista Records in New York. Evergreen's L.A. property was KKBT, 92.3 the Beat, an FM Urban station struggling from an attack by crosstown FM Power 106, a pop station that had started to behave a lot like KMEL.

Keith knew why. Until very recently Power 106 had been run by Jeff Wyatt—the programmer who had told *Billboard* that playing rap was "dangerous," who had told Hosh that what KMEL was doing would "never happen in L.A." Then Wyatt was gone, replaced by his own boss, Rick Cummings, the vice president of programming for Emmis Broadcasting, which owned Power 106 and New York's Hot 97. Just after the watershed 1992 Gavin Convention, Keith received a brief, remarkable letter from Cummings on Emmis stationery:

> *Dear Keith & Hosh:*
>
> *Just a quick note to tell you how impressed I was with KMEL—from the music to the language of the lines and*

---

[13]Both Keith Naftaly and Cameron Paul declined to discuss the specifics of the case for this book. However, Cameron Paul said the following: "I deeply regret how things ended with KMEL. I had a lot of bad counseling. If I had been more mature, and had thought things out better, I wouldn't have handled things the way I did. I got pushed in directions I wished I hadn't, and did things that I really regret."

*promos to the content between the records . . . it is a very
cool product. And fun for me to hear.*

    Hope you don't mind if I "borrow" a few things.

Rick Cummings

Less than a year after KDAY's end, rap was returning to Los Angeles
radio in a bigger way than ever.

Street Knowledge

There was no particular reason why Rick Cummings ended up being the man who created the first hip-hop format on pop radio.

On the surface Cummings wasn't much different from the radio programmers who had kept the door shut on Black music. He was White. He was from a small town in Indiana, not from some big, multicultural city like Keith Naftaly was. He liked rock and roll and hadn't heard a lot of R&B or rap. Cummings wasn't much of a music fan at all. In his youth he had wanted to be a sports announcer like Howard Cosell. When he saw how long those odds were, he became a talk radio jock. And when he got fired from a few stations for being insubordinate, he became a programmer. He could have ended up like the rest of them.

But Cummings had been lucky enough to find a mentor named Jeff Smulyan, a media entrepreneur with a progressive approach to management. Smulyan named his company "Emmis," which was the Hebrew word for "truth." He gave all his employees stock options, even secretaries and assistants. He created Emmis's "Eleven Commandments," an ethical count-down for how he wanted his people to conduct business:

XI. Admit your mistakes.
X.   Be flexible—Keep an open mind.
IX. Be rational—Look at all the options.
VIII. Have fun—Don't take this too seriously.
VII. Never get smug.

. . . and so on.

Once, when Cummings complained about a troublesome employee, Smulyan counseled compassion. "People get up in the morning wanting to do well," Smulyan told Cummings. "They want to do a good job. It's up to you to help them figure out how to do that."

Cummings took Smulyan's teachings to heart. He was open-minded. He was rational. He explored his options. And he wasn't afraid to take risks because Smulyan encouraged his autonomy, the very thing that most radio executives lacked. Which was why Rick Cummings was one of the luckiest radio executives in the country. He supervised all Emmis radio stations, flying from market to market, helping his programmers perfect their formats. "Here comes Cummings," they'd joke, "to drink and criticize."

But Cummings commanded respect. He was a formidable man with a deep, sonorous radio voice that shocked people when they finally met him in person, given that he stood only a pinch over five feet. Cummings's father and brothers were tall. But Rick had been born with osteogenesis imperfecta, or brittle bone disease. Most infants didn't survive it, but Cummings was fortunate to have a milder form of the genetic condition. Still, most of Cummings's growth energy as a kid went into repairing his easily broken bones. Cummings endured the worst of it—the pain, the cruel taunts from other children—and went on to have an accomplished career. He had in the 1970s been the program director for a little-known Emmis DJ named David Letterman. And, most important, he had pioneered the "rhythmic crossover" format in the country's top two markets, at KPWR-FM "Power 106" in Los Angeles and at WQHT-FM "Hot 97" in New York, by playing a mix of danceable music for a mostly Latino and White audience.

Cummings management had made Power and Hot the prize properties of the Emmis portfolio. But by the summer of 1991, the ratings at Power had collapsed, from a 6 percent share of the market the previous year down to 3.5. Cummings wanted to find out why. He flew from Emmis's headquarters in Indianapolis to Power's studios in Burbank.

First, Cummings called Don Kelly, the former programmer who preceeded Barry Mayo at WRKS in New York. As a consultant Kelly had launched Power 99's Urban format in Philadelphia, and in 1986 he had helped create Power 106 and brought on Power's current program director, Jeff Wyatt. For the current conundrum Cummings and Kelly decided to enlist the help of Coleman Research, a firm run by Jon Coleman, a former TV executive who had made a career in radio by bringing with him the open mind of an outsider. Coleman assembled a focus group at a special facility on Ventura Boulevard. There, Coleman's lieutenant, Pierre Bouvard, sat at a large rectangular table with over a dozen listeners from Power's target audience—Latina girls aged sixteen through twenty-four—while Cummings, Coleman, and Kelly watched and listened from behind a one-way mirror.

Bouvard asked the group what they thought of Power 106, and its signature "Latin freestyle" artists like Lisette Melendez, Sweet Sensation, and the Cover Girls—performers who were young Latinas just like them.

"Oh, Power 106," one of the participants said. "They play that whiny girl music."

Cummings's heart sank. Bouvard asked the next question: *So what kinds of music do you like?*

"Hip-hop!" she said. Suddenly the table came to life with talk of artists and songs that Cummings had no idea existed. Cummings turned to his consultant Don Kelly, the guy hired for his expertise in rhythmic music.

But Don Kelly looked absolutely perplexed. "Hip-hop?" he asked Cummings. "What's hip-hop?"

Now Cummings knew he was in deep shit.

Hip-hop, Cummings soon discovered, was merely "rap music" by another name. ("Rap you can dance to," said one of the girls in the focus group, devising her own definition.) And "rap" was a term that struck utter fear into programmers' hearts. Cummings understood why. The older and Whiter your audience was, programmers knew, the more appealing it was for advertisers. If your audience got too Black or too young, you couldn't monetize it. And "rap" was nothing if not synonymous with Black and young.

But the focus group changed Cummings's perspective. He realized that Power had been so focused on its freestyle and dance identity that it hadn't been able to see a huge change in its audience's listening habits. Latinas were now listening to rap. Power 106 and its program director, Jeff Wyatt, just flat out missed it.

Power had invested for years in its dance music image. Their slogan was "Dance Now." Their television spot featured colorfully dressed actors dancing in the streets (a stage set, actually), to DeBarge's "Rhythm of the Night," a six-year-old song. Clearly Power 106 was out of step. But leaving their old image behind meant creating a new one. Cummings had to be careful with Emmis's crown jewel.

First Cummings tested a few rap records in rotation just to see if the focus group was a fluke. It wasn't. The call-out research came back huge. Then Cummings commissioned two companies to confirm the findings. Both studies found that Latinos in Los Angeles had indeed moved on to hip-hop. Unfortunately the two reports proposed contradictory recommendations. One said that Power 106 should keep playing freestyle. *Forget the young generation*, it counseled, *and grow old with the audience you already have. When those listeners reach thirty-five or forty years of age, they'll still be listening to the Cover Girls and Exposé.* The other report, by Coleman, urged Cummings to get the freestyle stuff off the air immediately. Power 106, it said, was a "pass-through" format, meaning that it had to change every five years to keep itself current with a new generation of twelve-to-twenty-five-year olds. That meant playing hip-hop.

For Cummings the decision came down to numbers. If Power swung adult, it wouldn't have to change. But it would face a lot of competition for the adult audience. If Power skewed young and did it exactly right, it might make more money by being the only station serving the needs of a younger audience. Cummings understood that doing it right meant discounting adults altogether. Doing it right meant going all the way with rap, not "day-parting" it, but playing it morning, noon, and night. Cummings decided that he would take the riskier latter route.

It was a ride that program director Jeff Wyatt wasn't willing to take. He had already been a pioneer in programming Black music to mainstream audiences at Power 99 in Philadelphia. During the infancy of Power 106, Wyatt had been a staunch defender of the funkier music selections like Timex Social Club's "Rumors," even when Cummings worried that they were "too Black." Now Cummings seemed to be telling him that his selections weren't Black *enough*. In Wyatt's experience rap was polarizing. Programming rap risked alientating his core audience of females. He didn't think that Power had to change, and he resented Cummings' intrusion. Not long after the studies came back, Wyatt quit, telling Cummings that he was too burned-out to go through another format flip.

Now Cummings had to find somebody to fix the station, and fast. Emmis needed Power 106 more than ever, because the company was having problems. Smulyan had bought the Seattle Mariners, but his baseball venture had turned out to be a fiasco. There was a recession. Revenue had plummeted. Power 106, long the company's cash cow, had gone from first in the ratings to tenth. Emmis was faced with the prospect of cutbacks and firings. Cummings wondered if his company could continue paying him to fly around, drink, and criticize. He had just bought a big house in Indianapolis. His wife, Martha, had just given birth, and their tiny baby was in intensive care. Cummings waited until his son was healthy enough to bring home. Then in October of 1991 he flew to L.A. and checked into the Oakwood corporate apartments not far from Power's studios in Burbank. Cummings had decided to demote himself, and revamp Power 106.

Cummings had to program a rap station without knowing a thing about rap music. He knew only one person who did: his assistant back in Indianapolis, Michelle Mercer. She and her sister—both White girls in their twenties—knew every word to rap songs that Cummings was just now hearing about, like the Geto Boys song "Mind Playing Tricks on Me." Not only did Mercer like hip-hop, she was actually in Power's demographic. Having a White girl endorse the music eased Cummings's fears of veering too far from the mainstream. He made Mercer his music director.

Cummings and Mercer started adding rap tracks with abandon. By December 1991, Power 106 had more rap songs on its playlist than KMEL did— 16 to KMEL's 11. By February of 1992, around the time of the Gavin Convention, Power had 20 to KMEL's 10. At Gavin Cummings finally heard what KMEL was doing with rap. The more Cummings looked at Keith Naftaly's station, the more he saw a perfect model for the new Power 106. KMEL's *air staff* actually sounded like the music they played. He had seen KMEL's TV spots, which used shots of listeners across a broad ethnic spectrum. Most important, KMEL didn't sound like a Black station, nor like vanilla pop, either. KMEL was somehow using Black music, especially hip-hop, to knock down traditional racial and ethnic barriers, creating a perfect coalition of both inner-city and suburban kids. KMEL was unlike anything Cummings had ever seen in the business: a multicultural radio station. That, Cummings knew, was what Power 106 needed to be, too.

How did a radio station like KMEL develop such credibility and listener loyalty? Jon Coleman gave Cummings an answer. He called it the Image

Pyramid, a graphic guide to how great radio stations evolved. Unfortunately the Image Pyramid ran counter to the current conventional radio wisdom. Most stations placed emphasis on hiring popular disc jockeys and creating contests to boost their ratings. Coleman insisted that notion had it backward.

People listen to radio stations for music, he said, *first and foremost. So your first job is to get the music right.* Music formed the base of Coleman's pyramid.

Hiring credible air personalities is important, Coleman continued, *but secondary. Then come the contests and promotions. At the apex of the pyramid is community involvement, the point where stations can give to the community without seeming to pander because the station has done its homework. At that point the radio station becomes more than entertainment. It becomes an integral part of the community and its listeners' lives.*

Without ever seeing this pyramid, Keith Naftaly followed that model intuitively at KMEL.

For the first six months of his tenure, Cummings struggled to get the music right. He began playing Latino rappers like Kid Frost, Mellow Man Ace, and Lighter Shade of Brown. Cummings played 2nd II None, two Black rappers from South Central. Then the ratings came back. Power 106 had jumped from a 3.5 to a 5.0 share, tying KIIS-FM.

Charged, Cummings followed the pyramid. He made air staff changes. He fired some old jocks from Power's dance format, but kept Frank Lozano—a young Latino air personality. He hired Dave Morales from Wild 107 in San Francisco. Cummings had begun to formulate some community outreach, too—a "Stop the Violence, Increase the Peace" campaign to help get gang-bangers off the street.

But before they could launch the program, events outran Power 106.

On April 29, 1992 at 3:15 p.m. a jury in Simi Valley, California announced its acquittal of the four police officers on trial for the beating of Black motorist Rodney King. A few hours later, Los Angles was burning.

Many of Power 106's young listeners lived in communities that were suddenly under siege. Cummings cut his regular programming and booked a marathon show that included guests like Jesse Jackson and Arsenio Hall. Frank Lozano, the host, was petrified. He was a pop DJ not a talk-show host, and not particularly political.

After the riots it became clear that Power 106, despite its ratings, hadn't quite paid its dues. They weren't KMEL, and they sure weren't KDAY. One female caller, a teenage gangbanger, mocked Power's Polyannaish "Season of Peace" campaign in late 1992. "My parents are in *jail*," she said. "My mom was fourteen when she had me. My dad was eighteen. And they're in jail for *life*. I'm not *ever* going to see them again. It's so easy for people to say, 'Why don't you get out? There's a brighter side!' I've never *seen* that brighter side."

In the following months Cummings did his best to reach out to people who he thought were authentic, credible voices in the Latino community as well, like rapper Kid Frost. But when Frost began speaking, it didn't take long for Lozano and Cummings to figure out that the rapper, bedecked like a 1940s pachuco gangster, had little in the way of real street knowledge. Breaking a sweat, Frost turned to a friend he had brought into the studio with him. Manny Velazquez, a local crisis intervention worker, had recently intervened on Frost's behalf when he ran afoul of some real gangsters. Velazquez began speaking and the phone lines lit up. Cummings realized that Velazquez was the real deal.

After the show Cummings introduced himself. "If you want," Velazquez said, "I can come in and train your staff."

Velazquez returned and gave the staff a three-hour seminar on gang life in Los Angeles. He ended the session by offering to take them on a cruise of the neighborhoods in which he worked. Only Cummings and Lozano took him up on it.

Velazquez took them out on a Wednesday night. *The homies*, he figured, *won't be as crazy as they are during the weekend.* First Velazquez cruised past Sylmar Park, where members of two "party crews" were fighting.

Velazquez jumped out of his car and broke it up. Then he took Cummings and Lozano to a local taco stand on the corner of Van Nuys and Nordhoff, where big guys with low-riders were preparing for a car show. Cummings was fascinated, not just by the cars—which he had never seen up close—but by the fact that the guys kept switching between Power 106 and the Spanish-language station, KLAX, that had recently overtaken Power by playing "ranchera" music. Cummings pulled out a tape recorder to ask questions, while a man and a woman argued across the street. Suddenly the woman pulled out a gun and started shooting. Everyone ducked instinctively, except Cummings. Then, slowly, everyone rose and finished their food. Cruising again, Velazquez talked about gangs past and present until they spotted a wino lying on the sidewalk who had a huge bloody gash in his head. Lozano and Cummings turned white at the sight of it. Velazquez stopped to help.

At the end of the evening, Cummings turned to Velazquez: "How would you like to do this live on the air?"

On April 12, 1993, as Los Angeles awaited the verdict from the second, federal trial of the police officers who beat Rodney King, Power 106 debuted their new public affairs show, "From the Streets," hosted by Frank Lozano and Manny Velazquez.

The calls came in as before—angry, fearful, defeated. But this time Power 106 had someone in the studio who related to those voices. Velazquez was an alternative voice to the mainstream media, who looked to the police to quell any possible violence. "For them to say, 'We're gonna wipe out the bad guys' is ridiculous," Velazquez said. "The police are the ones who started the whole thing."

A few weeks later the first guilty verdicts in the King case were announced. No riots happened. As "From the Streets" became popular, Velazquez spoke a phrase that would become a refrain for the show, but might well have served as a motto for Power 106 and its approach to a young, multicultural audience: "Racism," he would say, "is an old-folks' disease."

Cummings had become convinced of the broad appeal of hip-hop. Joel Salkowitz, Cummings's friend and counterpart at Emmis-owned sister station Hot 97 in New York, wasn't so sure.

Hot 97 continued to play the dance and Latin freestyle music of the old Power 106, and now *its* ratings had begun to tank as well. Cummings suggested to Salkowitz that the same musical shift that had happened in L.A.

was now occurring in New York. Salkowitz, however, needed to be hit over the head a few times.

The first blow came when he was invited to spend a weekend at the Long Island beach house belonging to a friend of a friend, a union boss. After he arrived, the "kids" came by—all the young family cousins in their teens and early twenties—driving their muscle cars. They were all listening to rap. These were the kids that were supposed to be into dance music—Italians from the outer boroughs and suburbs. And yet they were rapping along with the same Black guys whom they would just as soon attack if one of those rappers were walking through their neighborhood.

Salkowitz didn't understand why these kids liked rap music. But then, he didn't get much about the tastes of youth. Salkowitz grew up with rock and roll. He was a radio nerd like Cummings, not a music guy. He barely tolerated the Latin freestyle on Hot 97. "Cowbell music," he called it at first. But Salkowitz understood its value to the station, and he largely left the music programming to his music director, Kevin McCabe. Once, when Salkowitz put an Elton John record on the playlist, McCabe threw a fit. Salkowitz didn't understand why the song would be totally inappropriate for the format.

Salkowitz got an occasional musical education from Vito Bruno, who promoted the Roxy after the club's founder Ruza Blue was pushed out. In the late 1980s, Bruno abandoned rap, like everyone else in the club scene had done, because of violence during the crack epidemic. Bruno then fostered the Latin freestyle movement with Club 1018, where he met Salkowitz during Hot 97's live broadcasts. As Hot 97's fortunes lifted in the late 1980s, the club prospered.

Bruno made it his business to keep Salkowitz informed. When Bruno saw house music gaining a foothold in the clubs, he convinced Salkowitz to start a "Saturday Night House Party" on Hot 97 with live broadcasts from Bruno's other club, the Tunnel. In 1992, after he sensed hip-hop's resurgence, Bruno took a chance and started a new club, Home Bass. He hired veterans like DJ Red Alert and newer guys like DJ Enuff and Funkmaster Flex.

Bruno, too, told Salkowitz that more White kids were listening to hip-hop. Salkowitz shrugged. So Bruno brought Joel out to 86th Street in Bensonhurst, Brooklyn, where the "greaseballs" cruised.

"Listen," Bruno said. The music coming from the cars sure wasn't Hot 97. It was hip-hop. Finally, Salkowitz was moved. Bruno suggested that he find a DJ to spin hip-hop on Hot 97 on Friday nights. He knew where Joel could find the right one.

Bruno knew a lot of DJs. Very few of them were stars. But Funkmaster Flex knew how to read a crowd. He could lift them at will. Bruno beckoned Salkowitz to Home Bass to see Funkmaster Flex in action.

"Flex," Bruno said. "Show him what you can do." Flex leaned into the turntable with his right arm, rubbing and releasing his next record, greeted with howls from the packed crowd. Flex repeated this feat, punctuating new hip-hop jams with old favorites like Run-DMC's "Peter Piper" or the Fatback Band's "I Found Lovin'," records he knew would detonate on the dance floor.

Joel Salkowitz needed no more convincing. In the spring of 1992, Hot 97 became the first pop station in New York to host a specialty rap show, featuring the mixes of Funkmaster Flex.

For his decision Salkowitz faced resistance both inside and outside the station. A few club promoters fumed that Hot 97 had given a chunk of its Friday night to a hip-hop DJ, especially when they had no intention of doing the same. Bruno explained how his peers in the business felt: "The life of a club has a few stages," he'd say. "It starts off trendy. Then you get the bridge-and-tunnel crowd. Then it's Spanish. Then it's Black. Then it's out of business." Most club promoters were adamantly opposed to any music that would darken the overall complexion of their crowds. Soon these promoters protested to the station's sales staff, who in turn rang the alarm with Hot 97's general manager Judy Ellis.

Ellis was in many ways the exact opposite of Joel Salkowitz. She was tiny. He was huge. She was impulsive and brusque. He was slow and cautious. Salkowitz considered Judy Ellis a bean counter, a "sales slug." And Ellis thought that Joel Salkowitz was the worst program director ever. He didn't command the respect of his troops, Ellis thought. He demonized the sales staff. He fought constantly with music director, Kevin McCabe. Even Salkowitz's young assistant, an on-the-ball Brooklyn girl named Tracy Cloherty, complained about her boss not getting things done. Ellis thought Salkowitz was madly jealous of other, successful programmers. On his wall Ellis spied a picture of a PD who had recently won fame for reviving pop station KKFR in Phoenix. The programmer's name was Steve Smith, the same guy who had battled Keith Naftaly in San Jose. Under Smith's picture Salkowitz had written UNDERWHELMED. It was exactly how Ellis felt about Salkowitz.

But she couldn't just fire him. Salkowitz was the godfather of Rick Cummings's children. And Cummings still ran programming for all of Emmis. Judy felt stuck. She kept asking him, "How are you going to turn this station around, Joel?"

One day Salkowitz asked Ellis for a meeting. When she saw Salkowitz march in with his club promoter friend Vito Bruno, Ellis got annoyed. She had asked Joel for solutions, for direction. And what was his answer? Give Funkmaster Flex a *second* night? Play rap on Saturdays, too? Vito Bruno was blathering about Hot 97 needing to play more hip-hop. *What he really wants*, Ellis thought, *is more promotion for his nightclub. This guy has been manipulating Joel for years.*

"We can't sell it," Ellis replied. "We will *never* be able to sell hip-hop. It's not going to happen. Thank you very much."

With that, she pointed Salkowitz and Bruno to the door.

Soon after, in early 1993, the next ratings book came out. Hot 97 was now dead last among New York's three pop stations. Ellis decided that it was either her or Joel. She placed a call to Emmis's president and Cummings's boss, Doyle Rose. "I can't deliver a radio station to you with this guy," Ellis declared.

When word got back to Rick Cummings, he knew he couldn't stand in Judy Ellis's way. She simply wanted her own guy in there. He believed in empowering his people to make their own decisions, just as Smulyan had empowered him. It was the Emmis way.

Still, Cummings thought that Joel was right. If Ellis would program more hip-hop, she could reverse her ratings slide. Given enough airtime and promotion, Flex could do for Hot 97 what Sway and Tech did for KMEL. Cummings himself needed that kind of credible hip-hop anchor for Power 106. He had asked Dave Morales to do a Friday-night rap show. But Morales could barely hold down his current shifts. Morales wasn't a real hip-hop head, either. Cummings was still looking for DJs who knew the music and could appeal to his listeners. Ideally, they would be Latino hip-hop junkies. Not the easiest combination to find.

Nick and Eric Vidal were like most teenagers in Bakersfield, California. They ate chili burgers and fries at Carrows. They played video games at the

7-Eleven. They were regular kids in all respects—except that they had the highest-rated show on the local pop station, KKXX, and produced songs for major rap artists at recording studios in Los Angeles, a hundred miles to the south. The Vidal brothers owed their peculiar pedigree to two factors.

First, the fickle frequency of 1580 KDAY—patchy even in Los Angeles during the day—came loud and clear over the San Gabriel Mountains at night. Back in the mid-1980s, Nick and Eric got their music education from disc jockeys like Greg Mack and Tony "G" Gonzalez, and they often stayed up past two a.m. to hear records by LL Cool J, Run-DMC, Eric B & Rakim, and Boogie Down Productions.

Second, Nick and Eric had Francisco Vidal for a father. A grade-school dropout, Frank Vidal founded a construction firm in the late 1960s. But Frank's real passion was partying and promoting. He had managed a pop music band from nearby Victorville called the Younger Half. Then he opened a teenage nightclub in Bakersfield—a squat building with a concrete floor that had to be repainted every weekend after dancing feet wore off the previous layer.

True to its name, Vidal's was a family affair. Frank watched for trouble-makers inside; his wife, Theresa, watched the door; and his two youngest sons, Nick and Eric, watched the DJ, Moses Aguirre. After the club closed, when Nick and Eric were supposed to be on cleaning duty, the twelve-year-old Nick played with Aguirre's equipment and records instead.

"What are you doing?" sixteen-year-old Eric complained. "Come help!"

When Aguirre found out and forbade Nick to touch his stuff, Frank Vidal fired Aguirre and hired Nick instead. He drove his son to Los Angeles to buy his own turntables and vinyl. Now Nick worked the wheels of steel on weekends and his older brother, Eric, operated the lights.

"Show me how to DJ," Eric asked his younger brother.

"Shut up, light man," Nick replied. Eric was forced to teach himself.

Nick and Eric Vidal became young maestros of all kinds of dance music—funk, freestyle, high-energy, and disco classics. But they reserved special reverence for rap, and for the best mix master on KDAY, whose turntable styles they emulated.

One evening, after DJ Tony "G" Gonzalez wrapped up his regular gig at Los Angeles club La Casa Camino Real, he was approached by an older man, smoking Marlboro reds and looking every bit like a Mexican mafioso. The man, who shook Gonzalez's hand and introduced himself as Frank Vidal, said that he had a nighclub in Bakersfield and that he would like Gonzalez to come DJ there.

Gonzalez accepted the offer politely, not wanting to offend Vidal—who could very well have been a connected guy—and the following weekend drove the hundred-plus miles to the middle of nowhere with his friend Jose. Gonzalez didn't expect to get paid. He figured it was some party for Vidal's kids, who called Gonzalez a few days before the gig and breathlessly asked if he needed anything for his upcoming set.

When Gonzalez got to Vidal's he was shocked. A long line snaked around the two-story club. Inside, Frank and Theresa Vidal greeted Gonzalez like a VIP and escorted him to the tiny DJ booth, where a kid, *a little kid*, was cutting, scratching, and mixing. Nick introduced himself, as did Eric. Once the famous Tony G from KDAY took the turntables, the brothers remained transfixed, taping his techniques with a video camera while their older sister Zina brought Gonzalez sodas. After the club closed, Nick and Eric moved the turntables and mixer to the middle of the dance floor. They begged Gonzalez to stay and DJ some more with them, just for fun. *What the hell*, Gonzalez thought. These were good country people. There were pretty girls around and the family was super nice. At the end of the long night Frank Vidal stuffed nearly $300 in Gonzalez's pocket, and the family saw Gonzalez and his friend off with hugs.

"Mr. Vidal, you can bring your boys to my club *anytime*," Gonzalez said.

Soon enough Frank Vidal was driving the distance between Bakersfield and Los Angeles on Friday nights. Gonzalez would sneak the young brothers in through the back of La Casa and hustle them up to the DJ booth. At midnight Tony G would step aside and Nick V would take the set and rock a thousand people, none of them aware that they were dancing to records spun by a thirteen-year-old kid. On other weekends Theresa Vidal woke before dawn and drove Nick and Eric to Gonzalez's house where they would spend the day scratching and mixing, and learning from Gonzalez and his fellow mix master Julio "G" Gonzalez how to make beats on a SP-1200 sampling drum machine. At midnight their mother would return to retrieve her kids. Gonzalez had never seen such dedicated parents. Gonzalez's mother even got used to having them around. *Los muchachos de Bakersfield*, she called them. *Los de la Baker*. Or, in English, the Baker boys.

After the fall of KDAY, Tony Gonzalez began producing records. He got the "Baka Boyz" their first production credit as well arranging for the Vidal brothers to produce a few tracks on Kid Frost's debut album for Virgin Records. Erik got his own car, and he and Nick shuttled back and forth to Los Angeles, racking up studio time with Frost, Mellow Man Ace, and other Latino hip-hop artists.

Lighter Shade of Brown, a Latino rap group from Riverside, California, asked Nick to be their tour DJ. But Nick was still in high school, so his father made Eric go along as Nick's chaperone. At Lighter Shade's show in Bakersfield, Frank Vidal spotted the new program director for local pop station KKXX, Steve Wall, in the crowd.

"That's my son," he said, pointing to Nick.

Wall invited Nick and Eric to the station for a meeting and then hired them to do a Saturday mix show, where they spun dance, R&B, and rap music. When the Baka Boyz started posting incredible ratings, Wall offered them a daily shift. The Vidals had to refuse, as their production career was taking them to Los Angeles more often. Nick and Eric were working with Ice Cube and his female protégé, Yo-Yo. In the fall of 1992 Steve Wall finally made Nick and Eric Vidal a better offer: He asked the two brothers to be KKXX's music directors. Wall, like Naftaly and Cummings, felt the coming of hip-hop. Who would be better to lead the charge for his station than two smart kids who had grown up on it? Nick was only nineteen, Eric twenty-three.

Now their Bakersfield-to-Los Angeles shuffle became a drag. It was a two-hour ride each way—straight to the foot of the San Gabriels, up through the steep Cajon Pass, and then through the mountains to the sharp decline into the San Fernando Valley. Nick and Eric set a new goal: Get the hell out of Bakersfield, and get on the radio in Los Angeles, on a station like Power 106.

One evening in early 1993, after an aborted studio session, the Vidals cruised around L.A. aimlessly. They didn't want to head home so soon. "Call Bruce," Nick told Eric.

Bruce Reiner, Profile Records' rotund, jovial pop promotions executive, was one of the many industry contacts that the Vidal brothers had made in the past few years. Reiner, too, had his eyes on Power 106. After years of struggling to get pop radio to play his records, Reiner felt a sense of relief now that Rick Cummings was programming the station. Reiner remembered begging Jeff Wyatt to play Profile's rap artist from Compton, DJ Quik. Quik was a local kid with a gold album, and Wyatt still wouldn't add his record. As usual, Keith Naftaly in San Francisco played it first. Reiner had the last laugh when Cummings took over and played DJ Quik's new protégé group on Profile, 2nd II None. Reiner had a new friend at Power, too: his drinking buddy Dave Morales. Reiner wanted Morales to meet the two boys from Bakersfield. Reiner had watched Nick and Eric's career grow. He felt they were destined for greater things.

So when Nick and Eric called, Reiner grabbed Morales and met them down at a Mexican restaurant called Antonio's. Reiner also invited his friend Harold Austin. Austin had been Hosh Gureli's replacement at KMEL. But Naftaly then transferred Austin to 92.3 the Beat in L.A. in preparation for his own arrival. Reiner had also urged Austin to consider hiring the Baka Boyz.

Austin couldn't stand being around Reiner and Morales together, especially when they drank. They called to the mariachi strolling through Antonio's with a guitar and requested "La Bamba." As they sang, Nick and Eric laughed, and Austin sulked.

After dinner they all stumbled out into the cool evening, the cars rushing past them on Melrose. A homeless man waddled up to Nick and asked him for money. Nick said he was fresh out, and then asked the bum if *he* had any spare change to give him. Morales laughed. "These guys are hilarious," he told Reiner.

Morales approached Nick and Eric. "This is going to sound so L.A.," he slurred, "but I'm gonna give your name to Rick Cummings. I think you'd be perfect for something we're getting ready to start on Friday nights."

Nick and Eric hoped he would remember his drunken pledge when they delivered their demo tape to him at the 1993 Gavin Convention. When they caught up to him, Morales was smashed again. "Put the tape in my bag," Morales shouted, and went back to partying.

On a Tuesday in late February their phone rang.

"Rick wants to meet with you guys," Morales said.

As they drove down from Bakersfield, Eric sensed his little brother's anxiety. "If we get the job here, cool," Eric told him. "If we don't, whatever, it's not a big deal."

When they met Cummings they almost laughed aloud. The man who loomed so large in their thoughts was about half Eric's size.

In his office Cummings listened to a minute of their demo before stopping the tape. Nick and Eric were a little too slick, talked a little too fast. "The energy is there," Cummings told them. "You just need to slow it down a bit." But Cummings knew that he had just stumbled upon a miracle: two impossibly young hip-hop fanatics who already knew something about professional radio. The Baka Boyz were a divine coincidence of youth and savvy. The Baka Boyz liked Cummings, too. "Buckshot Shorty," Nick dubbed him, referencing a popular New York rapper.

Cummings would start them with a Friday-night mix show devoted entirely to rap. There was, however, a point of contention. Power 106's mixes were all prerecorded. Nick and Eric wanted to do the show completely live, like Sway and Tech did. Cummings wasn't so sure about live mixing.

"What if the record skips?" he asked.

"Then it skips," Eric replied.

They called the show "Friday Night Flavas," though it technically began at midnight on Saturday morning. They borrowed some promotional artist "drops" and other production elements that Funkmaster Flex had been using for his show on Power's sister station. They converted Power's newsroom into a makeshift DJ booth. And in March of 1993, Power 106 launched the first commercial FM rap show in Los Angeles.

Cummings had conquered the Image Pyramid.

He had the community credibility with Manny Velazquez and his show, "From the Streets," and from another young female jock named Josefa Salinas who doubled as his unofficial community affairs director.

He had the air personalities. He had Lozano. He had Morales. And it wasn't long before Cummings gave the Baka Boyz a daily air slot, the overnight shift.

Most important, he had the music. Before the Baka Boyz, Cummings and Michelle Mercer were really flying blind when it came to picking rap records. Now they had two kids on staff who were bona fide members of the hip-hop community—DJs since childhood, schooled by KDAY's finest, who had evolved into producers working with the top artists in the genre. The Baka Boyz, in practice, programmed the station. They chose credible rap songs by EPMD, Digable Planets, Das EFX—exactly the kind of music that KDAY would have been playing if it were still around. What was more, the Baka Boyz' arrival at Power 106 coincided with a key musical moment in Los Angeles hip-hop: the release of NWA producer Andre "Dr. Dre" Young's first solo album, *The Chronic*. Its singles "Nuthin' but a 'G' Thang," "Dre Day," and "Let Me Ride" featured the debut of a dynamic young rapper named Snoop Doggy Dogg, and defined the new sound of Power 106.

But there was one last piece of advice from Jon Coleman that Cummings had yet to implement.

"Own the words," Coleman told him.

Over the years Coleman had found that the most valuable thing a radio station could do was to adopt the words that best described it. But these had to be the words that the *listeners themselves* used. Coleman learned this lesson when he consulted the very first classic rock station in Kansas City, KCFX. The station was big on its nickname, "the Fox," which meant nothing to listeners. When he asked the members of a focus group to describe KCFX, they said, "It's the classic rock station." Coleman went back to the station management. "You're no longer 'the Fox,'" he said. "You're 'the Classic Rock Station.'" In Phoenix, Coleman was able to turn a stalemate between two pop stations into a victory for the one that incessantly called itself "the Number One Hit Music Station."

So Coleman told Cummings flat out: *If you are going to be a hip-hop station, you are going to have to own the words.*

Cummings convened a weekend meeting at his house in Glendale, only a few minutes from Power's studios. In the backyard, over barbecue and beer, Cummings stood at an easel with markers and a white posterboard and asked his troops for ideas.

Dave Morales talked about how club DJs described the kind of music they spun. "They actually say, 'I play KROQ music,'" Morales said, referring to the L.A. radio station that former KMEL music director Kevin Weatherly had turned into an alternative/grunge cultural colossus.

"So why not 'Power music'?" someone else suggested.

Cummings wrote it down but replied that "power" wasn't the descriptive term they needed to own. "Hip-hop" was. What they needed was a slogan that would show that Power 106 was the home of hip-hop.

"Fuck it, then," Morales said. "Let's just say, 'Power 106: Where Hip-Hop Lives.'"

The new slogan for Power 106 was more than simple, more than effective. It marked the first time that a radio station anywhere in the world used the words "hip-hop" to brand itself. Not even KDAY and KMEL had done that.

The on-air spots promoting Power 106 as the place "Where Hip-Hop Lives" were supplemented by a huge billboard campaign. Along with the new slogan and a revamped, geometric logo, each billboard featured a different lyric from a signature Power 106 hip-hop song, handpicked by the Baka Boyz and the Power staff: *We be to rap what key be to lock. Check yourself before you wreck yourself. Strictly hardcore, keep the crossover.* When Greg Mack, the founder of KDAY's rap format, first saw one of the billboards, he nearly drove off the road.

In New York, Rick Cummings sat in Hot 97's conference room across from Judy Ellis, pointing to the pie chart on the screen in front of them.

"You see that, Judy?!" Cummings said. "You see that green slice?! That's what I've been telling you about!"

The slices of the pie chart represented the kinds of music preferred by Hot 97's core listeners—White, Latino, and Asian. And the biggest slice by far, in glowing green, represented hip-hop.

Cummings had flown to New York to discuss the results of Jon Coleman's study of the New York market. Coleman had confirmed that Hot 97 was facing a transformation of listener preference similar to the one Cummings and Power 106 had confronted in Los Angeles. As in L.A. there was a split in the New York audience. The older listeners continued to prefer dance music. The younger ones wanted to hear hip-hop. Now Hot 97 had to make a decision about its musical direction. Jon Coleman and Pierre Bouvard recommended embracing hip-hop as the new youth music to keep the station relevant.

Even with the new Coleman study, the popularity of Flex's show, and the evident success of Power 106, Judy Ellis chose to keep her own counsel. For Rick Cummings it was frustrating to watch. But Cummings suspected that Ellis wouldn't move unless she felt it had been her own decision to do so. He left New York and left Ellis alone. Ellis began a nationwide search for her new program director. Meanwhile the station limped along. Ellis put Joel's former assistant, Tracy Cloherty, in charge of the music for the time being. To Ellis, Cloherty was a kindred spirit: a hardworking, capable woman who wasn't afraid to speak her mind, who could match wits with any man in the corporate world.

For Rocco Macri, the station's young marketing director and the person who had first hired Cloherty as an intern, the changing of the guard at Hot 97 came as a relief. He liked Joel Salkowitz. But with Joel fighting Judy and the entire sales department, the atmosphere had been tense. Even though

Hot 97 had yet to find a new PD, at least now there was the promise of movement.

Finally, in September, after a long summer of interviewing candidates,
Judy Ellis found the person she wanted to hire as her new program director:
Rick Gillette, from Detroit pop station WHYT. That was when her phone
rang again. It was Joel Salkowitz's nemesis, Steve Smith.

"I've already found someone," Ellis told Smith.

Smith replied that he was ready to fly to New York to meet with her, "on
my own dime, if I have to."

Ellis liked Smith's passion. Best of all, she knew Salkowitz and Cummings didn't think much of him.

Come on in, Ellis said.

Steve Smith landed at JFK on a Saturday. As promised, he paid his own
way and stayed with an aunt on Long Island. He knew the gig was a long shot.
Judy Ellis told him that Rick Cummings didn't want him for the job. Smith
knew why: Years back, Smith had considered leaving radio altogether after
Cummings fired him. During Power 106's heyday as a freestyle dance station, Cummings wanted Smith to re-create Power's format at Energy 96.5,
Emmis's FM in Houston. Smith figured out quickly that it wasn't going to
work because Latinos in Houston listened to Tejano and Black music, not
Latin freestyle. The station bombed. Smith was canned and took it personally.

Steve Smith, like Salkowitz and Cummings, was a rock-loving White
guy. He didn't know anything about dance music. But he did know how to
watch, ask questions, and listen. While he was still in college in Phoenix, he
boosted the ratings of a tiny AM station called KUKQ by recognizing that
no one in town was serving the young Latino audience. After law school he
did the same thing at Y97-FM in Santa Barbara, doubling the ratings from
a 6 percent share to 12. Upon his arrival he spent hours walking up and
down State Street, Santa Barbara's main drag, talking to kids.

"What station do you listen to?" he asked. "What kind of music do you
like?"

Smith did it a third time when he flipped an easy listening station in San
Jose to rhythmic Hot 97.7, and it surged from a 2.5 to a 6 percent share, beating KMEL. Some listeners weren't so pleased. One woman called Smith to
complain that she missed how the beautiful music of Montovani would lull
her to sleep every night.

"Lady," Smith replied, "that's the *reason* we switched the format!"

After the Houston debacle Smith's salvation came from his hometown of Phoenix when he was hired by pop station Power 92. After a grueling three-year battle with two other pop stations, Smith led Power 92 to victory in 1993, in part because he made members of the Phoenix Suns de facto air personalities the same year that the team went to the NBA finals.

But New York was a hometown, too, for Smith. He had spent his child-hood years on Long Island, before his parents moved him and his little sister to Arizona. His sister's sudden death in a car accident provoked Smith to leave his law degree behind and seek his true calling in radio. And the big-gest calling in radio had always been its number one market, New York. Steve Smith flew to New York to meet Judy Ellis because everything he'd ever done in his life pointed him there.

Smith met Ellis at Hot 97's Broadway offices on a Sunday. Ellis reviewed the station's recent history, including the research that showed the increas-ing popularity of hip-hop among Hot 97's young core listeners. She asked Steve Smith what he would do.

"I have no idea," Smith answered. "But I'll tell you how I'll find out. I will go out into the city. I will talk to people on the street. I will talk to peo-ple on the subway. I will figure it out."

Every program director Ellis had interviewed thus far had trumpeted long lists of recommendations, men who talked to her as if she didn't know what the hell was going on with her own station. Now here was a guy who pledged, simply, to listen.

Ellis changed her mind, and hired Steve Smith.

In the fall of 1993 Steve Smith inherited a drifting, demoralized Hot 97. On his first day Smith walked into his new office to see a picture of *himself* tacked to the wall, left there by that office's previous occupant. Smith read the caption that had been handwritten under the picture: Underwhelmed.

As if to disprove Salkowitz's taunt, Smith took to the streets immedi-ately. In October 1993 countless young New Yorkers—mostly Black and Latino—were approached by a strange White guy with long, curly hair. "What stations do you listen to?" he asked. "Do you ever listen to Hot 97?" Smith heard a similar answer from a surprising number of people. *Only when Flex is on.* So Smith did the first, obvious thing. He put Flex on the air six nights a week. Judy Ellis, who had been so resistant to the idea of hip-hop with Salkowitz, dropped her resistance now that the recommendation was coming from her new hire.

Back on the streets the kids weren't buying the extra Flex time. *Hot 97 sucks. They're frontin'.* Meaning, of course, that Hot 97 was still perceived as a dance station merely trying to co-opt the growing popularity of hip-hop.

Either I go for this or I don't, Smith thought. It was abundantly clear that kids of all colors loved hip-hop. He didn't need Coleman Research or Rick Cummings to tell him that. Since being hired, Smith talked with Rick Cummings daily, sometimes for hours. The former adversaries had put aside the past. Ironically, Cummings was becoming a mentor for Smith, teaching him how a pop station could successfully embrace this African-American music form and win with everyone. It didn't take long for Steve Smith to declare that Hot 97 was going to become a hip-hop station. "You can't put one foot in," Smith told his colleagues and staff. "We've got to get in with both feet." When Steve Smith finally jumped, the depth of his commitment surprised everyone—not only Ellis, but Cummings, too.

Steve Smith already had Funkmaster Flex. But he wanted to grab the hip-hop mantle with a bigger name. Knowing nothing about rap, he turned to his new music director, Paco Lopez. "What's the biggest hip-hop show?" Smith asked, thinking he might poach a DJ or two from another station. The biggest hip-hop show wasn't on radio, Lopez replied. It was on MTV, hosted by Ed Lover and Andre "Doctor Dre" Brown.

"I'm going after them," Smith vowed.

The Baka Boyz were in town, and Cummings sent them to see Smith. As they walked down the street together, Smith revealed his plan.

"I want to get these guys Ed Lover and Doctor Dre to do my morning show," he said. "You think that's a good idea?" Nick and Eric glanced at each other and smiled wryly. *Yes,* they told Smith, *it's a good idea.* They had grown accustomed to reassuring their bosses of the obvious. Smith hired Doctor Dre and Ed Lover, now represented by the former manager of the Fat Boys, Charles Stettler.

Smith won points with Judy Ellis by seconding her better instincts. Ellis's assistant was a pretty Puerto Rican girl with a slippery Brooklyn accent. *If Hot 97 is going to be the number one station for young New Yorkers,* Ellis said, *then here is the voice of young New York.* Steve agreed and hired Angie Martinez as his overnight jock.

Out-of-work air personalities across the industry complained. *We've been working all our careers to get to New York,* they said. *Now some kid who's never done radio in her life gets a shot?* The trades ran stories on the new trend, typified by the Emmis stations, Hot 97 and Power 106: hiring street kids or entertainers with little or no radio experience at the expense of longtime professionals who had paid their dues. *Tough,* Steve Smith thought. *I'd hire some local kid who can relate to my listeners before I'd put some stupid, old White DJ from Dayton on the air.* Cummings and Smith were of one mind about this: "I can teach a comedian how to run a board," Cummings would say. "I can't teach a professional radio person how to be funny."

Finally Smith decided he had better learn about hip-hop history and culture. To that end, he sat for hours with some of the rap artists who visited the station, like Q-Tip from A Tribe Called Quest. Smith asked questions. The answers led him to some of the founders of hip-hop, people like Afrika Bambaataa and Grandmaster Flash. Smith did more than make these old-school artists his teachers. He hired them. Soon, these hip-hop icons were pulling air shifts, and stars like LL Cool J and KRS-One were making regular appearances at Hot 97. Flavor Flav of Public Enemy came on board to do morning traffic.

"The GWB is messed up, g!" Flav shouted over the helicopter noise.

Flavor, of course, couldn't see the George Washington Bridge, and was nowhere near a helicopter. Usually, he was calling in from home, on the days when he could be found at all. Dre played the helicopter sound effects in the studio.

Steve Smith had no idea that Flavor and Andre "Doctor Dre" Brown had done this kind of compelling radio ten years earlier with Bill Stephney at WBAU-FM on Long Island. For ten years, pop stations ignored rap, and Urban radio pushed hip-hop DJs like Red Alert and Marley Marl to the fringes of its weekly calendar. WBLS, once the "Black Liberation Station," had rarely played Public Enemy, and had seen fit to give Brown only a weekend mix show. But now, a decade later, here was the White guy at the pop station opening the door to the very creators of hip-hop—not just by playing the occasional song or two, but by embracing the artists themselves, their personalities, their genius. Steve Smith wanted hip-hop artists to feel at home at Hot 97. Power 106 invented the slogan, "Where Hip-Hop Lives." But Steve Smith at Hot 97 took it literally. Hip-Hop was born in New York. What better place for it to live?

The switch to hip-hop wasn't a foregone conclusion for some people at Hot 97, even for Judy Ellis. She may have hired Steve Smith to deliver her from ratings purgatory, but Smith's newfound zeal scared her. Ed and Dre were off to a rocky start, and Don Imus, the morning jock on crosstown sports-talk AM station WFAN, played excerpts of their screwups on his own show for laughs. The members of the sales staff brought up the perennial arguments against rap. Their advertisers wanted to buy airtime on a *pop* station. *Hip-hop* would scare them away. Hot 97 would surely be perceived as an Urban station, and thus make sixty cents for every dollar that pop station Z100 made. One day, Hot 97's head of sales, Jeff Dinetz, came into Steve's office and slammed the door.

"I want the truth," Dinetz said. "How long are we going to have to play this hip-hop shit?!"

Smith replied to both Ellis and Dinetz that it would take six months to a year to even know if Hot 97 was on the right track. "You don't even know who you are right now," Smith said, "because you keep changing who you are."

It took as much time to *de*program Hot 97 as it did to program it. Record promoters were still bringing Smith dance singles, asking why Hot 97 wasn't playing them. "Because we're a *hip-hop* station!" Steve barked. Still, Steve Smith was not the most knowledgeable person to pick rap records. When Smith selected a single by Jheri-curled Los Angeles rappers Rodney O and Joe Cooley for the playlist, Tracy Cloherty threw a fit. "You can't do that!" Cloherty yelled. She had to explain that New York kids thought most West Coast artists were corny. Smith didn't have the slightest idea about the difference between East and West Coast rap.

Again Steve listened. He liked Cloherty's feistiness. When Paco Lopez left Hot 97 for another job, Smith made Cloherty his music director. Cloherty, in turn, urged Smith to devote Hot 97 to records that would work for the New York audience—like the new song "Method Man" by the Wu-Tang Clan, a Staten Island crew who had put out their own self-produced single. For New York hip-hop fans who had cringed through the ascendance of West Coast rap—first NWA and now Andre "Dr. Dre" Young and his protégé, Snoop Doggy Dogg—the Wu-Tang Clan was an adrenaline injection into the heart of hip-hop. The East Coast was back, and Hot 97 led the charge.

The ratings started to tick upward, and the mood of the station was transformed. Whatever doubts marketing director Rocco Macri still held about the station's new hip-hop format were dispelled one night as he stood outside the Palladium before a "Hot Night" concert featuring the Wu-Tang Clan. Hot 97's listeners filed in, a multicultural cross section of White kids, Black kids, Latino kids, Asian kids.

It was just like the research said it would be.

In Los Angeles, the last relic from Power 106's dance era was Jay Thomas, Power's longtime morning man. Thomas was an anachronism: a middle-aged announcer in a station filling up with young Latino air talent serving up a playlist of hip-hop. Cummings knew he would eventually have to make a change in the time slot. But Thomas still pulled in big ratings. He was a television star, with appearances on the CBS sitcom *Murphy Brown*, and TV pilots of his own. Perhaps that was why Thomas began disparaging his radio career in the press.

"I sort of roll along and we end up making a bunch of money in the morning," Thomas told *Billboard*. "We're all in it for the loot."

Thomas was "phoning it in," almost literally. After Cummings caught him running prerecorded shows in the mornings, Thomas was tossed in a contract dispute. Cummings now had a chance to build a morning show that suited a station where hip-hop lived. First he tried Morales in the mornings. But Morales could hardly drag himself in for a six a.m. shift after his nightly routine of clubbing. Cummings put Frank Lozano in his stead. But by early 1994 it was evident to Cummings that the ideal Power 106 morning show would have to come from the two young brothers from Bakersfield. Shortly after Steve Smith had installed Doctor Dre and Ed Lover as the morning men on Hot 97 in New York, Cummings sprang an equally ballsy move on Power's listeners, as the Baka Boyz became Power 106's new morning team.

The Baka Boyz morning show jelled, thanks in part to a regular bit suggested by Adrian Miller, Friday Night Flavas' news and industry gossip segment host. Miller had grown up in St. Louis listening to Dr. Jockenstein do the nightly "roll call," where kids could call in and rap over the phone about themselves, their high school, their neighborhood. At Miller's suggestion, the Vidals took the roll call a step further, rapping back and forth with their callers over a Snoop Dogg instrumental.

One for the treble, two for the time, it's the roll call, who's on that line? the Baka Boyz would rhyme.

The caller would kick a couple of lines about themselves. And then the

Boyz would answer, *That sounds cool, and that may be, but where are you calling from, what city?*

After another couplet from the caller, the Baka Boyz would shout out to an audience that mirrored the sprawl of Southern California: *Compton's in the house! Pasadena's in the house! Northridge in the house! Hollywood's in the house...*

Before the Baka Boyz took the morning show, the only thing that stood between Power 106 and the number one spot in the Los Angeles market was the Spanish "ranchera" station, KLAX.

But the Baka Boyz' multicultural appeal had won Power 106 an entirely new generation of listeners. By the end of 1994, Power 106 finally tied KLAX at a 5.1 share. Power 106 would stay on top for a long time.

In New York, the news was even better. For the first time, Hot 97 beat all of its pop and Urban competitors with a 4.8 rating. Emmis's hip-hop format had produced the highest-rated music stations in the number one and number two markets in the country.

True to Rick Cummings's letter to Keith Naftaly, Emmis did indeed borrow a great deal from KMEL, including the concept of "Summerjam," which became an anchor event for both Power 106 and Hot 97. And Emmis owed a debt to KDAY, where the idea of a rap-dominated playlist was born. Soon after Emmis adopted the "Where Hip-Hop Lives" slogan and format, pop stations across America opened their playlists to rap. Now hip-hop lived everywhere.

As a result, the pop upsurge of MC Hammer and Vanilla Ice didn't turn out to be hip-hop's apocalypse after all. Hammer, who had developed an authentic fan base many years before his brief trip to the showbiz stratosphere, survived to make more modest hits; though he eventually faced bankruptcy when he failed to downsize his business operation to match his reduced sales. Vanilla Ice, who had neither fan base nor credibility before his superhuman debut, flamed out quickly. Pop radio embraced the artists who once labored in Hammer and Ice's respective shadows—like A Tribe Called Quest, Ice Cube, and Cypress Hill—so-called "hard-core" artists who now enjoyed wide audiences and viable careers.

The events were stunning for anyone who had worked in hip-hop just five years earlier. In the early 1990s, pop stations still played as little Black music as possible, and "rap" was regarded as the antithesis of "pop." Now "hip-hop" was synonymous with pop itself.

The men and women who brought hip-hop to American radio—people like Greg Mack, Keith Naftaly, Paulette Williams, Rick Cummings, Steve Smith, Joel Salkowitz, Judy Ellis, and Tracy Cloherty—did something even more profound. Without ever intending to, they basically ended the cultural segregation that had reigned in American radio since its inception in the early twentieth century. True, radio would continue to have a variety of formats featuring different kinds of music, and aimed at different audiences. But increasingly, those formats were determined less by the race of the performers, and more by the music itself.

The breakthrough at pop radio meant freedom. For decades Black artists had to water down their music to get exposure to larger audiences. Record executives and radio programmers on both sides of the racial divide filtered out artists and records that sounded "too Black" or "too street." Now that Black artists and street sounds were no longer anathema, the sounds of the Black streets spilled out of radios across America, unfiltered.

On one hand it was a joyous and just development. Young Black voices, at long last, could be heard on their own terms. On the other the sudden ubiquity of Black voices in mainstream media provoked a cultural reckoning unlike anything since the birth of rock and roll.

The reckoning would test every business that traded in hip-hop culture. Before it subsided, it would topple the leadership of the world's largest media corporation.

COPS & RAPPERS

Time Warner and corporate
America grapple
with gangsta rap
(1991–1995)

Side A
Truth

In 1881 Marshall Field founded the legendary department store in Chicago that bore his name. By the time Field's great-great-grandson Frederick "Ted" Field was born in 1952, the family's estate had grown to include the *Chicago Sun* newspaper, *Parade* magazine, and Simon & Schuster publishing. But when Ted Field came of age in the early 1970s, inheriting millions of dollars from his late father, Marshall Field IV, he wasn't interested the family business.

Field dropped out of college. He bought a Ferrari and roared down endless black ribbons of American road. Soon, Field's need for speed propelled him to race cars professionally. Because of this, some people called Ted Field a dilettante, a dabbler, a spoiled rich kid whose fortune insulated him from consequence. And, at first, he was.

In 1975, at the Riverside International Raceway in Moreno Valley, California—during twenty-two-year-old Ted Field's second-ever race—the engine on Field's Formula 5000 car died. A tow truck pulled in front of him. The truck driver affixed the tow rope to the car's roll cage, and told Field to hold on to the cord. The driver wasn't experienced enough to know that the roll bar's center of gravity was too high, and Field was too green to know that anything was amiss. When the driver took off, the nose of the car went under the tow truck and flipped over, trapping Field's left hand between the strap and the roll bar. As the truck accelerated to almost a hundred miles per hour over gravel and asphalt, Field's hand was crushed, the skin and flesh ground away under the car's five thousand pounds.

Field's left hand was reduced to a mangled, bloody claw. For two years thereafter, Ted Field endured constant pain. He likened the sensation to putting one's hand on a hot stove and leaving it there, day and night. It was an agony that his entire inheritance couldn't relieve.

Despite his physical torment, Ted Field kept racing, and got better at it. He founded and funded a racing team, and with his partner, Danny Ongais, went on to win "24 Hours of Daytona" in 1979.

He called his crew Interscope Racing—a name concocted by Field and his lawyer one day as they sat at the Blue Dolphin Coffee Shop in Newport Beach, California. Field envisioned a holding company that would have a large scope and combine interrelated enterprises. In the mid-1980s, that vision started to materialize.

When Ted Field left racing and came to Hollywood to produce movies, he was viewed as another know-nothing rich kid, an undeserving heir spending Daddy's money on showbiz dreams. It wasn't surprising, then, that Field's first movie told the tale of a group of smart, underestimated underdogs. Everyone *was* surprised when the film, *Revenge of the Nerds*, became a huge hit. Field's Interscope Communications went on to produce dozens of movies that grossed hundreds of millions at the box office, including *Outrageous Fortune*, *Three Men and a Baby*, *Cocktail*, and *Bill & Ted's Excellent Adventure*. By the 1990s, the supposed ne'er-do-well heir had doubled his grandfather's fortune, and had a personal net worth of at least a half billion dollars. Ted Field may not have chosen the family business, but he had his family's business acumen in his blood.

The dilettante accusation again dogged Field when he decided to move into the music business. Field's concept for Interscope Records began one week in late 1989, after he attended two inspiring concerts in Los Angeles— the Rolling Stones at the Coliseum, and Tone-Loc at the Hard Rock Cafe. Field broke into the recording industry the same way he entered film: by meeting with as many smart people as he could, like Clive Davis and Walter Yetnikoff. Ultimately, Field determined that the best way to get started was by putting the music first and enlisting some good A&R people. Lionel Richie convinced Field to recruit a young Black executive named John McClain. Based on a recommendation from a music industry lawyer named John Branca, Field hired a young talent executive named Tom Whalley who had been recently laid off from Capitol Records. Another adviser, Paul McGinnis, told Field that he had the perfect person in mind for him, a celebrated record producer who had worked with artists like Tom Petty, John Lennon, and U2.

"It's too bad he's already started his own company," McGinnis said.

Field asked McGinnis to set up the meeting anyway. As it turned out, Jimmy Iovine hadn't yet closed his production deal with Doug Morris, the head of Atlantic Records.

By bringing Field in on his Atlantic offer, Iovine scored a better deal than he could have alone. And in giving Iovine a minority stake in Interscope Records—about 20 percent—Field bought legitimacy in the music business, and distribution for his fledgling company through Atlantic's parent the Warner Music Group, the largest music conglomerate in the world, and a division of Time Warner.

Iovine brought in the company's first hit, from a young actor-dancer-turned-rapper named Gerardo Mejía. Gerardo's record, "Rico Suave," was a Latin-flavored pop-rap track along the lines of Tone-Loc's "Wild Thing." In early 1991, "Rico Suave" put Interscope on the charts. By the summer Interscope scored a second big "hip-pop" hit with "Good Vibrations"—produced by Donnie Wahlberg, the leader of the boy band New Kids on the Block, and performed by Wahlberg's younger brother, who called himself "Marky Mark." In the first few months of its operation, Interscope developed an industry reputation as the House that Bubblegum Rap Built.

A great many record executives might have contented themselves with this distinction, but Ted Field held the notion that he wanted to do "important" music. Field found his first candidate in a young rapper brought to his attention by Tom Whalley.

Tupac Amaru Shakur would have been born in jail had his mother, a Black Panther named Afeni Shakur, not been acquitted on over a hundred counts of conspiracy to kill police officers and blow up buildings around New York City. Tupac, a brown-skinned boy with long lashes and a wide smile, spent his childhood in Harlem, and then Baltimore, where he studied acting, dance, music, and poetry at the Baltimore School for the Arts.

He was an enlightened kid with a dark history. As his mother struggled with drug addiction, she moved her son to the Bay Area, where he balanced his vibrant intellectual life with a growing attraction to the "thug life," embracing the polarities in his growing repertoire of rhymes. Leila Steinberg—a local community activist, poetry instructor, and hip-hop promoter—looked after the young Shakur, and introduced him to Atron Gregory, the manager of one of the most successful hip-hop acts from the Bay, Digital Underground.

Gregory took Tupac on as his client, and secured a spot for Shakur with Digital Underground as a roadie and dancer during the promotion of their first Tommy Boy album. Within a year, Tupac was rapping on the group's tracks. But when it came time to shop Tupac's own demo tape, Gregory found no takers. Tommy Boy wasn't interested in the second-string member of Digital Underground. Finally, when Tupac was considering a move to Atlanta to run a Black Panther youth program, Gregory brought the demo to Tom Whalley at Interscope.

Whalley gave the tape to Field, who had lately been inundated with rappers' demos. But Field was struck by Tupac's cadence, his resonance, and his politics, especially on the song "Trapped," in which Tupac rapped about a growing frustration among young Black men with unchecked police brutality. "Hands up, throw me up against a wall, didn't do a thing at all," he said. "I'm tellin' you, one day, these suckers gotta fall."

"This is the most original voice I've heard," Field told Whalley. "We've got to sign this kid."

When Tom Silverman heard that Gregory had landed Tupac a deal with Interscope, he called him to complain.

"Why are you putting them in the rap business?" Silverman demanded.

"Because," Gregory responded, incredulous, "you guys wouldn't do the deal!"

It was a completely different Tupac from the young MC from Digital Underground who rapped about being harassed by girls, rather than cops. For Interscope, too, Tupac's "Trapped" was as far from Marky Mark's "Good Vibrations" as they could get. The lyrics, about killing cops to defend oneself, were brutal. But to Field, they represented truth. Tupac had, just before the release of his album, filed suit against the Oakland Police Department for beating him after an arrest for jaywalking.

Bringing Tupac Shakur's truth to Interscope would ultimately lead to consequences bloodier than Field's fateful day on the racetrack at Riverside in 1975.

In fact, all of the major record companies that were now dabbling in rap were about to take a very wild ride, and no conglomerate would have a more volatile encounter with hip-hop than Interscope's distributor and partner, Time Warner.

To many people who met him, Warner Bros. Records chairman Mo Ostin did not look like the man who signed Jimi Hendrix and the Sex Pistols. He looked like a bookkeeper. And, at first, he was.

During the 1950s, the man born Morris Ostrofsky was the controller of a jazz label called Verve. In 1960, when Frank Sinatra founded his own label, Reprise, the pop star tapped Ostin to run it. Sinatra's label offered up mild fare like Bing Crosby and Rosemary Clooney. After Reprise was sold to Warner Bros. Studios and merged with Warner's own struggling record company in 1963, Ostin began to show his prowess as a visionary record man, bringing in rock and roll acts like the Kinks and other signings Mr. Sinatra would surely have forbidden.

Ostin's steady hand and able ear helped build the combined Warner-Reprise—even as Warner's parent company, Warner Bros. Studios, was in 1966 sold by Jack Warner to a company called Seven Arts, and then in 1969 to an obscure corporation called Kinney that ran parking lots and funeral homes.

Kinney, however, had been assembled by a shrewd man, Steve Ross, who saw a hidden jewel in the movie studio's music operation; and in its capable executive, Ostin, whom he elevated to president. Within two years, Ross jettisoned the funeral parlors and parking lots and changed Kinney's name to Warner Communications, which now comprised, among other media properties, Warner Bros. Pictures, Warner-Reprise, and the recently purchased Atlantic Records. Warner Communications soon acquired another independent label, Elektra. Ross created the largest distribution company in the country to handle the three record companies' releases. He named it WEA, for "Warner/Elektra/Atlantic." In its debut year, WEA boasted a 22 percent market share, a lead that it rarely lost.

Although Warner Communications, Inc., was publicly traded—with interests in sports teams, video games, and cable television—Ross gave his executives lavish compensation and unusually free reign to do what they did best. At the end of the 1980s, the three chiefs of Warner, Elektra, and Atlantic—respectively, Mo Ostin, Bob Krasnow, and Ahmet Ertegun (who left daily operations to his lieutenant, Doug Morris)—enjoyed an almost entrepreneurial independence. Down the line, Ostin, in particular, afforded his own staff and artists the same kind of freedom that Ross gave him.

Ostin quietly built an artist-friendly empire in a sprawling wood-beam building on the corner of Warner Studios' Burbank lot, signing musicians like Prince and creating partnerships with outside producers and entrepreneurs like Quincy Jones, Seymour Stein, David Geffen, Frank Zappa, Chris Blackwell, and Irving Azoff. In the world of hip-hop, Ostin had missed out on signing Def Jam. But he made up for the loss by purchasing half of Tommy

Boy and signing Cold Chillin' Records; and he never took his eye off of Def Jam's young producer, Rick Rubin, who eventually brought his label Def American to the Warner-distributed Geffen Records.

Def American Recordings had done well as a hard-rock and heavy-metal label since its inception in 1988. Its earliest artists Slayer and Danzig sold records in the hundreds of thousands, and comedian Andrew "Dice" Clay brought Def American its first gold album. But Rubin's extreme tastes proved too much even for David Geffen, who asked that his company's logo appear nowhere on Clay's record. The relationship between Geffen and Rubin soured further in 1990 after Geffen sold his company to rival major MCA for a half billion dollars. Rubin feared leaving Warner's huge, efficient distribution channel. But the final split came after Rubin decided to sign his first rap act, picking up a group called the Geto Boys from a small independent Houston label, Rap-A-Lot.

As much as Rubin had distanced himself from rap in the years since his departure from Def Jam, the audacity of hip-hop's emerging "gangster" strain appealed to him as much as that first Schoolly D record had. He had even tried, unsuccessfully, to lure NWA away from Priority Records. But the gall of the Geto Boys easily trumped Eazy-E in their song, "Mind of a Lunatic," in which the group's front man—a three-foot, eight-inch midget named Bushwick Bill—took the character of a "peeping Tom" turned rapist. The woman pleads for her life, at which point the assailant gives her a rose, slits her throat, and watches her "shake till her eyes close."

"Had sex with the corpse before I left her," Bushwick Bill rapped. "And drew my name on the wall like 'Helter Skelter.'"

The Charles Manson reference might have pegged the Geto Boys' "Mind of a Lunatic" as the rap equivalent of a horror flick. But the folks at Geffen's manufacturer took the lyrics at face value, and refused to print the records. Rubin's contract compelled Geffen to either find alternate manufacturing and distribution, or release Def American from its contract. David Geffen chose the latter, sending a terse one-page fax to Rubin's Sunset Boulevard offices one morning in the early fall of 1990.

The split between Geffen and Def American occurred at an opportune time for Rubin. His old friend George Drakoulias had joined the label after a stint scouting talent for A&M Records, where he couldn't interest anyone in signing a bluesy rock band called Mr. Crowe's Garden. Rubin hated the group. But he wanted to work with Drakoulias again, so he signed them on the condition that Drakoulias get the band to change their name, and that Rubin's name be listed nowhere on the record. By the time of the Geto Boys controversy, Mr. Crowe's Garden—renamed the Black Crowes—had scored an MTV hit with their remake of Otis Redding's "Hard to Handle," and were selling hundreds of thousands of records. Geffen, by declining to release the Geto Boys' album, had to relinquish the Black Crowes' record as well, handing Rubin the perfect calling card to shop his label anew. By this time, Rubin had experienced a change of heart about the Black Crowes, slipping his name into new pressings of their album.

Ostin seized this chance to work with Rubin, rushing in to provide the young record producer with manufacturing and distribution for not only the Black Crowes but for the Geto Boys' album as well. Ostin did it because he *could* do it. Steve Ross never interfered with Ostin's business or questioned his judgment.

Ross's mind was on a bigger issue: completing the merger of Warner Communications and Time, Inc. The new company, Time Warner, was an unprecedented media behemoth, owning magazines, movies, music, books, and moving into the profitable business of local cable franchises. The merger instantly created an almost insurmountable corporate debt: $16 billion. The debt, as one Warner executive later recounted, turned the pleasure of raking in money into the *need* to rake it in.

But the industry was flush in the early 1990s—with millions of music lovers repurchasing their entire record collection on the new "compact disc" format. That prosperity insulated former finance guy Mo Ostin from the critiques of current bean counters like Ross's corporate music chief, Bob Morgado, a veteran of New York state politics with no previous experience in the entertainment business. Morgado resented that Mo Ostin, Bob Krasnow, and Ahmet Ertegun reported directly to Ross, and not to him. As long as Ross was in charge, Ostin was free to run his business the way he saw fit. But there was something that Mo Ostin didn't know yet about his benefactor.

Steve Ross was dying of cancer.

Rubin's enthusiastic espousal of the Geto Boys' misanthropy caused problems even for people who supported the group. *The Source* was set to run a full-page ad for the Geto Boys' album in their October 1990 issue, but their printer in Virginia balked at Rubin's chosen headline—"Play

Pussy, Get Fucked"—because it was, as they put it, "presented outside of any meaningful editorial context." They gave publisher Dave Mays an ultimatum: Remove the ad, or find another printer.

Over the next forty-eight hours, a spirited debate among the magazine's founders and staff ensued: By dropping the ad, wouldn't *The Source* be pandering to the voices of outsiders who had uneducated and often racist views of hip-hop? The headline, after all, was street slang that likely predated rap. And yet, were sexist slang and misogynist lyrics the kind of free expression that *The Source* wanted to stand behind? Eventually, Jon Shecter, Dave Mays, James Bernard, and Ed Young came to a decision: They would drop the headline from the advertisement and, in the next issue, run a feature on the phenomenon of "gangster" rap to probe some of the questions provoked by the emerging subgenre.

"The Gangsta Rapper" cover story—the first in any magazine ever—centered around an article by David Mills, the young Black journalist who made his name by reporting anti-Jewish quotes from Public Enemy's erstwhile spokesperson, Professor Griff. Mills's piece rightly traced the roots of gangster rap back to Schoolly D and KRS-One, acknowledging the latter artist's evolution. Mills outlined the hypocrisy of the consumer ("I paid money for *Criminal Minded*. I bought *Straight Outta Compton*. And I just purchased the *Geto Boys*. Am I following rappers to the brink, or am I the one who's pushing them there?"). He also decried the duplicity of the artists, arguing that the "horror flick" analogy contradicted their "we just report reality" defense.

"Gangster rap isn't about the reality of underclass America," Mills wrote. "It's about shock value."

Mills fretted over the future: "Like radiation exposure, it'll be years before we really know the consequences of our nasty little entertainments." And yet, even Mills admitted that gansgter rap had produced at least one great work of pop art: former NWA member Ice Cube's *AmeriKKKa's Most Wanted*.

The article's sidebars included Mays's lengthy explanation of *The Source*'s struggle with the Geto Boys ad, accompanied by a small reproduction of the original ad, its headline now appearing in "proper" editorial context. The editors also solicited quotes from a number of industry leaders and artists on the issue, from Tom Silverman ("I think people need to be shocked"), to Bryan Turner ("It's freedom of speech"), to Chuck D ("People worship the gangster . . . because it's against the flow. But that's only because the flow hasn't proven to be the right way for all Black people"). The editors gave members of the Geto Boys and NWA a platform to respond to the controversy and their critics.

"Whenever a person decides to kill somebody, and uses my album as an excuse, they're full of shit," Bushwick Bill argued. "It's something that was already within your heart to go out and do, and you just wanted a good excuse."

But NWA's Dr. Dre dropped any political pretensions.

"Bottom line: We ain't doing this shit to send out no messages," Dre said. "We in this shit to get paid. We don't want to start no controversy, we just make records that we like listening to and that we think others will like also."

Rubin had made the latter point himself in the media: *It's about art. Art doesn't need to be political to be worthy. Art, ultimately, is about what people like, whether gangster rap, or porn, or violent movies.*

Not everyone wanted to be in the business of "extreme" entertainment. As entrepreneurs like Rick Rubin partnered with executives at major corporations, they found themselves subject to the whims and wishes of people who had very different tastes and priorities.

Bob Krasnow surrounded himself with the finer things.

In the years he worked for Warner Bros. Records, from 1975 to 1983, Krasnow was an infamous bon vivant. He once billed Warner for a limousine he had hired to retrieve a Montblanc pen for him from a local jeweler. On company retreats, Krasnow wouldn't stay at the same hotel with the other execs if he deemed the accommodations too pedestrian. Along with Krasnow's impeccable taste came impatient tirades against colleagues and underlings, anyone who offended him or got in his way.

Krasnow's obnoxious behavior rankled the rank and file, but Warner Bros. Records chairman Mo Ostin put up with it all for one simple reason: When it came to "Black" music, there was no executive better than Bob Krasnow. The Jewish record man had, during his tenure with Warner Bros., single-handedly turned the company from what one executive called "the Whitest label in the world" into one with the best roster of Black artists in the business, signing George Benson, Chaka Khan, Funkadelic, and Bootsy Collins.

In 1983, Warner Communications had offered Krasnow the chair of

Elektra Records—home of rock bands like the Eagles, the Cars, and Queen—a label that had been performing weakly as of late. Many people in Warner's Burbank offices were pleased to see Krasnow go, and some whispered that he was being deliberately set up to fail.

Krasnow didn't. He seized the opportunity to turn Elektra into a dynamic label by infusing it with the power of Black music. Once again, he built from scratch a powerful new roster of R&B artists, including Anita Baker and Keith Sweat. And he scored a number of sophisticated rock hits, too: Metallica, Tracy Chapman, Simply Red, and 10,000 Maniacs.

Krasnow had been among the first major-label record executives to attempt to break into hip-hop. In 1984 he signed Grandmaster Flash, who, by then, had already made his last good record. Elektra lagged behind other major labels in closing deals with rap indies like Def Jam and Tommy Boy. But in 1989, Krasnow outdid them all. Elektra became the first major label with a credible in-house talent scout for rap music when Krasnow hired the twenty-two-year-old Dante Ross away from Tommy Boy.

Ross had been Tom Silverman and Monica Lynch's secret weapon in Tommy Boy's resurgence. Yet, despite his role in bringing Queen Latifah and Digital Underground to the label, Ross still made only $28,000 a year. As an A&R man, he didn't even have an expense account. Ross, known to hip-hop fans across the globe as "Dante the Scrub," was forced to supplement his income by bartending on weekends and selling weed out of the Tommy Boy offices.

In 1989, Ross's old friends the Beastie Boys recommended him for a job at their new home, Capitol Records—which had no one on staff from the hip-hop community. A&R executive Tim Carr offered Ross a gig with an annual salary of $60,000. Ross was torn between the money and loyalty to his current artists. So Ross and his lawyer, Andy Tavel, set up a meeting with Silverman to inquire whether there were some way that Ross could continue working with Tommy Boy at a level commensurate with his talents and contributions. Silverman was uncomfortable doing negotiations in the presence of his employee, so he asked Ross to step outside.

Although his company was half owned by Time Warner, Silverman still operated Tommy Boy as an independent label. So Silverman's predicament was indicative of the quandary facing many of his peers at the rap indies, like Cory Robbins and Steve Plotnicki at Profile, and Fred Munao at Select. The major labels had been signing more rap acts every year, driving up the price of talent. Where indies might offer $20,000 for an album, the majors sometimes offered several times that amount. Now that it seemed the majors would be competing for executive talent as well, Silverman decided that it would be foolish to outbid them.

A few minutes later, Andy Tavel emerged from the room and took his client aside. Silverman had offered Dante Ross a raise to $37,000 and use of a company credit card.

"He's never going to do the right thing," Tavel said of Silverman.

With the Capitol offer in hand, and another offer from Bryan Turner at Priority, Tavel suggested that he and Ross see what else was out there.

Bob Krasnow had read about De La Soul in *The New York Times*, and was eager to meet the man who signed them.

"De La Soul landed in my lap," Ross told Krasnow during their first meeting at Elektra. "I'm not going to lie to you. But I helped make them better."

"I respect you for telling the truth," Krasnow replied.

Krasnow liked this crazy street kid, with his blunt style and ghetto gold. The silver-haired executive eyed Ross's huge, three-finger ring.

"Let me see that," Krasnow said. Ross handed him the hunk of metal, and Krasnow slipped it on his hand.

"What do you think?" Krasnow asked.

"I don't know," Ross replied. "It's not really your style."

"Yeah," Krasnow agreed, handing the ring back to Ross. "I'm into diamonds."

In that moment, Ross decided he liked Krasnow, too.

Krasnow tripled Dante Ross's Tommy Boy salary, made him a director of A&R at Elektra, and gave him his own imprint. As such, he was the first person from the independent hip-hop industry to take a job on the staff of a major record company for the express purpose of imparting his hip-hop expertise to that label.

Things weren't easy for Dante Ross during that first year. Although Russell Simmons and Andre Harrell had gone out of their way to sing his praises to Krasnow, some of the Black employees at Elektra regarded Krasnow's new White rap A&R person cynically. But in Dante Ross, Krasnow saw something of himself: a White guy who understood Black music better than many Black executives did. So Krasnow told his staff to leave Ross alone and do their jobs. And when Ross's first record bombed, Krasnow looked the other way. Within a year, Ross built a well-respected roster that included a group called Brand Nubian—whose debut album garnered a rare "five mic" rating from *The Source*—and Leaders of the New School, a group of teenage Public Enemy protégés from Long Island, including a hoarse-voiced MC who called himself "Busta Rhymes."

Elektra's new rap releases sold a few hundred thousand copies each—respectable, but nothing to match their critical acclaim. The dense, somewhat cerebral nature of Ross's records didn't yield obvious hits, and Elektra's Black promotion staff didn't go beyond the call to promote them. Krasnow mulled his options. He could hire knowledgeable promotion people, or he could partner with another company to provide those services.

In early 1991, Krasnow heard that Fred Munao's Select Records was looking for a home. Krasnow asked Dante Ross what he thought. Ross liked Munao and gave Krasnow the thumbs-up.

Select's rap duo, Kid 'N Play, had nabbed the lead roles in a hip-hop movie called *House Party* from the independent New Line Cinema. But despite Select's success, Munao was still having cash-flow problems. If he was ever going to do a deal, now was the time.

Krasnow made the trip to Select Records in Manhattan's Flatiron District. Munao took him on a tour of an office that was cramped and chaotic. Employees scurried and music blasted. Krasnow walked though the halls, repeating, "I love it. I love it all."

Over the next few weeks, Krasnow courted Munao through meetings and extravagant meals. Munao and Gary Casson, Krasnow's executive VP of business affairs, began negotiations. Elektra arranged to buy 50 percent of Select Records for an advance in the low seven figures. The deal was announced in *Billboard* magazine on May 18, 1991.

Munao settled into the new arrangement with Elektra, setting up the new album from another respected rapper, Chubb Rock. Krasnow told Munao to call him anytime—even at home—if he needed anything or had concerns. Munao was welcome at Elektra and even attended some of Bob Krasnow's Monday meetings.

At those employee gatherings, Munao experienced Krasnow's high-minded talk of building a label with an "ethical culture." But Krasnow didn't always operate in a high-minded manner with his staff. Munao witnessed some of Krasnow's legendary abusive behavior. He just never dreamed he would be the target of it.

Once a year, Bob Krasnow took his staff on a weekend retreat to New York's Carlyle Hotel, the luxurious art-deco building where President John F. Kennedy had once maintained an apartment. There, away from the bustle of the Midtown office, Krasnow and his A&R team shared their new projects and talked about music in an elegant, relaxed environment. On a Sunday afternoon in the summer of 1991, just months after the Select deal was signed, Kransow invited Fred Munao to join them.

Munao was particularly eager to play a record that he had just released, the debut single by his first West Coast rapper. AMG was produced by Compton, California's DJ Quik, whose own debut album had just gone gold for Profile Records, without much radio or video play. Now that Quik had a following, it seemed given that AMG would ride his coattails. The single was already climbing the Billboard rap singles chart. Munao's job was to get Elektra excited about releasing the album.

Krasnow and the others in the room, around twenty of them, fell silent as the music began. From the speakers came a young man's monotone voice saying, "Bitch betta have my money!"—followed by a huge resonant boom and a lick from a fuzz guitar . . . repeating and repeating, building up to a crescendo as the voice intoned, "AwwwwwwwwWWWWWW SHIT!"

And then: "There ain't nothin like black pussy on my dick! Word to the motherfuckin' DJ Quik . . ."

Krasnow shouted over the music. "Take that shit off!" he said. "I don't have to hear that fucking crap!"

The CD was stopped. Munao froze. After a momentary hush that hung over the sumptuous conference room, Krasnow turned on Munao.

"You've got a lot of balls playing this in my meeting!" Krasnow bellowed, berating Munao as if he were an employee, and not the label head he had wooed just months earlier. "I am never putting this crap out! Where's your sense of moral obligation to society?" A few of the A&R people joined Krasnow in his outrage.

Munao defended himself: "Look," he began. "I grew up like most of you, middle-class. But I'm not about to impose my middle-class values on a piece of music that's coming from a community that I don't even know about. This is what they want to talk about! And this what they're buying!"

"*They?!*" How could Munao be so crass? Krasnow and the others decried the damage that a song like this would do to poor Black children. Munao looked in disbelief at the White executives who were now shouting at him.

"You know what?" Munao said, raising his voice, "you have Mötley Crüe talking about bending girls over and banging 'em up the ass, and shit like that! But that's okay, because they're White and it doesn't threaten you. But because my kids are Black, you can't handle it!"

The civilized conference became a shouting match. At one point, Mitchell Krasnow, Bob's son and A&R person, turned to his father and said, "Dad, why did you do this deal in the first place if you didn't want to put out these kinds of records?" This was the very question that Select's embattled chief was asking himself, so Munao thought that Krasnow's son was coming to his aid. He wasn't. Unbeknownst to Munao, Mitchell had been against Elektra's getting involved in rap from the start.

But one person did rise in Munao's defense. Dante Ross, Krasnow's new protégé, thought that Munao deserved better than what he was getting from Krasnow. So Ross spoke up, comparing AMG's juvenile, testosterone-fueled lyrics to the rhymes of 1970s black icons Dolomite or Flip Wilson.

It wasn't some heinous, misogynistic song, Ross argued. On the contrary, it was a goof.

Elektra VP of A&R Sue Drew listened with alarm as he spoke. Drew had remained quiet though the meeting. She felt bad for Fred, but she had been through enough of these Krasnow tirades to know that it was best to keep her head down. Since Ross had arrived at Elektra, she tried to look after the kid, help him navigate the treacherous waters of label politics. So she did the only thing she could do to save Dante Ross from himself, from falling out of favor with his one true benefactor at the label: She shot him a look.

Ross caught her glance.

Dante, her eyes said. *Shut the fuck up.*

The sprawling new empire of Time Warner comprised a bevy of classic, unrelated brands like *People* magazine, HBO, CNN, Atari, Lorimar, Franklin Mint, Warner-Elektra-Atlantic, Hasbro, and Chris-Craft. The culture of the new company was as confusing as the new Time Warner logo, which looked like a cross between an eye, an ear, and an unraveling ball of string. The laid-back Warner executives who thrived under Steve Ross's loose style often clashed with the stiffer, more buttoned-down Time alums.

Jenette Kahn was a Steve Ross person. Kahn ran DC Comics—home to those all-American brands Superman, Batman, Wonder Woman, Captain Marvel, and Flash—and was something of a wonder woman herself. After graduating from Harvard with a degree in art history, she founded three innovative children's magazines. In 1976, at only twenty-eight years old, Kahn became the publisher of DC, the youngest person and the first woman to run a division of Ross's Warner Communications.

Kahn knew Ross was ailing, and she wanted to do something to bring the two corporate cultures together. So she reached out to one of her new colleagues from the Time, Inc., side, Richard Stolley. In 1963, Stolley had been the reporter for *Life* magazine who negotiated with Abraham Zapruder to buy the film that captured the assassination of President Kennedy. In the 1970s, Stolley became the first managing editor for *People* magazine, and had since become Time, Inc.'s overall editorial director, a kind of éminence grise for the corporation.

Kahn and Stolley conceived an ongoing gathering called the "Time Warner Executive Forums." These seminars wouldn't deal with business issues, but rather focus on culture to enrich executives' understanding of the world. Kahn and Stolley brought their idea to Ross's second in command, a quiet, mustachioed Time, Inc., veteran named Gerald Levin, who threw his support behind the project.

One of the first subjects that Kahn wanted her fellow executives to explore was hip-hop. And who better to explain this cultural phenomenon to her colleagues but her friend Fab 5 Freddy, the man with the gift for framing things? Kahn, a chum of Andy Warhol's, knew Freddy from the New York art scene. Freddy, in turn, respected Kahn for her expertise and adored her aesthetic—her wild, fluorescent clothes and her quirky collection of furniture and paintings made Kahn the embodiment of the pop-art sensibility.

Kahn envisioned Freddy, onstage, dialoguing with a rapper. And Kahn happened to be friendly with one rap artist in the Time Warner family of record labels, someone she had met only recently. He was a charming, whip-smart guy, perfect to translate the street spirit of hip-hop for a roomful of clueless White executives.

Who, Kahn thought, *wouldn't love Ice-T?*

Ice-T's double life as a part-time rapper, part-time hustler ended in 1986, when he landed an album deal with Seymour Stein's Warner Bros. imprint, Sire Records. Sixty thousand dollars wasn't much compared to the money he had seen in his life, but now Tracy Marrow was earning a decent wage through full-time recording and performing. He named his first album, optimistically, *Rhyme Pays*.

Ice-T was the first rapper signed to Warner Bros. Records. Initially, it was not a great fit. Ice was an independent artist with a small but loyal street following, now under the care of one of the widest, and Whitest, labels in the world. Warner's Sire label had been the source of White interpolations of Black music from Blondie, Tom Tom Club, and Madonna; Ice-T was their first Black artist. At Sire's parent, the once-proud roster of soul and funk artists built in part by Bob Krasnow—Funkadelic, Chaka Khan, Prince and his protégé groups—had aged out of their prime. The Black promotion staff at Warner, led by Tom Draper, lacked fervor—except when it came to their opinions about rap music, which many of them despised.

Ice-T's path to success at Warner Bros. was forged by someone who had fire to spare. Jorge Hinojosa was a nineteen-year-old intern at Island Records' Los Angeles office when he met Ice-T. Every day, Hinojosa commuted four hours a day by bus to and from his mother's house in Riverside, sixty miles away. A fan of rock and new wave who had only recently come to know hip-hop, Hinojosa helped Ice-T book shows and shop his records to labels around Los Angeles. In return, Ice-T started introducing Hinojosa to everyone in the L.A. hip-hop scene as his manager.

Hinojosa loved Ice-T's complexity. The rapper came up with neighborhood thugs, but easily mingled with anyone in Hollywood, including up-and-coming stars like Madonna. He even had a rap called "New Wave Baby," about dating a White chick with pink hair. Like Hinojosa himself—half-Anglo and half-Bolivian—Ice-T was a man of color who defied stereotyping. At Warner Bros., Hinojosa used this to his artist's advantage.

With Warner's Black music department offering little help, Jorge and Ice-T decided instead to play to Sire and Warner's strengths with the growing "alternative rock" market, college-age White kids who often had some affinity for hip-hop. For these kids, White rap artists like the Beastie Boys were an easy sell. But occasionally, college radio would latch onto certain Black rap artists, usually those who leaned toward rock or punk sensibilities. It was, perhaps, the reason that Public Enemy's debut was embraced enthusiastically by White college radio even as it fell flat in the streets. So when East Coast rap radio DJs turned their back on Ice-T, college radio welcomed him. No major label had more credibility or capability with college radio than Warner Bros. Records.

With hundreds of artists on the Warner roster, Hinojosa still had to find some way to gain an edge for his client. Hinojosa did it by cultivating personal relationships with the Warner staff. Jorge and Ice-T relentlessly "worked the building," the headquarters of Warner Bros. Records—a sprawling, multistoried labyrinth of myriad departments. Jorge literally walked miles during his daily visits to various departments—promotion, artist development, publicity, production, creative services. Jorge was a notorious noodge, but people respected him, especially because the artist for whom he fought was so damn nice.

Many Warner Bros. employees had never met a rapper, much less one with song titles like "Pimpin' Ain't Easy" and "Grand Larceny." But Ice-T blew away every stereotype that the underexposed Warner staff might have held. He was so polite, they observed. He was so charming and articulate. He could hold forth in any conversation, whether it was about politics, sports, or rock and roll. He remembered your name. He recorded cool outgoing messages for your voice mailbox. To the outside world, he was the rapper Ice-T. But to the employees of Warner Bros. Records, he was their buddy Trace. Mo Ostin and his young president, Lenny Waronker, loved Ice-T. So did Seymour Stein, who signed Ice because his voice reminded him of Bob Dylan's. Sire's general manager, Howie Klein, an outspoken critic of Tipper Gore and her Parents Music Resource Center—which had recently begun fulminating about salacious lyrics from rap acts like 2 Live Crew—found Ice-T to be a kindred spirit when it came to the politics and culture of rebellion. Executives like Steven Baker, Warner's chief of product management, and Jo Lenardi, the head of alternative promotion, fought hard for the rapper's records; and the Warner rank and file would do almost anything for him.

Being with a huge label like Warner Bros. did have its advantages. In 1988, Warner Bros. landed the soundtrack for a new Dennis Hopper film about gangs in Los Angeles. But, as Steve Baker noted, Hopper's movie had an authenticity problem: It was a film about L.A. youth with no rap music in it. Baker convinced Hopper to hire Ice-T to do the title song for the movie, *Colors*. Hinojosa convinced the movie studio, Orion Pictures, to hire him to promote the film to the hip-hop market. Hinojosa, who had been borrowing money from his mother to survive, walked away with the biggest check he had ever received. He went back to Riverside and gave the $15,000 to her.

"Put this toward what I owe you," Hinojosa said.

Soon Warner's film division tapped their sister company's resident rapper for the lead role in a film from George Jackson, Doug McHenry, and Fab 5 Freddy called *New Jack City*. Ice-T played the part of police officer Scotty Appleton, opposite Wesley Snipes's drug dealer, Nino Brown. It was a role that Ice-T almost didn't take. He feared his street credibility could be ruined by playing a cop. Ice-T's fans—the people who knew every word to "6 'N the Mornin' "—had, whether guilty or innocent, spent their entire lives running from the cops and didn't much like them. Ice-T, a former Crip, told MTV's Kurt Loder why he struggled with the part.

"I hate cops," he said.

By 1991, Ice-T had become an unlikely multimedia success, in large part because of his partnership with Warner Bros. After *New Jack City* hit, more movie offers followed from Warner, roles in *Ricochet* and *Looters*.[14] His records now sold in the hundreds of thousands through the WEA distribution system. His latest album, *O.G. Original Gangster*, had gone gold and was inching toward platinum. The album showed Ice-T at his most musically diverse, including a heavy-metal song called "Body Count" that featured a backing band composed of Ice-T's muscled, metal-loving buddies from Crenshaw High School. Ice-T was the only rap act booked on the summer's hottest national package tour for alternative rock, the Lollapalooza festival, and he brought the "Body Count" players with him. Every day, Ice-T and his bandmates rocked the crowd. With a production deal already in place to produce new artists for Warner's Sony-owned rival, Epic—the rapper began to conceive of an entire "Body Count" album.

Sire's Howie Klein wasn't about to let this one get away, and he made the deal to bring the album to Warner. As a heavy-metal band, Body Count lacked the gravitas of revered groups like Slayer. But their music was fun, puerile, and pointedly political. On the lead single, "There Goes the Neighborhood," Ice-T made the band's ethos plain, taking the voice of a White rocker raging at the entry of guitar-playing "niggers" into his club. "Those Blacks want everything in the fuckin' world," he screamed. "That nigger plays so good, he took my motherfuckin' girl!"

The album was packed with these kinds of provocations. Ice-T played a cast of characters: a young White boy ranting about killing his racist mother in "Momma's Gotta Die Tonight"; a big Black dick taunting White supremacists in "KKK Bitch"; a ghetto everyman, issuing lethal payback to renegade police officers in the album's title track, "Cop Killer." All of these songs were tongue-in-cheek, over-the-top revenge fantasies, even if the latter tune seemed true to life in the wake of the recent beating of Black motorist Rod-

---

[14]The title was later changed to *Trespass*.

ney King by L.A. police: "I'm 'bout to bust some shots off. / I'm 'bout to dust some cops off. / I'm a cop killer, better you than me. / Cop killer, fuck police brutality!"

As Warner Bros. readied the album for release, one executive quietly raised his hand.

Russ Thyret was Warner's ruddy, jocular head of promotion. More than that, Thyret had brought Prince to the label. He embodied the open-door, artist-friendly ways of Warner. He was fiercely loyal to Mo Ostin. Russ Thyret, in short, was the consummate company man.

But Russ Thyret's father was a cop.

In one of the marathon promotion meetings that the staff liked to call "Korea"—because they dragged on as long and were as pointless as the 1950s conflict—Thyret told his colleagues that he respected Ice-T's artistic freedom. But he asked them to think, for a moment, with their hearts, and not their heads. *I understand that it's a third-person narrative*, he said, *but I cannot divorce myself from my own feelings about this song*. Thyret warned them: *When police officers and their supporters hear this, they will react*. Thyret and a few other execs asked, as they had with other controversial releases: *Do we really need to do this?*

Thyret spoke his peace. Ostin had never stopped his artists from speaking theirs. He hadn't backed down during an open revolt among the staff over a record by comic Sam Kinison, whom many considered homophobic and misogynist. But while many folks at Warner detested Kinison, there was near-unanimous admiration for Ice-T. Despite Thyret's warnings, there was no way Ostin was going to keep this record from coming out. Even so, the Warner execs asked Howie Klein to convey their concerns about the album's title track. At the very least, some retailers would refuse to stock the record. Would Ice-T consider taking "Cop Killer" off the record?

Howie Klein translated these trepidations to Hinojosa and Ice-T, but told them that personally he would be disappointed if Ice removed the song. It was the principle of the thing. Hinojosa and Ice, unwilling to jeopardize the ability to reach their fans, arrived at a compromise. They would change the name of the album from *Cop Killer* to *Body Count*, and let the most controversial song rest as an album track.

The video for the single "There Goes the Neighborhood" played in heavy rotation on MTV. College radio and some rock stations spun the record. By the spring of 1992, *Body Count* had shipped around 300,000 units, selling around 200,000 of those. Howie Klein thought it was a respectable, profitable showing. After a few months, unsold copies started returning to WEA, as they usually did when a record was slowing down.

In the rock world, the album was a minor blip on the radar screen. In the hip-hop community, *Body Count* barely existed.

When the riots hit Los Angeles in April 1992, Ice-T was deluged by calls from the news media.

"We definitely knew there was a lot of tension down here," he told the *CBS Evening News*. "We tried to explain it to people, but nobody wanted to listen."

While some journalists sought an explanation for the riots, others simply wanted a Black icon who would issue a call for peace. An anchor on L.A.'s KTTV asked Ice-T to do something to "stop the riots." The rapper refused.

"I hate to tell you I told you this was going to happen," he said. "It hurts me to see my neighborhood going up like this 'cause that's where I grew up. At the same time, I can't honestly say that if I didn't have this money in my pocket, and I wasn't who I was, that I wouldn't be there too."

In the days and weeks after the uprising, the news media discovered what the folks at Warner Bros. knew all along—that Ice-T possessed a perfect combination of street credibility and eloquence. In the midst of this, Jorge Hinojosa got a call from Jenette Kahn: Would Ice consider being a guest at the next Time Warner executive forum, to teach Time Warner executives the meaning and significance of hip-hop?

Kahn first arranged a meeting between Ice-T and Time Warner's acting chief, Gerald Levin. They walked into Levin's office at 75 Rockefeller Plaza as the executive was listening to Ice-T's new album. Of course, Levin wasn't a hip-hop fan. He couldn't even recall the names of the rap albums he'd bought over the years for his son, Jonathan. But he wanted to hear the music of the artist about whom Kahn had gushed. For Ice-T and Hinojosa, hearing their album in Levin's office was an icebreaker. The men had an energetic conversation.

Hinojosa had ulterior motives. This was a perfect opportunity to pitch Levin on a "synergy" deal—like the kind that another Sire artist, Madonna, had just negotiated—entailing not just a new recording contract, but a series of joint ventures with a host of Time Warner companies like Warner Pictures, HBO, Warner Books, and Lorimar Television. Madonna's deal, valued at nearly $60 million, was one of the richest in history.

Hinojosa felt he had an artist who was similarly multifaceted. Ice sold millions of records, and made successful movies. He had just negotiated both a deal with Kahn's DC Comics and a pact with HBO to do a show called *Ice-TV*. If Time Warner could do a synergy deal for Madonna, they could surely do a scaled-down version for Ice.

"We want to know that when Ice has any kind of creative impulse, that we have an outlet," Hinojosa proposed. Levin seemed game to the idea. They would talk about it when they saw each other again at the Time Warner Executive Forum, in June.

One morning in May 1992, senior corporal Glenn White reported for duty at the northeast substation of the Dallas Police Department. White was a patrol officer, and spent most of his day on the street. But he also worked part-time as the vice president of the Dallas Police Association, editing the DPA's monthly newsletter, "The Shield."

That morning, White's friend, Sgt. Ron Rose, approached White with a tip for the next issue. Rose produced a piece of paper containing the lyrics to a song called "Cop Killer," which Rose had photocopied from the CD booklet for the *Body Count* album, brought to the house by one of his fourteen-year-old daughter's friends.

"Holy shit," White said as he read.

Rose had done some research for White. The album had been released on Warner Bros. Records. Rose found name of its president, a guy named Lenny Waronker. He also found that Warner Bros. was part of a much larger company called Time Warner. Rose knew that Time Warner owned companies like *Time* magazine and Warner Bros. Pictures. But he was surprised to learn that they owned the Six Flags amusement park chain. That meant that every time he took his kids to Six Flags over Texas, he was, in some way, rewarding a company that profited from music that openly called for his own death.

"Can you let people know about this?" Rose asked White.

White obliged with an emotional plea. "Are you ready for this?" began the article on page nine of the May 29 issue of "The Shield," entitled, "New rap song encourages killing police officers."

"I urge you to BOYCOTT any and all Time Warner products and movies until such time as they have recalled this tape. . . . If we want this pulled from the record stores, we're going to have to make it happen ourselves. WE CAN DO IT!" White then printed Lenny Waronker's name, address, and phone number.

"The Shield" arrived in the mailboxes of thousands of active and retired Dallas police officers and other police associations across Texas. A few days later, White's phone rang. It was Eric Ramp of the Corpus Christi police, asking if he could forward White's article to a reporter at the local paper, the *Caller Times*. The reporter, in turn, called the state's largest police advocacy organization, the Combined Law Enforcement Association of Texas, or CLEAT.

Ron DeLord, CLEAT's cofounder and president, took the call. It was the first he had heard of any boycott.

DeLord, a forty-four-year-old lawyer and lobbyist in Austin, had come a long way from the scared twenty-one-year-old rookie cop he was in Beaumont, Texas. On his first day, he was given a pistol and badge, and—without any weapons training or knowledge of the penal code—put out on the streets to police a poor, mostly Black town near the Louisiana border.

"They're out of control down there," his fellow officers would say.

Along with the rest of the two-hundred-man, all-White department, DeLord made arrests and shuttled suspects into one of four segregated jail cells—White male, White female, Black male, Black female. It was 1969, four years after the passage of the Civil Rights Act. The force now had two Black police officers, but neither was allowed to arrest Whites. The signs above the segregated drinking fountains were still visible through a thin layer of whitewash.

It wasn't until many years later, when he was on his way to completing his law degree, that DeLord began to fathom the historical and economic forces behind crime: that poor people and Black people were more often victims than criminals; that the police were needed not as occupiers but to make sure the most vulnerable citizens could at least get to the corner store or their mailboxes safely. After he started CLEAT in the late 1970s, DeLord worked with a Black state senator named Royce West to fight for legislation mandating statewide technical, cultural, and racial sensitivity training for the almost sixty thousand peace officers in Texas, half of whom worked at least twelve months before receiving any instruction whatsoever. They waged their battle for most of the 1980s over the objections of most of the state's chiefs of police. The bill finally passed in 1987, the same year that DeLord received his license to practice law.

DeLord dedicated his career to uplifting the reputation of the Texas police. But by 1992, law enforcement officers across the country were on the defensive, reeling from accusations of brutality and racism in the wake of the Rodney King beating and subsequent riots. The Black community in general, and the rap world in particular, seemed to revile the police. First there was NWA with "Fuck the Police." Now this "Cop Killer" song, which DeLord hadn't even heard yet.

DeLord met with CLEAT cofounder John Burpo in their Austin offices on the morning of June 8 to discuss joining the boycott. Burpo saw an opportunity immediately. "There is a deep wound to the psyche of the police," Burpo said. "Now we've found a way to say, 'Enough is enough. This is too much. You cannot call for our death.'"

DeLord considered the situation with his Texan sensibilities. *You can kick a dog all you want*, DeLord thought. *But sooner or later the dog is gonna bite you.* Even with DeLord's racial enlightenment, the irony of his turn of phrase was lost on him—that young Black men might view themselves as the dogs in that folksy parable. Whatever the case, it would now be a dogfight.

DeLord's spokesperson, Mark Clark, reached out to Glenn White about joining the boycott, suggesting they do a joint press conference later that week. To Clark's surprise, White refused, saying he didn't have the time.

DeLord wasn't surprised. He and White didn't get along, and this seemed to be yet another volley in an ongoing pissing match. White had become national news. *Entertainment Tonight* had come down to Dallas to interview him, and *CBS News* flew White to New York to spar with a writer from *Spin* magazine. Now that DeLord was fielding calls from media outlets, the CLEAT executive presumed White was jealous that he was stepping on his turf.

DeLord went on alone. To prove a point about Time Warner, he booked the press conference in Arlington, the home of the Six Flags amusement park between Dallas and Fort Worth. The next day, DeLord got a call from Bob Bennett, the president of Six Flags, who argued that his family-oriented business shouldn't be held accountable for the actions of its corporate parent.

But DeLord wanted to emphasize that nothing would be off-limits—not Six Flags, not Time Warner's upcoming big summer movie, *Batman Returns*, nor their precious cable franchises, which police in Houston had already asked their city council not to renew. More police organizations rolled under CLEAT's tent, and by the day of the press event—June 11, 1992—even Glenn White and the DPA showed up.

With White standing nearby DeLord announced the planned boycott of Time Warner for the song "Cop Killer." The organizers called for an apology from both the artist and the company; for the song's removal from the *Body Count* album; and for group leader Ice-T to make a million-dollar donation to a community services program. DeLord set a deadline for the satisfaction of these demands: July 16, the date of the Time Warner shareholders' meeting in Beverly Hills, California. *The anticipation of an ass whipping*, DeLord calculated, *can be more powerful than the ass whipping itself.* If his ultimatum wasn't met, then police would pressure their pension funds to divest themselves of Time Warner stock.

"We're here to send a message to Time Warner, Inc., and its related companies," DeLord said. "We want them to have a wake-up call from the six hundred thousand police officers in this country."

That night and the next day, wire services carried the news from coast to coast. Tom Brokaw aired a segment on the boycott on *NBC Nightly News*. Major newspapers across the country reported the event. But almost every one of these stories committed a factual error.

"The artist is rapper Ice-T," said NBC reporter Jim Cummins. "His song is called 'Cop Killer.'"

The headline for the June 12 AP story read: "Police Organization Angry over Rapper's 'Cop Killer' Song."

Almost every major publication except *Billboard* magazine had misidentified both the proper creator and the genre of "Cop Killer." Hereafter, major media outlets, including the venerable *New York Times*, continued to misidentify *Body Count's heavy-metal* song as Ice-T's *rap* song. As a result, the controversy over "Cop Killer" became a referendum on rap music.

Back in Burbank, Warner Bros. president Lenny Waronker summoned publicity chief Bob Merlis to his office. Waronker motioned to a pile of envelopes, some addressed to "Lenny 'Cop Killer' Waronker," all containing letters demanding that Warner Bros. withdraw the *Body Count* album.

"Know anything about this?" Waronker asked him.

Merlis did. Margaret Wade, Time Warner's corporate publicist had tipped him to the rumblings of a boycott. Then, after the Arlington press conference, a tidal wave broke over the record company. Merlis fielded calls from furious cops and persistent reporters.

On Friday, June 12, Howie Klein phoned Jorge Hinojosa to tell him about developments. Hinojosa thought that the story might blow over by Monday. It didn't.

Over the weekend, the National Rifle Association—led by former actor and minor Time Warner shareholder Charlton Heston—joined the boycott. In Los Angeles, a Republican city council member running for Congress, Joan Milke Flores, introduced a resolution in calling for local retailers to voluntarily remove *Body Count* from stores. By Tuesday, June 16, the Los Angeles County board was considering a similar motion. That same day, Alabama governor Guy Hunt asked record stores in his state not to sell the album. On Wednesday, House Minority Whip Newt Gingrich sent an angry letter to Time Warner headquarters, signed by sixty members of the U.S. House of Representatives—mostly Republicans, many from Texas. The New York State Sheriffs' Association joined the boycott. And in an ominous development for Warner Bros. Records, two large record chains, Trans World and the Dallas-based Superclub, dropped the *Body Count* album from their collective twelve hundred stores.

To say the least, it was peculiar timing for Ice-T's scheduled appearance at the Time Warner Executive Forum.

Time Warner flew Ice-T and Jorge Hinojosa to New York. They were flying, emotionally, too: It was their first time on a corporate jet. This "Cop Killer" controversy was a fight and a spotlight for which they both felt ready. After they landed, the pair huddled with Jenette Kahn and Fab 5 Freddy at Sammy's Roumanian Steak House to strategize for the following evening. The New York tabloids were filled with news of "Cop Killer." Some Time Warner executives, in light of the events, had tried to spook Kahn, imploring her to bring security to the friendly dinner. But Kahn and her friends ate, and laughed, and listened to the owner, Sammy, blather drunkenly. All agreed that they had to address the controversy straight-on.

The next day, about two hundred suit-and-tie-clad executives—mostly men, nearly all of them White—gathered in the eighth-floor auditorium of the Time Life Building. Fab 5 Freddy took the stage, introduced himself, and gave what Kahn thought to be an extraordinary prologue about hip-hop. Next, he introduced the man sitting next to him, Ice-T.

Freddy got right to the point. "We really can't go forward without first addressing what's on everybody's mind, around the country and here in this audience. So . . . if you had a minute to address the police in Texas who started this whole thing, what would you say?"

Ice-T, the rapper Kahn picked for his communication skills, answered with just two words.

"'Fuck you.'"

A collective gasp issued from the audience.

In that uncomfortable aftermath, Freddy waited a few moments.

Then he said: "Well . . . supposing you had a few minutes more?"

The entire assembly, including Ice-T, exploded in laughter. The tension dissolved. For the next few hours, the executives sat, rapt, as the two hip-hop icons went on to have an informative and provocative discussion about the socioeconomic and political conditions behind "Cop Killer," the recent riots, and the roots of rap rebellion. The conversation continued as two dozen top executives, including HBO chief Michael Fuchs, joined Kahn, Freddy, Hinojosa, and Ice for a late dinner at the restaurant, 21. The whole event, Kahn observed with pride, had generated a tremendous amount of goodwill for Ice-T within the corporation.

The lightness of that evening gave way to a darker day for Gerald Levin. The chief executives of his own companies were calling him, angry and panicked. In Texas, there was talk of revoking the licenses of Six Flags and Time Warner's cable operations. Levin remained committed to defending Ice-T; but the meeting that Jorge Hinojosa had hoped to have with Levin about synergy turned instead into a discussion about how best to handle the spreading firestorm.

Hinojosa disliked Levin's plans to defend Ice-T along free-speech grounds. "It's not going to work," Hinojosa said. "What you have to say is this: This song is *not* about killing cops." Rather, Hinojosa continued, it was a work of fiction, no less than the upcoming Warner movie directed by Clint Eastwood, *Unforgiven*, in which the hero murders a sheriff.

"Instead of making the free-speech argument," Hinojosa said, "let's talk about what the song actually means."

Hinojosa walked out of 75 Rockefeller without his synergy deal. But on Thursday, June 18, Ice-T enjoyed the full support of a ballroom packed with young music-industry denizens at the opening session of the New Music Seminar.

"The ramifications of this are immense," he said. "Basically they're after all of us." Ice-T defended "Cop Killer" as an argument for the rights of man. "A cop cannot walk up to a man on the street and feel that he is so powerful that you will not retaliate, especially if he's wrong."

The next day, as conventioneers spilled out into Times Square for dinner, the electronic news ticker wrapped around the Allied Chemical Building alerted them to a stunning development:

Vice President Dan Quayle had mentioned "Cop Killer" in a speech, calling it an "obscene record."

Rap music had suddenly become a major tool in the 1992 presidential contest between President George H. W. Bush and the Democratic contender, Arkansas governor Bill Clinton. Just a few days earlier Clinton stunned the mostly Black audience at Reverend Jesse Jackson's Rainbow Coalition convention by denouncing Sister Souljah, who had spoken on a panel there the previous day.

Sister Souljah wasn't exactly a rapper. She made her debut to hip-hop fans a year earlier, on a song called "Buck Whylin," the newest in Public Enemy's cast of pro-Black propagandists. Not many knew that Souljah, born Lisa Williamson, was an accomplished activist, discovered while she was a student at Rutgers University by Bill Stephney and offered a place in the PE crew. By 1992, she had released an unsuccessful solo album through Sony that had pretty much sealed her fate as a rapper. In the wake of the riots, however, Souljah was a compelling voice for journalists seeking hip-hop oracles. But Williamson was angry and young, and once again, Black reporter David Mills of *The Washington Post* caught a member of Public Enemy in an unguarded moment.

"If Black people kill Black people every day, why not have a week and kill White people? . . . So if you're a gang member and you would normally be killing somebody, why not kill a White person?"

Clinton may have attacked Sister Souljah to show conservative, working-class White voters that, even as a liberal, he would look out for them—bashing a Black "rapper" made his point. Whatever the reason, Clinton had embarassed Jesse Jackson in his own house. Steaming, Jackson hastily called a press conference to challenge Clinton's remarks, saying that Sister Souljah "represents the feelings and hopes of a whole generation of people." *The Source* accused Clinton of using the same racial scare tactics to play to conservatives that George Bush had used in the previous election with his infamous "Willie Horton" advertisement.

But Souljah's story had little traction compared to the "Cop Killer" fiasco, which grew by the day. Quayle continued to reference the song on the campaign trail. President Bush himself denounced it. More retail chains, Hastings and Sound Warehouse, dropped the *Body Count* record. The city and county councils of L.A. passed the motions against "Cop Killer."

The Time Warner board battered Gerald Levin. Board members from the cultural world, like opera singer Beverly Sills, united in umbrage with the more "white-shoe" members to challenge Levin's leadership. *The principle,* they argued, *isn't worth the controversy. It's hurting the corporation.*

Levin also took a beating on the elite social circuit. At a party in the Hamptons, Levin was grilled by friends and socialites. *How can you defend the indefensible?* some asked. *You've let yourself get dragged into presidential politics,* others reasoned. *Why are you doing this to your company?*

Levin understood their perspective. To his White and well-to-do acquaintances, the police were protectors. But Levin understood something else. For another part of society, the police were a fear-inducing occupying army. Finally, on June 24, Gerald Levin articulated his arguments in a *Wall Street Journal* piece simply called, "Why We Won't Withdraw 'Cop Killer.'"

> We know that profits are the source of our strength and independence . . . but we won't retreat in the face of threats of boycotts or political grandstanding. In the short run, cutting and running would be the surest and safest way to put this controversy behind us and get on with our business. But in the long run it would be a destructive precedent. It would be a signal to all the artists and journalists inside and outside Time Warner that if they wish to be heard, then they must tailor their minds and souls to fit the reigning orthodoxies.

The following day, Gerald Levin received a note from his son, Jonathan—in his twenties now and studying to be a schoolteacher.

"That letter was the most courageous thing I have ever seen my father do," Jonathan wrote.

Levin wasn't the only one pushing back now. Many Black police organizations, like the National Black Police Association, refused to join the boycott, claiming solidarity with Black victims of police brutality. *Billboard* and some consumer newspapers weighed in with strong editorials supporting artistic freedom in the face of government or corporate censorship. When California attorney general Daniel Lungren wrote a letter to prominent record retailers in the state, asking them to "voluntarily withdraw" the *Body Count* record, the American Civil Liberties Union responded with a letter of its own, urging retailers not to "bow to the heavy-handed attempt . . . to dictate what music shall or shall not be sold in your stores." More chains like Camelot and Musicland were dropping the record, but critics of the boycott noted with glee that sales of *Body Count*'s album had spiked, moving nearly 100,000 units in the month since the controversy began. Politicians like U.S. Representative Maxine Waters lauded Levin and Time Warner for taking a stand.

But those inside Warner Bros. knew that the top-level executives at Time Warner were not so resolute. If Levin was looking for relief, corporate music chief Bob Morgado and a few others were fuming at Mo Ostin for putting the entire corporation in jeopardy. The shareholders' meeting was fast approaching, and Levin wanted to do everything he could to contain the conflict. Quietly, he sent his general counsel, Marty Payson, and Time Warner spokesman Tod Hullin, down to Texas to see Ron DeLord and Mark Clark.

They met at a restaurant in Houston on a Thursday morning, July 9, one week before the shareholders' conference. DeLord walked in, feeling confident. He remembered a quotation he had once heard, attributed to Napoleon Bonaparte: *Never interrupt your enemy when he is making a mistake.* And Levin had screwed everything up, simply by defending Ice-T on the grounds of freedom of speech. All DeLord had to say in the media to counter the First Amendment argument was this: "Would you put out a song called 'Nigger Killer'? 'Homosexual Killer'?" Against the obvious answer to that question, Time Warner's position looked all the more untenable.

For two and a half hours, the Time Warner execs and the Texas cops set the terms of engagement for the following week. There would be two meetings. On Wednesday, Time Warner execs would address a convocation of the boycott organizers. On Thursday, a certain number of the protesters, including DeLord, would be allowed to speak at the shareholders' meeting.

Through the negotiation, Payson and Hullin were genial. They didn't come to argue. In fact, DeLord got the notion that they were looking for a way out. They talked of a meeting with New York's powerful union chief

Bill Caruso the following day. They talked of funding some project in South Central Los Angeles, and of a PBS documentary on police relations with the Black community. Payson and Hullin agreed to keep the back-channel line of communication open.

But they still couldn't give DeLord what he wanted.

DeLord arrived in Los Angeles the following week to a scene of chaos and competitiveness. The NRA was attempting to hijack the cops' protest by inserting their own antigun control police group—the Law Enforcement Alliance of America, or LEAA—into the fray, holding their own press conference and marching down Wilshire Boulevard, over the objections of CLEAT. The representatives of LEAA also muscled their way into the Wednesday meeting that CLEAT had negotiated with the Time Warner representatives.

That same day, the Time Warner board of directors met in private. Beverly Sills, the opera singer and a member of the board, demanded that Time Warner not only disavow Ice-T, but also ban any further records critical of the government or police. Lenny Waronker rose in his artist's defense. He had been preparing for this moment for weeks, especially because he knew Sills was gunning for Ice-T. He had even called his childhood friend, singer-songwriter Randy Newman, for advice.

"How violent was opera back in the day?" Waronker asked.

"Very," Newman said, giving Waronker a whole history.

Waronker reconsidered getting into an opera argument with Sills. Instead, he used a comparison from Newman's career.

"Am I going to tell Randy Newman that he can't put out 'Short People,' because it might be misinterpreted that it's *Randy* who's against short people and not *the character* he's portraying?"

On July 16, Time Warner executives and stockholders arrived at the Regent Beverly Wilshire Hotel. They were greeted by nearly a hundred picketing, jeering police officers from seventeen different police groups—Ron DeLord and Glenn White among them—holding signs, some with the names of slain police officers, and others that read, TIME WARNER PUTS PROFITS OVER POLICE LIVES, and, YOUR RAP IS CRAP. The police were flanked by a phalanx of journalists and TV cameras. Just before the meeting began, a Rolls-Royce cruised by the protesters. And out of the window emerged Ice-T himself, giving the cops the middle finger as he rolled down the street. The "drive-by" appalled a number of Time Warner executives, including Levin, who didn't appreciate the provocation at their most vulnerable moment.

Inside, Jorge Hinojosa made his way to the men's room, where he spied Charlton Heston being coached by some representatives from the NRA.

"I know what I have to say!" Heston barked at them. Hinojosa kept his head down until a friend spotted him.

"Imagine that!" his friend bellowed. "Ice-T's manager!"

"Dude!" Jorge hissed. "Enough with the name check!"

A few minutes later, Hinojosa sat to watch the proceedings with Jenette Kahn and Courtney Sale Ross, the wife of absent and ailing chairman Steve Ross. Just in front of him, onstage, was Beverly Sills. Hinojosa knew that Sills had attempted to get Warner Bros. to drop Ice-T. *She stabbed a fellow artist in the back*, Hinojosa thought. *What a cunt.*

Traditionally at these meetings, shareholders and representatives of other interested parties are invited to make comments prior to the agenda items. The friends of the boycott ultimately dominated the day. Hinojosa watched as Charlton Heston rose to speak. To document his disgust, the famed actor began to recite the lyrics to "Cop Killer" in the same stentorian tones he used to portray Moses in Cecil B. DeMille's *The Ten Commandments.*

"Were that song entitled 'Fag Killer,' or if the lyrics read, 'Die Die Die Kike Die,' would you still sell that album?" Heston asked Levin and the board.

Things took a turn to the surreal when Heston plowed ahead, reciting the lyrics from a song that the police hadn't even made into an issue, "KKK Bitch." Heston read, "Love it when she sucks me though," he said. "Love it when she fucks me though." He concluded by asking the shareholders to censure the board.

It was Ron DeLord's turn to speak next.

"How do you follow Moses?" he said, before launching into a monologue that accused Jerry Levin and Time Warner of dehumanizing police officers for profit and compared them to Hitler's propagandist Joseph Goebbels. But even Heston and DeLord's speeches were upstaged by the testimony of two officers who had been badly disfigured after being shot in the face. Everything went quiet. DeLord could see Beverly Sills onstage, tears rolling down her face.

Speaker after speaker harangued the board. One asked, almost in disbelief, "Is there one person on the board who will stand up and say, 'Enough is enough'? Is there one person who will stand up and say, 'I agree with you'?"

Hinojosa's eyes bored into the back of Beverly Sills's head. Would she get up? As he realized that she would not, Hinojosa hated her even more. *At the end of the day,* he concluded, *the power she has with Time Warner is more important to her than her morals.*

Gerald Levin began to speak. Hinojosa could see he was sweating.

"What would it profit anyone if, in the name of pleasing everyone, the country's leading media and entertainment company ceased to risk saying anything worth listening to?" Many of Time Warner supporters and censorship foes leapt to their feet.

The meeting ended without incident. *Maybe,* Hinojosa thought, *we'll get through this thing after all.*

In the audience at the Regent Beverly Wilshire, two other record executives who had reason to be concerned waited for the outcome of the day's proceedings. Technically, Tom Silverman and Monica Lynch were vice presidents at Warner Bros. Records. But they had always felt like outsiders, and as Tommy Boy Records became successful outside the WEA distribution system, Silverman and Lynch stopped caring. Silverman long regretted selling his company to Warner Bros. for such a low price. Now he and Monica had discovered that there was another price to being in business with Time Warner.

The events of the past month had ended their sense of isolation. The problem began in June, when one of their artists, a Bay Area rapper named Paris, submitted his new album.

Paris, born Oscar Jackson Jr., was the son of a Black doctor from San Francisco. He attended Lowell High, the same honors school from which Keith Naftaly graduated. Even with his bourgeois upbringing, Paris styled himself as a Black Nationalist revolutionary rapper in the vein of Public Enemy. His first album, *The Devil Made Me Do It,* had sold respectably. He had a good fan base in the Bay Area, the support of KMEL, and had begun to win fans in other parts of America. For Tom Silverman, a second album was a given.

The finished master tape for *Sleeping with the Enemy* contained a song that Silverman and Lynch knew would be a problem in light of the "Cop Killer" controversy. It was called "Coffee, Donuts, & Death." Like Body Count, Paris rapped the homicidal fantasies of a man in whose world the cops can do anything to citizens that they please, and the courts do nothing about it. Yet unlike "Cop Killer," "Coffee" referenced a specific event as reason for revenge: The alleged rape of Nina Gelfant by Oakland Police officer Bernard Riley.

"Coffee, Donuts, & Death" was not the only song that gave them concern. Another track seemed devised for the sole purpose of pushing the foes of "freedom of expression" to their limit. It was called "Bush Killa," with Paris lyrically lying in wait on a rooftop, vowing to "lay low" and "keep it neat."

Tom Silverman wasn't a lawyer. But he understood that he had a record on his hands that could easily be interpreted as a direct threat to the life of George H. W. Bush, the president of the United States. That interpretation seemed encouraged by the album artwork, which arrived in Lynch's office not long after the masters. The cover featured the president, flanked by a Secret Service agent, smiling and waving as he walks past the U.S. Capitol building; while Paris, dressed in black clothes and ski cap, hides behind a nearby tree with a rifle, waiting for the president's approach.

Silverman and Lynch believed in the record's political value, but knew they would have a shitstorm on their hands if they released it. They would have to think about how to approach this.

They never got the chance. The next day, Monica Lynch arrived in her office to find the Paris artwork gone. It had been on her assistant's desk. Now her assistant was nowhere to be found. She and the artwork would never return to Tommy Boy.

A few days later, on July 2, 1992, the artwork turned up in a huge article in the *New York Post*, entitled, "Police Group: New Rap Album Urges Bush Slaying."

Apparently, Lynch's assistant's boyfriend and father were cops. They circulated the artwork, which had quickly made its way to the New York Sheriffs' Association—a main participant in the "Cop Killer" boycott—who fed it to the *Post*. But the worst of it was that the *Post* had caught Time Warner corporate spokesperson Tod Hullin completely by surprise.

Just a week after his boss Gerald Levin's defense of "Cop Killer" in *The Wall Street Journal*, Robert Morgado issued a statement that said the Paris album had not been released by Time Warner, and *would not* be released with the artwork described.

That was news to Silverman and Lynch. For his part, Silverman doubted the sincerity of Levin's fight for artistic freedom. Tom believed that Levin had simply painted himself into a corner by making a big show of supporting Ice-T in his internal executive seminars and in the media. Tom Silverman supposed that Levin would just as soon wish away these artists and their problems.

The police organizations came away from Beverly Hills empty-handed. Their July 16 deadline had passed. Ron DeLord had called for a national boycott, but hadn't come up with a plan for it. Some boycotters admitted the difficulty of a nationwide embargo and mass divestment. Representatives of the National Sheriffs' Association and the Los Angeles Police Pension Fund declared that they weren't prepared to call for divestiture. DeLord still held out hope that Time Warner would settle the matter with an apology. *Billboard* readied an article for press that would report the boycotters' "tactical disarray."

Despite this, a bunker mentality still hung over Time Warner corporate, as opprobrium and bad news continued unabated. The Philadelphia Municipal Pension Fund told *The Wall Street Journal* that they were prepared to sell $1.6 million worth of Time Warner stock. Two days after the shareholders' meeting, Las Vegas Police claimed that five Black teenagers had set upon two patrolmen, and that "Cop Killer" provided their motivation. Despite Levin's idealistic public declarations, Bob Morgado and others were indeed pressuring Mo Ostin to drop the song, and warning him to take every measure possible to make sure nothing like this ever happened again.

The Time Warner offices may have felt like a bunker, but it was the Burbank headquarters of Warner Bros. Records that were really under siege. Executives were deluged with outraged letters. Others received threatening phone calls. One executive was called a "nigger-loving Jew." And then came the bomb threats, in which the Burbank police would clear the building for hours—preventing employees from working—while the bomb squad investigated, and, in one instance, detonated a suspicious package. Hinojosa arrived a few times to see the entire Warner staff milling about the parking lot.

It was Friday, July 24, when Ice-T and Jorge Hinojosa arrived in Burbank for a strategy session with Mo Ostin, Lenny Waronker, Seymour Stein, Howie Klein, and Bob Merlis. Ice-T was visibly upset. Jorge had told him about the bomb threats, and that the folks at corporate in New York were putting a lot of pressure on the Warner record executives. Ice-T understood. Mo and Lenny had stood up for him. The employees at Warner Bros. had fought for him, too. Their livelihoods, even their lives, might be on the line.

This is my fight, Ice told them. *I don't want anybody else to get hurt. I don't want to be a one-issue artist anyway. I'm tired of being the Willie Horton of the moment. Take the song off.*

The executives couldn't believe what they were hearing. Klein could see that Mo and Lenny were sad, but unmistakably relieved, too.

No one tried to talk Ice-T out of it.

On July 28, Marty Payson, Time Warner's general counsel, placed a call to Ron DeLord.

"You're going to be happy. Ice-T is calling a press conference in thirty minutes," Payson told him. "I will call you afterward."

At the Ma Maison Sofitel in Los Angeles, Ice-T announced his decision to the media.

"At the moment, the cops are in a criminal mode," Ice-T said. "They've threatened to bomb the record company. I'm in the position now where I think Warner Bros. is taking the war for me. So, as of today, I'm gonna pull the song off the record."

Bob Merlis later announced that Warner would be recalling all the stock for the album, and that a revised album would be in stores within a month.

Surprised by the sudden turnabout, CLEAT's Ron DeLord rejoiced. "I applaud Ice-T's decision to pull the record," he told *Billboard*. "It's a first step to resolving the situation." The next step, DeLord said, was a public apology from Time Warner, and assurances that "they will be responsible in the future."

But then DeLord got another phone call. This one was from Phil Caruso, the head of New York City's Patrolmen's Benevolent Association, and one of the most powerful union bosses in the country.

"This is good enough," Caruso said. "You've won. Declare victory and move on."

DeLord hung up the phone and did exactly that. On August 3, DeLord issued a press release stating that CLEAT was ending the boycott.

The next day, Glenn White and the head of California's biggest police union, PORAC, complained that DeLord had given in too soon, that he had sold them out.

But even down in Texas, DeLord knew that when Phil Caruso said it was over, it had better be over.

The next day, at Warner's Burbank offices, Mo Ostin and Lenny Waronker convened an emergency summit of executives and rap artists from Warner and their partner labels.

From Tommy Boy came Tom Silverman. His artist, Paris, arrived with his lawyer, Michael Aczon. Atron Gregory—who managed not only Digital Underground, but another Tommy Boy group, Live Squad—was also in attendance, as well as Bill Stephney, whose new Stepsun label Silverman distributed.

Stephney's old boss, Rick Rubin, walked over from Def American's offices across the street.[15]

Tyrone Williams of Cold Chillin' arrived with his artist, Kool G Rap.

Jorge Hinojosa came, too. His client, Ice-T, showed up late.

Every artist in the room was on hand, because their lyrics represented a risk to Warner Bros. and the executives present, and because Ostin needed to let them know about the new reality for rap at his record company.

Ostin told the assembled that he and Waronker no longer had the freedom to release any record they pleased. After "Cop Killer," they had to be practical about the records a corporation like Time Warner could sell. Going forward, Warner Bros. would have to be vigilant about reviewing lyrics and artwork. If Warner deemed a record unfit for release, Ostin pledged that he wouldn't stand in the way of his artists' finding a new home for it somewhere else.

In the discussion that ensued, Tom Silverman lamented Time Warner's timidity. "An entity that controls this much of the media should be able to control some of the debate," Silverman said. A few executives offered suggestions for doing so, and Ostin said that he would do his best to defend the artists who needed defending.

After the meeting, Waronker invited Silverman and Paris back to Ostin's office, where the Warner chiefs informed them that they wouldn't be releasing Paris's new album.

Over the next few weeks, Warner dropped more rap acts for their lyrical content: Tommy Boy's Live Squad and RSO Crew, Cold Chillin's Kool G Rap, and Warner's Juvenile Committee.

Ice-T would remain on Warner. But the artist himself was gloomy.

"We're witnessing the creation of a police state," he had said in the meeting. "It's going to get a lot worse before it gets any better."

---

[15] As did the author.

Within days, Ice-T was proven right.

On August 13, down in Texas, a woman named Linda Davidson and her children filed a civil suit seeking compensatory and punitive damages from Time Warner; its subsidiary, Atlantic Records; Atlantic's partner label, Interscope; and Interscope's artist Tupac Shakur.

A few months earlier, Davidson's husband, Bill—a Texas state trooper—had stopped a Chevy Blazer with a broken taillight on the side of U.S. Highway 59 in Jackson County. Officer Davidson didn't know that the car had been stolen, nor that its driver, a nineteen-year-old Black gang member from Houston named Ronald Ray Howard, was loading his 9mm Glock pistol as Davidson approached the vehicle. Howard shot Davidson as the sounds of a bootlegged copy of Tupac's first Interscope album played in his cassette deck.

After Howard was apprehended, police found the gun and the cassette. In the months after the incident, as word got back to Davidson's widow that Howard was hoping to avoid the death penalty by claiming he was "brainwashed" by Tupac's music, Linda Davidson filed her suit against Time Warner. Jim Cole, her attorney, asserted that the defendants were negligent for selling music that incited imminent lawless action—an album in which at least six songs had lyrics that seemed to be "pages out of a cop-killing manual."

The media coverage that followed Davidson's filing revived the major players in the "Cop Killer" saga.

Vice President Quayle demanded the recall of Tupac's album and met with the Davidson family.

Ron DeLord weighed in, too. "In every other industry, companies are held liable for dangerous products they produce," he told the *Los Angeles Times*. "If it's illegal to produce physical pollution, it ought to be illegal to produce mental pollution."

Even Oliver North offered to help the Davidsons' case.

Supporters of the war on Time Warner subscribed to a very different version of the truth than Tupac or Ted Field promoted on their album.

Murder was the case, rap was the cause, and Time Warner was to blame.

Side B
Consequences

At *The Source*, Jon Shecter and James Bernard's new colleague, Reginald C. Dennis, had been tracking industry activity in the wake of the "Cop Killer" controversy. The problem was now bigger than Time Warner. Fear of another "Cop Killer" was spreading to other major labels, and rap releases were being affected across the board. At A&M Records, president Al Cafaro gave the rapper Intelligent Hoodlum a choice—remove the anticop song "Bullet" from his album *Black Rage*—or take the album to another label. At Hollywood BASIC, the rap label Funken-Klein ran for The Walt Disney Company after he left Red Alert Productions, Klein was forced to take an anticop song off of the Boo-Yaa Tribe's new release after he received complaints from their distributors.

Dennis was sardonic about the timing of all this. The presidential campaign was in full swing, coming right on the heels of the Los Angeles uprising, the greatest civil insurrection the United States had seen since the 1960s. Now, as all the righteous rage about racial oppression was making its way to wax via hip-hop, suddenly rap was under attack. The more political and rebellious the song, the more likely it was to be suppressed.

As Dennis discussed the "Cop Killer" aftermath with his colleagues at *The Source*, he prepared an editorial for the next issue.

"Mark July 28, 1992, on your calendars as the beginning of the end of rap music," he began. "On that day, when he 'voluntarily' removed 'Cop Killer' from the Body Count album, Ice-T allowed a devastating precedent to be set, opening the door for the widespread censorship of rap."

Dennis had barely finished writing when his phone rang. Mickey Bentson, a local promoter and associate of Ice-T, was the first to call. "I heard *The Source* was gonna dis Ice-T," he said. *How the hell did Bentson know?* Relationships between *The Source* "Mind Squad" and artists or their representatives were often cozy. Did someone in the office tell him? Or did a visitor overhear what Dennis was saying?

"You'd better check yourself," Bentson threatened.

Dennis was startled by Bentson's tone. *The Source* had always treated Ice-T with respect. They had given Ice the cover in advance of his lead role in *New Jack City*. They had given *Body Count* a positive review. Their last editorial was written in *support* of Ice-T. Dennis tried to reassure Bentson that his editorial was not a personal attack on the artist.

"Let us read the editorial," Bentson replied. "Then we'll see." Dennis refused. Bentson hung up.

Jorge Hinojosa called shortly thereafter.

"You weren't there," Hinojosa said in reference to the final negotiations with Warner Bros. "You didn't know what was going on." Hinojosa threatened to make things "very difficult" for Dennis if he ran the editorial. And why was *The Source* concerned anyway? Hinojosa wanted to know. "Cop Killer" was a *heavy-metal* song, he insisted. It had nothing to do with rap.

"Really?" Dennis said. Heavy-metal groups weren't facing scrutiny in the wake of Ice-T's decision. Rap artists were. Their albums were being rejected and their contracts terminated. What did Hinojosa have to say about that?

"I don't care about other artists," Hinojosa said. "I just care about Ice-T."

Back in Burbank, Howie Klein was boxing up a special gift to send to a friend in Washington, D.C.

Because of the controversy over "Cop Killer," the police and the Republicans had managed to revive a slowing record, sending it over the 500,000 mark in sales. The RIAA had certified Body Count's album gold on August 4. While he was ordering commemorative gold records for himself and the band, Howie requisitioned one more, for the man he felt had made it all possible.

Lenny Waronker walked in, and Howie showed him the plaque beneath the record. "This award is presented," it read, "to Vice President Dan Quayle."

"Jesus, Howie," Waronker said. "Can you at least wait until the election's over?"

After Mo Ostin and Lenny Waronker had made it clear that they didn't want Paris coming out on Tommy Boy, Tom Silverman felt a certain obligation to find Paris another home. At first, it looked like he had found one at Chris Blackwell's Island Records, which had long ago released the most famous "cop killer" song of all time, Bob Marley's "I Shot the Sheriff."

But Island had been sold to Polygram in 1989, and Blackwell no longer had the kind of freedom he once enjoyed as an independent. Polygram's chief, Alain Levy, received a sober assessment from his general counsel in London, Richard Constant, who wrote that Paris's lyrics could be viewed as an "incitement to violence against the President . . . and as such is probably criminal on the part of Paris and possibly on the part of the record company which releases the album and wholesalers and retailers who handle it."

Polygram was a public company, Constant said, with a duty to the community at large. "If we release the album, we will be seen as endorsing the views it expresses. By putting out the album we would be failing in this duty."

When Rick Rubin heard of his friend Tom's travails, he was moved to act. By the letter of his contract with Warner Bros., Rubin had the right to release any record he wanted at Def American, and he hadn't yet put his creative autonomy to the test. "I won't put out any record that's not good," he had assured Ostin during their negotiations. "But if it is good, I want to put it out."

Yet Rubin agreed to take on the Paris record without even hearing the music. Contrary to his pledge to Ostin, this wasn't a matter of personal taste. Rick simply wanted to do something for Silverman, and for an artist who was being silenced.

Rubin placed a call to a man he knew he could trust inside Warner Bros. Mark Goldstein was the second in command in the Warner business affairs department, charged with negotiating all of Def American's artist deals.

"I need to ask you a hypothetical question," Rubin began.

Uh-oh, Goldstein thought.

"If I wanted to release the 'Bush Killa' record, could I do that?"

"If anybody asks," Goldstein replied, "we didn't have this conversation, right?"

"Right," Rick said.

Goldstein reminded Rubin of one remaining constriction in his deal. Rubin indeed had the right to release any record on Def American—*as long as it didn't break the law to do so.* As far as the "Bush Killa" record was concerned, Goldstein believed it did. "Whether you release it as Def American or as a private American citizen, you're still in violation of that law."

Rubin wasn't so sure about that. He knew that there was room for interpretation. Marjorie Heins, the American Civil Liberties Union's watchdog for
arts censorship, thought so, too. Federal law forbade "any threat to take the life
of, to kidnap, or to inflict bodily harm upon the President of the United States."
But Heins knew that the courts saw a big difference between a fantasy narrative and a true threat. There needed to be a "determination to carry out the
threat," as one ruling said. "Political hyperbole" alone could not be penalized.

It was a risk that Rubin was willing to take. Rubin devised a plan to
shield himself and Warner: Create a shell company, complete with its own
offices and staff, and fund the whole operation. Rubin even had a name for
the new company, albeit a complete non sequitur: Sex Records. Rubin dispatched the head of his rap department[16] to the Bay Area to meet with Paris,
create a marketing plan, hire an operations person, and set up offices in
Oakland. Rubin got the artwork from Tom Silverman, and Def American
employees became involved in procuring outside manufacturing. Paris's
publicist just happened to be Bill Adler—Rubin's former colleague from the
Rush/Def Jam offices at 298 Elizabeth Street—and Rubin paid him to continue his work. The whole project had to be rushed out by mid-October,
before the elections, or the album would lose most of its political and commercial impact.

It wasn't long before Ostin got wind of what was going on at the Def
American offices across the street. He had asked Tom Silverman not to release the record, and here it was again, back in his house. Ostin informed the
Time Warner brass of his new problem. Within a day, he and Rubin were on
a plane to New York to face the Time Warner brass.

Gerald Levin and Bob Morgado informed Ostin and Rubin that they did
not want this record to come out. Rick made the case that he had the right
to put out any record he wanted. The meeting ended in a standoff.

On their way out of the meeting, Ostin begged Rubin not to force the
issue. "As a favor to me," Ostin said. Rubin knew that Ostin would stand by
him if he did, but that it might cost Ostin his job. In the end, Rubin chose
loyalty over any pretense of artistic freedom.

To Paris's utter frustration, his last opportunity to issue the record before the election had suddenly evaporated. Def American staffers were ordered to destroy any records and other materials related to Paris, lest the
Secret Service come calling. The artist's only consolation was a check for

---

[16]The author.

$100,000 to keep Sex Records going as his own independent label. The rest would be up to him.

Jorge Hinojosa lay in the infirmary at the Los Angeles International Airport with an intravenous drip in his arm. He was with his girlfriend, Madeleine, about to board a flight for Hawaii to take his first vacation in months, when he collapsed. The doctors told him he needed to rest. They didn't know the half of it.

Ice-T's multimedia career withered in the wake of "Cop Killer," and the synergy deals ended as other Time Warner companies walked away from him. *New Jack City* had been a huge hit for Warner Bros. But for some reason, the planned sequel—in which Ice-T would have reprised the role of police officer Scotty Appleton—died in preproduction. Even Ice-T's project with their good friend Jenette Kahn at DC Comics had been shelved.

By November of 1992, Hinojosa was, quite literally, sick and tired. The career of his major client was disintegrating. By his own estimation, Hinojosa was turning into a short-tempered, miserable son of a bitch. To make things up to his girlfriend, he booked a trip to Hawaii for Thanksgiving week. After collapsing at the airport, Hinojosa and Madeleine returned a few days later and made a new flight. But Hinojosa still felt awful, and he spent most of the time inside his suite with the shades drawn. "Go and lie by the pool," Hinojosa urged his girlfriend. "Get a tan."

While in his room Hinojosa got an urgent call from his L.A. office. Chris Albrecht, the head of programming for HBO, needed to speak with him right away. Albrecht was the executive in charge of *Ice-TV*, which had just wrapped production.

"We're canceling your show," Albrecht said.

Hinojosa was stunned. "You haven't even seen the finished product!" Hinojosa said, thinking the dispute creative. It wasn't.

"No, the show is really good," Albrecht continued. "If it were anybody else's show, it would air, and it would be really successful."

In disbelief, Hinojosa called Michael Fuchs, the head of HBO. "That's not the reason," Fuchs told him. "It's just not a good show for us."

Hinojosa hung up the phone. He could hear the surf pounding outside in paradise. Hinojosa knew he wasn't dying. But it felt pretty damn close.

———

On December 20, 1992, Steve Ross died of complications from prostate cancer. He was only sixty-five years old.

For Mo Ostin, Steve Ross's death meant the end of the old Warner Communications way of doing business, in which he, Krasnow, and Ertegun reported directly to Ross. The new Time Warner CEO, Gerald Levin, wasn't the fulsome, gregarious showbiz person his late boss was. Levin was more practical, less prone to afford the music group chiefs the kind of royal deference and autonomy Ross had extended to them.

Levin listened to the reasoning of his corporate music chief, Bob Morgado, who saw waste at Warner and Elektra. Morgado needed a way to rein in spending to increase profits, but he had no control. Ostin and Krasnow didn't report to him, as did Atlantic's co-CEO and Ahmet Ertegun's successor, Doug Morris. Morgado lobbied Levin forcefully for a clear chain of command.

Ostin feared Morgado's thirst for power and control. Morgado had openly questioned Ostin's value to the company, and punished Ostin's defiance by taking millions in expenses off of Atlantic's books to make the agreeable Doug Morris's company look more profitable.

"I don't trust this man," Ostin told Levin in a meeting with Morgado. Other Warner executives called Morgado "the smilin' Hawaiian," and alternately, "the lyin' Hawaiian."

Ostin's contract specified that he reported to Ross. But Ross was gone now, and the sixty-six-year-old Ostin's contract was up at the end of 1994. The prospects for Ostin getting what he wanted—a renewed contract with a direct report to Levin—depended greatly on Levin's perceptions about whether Ostin was an asset or a liability. To Morgado and others at corporate, the controversy over Ice-T and Paris seemed to point to the latter notion. To them, Ostin's preference for principle over profit hurt the entire corporation.

Unfortunately for Ostin, the fallout from "Cop Killer" continued.

Time Warner's most lucrative business—the local cable franchises—was still at risk. Police movements to block franchise renewal were still afoot in Houston and Indianapolis. Gerald Arenberg, the executive director of the National Association of Chiefs of Police, threatened to "create a living hell" for Time Warner's cable systems across the country. "Just about every time one of their trucks makes a call, it parks illegally. We could write parking tickets for every one of those violations."

Time Warner's magazines suffered when Chrysler dropped one of its high-end advertising campaigns because of Time Warner's continuing association with Ice-T. It was a largely symbolic gesture, but humiliating for many at Time Warner nonetheless.

Even with "Cop Killer" pulled from the *Body Count* album, Ice-T continued to pay the price for his words. The increased police presence at his shows across the country seemed more about intimidation than security. Local police organizations waged war on local promoters and venues that hired and hosted Ice-T. In San Diego, where Body Count had been asked to open for rock bands Guns N' Roses and Metallica at Jack Murphy Stadium, the police union demanded that Ice-T be dropped from the bill. The promoter promised that Ice-T would not perform "Cop Killer." Days later, Ice-T strolled onstage, read the police union's letter in the most sarcastic tone possible, stuffed the letter into his crotch, and then sang the song as thousands of kids, mostly young and White, sang along: "Die, pig, die!" In Pittsburgh, the ACLU intervened on Ice-T's behalf after off-duty police officers refused to provide security for the artist's show at the Metropol, forcing the show's cancellation.

Through it all Ice-T remained defiant. He got to speak his peace in *Rolling Stone*, where he graced the cover in a full patrolman's uniform, complete with billy club. He looked forward to some payback with the release of his next solo album, scheduled to hit stores on February 9, 1993.

But Warner Bros. had changed in the short year since the release of *Body Count*; their laissez-faire attitude toward production had been replaced with an eagle eye. This time it wasn't the lyrics but the cover art for Ice-T's new album, *Home Invasion*, that set off alarms in Burbank. In the center of the illustration sat a young White boy, cross-legged on the floor, listening to his portable cassette player through headphones. Around his neck hung an African medallion, on the floor beside him a stack of books with the titles *Malcolm X* and *Iceberg Slim*. Ice-T appears as a ghostlike figure emanating from the child's headphones. But around the child are three shadowy, hooded figures. One of them manhandles a scantily clad White woman. Another drives the butt of his rifle into a White man's bloody face. *Is the kid imagining these violent things as a result of listening to Ice-T? Or is the violence really happening in his room, while the child remains distracted by the music?*

The executives at Time Warner couldn't afford to leave any more room for interpretation of Ice-T's art. They assumed the worst, and sent word down to Mo Ostin that the cover was not acceptable. The release date of the album was pushed back.

For Jorge Hinojosa and Ice-T, the controversy over the artwork was an indication that they would never again enjoy artistic freedom while tied to Time Warner.

"You know this is never going to stop," Hinojosa told his client. Ice-T agreed, and he asked his manager to write a strongly worded letter to Mo Ostin and Lenny Waronker.

"In every instance when asked by Time Warner to make changes to his work," Hinojosa wrote, "Ice-T has capitulated and risked his artistic credibility. Ice-T is an artist, but because of the way he is being treated, he looks more like a corporate puppet. He has no desire to be anyone's puppet or token nigger."

Ice-T himself had asked his manager to use the racial epithet. Hinojosa continued:

"It is obvious by Time Warner's treatment of him and his work that he is viewed as a liability. That being the case, Ice would like a release for Body Count and Ice-T."

Hinojosa sent the letter on a Wednesday in late January 1993. He figured that Ostin and Waronker would need a few days to discuss it with corporate before they responded, so Jorge didn't expect to hear from them until the following week. That was good: Hinojosa wasn't looking forward to that confrontation. But on Friday, Hinojosa got a call from the art department at Warner. They needed him to come in and approve some artwork for another rap artist he represented there, the decidedly uncontroversial female rapper Monie Love. The last thing Hinojosa wanted was to run into Mo Ostin or Lenny Waronker in the hallways. But the building was so huge, the chances were slim. Hinojosa drove to Burbank, parked on the street, and walked along Warner Boulevard to the main entrance. The street was deserted, save for two people walking down the sidewalk toward him.

Mo and Lenny.

They approached wordlessly, and stopped. Waronker broke the silence. "Will you at least shake our hands?" he asked.

Hinojosa melted. "You know it was never about you guys," Ice-T's manager said. "They just don't want us playing in the same sandbox. As long as we do, we're all going to be miserable."

Later that day Hinojosa echoed that sentiment in an impromptu meeting with Warner executives, as they hashed out a deal that would let Ice-T walk away from his contract with his new album. The conference drew to a close, ending Ice-T's long, profitable, and mostly happy six-year relationship with

Sire/Warner Bros. That was when Hinojosa caught a glimpse of Howie Klein, their chief supporter and coconspirator at the label, as tears rolled down the defiant executive's face.

Hinojosa quickly secured his artist a pressing and distribution deal through Bryan Turner's Priority Records. The Priority deal allowed Ice to enjoy a much bigger share of the wholesale price of his records, but it meant that Jorge and Ice-T would have to pay for their own promotion or do it themselves. Hinojosa chose the latter.

Home Invasion—complete with the original artwork—was released on March 23, 1993. The debut of *Home Invasion* was less than auspicious. The album received some of the worst reviews Ice had ever garnered. "Sounds like a long, dull thud," said *Entertainment Weekly. Hustler* magazine dubbed Ice-T "Pussy of the Year" for removing "Cop Killer" from his album. In the rap press, Ice-T's war with *The Source* escalated after Ice cursed the magazine on the album's intro, and then issued a personal threat against Reginald Dennis in *The Bomb* magazine: "We beatin' the kid's ass on sight." *The Source* ran an editorial chronicling their long-standing support for Ice-T followed by the fallout from Ice-T's decision, entitled "Shooting Himself in the Mouth."

Ice-T's previous album, *Original Gangster*, had topped out at nearly one million. Now Hinojosa saw Ice-T's new album slowing down at around 500,000 copies. What the hell was going on? Bryan Turner provided a likely answer. Many large retail chains would no longer stock Ice-T's record. Those who would were not displaying it conspicuously in their stores, at the end caps of aisles. It seemed retail was embarking on its own, silent boycott of Ice-T.

Home Invasion debuted on the Billboard charts at number fourteen, and limped downward.

While the family of Texas state trooper Bill Davidson awaited the trial of accused killer Ronald Ray Howard, whose lawyer blamed a cassette of Tupac Shakur for putting his client in the mood to murder, Interscope moved further into the gangster rap business.

John McClain, Ted Field's specialist in Black music, heard that erstwhile NWA producer Dr. Dre was still looking for a label deal in the wake of his departure from Ruthless Records. Dr. Dre and his new partner, Suge Knight, had planned to make the deal for their new record company, Death Row Records, through Sony Music, which had just released "Deep Cover," Dre's contribution to the movie soundtrack of the same name. The song featured verses from a young, gangly protégé named Snoop Doggy Dogg.

"Yeeeeah, and you don't stop," said Dre.

"'Cause it's one-eight-seven on an undercover cop," responded Snoop.

And even though its refrain was just as much a "cop-killer" song as Body Count's—"187" referring to the police code for murder—the song garnered nowhere near the notoriety of Ice-T's creation. Dre had an excuse after all: "Deep Cover" *had* to be about cops because the *movie* was about cops.

"Deep Cover" elecrified dance floors from the West to East coasts and proved Dr. Dre's viability as a solo artist. But in the wake of Knight's alleged extortion of Eazy-E, Jerry Heller claimed that any releases signed by Eazy were done so under duress and that Dr. Dre was still very much under contract to Ruthless. Heller sued Death Row and Sony for millions of dollars.

Not many record executives would touch a producer who came with such legal entanglements. But Ted Field felt strongly about working with such a reputable name in hip-hop, and Jimmy Iovine believed he could extricate Dre from his current quagmire.

First, Iovine called Jerry Heller. Iovine was both respectful and frank. "Dre is never going to make another record for you," he told Heller. Instead of Heller's holding Dre's career in permanent limbo, and losing money, Iovine urged Heller to settle for a piece of Dre's contract moving forward. Heller agreed. Ruthless would own a percentage of Dr. Dre's contract with Death Row/Interscope. In the event that the Interscope deal ended, Dre's production contract would revert to Ruthless.

But Iovine had another problem. Dr. Dre was not only signed to Ruthless Records; he also had an airtight "side letter" with Priority Records as a member of NWA. Bryan Turner would also need to see some money out of the deal. Iovine and Turner negotiated an arrangement that benefited all parties: Priority Records would manufacture and sell the record through its pressing and distribution deal with CEMA. Turner would get a nice fee for every record sold, and Interscope would avoid any potential lyrics-related problems with releasing the record through WEA, Warner's distribution arm.

Ted Field was impressed yet again by his partner. Jimmy Iovine swept in and created a situation in which everybody won.

Dr. Dre's finished solo album, *The Chronic*, hit record stores just in time for Christmas 1992. Fans and critics greeted the album with widespread acclaim, including a four-and-a-half-of-five "mic" rating in *The Source*. Dre called his refined sound "G funk," or "gangsta funk"—a smoother sonic take on gangster rap.

The Chronic, which quickly hit a million units in sales on its way to an eventual triple-platinum certification, was not only another triumph for Interscope; it was an auspicious debut for Death Row Records. Suge Knight had moved his fledgling company into a suite of offices in Interscope's building on 10900 Wilshire Boulevard. It was an odd coupling, as the building was owned by David Murdoch, a top fund-raiser for the Republican party, and featured a conservative eating club on the top floor. Suddenly rappers and Knight's entourage—many of them from notorious Blood gang sets—were riding the elevators and milling around the lobby. One day dozens of low-rider cars circled the building and parked in the garage. Field received a few letters of protest from the building management, but he quietly enjoyed the waves he made.

As anticipation built for Death Row's second release—Snoop Doggy Dogg's first solo album—Interscope's own hard-core rap artist, Tupac Shakur, prepared his follow-up.

In the year and a half since the release of his first album, Shakur had begun a budding acting career with a breakout starring role in *Juice*, a film by Spike Lee protégé Ernest Dickerson. John Singleton tapped Shakur to be the leading man of his love story, *Poetic Justice*, opposite Janet Jackson. Still, Shakur's personal tumult continued. In October 1993, Shakur got into a traffic altercation with two off-duty police officers in Atlanta. The officers pulled their guns and Shakur pulled his. A shoot-out ensued, sending the officers to the hospital with nonlethal wounds. Shakur was arrested and released on bail shortly thereafter.

Before his Georgia strife, however, some cold consolation came from Texas. On June 8, 1993, Ronald Ray Howard was convicted of murdering state trooper Bill Davidson, despite the argments of his lawyer shifting responsibility for his actions to rap music:

"We've got lots of kids out there who are being influenced by violent 'gangsta rap music,'" said Allen Tanner. "They've built up a hatred. . . . These kids are starting to fight back. I think this music brainwashed Ronald Howard."

The jury didn't buy it. Neither, apparently, did Howard himself. During the second, punishment phase of his trial, Howard disavowed his lawyers' arguments about rap music in tearful testimony to the court, speaking instead of his own brutal childhood: beatings at the hands of his father, his parents' split, school fights, nightly neighborhood violence. Rap music, he said, actually provided him rare comfort and solace.

After six days of deliberations, a jury with only one Black member gave Ronald Ray Howard the death sentence. Jurors later revealed their agreement that rap music might have affected Howard's actions; but in the end, they determined that rap lyrics were not a sufficient mitigating factor.

Neither, alas, were child abuse, poverty, and racism.

In Los Angeles, Khalid Shah awoke one Sunday morning in the fall of 1993 to a phone call from his friend Muhammad Nassardeen.

"Flip on Power 106," Nassardeen said.

Shah and Nassardeen, both activists in the vast Black expanse of South Central, had already been talking in the past few weeks about the sudden surge of "gangsta" rap on the popular radio station. Nassardeen had been disturbed when he discovered his daughter listening to it. But Shah couldn't believe what he was hearing now, on a Sunday morning, no less, as Dr. Dre and Snoop Dogg's voices traded lines: "Rat-tat-tat-tat tat ta tat like that, and I never hesitate to put a nigga on his baaaaaack!"

As a teenager in East L.A., back when his name was Robert Watkins, Khalid Shah flirted with gangs. As an adult, he devoted his life to saving other kids from them. Shah had been alarmed by the rise of Eazy-E and NWA as popular icons in the Black and Latino communities where he worked. It was bad enough that NWA had become successful without the media's help. Yet here was the voice of NWA's producer and heir apparent, Dr. Dre, rapping uncensored on the most powerful radio station in Southern California. What he was saying didn't even have the redeeming virtue of being protest music, like NWA's "Fuck the Police." Instead, the singsong chorus to this song encapsulated the exact mentality that Shah had been battling for years: *Don't pause to think. Just shoot.* Shah wondered whether this behavior had become so commonplace that it was acceptable to broadcast it for general consumption. *What would happen to the next generation of kids if they grew up listening to this stuff—not passed from hand to hand on cassette tapes like NWA, but on their radios, all day long?*

A few days later, Shah, Nassardeen, and almost a dozen others gathered at the Inglewood offices of their organization, Stop the Violence-Increase the Peace. The name had ironically been inspired by the same conscious hip-hop effort from which Power 106 had named its first community service campaign.

Rap artists were not their enemy, Shah told the assembled. The wholesale broadcast and promotion of gangster rap was. Power 106 had been playing more gangster rap than any other station in town, and more Black and Latino kids were listening to it than ever.

Shah and the others resolved to open a dialogue with the heads of the station to let them know how they felt. Shah didn't know much about radio, nor whom to contact. But he eventually divined enough information to leave messages for program director Rick Cummings and general manager Doyle Rose.

Cummings and Rose didn't return repeated calls. So Shah and Nassardeen, with the help of their board chairman Anthony Samad, assembled a new meeting at the offices of Los Angeles's Black newspaper, the *Sentinel*, where Samad was a columnist. There, with representatives from the local chapter of the NAACP, Shah determined that they needed to take the next step to get Power 106's attention: They would picket the station and boycott its advertisers.

First, Shah drafted a petition and sent volunteers out into the street corners and shopping malls to get signatures. Next, Shah made a list of Power 106 advertisers and contacted each of them—local companies like Adray's and In-N-Out Burger, national sponsors like Ford, AT&T, and Budweiser. Then, one day in November 1993, Shah and a few dozen community activists and volunteers from South Central Los Angeles rode to Burbank and formed a picket line in front of the sleek office building on 2600 West Olive that housed Power 106's offices.

Josefa Salinas had just finished her air shift when Rick Cummings came for her.

Salinas was not only a DJ. She was also the closest thing Power 106 had to a community affairs director, whom Cummings had poached from a local urban station, KACE, after he heard that Salinas had been responsible for pulling off a huge benefit concert called "Jam for Peace" featuring Tupac Shakur. Since arriving at Power, Salinas had begun work on a benefit CD called *Straight from the Streets* that would channel funds to community organizations. Best of all for Power 106, Salinas was a woman of color who could be a credible ambassador to those organizations. So Cummings sent Josefa Salinas downstairs to deal with the protesters.

Salinas emerged from the building, walked up to Khalid Shah, introduced herself, and invited Shah and a few of the protesters up to the offices to talk. She escorted them into the lobby, up the elevators to the eighth-floor suite of offices, and into Power 106's conference room. There, she introduced the group to Rick Cummings and general manager Doyle Rose.

Damn, Shah thought. *So this is what it takes to get a meeting with these guys?*

The mood was cordial, but tense. Cummings did most of the talking. He and Rose seemed bewildered at all the controversy. Cummings passed around press packets for the station, and explained the station's journey from dance music to hip-hop—the changing demographics of the genre's appeal, the need to own hip-hop to secure the station's future with young listeners. The music on the station, Cummings said, had been demanded by the kids themselves, recommended by in-house experts like the Baka Boyz, and confirmed through call-out research. Cummings wanted to know what the protesters found so distasteful. The kids, after all, weren't complaining.

Many of the protesters in the room were the parents of those kids. They passed around their own packet of information, containing the lyrics to many of the songs that Power 106 played, like Dr. Dre's "Let Me Ride" and Snoop Doggy Dogg's first solo single, "What's My Name?" They fumed about the open broadcast of words like "nigga," not only in prerecorded songs, but also live on the air by personalities like the Baka Boyz, who weren't even Black. They complained about how some songs referred to women and girls as "bitches" and "hoes." They wanted to know what made that kind of language acceptable to Cummings and Doyle.

Salinas silently concurred with Shah and the protesters. She had been given more than a few moments of pause while listening to Power 106 lately. But she didn't program the station. Cummings listened without being defensive, but didn't exactly yield either. He promised Shah that Power 106 would give the lyrics question serious consideration. They would take the issue to the listeners themselves in an on-air forum. If the listeners wanted Power to remove particular songs or words, they would do what the audience asked. After that, Cummings promised, they would meet again.

On December 3, 1993, Lozano and Salinas cohosted the on-air "town hall meeting" that included artists like Chuck D. During the broadcast, Lozano expressed his own belief that words were fluid and could take on different meanings. Queen Latifah had a pro-woman song called "U.N.I.T.Y." with the refrain, "You gotta let 'em know / You're not a bitch or a ho." Would Power 106 not be able to play that song anymore? Once edited, would it make any sense? Lozano had illustrated the point on his morning show a few days before, playing the song "Heigh-ho" from Disney's *Snow White and the Seven Dwarfs*, bleeping out every occurrence of the "offending" word, "ho."

In the end, there seemed to be a consensus among Power's young listeners that certain words weren't appropriate for public broadcast. Five days later, Cummings and Power 106 issued a statement to the press: The words "nigga" "bitch," and "ho," when used in a negative context, would be deleted or masked. "Although we believe in the freedom of expression of our musical artists, we also believe that no good purpose is served by airing these words," Cummings wrote. "Artists should have the right to represent their perception of today's society. However, we cannot be certain that the youngest part of our audience is capable of discerning between artistic interpretation and endorsement."

Shah was pleased with the outcome, and promptly ended the boycott. But some on the Power staff remained bitter. Lozano told a reporter for a local newspaper that the three-word ban in no way addressed the real problem: the social conditions that gave rise to such a lack of consciousness. In the hallways at Power, a stray curse was enough to ensure a mocking warning from air personality Dave Morales: "You'd better watch it, or I'm going to report you to Khalid Shah." Rumors flew around the station that Shah had merely been looking for a handout, that he had been bought off by the station management. He hadn't. Yet Cummings ensured Shah's continued voice on the station by inviting him to participate in more on-air forums, and on "From the Streets," which Morales now cohosted with Manny Velazquez.

Of all the people at Power, Velazquez was the only person who knew Shah before the boycott. They had met years before at a community event in South Central through Tony Barbone, Manny's mentor. Velazquez saw Shah as a bit of an opportunist—sincere about helping the community, but just as determined to leverage power for himself and his organization within the entertainment business. Shah had a concert promotion company, K-ROC, and had recently done a show cosponsored by KPWR's rival, 92.3 the Beat. Now Velazquez felt Shah was trying to muscle Power 106.

Velazquez believed that Shah had never even listened to the station and told him so. Power 106 had brought the leaders of the Latino gang truce on the air, Velazquez argued. Did KACE do that? Power 106 had brought on the group who had done the same thing for the Black gangs, the Bounty Hunters from Jordan Downs. Did 92.3 The Beat do that? Did Shah have any idea about the peace concerts that Power 106 was throwing at high schools? The answer to all these questions, from Shah himself, was no.

Still, to Shah and his fellow activists, Power 106 was trying to have it both ways: equivocating when it came to lyrics and then trying to make up for broadcasting questionable content by doing community outreach. The result was an ideological muddle.

As word passed around the industry about the change in Power's policy, other stations followed suit. Labels began to "backmask" more than just the obligatory seven words traditionally banned by the FCC ("shit," "piss," "fuck," "cunt," "cocksucker," "motherfucker" and "tits"), and added to them the new unholy trinity of hip-hop: the "n-word," the "b-word," and the "h-word." Whatever the labels didn't clean up, Power's production staff did the rest.

The resolution of the lyrics controversy did not spell the end of Power 106's problems. Months later, Doyle Rose and Rick Cummings readied a new outdoor advertising campaign promoting their dynamic new Baka Boyz morning show to Los Angelenos. The billboard slogan derived from a song called "2 Fat Mexicanz" that Nick and Eric Vidal sang several times during their shift.

Initially, Cummings misunderstood what the Vidal brothers wanted.

"Two P-H-A-T Mexicans, right?"

"No," they told him. "Two F-A-T Mexicans."

Cummings worried about the repercussions of the spelling. Ignoring his own instincts, Cummings deferred to his morning team. They were the experts in the hip-hop market. He was not.

When the "2 Fat Mexicanz" billboards appeared across the Southland, featuring the Baka Boyz in a variety of naked poses—on the toilet holding a pizza box, standing with a surfboard covering their privates—public revulsion came swiftly. Los Angeles city councilman Mark Ridley-Thomas called for Power 106 to replace the billboards immediately; Edward Pizzorno, the mayor of Montebello, decried the revival of "a negative stereotype that the Mexican community has been trying to bury for many decades"; Ron Wakabayashi, the executive director of Los Angeles County's Commission on Human Relations, spoke of "great outrage" from residents of all backgrounds.

"While your strategy seeks to be amusing," he wrote to general manager Doyle Rose, "it comes at a great social expense."

A collective of Mexican-American community activists demanded that Rose come to their next general meeting and discuss the campaign.

As calls and letters flooded Power 106, Rick Cummings turned once again to his in-house community activist, Manny Velazquez, for help.

Velazquez went to the meeting with Rose and Cummings, and defended the Baka Boyz vigorously. He had family in Bakersfield, so he possessed a visceral understanding of the forces that created Nick and Eric Vidal. To Velazquez, the brothers, both barely into their twenties, were part of a new generation of kids who had gone to integrated schools and grown up with friends of all ethnicities, far from the tensions of Los Angeles. Thus they possessed a certain degree of flippancy about matters of race and culture. Liberated from the weight of history, they didn't care what the songs said as long as they sounded good. The people who reviled the Baka Boyz and Power 106 were generally older, more sophisticated people who had come of age during the Chicano power movement and who had vivid memories of the struggles of activists like César Chávez. They were nationalists, like the members of the Chicano Moratorium. They had no idea how hip-hop had become so powerful among young Latinos. They didn't listen to the station and had never heard the Baka Boyz. They didn't understand them and they didn't care to.

The casual way that controversial lyrics and ad slogans issued forth from Power 106 bespoke either carelessness or cluelessness. As they embraced hip-hop, Rick Cummings and Emmis suddenly found themselves in a curious position for which they were altogether unprepared.

For years pop radio had excluded the work of Black artists. For years Black radio had ignored the preferences of its younger listeners. Now for the first time in American history pop radio was programming radio for kids of all colors and taking its cues directly from young Black and Latino DJs like the Baka Boyz in L.A. and Funkmaster Flex in New York.

Most hip-hop DJs were not particularly political people, even in an age of strident hip-hop politics. The Baka Boyz and Flex didn't have many qualms about lyrical content; they just wanted to play hot music. At Black radio stations, their voices and choices would not have mattered because most programmers at those stations didn't listen to their mix-show DJs anyway. Black programmers, who were most likely to grasp the full cultural impact of rap lyrics and imagery, squelched it instead; many of them derided political artists like Public Enemy as "angry" and "negative."

But at pop stations geared toward teens, no one second-guessed the musical selections or the DJs, at least not at first. The downside of the DJs' musical freedom was the lack of any filter. In heeding the tastes of the kids, pop programmers uncorked hip-hop's creative geyser at the very moment that the culture itself was shifting. As hip-hop was becoming more successful, fans' quest for the "righteous" was being surpassed by their thirst for the "real." The music began to shed its political pretense in favor of cynical street tales, symbolized by the emergence of Death Row Records. In Los Angeles, Death Row's advent coincided with the birth of Power 106's "Where Hip-Hop Lives" format. The tenor of the music began to change, and the newfound openness in pop radio amplified its reach. Possessing little understanding of the cultural context of the music while rationalizing their musical offerings by pointing to call-out research and higher ratings, White executives like Cummings suddenly became lightning rods for criticism from the elders of the Black and Latino communities.

The lyrics had come from the streets. Some people thought they should have stayed there.

In the fall of 1993, the Congressional Black Caucus held its twenty-third consecutive "Annual Legislative Weekend" in Washington, D.C. From around the country, activists, academics, actors, and musical artists convened with politicians and lobbyists to network, strategize, and discuss the latest issues facing Black America.

Dionne Warwick, pop singer of fame in the sixties and seventies, and now "infomercial" host for the much-mocked Psychic Friends Network, had come to moderate a forum on AIDS. But she also had another mission: to muster a coalition of Black women to do something about misogyny and obscenity in rap lyrics.

Women within the hip-hop community had been worried about this phenomenon for some time—especially as Afrocentric rap crews like the Jungle Brothers and De La Soul were eclipsed in popularity by gangsta rap collectives like Death Row, who cultivated a defiantly crass aesthetic. *The Source* writer dream hampton and artist Queen Latifah were among many in the hip-hop community who observed that the culture was quickly losing its balance and that the lyrical din was becoming increasingly oppressive to young women.

Latifah and hampton raised their voices out of love. They spoke not against hip-hop, but against the darker forces within it.

Warwick didn't listen to rap music. Neither did the team of concerned women she assembled. And the person Warwick enlisted to lead their charge knew nothing about hip-hop at all, save for the bits of lyrics that she had been fed by Warwick and others.

Cynthia DeLores Tucker was only too happy to take up the fight. Tucker had been seeking public redemption for over fifteen years, since she was fired from her position as Pennsylvania's commonwealth secretary in 1977. She had been the first African-American woman to hold that office in any of the fifty states. A former civil rights activist who once marched with Dr. Martin Luther King Jr., Tucker had once been considered for a national cabinet post in the Carter administration. But during her tenure as commonwealth secretary in the 1970s, Tucker developed a reputation for greed and vanity. She and her husband were branded as slumlords in Philadelphia, where they owed $25,000 in taxes on a dozen poorly kept buildings. The governor who appointed her, Milton Shapp, reprimanded Tucker for failing to report thousands of dollars in honoraria for public speeches. Finally, an investigation by the state's attorney general found that not only had Tucker occasionally used state employees to write her oration, but that she had made 150 speeches in twenty-eight months and collected $65,000 for them—nearly double her state salary. Shapp, in a sharply worded termination letter, accused Tucker of using her office as "a clearinghouse for your personal moneymaking activities."

Tucker's unrepentant response had become legend in Pennsylvania: "Maybe it is wrong," she said. "But it is a way of life."

Tucker reemerged in the mid-1980s when she and Shirley Chisolm helped found the National Political Congress of Black Women. As memories of her political imbroglio faded, her standing increased. But Tucker's sense of entitlement nearly always proved self-destructive. In 1992, during her attempt to unseat another Black politician, U.S. Representative Lucien Blackwell, she criticized him for not hiring any Black women, while emphasizing that he had retained a "Jewish" female staffer from his predecessor. Tucker's remark may have cost her the election.

Tucker sat on the board of the NAACP and had raised over a million dollars for them. In the search for a new executive director for the organization, Tucker was passed over for Dr. Benjamin Chavis. She had to content herself with her current station, where she engaged in mild, low-profile chastisement of the new Clinton administration for any perceived slight to Black women. That is, until Dionne Warwick and her sidekick friends network offered Tucker a new crusade.

In December 1993, Tucker called a press conference in Washington, D.C. Flanked by former mayor Marion Barry, Tucker unveiled an illustration of her enemy: the cover of the debut album by Death Row/Interscope rapper Snoop Doggy Dogg, which featured a cartoon of a naked woman with a dog's tail—a bitch looking for a bone. She also unearthed the lyrics for the then-three-year-old horror song by the Geto Boys, "Mind of a Lunatic."

"If that isn't pornography," Tucker said, "I don't know what is."

Tucker and her organization began their campaign three days before Christmas in 1993, when they blocked the entrance to a Nobody Beats the Wiz record store in Washington, D.C., Tucker and comedian and activist Dick Gregory were arrested. After the New Year, she got herself jailed briefly again for picketing a Sam Goody across town.

Almost immediately, Tucker used her newfound press pulpit to strike back at her enemies. Ben Chavis now presided over the NAACP, and Tupac Shakur had been nominated for an NAACP Image Award for his role opposite Janet Jackson in John Singleton's latest film, *Poetic Justice*. To Tucker, Shakur's recent arrest for sexual assault in New York confirmed that he was a misogynist gangster rapper—his female-affirming songs like "Brenda's Got a Baby" and "Keep Ya Head Up" notwithstanding. Tucker embarrassed Chavis, a strong supporter of hip-hop, by calling for a boycott of her own organization's award show.

Chavis was young and knew hip-hop. Tucker was older and didn't. Chavis thought rap's positives outweighed its negatives. Tucker believed the opposite. The battle was just the latest in the long war between the civil rights and hip-hop generations.

As a people's movement, her campaign against the music faltered. At her Martin Luther King Day picket of a Philadelphia Tower Records, no one showed up but the police. But her point of view started to gain political momentum. Jesse Jackson's Operation PUSH called for a "thirty-day fast" from explicit, violent rap music. And in February 1994, the U.S. Congress held the first-ever public hearings on the perils of rap music, each called by Black female legislators from Chicago: Representative Cardiss Collins in the House, and Carol Moseley Braun in the Senate.

"The record industry is out of control," C. DeLores Tucker told the House committee. "If it has to be regulated, so be it."

During the House hearing, Tucker got a strong rebuke from one female rapper. Yo-Yo had been introduced to the world by Ice Cube in their classic battle-of-the-sexes song, "It's a Man's World," in which Yo-Yo, born Yolanda Whittaker, gave as good as she got.

"There was violence before rap and there will be violence after rap," Yo-Yo said. "This is a time for everyone to take responsibility for their own actions. Rap should not be made the scapegoat."

Also testifying before the House was Nelson George, the author of perhaps the very first newspaper article on hip-hop back in 1979, and now a successful Hollywood screenwriter. Even though George's movie—a Chris Rock vehicle called *CB4*—lampooned gangster rap, George defended the genre.

"The question we should really address is not what is the impact of gangsta rap," he said. "But, rather, why does a wide cross section of young America find it so enjoyable?"

Representative Maxine Waters, who represented the South Central district from which so much gangster rap came, stood by her constituents:

"These are my children," Waters said. "I do not intend to marginalize or demean them. Rather, I take responsibility for trying to understand what they are saying. . . . Let's not lose sight of what the real problem is. It is not the words being used. It is the reality that they are rapping about."

Representative Collins disagreed. "In my view, the lyrics are not acceptable for whatever reason," Collins replied. "People are complaining. Yet no one in the industry seems to be listening and taking the complaints seriously. Let one thing be clear today: Congress is listening."

No rappers came to the five-hour Senate hearings. Luther Campbell of 2 Live Crew canceled his appearance because he claimed the senators didn't know enough about the subject and were interested in investigating only Black artists.

But a young Black professor from Brown University named Michael Eric Dyson got a standing ovation from the gallery when he decried Tucker and other antirap activists as "petty, bourgeois Negro intellectuals" who condemned obscenities in the art of disenfranchised Black youths while tolerating the obscene conditions under which they lived.

But C. DeLores Tucker's demand that the government use its "full authority . . . to restrict access of such music and videos to minors" had moved Moseley Braun and others to renew the call for stricter labeling.

Tucker, so long outcast, had become a political power once more.

Warner Music chief Bob Morgado won a big battle in his war for full control of all three major companies in his group: Gerald Levin had denied Mo Ostin's request to remain outside of Morgado's chain of command.

If Levin's refusal upset Ostin, it was nothing compared to Morgado's next abomination: elevating Atlantic's cochairman Doug Morris to run all of Warner Music's U.S. operations, effectively making a recent junior executive the boss of Ostin and Elektra chief Bob Krasnow.

Ostin announced that he would be resigning when his contract expired at the end of 1994, and Krasnow took a buyout of $7 million. In their stead, Morris placed his own lieutenants: Atlantic president Danny Goldberg at Warner Bros., and Atlantic Black music chief Sylvia Rhone at Elektra. The mood at Warner's Burbank offices was especially bitter: Ostin, a gracious executive whose company held the biggest market share of all the Warner labels, had been hustled out the door, replaced in a coldhearted corporate coup.

Then things got really bizarre. Doug Morris realized that the man who elevated him to his lofty new position had little inclination to actually let him run the show. So Morris threatened a walkout of the chief executives of all three companies, all loyal to him. Gerald Levin could not afford another shakeup at the music group, so he sided with Morris, and fired Morgado.

In Morgado's place, Levin brought in another nonmusic executive: Michael Fuchs, from HBO. Fuchs made the rounds of the three labels to introduce himself.

He did not make a good impression. During Fuchs's speech to the shell-shocked executives of Warner Bros. Records, one employee started counting how many times Fuchs said the word "I." The tally passed a hundred.

Truth be told, Fuchs didn't think much of the music industry, which he called a "nasty business," filled with people of meager intellect and little financial acumen. People who worked in movies and TV at least had to know how to read and manage budgets, Fuchs concluded. Furthermore, Fuchs despised the joint-venture deals that Warner gave to people like Ted Field, Jimmy Iovine, and Rick Rubin. The contracts gave Time Warner too little control. Fuchs came from HBO, where he always had "final cut" on any movie or program. *And fuck you if you don't like it*, Fuchs believed. Then there were the lavish executive contracts given to people like Morris and Goldberg. All these guys did, Fuchs thought, was sit in their offices and call each other a hundred times a day.

Fuchs, unlike Morgado, didn't think much of Morris, nor the sweet deal he had given to his friends Jimmy Iovine and Ted Field. And he resolved to do something about it.

After the debacles with Tommy Boy and Def American, Paris finally landed a distributor for his album, *Sleeping with the Enemy*—albeit *after* the defeat of George H. W. Bush in the presidential elections of 1992.

INDI, a conglomeration of three regional distributors who merged to survive in a shrinking market for indie labels, debated whether to release Paris's album. Chris Joyce, INDI's general counsel, didn't believe his record broke the law, as Time Warner's and Polygram's lawyers did. From a business perspective, if INDI wasn't going to be a viable alternative to corporate timidity and censorship, how could they really stake a claim in the music marketplace if they didn't release it? *Sleeping with the Enemy* was exactly the kind of record for which INDI existed. A deal was struck. Sex Records, now renamed Scarface Records, received a six-figure advance against preorders of around 200,000 units. Michael Eric Dyson even contributed to Paris's media campaign, ghostwriting the rapper's op-ed piece in the *Washington Post*.

Throughout 1993, with his record selling and some reorders coming in, Paris started to see his exile from the majors as a blessing. This time, instead of getting an artist's cut, around $1 from every record he sold, he now got a wholesale cut, $6 to $7. He could make a career of this, and wouldn't have to answer to anybody. He could turn Scarface into a real record label.

He moved Scarface to bigger offices, hired more people, and started putting out records by other artists through the INDI system. But within a matter of months, Paris stopped receiving checks. Over the phone, Chris Joyce explained that the six compilation albums of Miami "bass music" that Scarface had released had been overmanufactured and overshipped. Now those records were coming back. Scarface, in the parlance of the record business, was "upside down." Meaning that the record company owed money to INDI—over $200,000, in fact—rather than the other way around.

Paris wasn't trying to hear it. By his count, his album sales had accumulated for him at least a half million dollars in credit. There was no way that the manufacturing and shipping of less than 100,000 units could have eliminated that. Given INDI's refusal to pay him, Paris wasn't trying to give them his next album either. So Paris made the trek to Los Angeles and struck a new deal for Scarface Records with Priority Records. Bryan Turner's partner, Mark Cerami, made a courtesy call to INDI to let them know. Now INDI was in a bind. Without Paris's next album, they would be in the hole for hundreds of thousands of dollars. Joyce sent a cease-and-desist letter to both Scarface and Priority.

Joyce stopped returning calls, and Paris burned. But he knew how to catch him. All of these independent record people came to the annual convention of the National Association of Recording Merchandisers, which was being held this year, coincidentally, in San Francisco, at the downtown Marriott. On March 19, 1994, the opening day of the convention, Paris and a friend scoured the hotel for executives from INDI. No sign of anyone. Paris headed through the lobby toward the front doors. And there he was, Chris Joyce, with a bunch of other INDI execs and their dates, returning from a dinner thrown by another client, American Gramaphone.

Paris walked up to Joyce. "What's up, Chris?" he said.

Joyce, it seemed, didn't acknowledge him.

Paris stepped closer. "*What's up, Chris?*" he asked again, louder. "What's up with my money? Why don't you return my phone calls?"

Joyce replied that he hadn't heard from Paris since November. Joyce began to reiterate INDI's position: Paris owed them money, not the other way around.

Paris raised his voice again: "Where the fuck is my money, motherfucker?!"

Joyce told Paris that he wouldn't have an argument with him in the lobby. "If you want to talk, call me at the office on Monday. Good night, Paris."

Joyce turned to walk away. Yet again, Paris felt dismissed: Tommy Boy, Warner, Polygram, Def American, and now INDI. Joyce was yet another White gatekeeper standing in his way. Was this little bitch smirking at him? Paris cocked back and punched Joyce in the eye. Joyce fell to the ground and Paris began kicking him hard in the ribs. Everything happened so fast, Joyce's colleagues took a few moments to react. Rick Hocutt, the West Coast branch manager for INDI, thought Paris was about to kick Joyce in the head. He started toward Paris. The rapper and his friend ran out of the building. Joyce lay on the floor, an open wound in his forehead leaking blood into his eye.

Paris jogged away, feeling exhilarated. *I served that motherfucker's ass. My name will ring out after this.* He and his boy laughed all the way home.

The police came for Paris at the offices of Scarface Records, but the rapper wasn't there. Paris hid out and had his lawyer negotiate a deal for his surrender. The San Francisco DA's office was charging him with attempted murder. Paris's attorney negotiated the charges down to two counts of misdemeanor assault.

At the trial, Rick Hocutt and others from INDI arrived to give Chris Joyce their support. Under questioning from his own lawyer, Paris attempted to paint the altercation as a fair fight. Joyce, he claimed, had called him "nigger" and taken a swing at him. Joyce emphatically denied Paris's account. Witnesses confirmed Joyce's accusations.

But the most damning testimony to Paris's character came from Paris himself. Priority had just released the rapper's new CD *Guerrilla Funk* the week of the trial. The district attorney played the album in open court, and distributed the lyrics to the jury.

Paris's slowed-down voice chuckled over a gangster-funk dirge, taunting sellout rappers and "punk-ass pigs." Paris concluded with this:

"Oh, and uh, Chris Joyce, how you feel? I ain't forgot you, motherfuckers."

The jury returned guilty verdicts on both counts. Oscar Jackson Jr. was sentenced to fifteen days of community service. Joyce had the option to pursue a civil case. But his bruises were gone and his scars healing. He wasn't even sure whether Paris had any money that would make a new trial worth the time and trouble. He decided to put the episode behind him.

Paris, the honor student and son of a San Francisco doctor, served his time with a bunch of other young Black convicts, picking up trash in a park. Some of the guys knew who he was. He even caught up with an ex-girlfriend on one of his excursions. His whole career had been about serving his community.

This, he thought, *was nothing.*

———

C. DeLores Tucker roared out of the 1994 Congressional hearings with a vengeance, turning first on Benjamin Chavis—the executive director of the NAACP who refused to rebuke Tupac earlier that year. Chavis was now vulnerable due to troubles of his own making, having authorized secret payments of almost $100,000 to settle a sexual harassment suit with a former NAACP employee. Tucker pushed the NAACP board to oust Chavis, which they did in August 1994.

Then Tucker led a drive to depose the NAACP's chairman, William Gibson, for fiduciary neglect and fraud. Gibson was canned in February 1995, and Tucker's choice, the widow of slain civil rights leader Medgar Evers, was installed.

While Tucker flexed her new muscle in the NAACP, she continued her offense against the offensive with a newfound ally. Although Tucker was a lifelong Democrat, she found much in common with Republican William J. Bennett, the former secretary of education under President Ronald Reagan who had recently embarked on a cultural crusade of his own with the publication of *The Book of Virtues*, in which he espoused timeless values like compassion, responsibility, friendship, courage, perseverance, and faith.

Like Tucker, Bill Bennett saw none of those virtues in rap music. Bennett first discovered Tucker in a *U.S. News & World Report* opinion piece, in which she condemned Time Warner for its involvement in gangster rap. Bennett saw an opportunity to reach across racial and party lines to combat "cultural garbage." Bennett's wife and Tucker shared a common acquaintance—Barbara Wyatt, the president of the Parents Music Resource Center. Wyatt brokered a meeting between the two in the spring of 1995, and the partners began planning a new campaign—not to petition the government this time, but to exert financial and political pressure directly on record companies. Though all six of the major labels dealt in rap music in one way or another, only one of them, Time Warner, remained American owned, and thus uniquely susceptible to political pressure.

Taking a cue from Ron DeLord and the 1992 "Cop Killer" boycott, Tucker and Bennett built a multipronged media blitz designed to create maximum discomfort around Time Warner's annual shareholders' meeting on May 18, 1995, at the New York City Center auditorium. They readied a television commercial decrying the corporation's involvement with "music that celebrates the rape, torture, and murder of women."

"Is anybody at Time Warner embarassed by these lyrics?" Bennett said in the spot. "Will the executives of Time Warner stand up and say these things in public?" Bennett and Tucker promised to air the spot in New York, Los Angeles, and San Francisco if Time Warner didn't accede to their ultimatum: Get out of the rap business.

As he had in 1992, Gerald Levin opened the floor to shareholders— whether major or minor. And with her own purchase of ten shares of Time Warner stock, Tucker had bought herself the right to speak. Levin stood silently onstage as Tucker made a seventeen-minute-long speech.

"You are destroying not just a generation," she told him, "but a race of people." Responding to Levin's attempt to minimize Time Warner's hip-hop footprint as just "8 percent of the market," Tucker responded: "Even 1 percent is too much when we weigh it against the value of life lost because of its violent messages." She blasted Levin for Time Warner's recent purchase of an additional 25 percent of Interscope, which pumped nearly $100 million more into the very company that, she proclaimed, "Time Warner needs to get out of business with immediately."

Bennett brokered a face-to-face parlay with Levin, Michael Fuchs, Doug Morris, and Time Warner president Richard Parsons, in private quarters at HBO's 42nd Street offices after the public shareholders' meeting.

Tucker was particularly strident behind closed doors.

"Stop peddling that music to children!" Tucker yelled. "No one wants their kids being told to suck somebody's dick! Nobody.... No child should be told to do the things these lyrics are telling 'em to do!"

Tucker not only reiterated her demand that Time Warner divest itself of Interscope, she also insisted that Fuchs and Morris read the lyrics to the now five-year-old Geto Boys song, "Mind of a Lunatic."

"I'll give you a hundred dollars to read it!" she told Fuchs.

When he refused, she stormed out of the meeting. Gerald Levin coaxed her back in. Levin reiterated that Time Warner would lead an industry-wide "standards and labeling" effort. That wasn't enough for Bennett, who asked Levin "whether there is anything so low, so bad that you will not sell it?" Levin insisted that he was sensitive to the issues Bennett and Tucker raised: His own son, Jonathan, after all, was a teacher in an inner-city public school. Finally, when Bennett called Levin's offer "baloney," it was Levin's turn to walk out in a huff.

After the meeting, Bennett and Tucker parted ways to double their effectiveness. Tucker addressed the NAACP board, while Bennett appeared on *Meet the Press*. Bob Dole, the chief contender for the 1996 Republican presidential nomination, echoed their talking points on the floor of the Senate.

"Time Warner," Dole said, "is now on the cutting edge of the misogyny business."

On June 2, Bennett's and Tucker's names appeared side by side above a *Wall Street Journal* op-ed piece entitled "Lyrics from the Gutter."

"When we read the lyrics to Time Warner executives and asked if they thought them offensive and ought not to be sold to children, we were told that it was a 'complex issue,'" they wrote. "It is not a complex issue. There are things on which reasonable people will disagree. But some lyrics of these songs are beyond the pale."

Bennett and Tucker asserted that their appeal had "fallen on deaf ears." But within Time Warner, the renewed focus on rap lyrics had rocked the company. Board member Beverly Sills's long-standing opposition to rap music was amplified now by another director, Henry Luce III, the son of the founder of *Time* magazine, who now spoke publicly of his opposition to Levin's lack of action on the issue.

Michael Fuchs listened. He had been on the job only a few weeks, but he had determined that Interscope wasn't making Time Warner enough money to be worth the trouble of having to put out everything Field and Iovine wanted to release. He told the board that he would get rid of the troublesome venture. Before he did that, he had to deal with the one person who would surely stand in his way.

On June 21, 1995, Fuchs summoned Doug Morris to his office and showed him a press release. The headline read, "Doug Morris Relieved of Responsibilities at Warner Music Group." Morris was escorted to his office by security guards to gather his things, and then out onto the street.

With Morris out, Fuchs made his intentions known to Ted Field and Jimmy Iovine: Not only was he going to cancel the recent deal to purchase an additional 25 percent of Interscope; he wanted to sell back to Field and Iovine the 25 percent that Time Warner already owned.

Fuchs set a price, and the Interscope executives agreed. Then Fuchs decided that he hadn't asked them for enough money, and raised the price.

Allen Grubman, Interscope's negotiator, was apoplectic. "I represent forty-eight of the top fifty people in the record business," Grubman told Fuchs. "In all my years, no one has ever reneged on me. This is too small a business to act that way."

"Allen," Fuchs replied, "I've been in the entertainment business for a while, too. What do you think I've been, a fucking *butcher*? I'd like to have a dollar for every time *you* reneged on someone."

The negotiations ground on through the summer.

In a statement to the media, C. DeLores Tucker cited her hand in Doug Morris's departure: "The firing of Doug Morris is a major victory for those of us who asked Time Warner chairman Gerald Levin to stop putting out pornographic music. Doug Morris was the biggest supporter of this smut at the company, and now he's gone. I predict that Interscope Records will fall next."

Indeed, since her first meeting with Time Warner, Tucker had been making curious pronouncements. She sounded less like an activist, and more like a record executive.

"My office is full of albums of those young people that have positive messages to give," she said. "Some of these poor kids . . . will get some contracts."

A reporter asked her: "You really think that's going to happen?"

"I *know* it will happen," she responded.

Tucker—no stranger to using public station for private gain—was intimating that she had access at Time Warner that would enable her to start her own record company.

In early July 1995, Tucker invited Suge Knight and his lawyer David Kenner to the National Political Conference of Black Women's convention in Seattle. Until that point, Tucker had never met Knight and had issued nothing but condemnation for Death Row. But at the meeting, Tucker was cordial. She appealed to Knight's sense of racial solidarity: Couldn't they both work to create more positive messages for African-American youth? Knight replied that he would like to, but that positive messages didn't sell.

That's because they're not marketed correctly, Tucker replied.

Tucker assured Knight that his distributor, Interscope, would soon be cut loose from Time Warner. In its place, Tucker would be launching her *own* joint venture with Time Warner, promoting artists with clean lyrics and positive messages. Death Row could avoid certain limbo and possible financial failure if Knight were to allow Tucker to broker a new deal with Time Warner through her company. Knight would have to jettison gangster rap, of course. Knight later recounted that Tucker offered him an astonishing windfall if he went along with her: an $80 million advance and the installation of not one, but two new recording studios.

Tucker arranged for her office to write a legal release for Knight to sign. Drafted on NPCBW letterhead and sent to Kenner in advance, it read:

> I [Knight] hereby designate and authorize the [NPCBW] to negotiate an acceptable contract relationship with Time Warner Inc. regarding the production and distribution of [Death Row] music products. I hereby understand that the above arrangement is based on the fact that my company will cease and desist from the production and distribution of misogynist, obscene and pornographic music. . . . This authorization is submitted to demonstrate my good faith in cooperating with the [NPCBW] in every way possible to reverse the negative trends in African-American music.

Tucker had the letter faxed to Kenner, and she invited him and Knight to a special meeting at Dionne Warwick's Los Angeles home on August 8, where another special guest would be in attendance: Warner Music Group chief Michael Fuchs. They could seal the deal then.

Fuchs had accepted an invitation to the same meeting on very different presumptions.

Warwick had cold-called Fuchs in his New York office. She'd told him that she'd known Suge Knight "for ages" and that Knight wanted to meet him in person. Fuchs had heard that Knight didn't like him very much—he'd even heard rumors that Knight had put a "hit" out on him. Perhaps a face-to-face meeting would be a good idea. He could tell Knight why Interscope had become so problematic and why Time Warner had to back out of the deal.

On the day of the meeting, Fuchs arrived, but Tucker and Knight did not. Fuchs, starving from the long flight, ordered deli sandwiches, waited a few more hours, and then left.[17]

Fuchs, of course, knew nothing about C. DeLores Tucker's plans to develop her own company. Contrary to her public and private statements, Fuchs had never offered her any deal; nor was he planning to.

---

[17]Dionne Warwick says that she did call Michael Fuchs once, but denies that this meeting ever took place. "Michael Fuchs never came to my house," she said.

Knight, for his part, refused to sign Tucker's inducement letter, and he had Kenner send the NPCBW a reply through Dionne Warwick, rejecting the deal.

After the latest encounter with Tucker and her organization, Knight and Kenner informed Ted Field and Jimmy Iovine of the back-channel deal.

Field and Iovine immediately halted negotiations with Fuchs and slapped Tucker and the NPCBW with a tortious-interference lawsuit, alleging that she attempted to induce Death Row to breach its deal with Interscope. The Interscope suit was followed closely by a similar sally from Death Row, which named Time Warner, Gerald Levin, and Michael Fuchs as a codefendants.

When the news of the lawsuits broke, Tucker called them "frivolous" and an "effort to cloud the real issue." But while she vigorously disputed Knight's claim that she had discussed money with him, she couldn't deny that she had commissioned a letter that appeared to induce Knight to break his deal with Interscope, while aggrandizing her own organization.

Suddenly, Time Warner began politely backing away from Tucker. "Any efforts . . . by Ms. Tucker with Death Row Records were undertaken by her acting as a well-intentioned volunteer, without any authorization from Time Warner, Warner Music, Gerald Levin, or Michael Fuchs," a corporate spokesperson said.

Nearly two decades after her disgrace in Pennsylvania, Tucker had bounced back into the political spotlight only to discredit herself once again—squandering her station by blurring the lines between profit and nonprofit, between public trust and personal gain.

In one sense, Tucker had succeeded. She had provoked Time Warner to sever ties with Interscope. But Tucker trashed her own political standing in the process.

In the final negotiations between Time Warner and Interscope, Ted Field and Allen Grubman sat across from Michael Fuchs for a face-to-face discussion.

Fuchs's readiness to terminate the relationship between the two companies stemmed from Interscope's refusal to give Time Warner any control over the label's releases. Iovine and Field wouldn't allow corporate to hear the much-discussed album from Snoop Dogg protégés Tha Dogg Pound; so Fuchs ordered it dropped from the schedule.

But more than issues of autonomy, Fuchs was bothered by Field's posturing. Fuchs observed the multimillionaire trust-fund baby making a big show of defending ghetto rappers, calling criticism of gangster rap "racist" and telling newpaper reporters that anybody who wanted to censor hip-hop could "kiss my ass." Field got Bob Dole to vilify him on the floor of the United States Senate. Now, in their latest meeting, Field was sermonizing to Fuchs about artistic freedom, integrity, and truth. It was too much.

"You can't *possibly* believe in this music, given where *you* come from," Fuchs declared.

"I do," Field replied. "I relate to it. I feel its pain."

"You feel its *pain*?" Fuchs almost sneered. What could Field, who had been pampered all his life, know of pain?

To answer Fuchs, Ted Field raised his left hand. Field slowly began unwrapping the brown elastic bandage that he had worn nearly every day since his racing accident in 1975. Field unraveled the dressing until he revealed the disfigured hand beneath it: white, pulpy skin, fingers ground to stumps, thumb and lone finger functioning as not much more than a rudimary pincer. Once, at a business meeting, a doctor had approached Field, taken one look at the damage, and said, "Tell me that happened *after* they invented nerve blocks."

Field replied that it hadn't.

"You poor man," the doctor told the millionaire.

Now Field held his mutilated hand before a silenced Fuchs.

Take a look at that, Field said. *That's pain.*

In early October 1995, Time Warner announced that they had sold their 50 percent stake in Interscope back to Field and Iovine for $115 million.

Some in the music industry speculated that Interscope's upcoming gangsta rap releases would return to Priority Records for distribution—gangsta rap's original home. Others talked of a possible deal with Polygram. It wasn't such a bad thing to be looking for another distribution deal when you had hit records.

In ridding Time Warner of Interscope, Michael Fuchs might have thought himself free and clear as well. He wasn't. His war with Doug Morris had alienated him from the entertainment executives across the company. The prospect of Fuchs as heir apparent to Gerald Levin scared Bob

Daly and Terry Semel, the Warner Pictures co-chiefs who would have to report to Fuchs under the proposed structure. Daly and Semel balked, and Levin blinked.

Levin offered Fuchs a transfer to run Turner Broadcasting in Atlanta. Fuchs exploded, saying he didn't want to be moved around like a piece of furniture. Levin fired Fuchs on November 15, albeit with a severance package of $60 million.

Many longtime executives in the three major labels of the Warner Music Group might have celebrated Fuchs's departure as karmic payback, just as they applauded Bob Morgado's exit, but few were left to enjoy the moment.

Mo Ostin—the man who built Warner Bros. Records, who signed Tommy Boy and Cold Chillin' and supported Ice-T—was gone.

So, too, was Bob Krasnow, the man who revived Elektra Records, and gave Dante Ross a job doing rap A&R.

Also gone was Doug Morris, the longtime leader of Atlantic Records and the champion of Interscope.

Morris had since taken a job running rival MCA Music. Within months of his arrival, Morris gave his old buddies Ted Field and Jimmy Iovine a new distribution contract, buying 50 percent of Interscope for a reported $200 million, giving an instant $90 million windfall to Field and Iovine. William Bennett and C. DeLores Tucker issued statements decrying the move, but their clout had evaporated considerably. The reality was insurmountable: Hip-hop chased from one label would simply land at the next.

Back at Warner Music Group, a new slate of executives tried to regain their labels' footing in a marketplace where hip-hop was more, not less, popular than ever before, and the staff struggled to make sense of the carnage at what had once been the greatest record conglomerate on earth.

Tommy Boy's latest hit seemed to portend the end of the gangster rap era.

"Gangsta's Paradise" was recorded for the soundtrack of a Michelle Pfeiffer movie called *Dangerous Minds*. To a sample of a Stevie Wonder song, rapper Coolio issued a repudiation of gangsterism that only a real former gangster could. The song went to number one on the pop charts, and the album went double platinum for Tommy Boy.

Even though Tommy Boy was having a profitable run, Silverman was considering leaving the company he had built. He had sold Tommy Boy to Warner long ago. His contract was almost up. If he wanted to, he could walk away, form a new company, and take all of his executives with him. Tommy Boy had become very profitable for Time Warner. If they wanted him to stay, they would have to give him back some equity.

But every time Silverman started negotiating with someone, they got fired. First Mo Ostin. Then Lenny Waronker. Then Danny Goldberg. Now he was dealing with Russ Thyret.

During this long process, with the majors driving up the price of making and marketing hip-hop records, Silverman knew that if he wanted Tommy Boy to remain competitive, he would have to expand. With that in mind, in the previous year he had set his sights on a fellow rap indie label, Profile Records.

Although they never again experienced the heights of Run-DMC's triple-platinum *Raising Hell*, Profile continued to do well. Artists like DJ Quik, 2nd II None, and Nine had hits, and Run-DMC had even enjoyed a comeback in 1993 with a song called "Down with the King."

Steve Plotnicki and Cory Robbins never sold Profile to a major label—although they came close to a deal in the early 1990s with Polygram. Instead, Plotnicki and Robbins believed that it might be possible to *become* a major. Plotnicki engineered the creation of a national distribution network called Landmark, which, in turn, came to distribute not only Profile's releases but records from other independents, like Tommy Boy and Select—which Fred Munao had recently brought back from the Time Warner fold.

Then Robbins and Plotnicki began to bicker. Plotnicki needed Robbins to deliver more records to feed their distribution network, and he felt that Robbins wanted the company to remain small. *We can't compete*, Plotnicki said, *doing business the way we used to*. Robbins, for his part, thought that Profile's recent peak of seventeen albums a year was plenty, even for some majors.

Robbins suspected that Plotnicki's anger was about more than just business. Robbins was still wealthy, single, dating lots of women, and hanging out every night. Plotnicki was married, and Robbins thought that Plotnicki was jealous of his life. Eventually, the partners stopped talking to each other.

Silverman saw his friend Robbins in distress and Profile as obtainable. Silverman offered to buy them out for $10 to $12 million. His plan was to hire Robbins to stay on and run the company. Hearing that, Plotnicki insisted that he get more money out of the deal than Robbins. Talks broke down, and Robbins, seeing no alternative for himself, sold his 50 percent of Profile Records and his interest in Landmark to Plotnicki for just $2 million in cash and $1.5 million in promissory notes.

The following day, Tom Silverman and Fred Munao sued to force Plotnicki's Landmark into bankrupcy, claiming that the distributor hadn't paid them. Plotnicki countered that Silverman was suing for revenge, after failing to buy Profile. The judge believed Plotnicki and rejected Silverman and Munao's petition.

The legal battle proved fatal for Landmark, which closed its doors soon thereafter.

But the judge's ruling also set the stage for Steve Plotnicki to go after Silverman for damages, which he did, casting Tommy Boy as the wily hand of Time Warner out to crush a small, vital competitor. Tommy Boy, in suing to recover just $30,000 from Landmark, was rumored to have been forced to pay over $20 million in damages and legal fees.

Silverman's hits were enough to cover its losses, but within a few years he left Time Warner and the rap business, moving back into his original bailiwick, dance music. Cory Robbins returned to dance music as well with his new company, Robbins Entertainment, and eventually had to sue Plotnicki to deliver on his $1.5 million note. Plotnicki ran Profile successfully for a few years before selling it to Arista for a reported $12 million. The entire episode brought another meaning to the term "gangsta rap."

On May 30, 1997, Jonathan Levin, the son of Time Warner CEO Gerald Levin, was brutally murdered in his Upper West Side apartment. The younger Levin was a public schoolteacher in the Bronx. One of his students discovered that he was the son of a rich man, and thought Jonathan Levin was rich, too. Corey Arthur went to Levin's apartment, tortured him for his automatic teller machine pass code, and then shot him.

In the aftermath, Gerald Levin was disconsolate, as any father would be. Some of Levin's adversaries—the cultural conservatives who blamed Levin for Time Warner's spewing what they called violent, misogynist filth— whispered that the loss of his son to violence was, perhaps, karmic payback. After all, the kid who killed Levin's son was Black and likely listened to rap.

But for Levin the tragedy was beyond comprehension. His son's teaching philosophy had been, "Nobody is beyond redemption." Like the teacher

Michelle Pfeiffer portrayed in *Dangerous Minds*, Jonathan used every tool at his disposal to communicate with his students, especially hip-hop. He had even been criticized for using rap music to teach. Jonathan was a heroic figure in his father's eyes, a person who knew that hip-hop wasn't the problem. Inequity was the problem. Poverty was the problem. Addiction was the problem.

Jonathan Levin had supported his father throughout the "Cop Killer" episode, when every law enforcement officer across the country reviled the name of Gerald Levin. So, for Gerald, the ironic thing about losing Jonathan to murder was, in its aftermath, the supportive and sensitive demeanor of the men and women who worked for the New York City Police Department.

ALBUM SEVEN

KEEPING IT REAL

The branding of hip-hop and the rise
of the superempowered artist
(1993–1999)

Credibility

For the artists in the Time Warner family who didn't rap about cops, guns, and gangs, cultivating a squeaky-clean image didn't necessarily guarantee the corporation's favors; nor did it assure success. In 1991, two cousins from Staten Island learned that the hard way.

Robert Diggs, who called himself "Prince Rakeem," was only twenty-one years old when he got an offer from Tommy Boy Music to release his self-produced single, "Ooh I Love You Rakeem." It was a rather tame, happy-go-lucky song about how he had "too many ladies," and needed to "learn to say no."

Diggs deal was secured by his manager, Melquan, who also landed a contract for Diggs's older cousin, Gary Grice, twenty-five, at another Time Warner label, Cold Chillin'. Grice, who performed as "The Genius," recorded an album filled with intricate battle rhymes. "After you melt, you start dripping like water. Then you can say this was a goddamn slaughter," he rapped in the song "Phony as Ya Wanna Be."

But The Genius himself adopted a fraudulent identity to promote his record. In 1991, with radio play still hard to earn, one of the best ways to wedge a rap artist onto the playlist of a Black station was to flavor a single with "new jack swing," the prevailing R&B style of the time that blended hip-hop beats with conventional musicality. In the case of The Genius, Cold Chillin' commissioned a single called "Come Do Me," with music and lyrics that had almost nothing to do with the talents and strengths of the artist they signed. "Your soft warm little voice is very pleasing," he rapped. "And your tight miniskirt is kind of teasing."

Tommy Boy and Cold Chillin' invested in videos for their new artists, colorful confections as inoffensive as they were ineffectual. After the records shipped, where they remained unplayed in DJs' crates and lay unbought in record store bins, Tommy Boy and Cold Chillin' dropped Prince Rakeem and The Genius from their rosters.

The truth was that the concocted hip-hop personas of these two artists were diametrically opposed to the real lives of Robert Diggs and Gary Grice, two young MCs who had grown up in New York City's worst neighborhoods and experienced the streets' terrors from a very young age. If any MCs had stories to tell, these two did.

Robert Diggs ultimately decided that he and his cousin weren't going to be able to tell those stories within the context of a record deal with a major label—or any label, for that matter. For his second act at the age of twenty-two, Diggs resolved to own his words, his music, his image, and himself. His authority would secure his authenticity. Whomever he eventually did business with would have to deal with him as a sovereign, not as an artist.

When that time came, Diggs's entrepreneurial vision would lead the way in transforming not only the music business, but American business itself—from an age in which hip-hop had to sell out to gain access to its audience, into one where some of America's major corporations sought the imprimatur of authentic hip-hop to market their products and services to a new, multi-cultural generation of Americans.

Robert Diggs saw his first shooting while playing with his older brother Mitchell outside his mother's new home in Brownsville—a section of Brooklyn that had plummeted from working-class community to burned-out ghetto over the course of the 1960s and 1970s.

Diggs's mother, Linda Hamlin, whom everyone called "Miss Linda," had eleven children—eight boys and three girls. To get them away from the streets, she had sent the kids down to North Carolina for a time, where they lived with relatives. But when Hamlin discovered that the New York State Urban Development Corporation was building brand-new, subsidized, suburban-style town houses in Brownsville, Hamlin hastened to rent one of the units. The thirty-nine low-slung buildings of Marcus Garvey Village were supposed to be the solution to the disaster of the ubiquitous high-rise housing project. But social architecture couldn't shield the children of Marcus Garvey from the reality of Brownsville.

Robert and Mitchell—seven and eight years old, respectively—still had to leave Marcus Garvey to walk to school and to the store. Every time Mitchell lugged the family's clothes to the Laundromat, he had to cross Amboy Street, where kids would rob him of his cash and coins before he reached his destination. Mitchell was a short, slight kid with a lazy eye, apparent weaknesses that galvanized his tormentors. To survive in Brownsville, Mitchell had to learn to box. Once, his younger brother Robert had come back home after being mugged by some teenagers. Miss Linda grabbed Robert in one hand and a butcher knife in the other to go looking for them.

Even on their mother's front stoop, it wasn't safe. While he and Robert played, Mitchell glanced at the park across the street. It was a sunny day, with swimmers in bathing trunks walking to and from the Betsy Head Pool on Dumont Avenue. A vendor sold hot dogs from a cart on the sidewalk. Then Mitchell saw one guy grab the hot dog for which another fellow had apparently just paid. Mitchell and Robert looked on as the two men argued. One more fight of many. Suddenly, one fellow lifted a silver handgun with a pearl handle and shot the other in the torso.

When Miss Linda heard the shot, she did two things. First, she ran outside and grabbed her sons. And not long thereafter, she made arrangements for Robert and Mitchell Diggs to live with their grandmother on Staten Island.

The least urbanized, least populated, and most isolated of New York City's five boroughs, Staten Island was a world away from Brooklyn. Its streets were largely quiet, its homes modest but well kept. The Diggses' grandmother Ethel kept a small flat above a hardware store on Jersey Street in Staten Island's New Brighton neighborhood. Mitchell liked the change of scenery, and concentrated on his studies at P.S. 31. Robert went back to Brooklyn every chance he got, to see his mother, sisters, and his favorite cousins, Russell Jones and Gary Grice. Soon Grice would relocate to Staten Island as well.

The Diggs brothers discovered that Staten Island had mean streets of its own. In a borough that was home to a large, working-class Italian-American population, the Black poor were cordoned off into tiny ghettos. The communities of Stapleton and Park Hill were bounded on two sides by hills dotted with the homes of the wealthy; on the third by an expressway; and on the fourth by an Italian neighborhood where the local kids literally drew lines in the street, beyond which Black kids might get a beating if they crossed. Stapleton was dominated by a high-rise housing project as rough as any in Brooklyn, built with outdoor hallways so police could easily monitor comings and goings. Nearby Park Hill had subsidized apartments that were barely a cut above that. The whole community was like a prison, an island on an island.

For a while, Mitchell was bused to a school in the all-White neighborhood of Rosebank, and faced a fusillade of eggs, sticks, stones, and bricks from White children on his way. Mitchell and Robert's mother eventually engineered a kind of détente with the Italians of Staten Island after she moved from Brooklyn and reunited the entire family in a small house on Laurel Street. Linda Hamlin and her mother, Ethel, ran a restaurant across the street from the nearby Stapleton projects that served as a front for a mob-run numbers operation. While Ethel cooked in the front, Miss Linda tallied the daily wins and losses in the back, under the protection of a neighborhood enforcer nicknamed "Fat Larry."

To the Diggs brothers, he was *Uncle* Larry—a gruff, friendly presence in their daily lives. He was one of the richest men they had ever seen, sporting fat diamonds and driving a Lincoln Continental. Uncle Larry provided Hamlin and her family with a security that was both financial and physical. At I.S. 49, the Italian kids didn't jump Mitchell anymore. They knew whom he was with.

One day after school, while Mitchell was sitting in the restaurant, Uncle Larry took him aside.

"You're not going to be sitting around here looking at your mother every day," he said. "You're going to work."

So Uncle Larry got Mitchell a job with one of his construction crews. Soon Mitchell was bringing home over $300 a week. But that was nothing compared to the money that Mitchell helped Miss Linda count in the back room, stacks of bills sometimes totaling thirty or forty grand.

Despite her illegal trade, Linda Hamlin kept strict rules for her eleven kids. Generosity was mandated. You took one slice of bread out of the refrigerator, not two, if there wasn't enough for everybody. Theft was out of the question. At the house, every child had a rigorous schedule of cleaning assignments: rinsing dishes, scrubbing pots until they gleamed, mopping the floors, scouring the bathtub. Hamlin's own fastidiousness came in handy one day when the police raided the restaurant and found not a scrap of paper to incriminate her.

By the time the numbers operation closed, Linda Hamlin had sold the restaurant and saved enough to relocate to a home in Steubenville, Ohio, where she could stretch her money. She left Mitchell and Robert, now in high school, the keys to an apartment of their own in the Stapleton projects so they could finish school in Staten Island. But after Hamlin's departure, the two Diggs brothers had other things on their mind. For Mitchell, it was money. For Robert, it was music.

Mitchell's first hustle was harmless enough—hawking newspapers to commuters on the Verrazano-Narrows Bridge with his friends, Oliver "Pook" Grant and Corey "Shallah" Woods. Mitchell could pull down a few hundred dollars a day this way. But the streets surrounding the Stapleton and Park Hill projects offered a more lucrative trade. Pook jumped into drugs just as the crack wave hit Staten Island, and brought Mitchell into his organization. Mitchell used a new, legit job working a food stand at the base of the Statue of Liberty to provide some cover for his earnings, allowing him to open up a bank account and get a credit card.

Some of his income went toward buying music-making equipment— turntables, keyboards, samplers—for his younger brother Robert, who had formed a group with cousins Russell Jones and Gary Grice called All in Together. Robert dabbled in the drug trade, too, living between the polarities of thuggery and spirituality: going to park jams and house parties and ending up in fistfights; taking in kung fu movies on 42nd Street with cousin Russell Jones; absorbing the lessons of the Five Percenters, the followers of a Black Musilm offshoot called the Nation of Gods and Earths.

The Five Percent "Supreme Mathematics" promised power deriving from knowledge of self. The Diggses' tight-knit circle of family and friends conferred new names upon one another, sometimes trading them back and forth. Robert became "Rakeem." Mitchell became "Divine." Jones became "Ason Unique." Grice became "Justice." Rakeem gave Oliver "Pook" Grant the mononym "Power." Rakeem and his comrades built their own code, their own ethics, their own language, and their own lore.

Mitchell Diggs's unconventional, ungoverned lifestyle came to an end when, at the age of nineteen, he was caught by narcotics officers with thousands of dollars in marked bills. Diggs was convicted of conspiracy, and faced between eight and twenty-four years in prison. Then he got lucky. A judge gave him one year in a mild rehabilitation program.

A few years later, as his rap career got started, Mitchell's brother Robert would also come close to falling into the abyss of the criminal justice system.

Prince Rakeem's first record, "Ooh I Love You Rakeem," was marketed in the typical way that Tommy Boy Music handled new artists' projects. *Commit only to a single. Put some money into a relatively inexpensive video. See how it does. If it pops, pick up the album option. If it doesn't, consider dropping the artist.*

Monica Lynch liked Prince Rakeem. After his first single tanked, she wanted to hear something that made her believe a second release would be worth the investment. But after Rakeem dropped off the charts, he dropped out of sight. She heard that he was somewhere in Ohio. She didn't know why.

The truth was that, after the long buildup and quick evaporation of his record, Robert Diggs was desperate. Broke and angry, he began dealing drugs and plotting petty capers. But Diggs was a small-time player in a game with established contenders. Faced with too much competition in New York, Diggs and a friend, Dennis Coles, decided that they would set up shop instead in Linda Hamlin's adopted hometown of Steubenville, Ohio. For a time, Diggs made money. But then he got into a shoot-out after being ambushed by a local crew. One of the bullets from his gun ripped into the leg of a kid named Willie Walters. Diggs ended up in jail, charged with felonious assault and attempted murder. At the trial in the spring of 1991, Diggs faced a prosecutor named Chris Becker who sought to put Diggs in prison for eight years. Only Diggs's frank testimony saved him from that fate. The jury acquitted Diggs, as Linda Hamlin watched from the gallery.

"This is your second chance," she told her son.

Back on Staten Island, Robert "Rakeem" Diggs returned to his Five Percent lessons, and gathered himself in the way of the mystic martial artists he idolized. Every day, Rakeem walked the island—past the projects and the Victorian houses, past the bridges and ferries and the great green lady in the harbor, the Mother of Exiles lifting her golden lantern to the sky.

With each step his new vision slowly emerged: Rakeem would become the Father of Exiles. He conceived of a fellowship of MCs, the "tempest-tost" from across the boroughs, the wretched refuse of the recording industry. It would be him and "The Genius"—his cousin Gary Grice; from Brooklyn, their other cousin Russell "Ason Unique" Jones; from Stapleton, his partner in crime Dennis Coles; from Park Hill, Rakeem's young sidekick Clifford "Shaquan" Smith, whom Rakeem dubbed "Method Man" for the amount of weed or "meth" he smoked; Divine and Power's running buddy Corey "Raekwon" Woods; Jason "Inspectah Deck" Hunter; and Lamont "U-God" Hawkins.

He had been making music with these guys for fun. Now it was time to get serious.

Unifying this disparate group of Staten Island guys wouldn't be easy. Stapleton and Park Hill, after all, were bitter rivals. Coles had once shot up the house of Divine's friend Oliver "Power" Grant. But Rakeem and Divine had floated between these two worlds since they were kids, and their various homes and apartments had always been places where their far-flung friends could congregate over their mutual love of hip-hop and kung fu flicks like *Five Deadly Venoms* and *The 36th Chamber of Shaolin*. Coles had even lifted his MC name, "Ghostface Killah," from the villain of a 1979 movie called *The Mystery of Chess Boxing*. Rakeem's friends obsessed in particular over a school of unbeatable Chinese swordsmen from the temples and monasteries of Wudang Mountain, as portrayed in the movie *Shaolin and Wu-Tang*. Coles had taken to using the term "Wu-Tang" as an adjective: "That's *Wu-Tang*"—meaning unbeatable, fly, the hardest shit. Rakeem and his friends had been calling themselves "Wu-Tang" for years. He even used the term to name one of the remixes on his Tommy Boy 12-inch.

Rakeem realized that his crew already had a name and a unifying mythology. Stapleton and Park Hill were nothing more than the Shaolin monks and the Wu-Tang swordsmen, uniting to fight their oppressors, the Manchu of the record business. Henceforth, Rakeem referred to his borough as "Shaolin," and his crew as the "Wu-Tang Clan."

Rakeem approached Monica Lynch and her staff at Tommy Boy about his new concept. At first, it seemed to Rakeem like they were interested. Tommy Boy had even run an advertisement on the back page of *The Source* listing the Wu-Tang Clan as part of their roster. But the prospect of funding a full album from a supergroup of nobodies dissuaded Tommy Boy from exercising its option, and the label informed Rakeem that their relationship was over.

The songs that Rakeem recorded in the studio of the house he now shared with Divine on 298 Morningstar Road were nothing like the safe, corny rap he recited for his former label. "Rugged and Raw" was more than simply the name of a track he had done with cousin Russell Jones, who now rapped under the MC name of "Ol' Dirty Bastard." It was now an ethos, lyrically and musically. Rakeem and "Ghostface Killah" Coles recorded a mournful tale of watching family and friends die from violence and disease called "After the Laughter Comes Tears." Rakeem's musical backing was pasted from grainy, low-resolution samples that added to the "dirty" feel of the song.

Monica Lynch had been right about one thing: It was incredibly difficult to maintain a rap group with eight MCs, much less get them all on the same song. But Rakeem had grown up in Miss Linda's house. He was used to having a big family. Rakeem managed to squeeze them all into the four minutes and thirty-four seconds of "Protect Ya Neck," a breakneck showcase of each rapper's skills and personality: Inspectah Deck's precision, Raekwon and Ghostface Killah's slang, Rakeem's righteous anger, Method Man's creativity, and Ol' Dirty Bastard's insanity. And at the end of the song, The Genius let loose a verse of vengeance against the hip-hop business in general and his former label in particular. "For example, who's your A&R? / A mountain climber who plays an electric guitar?"—"mountain climber," he said, as in "White guy." "But he don't know the meaning of dope when he's lookin for a suit-and-tie rap that's cleaner than a bar of soap."

Rakeem and The Genius had returned from the record business to the grime from which they came and emerged purified, with new names to commemorate their resurrection: "the RZA" and "the GZA."

The RZA convinced his comrades to sign with his company, Wu-Tang Productions.

"Give me five years," he told them, "and I will take us to the top."

In reality, the RZA knew little about the record business. He took up another collection from Divine, Power, and Ghostface to press up an initial run of ten thousand 12-inch singles at Disc Makers in South Jersey and some more to finance a low-budget video. The Diggses' cousin John "Mook" Gibbons and Oliver "Power" Grant did their best to get the record into stores around New York like Rock and Soul and Beat Street while Divine kept track of billing, sales, and collections. Divine worked with lawyer Bill Warren to incorporate their company and draw up contracts for each of the MCs.

The 12-inch single for Wu-Tang Clan's "Protect Ya Neck" might have gone the way of so many other self-produced singles in rap history had it not been for the favors of a few sympathetic young supporters with jobs inside the industry.

RZA gave his record to another Staten Island MC named Schott Lee Jacobs, who rhymed with a group called Legion of Doom. Jacobs, in turn, was friendly with Matteo Capoluongo—Matty C, who ran the news section of *The Source* and wrote "Unsigned Hype"—the monthly column reviewing the demo tapes of unsigned rappers that had developed a remarkable track record. Many of the groups that Capoluongo featured had landed record deals: the Poetical Prophets were signed to Island as "Mobb Deep." A Chicago rapper called Common Sense secured a contract with Relativity Records. An East Bay MC named Saafir got plucked by Quincy Jones's label, Qwest. A mention in "Unsigned Hype" could be a life-changing event for an aspiring rap group.

Capoluongo featured Jacobs's group in his column, and Legion of Doom received an offer from a Philadelphia label called Ruffhouse. When the deal didn't pan out, Jacobs decided to pursue an industry job, and remained in touch with Matty C.

The day that Jacobs arrived with a pressing of "Protect Ya Neck," Capoluongo snapped into his reflexive role as advocate of the underdog artist. Since the Wu-Tang Clan already had a record out, they didn't quite qualify as "unsigned." Capoluongo gave the single to *Source* staffer Reggie Dennis, who had started his own section called "The Singles File," and he gave Wu-Tang an enthusiastic mention.

Meanwhile, another Staten Island native used his inside position to help his homies in the Wu crew. Michael McDonald worked for Bill Stephney's promotion company, located in the offices of Stephney's Tommy Boy–distributed label, Stepsun. But back on Staten Island, McDonald was known by another name—LASK, an infamous graffiti artist well-known to the borough's hip-hop community, RZA included.

It had been McDonald who guided Mook and Power to local record stores. McDonald knew how to promote records nationally, as well. He had the mailing lists of DJs and retailers at his fingertips but didn't want to risk mailing the Wu-Tang Clan's records from Stepsun. He called Sincere Thompson, a sympathetic friend at the major label Polygram, where a spike in postage expenses wouldn't be noticed. One evening, McDonald, RZA, and a few other Clan members joined Thompson at Polygram, slipping the Wu-Tang's 12-inch into a mailing for one of Thompson's artists. Schott Jacobs, who had taken a job with another small label, did the same. The Wu single hit the mailboxes of important DJs, retailers, and tastemakers across the country. Between the efforts of McDonald, Thompson, Jacobs, and Capoluongo, DJs from coast-to-coast—including Funkmaster Flex at Hot 97 in New York and the Baka Boyz at Power 106 in L.A.—began banging the Wu-Tang Clan on their mix shows.

By that time, the executive board of Wu-Tang Productions—RZA, Divine, Power and Ghostface—decided the job of distributing their record and capitalizing on the growing interest was simply too big for them. The industry buzz on Wu-Tang was growing, and representatives from record companies were calling. But how could they make another deal with the devil without getting burned?

RZA shared his idea with Matty Capoluongo on a visit to the offices of *The Source*: He would sign the Wu-Tang Clan not to one label, but all of them. In other words, any contract that the Clan made with a record company would have to give him the freedom to sign each individual member of the group to another label of his own choosing.

Capoluongo listened to RZA as they sat in the fire stairwell near *The Source*'s suite on 594 Broadway with Wu-Tang members Method Man and Raekwon. Capoluongo didn't know too much about the music business either, but he did know that he had never heard of a record company agreeing to the kind of contractual arrangement that RZA sought.

Indeed, when record companies conscripted acts with multiple members, each member of the group had to sign the contract to make it legal. In that contract, each player was subject to a "leaving member" clause—meaning that if he left the group, or wanted to release a solo album, he would still be under contract to the company for any recordings he wished to make—much like the arrangement Priority Records had with Ice Cube as a leaving member of NWA. The "leaving member" would be bound by the terms of the contract he originally signed as a part of the group, a contract that often set much less favorable terms for members as solo artists.

Capoluongo told RZA that he had a hard time conceiving that any record label that spent money promoting the nine members of the Wu-Tang Clan would willingly forfeit the rights to exploit the members' solo careers.

As it turned out, record labels were more interested in picking up individual members of the group than the Clan as a whole. RZA told Capoluongo about the offers he had already received. Because of the "Protect Ya Neck" video, Russell Simmons and Lyor Cohen of Def Jam had determined that Method Man was the star of the group, and offered RZA $180,000 for Meth's services. Dante Ross at Elektra had made a similarly priced offer for another member who more suited his edgier taste, Ol' Dirty Bastard.

In fact, the only company that had made an enthusiastic offer for the entire group—and seemed desperate enough to agree to RZA's terms—was a small label distributed by RCA called Loud Records.

As a hip-hop fan and *Source* critic, Matty C had already dismissed the few artists on Loud's roster. He was even less impressed by the person who ran the company, a hustling, marble-mouthed record promoter named Steve Rifkind. Capoluongo had met him a few years back when Rifkind came into *The Source*, hawking a tame West Coast rapper for Disney's Hollywood Records.

Matty raised an eyebrow at the mention of Rifkind.

"You're talking about this long-haired blond dude, coming in here with Jheri-curled Hi-C? *That's* who you want to fuck with?"

Capoluongo was emphatic. The Wu-Tang Clan—raw and uncut—were the epitome of hip-hop purity. Rifkind, on the other hand, seemed dirty. Wasn't he just another hip-hop dick rider, promoting any artist for as long as the pay was right?

In a national scene overrun by West Coast gangsta rap, people were already calling Wu-Tang the saviors of East Coast hip-hop. Capoluongo couldn't see them partnering with the California-based Rifkind. It didn't seem like a good fit at all.

In reality, Steve Rifkind and the Wu-Tang Clan were a perfect match. Both the young Jewish music entrepreneur from Long Island and the young Black posse from Staten Island shared an important common ethos: Business was about keeping it in the family.

The Rifkinds' run in the entertainment business began in the mid-twentieth century with a young boxer from Brooklyn named Harry Rifkind. "One Punch Harry" got his nickname for a simple reason: He hit you once, and that was it. Outside the ring, Harry Rifkind was a straight kind of fellow, a mensch who didn't gamble or drink. Tough guys loved him. After Harry Rifkind hung up his gloves, music impresario and Genovese ally Morris Levy took Harry under his wing, eventually hiring him to manage nightclubs like the Roundtable in Manhattan and the Boulevard in Brooklyn.

Harry Rifkind had two sons—Jules and Roy. When Jules was a prelaw college student fresh from a stint in the army, Harry helped him procure the entertainment for a student ball. Jules made a terrific profit by spending only a fraction of the budget he was given.

Fuck becoming a lawyer, Jules Rifkind thought. *This is a great fucking business.*

Jules Rifkind's big break came after a chance meeting with New York's top Black DJ. In the mid-1950s, Tommy "Dr. Jive" Smalls broadcasted from

WWRL with the likes of Jocko Henderson. Smalls asked Rifkind to help him build a new artist management company, and the partners quickly assembled one of the best rosters of Black performers in the country: the Shirelles. Tommy Hunt. Flip Wilson. At Smalls's Midtown Manhattan office, the twenty-two-year-old Rifkind opened dozens of white envelopes from record companies, in which he found not only the latest 45 rpm singles, but thousands of dollars in cash, of which Smalls gave Rifkind a cut.

What a fucking business this is, Rifkind concluded.

Rifkind and Smalls's partnership ended after Smalls and Alan Freed were caught and convicted of payola. It was a common practice in American radio, yet the main targets of the government's wrath just happened to be the top two DJs purveying Black music to White youth. Jules Rikfind thus became an accidental revolutionary: He launched one of the first interracial partnerships in the music business with Tommy Smalls. As he rose in the industry—first as head of promotion at MGM Records, next as general manager of Bang Records, then at ABC Records—he hired Black executives. Rifkind's fluency with R&B and the respect for him among Black musicians yielded benefits: Spring Records, the venture that he and his brother Roy launched with Polygram; his strong relationship with James Brown; his friendship with Frankie Crocker; and ultimately, the landmark Fatback Band record that first brought the sound of the MC to commercial radio.

Jules Rifkind and his wife, Eleanor, had three sons—Steven, Robert, and Jonathan—settling down in a predominantly Jewish neighborhood in Merrick, Long Island. But their home life was always filled with Black music, whether it was Millie Jackson cursing up a storm on the living room turntable, Frankie Crocker bearing gifts at Steve's bar mitzvah, or the Fatback Band playing at Jon's five years later.

Rifkind's eldest son had no intention of following in his father's footsteps. At Kennedy High School, Steven struggled with a learning disability and with his temper as well; he was expelled for a time after getting into a fight with the principal. Steven described his two interests in his father's blunt manner: *basketball and pussy*. The long-haired, five-foot-eleven point guard for the varsity team had dreams of playing for UCLA. When he couldn't get a ball scholarship, Steve spent some time at Hofstra University, and then forgot about college altogether. Upon Steve's graduation in 1980, Jules got his son an internship in the promotion department of an independent label, A&M Records. It was an unwitting homecoming for Steve: As an infant, he had been carried by his parents to California, where Jules helped the label's founders, Herb Alpert and Jerry Moss, score their first hit with "The Lonely Bull."

Steve Rifkind was so good promoting records for A&M that his boss, Charlie Minor, offered him the label's regional promo job in Detroit. Steve turned the offer down. By this time, he was helping his father and Uncle Roy at Spring Records, and had picked up a client of his own, promoting a record called "Smerphies Dance" by the rapper Spyder D, for a tiny label called Telestar. Rifkind was only nineteen years old, but he got the record played on New York's number one radio station, WBLS. Rifkind had an inside track: The station's program director, Frankie Crocker, was practically family.

Steve Rifkind and Crocker had a weekly ritual. Every Thursday, Rifkind would bring Crocker a box of Popeyes fried chicken, and Crocker would play Rifkind's records—taking care to announce Steven as the promoter. In the summer of 1982, Rifkind quickly amassed a client roster of over a dozen records a week, at $300 per record per week, raking in tens of thousands of dollars because of Crocker's public endorsement.

Jules Rifkind worried that Spring's records weren't enough of a priority for his son. By the summer of 1986, the friction with his father, a gig co-managing R&B boy band New Edition, and a beautiful woman led Steve Rifkind out of Spring's offices, out from under his father's wing, and all the way to Southern California.

Rifkind started hustling up promotion work for himself in Los Angeles. Flipping through the pages of *Billboard,* he spied a review of an album by Mellow Man Ace, a rapper who happened to be on a local independent hip-hop label he'd never heard of called Delicious Vinyl.

Mike Ross was sitting in his office on Melrose and Gardner when Steve Rifkind walked in off the street and introduced himself. Ross found Rifkind instantly entertaining. The record promoter carried himself like a mob boss as he spun tales of his industry pedigree in his mumbly New York accent.

"I can help you guys," Rifkind claimed. "Are you calling retail?"

"Calling retail?" Ross replied. "What do you mean?"

Rifkind sat with Ross and explained why Delicious Vinyl needed his services. *Billboard* compiled its weekly charts from reports filed by a select number of retailers. Rifkind knew who those retailers were. He had relationships with them. And he'd call them every week, making sure they had whatever they needed to ensure that Delicious Vinyl's records would be well ranked. Ross cut Rifkind a barter deal: retail promotion for free office space.

Rifkind, with his experience promoting records to Black radio, helped Delicious Vinyl get to a few key "Urban" stations as well. And when Rifkind's friend Rick Krim was named vice president of talent and artist relations for MTV, Rikfind added video promotion to his repertoire; he was instrumental in getting Tone-Loc's "Wild Thing" and Young MC's "Bust a Move" videos added to MTV.

Retail, radio, and video—Steve Rifkind had command of the three main avenues of promotion in the record business. Rifkind offered these services to small labels like Delicious Vinyl, labels that couldn't afford their own promotion staff. Some rap labels, however, had adopted a fourth promotional path, created out of necessity when traditional routes remained closed to them. Radio and record stores weren't the only way people heard new music, after all. Steve Rifkind became more familiar with this "fourth way" when he partnered with the three Los Angeles–based promoters who honed their alternative promotion hustle working records for Macola.

Doug Young, with his partners Lionel Ridenour and Jeff House, had developed an exhaustive daily routine. His Suzuki Samurai loaded with product, Young began his mornings in Palm Springs, a hundred miles from Los Angeles. From there, he would work his way toward the city along the 10 or the 60 freeway corridors—stopping not only at record stores, but barbershops, bars, nightclubs, gang hangouts, and hot street corners along the way. Young paid special attention to the swap meets at Crenshaw, Roadium, and Slauson—completely off of the major labels' radar but so important to the spread of rap music. After he finally hit the beach, Young doubled back and hit the cruiser spots along Hollywood, Crenshaw, and Whittier, throwing the latest cassettes into the cars with big sound systems. All the while, his partners Ridenour and House helped Young cover more territory.

Rifkind and his young assistant Fabian "Fade" Duvernay joined forces with Ridenour and House, sharing clients and splitting work. While Rifkind and Duvernay worked the phones, the promoters rode the freeways and walked the streets. The effectiveness of this "street promotion" became manifest to executives at Capitol Records after Young, Ridenour, and House worked some of their first rap records for them. In 1989, Capitol offered to formalize the relationship with the three promoters, asking them to help them form a "street awareness team." A few other labels like Def Jam were using their own nascent networks of "street promoters" in cities across the country, usually young rap DJs at college stations who distributed flyers, promotional cassettes, and stickers in exchange for coveted label logo swag like T-shirts and jackets.

For Steve Rifkind, the whole concept reminded him of what his father used to do at Spring Records. Jules Rifkind pioneered the idea of hiring professional basketball players—who really had nothing to do in those days when they traveled but sit in their hotel rooms—to carry records to cities far and wide. Jules put a few of the New York Knickerbockers on his payroll, including Earl "the Pearl" Monroe. To Steve, deputizing college students and hustling scenesters in locales across the country didn't seem like a strange concept at all.

Soon, Steve Rifkind started to cobble together his own national network of young rap fanatics; he was, perhaps, the first independent record promoter to do so. Rifkind sensed an opening: He could sell his ready-made team's services to small rap labels on a record-by-record basis, or on a retainer. But the biggest opportunity lay in major labels—some of which had signed rap artists and brought on rap A&R people but had zero hip-hop promotion expertise to protect their investment.

In the spring of 1990, Rifkind booked a flight to spend Passover at his parents' house on Long Island, intending to use his trip back home to drum up some business with the New York–based labels for his new promotion company. With $3,000 of his $15,000 in savings, Rifkind printed up color brochures for his business—called SRC, for Steven Rifkind Company—detailing his services in national video promotion, college, and mix-show radio, retail promotion, and how all of these services would be augmented by his local "street teams." Rifkind booked appointments with a number of promotion executives at major and independent labels. Suffering from a painful sinus infection and fresh off a flight that had only made it worse, Rifkind made his rounds. One by one, he got records from labels like Jive, Chrysalis, RCA, and Elektra—where Jules had secured a promotion internship for Steve's little brother Jonathan. By the time he boarded the plane for his return trip to Los Angeles a week later, Rifkind had turned his $3,000 investment into $150,000 in billing.

Delicious Vinyl had moved to new digs on Sunset Boulevard, and Rifkind took over their Melrose offices. Young, Ridenour, and House had been replaced by a rotating crop of young promoters, including a young club DJ named Paul Stewart. Rifkind chain-smoked and jawed on the phone from the time businesses on the East Coast opened until long after the sun had set on the West Coast. Soon, he landed his biggest client yet—a new label called Interscope Records, which offered SRC a monthly retainer of $15,000 to promote pop rap acts like Gerardo and Marky Mark, and an edgier artist named Tupac Shakur.

A booking agent friend, Jerry Ade, marveled at Rifkind's roster of clients.

"If you are working all these records," Ade remarked, "you should have your own label."

Jules Rifkind's lawyer, Paul Marshall, had his hooks into a new multimillion-dollar venture with RCA being headed by Island Records' former head of promotion, Lou Maglia. Maglia gave a small production deal to Steve Rifkind, who began using his promotion company's "street team" to find talent. His first signing was a lightning-fast rapper from Chicago named Tung Twista—clocked at 11.2 syllables per second by the *Guinness Book of World Records*, a marketing ploy engineered in part by Rifkind himself.

With two companies to manage, Steve Rifkind needed help. He turned to a childhood friend from Merrick. Rich Isaacson had gone to high school with Steve and ran through Studio 54 with him during Rifkind's days as a member of Frankie Crocker's entourage. Isaacson was now a junior associate at a corporate law firm in Manhattan and hating every minute of it. Isaacson took a job at half his current salary just to get in on Steve's showbiz life, trading fourteen-hour days spent cooped up in a fluorescent-lit high-rise for an office with a sunny terrace that overlooked trendy Melrose Avenue.

Just as Isaacson settled into his new job and a room at Steve's duplex in the Valley, Interscope canceled SRC's lucrative monthly retainer. Suddenly, the laid-back routine that Isaacson expected became a tense, daily grind to drum up more work. Every morning, the two of them left the house at seven a.m., stopped for coffee, and made it to the office by eight—an unheard-of arrival time for most music-industry types on the West Coast, but essential for Rifkind's East Coast contacts. They would work until the sun fell, and before they left the office, Rifkind would diligently make his call list for the next day.

While Rifkind concentrated on business development, Isaacson took charge of the street team. Creating a reliable field staff out of teenagers and twenty-somethings with little or no professional experience seemed a daunting prospect, especially when so many members of the team also worked for other label clients. Isaacson solved part of the problem by putting his far-flung street promoters on a monthly retainer of $100 to $200 a week. The modest but steady pay gave SRC an instant advantage over record labels that usually paid the promoters on a project-by-project basis; and it gave Isaacson both credibility with his team and the right to bust their balls if need be, especially if they didn't turn in the weekly reports that Issacson demanded every Tuesday. Isaacson checked up on his team, too. If, say, his San Francisco guy reported that he went to T's Wauzi Records that week, Issacson called the store to make sure. Gradually, Isaacson winnowed out the deadbeats, and doubled down on the people who turned out to be professionals, like a hip-hop-loving Indian-Swedish-American social work student named Ranadeb "Jellow" Choudhury in Chicago, and a rap-obsessed Korean graduate of Georgetown University in Washington, D.C., named Duk-Ki Yu. Isaacson could never truly know, of course, what guys thousands of miles away were doing with their time. But he created a system to minimize the amount they could bullshit him. If these guys were going to fuck someone over, he'd be fucked the last, and the least.

Up the chain, Issacson served his label clients—who paid SRC an average of $15,000 for the life of a given single—with regular, reliable progress reports. If Isaacson could keep at least four clients at any one time, the business could make money.

Of all the labels they served, SRC's committed street team benefited one in particular: Steve Rifkind's Loud Records. But by the time Rifkind and Issacson worked the Tung Twista album up to the 50,000-unit threshold that would trigger a disbursement of marketing money from Zoo Records, Lou Maglia's label had run out of money, and Loud Records was out of a deal.

The day after they got the bad news, the two partners flew to Atlanta to attend the Jack the Rapper convention. Rifkind threw a tantrum in the offices of Joel Katz, a high-powered music attorney based in the Southern city.

"Fuck Lou Maglia! He lied to me!" Rifkind ranted, punching the wall. "I'm going to smack the shit out of him!"

Isaacson was freaking out, albeit more quietly. He had given up a career in law for a job that now seemed to be a dead end.

Rifkind and Isaacson were saved by the power of family. Katz happened to be Jules Rifkind's attorney. Jules and Eleanor Rifkind happened to be in town to visit Steve's little brother Jon, who happened to work in Atlanta as a regional promoter for Elektra. Jules and Jon happened to be in another part of Joel Katz's office at that very moment, unbeknownst to Steve, selling the idea of Loud Records to Ron Urban, who happened to be the senior vice president of operations for Zoo's parent, RCA Records. RCA happened to be notoriously weak in Black music and had next to no presence in hip-hop.

Ron Urban met with Steve Rikfind that night, and Rifkind walked away with a better production deal than he had before.

In early 1993, the new Loud/RCA venture released two records, one by an L.A.-based rap group called Madkap and another from a rapper/singer named HanSoul. Neither caught fire. But in the summer, Loud scored its first true hit with a group called Tha Alkaholiks, whose song "Make Room" was broken by the Baka Boyz on Power 106 in Los Angeles. Although the song never made it beyond the West Coast, suddenly Loud was moving hundreds of thousands of rap records through RCA's distribution channels. RCA president Joe Galante called Rifkind and Isaacson to arrange a lunch date.

Loud Records' roster didn't have currency in New York, still the largest market for rap music in the country. As a start, Rifkind and Isaacson decided to create a beachhead there, renting an apartment in Manhattan for themselves for their monthly visits to RCA headquarters and taking a small office there.

It was around this time that Steve Rifkind's A&R kid, Trevor Williams, handed Rifkind the first Wu-Tang Clan single. Williams had gotten the 12 inch from a DJ in Lansing, Michigan, named Jason Staten. Staten had been introduced to RZA by Sincere Thompson, and he promoted the Wu-Tang Clan to Midwest radio and sent the single to all the record executives he knew. After a few listens and repeated urgings from Staten and Williams, Rifkind recognized the sound of credibility for his fledgling label.

Getting in touch with the group's leader, the RZA, was a challenge. The number listed on the label of the Wu-Tang 12-inch didn't have an answering machine, and RZA was never there. He didn't have a cell phone either. Back in New York for his thirty-first birthday, Rifkind worked out of his office at RCA. The RZA eventually showed up with at least a half dozen other members and associates of the Wu-Tang Clan, all crowded into Rifkind's tiny room. As Rifkind played the 12-inch on his stereo, the door to the office flew open. Some kid Rifkind had never seen before—maybe he worked in the mailroom—poked his head in.

"That's that shit!" he shouted. Then the kid was gone.

Rifkind wanted more than anything to conquer New York. The kid had just told him that signing the Wu-Tang Clan was the right way to do it.

Rifkind didn't care too much that RZA insisted on reserving the rights to his members' solo deals. Ol' Dirty Bastard was already gone—signed by Dante Ross to Elektra with the caveat that the rapper could record for the

Wu-Tang Clan, wherever the group landed. But getting RCA to agree to such an unorthodox arrangement was difficult for Rifkind and Isaacson. Joe Galante and the rest of the White male executives at RCA derided the "Chinese rap group." Perhaps because none of the brass believed that this "Wu-Tang Clan" would ever sell more than a handful of records, RCA agreed to Rikind's proposed compromise: waiving the sacrosanct leaving-member clause of RCA's standard contract provided that Loud Records have the right to match any solo offer made by another record label. In return, the RZA agreed to a relatively small advance of $60,000 for the single and album.

The first test of the Wu-Tang Clan's new contract came even before RCA's legal department had finished preparing it. Def Jam had offered $180,000 for Method Man. This kind of money was way beyond what Rifkind had the right to extend under Loud's production deal, and he implored business affairs at RCA to make an exception to let him match Def Jam's offer. RCA refused.

By the time the Wu-Tang/Loud deal was done, Rifkind had lost the rights to the solo careers of what many people regarded as the best two MCs in the group. In return, however, he gained the hottest rap single in New York—rereleased on Loud with a new B-side called "Method Man," which shot to the top of Hot 97's weekly playlist—and the rights to the most anticipated rap album in the country.

But the winner of the Wu-Tang feeding frenzy wasn't Loud, nor Def Jam, nor Elektra, nor any label. The real victors were the members of Wu-Tang, and RZA as their producer in particular. Wu-Tang not only kept the right to determine the destinies of its members individually, but—fatefully—they also retained their *brand*: their name, their merchandising, and their publishing. Never before had hip-hop artists negotiated the kind of autonomy that RZA did. Never had record companies been played so deftly against one another, not just to the Wu-Tang Clan's benefit but to their own. Whenever Hot 97 played Loud's "Method Man" record, they advertised a Def Jam artist. It was in Def Jam's interest, and Elektra's, too, that Loud's Wu-Tang project succeed; both majors had, in fact, invested more money than Loud. And, eventually, when Def Jam and Elektra released their Wu solo artists, it would be in Loud's interest that they succeed as well. No matter who promoted what, they were all promoting the Wu-Tang Clan. The situation was so wonderfully balanced, so Eastern in its deflection of opposing forces into a greater, peaceable union, that it could well have been the plot from one of the martial arts movies that gave RZA his inspiration or from the *Tao Te Ching* itself.

At the end of 1993, the Wu-Tang Clan's first album, *Enter the Wu-Tang (36 Chambers)*, was released on Loud/RCA. By early 1994, it had been certified gold, Loud's biggest record ever. By May, it had shipped over a million copies and went platinum.

In the wake of the Wu-Tang Clan's success, the solo rights of the Wu's members were quickly bought up. GZA, who had once toiled in obscurity for Cold Chillin'/Warner Bros., picked up a much richer contract from Geffen. RZA signed to Island Records, and participated in still another collective of MCs on the label, called the Gravediggaz. Ghostface Killah signed to Sony. Before long, RZA's crazy vision for his cast of castaways became reality: Every major label except one—Capitol/EMI—now had some stake in the Wu-Tang Clan's success.

The Wu-Tang Clan became the first hip-hop group to reverse the relationship between record companies and artists. The members of the Wu weren't branded like property with label logos. Quite the opposite: The labels themselves sought out the mark of the "W." The Wu-Tang logo, like the "rough, rugged, and raw" production style of the RZA, became a valuable emblem of authenticity, worth millions of dollars to any company that bought into the Wu franchise.

Wu-Tang represented authenticity on a musical level. Steve Rifkind's street teams offered that same authenticity on a promotional level. Hip-hop's sense of cool didn't descend from above, like some consumer product concept created in a corporate lab, blasted out by television commercials. It bubbled up from below, via word of mouth, cassette tapes, CDs, and vinyl passed from hand to hand, and on flyers and stickers left behind in trusted venues like bars and barbershops. Rifkind's SRC sold that street conduit and street credibility to its corporate-label clients.

In so doing, both the RZA and Steve Rifkind began to show corporate America how to hustle, the hip-hop way.

In the summer of 1993, the Wu-Tang Clan was featured in a new magazine dedicated to hip-hop culture. The publication was created not by fervent fans of the music, but by one of the largest publishers in the world, Time, Inc.—now a division of Time Warner.

The debut marked the first time that an American corporation had attempted to create its own hip-hop brand from scratch. The problem with creating a credible magazine, however, was that no one in the company knew anything about hip-hop.

Gerald Levin didn't. The Time Warner CEO had inherited the Quincy Jones–led project from his former boss, the late Steve Ross.

Robin Wolaner didn't. The self-proclaimed "tone-deaf" chief of new magazine development knew little about pop music, much less rap. But she did know how to start magazines. She founded the hugely successful title *Parenting* in 1986, and launched *Martha Stewart Living*.

Gil Rogin didn't. As editor of *Sports Illustrated*, Rogin had invented the swimsuit issue. Now, as one of the top executives in the building, the sixty-two-year-old Rogin had license to say just about anything that came to his mind.

"What the fuck are we gonna do?" Rogin asked Greg Sandow, the music editor of *Entertainment Weekly*. "We have a deal with Quincy Jones that says he can do anything he wants. And he wants to start a *rap* magazine." Sandow offered some help and advice, but was stunned during a meeting with Time, Inc., executives when one of them asked directly, "Do we really have to put Black people on the cover?"

Even Quincy Jones didn't know hip-hop that well. The legendary record producer had himself created some of the musical foundation for the culture. But Jones was a newcomer to rap music, just beginning to familiarize himself with the canon, collaborating with rap artists for the first time for his album, *Back on the Block*.

In fact, the only hip-hop expert on the development team for Time Warner's magazine was Russell Simmons. But Simmons' role on the team was nebulous. Jones had offered Simmons a cut of his 25 percent stake in the magazine in return for Simmons' advice and unimpeachable imprimatur. They had signed a MOU, or memorandum of understanding, but a formal agreement had yet to be finalized. And their visions weren't quite aligned. Simmons had championed the acquisition of *The Source* and brought the owners to the table. Jones ultimately wasn't interested in trying to reshape someone else's property. Now that Jones had decided to do his own title, Simmons remained emphatic about his creative convictions.

But no one on the project besides Quincy Jones knew or cared who Simmons was. Gil Rogin didn't understand why they needed Simmons in the first place, and he had little idea of the vast difference between Jones's and Simmons's cultural specialties. Robin Wolaner detested Simmons, whom she considered a boor. But he was Quincy's guy, so her favorite candidate for editor in chief had to pass muster with him.

Twenty-seven-year-old Jonathan Van Meter, a gifted feature writer and assistant editor at *Vogue,* had been referred to Wolaner by a cultural editor at *The New York Times* named Adam Moss, who had been Van Meter's mentor at another magazine.

"He's gay and he's White," Moss described. "But in his heart, he's a fourteen-year-old Black girl."

Rogin, too, had heard about Van Meter—praised by Monica Lynch, the president of Tommy Boy Music, and by Jane Pratt, the young founder of *Sassy* magazine, who consulted on the project for a time.

Rogin called the young prospect in for a meeting. Van Meter was miserable at *Vogue.* He realized the immensity of the opportunity before him, and said all the right things. He had been wanting to create a magazine about dance music and pop culture, and the places where Black and White tastes intersected. He knew what the magazine would look like. He was close with all the young Black writers who worked at every magazine in New York— there were only one or two at each publication—so Van Meter told Rogin that he knew whom to hire. Van Meter echoed something that Sandow told Rogin: Remaking *The Source* would be a mistake. *Too male, too musically narrow.* Think of the new project not as a rap magazine, but as an urban youth culture journal—one that would embrace rap and R&B, males and females, Black and White.

Van Meter's first meeting with Russell Simmons, however, did not go well. Simmons didn't know who Van Meter was, nor why Time, Inc., picked him.

"I know all about hip-hop and dance music," Van Meter assured Simmons.

Simmons told Van Meter that his statement was ridiculous, like lumping break dancing and ballet together.

Lurking beneath Simmons's rebuke was an implication about the prospective editor himself. Van Meter was gay and White, and Simmons worried how that would be perceived by the Afrocentric and homophobic factions of the hip-hop community. Frankly, Simmons worried about how he *himself* might be perceived being associated with the magazine. But also worrying Simmons was the *cultural sensibility* that might come with Van Meter's race and sexual orientation. With Van Meter's outlook, Simmons believed the magazine would be just another reflection of "downtown" culture—a mélange of multicultural music and fashion with the agenda set by "cool" Whites. Simmons told Van Meter that if he wanted the job, he would have to make sure to recruit people who knew the difference between hip-hop and dance, between uptown and downtown, between Black innovation and White appropriation.

But after Van Meter began assembling a roster of editorial talent for the test issue of the magazine—which now had a name, *Volume*—word trickled to Simmons about Van Meter's new hires, many of them Black and gay. The senior editor, Scott Poulson-Bryant—who had worked for Simmons as an outside publicist for LL Cool J—was someone whom Simmons had long suspected was gay. Simmons simmered: Where on the staff were the people who largely determined the core aesthetic of hip-hop: straight Black men? Simmons's vision, however, was selective. Van Meter had also convened a diverse panel of Black freelance writers whose authenticity couldn't be disputed, like Kevin Powell, Greg Tate, Nelson George, Lisa Jones, Charles Aaron, Michael Gonzales, Tricia Rose, Ben Mapp, Havelock Nelson, Joan Morgan, and Bonz Malone.

Simmons was neither eloquent nor subtle about his opinion of Van Meter.

"He's a faggot!" Simmons shouted at Gil Rogin.

"Yes, he's a faggot," Rogin replied. "But he's *our* faggot."[18]

Simmons's words rolled off Rogin's back. But even when Simmons tempered his language for Robin Wolaner—calling Van Meter "too fancy"—Wolaner was appalled. She told colleagues that she thought Simmons was either a homophobe or a repressed homosexual. The argument broke into the public eye in January 1992, when Simmons discussed Van Meter's sexual and cultural orientation while being interviewed by Frank Owen, a renowned music writer for *Spin* and *Newsday*.

Van Meter allowed Owen to "out" him in his *Newsday* article, but as his sexuality became a matter of industry debate, Van Meter kept his head in the work, and Simmons at bay. No one, least of all Simmons, could seem to understand that he couldn't recruit the best and brightest of hip-hop journalism quite yet, because he was just hiring nine people for a few months to prepare a test issue. Few gainfully employed editors—Black or White—would come work for him without the promise of a permanent job.

As Van Meter began to assemble layouts and distribute the work to the executive team, Simmons became more vocal about the direction of the

---

[18]Through a publicist, Simmons said he "never used that word." Simmons has been quoted in a book about Def Jam's history using the same epithet in an unrelated instance.

magazine. Robin Wolaner arrived at a creative meeting to find that Russell Simmons had brought a friend to critique the content—the editor of another magazine whom Wolaner also despised. For Wolaner and Rogin, Simmons had crossed a sacred line: *One does not give advance looks of editorial content to outsiders.* The incident was their excuse to inform Quincy Jones that Simmons's behavior had become intolerable.

Jones didn't need to be told. He already didn't like that Simmons seemed to be taking credit for the magazine. After Simmons went public with his criticisms of Van Meter, Jones paid an angry phone call to the rap impressario.

"Guitar players don't write *Rolling Stone*," Jones said, "and football players don't write *Sports Illustrated*." It was Jones's way of telling Simmons that he shouldn't expect that a hip-hop magazine would be staffed by people who fit the profile of the average rapper.

"Why don't you just keep your mouth shut?" Jones snapped. After Simmons and Jones argued, Jones told Simmons that he could just "forget about it"—"it" meaning their proposed partnership.

In May 1992, four months before the first test issue was due on newsstands, Russell Simmons made his exit public in a brief press release, stating that he decided to leave *Volume* because it had morphed from a hip-hop magazine into something more diffuse, "a publication for a generation that has been influenced by hip-hop." In conversation, Simmons cited an example of the editorial drift—a sell piece for *Volume* intimating that White pop icons like Madonna and Sandra Bernhard were part of hip-hop culture.[19]

While Van Meter built *Volume*'s editorial under Rogin's counsel, Robin Wolaner hired *Parenting*'s publisher, Carol Smith, to fill the test issue with advertisements. But Smith found resistance to the idea among her sales staff.

"Negroes don't buy cars," said Time, Inc.'s field manager in Detroit.

Smith pressed on, collaborating with Van Meter to produce a gleaming, metal-covered media kit that explained *Volume*'s ethos. Smith's sales spiel was straightforward: *What* Rolling Stone *was to the 1960s,* Vibe *is to the 1990s.*

To Smith's utter delight, she didn't have to fight. Advertisers got it immediately. Levi's jeans came in for full-page ads. So, too, did Nike and Ver-

---

[19]Simmons denies he was ousted, maintaining that he departed of his own accord because he believed that the new magazine would hurt his credibility.

sace, Body Glove and Van Grack. Time Warner companies filled ad space, too. Smith sold fifty-four pages at full price, so quickly, in fact, that she had to close the book early. Though Dave Mays at *The Source* had found it nearly impossible to sell ad space to corporate sponsors, these same advertisers apparently had no problem buying the concept of the hip-hop consumer when it was presented to them by the world's largest media corporation.

All seemed set for *Volume*'s September street date, when word came from Time, Inc.'s legal department that a small British periodical—also called *Volume*—had the rights to use its name in America. Van Meter and his staff had to quickly rename and redesign their magazine.

The new moniker came from Scott Poulson-Bryant, the magazine's senior editor. Since *Volume*'s inception, Poulson-Bryant had been the target of much industry chatter. After Russell Simmons's public rant about gays on the *Volume* staff, Poulson-Bryant—who was not yet "out" as bisexual—avoided both Simmons and the subject. Some Black journalists and media people were asking why Poulson-Bryant wasn't the editor instead of Jonathan Van Meter. Poulson-Bryant, for his part, didn't care what his title was. Of anyone on staff, he knew the most about hip-hop. He would make his mark that way.

Poulson-Bryant had attended the same high school as Public Enemy producer Bill Stephney. He'd gone to Brown University with *The Source* co-owner James Bernard. For the *Village Voice*, he'd written the first major piece about the downtown gay phenomenon that would soon go on to worldwide fame: voguing. He'd become *Spin*'s first dedicated hip-hop columnist. Through it all, Poulson-Bryant envisioned that he'd someday start his own magazine. But instead, he had been recruited by Van Meter and given up his full-time job at *Spin* just to work on the test issue of *Volume*. Now that the magazine needed a new brand, Poulson-Bryant suggested the one he had been saving for his.

"Call it *Vibe*," he told Van Meter.

Hours later, Van Meter called him back.

"Quincy likes it," he said.

Two hundred thousand copies of the test issue of *Vibe* appeared on newsstands across the country on September 14, 1992. On the cover, the bare-chested rapper Treach of Naughty by Nature. Inside, page after full-color page of beautifully designed, written, and photographed glimpses of hip-hop culture. Van Meter had achieved his main objective: to create a hip-hop magazine irreproachable in its quality. To make hip-hop—and, by extension, people of color—look beautiful.

Not everyone agreed that *Vibe* was, in fact, a hip-hop magazine. David Mills, the Black journalist who took down two Public Enemy mouthpieces—Professor Griff in 1989 and Sister Souljah in 1992—wrote a long profile in the *Washington Post*, calling the 144-page issue "spectacular," but also intimating that "Van Meter's wide lens on hip-hop" was, perhaps, too broad. Mills noted articles on Madonna, Naomi Campbell, Sandra Bernhard, club diva Martha Wash, and dance music legend and gay icon Sylvester. "What's that stuff doing in a hip-hop magazine?" he asked.

Mills quoted Russell Simmons predicting that *Vibe* would "never, never in a million years" be as respected by the hip-hop community as *The Source*, whose editors Simmons noted came "from all walks of life" and "who are honest in their commitment to hip-hop."

Furthermore, Mills—who wrote on occasion for *The Source*—scared up a squabble between the editor of that magazine, Jon Shecter, and the new White kid on the block, Jon Van Meter.

"I feel that I take more shit for being gay than he does for being a wannabe," Van Meter told Mills, noting Shecter's Harvard education and "privileged" background. "I think I am closer to the aesthetic of rap than he is, because I'm lower-middle-class, big family, grew up on the edge of a black neighborhood, went to a [lousy] high school."

Mills got Shecter's response: "While he was voguing or listening to the Village People, I was listening to UTFO. I never claimed that I was a product of the ghetto. But I'm definitely a product of this music."

After complicating things, Mills added: "Told you it'd get complicated."

Before the coming of *Vibe*, *The Source* partners held the slim hope that Time Warner's efforts to launch a hip-hop magazine would, instead of crushing them, somehow validate the niche market to the advertisers they hadn't yet been able to touch.

To the delight of Dave Mays, Jon Shecter, Ed Young, and James Bernard, that was exactly what seemed to be happening. Instead of bullying *The Source*, Time Warner boosted them. In 1993, Nike and Reebok booked their first ads in *The Source*. Clothing advertisements were way up, thanks in part to the efforts of new fashion editor Julia Chance, who moonlit at *The Source* while spending her days working at a trade publication called *Sports Style*. Chance assembled fashion spreads that included the first national coverage of brands like Cross Colours and Karl Kani and launched the career of model Tyson Beckford, a kid on the street whom *The Source*'s designer, Eric Council, had met fortuitously while walking with Jon Shecter in nearby Washington Square Park.

Julia Chance noticed something disturbing, however, when she called one particular clothing company for samples. Timberland boots had become, by far, the favorite footwear of the East Coast hip-hop set—mentioned in lyrics and worn on album covers. At *Sports Style*, Chance had no problem tapping Timberland for merchandise. But when she attempted to get the company to fork over samples for *The Source*, they refused. Timberland didn't feel that the readers of *The Source* were the type of consumers they wanted. The situation was all the more vexing because *The Source* had just given the company a free advertisement for their public service campaign, "Give Racism the Boot."

Chance vented her frustrations to *The New York Times* in an article about Timberland's growing urban popularity called "Out of the Woods."

"I think that they think that if their clothes are celebrated in the black, urban community, with all its ills, that it will cheapen their brand names," Chance said. "Now some of these companies are saying our dollars don't count."

Timberland's thirty-three-year-old chief executive officer, Jeffrey Swartz, insisted that the urban market comprised only 5 percent of the company's sales—even though overall sales for the first nine months of 1993 had somehow grown by 46 percent over the same period in 1992. But Swartz enraged the hip-hop community when he told the *Times* that Timberland's target market would remain "honest working people." The *Times* and *The Source* received letters calling for a boycott.

"Companies like Timberland only have love for our money and in turn we become walking billboards for them," wrote one *Source* reader. "Tell Mr. Swartz and others like him . . . I'll buy my boots elsewhere."

In the midst of the discord, Julia Chance started getting calls from the formerly hesitant footwear firm. In the coming years, more companies— like the designer Tommy Hilfiger—would come to value their young Black consumers by advertising in *The Source* and *Vibe*.

Vibe **not only resonated with advertisers** but with consumers as well. The test issue of the corporate concoction had an extraordinary sell-through rate of 45 percent. Time Warner green-lit the magazine and released the funding for its first regular issue, scheduled for publication in September 1993, one year after the test hit stands. Carol Smith hired a white publisher, John Rollins, to replace her, and a Black businessman, Keith Clinkscales, as chief operating officer. Meanwhile, Van Meter began hiring his permanent staff. As music editor, Van Meter lifted a young White writer from *Rolling Stone*. Alan Light, who had written his college thesis at Yale on the Beastie Boys, had become *Rolling Stone*'s very first in-house hip-hop fanatic. Light saw *Vibe* as a home for *all* the Black music that wouldn't find a home at either rock or rap magazines—new hip-hop-influenced R&B icons like R. Kelly and SWV, Mary J. Blige and Jodeci.

Van Meter polled his staff writers about the stories and figures they were passionate about covering in the first year. The people they chose would come to define both *Vibe* and hip-hop in the coming years.

Kevin Powell suggested Death Row rapper Snoop Doggy Dogg and Interscope artist Tupac Shakur, who intrigued Powell in part because of his family's legacy: the Shakurs—Afeni, Mutulu, and Tupac's godfather Geronimo Pratt were revolutionary royalty.

Scott Poulson-Bryant mentioned that he wanted to write an article about a talent executive at Andre Harrell's Uptown Records. Van Meter didn't understand. This was a *consumer* magazine, not an industry trade. Who cared about some A&R guy?

Poulson-Bryant tried to explain that *this* A&R guy was different. He was just twenty-two years old. He had started at Uptown as an unpaid intern. Now he was the label's virtual creative engine—producing and remixing music, styling album covers, and directing videos. He was helping to define a new aesthetic called "hip-hop soul" with his artists Mary J. Blige and Jodeci. He threw hot industry parties regularly. He was as much a personality as the artists he shepherded and in some ways more controversial. At one of his recent events—a celebrity basketball game—nine people had been killed in a stampede.

Jonathan Van Meter warmed to the idea, and gave Scott Poulson-Bryant his blessing for the unorthodox feature. In turn, Poulson-Bryant set about writing the article on Uptown Records' wunderkind, Sean "Puffy" Combs, the man-child who would become hip-hop's greatest one-man brand.

Scott Poulson-Bryant trailed Combs everywhere: Uptown's offices, the recording studio, his home, artists' apartments, parties, and more. Poulson-Bryant met Combs's mother, Janice, as she cooked for her son and his two assistants at Combs's split-level house in Westchester.

Over the course of a month, the writer began to piece together the life of the young executive. Janice Combs had raised her children by herself after her husband Melvin's death in 1972, when Sean was just three years old. She had moved Sean and his sister, Keisha, from Harlem to the suburb of Mount Vernon as Sean reached his teens, where he attended Catholic school and played football.

Janice Combs called her son a "ham," and talked about Sean's early lust for the limelight. He'd modeled in *Essence* magazine as a child; and in high school, he'd been a dancer in videos for Diana Ross and Fine Young Cannibals. Poulson-Bryant collected anecdotes like the "pool story." The way Sean told it, he'd gotten upset after the move to the suburbs, where the White kids across the street wouldn't invite him to swim in their backyard pool. Sean asked his mother to buy him a pool, too, which she did. Now that he had the biggest on the block, the kids would have to beg *him* for access. It was young Sean's sense of entitlement and short temper that earned him his nickname, "Puffy."

When Sean graduated, he went off to Howard University. Janice Combs had succeeded where so many single mothers of young Black men had failed: She kept her son off the streets and got him to college. But Janice and Sean Combs didn't share with Poulson-Bryant the one story that would make that feat seem all the more miraculous.

Sean's father hadn't died in an automobile accident, as they had told Poulson-Bryant. "Pretty Melvin" Combs was a midlevel drug dealer in the Willie Abraham crew in Harlem. He was a bon vivant, a nice guy, known to many of the big players and hustlers in 1960s Harlem, like Nicky Barnes and Frank Lucas. Combs had been shot dead one night in a parked car on Central Park West, shortly after he had been arrested for drug possession. Someone in Abraham's organization apparently thought that Melvin Combs had flipped, or was about to.

Sean Combs spent much of his childhood wondering about his father, and had only just begun to fathom who he had been. Perhaps that was the source of Combs's fascination with all things ghetto, despite his mostly suburban upbringing. "Puffy" the petulant child was becoming "Puff Daddy," the young man in search of his inner hustler, the backyard-swimming-pool kid in search of his street credibility. Where better to find it than Uptown?

At Howard, Sean "Puffy" Combs focused not on academics, but on the social scene, promoting parties on weekends. Combs burned for the spotlight—although he hadn't yet decided which way he leaned, "show" or "business." Then a rapper from Combs's adopted hometown of Mount Vernon named Heavy D told Combs that he would try to get him an internship with Uptown Records.

Heavy D had been Andre Harrell's inspiration for founding Uptown. Harrell first brought the overweight rapper to Russell Simmons, touting Heavy D as not only a star, but a *sex symbol*. Simmons thought Harrell was out of his mind. Harrell left Rush, parting amicably with Simmons after Harrell secured a modest production deal with MCA Records. When Heavy D's first single, "Mr. Big Stuff," became a hit, Simmons was happy for his friend.

The success of "Mr. Big Stuff" was due in part to the young producer that Harrell had signed to Uptown named Teddy Riley. At only seventeen years old, Riley had produced a song called "The Show," the Doug E. Fresh record that launched the career of sidekick Slick Rick and, more important, introduced a new kind of musicality into hip-hop production. Conversely, Riley's three-man singing group, Guy, slipped hip-hop break beats into R&B. Uptown Records became the first home of Teddy Riley's new style, called "new jack swing."

Andre Harrell and Uptown established a counterpoint to Russell Simmons and Def Jam. While Simmons sold street culture to suburban White audiences, Harrell sold a smooth, upscale take on hip-hop to Black America. Harrell called his more mature outlook "ghetto fabulous." It was the same aspirational impulse that had been around since Harlem's residents first turned their eyes up toward Sugar Hill. And it was everything that the young, highly ambitious, Harlem-born son of Pretty Melvin Combs wanted to be.

Sean Combs impressed Andre Harrell. He wore a red tie, a crisp white shirt, and respectfully called him "sir." When Harrell offered him an internship, Combs sacrificed sleep and cash to do it: rising before dawn on Thursdays, catching Amtrak to make it to Uptown's New York offices by ten a.m.; working Thursday and Friday; and returning to Washington, D.C., for his weekend parties. When the commute got too tedious, Combs sacrificed his Howard University education altogether. When sent on errands, he ran them, literally—necktie flapping behind him. He absorbed everything he could in the office and at the recording studio.

Combs assisted A&R man Kurt Woodley in setting up two artists that he had just signed: a young siren named Mary J. Blige, and a group of four singers from down South who called themselves Jodeci. When Kurt Woodley suddenly received a job offer he couldn't refuse from Columbia Records, Combs took Andre Harrell to lunch and asked for Woodley's job. Harrell gave it to him.

Combs adopted Woodley's acts, but directed their production in his own way. His remix for Jodeci's "Come & Talk to Me" defined his approach: smooth R&B melodies and harmonies over hard, recognizable beats from rap classics; Teddy Riley's "new jack swing" updated for a younger generation. It was "hip-hop soul."

Combs brought his visual aesthetic to bear on his acts as well. Harrell noted that Combs could wear boots, jeans, and a baseball cap and still look "fashion forward."

"Dress Jodeci the same way you dress in the office," Harrell told him.

In 1991, as Jodeci became a cultural phenomenon, their executive producer "Puff Daddy" began making his name, too. He began promoting a popular party called "Daddy's House" at a Manhattan club called the Red Zone, where everyone who was anyone in the industry went to see and be seen. Then came the night of December 28, when Combs and Heavy D cosponsored a celebrity basketball game as an AIDS benefit, on the campus of City College, up on Sugar Hill.

The event attracted a crowd that exceeded the capacity of the gymnasium. As the game began, thousands of young people who still hadn't gotten in pushed those ahead of them into a virtual funnel caused by a stairwell and a wall of four doors, only one of which was open. Dozens of people were squeezed, trampled, and crushed. Within minutes, nine people were dead and twenty-nine injured.

In the aftermath, Combs was vilified in the local media. With public statements and press conferences, Combs told his side of the story: how he begged police officers to control the crowd, pulled people to safety, and administered CPR. A representative for Uptown Records told *The New York Times* that Combs had been placed on "indefinite suspension." He hadn't, though he had taken some time off at the behest of Andre Harrell.

Combs's salvation came with the release of Mary J. Blige's 1992 debut album, *What's the 411?* Again, Combs commissioned productions that featured singing over stark break beats. Uptown dubbed Mary J. Blige the "Queen of Hip-Hop Soul," and her record broke triple platinum. Blige became the paragon for a new musical paradigm, and Combs was celebrated as its maestro.

Scott Poulson-Bryant summed all of this up in a huge, seven-thousand-word piece for the September 1993 issue of *Vibe* magazine. Just before the book was set to go to the printers, Poulson-Bryant received word that made him call, literally, to stop the presses.

Combs had just been fired.

Though Combs himself hadn't discovered the artists to whom his name was now attached, he got the credit for their success. Andre Harrell, never averse to the spotlight himself, let Combs shine. Combs sought to negotiate his own production deal within Uptown, but one lawyer, Andy Tavel, the former in-house counsel for Def Jam, declined to represent him. Tavel thought Combs's proposal was aggressive to the point of being disrespectful and insulting to Combs's benefactor, Harrell.

Combs found another attorney, and arranged for a place to put the artists he wanted to sign who didn't quite fit the "grown and sexy" Uptown sound and image. Chief among these was a young MC named Christopher Wallace—brought to Combs's attention by Matty C, who featured the rapper in his "Unsigned Hype" column in *The Source*.

Wallace went by various sobriquets: Biggie Smalls, the Notorious B.I.G., Biggie or, simply, Big. In his booming baritone, Biggie rapped rough rhymes about drug selling and delinquency on the streets of his native Brooklyn. Combs got Biggie exposure by putting his first record, "Party and Bullshit," on the Uptown soundtrack album for Ted Demme's first feature film— *Who's the Man?* starring Doctor Dre and Ed Lover, produced by Charles Stettler, and featuring cameos from an all-star cast of rappers.

But in the wake of the "Cop Killer" and gangsta rap controversies, Al Teller and other executives at MCA were less than enthusiastic about the prospect of releasing an entire album from Biggie, even if sequestered on Combs's imprint, now called Bad Boy Entertainment. Harrell, too, wasn't sure that he could stand behind Biggie. He had never released records about gunplay and street hustling; even Jodeci's song about having a child out of wedlock, "Forever My Lady," had given Harrell pause.

Harrell faced other pressures. MCA executives worried that Uptown's spending was out of control, and they pressured Harrell to hire someone to mind the store. He chose Mark Siegel, an agent at ICM who represented many of Uptown's acts, as his first general manager. Years back, Siegel had booked shows for Harrell and Alonzo Brown when they were known as "Dr. Jeckyll & Mr. Hyde."

Harrell took care to introduce Siegel to Combs, knowing instinctively that Combs saw himself as Andre's heir apparent.

"This is my consigliere," Harrell said, motioning to Siegel. "You're not ready for that."

Predictably, Combs felt betrayed, making his displeasure known by simply ignoring the new general manager.

Mark Siegel's first order of business was to get the Uptown staff's Diners Club cards turned back on. He discovered that MCA had sent the employees reimbursement checks to cover their credit card bills, but that many of the staff hadn't used the money to pay them off. Siegel extracted a favor from MCA: They would pay the cards off directly—to the tune of another $190,000—provided that Uptown recover the money by garnishing the wages of its employees. Among them was Sean "Puffy" Combs, who complained that Siegel was "stealing" money from him.

Harrell had warned Siegel that everyone at Uptown would hate him because it was Siegel's job to be "Mr. No." But Combs's loathing quickly metastasized into open war on Siegel—whose entry into Uptown's self-assured and exclusively Black atmosphere was jarring, for Siegel was neither ghetto nor fabulous.

"Don't give me your opinions on none of my records," Combs hissed at Siegel, in front of the entire staff. "Shut the fuck up. I don't even want to hear you talk."

Harrell was coproducing a TV show called *New York Undercover*, and trying to get into movies. He needed Siegel to be able to run the office in his absence, and Combs's constant agitation was making that impossible. So Harrell and Siegel invited him for a sit-down in the Uptown offices to see if they couldn't talk out their problems, once and for all.

"Why don't you go first, Puff?" Siegel said. "I've obviously offended you, and I bother you."

"I ain't got nothing to say," Combs replied.

"Okay," Siegel said. "I'll go. I think you act crazy. But I don't think you are actually *that* crazy. . . ."

Combs stood suddenly.

"Who the hell are you to psychoanalyze me? Fuck this bullshit!"

Thirty seconds into the meeting, Combs stormed out. Harrell looked at Siegel.

"That's it, he's out of here," Harrell said. "I can't take it."

"Are you sure?" Siegel replied, suggesting the three meet again after Combs had calmed down. Harrell shook his head. Combs's disrespect had spilled over into outright rebellion against them both, and that was a capital offense.

Harrell exited. A few minutes later, Siegel heard a knock on his door.

"Come in," Siegel said. It was Combs.

"Yo, b, can I talk to you for a minute?" he asked Siegel. Combs sat down, crying, contrite.

"I know I was trying to fuck with you, man," Combs said. "But now I realize you're the only one who can save my job. Could you talk to Andre?"

"You've got to be kidding me," Siegel said. "You were so rude to me. You flipped out on me. Now you want me to go save your job?" In Siegel's mind, this twenty-four-year-old, no matter how much he had accomplished in his short career, wasn't worth the trouble he caused. Combs didn't come close to matching the genius of the great Andre Harrell.

"You're better off now," Siegel assured Combs dryly. "You're talented. I'm sure you'll do great. You'll probably be a superstar."

Sean Combs camped out on the doorstep of Andre Harrell's apartment to plead for his job. Harrell wouldn't let him inside. But Combs had one more father figure to whom he could turn.

Bert Padell was a name that many rap fans knew well because the legendary business manager seemed to be credited on the back of every other hip-hop album cover. Padell's entrée into the rap business came through Russell Simmons; for many years, he had managed the accounts of Def Jam and Rush. The diminutive Padell welcomed artists into his huge office with its walls and desks covered with memorabilia from when he was a batboy for the New York Yankees, and sent them away with autographed copies of his self-published books of poetry. Every year, he taught a well-attended class on the pop music business at Manhattan's The New School. In 1991, a young intern from Uptown Records named Sean Combs had been seated in the front row.

Now Padell comforted the distraught Combs. He'd make everything right. He'd reason with Andre. Padell called Harrell, whom he also represented, asking Harrell to give the kid another chance. Harrell—who had offered to keep paying Combs's salary while he found his footing—again refused.

"Don't worry," Padell reassured Combs. "We'll get something going."

Padell started making calls while the music industry was still abuzz over Combs's high-profile termination. Scott Poulson-Bryant's *Vibe* article— slightly modified to account for Combs's firing—had just hit newsstands, multiplying the mythology of "Puff Daddy," the glossy magazine molding a new glossy superstar. In the minds of many in the business, it wasn't so much a question of whether Combs would get a new deal, but where.

At the headquarters of EMI Records, Combs made his case before label heads Daniel Glass and Fred Davis. Together, they discussed the possibility of Combs coming on board as head of Black music, and bringing his label, Bad Boy, with him. Glass and Davis, however, knew little about hip-hop, so they brought in their "kid" who did—a twenty-five-year-old White guy from Long Island named Rob Stone.

Like Combs, Rob Stone had made a name for himself at a young age. As one of the new breed of promoters focusing on crossover radio stations like Power 106 and KMEL, Stone was the record business counterpart to innovative radio programmers like Keith Naftaly and Hosh Gureli. Stone made friends with Steve Smith while he was still a program director in Phoenix by throwing seven of the eight CDs he had brought from EMI into Smith's trash can.

"These are garbage," Stone said, holding the remaining CD in his hand. "Here's the record you should be playing."

Stone spoke the new programmers' language. He showed them that he not only understood music, but that he knew *which* music was right for their stations. Stone was one of the first national radio promotions people for major labels who had grown up on hip-hop. Combs sensed this in the meeting, as he gestured to Stone repeatedly, looking for support when asked about EMI's moribund superstar, Vanilla Ice.

"*Rob* knows I can't mess with that dude," Combs said.

As Combs extolled his personal and professional value, Stone became exhilarated. Combs's confidence was contagious.

"I have the textbook," Combs declared. "And I'll show it to anyone. But no one can do it like me. No one has respect in the streets like me. When people hear my voice, they're gonna know that the record's hot."

After the lively discussion, Combs rose. But just before he left, he turned back toward Stone and his bosses.

"When you get in the room where you decide what you're gonna pay Puff, just when you get to that number that you think is gonna make Puff happy, get ridiculous on top of that."

Stone thought: *This guy is incredible.*

The executive with two of the best ears in the music business agreed. Clive Davis had brought rock music to Columbia Records in the 1960s. He had founded Arista Records in the 1970s, and by the end of the 1980s, he had built a roster that included Whitney Houston, Aretha Franklin, and Toni Braxton. But for all his expertise with Black divas, Davis had never been able to hear hip-hop. But after his first meeting with Sean "Puffy" Combs, Clive Davis called Burt Padell and told him that he was ready to make a deal. Shortly thereafter, Andre Harrell called Davis and vouched for his protégé, just as Russell Simmons had once vouched for Harrell.

The production contract Padell negotiated for the young record executive was impressive, especially for a client who had produced hit records, but never signed one: $1 million in overhead each year, recording funds for Combs's first round of artists, and a nonrecoupable $1.5 million loan to create a recording studio, one that didn't have to be repaid until the studio was opened to the public.

In early 1994, Combs opened Bad Boy's new offices on 19th Street, and spent hundreds of hours at Manhattan's The Hit Factory, recording the debut albums for his initial salvo of rappers, the Notorious B.I.G. and Craig Mack.

As Combs worked to launch his new stars, the stars aligned around him. Arista Records, as it just so happened, was looking for a new crossover promotion person. They hired Rob Stone, who, as it just so happened, was recommended for the job by Hosh Gureli, now working for Arista. On the Black promotion side, Lionel Ridenour and Jeff House, Rifkind's former street team partners, complimented Stone. Stone had become even friendlier with Steve Smith after Smith had taken the PD job at Hot 97, which, as it just so happened, had recently adopted its "Where Hip-Hop Lives" slogan and format. And Stone just so happened to be the guy taking Smith around to the clubs and street corners in the five boroughs and beyond, helping the incoming programmer get a feel for the variant rhythms of the New York market.

"You need to know Puffy," Stone told Smith.

Combs sent a car to pick Smith and Stone up at Hot 97, which whisked them to the Bad Boy offices. After Stone made introductions, the three of them—promoter, producer, and programmer—sat down at a linen-covered table in Bad Boy's conference room and were served a three-course Italian meal by two older Italian gentlemen in suits and aprons.

Steve Smith had already voiced his discomfort with the situation, going to a label for a fancy lunch. *I'll meet him,* Smith said, *but I'm not doing any favors.* Rob Stone could tell that Combs was anxious, too. Each of them had so much at stake in their new enterprises.

Nobody touched their plates. Instead, Smith talked about building Hot 97's audience. Combs talked about establishing Bad Boy. And then they listened to some music. "Juicy" by the Notorious B.I.G. A track that Puffy had produced for a new Arista artist, a sixteen-year-old kid named Usher Raymond. But the record that stimulated Smith's sixth sense as a programmer was the song by Craig Mack called "Flava in Ya Ear."

That, Smith thought, *sounds like it belongs on my station.*

By the fall of 1994, Craig Mack's "Flava in Ya Ear" had become a Top 10 Billboard pop hit and certified platinum. The Notorious B.I.G. remained a slower-burning underdog favorite of mix-show DJs until the beginning of the next year, when his second single, "Big Poppa," also zoomed into the Top 10 on the pop chart. Bad Boy Entertainment's first two albums, *Funk Da World* by Craig Mack and *Ready to Die* by the Notorious B.I.G., went gold and platinum, respectively. And in many of Bad Boy's records and videos appeared a novel sight: the owner of the label himself, Sean "Puff Daddy" Combs. Appearing beside his own stars, Combs was a star himself.

For some people in the hip-hop nation, Combs's flamboyance was fraudulence. The rise of Bad Boy seemed to usher in a new era in which authenticity and credibility were defined less by artistry and more by access to power, whether in the street or the boardroom.

For Hot 97, Bad Boy's artists formed the slick flip side to the raw Wu-Tang ethos that Steve Smith and Tracy Cloherty had initially embraced. Wu-Tang was about "keeping it real." Combs sold a fantasy, grafting Uptown's bourgeois flashiness onto dramatized visions of street turmoil. Bad Boy represented a new kind of heat, coupling genuine hip-hop with higher-than-ever commercial aspirations—a hustle on a whole new level.

One year before the debut of Bad Boy, Poulson-Bryant had written the following, prescient words:

As hip-hop makes its mad dash toward the finishing line of high capitalism, it will need a hero.

Thereafter, whenever Combs saw Poulson-Bryant in public, he would point at the writer.

"This nigga made me!" he'd say.

The battle over branding and authenticity would soon take down the editorial regimes at both *Vibe* and *The Source*—the former because it wasn't credible enough and the latter because it insisted on its credibility above all else.

Jonathan Van Meter's first year as editor of *Vibe* proved difficult. He was only thirty years old and managing a staff of people even younger than him, many of whom had never worked a full-time job. He struggled to enforce regular hours, chain of command, and office decorum. Sell-through varied from issue to issue, disappointing the executives at Time, Inc. Faced with flagging newsstand sales, Van Meter arranged a cover story that he expected would be a double coup: Madonna interviewing the Madonna of basketball, Dennis Rodman.

The editorial crew, led by Scott Poulson-Bryant, revolted. They asserted that it was a mistake to put a White woman on the cover, especially with Eddie Murphy and Spike Lee in the same issue.

"This isn't a democracy," Van Meter told Poulson-Bryant. "You're not unionized. This isn't the *Village Voice*."

When Poulson-Bryant persisted, Van Meter fired him in front of the entire staff.

As the young editor walked away, Van Meter realized he had made a terrible mistake. The office was in an uproar. The young editorial assistant, Mimi Valdes, was wailing as if a close family member had been shot. Van Meter found Poulson-Bryant as he packed his things, told him he was still on staff and offered to talk things over when they had both cooled down.

Ultimately, Van Meter's undoing came not from mutiny, but from his own defiance. If the editorial staff's reaction to the Madonna cover was bad, it was nothing compared to that of Quincy Jones.

Jones had, until this point, been largely agreeable and unintrusive on Van Meter's editorial purview. But Jones revealed that he had caught a lot of flak from his Black confidantes about *Vibe*'s last cover, featuring the Beastie Boys. To go from a bunch of White rappers one month to a White pop star the next would be a betrayal of the magazine's core mission, he said, especially when *Vibe* had features on Black icons in the current issue.

Van Meter couldn't conceive of taking one of the biggest American superstars off the cover of his magazine just because Spike Lee was complaining. He wouldn't and told Quincy Jones that he was keeping things as they were. Jones replied, "Over my dead fucking body." The conversation descended into a screaming match that ended with Van Meter shouting, "I quit!" He slammed his phone down so hard that it shattered, swiped everything off of his desktop onto the floor in a fury, stormed out of the office, and stomped home.

When it became apparent to Gil Rogin and Robin Wolaner that Jones would not budge, they commiserated with Van Meter on his fate, both in their own inimitable way.

"Who elected him the king of the Blacks?" Rogin spat, referring to Spike Lee, whose pique reportedly sparked the entire episode.

"Get as much money as you can," Wolaner counseled.

One year after Russell Simmons's departure from *Vibe*, Quincy Jones finally understood Simmons's fears about having a hip-hop magazine led by Van Meter. Upon reflection, Wolaner, too, had to admit that Van Meter was not the right person to edit *Vibe*. She called his aesthetic too "precious." She might have used the word "fancy" had Simmons not said it himself.

Ultimately, Van Meter did not understand one fundamental fact: No matter how big Madonna was, no matter how many magazines she sold, she had no place on the cover of a magazine supposedly dedicated to hip-hop, a culture that determined its own superstars and icons.

The deposed editor in chief sequestered himself for months after his resignation, depressed. But the template that Van Meter created at *Vibe* emerged as a clear counterpoint to *The Source*. In the pages of *Vibe*, hip-hop culture was more than simple fealty to the "four elements" of rapping, deejaying, graffiti, and dance. Hip-hop was also about the openness and diversity of its fans and followers. Hip-hop loved R&B. Hip-hop had its favorite movie stars and TV shows. Hip-hop had its own outlook on fashion. Hip-hop had women, and yes, gay and lesbian acolytes. *Vibe* was a place for them all, an emerging urbane, multiracial generation from various backgrounds whose tastes converged in one culture, hip-hop.

After Jon Shecter helmed over forty consecutive issues of *The Source*, he decided he needed a break. Over the grumblings of Mays, Shecter decided to take a sabbatical, renting an apartment in Philadelphia to begin work on a screenplay. James Bernard temporarily assumed the duties of editor in chief.

The furlough didn't last long. When Shecter received a copy of the next *Source* issue in the mail, the first things he noticed were the typos. Then he read Reggie Dennis's column, in which Dennis wrote that he had heard the rap group Cypress Hill had burned an issue of *The Source* onstage because they didn't like their album review in a recent issue. Dennis responded: "You wouldn't want me to cross the line and make a comment about your setting fire to your green cards by accident, now, would you?"

Shecter was furious. To him, both Bernard and Dennis seemed so eager to engage in beef with artists. He felt that they had deliberately goaded Ice-T during the "Cop Killer" controversy the previous year. Now came this gratuitous, racist attack on a group that Shecter considered to be his friends, completely destroying the goodwill he had built over the last couple of years. When Shecter confronted Bernard and Dennis, they cited something akin to the code of the street as their rationale: *They dissed us, so we dissed them.*

Shecter cut short his leave of absence after only three months, but the rift between him and his fellow editors grew. Beneath the split lay a fundamental difference in philosophy. Shecter conducted himself as a humble fan. He had founded *The Source* to boost the rap industry. While Shecter wasn't opposed to critique, he felt that Bernard and Dennis had become meanspirited. *The Source* was supposed to be a unifying force, not a divisive one.

For their part, James Bernard and Reggie Dennis felt that the issues at hand in hip-hop—censorship, ignorance, injustice, oppression, violence—superseded Shecter's niceties. Their job was to challenge artists, not cheerlead. *The Source* had now become an important institution in the community. The editors and writers had a voice as powerful as the rappers they covered. They needed to use it. To them, Shecter was apolitical in a time of political significance, and weak in an era that required strength.

Even Shecter's oldest friend at *The Source*, Chris Wilder, thought Shecter didn't understand what some of his colleagues were going through. At the clubs and in the streets, it was Wilder who would get icy looks and take sucker punches from artists who didn't like their latest review in *The Source*. A White boy like Jon Shecter was never going to catch that kind of hell, and Wilder told him so.

"You don't understand," Wilder would say, "because you're White."

Shecter heard this often enough that he began to consider whether he was the right person to run *The Source*'s editorial. Maybe a Black person should be editor in chief. He was beginning to feel like a stranger in his own house.

Strife at *The Source* wasn't limited to the editorial side. Dave Mays's attempt to produce a "*Source* Awards" show alienated old-school artists, enraged longtime friends like KRS-One, and would have bankrupted the company had Ed Young not directed some of the magazine's monthly income to another account, one he vowed to keep as a safety fund for an occasion such as this.

Mays's side hustle as manager of rap group the RSO Crew was beginning to interfere with life at *The Source*. His clients, led by rapper Raymond "Ray Dog" Scott, had been a fixture of Mays's life since his days in Boston. But Scott and his friends were becoming increasingly strident in their demands for coverage in the magazine and ever more disruptive around the office, treating *The Source* as their hangout and playground.

Matty Capoluongo returned to his desk one day to find that a number of his records had been stolen by a member of the RSO Crew. Capoluongo had been feeling the growing tension around the office, and this incident provided more impetus for him to reconsider his continued presence at the magazine. His track record with his column "Unsigned Hype" more than qualified him for an A&R position in the music business if he so chose. His friend Schott "Free" Jacobs had landed a job at Loud, and soon "Matty C" came to the attention of Steve Rifkind. Capoluongo had once disparaged Loud's founder. But now he admired Rifkind for the chance he took on the Wu-Tang Clan and for finally shaving his long blond hair.

The Source had become a breeding ground for executive talent. Rob Tewlow left to do A&R for Big Beat Records. Chris Wilder took a job as a copywriter for Sony Music. Brett Wright had gone, too, first to Uptown, and then to Loud. After Rifkind offered him a full-time A&R job, Capoluongo joined their ranks as a *Source* alumnus.

The end of Jon Shecter's and James Bernard's days at *The Source* came soon thereafter. Leaning heavily across the traditional church-and-state-like divider between the business and editorial halves of his journalistic enterprise, publisher Dave Mays repeatedly asked Shecter, Bernard, and Dennis to give coverage to the RSO Crew. The editors refused. After all, RSO's biggest mouth, Raymond Scott, had openly threatened to "put niggas in body bags" if RSO didn't get a satisfactory review.

Mays was furious. He felt that Bernard and Dennis were unprofessional, alienating the entire rap industry with their editorial agenda. He thought they were denying proper coverage to deserving artists out of spite. And he didn't think much of the high-minded concept of separation between publishing and editorial. *Major media corporations influence the editorial direction of their properties all the time,* he thought. So Mays decided to take matters into his own hands with a bit of subterfuge. He reserved four pages of the next issue for a large advertisement. Mays made the printer insert his own article about the RSO Crew into those four pages.

When the magazine came back from the printer, James Bernard and Jon Shecter convened a meeting of the editorial staff. Together, they decided that if Mays could not be shamed into leaving, that they themselves would have to go. Bernard transmitted a public mass resignation letter, sent via facsimile to every single phone number on *The Source*'s five-thousand-strong contact list. Within minutes, the entire hip-hop industry knew about the schism at the magazine of hip-hop music, politics, and culture.

If any of the editors thought that the walkout would cripple *The Source*, provoke an idealistic industry-wide boycott, or force Mays out, they were wrong. Few in the industry cared about *The Source*'s editorial integrity enough to stop advertising. In the end, it came down to numbers. Mays owned 40 percent. Shecter and Bernard, together, held 45 percent. The balance of power fell to Ed Young, who retained the remaining 15 points. Young thought that what Mays had done was wrong. But Young was even more incensed by Bernard's fax, which in his mind could have sunk the whole business. Young sided with Mays, and *The Source* partners began to battle over the terms of a buyout. After a long stalemate, Jon Shecter found someone to mediate the dispute, a person who had a good relationship with both Shecter and his estranged partners.

Dave Mays was sitting in his office at *The Source* when he got the call from Lyor Cohen.

"Hey, Dave," Cohen began. "I've got some great news."

"Oh, yeah?" Mays replied. "What is it?"

"I'm your partner!"

Mays paused a moment. "What are you talking about?" he said.

"I just got the stick from Jon and James," Cohen said.

"*What?!*" Mays cried. "You can't be serious!"

But Cohen *was* serious. He told Mays that he and Russell Simmons had purchased an option on Shecter's and Bernard's shares for $150,000.

Mays couldn't believe Cohen's audacity. Cohen was trying to make it sound like he was doing him a big favor. After all, Cohen intimated, the shares could have gone to God knows who, an Arabian sheik or somebody like that.

You're lucky that I'm your friend, Cohen said.

Mays told Cohen that he didn't consider the move a friendly act at all. And Cohen was much too wily to keep as a partner.

When he saw Cohen's paperwork, Ed Young agreed. Cohen had engineered the situation perfectly. If Mays and Young wanted to get rid of Lyor, they would have to pay him to relinquish his option—at a price somewhat higher than Cohen paid for it. Mays and Young had to take out a bank loan to cover the cost.

The transaction preceded the resolution of the entire conflict, when Young exited *The Source* and compelled Mays to buy the rest of his partners out. Shecter and Bernard eventually received $1.5 million collectively for their shares.

The *Source* and *Vibe* brands carried on. Dave Mays hired a new crop of editors and writers. Few were surprised when Time Warner hired yet another White man to run *Vibe*. Gil Rogin and Robin Wolaner's boss, Bob Miller, promoted music editor Alan Light to acting editor in chief, with the mandate to get newsstand sales up quickly in the next three issues, or the magazine would be shut down.

Light, however, turned out to be quite effective. Bringing in respected Bay Area–bred music journalist Danyel Smith to fill his vacated music editor chair, Light scrambled to salvage the current issue and prepare the next one. Light had been cultivating a scoop for months: trying to convince the press-shy Prince to give his first interview in five years to *Vibe*. Just when Light took the reins, Prince said yes. The issue sold well. Danyel Smith's cover story on Janet Jackson sold the next issue, too. Light's third cover did even better, featuring the members of the hip-hop/R&B girl-group TLC in fire-fighting regalia—a reference to member Lisa "Left Eye" Lopes's recent arrest for arson after burning her ballplayer boyfriend's house down. And on the fourth cover, *Vibe* broke the story of R&B singer R. Kelly's secret marriage to his underage protégée, Aaliyah.

None of these *Vibe* covers featured hip-hop artists. But they were the kinds of figures who fascinated the hip-hop generation. Light and Smith forged a commitment to report the stories in the "Urban" music world that no one else—not *The Source*, not *Rolling Stone*—would or could cover. And although *Vibe* maintained a strong commitment to covering the important issues and cutting-edge artists of hip-hop, the stories that actually sold magazines weren't the artist profiles, fashion spreads, or long think pieces.

They were about drama.

Tupac Shakur came to New York in late 1993 for the filming of a new movie, *Above the Rim*—penned and produced by Will Smith's comanager, Jeff Pollack. Shakur was set to play the role of a drug dealer named "Birdie." Shakur researched his character by surrounding himself with real New York hustlers. His friend Biggie Smalls had himself been a small-time dealer on the streets of Brooklyn before signing to Bad Boy. Biggie told Shakur his stories, and Shakur returned the favor by imparting some wisdom about the record business. Ultimately, though, Shakur was looking for a more prominent role model. He found one in "Haitian" Jack Agnant, a Brooklyn hustler of some renown.

Tupac Shakur already possessed stellar qualifications. He had been raised by Black revolutionaries. He had attended drama school and starred in major motion pictures. His albums had already sold millions. Shakur was nothing if not legitimate. But Shakur sought another kind of credibility instead—street credibility. In the case of artists like the Wu-Tang Clan, "keeping it real" meant staying true to both their lowly past as well as their raw artistic aspirations. But with Shakur, "keeping it real" seemed to mean devaluing his personal achievements, gifts, and experience in favor of a lower order in which his stature was measured by money, violence, brutality, and blind loyalty.

The respect Shakur sought from men like Agnant was not forthcoming. While keeping their company, Shakur was arrested for the sexual assault of a young woman in his Manhattan hotel room, a crime for which people in Shakur's circle believed he was taking the fall. The case went to trial in New York. On the evening of closing arguments, Shakur was called to a recording session at Quad Recording Studios for an artist named Little Shawn. Upon entering the lobby, Shakur was shot five times. In shock, Shakur took the elevator to the studio, where, coincidentally, his friend Biggie was working on his own material, his producer Sean Combs and Combs's mentor Andre Harrell in attendance. All were slow to realize their comrade had been attacked and was seriously injured. Shakur, fearing for his life, left the hospital after only fifteen hours. Two days after his shooting, Shakur appeared in court to hear the jury's guilty verdict.

Awaiting sentencing in the city jail on Rikers Island, Shakur gave an exclusive interview to Kevin Powell for *Vibe* magazine. In the sit-down, Shakur implicated Biggie, Combs, and Harrell in the ambush, although he was unclear about the motive for such a betrayal. Powell's interview, which appeared in the April 1995 issue, set the hip-hop world on fire. Combs and Biggie vehemently denied their involvement, but made a decision not to fuel the firestorm with more words.

Shakur was eventually transferred to the Clinton Correctional Facility in Dannemora, New York, to serve his four-and-a-half-year sentence, while his manager, Atron Gregory, worked with lawyers to secure an appeal and bail.

Someone else, however, was interested in helping Tupac. Death Row Records CEO Suge Knight flew to New York to meet with Shakur, offering to post bond for Shakur's appeal if the rapper would shift his contract to Death Row from Interscope, Death Row's parent company. While in New York, Knight swung by the second-annual *Source* Awards at Madison Square Garden. Onstage, Suge Knight mocked the people on whom Shakur had turned his venom:

"Any artist out there that want to be an artist and want to stay a star and don't want to worry about the executive producer all up in the videos, all on the records, dancing—come to Death Row!"

The crowd gasped and jeered as they realized what Knight was saying, and about whom he was talking. Combs's flashy ways were despised by many in New York. But Knight's disrespect was so overt and audacious that it sparked in some attendees a patriotic reflex. Minutes later, Sean "Puffy" Combs took the stage, and the high road.

"I'm the executive producer that the comment was made about a little bit earlier," he said. "Contrary to what other people may feel, I'm proud of Dr. Dre and Death Row and Suge Knight for their accomplishments. I'm a positive Black man, and I want to bring us together, not separate us."

The public confrontation between the heads of two of the hottest record companies in hip-hop was dramatic enough. But the fact that one label represented the commercially dominant West Coast and the other a newly resurgent East Coast added an entirely new dimension to the conflict, reigniting a battle that had been dormant for several years.

In hip-hop's new ascendant brands, something had been lost. Companies like Def Jam and *The Source* that had been founded to represent integrity had been upstaged by brands like Bad Boy and Death Row that strove mostly to represent their own high standing. And the measure of authenticity in this new battle would not be level of skill, but who remained standing after the bullets flew.

The first shots of this war were fired from the pages of *Vibe* magazine. They echoed at the *Source* Awards. And they would ultimately reach their deadly mark in *Vibe*'s house.

Side B
Equity

T ravis Knight, a teenager from Beaverton, Oregon, dreamed of becoming a rap star. He called himself "Chilly Tee."

His dreams might have remained just that had he not been the son of Phil Knight—the founder and chairman of Nike, the largest sportswear company in the world.

His father's connections in the entertainment world led Travis to an album deal at MCA, where Public Enemy cofounder Hank Shocklee had taken an A&R job after folding SOUL Records, the label he started with Bill Stephney. Shocklee took on Knight's project, and produced an entire album for the young White rapper called *Get off Mine*, which included tracks like "Audi Like Jetta," "Krisis of Identity," and a nod to Travis's dad called "Just Do It." As MCA readied the album for release, Shocklee informed the Knights—elder and younger—that if they wanted to ensure the absolute best shot at success for their record, they needed to enlist the help of the premier independent promoter in the rap business.

Steve Rifkind had just left a meeting at BMG Publishing when he retreived a message on his voice mail.

I'm Howard Slusher, special assistant to Phil Knight, the chairman of Nike. I need to see you tomorrow.

Rifkind soon learned that this "special assistant" was no secretary. Slusher had once been the most powerful and feared sports agent in the business—so reviled that team owners and rivals dubbed him "Agent Orange." Now Slusher worked for one client only, with a name that Rifkind instantly recognized.

Within days, Rifkind found himself on a plane to Oregon and then in the home of the Nike founder, where Knight introduced him to Travis and enlisted Rifkind help for his son's rap career. Rifkind, in turn, told the Knights about his street team, and invited Knight and son to visit his headquarters in Los Angeles. As Phil Knight walked through SRC/Loud's suite of offices—music blaring, piles of records on the floor, kids stuffing stickers, posters, and T-shirts into envelopes and working the phones—he broke into a smile.

"This is just how I used to sell shoes," Knight told Rifkind and Rich Isaacson.

But Knight also sensed that Rifkind and his band of street promoters had developed something new: techniques and expertise that tapped into a cultural shift among American youth.

"I have to bring you guys to my marketing people," Knight said.

Within weeks, Isaacson called the ten leading members of his street team and offered them the field trip of a lifetime. Nike flew everyone in—Jellow and his partner, Jaybird, from Chicago, Duk-Ki from D.C., J. C. Ricks from the Bay Area, and so on. In Beaverton, the street team was treated to a tour of the Nike campus and a sumptuous dinner. The next day, SRC's young associates sat down with the heads of global marketing for Nike, where they explained their methods to the rapt panel of corporate executives and fielded questions. For their trip home, each team member left with a duffel bag full of the latest Nike gear, and something more valuable: the epiphany that their work had worth in the world beyond the music industry.

For all their skills, Steve Rifkind and his street team couldn't make a star out of Chilly Tee. But Rifkind secured a continuing relationship with Nike, the first corporate client for the Steven Rifkind Company.

Both Rifkind and Isaacson sensed their arrival at a crossroads. The music industry was lucrative, but finite. More record companies were hiring the right people to promote their hip-hop records. SRC's own Fabian "Fade" Duvernay had jumped ship to Interscope. As record companies got smarter and stronger, they needed SRC less. If the company were to grow—from hundreds of thousands of dollars to millions in billing—they would need to move beyond music. SRC's methods, born of hip-hop, could be used to market any credible product, and impart credibility to products as well.

First, Rifkind turned his pitch machine on Hollywood. Movie mogul Bob Weinstein of Miramax bit first, hiring SRC to promote two movies to the hip-hop audience. Rifkind and Issacson soon made inroads at other studios, like New Line and MGM. Rifkind augmented his push by hiring publicist

Laura Cathcart to do a round of media. In the late summer of 1994, Cathcart landed Rifkind an article in *Billboard* and a front-page feature in the business section of the *Los Angeles Times*.

"To be hip in urban America, a new product's gotta have street buzz," the *Times* article began. "Enter the Street Team."

The capital letters indicated that Rifkind was now branding his marketing squad for corporate consumption. Rifkind's lawyers had even begun the process of trademarking the term. This news elicited smirks from the music-industry promoters who had assembled "street teams" before Rifkind entered the game. Some of Rifkind's friends in the industry mocked his outreach to corporate America, reducing his business plan to three words: "Niggaz with Flyers." But Rifkind won grudging acknowledgment that he had indeed taken this thing to another level, selling the concept of "street" to people who had no idea what the "street" was.

"You can't reach America's youth with off-the-mark radio ads or insulting television commercials," the newly coronated street promotion specialist told the *Times*. "You have to reach them where they live: clubs, parties, and barbershops."

A new crowd of corporate clients were listening.

As SRC expanded, so did Loud Records. After the A&R additions of Matty Capoluongo and Schott "Free" Jacobs, Rifkind hired his brother Jon to handle radio promotion. Loud had truly become a family affair.

It disturbed Rifkind, then, that so much of the Wu-Tang family made its home elsewhere. However, one Wu project remained within reach. Rifkind resolved to keep it.

Rifkind and his staff decided that the Raekwon solo album that the RZA had just produced was the best album that Wu-Tang had ever done. But Rifkind and Isaacson knew that they faced a fight in procuring the money needed to secure the album. RCA's business affairs department had resisted Rifkind's entreaties for larger artist advances. Their negotiations wouldn't be any easier now that RCA president Joe Galante had taken another job in Nashville, leaving Loud no counterbalance against the by-the-book demeanor of RCA's chief lawyer, Carol Fenelon, charged with reducing the company's overall expenditures during a protracted sales downturn.

Isaacson's interactions with Fenelon were always unpleasant. Once over breakfast, Isaacson had asked her to advance Loud more money.

"It would be nice if you didn't have your hand out every time I saw you," Fenelon replied.

Isaacson was offended. The Loud brand was the best thing that the ailing RCA Records had, the only label partner moving units and making noise. Yet Fenelon was always on them about spending beyond their budgets. RCA was tightening their belt and choking the success out of Loud in the process.

Isaacson figured that Fenelon might soften if she met RZA face-to-face. Once she did, Fenelon would understand that RZA was a businessman and an honorable partner who could deliver for them. Back in Los Angeles, Isaacson arranged the summit at RCA's headquarters in New York, but fell ill just prior to the trip. Before the meeting, Rifkind and his attorney Jamie Roberts—the son of Steve's uncle Roy Rifkind—lunched with RZA, Divine, and their attorney Tim Mandelbaum to discuss their negotiation strategy. Then they marched up to the thirty-sixth-floor conference room of the RCA offices where Isaacson was on speakerphone.

Isaacson was wrong about Fenelon. Despite the artist's presence, the RCA executive dug her heels in even though RZA and RCA were just $20,000 apart. Rifkind knew he was supposed to be on Fenelon's side—giving the artist less and reducing his exposure. But he thought that Fenelon was being shortsighted and deliberately obstinate. The Wu-Tang Clan had made millions for RCA. Method Man's first solo single for Def Jam, "All I Need" featuring Mary J. Blige, was already climbing the charts. His album was poised to sell millions. What more proof did she need that the Wu-Tang phenomenon was real?

The discussions turned tense after Fenelon argued that the problem was not RCA's stinginess but Loud's profligate spending. She intimated that Loud had cannibalized its own artists' recording funds. The RZA turned to the assembled executives.

"Get yourself another nigger. I'm out of here."

The RZA and Mandelbaum left, and Rifkind exploded.

"Carol, just give him the fucking money already!" Rifkind spat, pacing back and forth. "It's going to cost us in the long run. You're fucking up my relationship with my best artist! You're fucking up my company over nothing!"

Fenelon had reached her limit. "Now you listen to me, Steve Rifkind," she began.

As Fenelon scolded Rifkind, the grandson of One-Punch Harry grabbed a chair and heaved it across the table. It barely missed Fenelon.

Three thousand miles away, Isaacson heard a crashing noise and a woman screaming via speakerphone. *What the fuck just happened?* Frozen, Isaacson tried and failed to stifle a laugh.

Back in New York, Fenelon had run from the room, shaken. Steve Rifkind was escorted out of the RCA building by security guards.

In the wake of Rifkind's RCA fracas with Fenelon, Strauss Zelnick, the chief of BMG North America, offered Fenelon consolation—a nicer job as head of business affairs for Arista—and Rifkind some advice: *Be a businessman, not a gangster.* Weeks later, Method Man's album debuted, selling 120,000 in just the first few days of release. Because of Method's monster smash, Zelnick intervened on Loud's behalf and got the Raekwon deal with the RZA done—albeit at a markedly more expensive price tag than Fenelon could have negotiated weeks prior.

Many fans called Raekwon's album *Only Built 4 Cuban Linx . . .* by another name, "the purple tape," on account of the cassette version's clear, amethyst-tinted shell. But the packaging of Raekwon's album possessed another peculiarity. The album artwork had an extra panel that featured a collage of Wu-Tang Clan clothing products.

The design of this minicatalog looked like the job of an amateur; but the clothes it displayed were well-done: hockey jerseys emblazoned with the huge Wu-Tang "W" logo, in red and black or black and gold; a "Wu-Tang Warriors" baseball jersey; Wu-Tang logo T-shirts, sweats, and hoodies of all colors; Wu-Tang caps and socks, skullcaps, and sweatbands; even a T-shirt with WU-WEAR STATE UNIVERSITY in collegiate block lettering, and smaller sizes that read, WU-WEAR FOR KIDS. On the back of the panel, an order form directed all money orders to a post office box in Staten Island, care of "Wu-Wear."

The nascent mail-order clothing business was the brainchild of Oliver "Power" Grant, one of the Wu-Tang's four executive producers. Grant's investment and support had been crucial in the early days. But as record company support staff got involved and marketing budgets grew, Grant began looking for other ways to grow the Wu-Tang business.

Clothes were a natural hustle for Grant. Back when he was known as

"Pook," Grant earned hundreds of dollars every week—whether by selling newspapers with Divine on the Verrazano-Narrows Bridge, or by saving the subway tokens and tips he earned as a messenger—and spent it all on fresh gear: kicks, jeans, shirts, jackets, and more. Every morning, after a commute by bus, ferry, and subway to Brooklyn's George Westinghouse vocational high school, Grant arrived looking right. He had to. In the mid-1980s, the school was a veritable fashion show. Grant's schoolmate, a rapper named Trevor Smith whom Chuck D of Public Enemy would eventually dub "Busta Rhymes," always came dressed in fresh slacks, shoes, and shirts. Another kid with rap aspirations in Grant's shop class, Shawn "Jay-Z" Carter, talked slick while he sported duck-billed Polo hats, Polo goose-down jackets, and Bally shoes. In later years, another fashion-conscious rapper, Christopher "Biggie" Wallace, would walk Westinghouse's halls. In a generation disregarded by mainstream society, "fresh gear" was a way for kids to say, emphatically, "I'm here."

Carter was in woodworking class the day that Grant came in dipped from head to toe in Coca-Cola wear—which, along with Benetton, was the latest craze for New York schoolkids. Brands mattered. The tall, brown-skinned Grant rocked his red Coca-Cola pants, red-and-white diamond-checked Coca-Cola shirt, matching red-and-white Charles Barkley Nikes, and around his neck, a thick gold cable.

Grant was "fresh to death," in the parlance of the day—that is, until the kid next to him started playing around with a big container of Elmer's glue, and ended up squirting the white ejaculate all over Grant's expensive gear. Now Grant's eyes reddened to match his clothes. He grabbed the bottle of Elmer's, poured the contents on the kid's head, and punched him in the face. If only Westinghouse's dean hadn't walked by during the altercation, Grant might not have had to pay such a high price for his clothing obsession.

Expelled from Westinghouse, Grant faced matriculation at the nearest Staten Island school. He had grown up hearing the stories about New Dorp High, a White school in a mostly Italian neighborhood.

They be throwing rocks and bottles at niggas, people said. *Tipping buses over and shit. Beating niggas' asses, chasing them home. Race riots and straight-up brawls.*

Grant imagined his daily commute back from New Dorp to Park Hill akin to something out of the legendary gang movie *The Warriors*, trying to make it back home through enemy territory.

In reality, New Dorp wasn't that bad. If anything, the school was boring.

Compared to Westinghouse, Grant didn't think too much of the faculty at New Dorp, nor they of him. Grant passed the time with a new running buddy—a squat Black kid named Corey Woods who called himself "Shallah," but would eventually be known by the MC name "Raekwon." Grant and Woods . . . Pook and Shallah . . . the two friends ultimately spent less time in class, and more time in the pursuit of extracurricular profits.

While he was still a messenger, Grant got his start selling weed in front of his building in the Park Hill projects. Then a crew of older kids moved in, running crack throughout Staten Island. In a bold move, Grant approached one of them, respectfully, and asked for his first package. It was simple math: Work all week for $300, or three hours for the same money. After dropping out of New Dorp, before he was even sixteen years old, Grant bought his first ride—a 1986 Audi Quattro, in satin black with chrome wheels. Grant's father, who rode the ferry every day to work at Chase Manhattan Bank, saw his son washing the car by the fire hydrant on the corner.

"Whose car is that?" Grant's father asked.

"Who you see washing it?" Grant answered.

Grant's father said nothing. His son was way too old for beatings, and he already had everything they could give him, things that most of his friends didn't: A two-parent, two-income home. Four grandparents. A stable family life filled with love and holiday rituals. Oliver Grant's descent from his modest but comfortable background into the crack game was simply a measure of how addictive the drug was to both its buyers and sellers. One taste of crack made you a fiend. One taste of crack money made you a dealer. It was the beginning of what Grant later called his "blackout period."

Grant eventually put almost two dozen people in his Park Hill–based organization, including Raekwon and Divine. He had his hands in other neighborhoods, like New Brighton and West Brighton. As he got older, Grant traveled to places like Sacramento, California, and Jacksonville, Florida, to set up shop for brief periods. Still, Grant's hustle wasn't about the acquisition of endless wealth and ever more territory. It was about having fun, buying some nice gear, and always having enough money in his pocket. He just had to be careful.

Grant never got caught with drugs. What he got "knocked" for was a gun charge—pulled over on Linden Boulevard in Brooklyn by undercover cops on the way to his girlfriend's house. In the holding cell, he prayed.

If I get out of this, he vowed, *I'ma do the right thing.*

Grant did get out, eventually receiving probation for weapons possession. As for the game, Grant didn't quit. But he did ease back a bit, with the nagging feeling that he needed to get out of the street. The year was 1990. He was just twenty years old.

They had a saying in Park Hill: *You win the game when you get out the game.* Grant moved away from Staten Island and rented a studio apartment in Queens. It was just his first step at disengagement, though he would still drive back to the old neighborhood daily. One day in 1991, as he stopped at the corner of Targee and Broad streets near the Stapleton Projects, he spied Divine's white Acura sliding up next to him. Divine's brother Rakeem, was in the driver's seat.

Rakeem had been trying to find Grant to thank him for putting up the bail money that freed him during his legal ordeal in Steubenville, Ohio. Now "Rah" needed more help to get on with his life, some cash for musical equipment. Prince Rakeem's hip-hop dreams quickly became a mission for Grant—who bought Rakeem a roomful of equipment and, with it, the possibility of a new career for himself, too.

To leave the past, they rebranded themselves. Thus Rakeem became RZA, Mitchell became Divine, and Oliver "Pook" Grant became Power.

As the Wu-Tang Clan exploded, Power tried to be as useful as possible. He didn't rap. He didn't produce. Nor was he the guy, like Divine, who was going to post up in the office all day. Power liked to move around. He parlayed, he politicked, he pinch-hit.

Power, therefore, had the time and the presence of mind to request that he control the clothing budget for Loud Records' first Wu video, "Method Man." Power took the money, bought some solid-color T-shirts, and paid a friend who worked in a Queens silk-screen shop $100 to let him in after hours to press the shirts up with the Wu-Tang logo.

Power found that the mark of the "W"—initially hand-drawn by RZA's friend Mathematics for the first 12-inch—began to cast a mystical power of its own. On the set, group members, crew, and hangers-on fought over the shirts. After the video was broadcast into homes across America, people "sweated" Power even harder. The Wu-Tang Clan was poised to tour, so Power invested some of his own money and silk-screened some more "W" tees. Half he sold; half he gave away. The idea was to make enough money to cover the cost of a slightly larger run the next time he went in.

Power had also assumed responsibility for the Wu-Tang Clan's fan club, and his post office box in Staten Island was inundated with mail. But shortly after *Enter the Wu-Tang (36 Chambers)* was certified platinum, Power made the fateful mental leap of the entrepreneur: He didn't have a million *fans.* He had a million *customers.* If he could get just ten thousand of them to spend $20, he would have a good little business.

Around this time, Power was approached by a young man named Michael Clark. Clark had done merchandise for a popular Def Jam group called Onyx, and offered to do the same for Wu-Tang. Power told Clark that he was tired of T-shirts. He wanted do something more distinctive—hockey jerseys. Clark brought Power a stack of catalogs to pick styles. Power said that he already knew how to silk-screen. He wanted the next level: embroidery. Clark took Power to a shop in Williamsburg full of machines, and introduced him to the owner, Simon, who made an embroidery disk out of the "W" logo and Power's own handwriting, "Straight from the grains of the Shaolin soil."

Slowly, Power accumulated samples—jerseys, T-shirts, headbands, caps—until they filled the living room of his small studio apartment in Queens that he now shared with his girlfriend and infant son. After he secured Raekwon's and RZA's blessing for the extra real estate on the cassette and CD versions of *Only Built for Cuban Linx . . .* , Power photographed his merchandise and put together the order form.

Even before Raekwon's album dropped, Power was fulfilling orders from fans who had seen the Wu-Tang merchandise on flyers that he handed out at concerts and clubs. Watching a mailbox for dribbles of cash wasn't Power's idea of fun. He had already been a messenger. Power wanted people to come to him. What he needed—what any dealer of product needed—was a *spot.*

The idea of opening up a store wasn't new to hip-hop artists. Naughty by Nature, a Tommy Boy act, had a place in New Jersey called Naughty Gear, selling their own branded shirts, hats, and sundries. Power had gone there once. He liked the store, but thought their clothes were corny and shoddy. He'd make sure that Wu Wear wouldn't have that problem.

Grant was already getting tired of Michael Clark's catalogs. *These are garbage,* Power said of the designs. None of the clothes suited the loose-fitting style that he and his friends preferred. He needed custom work done. Slowly, he and Clark found ways to piece together a unique Wu-Wear ensemble—buying cash-and-carry T-shirts from Eisner Brothers on Essex and Delancey;

hiring a West Indian tailor named Linden to cut huge bolts of camouflage fabric for shorts and pants and to sew Wu-Wear tags into their merchandise. All told Power spent $50,000 to stock the new Wu-Wear store on 61 Victory Boulevard in Staten Island, halfway between the Stapleton Projects and the ferry at St. George Terminal. The shelves of the eight-hundred-square-foot boutique were laden with with caps, shorts, shirts, and jerseys. The wall behind the counter was decorated with graffiti, and on the floor, a giant Wu-Tang logo. Power was ready.

Some members of the Clan, however, weren't so supportive.

"Wu-Wear?!" U-God exclaimed. "Ain't nobody going for that shit."

Aiight, Power thought. *Nigga's got jokes.*

In one respect, Power's "Wu-Wear" idea was an easy target. The history of artist-run businesses was, by and large, a history of failure. Hadn't one of the greatest groups of all time, the Beatles, launched a colossal, multifaceted flop called Apple Corps? Artist-branded products—whether Teddy Pendergrass's Teddy Jeans or Reggie Jackson's Reggie candy bar—tended to be novelties, spiking early and fading with the star itself, sometimes even sooner. Hip-hop wasn't much different. Run-DMC's Adidas deal came just a year before the crew's cultural cachet evaporated.

If Power second-guessed himself, his doubts evaporated on Wu-Wear's opening day in early August 1995. Hot 97's Wendy Williams trumpeted Wu-Wear's debut on air, and came down to help Power celebrate. A line of 150 people snaked around the block.

A few weeks later, Power checked the post office box. Hundreds upon hundreds of envelopes—some with money orders, others with straight cash—had arrived within a few weeks of Raekwon's album release. Power quickly fell into a new, tedious routine: Visiting the post office every other day. Lugging basket after basket of mail back to his spot. Separating the fan mail from the money mail. And fulfilling all of the orders from the store.

In the months thereafter, Wu-Wear received a parade of first-time visitors—kids and adults from the neighborhood, local Wu-Tang fans, industry people, not to mention the stunned, formerly dubious members of the Clan itself. But no visitors were more impressed by what Oliver "Power" Grant had accomplished than Grant's family. His grandmother came away with some Wu-Wear socks. His mother told him that she was proud. His father didn't say much, but Oliver recognized the look in his dad's eyes as one of happiness and, perhaps, relief.

Power was relieved, too. After six years of supporting the dreams of the team and playing the background of the Wu-Tang Clan, Power felt that he finally had *his* own solo album.

Power saw a definite progression in Wu-Wear's clientele. People were calling, asking for directions to the store from places like Virginia and Carolina. Then came the European and Asian tourists, Japanese entrepreneurs arriving with thousands of dollars in their pockets to damn near clean the store out. Power could barely keep up with that kind of demand, but it showed him that a simple storefront couldn't possibly serve all of his potential customers.

As if on cue, into Power's store came a man named Steve Schneider. Schneider owned a clothing distribution company called Urban Sales. He'd heard of the new Wu-Tang enterprise and had a mutual friend bring him to Wu-Wear for the first time. Introduced to Power, Schneider couldn't stop complimenting Power on the clothes, the setup, the whole operation.

If you're thinking about wholesaling, I can help you, Schneider said.

When he first started making Wu-Tang T-shirts, Power thought of them as artist merchandise, nothing more: items to hawk at concerts or give away for promotion. The store and the mail-order business were just more aggressive ways to sell that merchandise. But the influx of bulk buyers from foreign lands and now the words of Steve Schneider made Power think, for the first time, that what he had wasn't so much artist-branded merchandise as it was a clothing line.

Power's business models were Ralph Lauren and Tommy Hilfiger. Perhaps Wu-Wear could inspire that same kind of loyalty among cool, fashionable kids in the hip-hop generation? But when he shared his thoughts with RZA, the abbot of the Wu-Tang Clan planted another seed in Power's mind.

"You could make your shit like Nike," RZA said.

In other words, Wu-Wear could be more than a clothing boutique, more than a designer label. The Wu-Wear mark could be all-American, ubiquitous—transcending lines of race, culture, ethnicity, and income even better than the Wu-Tang Clan itself.

Now this White guy, Steve Schneider, was willing to help. After Power visited Schneider's office in Manhattan's Garment District, he signed a lease for some office space at the Fashion Atrium on Seventh Avenue and 36th Street. Power didn't have an official agreement with Schneider yet; nor did he have relationships with the manufacturers, brokers, and buyers that Wu-

Wear would need to be in business. But the average daily take at the Staten Island store was enough to cover the monthly rent, so why not?

It was Power's way of saying, "I'm here."

The Men's Apparel Guild in California, or MAGIC, first held their conference in 1942, in Palm Springs. As the menswear market exploded in the years following the Second World War, the annual MAGIC show attracted clothing manufacturers and retailers from around the country and the globe. By the 1970s, MAGIC had become so huge that the convention had to be moved out of state, to Las Vegas, to accommodate the needs of exhibitors and visitors. MAGIC was the place where established companies displayed their collections, and where new clothing lines tried to make an impression.

Urban Sales had a booth at MAGIC, and Steve Schneider invited his new friends at Wu-Wear to share his space. In February 1996, Power and Michael Clark arrived in Las Vegas with garment bags packed with T-shirts slung over their shoulders. Power walked around the exhibition and got his first look at the workings of the fashion industry. Schneider's spare display featuring Wu-Wear's little crop of shirts paled in comparison to the huge, professional Karl Kani showcase. Still, Power returned to New York with hundreds of thousands of dollars in orders, and a profound determination to turn Wu-Wear into something more.

Schneider introduced Power to Bob Safian at Courtside, a clothing manufacturing company in Manhattan capable of churning out the kind of quantities that Wu-Wear needed. Power worked out a deal with Safian and Schneider. Urban Sales would market the clothes. Courtside would manufacture and collect, returning the profits to Wu-Wear, which would give a 7 percent fee to Urban Sales.

In 1996, with Schneider's help, Wu-Wear started to appear in urban apparel stores across the country, including chains like Dr. Jays and Up Against the Wall.

As the business grew, Power promoted Michael Clark to be his VP of operations, and brought in a young FIT student, Cynamin Jones, as Wu-Wear's official publicist. Power began to expand Wu-Wear's retail operation, mainly by enfranchising key people in the extended Wu-Tang family to open their own businesses. In August 1996, Tarif and Jihad Michael opened the Wu-Wear store on Peachtree Street in Atlanta. In May 1997, another Wu-Wear store opened in Hampton Roads, Virginia. A one-thousand-square-foot store was being built in Philadelphia, too. For Power, the arrangement was merely an update of how smart players used to work their thing on the streets: sell product in bulk to dealers with the best real estate, rather than controlling the spots yourself—thereby eliminating your headaches, overhead, and liabilities.

Headaches found Power anyway. Members of the group and the extended Wu-Tang family—many of whom Power felt had been dubious and disrespectful to his Wu-Wear dream—now entered his stores with a sense of entitlement, taking whatever they wanted of his inventory without paying. Then there were the bootleggers, seemingly on every sidewalk and in every puny stall in New York, selling fake Wu-Tang and Wu-Wear gear. When Power ran up on these guys, he let them know with a steely gaze that they needed to surrender their goods and close shop immediately. He always tried to restrain himself and avoid a physical confrontation. But a few of the guys in the Wu-Tang circle would go "buck-wild" immediately. The Wu crew caught a lot of cases over bootleggers, and Power had to keep bail money at the ready.

Whether real or fake, every kid in New York sported the mark of the "W" on some piece of clothing, or so it seemed to Carmine Petruzello, the forty-year-old vice president of the men's, young men's, and boys' collection at Macy's Merchandising. Petruzello didn't know too much about hip-hop. He came from Pelham Parkway in the Bronx. Back in the 1970s, he and Sal Abbatiello had been friendly. Abbatiello went off to run the Disco Fever, and Petruzello went into the fashion industry. But nearly twenty years after Abbatiello first saw the commercial possibilities of hip-hop performance, Petruzello spotted his own opportunity in hip-hop fashion.

Petruzello's job was to set the buying strategies for all the Macy's divisions across the country. Over the course of the 1990s, he had watched the ascent of urban brands like Cross Colours. Kids were lunging for this stuff; and because these brands weren't in Macy's, the chain stores like Dr. Jays were getting all of that business. The urban clothing lines had shorter life spans, and young consumers were fickle. But if Petruzello could figure out a way to create "destinations" for these brands—ministores within Macy's—while being nimble enough to handle their volatility, the company might be able to create a larger market for this stuff.

In late 1996, Petruzello—the chief strategist for men's clothing at the largest department store chain in the world—phoned Power at Wu-Wear and asked to meet him.

"I wish I had a dollar for every kid I've seen wearing a Wu-Wear shirt," Petruzello told him.

In the first months of 1997—just four years after Power silk-screened his first Wu-Tang T-shirt, and less than two years after he opened the first Wu-Wear store—Wu-Wear became the first urban brand to get a window display in Macy's flagship Herald Square store, ground zero of mainstream American retail.

This miracle on 34th Street was part of a larger move by Macy's to bring in young, hip-hop-inspired clothing lines like FUBU and Mecca, two other lines run by young Black entrepreneurs bred on hip-hop. Petruzello soon put Wu-Wear into at least a hundred Macy's locations around the country and, on a larger scale, opened the door for all the urban lines to compete with the big boys of American fashion.

On one level, the rise of Wu-Wear added another dimension to the Wu-Tang Clan's seeming ubiquity, as White teenagers across America got to wear their allegiance on their sleeves. On another level, Wu-Tang became the first group in hip-hop, and perhaps in all of pop music, to not only launch themselves as a successful American brand outside of the entertainment industry, but to *own* that brand.

Power imagined that somewhere in America, a kid was arriving at school, sporting his new Wu-Wear outfit as proudly as Power had once worn his Coca-Cola pants and shirt, his way of saying, "I'm here."

When John Pemberton, a Confederate Civil War veteran and Atlanta pharmacist, invented Pemberton's French Wine Coca in 1885, he was trying to create a concoction to cure depression and addiction. He had no idea that he would be giving birth to an entirely new consumer product: the soft drink. An Atlanta businessman bought the rights to Pemberton's drink, now renamed "Coca-Cola," and to the drink's logo, written in Edwardian script by Pemberton's associate, Frank Robinson.

As Coca-Cola Company grew nationally through an ingenious bottling franchise system, the company saw the need to protect their product against imitators. They did it by branding their product with distinctive packaging, and launching an advertising campaign that highlighted the importance of authenticity, with slogans like "Demand the genuine," "Accept no substitutes," and "It's the Real Thing."

Throughout the twentieth century, Coca-Cola pioneered the use of advertising to turn its local drink into a global brand. In turn, anything that happened in the world of advertising and marketing, Coca-Cola usually did first. Coca-Cola launched its outreach to Black America in the 1950s when a businessman named Moss Kendrix offered to consult the company on cornering the Negro market, garnering the goodwill of the community with smart advertising and associations with the right celebrities. Coca-Cola also pioneered the use of pop music in its advertising when they created a TV commercial in the early 1970s called "Hilltop." The song that came out of that commercial, "I'd Like to Teach the World to Sing," became a Top 10 pop hit in the U.S. and number one in the U.K.

Coca-Cola, more than any other company, invented American branding. That was why generations of young marketing executives clamored to work for the company. It was why, on one morning in 1991, several dozen college seniors gathered at an informational session about employment at the company's Atlanta headquarters. Most of those present wanted to work with Coca-Cola's flagship brand, Coke Classic. All except for one: a young Black MBA student named Darryl Cobbin.

Cobbin hailed from Detroit, the place where America made things, whether cars or music. But he had fallen in love with *marketing* things as an MBA student at Clark Atlanta University. As he approached graduation, Cobbin set his sights on Sprite—a small brand with only 3 percent of Coca-Cola's overall sales—because he felt it was the only brand that was doing things a little differently. One of the things that impressed Cobbin about Sprite was that it had been the only product in the Coca-Cola family to do any kind of marketing with hip-hop in it—from a Kurtis Blow Sprite spot in the early 1980s, to recent commercials with pop-friendly rappers like Heavy D and Kid 'N Play.

Cobbin's enthusiasm got him hired at Sprite as a junior brand manager under another Black executive, Steve Horn. As Cobbin got a feel for the place, he looked for ways to grow the brand.

The traditional consumers of Sprite had been and still were mothers and children. Cobbin also understood that the soft-drink industry was experiencing its biggest growth among young people in their teens and early twenties. If Sprite were to grow, Cobbin would have to break into that market somehow. But Sprite had little profile among teenagers and young adults. To convince the higher-ups that Sprite even had a chance with the youth market, Cobbin would need proof.

So Cobbin taught himself how to use Coca-Cola's powerful Metaphor computer system, developed specifically to crunch numbers for the consumer products industry. What he discovered about Sprite encouraged him: high velocity—meaning higher sales—in areas with high concentrations of minorities, African-Americans and Latinos. It told him that Sprite's occasional forays into Black-targeted advertising were working, and that there was room for growth among a very influential, trendsetting segment of consumers.

When Darryl Cobbin, armed with his data, told the top marketing executives at Coca-Cola that he wanted Sprite to become the dominant beverage of young people across the country, they greeted him with skepticism. Cobbin was cross-examined by the head of North American marketing and by senior members of the bottling organization. *Why are you interested in the youth market? There's still room for growth among mothers and children. Why not steal some more moms and kids from 7UP?*

The question pointed to another obstacle for Cobbin. The Coca-Cola Company structured itself by "flavor profile." Sprite inhabited the "lemon-lime" category. Its customary competitors were 7UP and Mountain Dew. Lemon-limes never competed against colas—it was tantamount to pitting an office softball team against a major-league baseball franchise. But that was exactly what Cobbin wanted to do. He saw the "lemon-lime" lane as an artificial limiter to Sprite's growth.

Cobbin had crossed a line. The company was built on the success of Coke. It was the lead brand, with over 60 percent of the company's volume. Diet Coke accounted for another 15 to 20 percent. Every other brand in the building was *supposed* to be subservient to Coke, which, by definition, aimed to be the dominant brand in every demographic. Yet here was Sprite, with its measly 3 to 5 percent, wanting to launch a campaign to challenge colas, to challenge Coke itself, for one of those segments. In the building, the notion was heresy.

Cobbin's numbers and his argument were sound enough to secure him a relatively small budget to go after consumers in their teens and twenties, along with an admonition not to lose any ground against 7UP. Nobody really believed the campaign would amount to anything.

But Darryl Cobbin had a powerful weapon. He knew that hip-hop had become the ascendant—no, *transcendent*—culture for young America, not only among Black and Latino youth, but among White kids as well.

Cobbin saw an uncanny correlation between the attributes of his brand and the values of hip-hop. In focus groups, consumers consistently described

Sprite using words like "cool," "crisp," "clean," and "clear." *Weren't these also terms used to describe excellence in hip-hop?* Cobbin thought. "Cool" was still employed to denote calm under pressure, trusting your instincts, displaying style and excellence. In hip-hop, as with the Black community as a whole, the words "clean" and "crisp" related to fashion: *You're dressed well from head-to-toe; your shoes are nice, your jeans are nice, your shirt is nice, your cap is nice.* The biggest connective word for Cobbin was "clear": no additives, no bullshit. Sprite had no caffeine—or, in the language of hip-hop, no "hype." Hip-hop was, at base, about "keeping it real." Cobbin relayed these ideas to Sprite's general market advertising agency, Lowe Lintas & Partners, which came back with a three-part slogan:

Image is nothing.
Thirst is everything.
Obey your thirst.

Cobbin wanted to use hip-hop music and artists as the hub of his campaign. Usually, big consumer brands and their ad agencies chose artists with the broadest appeal. But that practice often resulted in the most tepid and least credible acts being tapped; MC Hammer's deals with Pepsi and KFC were a prime example. More than anything, Cobbin wanted credibility. He wanted artists who demonstrated Sprite's understanding of the art, regardless of commerce. He didn't want Kid 'N Play because they were cute. He wanted Brand Nubian because they were cool.

Not only did Cobbin want the right hip-hop artists, he wanted to use them in a *way* that was hip-hop. He detested the way corporations turned artists into hucksters: *Hey, do that song you do, but could you rework the lyrics to make it about Sprite?* Cobbin would simply ask the artists to be themselves. Mentioning Sprite was secondary. Associating Sprite with their unique creativity was primary.

Cobbin's requests confounded even the trendiest ad men and women. Burrell Communications in Chicago was Sprite's agency for the African-American market, the "go-to" firm when corporate America needed to sell Black folks their products and services. Coke and Sprite were long-term Burrell clients. But Cobbin's account executive had no idea what Cobbin was requesting when he asked that they get someone named "Primo" to do the beats for his radio spot. He had to clarify: *DJ Premier, the producer and DJ of Gang Starr.*

Cobbin concluded his conversation and hung up. Minutes later, Cobbin's phone rang.

"Who are you?" a male voice on the other end asked.

"I'm Darryl Cobbin; I'm the assistant brand manager for Sprite—"

"No, no, no," the voice interrupted. "Who. *Are*. You?"

Cobbin was dumbstruck. The man continued.

"I'm Reginald Jolley. I'm creative at Burrell. Did you just tell someone to 'Go get *Primo*'?"

"Yes," Cobbin said.

"Who the fuck *are* you, man?!"

Cobbin discovered that Reginald Jolley—a twenty-four-year-old former graffiti writer from the West Side of Chicago who transformed himself into an illustrator and graphic artist—was his analog at Burrell: the only guy in his company who understood hip-hop culture. The previous year, Jolley suggested EPMD protégés Das EFX for a Sprite spot. His bosses at Burrell thought that the rappers looked "scary." They insisted on the kiddie duo Kris Kross instead. So Jolley was excited to finally discover someone else in the business who knew what he knew—and an executive at Coca-Cola, no less! As they spoke, Jolley could scarcely believe what he was hearing: Cobbin talking of hiring Rakim for a radio spot.

"You know about *Rakim*?" Jolley cried.

"Yes, Reg, I know about Rakim," Cobbin replied.

Together, Cobbin and Jolley devised a series of TV commercials that featured artists Pete Rock & C. L. Smooth, Grand Puba from Brand Nubian, and Large Professor from Main Source, not performing to the camera, but freestyling in the recording studio over the classic break beat "Impeach the President" by the Honeydrippers. For a radio spot, Jolley plucked an obscure rapper from his hometown of Chicago named Common Sense to rap over a beat by an even more obscure producer named No I.D.

The "Obey Your Thirst" campaign took the hip-hop community by surprise as it rolled out in March of 1994. It was low-key. It was smart. It was novel. *The Source* lauded the commercials. Fans lunged for their VCRs to record them. But the numbers showed the full picture. In just nine months, Sprite's sales grew an astounding 9 percent, compared to nearly flat growth in the previous year. The corporation hadn't doled out any incremental money to supplement the initial budget either, so it *had* to be Cobbin's marketing.

By 1995, more money started flowing from Coca-Cola to Cobbin's Sprite campaign. In a meeting between Burrell and Coca-Cola executives, Jolley proposed a new chapter of the campaign by handing Cobbin a copy of *The Source* with a mock advertisement: The page was pitch-black, except for a few words scrawled in Sprite green-and-white: "KRS vs. MC Shan. Let's Settle This." Cobbin got the significance immediately: Sprite was about to create a historic event in hip-hop culture. Jolley described his idea: a TV commercial that presented a long-awaited rematch between old foes, with Red Alert and Marley Marl serving as corner men.

No one else in the room knew what Jolley and Cobbin were talking about. But Coca-Cola trusted Cobbin now, as Burrell did Jolley. For all intents and purposes, it was all on them.

Cobbin and Jolley called themselves "Batman" and "Robin." And the caper on which they embarked, "Obey Your Thirst," made Sprite the fastest-growing soft-drink brand in America for two years straight. It not only crushed 7UP. Its growth curve beat both Pepsi and Coke. The base volume of Sprite—the hard number of bottles and cans sold—tripled in three years, from 5 percent of Coca-Cola's business to nearly 15. In those years, Sprite was responsible for 40 percent of the Coca-Cola Company's overall growth. And true to Cobbin's prediction, Sprite became the dominant brand among young people—not just Blacks and Latinos, but White kids as well.

Darryl Cobbin knew what he was doing even if he never articulated it. When Cobbin booked time for his TV spots, he bought around pop music programming, irrespective of the ethnic composition of the audience. Just as the lemon-lime soda wasn't going to stay in its lane but rather compete directly with colas, hip-hop would be matched against pop music on its own terms. Both Sprite and hip-hop would win. Not by crossing over. But by taking over.

Cobbin liked to think that "Obey Your Thirst" sent a clear message to corporate America:

It's okay to work with this culture, Proctor & Gamble.

It's okay, Ford Motor Company.

It's okay, IBM.

Because this great American brand aligned itself with hip-hop.

And it's beating everybody.

On October 12, 1995, Tupac Shakur walked out of Clinton prison in Dannemora, New York. If you read the pages of *Vibe* and *The Source* in the weeks that followed, Shakur's release was rumored to be the result of intervention from Death Row Records CEO Suge Knight—who reportedly posted Shakur's bail in return for Shakur's move to Death Row.

The rumors were wrong.

Atron Gregory had been looking out for Tupac Shakur since Shakur was seventeen years old. Unlike many artist managers and music entrepreneurs, Gregory didn't try to choke every dollar out of his artist. When Shakur wanted his publishing rights back, insisting that he didn't know what he was signing, Gregory simply tore the contract up. When Shakur got upset that Gregory had other management clients, Gregory ceded his management contract to Shakur's uncle, Watani Tyehimba. After 'Pac caught the sexual assault case and Watani wanted Gregory back, he returned for half the rate he was making before. Gregory tried to get Shakur different legal representation when everyone said that Afeni Shakur's Black Panther lawyer, William Kunstler, wasn't the right man for the case. Gregory sat with Shakur as he threatened suicide, a pistol in each hand, pointing one at each temple. Gregory kept 'Pac's friends and family in motel rooms in Dannemora so Shakur could spend as much time out of his cell as possible. Gregory worked with Shakur's legal team to successfully secure the rapper's appeal. And Gregory put together the bail package to spring Shakur from prison.

He knew that Shakur wanted to sign with Knight. When Gregory visited Dannemora, Shakur had told him so. *You don't need Suge*, Gregory countered. Sitting in jail, all Shakur saw on TV was Biggie, in video after video. *You're selling better than him*, Gregory insisted. But Shakur didn't care. Shakur was convincing himself that his shooting was some Bad Boy plot to clear him out of the way so Biggie could take his place. It was ridiculous. 'Pac knew who set him up. *Everyone* knew. And it wasn't Big; it wasn't Puff. Now Shakur felt that the only one who could protect him was Suge.

Gregory wasn't mad at Shakur. Nor did he fault Suge Knight for being the predator he was. But Gregory seethed at Jimmy Iovine's back-channel machinations. In Gregory's judgment, Iovine had engineered Shakur's move to Death Row—arguably transgressing Shakur's production deal with Gregory—because Iovine thought Knight could control Shakur. Gregory had half a mind to slap Iovine with a tortious-interference lawsuit.

"I'm so sorry," Shakur's aunt told Gregory. "He knows he's making a deal with the devil."

Atron Gregory decided to get paid out of the recording contract by Interscope, and that would be it. He hoped Shakur knew what he was getting himself into.

Upon Shakur's release, Suge Knight flew his new artist to California, and put him directly into Can-Am recording studio, where he began taping the tracks that would comprise his Death Row/Interscope debut, a double-album called *All Eyez on Me*. Shakur recorded a song with Dr. Dre—a paean to West Coast hip-hop called "California Love." The album and single dropped in February 1996, and would go on to sell more than four million units.

At liberty and under the aegis of Death Row, Tupac Shakur escalated his war of words with Biggie, Bad Boy, and the East Coast. At the Soul Train awards in Los Angeles, Shakur leaned out of a car and taunted Biggie and Bad Boy's entourage, provoking a feverish drawing of weapons on both sides. In interviews, Shakur intimated that he'd had sex with Biggie's wife, Bad Boy artist Faith Evans; and in June 1996, he released a song called "Hit 'Em Up" where he made that assertion explicit, along with calling out several other East Coast artists.

The back-and-forth became the talk of radio DJs and magazines. But no media outlet covered the stories better or had more access than *Vibe*. In February 1996, coinciding with the release of Shakur's album, *Vibe*'s "Live from Death Row" cover featured the faces of Shakur, Knight, Dre, and Snoop Dogg, with Tupac predicting that the East Coast–West Coast war was "gonna get deep." Then, in September, *Vibe* scored another exclusive: Sean "Puffy" Combs and the Notorious B.I.G. speaking at length on the problems with Shakur and Knight. Again Combs and Biggie denied any ill will, incredulous that Death Row seemed bent on inflaming the situation at every turn. The article was accompanied by a time line labeled "Death Row vs. Bad Boy." But on the cover, the bold headline read "EAST VS. WEST."

A few weeks after *Vibe*'s issue hit newsstands, Tupac Shakur was shot by an unknown gunman while riding in a car with Suge Knight on the Las Vegas strip. He died of his wounds six days later.

Shakur came from the Bay Area. But after his death it was Los Angeles that got angry.

Harold Austin—the successor to Keith Naftaly as program director of 92.3 the Beat after Naftaly left to take an A&R job at Arista Records—felt the dark mood in the calls that came into the station. Although it seemed likely that Shakur was killed by members of a Los Angeles gang hostile to Suge Knight, many people seemed to think that Sean Combs and the Notorious B.I.G. had something to do with the shooting.

Austin tried to be faithful to his listeners. He was proud that a commercial station like the Beat could mirror the mournful, sometimes mad mood of the people. The Beat stood for its community, too, with promos and bumpers that shouted, "Representing the Best Coast, the West Coast," and "There's Only One Best Side, the West Side" running alongside the slogans that Naftaly exported from KMEL, "No Color Lines" and "Peace in the Streets."

About six months after Shakur's death, Harold Austin woke at four a.m. to the ringing of his phone

"Harold!" the voice said. "It's Rob Stone. Are you awake?"

"It's four in the morning," Austin said.

"Did you hear what happened?" Stone sounded agitated. "Harold, Biggie got shot. Biggie's dead." Austin sat up in his bed as Stone described what had happened.

Biggie had come to town to promote his new album, *Life after Death*. The double CD featured a sly remake of LL Cool J's "Going Back to Cali"—which sounded either like a peace offering to the West Coast in the wake of Tupac Shakur's death or a smug provocation, depending on how one was predisposed to hear it. Biggie and Sean Combs did seem at ease in Los Angeles, holding court at *Vibe*'s after-party at the Petersen Automotive Museum following the Soul Train Music Awards on March 8, 1997—a celebration attended by throngs of hip-hop celebrities, executives, and entourages. As Biggie and Combs left the party, a car pulled alongside the rapper's rented green GMC Suburban, and a gunman pumped seven 9mm bullets into his body. Twenty-four-year-old Christopher Wallace, The Notorious B.I.G., was pronounced dead at Cedars Sinai Hospital less than an hour later. Combs and the Bad Boy family were outside the emergency room, inconsolable.

Stone told Austin that Steve Smith had stopped regular programming at Hot 97 in New York and had called all his jocks back into the station for an on-air forum. At Power 106 in Los Angeles, the Baka Boyz were already on the air talking about Biggie's murder. But the Beat was still playing romantic ballads for Saturday night lovers.

"Helllloo?" Kevin "Slow Jammin'" James said luxuriantly when he answered the hotline. "Everything ohhhhhkaaay?" Austin told him about Biggie's death.

"Ohhhhh," James sighed. "What do you want me to do?"

It was a Sunday morning. Harold Austin sprang into action, calling the host of the Beat's community affairs program, Dominique DiPrima, to get down to the station right away. Austin and his girlfriend, air personality Lisa

Canning, sped to the Beat as well. Canning relieved DiPrima, playing Biggie's music and taking listener calls, while Austin listened from his office.

"So how do you feel about Big's death?" Canning asked one caller, who sounded to Austin like a dude from the 'hood.

"I'm glad that nigga's dead," the caller said.

"Excuse me?" Canning replied.

"That nigga had it coming."

"Please don't use the 'n-word.'"

"Fuck that."

In his office, Austin froze.

It's been six months since 'Pac died, the listener continued. *This fool come rolling here large, living it up. It was only a matter of time before we capped his ass.*

Austin leaped from his seat and ran into the studio just as Canning ended the call and segued into a song.

"How could you put that call on the air?!" Austin shouted.

"We're *live*," Canning replied.

"You should have dumped the call as soon as he said that! That was so irresponsible!" Now Austin wasn't Canning's boyfriend, but her irate boss. Canning shot back.

"I have news for you," she said. "L.A. is not exactly mourning Big."

The next morning, Austin came into the office early, at eight thirty, just to get a jump on the day's work. His assistant, Emily, was there already.

"Russell Simmons called you. Twice."

A few minutes later, Austin's general manager came to tell him the same thing. Then Emily poked her head into Austin's office: Russell Simmons was on the line for him right now.

"Hal!" Simmons began. Simmons pronounced his name so fast, it never came out as "Howard."

"Hal! I was with that nigga, man! That nigga was drinking champagne at my *table*! That nigga was on top of the world. He left, next thing you know, he got shot! I can't believe this shit!" Simmons was distraught.

"Hal, you're *contributing* to this shit!" he said.

"Wait a minute, Russell . . ." Austin replied.

"NONONONONONONO! LISTEN TO ME! I just got off the phone with Keith Clinkscales at *Vibe*! I just tore that nigga a new asshole! Because that motherfucker is *fueling* this shit so much on his covers! 'East vs. West' . . . 'Puffy and Bad Boy vs. Suge and Death Row' . . . THAT SHIT IS

IRRESPONSIBLE! Hal, I listen to your station, and I hear this 'West Coast, best coast' . . . THERE IS NO SHIT LIKE THAT! And *Lisa*, of *all people*, my *girl*, has some idiot blasting on the air. You're running one of the biggest stations in the country! You have so much influence! You can't do that kind of radio!

"Hal, I got niggas calling me like, 'Russell, what the fuck are you still doing in L.A.? Get on a plane now! It's not safe!' It's motherfucking 1997! I can't believe a Black man can't walk anywhere he wants in America! I'm gonna stay. But I'm scared, Hal. I'm scared."

After Austin got off the phone, he went to his production people who programmed the equipment where the music, commercials, and promotional spots were all stored in digital files. Austin ordered them to dump all of the "West Coast" drops.

"Take those things off of the system," Austin said. "I don't want anyone to play them anymore."

The deaths of Tupac Shakur and Christopher "Biggie" Wallace were hard on the editors and writers of *Vibe* magazine, too, people who had come to know the artists through covering them, like Kevin Powell, and Danyel Smith, who had a long-standing friendship with Tupac that preceded her tenure at *Vibe*.

In the aftermath of Biggie's murder, the cover of *Vibe* featured a photograph of the Notorious B.I.G. in profile, along with a headline that read, "When Will It End?" Many people, like Russell Simmons, felt the cover was the ultimate in hypocrisy. *After* Vibe *complicated things by reporting, they reported how things were so complicated.* But *Vibe* was only the most visible party to a duplicity that implicated the entire industry—the radio DJs who reveled in gossip of the East-West war and then lamented about the bloodletting on air; the artists who fed the conflict with their lyrics and then spoke of peace; the executives who distributed the music and then paid for funerals and posthumous tributes.

The fortunes of many businesses throughout American history were forged in blood. The titans of the hip-hop business in the mid-nineties were no exception.

In the wake of Shakur's death, Death Row Records sold Tupac Shakur records in the tens of millions, including a mysterious album that Shakur recorded under the name "Makaveli," whose lyrics seemed to presage his death.

Sean Combs had been tussling with Biggie's lawyers before his death. They wanted the return of Biggie's publishing, which Combs had bought for a figure that seemed painfully low in light of the artist's eventual success.

"I will never give it up until I'm dead and my bones are crushed into powder," Combs told Andy Tavel, the same attorney who declined to represent Combs in his negotiations with Harrell. "*You* people taught me that."

But following Biggie's shooting, Combs mourned his artist and friend in a song called "I'll Be Missing You," featuring Biggie's wife, Faith Evans, and other Bad Boy artists. In the video, Combs walked through surreal green fields and twirled in the rain. Whether dancing away his pain or dancing on Big's grave, Combs was dancing his way into a new career as his own record company's flagship artist. Puff Daddy & the Family's first album, *No Way Out*, went on to sell seven million copies. With "All about the Benjamins" as Combs's follow-up track, and continuing singles from The Notorious B.I.G.'s *Life after Death*, Bad Boy songs comprised 39 percent of the number one records on the Billboard Hot 100 in 1997.

In the years of Bad Boy's and Death Row's dominance, *The Source* had risen to become the number one music magazine on American newsstands, supplanting *Rolling Stone*. And the circulation of *Vibe* magazine, bought from Time Warner by former Time, Inc., honcho Bob Miller in 1995, reached 450,000 copies in 1997. With that clout, *Vibe* pulled an unprecedented power move: purchasing the alternative rock magazine *Spin*, for $43 million. This was an ironic twist on America's cultural history: a hip-hop magazine becoming the "parent" to a rock publication.

As turntables turned, tables turned, too.

Rob Stone buckled himself in for a six-hour flight to Los Angeles, scrounging in the seat pocket in front of him for something to read.

He pulled out not a copy of the in-flight magazine, but an issue of *Brandweek* that another passenger left behind from a previous trip—a special edition spotlighting "Marketers of the Year" for 1997. Thumbing through the magazine, Stone stopped cold on page sixty-two. Standing astride a two-page spread was Darryl Cobbin, honored for his work with Sprite as "the most important person to have wrapped his mind, soul, and spirit around the lemon-lime soft drink," nearly doubling the soft drink's market share using "a hip-hop attitude."

So this *is the guy!* Stone realized. He had never known who was behind those amazing "Obey Your Thirst" commercials. Just last year, he had seen the most incredible new Sprite campaign: Rappers Nas and AZ re-creating and updating the famous Double Trouble "Stoop Rap" from the classic hip-hop movie *Wild Style*. "Here's a little story that must be told," they rapped, "about two players rockin' all the ice and gold."

Stone read on. Cobbin's use of hip-hop to transform Sprite into the key youth beverage convinced Coca-Cola to shift the company's crucial NBA sponsorship from Coke Classic to Sprite. Cobbin himself had to talk NBA chairman David Stern through the wisdom of the switch. For his efforts, Cobbin had recently been promoted out of Sprite altogether, to senior manager of the global sports marketing group.

The story of Darryl Cobbin riveted Rob Stone, because Stone wasn't just a record promoter anymore. After a label bidding war for his services among Arista, Columbia, and Motown—where Andre Harrell had just been hired to helm and revive the fading brand—Stone decided to strike out on his own. A chance meeting with Jon Rifkind at the Jack the Rapper convention had led him to form a new company with Steve Rifkind called Cornerstone.

The idea was for the Steven Rifkind Company to handle the world of street marketing, and Cornerstone the realm of radio promotion—working together to use the power of hip-hop for corporate clients both inside and outside the music industry. Stone would also join Rifkind's companies as a vice president at both SRC and Loud. But Rifkind was doing huge things: launching his Street Team worldwide and preparing to sell an interest in SRC to Lowe—the same advertising agency that came up with the "Obey Your Thirst" slogan. These projects distracted Stone, who wanted to concentrate exclusively on his own business. Rifkind and Stone split amicably, and Stone moved his company to new offices on 23rd Street with a new partner, Jon Cohen. After reading the article on Cobbin, Rob Stone knew he had to make Sprite a client.

Stone assembled a package for Darryl Cobbin that he hoped would convey Cornerstone's value. In the envelope, Stone placed Cornerstone's first "mix CD"—a sponsorable collection of new music blended by DJ Supa Dupe to be sent to every important radio DJ and programmer across America, and a T-shirt that read, "DJs Are the Cornerstone of Hip-Hop," manufactured by up-and-coming hip-hop clothing company Mecca, cosponsored by a brand new hip-hop magazine called *XXL*, founded by *Source* alumni James Bernard and Reginald Dennis.

Stone sent his parcel and followed it with a couple of calls to Cobbin's office, with no response. Then, a few weeks later, Stone's phone rang.

"I think you're onto something here," Darryl Cobbin said after introducing himself. Cobbin wanted Stone to describe Cornerstone's "point of difference."

Point of what? Stone thought.

"What makes you different from any other agency out there?" Cobbin explained.

Stone answered by reciting Cornerstone's list of services: sending music to a network of DJs across the country, working the streets and clubs, getting records played. . . .

"No," Cobbin interrupted. "What you have are *conduits to the masses.* You have voice boxes in each market that can speak to today's youth."

Stone hurriedly took notes as this total stranger described Cornerstone's business plan better than Stone himself ever had. He had called for a client, and ended up with a mentor.

"If you want to do business with Coca-Cola," Cobbin said, "you're going to have to learn to speak this way."

Cobbin explained that he no longer worked for Sprite, and that he had bequeathed the day-to-day brand management to one of his personally groomed protégés—a savvy young marketer named Rohan Oza. Cobbin gave Stone some pointers on pitching Cornerstone to Oza.

"Off the record," Cobbin continued, "if he doesn't hire you, I'm going to give you the number of a friend of mine at Mountain Dew."

Stone found that Rohan Oza didn't need too much convincing. Oza wasn't a hip-hop aficionado like Darryl Cobbin or Reginald Jolley; but Cobbin had taught him a lot, and his former boss's recommendation of Cornerstone was enough to secure the firm Sprite's business.

Rob Stone proposed an ambitious event to capitalize on Sprite's credibility with the hip-hop generation: a Sprite DJ summit, flying the top twenty jocks from around the country into Las Vegas for the upcoming Billboard Music Awards. At the MGM Grand Hotel, Sprite set up a radio studio beneath the new Studio 54 dance club, where DJs could broadcast live interviews with big-name artists like Snoop Dogg, who made the rounds for the jocks in the Sprite suite.

With Cornerstone's help, Oza got to know America's top hip-hop DJs personally, and began to see them just as Stone did: as trendsetters and weathervanes in their respective markets. Oza also came to rely on them for honest feedback about the Sprite brand. Sprite gave DJs access and respect. In return, the DJs gave Sprite their goodwill, as well as copious mentions on the radio. And Stone tapped into a continuing stream of Sprite projects.

The Sprite DJ summit marked the climax of the latest Sprite ad campaign. It was Reginald Jolley's most preposterous idea yet: a series of five linked commercials, crafted in Japanese-style anime, to re-create the classic "Voltron" story with a hip-hop twist.

Again, his colleagues at Burrell had been doubtful. Why five commercials? Why Japanese animation? And why, for God's sake, did he want Japanese subtitles, too? What did it all mean?

Jolley explained the story line. The evil King Zarkon comes to Earth to destroy hip-hop culture. Four rap acts from the four corners of America try to defeat Zarkon: From the East Coast, Fat Joe; from the South, the Goodie Mob; from the Midwest, Common; and from the West Coast, Mack 10, each piloting a mechanical "lion" equipped to fight Zarkon's "Robeast."

Jolley continued: One by one, all four lions are defeated. Then, descending from the sun, a fifth lion emerges, piloted by the founding father of hip-hop culture, Afrika Bambaataa. As he did in the Bronx of the 1970s, Bambaataa counsels the young lions: *What you need is unity. You can't save hip-hop if you don't band together.* In the fifth and last commercial, the four lions from the four regions join forces, each transforming into a section of a new, larger being called Voltron. In the final moments, Voltron defeats King Zarkon. Hip-hop lives.

Jolley's narrative didn't mean much to the executives at his agency. But Jolley knew that hip-hop fans would understand. The hip-hop nation had just come through a senseless civil war in which two young "lions," former friends, had become enemies. Both, in turn, were killed. For hip-hop to survive, the petty regionalism would have to cease. And who better to broker the new solidarity than the man who helped define the four elements of hip-hop culture? The spots were imbued with spiritual meaning for the perceptive disciple of hip-hop: The lions formed the limbs of Voltron as Arm-Leg-Leg-Arm-Head, the Five Percenters' phonetic code for A-L-L-A-H.

Rohan Oza backed Jolley, despite skepticism at both Burrell and Sprite over the young creative executive's potential folly. What did this have to do with branding? Why should a soda company try to make some profound statement? Why would anybody even embrace this kind of message coming from Sprite?

"Because," Reginald Jolley said. "We matter now."

The Voltron spots began airing in August 1998. Like the earlier "Obey Your Thirst" campaigns, the new commercials were received with enthusiasm by many in the hip-hop community, and discussed in *The Source* and *Vibe*. The final spot aired during the Billboard Music Awards in Las Vegas, in tandem with the DJ summit. Rohan Oza felt a chill of energy and a surge of pride as he saw the DJs react.

Times had indeed changed. In the traumatic aftermath of the deaths of Biggie and Tupac, the moral uplift was provided not by a collective of artists— as it had been with the Stop the Violence Movement and *We're All in the Same Gang* records in the late 1980s—but by a young creative director at an advertising agency representing the archetypical corporate American brand.

The year 1997 was the high-water mark for the Wu-Tang Clan and for Wu-Wear as well.

On June 21, 1997, Loud/RCA released the Wu-Tang Clan's long-awaited second album. Many industry watchers had doubted that the Wu-Tang Clan could reconvene, given the members' success individually. This was a matter of extreme importance to Steve Rifkind and Rich Isaacson at Loud Records. The execution of their new joint-venture agreement with RCA Records and its parent conglomerate, the Bertelsmann Music Group, depended on their delivery and release of the next Wu-Tang album by June 30, 1997; Strauss Zelnick, the CEO of BMG North America, needed to make his numbers by the end of the company's fiscal year. Rifkind, with the backing of Zelnick, dangled a lucrative advance before the group as an incentive: $4 million, payable upon delivery.

Wu-Tang Forever debuted at number one on the Billboard Top 200 album chart, and sold over 650,000 copies in its first week. With several Wu-Tang members now solo stars, the album had been difficult to make; and the launch was marred by the late delivery of the video for the first single, "Triumph." The $1 million special-effects-infused opus directed by Brett Ratner premiered on MTV more than one month after the album's street date. By then, the album's sales had dropped considerably.

The Wu-Tang Clan virtually disintegrated over the course of their summer tour with rock group Rage Against the Machine. By September, the RZA pulled the group from the tour's remaining dates, and resigned himself to the prescience of his five-year prediction. The Wu-Tang, as a cohesive group, was over.

Oliver "Power" Grant's grand fashion experiment had reached the $10 million mark in sales. Wu-Wear sold in department stores across the country and appeared in fashion spreads in consumer and trade magazines from *The Source* to *Sportswear International*. Standing at the threshold between his small-business past and big-business future, like many American entrepreneurs, Power was having all kinds of trouble making the transition.

Power's stores were closing because of mismanagement. His relationships with Wu-Wear's manufacturers were fraught with disagreements over cash advances and delivery. Power increasingly blamed his lieutenant, Michael Clark, for driving a wedge between him and the executives at Wu-Wear's suppliers. And Power had troubles focusing on the business at hand, especially when his hands were still managing other Wu-Tang affairs and pursuing new opportunities. Director James Toback came to meet with Power about licensing some Wu-Tang Clan music for his new film. Toback came out of that meeting convinced that he had just found the perfect leading man.

Toback's script for *Black and White* was a screed on the White worship of Black culture. In its portrayal of Black-White interactions as mostly pathological, it aimed a cynical eye at the very phenomenon that made Wu-Tang and Wu-Wear successful. Power, cast as the film's protagonist, "Rich Bower," made his big-screen debut alongside a stellar ensemble cast that included Ben Stiller, Robert Downey Jr., Elijah Wood, and Mike Tyson. Along the way, Power got to have mock sex with Bijou Phillips and lock lips with model Claudia Schiffer. Compared to the rag trade, Hollywood was heaven.

Wu-Wear blasted open the breach for new "urban" apparel lines in major department stores, but it couldn't hold its new territory. The company was quickly outpaced by other players in the space, like FUBU, which—despite their "For Us By Us" moniker—vaulted to the $200 million sales level in 1998 largely because of an investment from the Korean firm Samsung.

The eclipse of the Wu-Tang Clan was symbolized at the 40th Annual Grammy Awards on the night of February 25, 1998, after Puff Daddy's *No Way Out* bested *Wu-Tang Forever* for Best Rap Album of the Year. Just as singer-songwriter Shawn Colvin was about to accept her award for Song of the Year, Ol' Dirty Bastard leaped onstage and seized the microphone:

"I went and bought me an outfit that costed me a lot of money today, 'cause I figured that Wu-Tang was gonna win," he began, white silk scarf swishing over his maroon coat. "I don't know how y'all see it, but when it comes to the children, Wu-Tang is for the children. We teach the children. Puffy is good, but Wu-Tang is the best. I want you to know that this is ODB and I love you all. Peace." With that, Ol' Dirty Bastard was hustled off the stage.

Half of the hip-hop nation, those who kept it real, cheered this bit of musical mutiny in rap's increasingly scripted and slick odyssey into the mainstream, while the other half, who kept it right, winced. However cringe-worthy the moment for the hip-hop nation's growing adult population, Wu-Tang did indeed teach the children of hip-hop and America a powerful lesson by igniting the entrepreneurial fires of hip-hop artists, and young Black artists in particular. The members of the Wu were once branded slaves of the music business until they snatched the branding iron, turned it on their corporate masters, and seared the mark of the "W" onto them all. The multipronged success of the Wu-Tang Clan carried with it an implicit message: You didn't need to beg corporate America for anything. If you were yourself, if you "did you," corporate America would come knocking on your door.

It was a teaching that even Sean "Puffy" Combs, who kept it rich, took to heart. It was a lesson in liberty, straight from the island upon whose children the green lady of the harbor kept her ever-watchful eye.

Despite the unprecedented success and autonomy won by the Wu-Tang Clan, most recording artists still lived in the Dark Ages.

For years, Bert Padell had described this sad state of affairs to the students who attended his pop music business class at The New School. Record contracts, he taught, were unconscionable things. The average new artist generally received a royalty rate of between 10 to 12 percentage points of the retail sales price of a record. A great many things were deducted from the artists' share: cash advances, the recording funds (including payments to all producers and recording studios), packaging costs, "breakage" deductions (an anachronism from the days when records were made from brittle shellac), and often half of the costs of video production and independent promoters. Whatever royalties an artist eventually earned were carved up further—15 to 20 percent to the manager, 5 percent to the lawyer whom the artist couldn't afford to pay at the hourly rate, another 5 percent to the business manager or accountant. A new artist, even if their debut album were certified gold at over 500,000 copies sold, might not see any royalties beyond their initial advance, depending on how much the record company spent in recoupable promotion to get the album to that level of sales.

Artists did have other ways to make money—publishing royalties from record companies for the use of the songs they wrote; and merchandise sales of T-shirts, posters, and artist swag. Alas, Padell continued: Record companies often grabbed half of the publishing and merchandising rights of new artists, especially those desperate to get their foot in the door with a record label.

Of course, record companies had good reason to minimize the risks they took with new signings. Most new artists sold next to nothing. So the sales of successful artists had to subsidize the overhead costs of the record label and the bad investments that the company made on artists who, more often than not, turned out not to be successful. The attitude of most small record entrepreneurs, whether straight-up businessmen like Steve Plotnicki or music-loving producers like Rick Rubin, was that artists shouldn't expect money until they made money. As soon as they scored their first hit, most artists and their representatives swooped in to renegotiate their initial deal, and most record companies acquiesced. The reigning ethos of the music industry remained: *You suffer until you sell.*

In 1992, one year after Sean "Puffy" Combs first sat in the front row of Bert Padell's classroom, another student absorbed Padell's lessons and stories—not with excitement, but with outrage. In the years to come, this young woman, like Combs, would go on to change the rap business, albeit in a very different way.

If not for the baggy Cross Colours outfits and Timberland boots she wore, few on first glance would have taken Wendy Day for a rap fanatic. She was White, overweight, and, at the age of thirty, old for a hip-hop head. The juxtaposition of her plain middle-American looks with her vociferousness about rap music and conspicuous clothing was so jarring—especially for Black people—that few knew what to make of her. Day had studied at Temple University with Dr. Molefi Kete Asante, the author of the book *Afrocentricity* and the leading propagator of the cultural movement that gripped hip-hop in the late eighties and early nineties. At an African studies seminar at The New School, Wendy Day met a young hip-hop writer named Kevin Powell, and afterward suggested they remain in touch. Powell demurred. He didn't trust that Day was for real.

If it was hard for others to peg Wendy Day, it was tricky for Day herself. For starters, she didn't know who her parents were. At two months of age, she had been adopted by a working-class couple in Cheltenham, Pennsylvania, a suburb just north of Philadelphia. Her adopted father, James Day, was a postman; her mother, Ruth, a homemaker. Cheltenham, despite the Anglo-Saxon name, was an opulent, overwhelmingly Jewish community—adding ethnic, religious, and economic aspects to Day's childhood isolation. Her friends got TransAms for their sixteenth birthdays. Wendy got a watch. All Wendy Day wanted to do when she grew up was make money and spend it.

The day after her high school graduation, the seventeen-year-old Day moved to an apartment in downtown Philadelphia. She worked as a sign painter by day, and went clubbing by night. At a Psychedelic Furs concert in 1980, Day was astonished by the opening act: a bunch of Black guys who rhymed to the beat of records that a fast-fingered DJ spun on the two turntables behind them. At the first sight of Grandmaster Flash & the Furious Five, Wendy Day became a hip-hop disciple. She collected every rap record and bootleg tape she could find. Day made a routine weekly visit to Sound of Market, a downtown record store where the Saturday salesperson, a part-time DJ, slid her dubbed cassettes of New York hip-hop parties and battles.

After a few years, Day had made a life for herself in Philly—enrolling in the graphic design program at the Moore College of Art. But then, on a Friday-night road trip to New York City with a few friends, she heard the Mr. Magic Rap Attack show on WBLS. A few days later, she returned to Philadelphia, dropped her classes, quit her job, packed her stuff, and moved to Manhattan.

Day quickly cultivated a new nightly routine to satisfy her hip-hop fix—going to clubs like the Palladium, the Latin Quarter and the World. She funded her lifestyle by selling magazine advertising for a company called Media Network, a lucrative job that gave her more than enough income for an apartment in SoHo, and a burgundy BMW 325. Money flowed through her.

She pampered not only herself but the people around her. When Day learned that her friend's father, a Canadian engineer named Louis Boulanger, had decided to try importing a French liquor called Aravis into North America, Day collated reams of consumer research available to her at Media Network—including state-by-state demographic information on alcohol consumption. On a trip to Montreal, she dropped the study on his desk. Boulanger offered to double her salary if she came to work for him. In 1987, Day left her hip-hop lifestyle to sell liquor and make bread in Canada, taking night classes in the MBA program at McGill University. Three years later, Boulanger sold his company, Aravis, to Seagram.

"You've made me a very wealthy man," he told Day. As a parting gesture, he gave Day a half million Canadian dollars, which came to about $450,000 when converted back to American currency.

Day returned to New York City, her bank account bursting. But her attitude toward money had shifted polarity. She was divorcing a man whom she had determined was a leech, and she figured her greed had attracted that energy. Capital had given her independence. Now she wanted to use that freedom to pursue a life with meaning. At Bert Padell's music business seminar, hearing the tales of rap artists reduced to virtual indentured servitude, Wendy Day found her mission.

After one class, Day approached Padell. She wondered who was there to help these rap artists when the records failed or the money ran out. Padell said that he tried. Unfortunately, a larger reality was in play.

"There's no money in helping people," he said.

It sounded like a perfect job for someone with a newfound contempt for cash.

That night, back at her flat on 14th Street, Day wrote the business plan and designed an Afrocentric-flavored logo for a nonprofit organization that she dubbed the Rap Coalition, to which she pledged her life and newfound fortune.

The purpose of the coalition, Day wrote, was three pronged. The critical objective was legal support: to introduce rappers to powerful attorneys who would break their contracts. The second was dispensing information— teaching rappers how not to get "jerked" by the music industry. Last, not least, was fostering unity.

She was, in essence, trying to start a rappers' union. For advice, she cold-called Dave Mays, the publisher of her favorite magazine. After three months of ignoring her, Mays finally took the call. Mays didn't think that a union would work, given the nature of the record business and the competitive behavior of rappers in general. But Mays referred her next to one guy he knew who had experience in unionizing. *Source* partner James Bernard spoke to Wendy Day by phone one day in the spring of 1992. Bernard gave her one piece of advice that stuck with her: *If you're really going to do this, never under any circumstances take money from record labels to do anything.*

Beyond the philosophical debate over whether the Rap Coalition could even accomplish its mission, Wendy Day faced two more tangible problems: She had never seen a record contract in her life, and she didn't know any rappers.

That changed one night a few months later when a rapper-producer who called himself Dasez—he pronounced it "Dizzazz"—walked into a bar on 23rd Street in Manhattan. Dasez had just come from a studio session with Run-DMC, producing a track for their latest comeback album, *Down with the King.* And there, at the bar, was a plain kind of White girl wearing a Run-DMC sweatshirt. Dasez was intrigued, so he struck up a conversation with the woman, who introduced herself as Wendy Day.

After she described her concept for the Rap Coalition, Dasez divulged his own situation. He was one-half of the rap duo "Dasez Tempo"—so named by Russell Simmons, who had signed them in 1989 to Def Jam, through a production deal he had given to former Run-DMC producer Larry Smith. Four years later, Def Jam still hadn't released a single record by Dasez Tempo. Simmons said he believed in them, but he kept telling them to wait.

After his conversation with Day, Dasez decided that he would rather have Def Jam be a springboard for him than a graveyard and asked for her help. Day went to Bert Padell for a referral to a good lawyer. Padell sent her to Tim Mandelbaum—the attorney who would, in a few years, represent RZA and Wu-Tang Productions. Offering his services pro bono, Mandelbaum negotiated the release terms with Def Jam. Meanwhile, Dasez began lining up a new deal. His friend Brett Ratner, the former manager of BMOC, was now a successful video director for Def Jam and other labels. Ratner had a new production entity with Sire/Warner Bros., and wanted to sign him. Mandelbaum offered to represent Dasez in the new deal, for 10 percent of his advance.

Day had no experience negotiating deals, but this didn't sound right to her. She had heard that *five* percent was supposed to be the standard lawyer fee. She wondered if Mandelbaum was trying to recoup his losses from the pro bono work on the back of Dasez Tempo's new deal.

Day got nervous and visited Padell, divulging her trepidation about the turnaround deal. She had barely finished speaking when Padell was already on the phone to Mandelbaum, screaming and calling him a snake; all this vitriol on her behalf when she was only asking a simple question.

Oh, my God, Day thought. *I am already finished in this business.*

She understood that Padell was just trying to prove that he was on her side, probably because he believed that she might bring him clients one day, too. The whole business operated this way, shuffling artists from one bad deal to the next. A big shell game, she thought, with the artist as the pea.

Soon, Wendy Day found another act to liberate, this time a rock-rap hybrid group called the Kemelions, signed to Zoo Records, the same moribund company from which Loud Records jumped. She befriended another lawyer who had spoken in Padell's class, Andy Tavel, the former head of business affairs for Def Jam. Tavel not only helped secure the Kemelions' release; he spent hours on the phone with Day, teaching her how to read contracts—line by line, clause by clause. Explaining to her that it wasn't just about the things in a contract that were *bad*, but also what was *missing*. Tavel and Day began an unofficial partnership, working together to break bad deals.

Day used her new knowledge—and her cash reserves—to produce and promote the first Rap Coalition events. She threw monthly panel discussions at NYU and free seminars for aspiring rappers on how to protect themselves against rapacious deals. She papered neighborhoods with flyers, and sent announcements to trade and consumer magazines. She wrote pieces for *The Source*, *Vibe*, and a growing crop of smaller rap magazines like *The Bomb*, *Rap Pages*, *Rap Sheet*, *Flavor*, and *Beat Down*. She sat on panels at music conventions like CMJ.

Her seminars and writings tapped into a reserve of mistrust and anger among established and aspiring hip-hop artists for the executives and management of the very industry to which they belonged, or hoped to. Even successful acts seemed to have a beef with the companies who distributed their work. Q-Tip of A Tribe Called Quest had rapped: "Music industry rule 4080: Record company people are shady." That broad brush painted and tainted everyone at Jive Records who had ever worked on their behalf—not just the label heads Barry Weiss and Ann Carli, but people like Jive A&R man Sean Carasov, the former Beastie Boys tour manager who had signed Tribe to the label.

What was Tribe's actual complaint? Did Jive Records swindle or scam the group? Q-Tip's song never said.[20] But his slogan was taken as truth

---

[20]Sean Carasov and Ann Carli took the "4080" lyric in good humor. Carasov figured that all artists become disillusioned with their label at some point. Carli even printed up T-shirts with the slogan as a promotional item.

But the tale of Tribe's journey into the music business illuminates some of the group's grievances. The members of A Tribe Called Quest were teenagers when they signed a production and by so many artists, journalists, and fans. One publisher even named his rap magazine *4080*, in tribute to Q-Tip's axiom. Day wrote for that magazine, too.

Thus some music executives greeted Wendy Day's work on behalf of aggrieved artists with skepticism. To work at a record company was to know that *every* artist thought they were getting jerked: If DJs didn't like the record and programmers didn't play their single; if people weren't coming into stores to buy the album; if the artist blew through his or her advance and had no sales to warrant an additional one, it was the record company's fault. And if the record actually did become a hit, and money flowed, well, then the artists did it all themselves.

---

management deal with Red Alert Productions. And Red Alert Productions was itself a partnership with Rhythm Method Enterprises, the company owned by Hank Shocklee, Chuck D of Public Enemy, attorney Ron Skoler, and Ed Chalpin. After Rhythm Method dissolved, Skoler and Chalpin remained, negotiating Tribe's $500,000 deal with Jive Records.

Group members Q-Tip, Phife and Ali Shaheed Muhammed didn't understand what "publishing" was, nor what it meant that Jive had bought half of it. They didn't realize that their management company—which also provided their legal representation—was due 30 percent of each royalty advance for the duration of their deal. As far as the group was concerned, they were grateful to Red Alert for putting them on, ecstatic to get a deal on a label they respected for what sounded like a lot of money, and excited to begin recording. It was only after their first album was released and they began reviewing the budget for their second that they became aware of the tangle of deals to which they were bound.

The group decided that although their benefactor DJ Red Alert had the best intentions, he wasn't savvy enough to guide them. They followed their day-to-day manager Chris Lighty to his new position at Rush Artist Management and retained lawyer Ken Anderson to negotiate their release. DJ Red Alert was hurt but willing to relinquish his contract with the group, as was Ron Skoler. Red Alert's business partner Ed Chalpin was not.

Thus began a year and a half of legal maneuvers. Tribe's new manager Lyor Cohen demanded more advances from Jive to foot the group's legal expenses, threatening to keep the group from recording if Jive didn't fork over more cash. Clive Calder himself eventually helped negotiate the settlement between Chalpin and the group by paying Chalpin's 15 percent out of Jive's share rather than Tribe's.

Despite Calder's intervention and his label's successful promotion of the group, A Tribe Called Quest had begun to sour on Jive Records. Calder's save had come with a price: one additional album due to Jive. As they became successful, Tribe suspected that Jive invested more money in their pop acts, and they believed that Jive viewed rap as music to be promoted as cheaply as possible. They were insulted by the difficulty of getting advances when their royalty account was in fact recouped.

Shadiness abounded in Tribe's long industry quest. But it was the "record company people" who shouldered the blame. The group never enumerated the previous 4079 rules.

As it turned out, Day rarely exposed financial "smoking guns" in rap artists' dealings with established record companies. More often, she simply found poorly negotiated contracts binding ill-represented artists to labels where they languished for two main reasons—loss of label interest or lackluster promotion.

While these situations could be career killers for great artists, Wendy Day discovered that the foremost foe of the neophyte recording act was not the record company at all but the ubiquitous middlemen: managers who were really just the friends or family of the artist, with no industry experience at all; managers who signed artists to their own production entities, effectively double-dipping in their client's income; producers who took huge chunks of the artist's advances while producing little or nothing (as Jive Records executives believed was the case with A Tribe Called Quest and Red Alert Productions); lawyers who charged unconscionable percentages and finder's fees. In the end, Day was less concerned with getting artists off of Def Jam, for example, and more with getting them away from, say, Bob the drug dealer's so-called "label."

As Day freed more artists, she felt a growing unease about the accomplishments of the Rap Coalition. One evening in 1995, she was with a rapper named Preacher Earl, who was throwing a party to celebrate his release from Strictly Rhythm Records.

He is so happy, Day thought. *But what is he going to do now? Get a job at Burger King?*

She felt like she hadn't helped Earl at all. Thereafter, Day decided that she needed to do more than get rappers out of bad deals. She needed to help them get better ones.

Now that the Rap Coalition was three years old, Day had the industry connections to do it. She had an advisory board that included artists like Chuck D and Tupac Shakur. She had won allies within the record companies themselves—sympathetic employees who would leak the better contracts to her, so she could see how far record companies were willing to bend for the artists with better representation and bigger prospects.

Day found a new paradigm in the deal that Barry Weiss at Jive Records cut with a rapper named E-40. Earl "E-40" Stevens was a rapper from Vallejo, California, who found he could do just fine without a record company. With the help and advice of his uncle Saint Charles Thurman, E-40 funded his own recording and manufacturing, and sold his cassettes and CDs through a local wholesaler called City Hall Records, and via Thurman's distribution company, Solar Music Group. E-40 sold tens of thousands of albums in the Bay Area to a local fan base thoroughly devoted to home-grown artists, through college radio play and word of mouth—as did other Bay Area–based rappers like Mac Mall, Master P, and Rappin 4-Tay. As word spread to other parts of California and the Southwest, E-40's album sales edged toward the 100,000 mark.

Independent and major labels got word of E-40's success and offered him deals. But E-40 and Saint Charles didn't see how they would benefit from a situation where they would make $1 to $2 per unit when they already made close to $7 or $8 on their own.

When E-40 and Saint Charles visited Barry Weiss at Jive's New York offices, the legend was that he wouldn't let them leave his office until they signed a deal. In truth, Weiss just made them a dignified, intelligent offer. Whatever they usually made by selling their records themselves, he would give them as an advance. The deal was simple. Every time E-40 delivered an album to Jive, Weiss would pay him $1 million. Essentially, Weiss was pay-ing E-40 *not* to distribute his own record but to give Jive the privilege in-stead. In return, Jive would take E-40's sales national, past his 100,000-unit ceiling.

Wendy Day learned a valuable lesson from the deal. Some groups signed directly to Jive, sold over 100,000 units, and made no money. But E-40 sold 100,000 before he ever got to Jive, and got millions in return.

The difference, Day knew, was leverage. E-40 was a businessman coming *into* the negotiations. You just couldn't bullshit him.

The Bay Area seemed to breed saavy, independent rap entrepreneurs. As it happened, the first artist deal that Wendy Day would help forge was for another Bay Area artist in the orbit of E-40 and Saint Charles. His name was Percy Miller, but he called himself Master P.

Master P wasn't from the Bay Area at all but from the Calliope housing project of New Orleans. Like so many others looking for a way out of the ghetto, Miller turned to sports—winning a basketball scholarship to the University of Houston. But Miller's path to the pros was blocked after a severe knee injury. Resolved not to return to "Callio," a dangerous neigh-borhood in one of New Orleans's most impoverished wards, Miller flew to the Bay Area to move in with his mother and younger brother, Kevin.

Living in Richmond, California, was like trading one ghetto for another.

Miller, however, had one advantage: a $10,000 insurance settlement from the death of his grandfather. Miller could have done a lot of things with that money, but he chose to open up a business—a record store, to be exact, because it sounded like fun, and Miller liked music.

In 1990, Miller negotiated a deal with the owner of an abandoned building on San Pablo Avenue: three months' free rent in exchange for fixing up the storefront. After sinking some money into renovation and cleanup, Miller went into another local record store, Jones & Harris, and asked where they bought their inventory. When the twenty-one-year-old Miller walked into The Music People, a distribution and record company in Oakland, he looked so young that the staff thought that he was setting up an account for his parents' business. But they took Miller on as a client, and within weeks, No Limit Records was open to customers. To get through those first cash-strapped months, Miller, his new wife, Sonya, and their baby son, Percy Junior, lived in the back of the shop.

Miller sold the tapes of East Bay favorites like Spice 1, Too Short, N2Deep, and Tupac. Before long, he began to sell his own recordings—distinguishing himself from the crop of local rappers with his lugubrious Southern drawl and his mouthful of gold teeth. Music People's in-house record label, In-a-Minute, picked "Master P" up for distribution. Soon, Miller booked himself on a tour, at the bottom of a bill that began with Tupac, Too Short, and N2Deep, while Sonya stayed behind to tend shop. Saint Charles Thurman took Miller under his wing, distributing his records through Solar and taking him on swings through the American West.

On one of these tours, Miller met a college DJ at Gonzaga University in Spokane, Washington, named Tobin Costen. The two young men hailed from different provinces of the Black American experience—Miller from the slums of New Orleans and Richmond, Costen an army brat who had seen the world at a young age. But both played basketball and loved rap music, and they became fast friends. Costen took care to introduce Miller to his local network of DJs and promoters. When Costen graduated and moved down to the Bay Area, Miller offered him a job—not at the No Limit store, but at his new No Limit label. Miller was quickly transitioning from retail to recording.

In 1994, Costen joined Miller in his shoe-box office in Oakland. Together, they booked marathon recording sessions for Master P, his brother Silkk the Shocker, his wife, Sonya, their group, Tru, local producer E-A-Ski, and rapper Dangerous Dame. In assembly-line fashion, Costen and Miller

would assign these tracks to albums—whichever one needed a hit, whichever one was already being presold to distributors and retailers—and rush
them into production. They kept the albums coming, as the promise of a
new release was often the only way to get paid for the last one. They launched
themselves into tours, not only around the West Coast, but down South—
Louisiana, Texas, Arkansas, the Panhandle—where they could get more
bang for their buck on the road and with radio time-buys. Costen marveled
at Miller's relentlessness. Master P was never too good to make a radio or
retail call, never too busy to talk to fans, never too tired to jump out of bed
and make the next item on the itinerary.

After a year of working together, Miller and Costen turned No Limit
Records into a powerful sales machine. Each release could be expected to sell
roughly 150,000 copies, exclusively though independent channels. No Limit
billed more than $900,000 in the first twelve months of Costen's tenure.
Still, none of it was easy. Costen and Miller were always waiting for a check,
always short on cash.

No independent label could move those kinds of units and not receive
offers from larger companies trolling for emerging talent. Most wanted to
sign Master P, the artist, not No Limit, the label. Bryan Turner's Priority
Records, however, seemed willing to offer them what they wanted: a pressing and distribution deal where No Limit would own its masters and take
the lion's share of the wholesale price.

This kind of dealmaking was way above anything that Costen could
comfortably handle himself. But through his old friend Poepan, a rapper in
the group the Kemelions, Costen had heard of someone who might be able
to help—a real-life guardian angel for rap artists.

"You helped my friend out of a fucked-up deal," Costen told Wendy Day.
"I think I need your help."

Costen was suspicious because the deal had been brokered by E-A-Ski—
Master P's producer, who had recently jumped to Priority himself. Day
thought that Costen had every reason to be wary. Wherever there was a
middleman, shadiness abounded.

Day found No Limit a good attorney, who promptly leaked Day the contracts for perusal. Day looked for signs of the usual contractual shenanigans.
She couldn't find any. With a few tweaks, Day put her imprimatur on the
new distribution contract between Priority and No Limit—one that accorded an astonishing and in some ways unprecedented set of deal points for
such a small, artist-run label: headache-free sales, distribution, and billing

by a truly national network, CEMA; an advance of $375,000 for every album against 75 percent of the wholesale price, leaving Priority just 25 percent to split between itself and CEMA; and most important of all, No Limit would own its masters, meaning that if the deal ended, Master P could take his back catalog with him.[21]

The Priority–No Limit deal in 1995 set Percy "Master P" Miller up to sell more records than ever before—which he did, exponentially. *Ice Cream Man* was his first album to go platinum.

The following year, Day brokered her next big deal between Atlantic Records and a small Chicago production company called Creator's Way—which now had the former Loud artist Tung Twista under contract.

Day negotiated a joint-venture agreement between the two companies that split profits fifty-fifty. It was the kind of deal that other companies had to sell millions of units in order to merit. But Day and her legal team—Andy Tavel and Peter Thea—won the deal because Creator's Way didn't need, nor did they want, an advance. The three partners had their own money—street money, by Day's estimation. They would begin the deal without any debt to Atlantic, and Atlantic would be risking little and gaining a hot artist in the bargain.

When the Creator's Way deal was made public, Day got a lot of press coverage. *The Source* called it "the best deal in the history of Black music."

But after Twista's album was finally released, Day wasn't so sure about that superlative. Once Twista's record, *Adrenaline*, had sold about 250,000 copies, she saw Atlantic shift priorities to the new album by R&B singer and TV star Brandy. Day learned whiy: The label had spent millions on Brandy and needed to make good on their investment. Once Twista's record had recouped its marketing expenditures, Atlantic wasn't too worried about promoting it. Day stored that information for her next deal.

Despite her transition from deal breaker to deal maker, Wendy Day's reputation remained pristine. The Rap Coalition operated as a nonprofit. Day never asked for, nor received, any remuneration for her work on behalf of

---

[21]Bryan Turner has a different recollection of this deal from those of Tobin Costen and Wendy Day. Turner recalls that he initially did a distribution deal with Master P for no no money up front. Costen ridicules this notion, saying that Master P was already being pursued by major labels and that he never would have signed without an advance.

Master P and Creator's Way—even though those deals had accorded millions of dollars to the artists involved.

But in her drive to enrich rap artists, money had become a problem for Day herself. By 1997, she had long since depleted her initial half-million-dollar fortune. Initially, Day supported her work at the Rap Coalition by running the volunteer program at a culinary school in Manhattan. Occasionally, she would accept a $1,000 fee to file artists' publishing paperwork. She had determined not to take money from artists' record deals, nor fees from anyone who might be connected to the drug trade. But her strong moral sense did not extend to corporations: Day had run her company for five years on bootlegged cell phone chips.

Day had come to rely increasingly on infusions of cash from her mother, who now worked as a bookkeeper back in Pennsylvania.

"I just want you to know," Day's mother told her, "that I've lent you more money in these past two months than I've made at my job."

Day woke to the fact that she had borrowed $70,000 from her mother over the past three years. And to the realization that she had the same ambivalent relationship to money that many of her artists had—a simultaneous contempt and obsession that made it impossible for her to sustain herself.

The Rap Olympics was one of the first enterprises that Day invented to start making some kind of income. She had enlisted some sponsors to help subsidize her concept: bring lyricists from all over the country to compete against one another in a rap battle in Los Angeles, well attended by A&R scouts.

Some of the participants in this contest were rappers whom Day had known for years. Some were artists she had extricated from bad label deals. But one MC—who eventually made it to the final round—Day had met only recently. In truth, she hadn't wanted to meet him at all.

Day was in Detroit for a music convention with a young Chicago rapper named Rhymefest, who pointed to a White kid with brown hair, reciting lyrics in a cipher of MCs outside the Atheneum Hotel.

"You should pay attention to this White boy," Rhymefest said. "He's incredible."

As Day and Rhymefest walked back to the car, Rhymefest handed her the White rapper's cassette. Day promptly threw it on the floor.

"That's fucked-up," Rhymfest said, immediately sensing the reason behind his friend's resistance. "He's White. You're White. You should listen to him."

"Why would I listen to a tape just because somebody's White? That's stupid."

The conversation had turned ironic. The American music business had traditionally been about selling Black art in a White package for White consumption. Now a White fan of Black music was being chided by a Black artist for not being open to White appropriation of Black art. As if the conversation hadn't already veered into the bizarre, Rhymefest then said the following:

"You know how hard it is being White in the rap industry, so you should give him the benefit of the doubt."

Day had made a career, though hardly a lucrative one, on the premise that rap artists, mostly Black, continued to be the victims of mostly White corporate exploitation. In her zeal to combat White supremacy Day had unwittingly fashioned for herself a supremacist role: that of the White savior.

But the quest for Black empowerment in the music industry—whether from the Wu-Tang or via Wendy Day, whether by Master P or Puff Daddy—was bearing fruit. Black artists of previous generations had rarely been able to negotiate the kind of equity that this new crop of hip-hop artists had. Despite the long history of White appropriation of Black art in America, hip-hop had yet to be overrun by White artists who obscured the genre's true cultural origin—as had jazz and rock and roll. Maybe hip-hop was different.

Day popped the cassette into the car deck and gave it a listen. It was phenomenal. Eminem was one of the best rappers she had ever heard. Even if he *was* White.

Eminem's journey to the center of pop culture was assisted by the patronage of rap's greatest producer.

Andre "Dr. Dre" Young's partnership with Suge Knight had turned toxic. Years earlier, Jimmy Iovine had liberated Dr. Dre from his ties to Eazy-E, Jerry Heller, and Ruthless. Once again, Iovine made things right—acting as the intermediary between Knight and Dre, allowing Knight to keep the Death Row masters and Dr. Dre to walk away with his freedom and a new multimillion-dollar joint venture called Aftermath Entertainment.

Dre signaled his legal liberation and spiritual rebirth with a single, "Been There, Done That," in which he lamented, rather hypocritically, the rappers who talked about guns and "hard bullshit." Few were buying it, figuratively and literally. "Been There, Done That" appeared on Aftermath's first release,

Dr. Dre Presents the Aftermath, a compilation album meant to showcase the new label's roster. The album sold a million copies—hardly an impressive debut when compared to Death Row's own three-million-plus launch with *The Chronic.* None of the featured Aftermath artists went on to success. For several years, Dr. Dre's Aftermath Entertainment failed to break a new act, rap or otherwise.

Yet again, Jimmy Iovine made things right.

Two of Iovine's employees, Evan Bogart and Dean Geistlinger, were in the audience at the Rap Olympics in Los Angeles as Eminem sliced his way through several MCs to reach the final round. And even though Eminem lost the championship to a local lyricist named Overdose, Bogart and Geistlinger approached the dejected rapper and asked for a demo.

Jimmy Iovine had passed on Eminem twice already when his demo was sent at separate times by Wendy Day and Eminem manager Paul Rosenberg. But this time, Iovine played the CD for Dr. Dre when the producer visited his house.

"What the fuck is that?" Dre asked. "Gimme that!"

Fortuitously, Eminem stayed in town after the Rap Olympics, making a fiery national radio debut with a live freestyle on Sway & King Tech's "Wake-Up Show," now broadcast on Los Angeles's 92.3 the Beat, and simulcast on San Francisco's KMEL and nineteen other stations around the country.

Day got a call from Eminem a few days later. Dre had found him and was keeping him up in a hotel. They were recording. It was all good.

Aftermath Entertainment offered Eminem a recording contract. For advice during the negotiations, Paul Rosenberg turned to Day, who had tried in vain to land Eminem a deal with Interscope the previous year. Jimmy Iovine passed.

Now Aftermath/Interscope were offering close to a half-million-dollar advance. While Rosenberg monitored the negotiations, Day focused on her forte: helping artists get rid of their middlemen. In this case, Eminem had been signed to a long-term production contract by two Detroit producers called the Bass Brothers. Now that Eminem had Dr. Dre, she didn't see why the small-time producers deserved an ongoing piece of Eminem's career.

"I found a clause in the contract where you can get rid of your production crew," Day told the artist. "Just cut them a check for a hundred thousand dollars and move on."

"No," Eminem replied. "They believed in me when I didn't have shit. They're staying in there."

Day was impressed again by the young rapper from Detroit.

Soon, the rest of the world would be talking about Eminem as either the new hot MC, the new White rapper, or the next Elvis, depending on whom you asked.

And the industry, too, would be talking about Wendy Day, as she prepared to negotiate her biggest artist-empowering deal yet.

Around Memorial Day of 1997, Day went to New Orleans for a convention. She stopped by Peaches, one of the best local record stores, to find out what was hot, and landed on a CD by an artist named Pimp Daddy. After a listen, Wendy Day liked the album enough to seek out the proprietors of Pimp Daddy's label. Day ended up wandering the Magnolia Projects of uptown New Orleans—a strange White lady asking anyone if they'd heard of Cash Money Records.

After an hour of searching, she gave up and flew back to New York. Weeks later, Cash Money Records found her, referred, quite coincidentally, by a mutual friend, a street promoter in Houston.

"They're a little hard to work with," he said. "But they've always paid me."

Day flew back to New Orleans and met the owners, two brothers named Bryan and Ronald Williams, who went by "Baby" and "Slim."

The Williams brothers told Day that they were interested in getting national distribution for their local product; and Day told the Williams brothers that she knew how to set them up for the right deal and nail it down. Because Day had already decided to stop working for free, she struck an agreement with Cash Money Records: 5 percent of any advance would go to her as a finder's fee, and 5 percent would go to the attorneys she recommended for the job, Andy Tavel and his partner, Peter Thea.

Wendy Day began executing her plan. Cash Money's albums typically sold between 5,000 and 25,000 units. Their distributor covered only the Southwest, so Day introduced Cash Money into other markets where she knew they would sell as well: the Midwest and the West. Within months, Cash Money's new release, the Hot Boy$, became their hottest ever, surpassing 75,000 copies sold. They were ready.

Wendy Day drafted an impressive business plan for Cash Money Records, and an audacious deal proposal for such a small label. Cash Money wanted an 80/20 pressing and distribution deal—the most lucrative for them, the least lucrative for the distributor. But they also wanted something virtually unprecedented. Before any records were sold, Cash Money wanted a multimillion-dollar advance on sales. Advances of this magnitude were unheard-of for P&D deals. But Day had learned that big investment ensured big promotion.

When Day, Andy Tavel, and Peter Thea began transmitting their offer to executives at major labels in September 1997, Thea got a call from Mel Lewinter, the chief of finance for the Universal Music Group.

Are you kidding me? Lewinter said. The executive could have laughed it off. But he was actually offended. *What was the business coming to when virtual unknowns felt they could ask for this kind of deal?*

Jocelyn Cooper, senior vice president and special assistant to Universal Music Group chairman Doug Morris, thought differently.

At twenty-nine, Cooper became the first African-American woman to run a major publishing company. At thirty-one, she had been hired by Doug Morris to do A&R, and not simply for Black artists and audiences, as many Black executives were often pigeonholed. Cooper despised the constraints of racism, both bald-faced and insidious. She was, in fact, much like her father, Andrew Cooper—a journalist and publisher of a Black newspaper who once sued the state of New York to shatter the gerrymandered district lines in Brooklyn that neutered Black voting power. Because of Andrew Cooper, the 12th Congressional District was created, and in 1968, Shirley Chisholm became the first Black woman elected to the U.S. Congress.

Jocelyn Cooper shared a similar passion for kicking down barriers. What she most wanted to do was use her power in the music business to extend to Black entrepreneurs the same kinds of opportunities and arrangements that the White boys gave one another all the time. And for the life of her, she couldn't understand why other Black executives didn't—not Universal's head of Black music, Jean Riggins; not even Sylvia Rhone at Elektra.

Accordingly, Cooper gave a P&D deal to a small Houston rap label called Suave House. It wouldn't make Universal nearly as much money as a joint venture or production deal, but it didn't cost Universal much either. And most important, market share meant more to Doug Morris now than profits. Suave House would benefit Universal by simply putting millions more records into Universal's system.

Cooper knew about Cash Money Records. She had gone to New Orleans herself and brought CDs back for Universal's research director, Marc Nathan. Nathan championed the label in the building, and Cooper sent her second in command, an A&R representative named Dino Delvaille, down to New Orleans to find and meet the label heads.

Delvaille came back with a story: Picked up at his hotel by two hulking guys in a Hummer; dropped off at a convenience store, where the two gentlemen asked him to transfer into another car; speeding twenty minutes out of the city to a house surrounded by a half dozen other luxury cars; escorted into the barren residence that served as a recording studio; seated at a table to wait; and joined by a muscled, tattooed man who casually laid a Glock pistol on the table between them before he spoke.

"You want to do business with us?" Bryan "Baby" Williams said.

"Yes," Delvaille replied. "I do."

Cooper eventually connected with Andy Tavel and expressed interest, but she, too, was taken aback by the magnitude of what these New Orleans guys wanted.

"This is crazy," she exclaimed.

"I don't disagree that it's crazy," Tavel replied. "But this is what these guys want, and if you don't give it to them, Sony will. And I have no control over that part of the deal."

It was true. Cash Money had retained a second lawyer, Tim Mandelbaum, to do simultaneous negotiations with Sony Music—essentially pitting two sets of lawyers against each other in a race to see who could clinch a deal first.

Within Universal Records, an internal battle raged, pitting the deal's advocates—Jocelyn Cooper, Marc Nathan, and Dino Delvaille—against three powerful opponents: Mel Lewinter, his lieutenant, David Ellner, and Jean Riggins. The tiebreaker was the chairman, Doug Morris, who ultimately gave Cooper his blessing for the Cash Money deal for the same reason he approved Suave House: Market share was more valuable than profits in the paramount effort to drive parent company Seagram's stock price higher. It was a deal that Sony ultimately couldn't match.

The day that the contract terms were ironed out, Wendy Day could scarcely believe that Universal agreed to them. A $3 million advance against Cash Money's 80 percent share of the wholesale price, plus a $1.5 million credit line per album, of which Cash Money agreed to deliver six per year. It was the best deal she had ever done.

On June 18, 1998, Universal Records announced its landmark distribution and marketing deal with Cash Money Records, for its roster of virtual unknowns: Big Tymers, B.G., Juvenile, and a sixteen-year-old rapper named Lil Wayne.

The industry and hip-hop community were beside themselves over the magnitude of the Cash Money deal. Russell Simmons, who also tried to tempt Cash Money with a standard production contract, was beside himself—not with envy, but admiration.

"The fact that Universal financed Cash Money Records just so they could press and distribute them is unbelievable," he said. Simmons had to sell millions of albums before he earned such an advanced deal. Cash Money had done it by simply walking through the door.

Simmons thought Cash Money had achieved the impossible by not knowing that they were asking for the impossible. Their ignorance, he presumed, was their strength. But the Williams brothers knew, because Wendy Day had taught them.

"Wendy, we have a problem."

Peter Thea reached Day by phone while she visited with friends in Chicago. Ronald "Slim" Williams had come to Thea's New York office to sign the two letters that would direct Universal to pay the 5 percent portions of Cash Money Records' advance to the lawyers and Day, respectively.

The problem: Williams had signed the lawyers' letter. He had refused to sign Day's.

Day had a premonition about all of this. She hadn't bothered to do her due diligence on the Williams brothers before she jumped in on their behalf. Over the course of the past months, she'd heard some unsettling things. Her friend who had vouched for the Williams brothers wasn't getting paid. She'd been told that the Williams brothers stiffed the Fruit of Islam, who had done some security work for them. Worst of all, Day realized she might have broken one of her commandments in taking the Cash Money project, after she'd heard whispers that the Williams brothers had made a lot of money running heroin into the projects of New Orleans. She couldn't be sure whether the tales were true. But she silently dropped any plans for helping them with their label. She just wanted her money, and wanted out.

For days, she tried to reach the Williams brothers, but they wouldn't take her calls. Finally, Thea managed to get Slim on the phone for her. Day told Slim that she had consulted a litigator, who told her that her contract actually entitled her to 5 percent of the entire deal's value, not just the advance. But she just wanted her money from the advance, nothing more.

Slim laughed. "I don't know if you're really, really nice or really, really stupid."

"Damn, I'd like to think that I'm nice," Day replied. "I did a lot of work for you guys. I flew you around at my own expense."

When Day returned to New York, things got worse. She got evicted from her apartment. Then came the day a friend at Elektra Records notified her that the Williams brothers were sitting in Sylvia Rhone's office, and another told her that they were en route to Tommy Boy Music. Wendy Day couldn't believe it.

These guys already have an exclusive deal with Universal, and they're trying to get another deal somewhere else.

She faxed the first and last pages of the Universal deal to Elektra and Tommy Boy, to quash any shenanigans and preserve her reputation. She wanted no one saying she had any part in this duplicity.

When two well-dressed gentlemen came into his office brandishing pistols, Andy Tavel thought it was a joke.

After all, it was his partner, Peter Thea's last day at the firm, having accepted a senior management job at Jive Records. He'd seen all kinds of practical jokes and stripper-grams over the years. Never a pistol-gram; but then again, this was hip-hop.

"Somebody didn't get paid," one of the gentlemen said calmly. "Where's the money?"

Tavel smiled.

"Well, Peter's the guy with all the money," Tavel said, pointing them to his partner's office.

Tavel didn't know that these two men had tied up his receptionist in the lobby. He didn't know that one of his employees was cowering in the bathroom. When he heard another staff member crying, it dawned on Tavel that it was the real thing. The gunmen were in Thea's office, where the lawyer was on the phone, attempting to purchase tickets for a Broadway show.

"Just a minute," Thea said, putting up his hand.

"Yo, this is serious! Somebody didn't get paid. Where's the money?"

Both Tavel and Thea knew who that somebody was. Tavel tried to reason with them.

"We don't hold the money. We don't control what our clients do," he said.

"Give us your wallets," one of them said.

Thea, Tavel, and the rest of the firm obliged.

"This person better get paid," one of the gunmen said. And then the two intruders left by the stairwell.

The police came to take a report. In the surreal aftermath, Tavel discovered that his associate Rose Meade Hart not only knew that the intruders were brandishing TEC-9s, but that she also knew the difference between a straight clip and a banana clip. The police found the firm's wallets in the stairwell. These men hadn't come to harm or rob anyone. They had come to send a message.

Thea was convinced that Wendy Day had sent the gunmen. Andy Tavel disagreed; Day was a friend, and still an active client.

"I don't believe that Wendy would put our lives in jeopardy," Tavel said.

Thea called her, screaming. Day denied that she had anything to do with the incident and agreed to meet them at the police station to look at mug shots. She arrived at the precinct with a new artist in tow—a rapper from Atlanta named David Banner. Tavel wanted to know what she thought had happened.

Wendy Day reiterated that she didn't send anyone. It didn't make any sense, Day said. *Why would I send guys with guns to Cash Money's lawyer's office in New York? Who also happen to be my lawyers, whom I like very much? If someone wanted to get at the money, they'd go to New Orleans. Or catch the Williams brothers on the road.*

Day floated the possibility that Cash Money itself sent the gunmen. The Williams brothers had recently made her a settlement offer of $75,000. She had refused to take the money on principle. The incident might have been a way of forcing her hand. But that didn't make much sense, either. Tavel and Thea were Cash Money's lawyers, too.

Day acknowledged that she had told a lot of people about Cash Money's betrayal. And she had a lot of sympathetic ears now in the rap business. It was possible that one of these people, without telling her, tried to do Day a solid by sending a message. That was the story that Tavel believed. Thea, for his part, never spoke to Day again.

Wendy Day, the woman who had spent her own personal fortune to empower rap artists and entrepreneurs so they could make a living for themselves, eventually sued to recover the first deal-making fee she ever charged.

It took her three more years and over $12,000 in legal fees to recover the $150,000 that Cash Money owed her.

The No Limit deal was paying off for Bryan Turner. Priority Records garnered seventeen gold and platinum certifications in 1997; over half of them were from No Limit. The sheer quantity of No Limit product moving through the system elevated Priority's overall share of the American recorded music market to 3.3 percent, startlingly high for an independent label. With Capitol-EMI's market share at about 8 percent, Priority accounted for more than a third of the major label's business.

Turner had sold the first half of Priority to EMI in 1996 for a little over $70 million. It was a good time to sell the second half, given that the price would be contingent on Priority's overall sales, and because 1998 turned out to be Master P and No Limit's monster year. Twenty of Priority's twenty-two certifications were No Limit releases, from seven different artists, including Master P (three multiplatinum albums, over six million units sold, including a million-plus-selling single, "Make Em' Say Uhh"), Silkk the Shocker (platinum), C-Murder (gold), Fiend (gold), and Young Bleed (gold). In return for the little company founded on compilations, California Raisins, and gangsta rap, Turner and his partner Mark Cerami pocketed another $65 million in cash.

One of No Limit's bestselling albums of 1998 came from its first superstar signing. Snoop Dogg, too, had left Suge Knight and Death Row Records with his life and career intact. Free and clear, the multimillion-selling artist could have picked any major label he wanted. But Snoop Dogg chose to be on No Limit, partly because of the strength and security that seemed implicit in joining a family of tough, street-savvy guys, a hedge against possible retaliation by Knight and Death Row; but mostly because Master P offered Snoop Dogg a man's deal, a share of the profits and the freedom to walk away from the situation at any time. Snoop Dogg's first album for No Limit/Priority, called *Da Game Is to Be Sold, Not to Be Told*, went double platinum. All told, No Limit sold over twenty million records in 1998.

Master P had diversified into films. His first self-produced movie, *I'm Bout It*, was issued solely on videotape and the new digital video disk format. *I'm Bout It* debuted at number one on the Billboard video chart, garnering double-platinum certification from the RIAA, rivaling many major movie studio releases. No Limit Films produced two new pictures: *MP Da Last*

Don, which went straight to video, and *I Got the Hook Up*, which was picked up by Miramax's Dimension Films for theatrical release. *I Got the Hook Up* cost a lot more to make than *I'm Bout It*, and looked it. But the $3.5 million price tag was more than covered by the film's $10.3 million gross. Just as he had with music, Master P had entered Hollywood through the back door, and now had the run of the place. Trimark Pictures signed No Limit to a $10 million, five-picture deal.

Between No Limit Records and No Limit Films, Master P grossed over $160 million in 1998 alone.

Percy "Master P" Miller began an unprecedented horizontal expansion: a clothing line, phone-sex lines, real estate, and toys, like a No Limit bicycle and Master P dolls (you could actually make 'em say "uhh"). Not all of Master P's ventures were successful. Miller's millionaire status meant that he could virtually buy his way back into the career that he wanted in the first place. Announcing his retirement as a recording artist, Miller got a position as point guard for the Continental Basketball Association's Fort Wayne Fury. He didn't need the extra $1,500 a week, but his brief pro career gave his fledgling No Limit sports management division instant credibility. Miller signed both Boston Celtics guard Ron Mercer and University of Texas running back Ricky Williams as clients. But Miller and No Limit were roundly criticized in the sports world for negotiating what many thought was a very bad deal for Williams with the New Orleans Saints.

Miller may have been better at advocating for his own interests than for those of his clients. But his insistence on autonomy and willingness to invest in himself not only set a new standard for the music industry; it actually fostered a new one. After Master P's straight-to-video successes with *I'm Bout It* and *MP Da Last Don*, an alternative avenue of promotion and sales opened up for hip-hop artists in particular—especially as American consumers adopted the new DVD technology. "Street DVDs," as they came to be called, shortly became a multimillion-dollar industry unto themselves.

Percy "Master P" Miller's entrepreneurial spirit and his $56.5 million income for 1998 earned him another place in history. The following year, Master P cracked into *Forbes*'s annual list of top-earning entertainers, debuting at number eleven. Master P outearned established celebrities like Robin Williams, Celine Dion, Mel Gibson, Garth Brooks, and Eddie Murphy.

At number sixteen, just five paces behind Master P, entered Sean "Puffy" Combs, with earnings of $53.5 million, a figure buoyed by a $40 million payment from Arista Records as an advance against income from its new fifty-fifty joint venture with Bad Boy Entertainment, negotiated in part by Combs's new manager, former Warner Bros. Black A&R chief Benny Medina.

Combs, like Master P, had become a master of diversification, a one-man brand. His Manhattan restaurant, Justin's, was nearing its third year of profitability, and Combs was planning to open a second eatery in Atlanta. Combs had just launched an upscale urban-lifestyle magazine, *Notorious*, and begun a clothing line.

From the start, Sean John was different from many of the hip-hop clothing lines because Combs picked a professional to run it. Jeff Tweedy had worked for Ralph Lauren and Karl Kani. The D.C. native had featured Combs in a Kani print ad when Combs was just an A&R man for Uptown. Tweedy knew how to design a full line, knew how to manufacture and market it, and had gotten Kani into the largest department store chain in the world, Federated. Before the launch of Sean John, Tweedy flew to Asia with a PowerPoint presentation to create direct relationships with manufacturers. Using Ralph Lauren as their business model, Tweedy and Combs started their line in 1998 with eight styles, including a velour suit that sold, Tweedy remarked, "like crack." Combs wore a black cap with a white Sean John logo on *Saturday Night Live*. The next week, the caps were sold out. Between Combs's aggressive marketing and Tweedy's retail experience, the line grew quickly. By 1999, Sean John had placed inventory into Federated chains Bloomingdale's and Macy's, and Tweedy predicted that Sean John's sales would hit $30 million in the next year.

"Two twenty-eight-year-old kick-ass entrepreneurs" is what *Forbes* called Percy Miller and Sean Combs. Ultimately, they were something more: the embodiment of the superempowered artist, two one-man brands, the fulfillment of the RZA's vision of self-determination and ownership—not just for hip-hop artists, not just for Black artists, but for all American artists.

In the coming new millennium, the success of Percy Miller and Sean Combs would mark the beginning of an unprecedented spike in Black American entrepreneurship.

The revolution no longer needed to be fought. It could, perhaps, be bought.

Miller and Combs were joined on the *Forbes* list by a third person from the world of hip-hop. Edging out A-list actor Jim Carrey at number thirty-eight with earnings of $34 million was a rapper named Will Smith.

Smith's branding as a marquee movie actor had begun modestly in 1993 with an adaptation of a cerebral Broadway play called *Six Degrees of Separation*. As his TV series, *The Fresh Prince of Bel-Air*, moved into its final season, movie scripts started flowing into Smith's managers at Handprint— the partnership between Jeff Pollack, Benny Medina, and Smith's longtime road manager and right-hand man, James Lassiter. But after perusing the offerings, it was clear that Hollywood saw Will Smith not as an actor, but a *Black* actor.

"You're Tom Hanks," Pollack told Smith. The Handprint partners refused to sell Smith into "Black roles," period.

Then a friend of Pollack's, a writer-producer named Dean Devlin, gave Pollack a copy of a script that he had just sold to 20th Century Fox, a big-budget science-fiction flick about an alien attack on America. Pollack read it and suggested that Smith would be perfect for the part of an air force pilot who becomes the unlikely hero, a role that required a delicate balance of macho grit and comic inflection.

Devlin agreed. The powers above Devlin, however, did not. Michael Ovitz's CAA had "packaged" the movie, and wanted an actor like Billy Baldwin or Val Kilmer in the role. But Devlin and his cowriter, director Roland Emmerich, had negotiated complete casting autonomy as long as they kept their budget under $70 million. Contractually, no one could stop them from hiring Smith.

Then Pollack received a call from the president of Fox Pictures, who offered Pollack's client a sweet deal: Will Smith could have a role in any Fox movie he wanted. Just pick a script. All he would have to do in return was relinquish his role in Devlin and Emmerich's movie.

Pollack smiled. Fox had been like any other studio, tendering Smith only roles written expressly for Black characters, shying away from giving Will any leads. Now they were offering Smith a role in another movie they had, until this moment, refused to give him. The president of Fox was trying to horse-trade Will Smith out of the role of a lifetime: an action hero in a summer blockbuster.

"Here's what's happening," Pollack replied. "You just don't think a Black man can save the world."

Will Smith stayed in the picture, and *Independence Day* made Smith the star of the highest-grossing movie of 1996, at $306 million in the United

States, and almost a billion dollars worldwide. The following year he costarred with Tommy Lee Jones in *Men in Black*, which outearned every movie that year except for *Titanic*.

America had a new leading man, one who would go on to save the world many times over.

ALBUM EIGHT

AN AMERICAN DREAM

Hip-hop cashes out

(1999–2007)

Side A
Building

A t the end of the twentieth century, hip-hop continued to generate ever more auspicious "firsts."

In the 1999 Recording Industry Association of America's annual consumer survey, the rap/hip-hop genre reached its highest market share ever, 10.8 percent, tying country music as the number two genre in American music, second only to rock. But the numbers hid the culture's true pervasiveness. Much of contemporary R&B was nothing more than sung vocals over hip-hop tracks. Rock, too, had slowly been absorbing hip-hop's influence, with hip-hop hybrids like Sugar Ray, Sublime, Rage Against the Machine, Limp Bizkit, and Fatboy Slim. Two rock stars even began their careers as rappers—Everlast and Kid Rock.

In 1999, rapper/singer/actress Lauryn Hill became the first hip-hop artist to win the Album of the Year award at the Grammys. That same year, a White rapper became the first to take the award for Best Rap Album, Eminem. It was a stunning reversal of racial roles—the Black artist taking the top honor in the traditionally "White" category, and the White artist doing the same for the normally "Black" award. The turnaround symbolized the sunset of racial politics in American music. For over a decade—from the debut of the Beastie Boys to Vanilla Ice and now Eminem—the emergence of successful White rap acts engendered dire prophecies of a White takeover of hip-hop. In each case, it never happened. In the new cultural order of the hip-hop generation, White-skin privilege yielded less advantage than at any time in history.

In 1999, *Time* magazine ran a glowing cover story called "Hip-Hop Nation," an unwitting throwback to the landmark *Village Voice* article a decade earlier. The author, Christopher John Farley, wrote with affection about the culture, interviewing Russell Simmons, Lauryn Hill, Sean "Puffy" Combs, and Master P, among others. While Combs predicted the political influence of the music ("In five years," said Combs, "if Master P and I endorse a presidential candidate, we could turn an election. Hip-hop is that deep"), Farley noted something novel about the art form's relationship to commerce. "Hip-hop," he said, "is perhaps the only art form that celebrates capitalism openly."

Indeed, by 1999, a few rappers had cracked into the *Forbes* list. But the revenues of Master P, the flash of Combs, and the box-office returns of Will Smith all paled in comparison to a single, less conspicuous deal.

In April, Russell Simmons and Lyor Cohen finalized the sale of the remaining portion of their company, Def Jam Recordings, Inc., to the largest record conglomerate in the world, Universal Music Group.

When Simmons and Cohen emerged, they were collectively $135 million richer. And Def Jam, the profitable business they had just sold, was placed on a par with the other legendary, iconic labels in the Universal family— Island, Interscope, Geffen, A&M, and Motown.

Def Jam had just become the first hip-hop label elevated to the status of a major and the first *hip-hop* brand to become a fully *corporate* brand.

The sale of Def Jam was the biggest hip-hop business deal in history, dwarfing anything that came before it, including the sale of the first 50 percent of Def Jam to Polygram in 1994 for $33 million. Universal valued the entire company at $325 million.

The deal was all the more astounding because, in the early 1990s, Def Jam was essentially a liability for Russell Simmons—$17 million in debt to Sony Music, with an aging roster and sagging sales.

How that deficit was transformed into a multimillion-dollar asset is the story of an extraordinary group of individuals: Russell Simmons; his second partner in Def Jam, Lyor Cohen; and the team of people they attracted.

It was this extended family of executives, entrepreneurs, artists, producers, handlers, and hustlers who would—in the next ten years—build businesses worth many times the record amount for which Def Jam had just sold and take their place among the most powerful figures in American culture.

When Chris Lighty first met Russell Simmons back in 1989, he wanted nothing to do with him.

Lyor Cohen needed Simmons's help to persuade the nineteen-year-old artist manager to join Rush. To do that, Cohen had to bring Lighty not to Rush's offices on 298 Elizabeth Street, but to a place where Simmons would more likely be found.

Cohen led Lighty to Nell's—a restaurant-cum-nightclub on 14th Street that served as Simmons's de facto workspace. Lighty, a kid from the South Bronx, had seen lots of bizarre, twisted things in his life. He had hung out at the Roxy and the Funhouse as a teenager and up at S&S with the old-school drug dealers. But he had never witnessed a scene like Nell's. The club was filled with White people wearing crazy shit. Someone was carrying a live snake. And in the middle of it all was Russell Simmons, shouting over the music, blathering incessantly in his ear, making absolutely no sense. Before Simmons was finished with one sentence, he was already in the middle of the next. This was the Russell Simmons who created Run-DMC? Lighty thought. *The Russell Simmons who founded Def Jam?* It was like someone pulled the curtain back on the great and mighty Oz.

Lighty turned to Simmons and said directly, "I don't care who you are or what you've done. I'm not fucking with you."

Cohen was mortified. The idea was for Russ to massage the guy, and all he ended up doing was rubbing him the wrong way. Lighty's reaction only confirmed Cohen's intuition that Lighty was the serious person that the guys in De La Soul had claimed he was.

You need to fuck with Chris, they said.

Since he was a teenager, Lighty had worked for DJ Red Alert. He carried crates of Red's records to the DJs many club gigs. He passed up a basketball scholarship at the Universty of Nevada to be a road manager for Boogie Down Productions. As Red Alert Productions faltered, Lighty took on most of the day-to-day responsibilities of handling Red Alert's groups, the Jungle Brothers and A Tribe Called Quest. Lyor Cohen wanted those groups and needed to co-opt Lighty before he could become a serious competitor. Moreover, Cohen needed real help around an increasingly chaotic office, still populated by people he could neither count on nor control. Lighty's street knowledge, work ethic, and temperament might come in handy. Lighty was calm, but completely capable of carnage. He was, in a word, *restrained*.

Chris Lighty grew up in the Castle Hill section of the South Bronx with his younger brothers Dave, Mike, and Jonathan, and his sisters Nicole and Hannah. His father Steve split when Chris was young, and his mother Jessica kept the family afloat on secretarial work and food stamps. When the relationship with her next husband went south, Jessica did, too, packing up the house and moving to Maryland. But Chris—enrolled at Samuel Gompers vocational high school and hanging out with the Zulu Nation DJs at the Bronx River Projects—wanted to stay in New York, so he bunked with his friend from Gompers, Darryl, in another housing project nearby.

Two good-looking light-skinned teens under little supervision, Chris and Darryl loosed themselves upon the streets and projects of the Bronx. Whenever they weren't helping DJ Red Alert, they were usually involved in something dangerous or downright criminal. Red gave them a nickname—"The Violators"—for the usual routine that Chris and Darryl ran at Union Square, scanning the club for the flyest girls and quickly peeling them away from whoever brought them. *You come into the spot with a nice-looking girl and a sandwich*, Chris would say, *we'll eat your sandwich and take your girl.*

If, say, you were the unfortunate fellow being "violated," you could try to fight back. Chris and Darryl were good with their hands, and they had backup—three tough guys from Bronx River named Chris Ali, Big Rod, and Hands, whom everyone called Black Jesus because of his long Jheri curl. After a melee in Union Square wherein the five Bronx brawlers fought off a much bigger troop from Brooklyn (led by a trio of thugs who called themselves "Pig," "Dog" and "Horse") the Violators attained mythic status and the duo quickly became a quintet. They provided protection for DJ Red Alert as he moved between his home, nightclubs, and the radio station. No one in New York dared beef with Red Alert for not playing their record for fear of the Violators. And if the Violators ever got into real trouble, they could—and did—call on Chris Lighty's father, an FBI agent, to straighten things out.

They called Chris Lighty "Baby Chris" for his pretty-boy looks and to distinguish him from the older Chris Ali, but the nickname also described Lighty's attitude. "Baby Chris" was interested in girls and thrills, not in creating a fearsome reputation. If he could talk his way out of a confrontation, he would. One weekend at the Latin Quarter nightclub in Times Square, another kid from Brooklyn, an associate of Big Daddy Kane's named Hawk, loudly challenged Lighty to a man-on-man fight.

"Walk around the corner with me," Hawk goaded him.

Baby Chris told Hawk that he wasn't interested. Later that night, Chris Ali and Big Rod took Baby Chris up to Red Alert's place in Harlem for an official reprimand.

"If you ever let someone chump you again," Chris Ali said, "*I'm* going to fuck you up." Chris Ali knew that the Brooklyn kids hated the cocksure Lighty, and their harassment would worsen, creating problems for the entire crew unless the kid stepped up.

Lucky for Chris Ali, Baby Chris was a fast learner. The next night at the Latin Quarter, Lighty ran directly up to Hawk and punched him in the face. The fisticuffs turned into a full-scale riot. When Chris Ali followed the fight out the front door, it seemed that all of Brooklyn was outside armed with knives and chairs they had taken from the pizza parlor next door. Now it was Chris Ali's turn to call for backup—the "55" crew, so named for the building at 1455 Harrod in Bronx River. They came within fifteen minutes with guns and sprayed the street with bullets.

The legendary Latin Quarter shut its doors not long thereafter. The Violators thus embodied the paradox of hip-hop. The same crew that wore the mantle of peace, unity and anti-violence promoted by their associates in the Zulu Nation and Native Tongues were an integral part of hip-hop's cycle of violent one-upmanship. The same crew that held decent jobs by day—Chris Lighty worked as an electrician for Metro North, and a few of the other Violators worked for the MTA—sold drugs for extra cash and flash.

The Violators' illicit activities provided the resources to make Red Alert and his artists' lives a little easier: money, cars, connections, weapons. But Red Alert saw something in Chris Lighty that was of a higher caliber than the rest of the crew. Lighty was a chameleon—he could be a hoodlum, but he would rather be a diplomat. Lighty's reluctance to use force worried Chris Ali, but it reassured Red Alert. Because Lighty was always the most level-headed and business-minded of the crew, Red put him out on the road with Boogie Down Productions, and then made him tour manager for the Jungle Brothers.

Lighty became the trio's virtual fourth member. The rest of the Violators became their transportation, their roadies, and their entourage. In fact, Red Alert and the Jungle Brothers mentioned the Violators so much in song and on the radio that some people thought that they were the next Native Tongues spinoff group. Virgin Records offered them a deal. Funken-Klein, manning the phones at Red Alert Productions, once had to convince a European A&R executive that the Violators weren't rappers, but bodyguards. It

was not an accurate description. The Violators were "security" only inciden-
tally, and certainly not a gang. More than mere muscle, they were simply
five friends who worked, partied, hustled, and fought out of loyalty to Red
Alert and to each other.

As an artist manager, Chris Lighty began exercising a different set of
muscles. The "JBs" scored their first real hit not in America but in Europe;
not with a hip-hop record but with a dance track called "Girl, I'll House
You." Lighty, the kid from Castle Hill, toured the world off of that record.
In 1989, when the single's success attracted the attention of Warner Bros.
Records, Lighty witnessed the negotiation of what might very well have
been the most expensive hip-hop signing at a major label to date: $1.6
million.

Of course, the deal was expensive because the Jungle Brothers' existing
contracts had to be bought. Lighty witnessed the $1.6 million advance cut
into huge chunks: $800,000 to Warlock, their current label; $300,000 to
Idlers, their production company. By the time Red Alert and Rhythm
Method had taken their management fee and the recording costs had been
deducted, the four members of the Jungle Brothers each received personal
advances of $50,000. Lighty was appalled. The businesspeople had just
chopped up a million and a half, while he and his bandmates still had to do
all the work of recording and touring.

After this experience, it didn't matter how many A&R people called for
a demo tape from the Violators. Chris Lighty decided he would never be an
artist. He wanted a bigger piece of the sandwich.

A few days after the botched meeting with Russell Simmons at Nell's,
Cohen pitched to Lighty again at Rush's Elizabeth Street offices. On its face,
Cohen's deal wasn't very generous: a smaller percentage of his clients' earnings in return for bringing them into the Rush fold. But Lighty knew that
he needed to learn some things to take his career to the next level. He felt
Simmons couldn't teach him anything, because there was no way Simmons
himself ran this company. This tall White man with the strange accent was
obviously the guy who did. It didn't take long for Lighty to figure out that
Cohen wasn't a regular White man, but an Israeli. Then he found out
that Cohen wasn't really Israeli, either, as most people thought. In reality,
Lyor was some other shit.

Cohen made big deals that brought in big money, and leaped at new ideas if he sensed that they might be lucrative—like setting up new "900" phone numbers for each artist in the Rush stable, where fans could call and hear special messages from their favorite artists at a rate of $2 per minute. But with every leap, he skipped some of the details. Cohen didn't read contracts. Lighty read them religiously. Cohen didn't pore over the books. Lighty made it his business to account for every penny. Cohen cared not for people's feelings when winning was at stake. Monica Lynch banned Cohen from Tommy Boy Records' offices after Cohen berated low-level employees and threatened to have them fired. Lighty was calm and personable. People liked him.

Throughout his early tenure at Rush, Lighty continued to supplement his entertainment business income with profits from the Violators' ongoing drug hustle. Cohen saw it all: Lighty's jewelry, his clothes, his Audi, the packages of money coming in from friends driving up to Elizabeth Street in their BMWs. Then came the evening that Lighty himself was violated. He was on line with Darryl outside the nightclub MK waiting to get into a birthday party for Queen Latifah when a kid walked up and slashed his cheek with a razor. The assailant ran into the club; Darryl and the bleeding Lighty gave chase and beat him down—just another thug from Brooklyn with a beef. The ensuing skirmish created a stampede of patrons fleeing the club. In the crush of people, Latifah's mother—Rita Owens—was injured. That evening, Lighty found himself up at Red Alert's place again, apologizing to Latifah even before he went to the hospital for stitches.

For Lighty, the incident was a sobering end to his youth and vanity. For Lyor Cohen, the time had come to give his protégé an ultimatum.

"You have to make up your mind," Cohen told him. "Are you going to be *that* guy, or *this* guy?"

Lighty told Cohen that he would give up the hustle and tussle in exchange for a salary. Shortly, Lighty assembled the Violators and told them the news. From that day forward, he would be their friend, but not their partner. Darryl was upset; they were just beginning to build their organization. Chris Ali was offended; he had wanted to be in business with Lighty. He had been shot at a club, spent over two months in the hospital, and received a three-digit settlement check from the club's owners, a check he wanted to give to Lighty.

"Russell and Lyor's money is longer than yours," Lighty told him.

Lighty had just bet his future on Lyor Cohen at a time when Cohen's own future in the business was far from certain. As rising insurance rates and skittish venues led to the decline of rap tours, rap management was becoming far less lucrative. Rush was bleeding, loaning money to its own artists to help them get by. And Cohen's first foray into the record business—a new company with Russell Simmons—was an unmitigated disaster that was quickly drowning the entire empire in debt.

Two years after their bloodless separation, Russell Simmons and Rick Rubin had succeeded in preserving their friendship, though their lawyers still hadn't hammered out a settlement. They saw each other whenever Simmons was in Los Angeles or Rubin was in New York. On one such occasion, as they sat down for a meal, Simmons talked business. Technically, Rubin still owned half of Def Jam. But Rubin listened with dispassion, more as an amused friend than an interested party.

"It's horrible," Simmons lamented. "I'm losing so much money."

Def Jam was hemorrhaging in part because of a business move designed to enfranchise Lyor Cohen. Rush Associated Labels (its abbreviation, RAL, also nicely signifying "Russell and Lyor") had been created to give Cohen a stake in new music signings.

The core of RAL's strategy was to give production deals—small imprints— to artists and producers in the Def Jam/Rush family. At first this seemed to be a smart idea. Artists and producers, not A&R people, had long been the primary funnels through which new signings came. Prince Paul of Stetsasonic, for example, brought De La Soul to Tommy Boy. The members of Run-DMC and Original Concept had introduced Public Enemy to Def Jam. It was good business to incentivize good ears. But giving a bunch of artists their own "vanity labels" without regard for creative oversight or business acumen invited mediocrity and failure. And the two people supervising these deals were Simmons, whose track record as an A&R person for Def Jam wasn't outstanding, and Cohen, who had no experience making records at all.

Chuck D of Public Enemy began his own label, PRO Division, and put out the first solo album of his DJ Terminator X. Prince Paul launched Dew Doo Man Records for his new protégés, Resident Alien. Ed Lover won a deal for No Face Records, featuring the girl group Bytches with Problems, and his own group, No Face (which Ed Lover had to leave because of MTV's insistence that he choose either a career as an artist or his job as the host of the *Yo!* show). Jam Master Jay helmed JMJ Records, signing the Afros and

Fam-Lee. And Sal Abbatiello relaunched his successful Fever imprint under the aegis of RAL, with Latin freestyle acts like Lisette Melendez.

The Def Jam label was now reduced to just one of many imprints under the RAL umbrella. Few new signings happened on Def Jam proper—mostly Simmons's signings, mostly failures. The new "associated labels" didn't fare much better. The minor successes of singles like Terminator X's "Buck Whylin'"—the song that introduced Sister Souljah to the world—lay buried under an avalanche of unsold vinyl, CDs, and cassette tapes from other projects. The labels of RAL yielded only one breakthrough artist—Onyx on JMJ Records—and two high-priced acquisitions of established artists—Nice & Smooth and EPMD—both refugees of the defunct Sleeping Bag Records. EPMD was responsible for the career of another hit signing to RAL, their protégé Redman, one of the shining lights in an otherwise dark 1992 and a signing that Lyor Cohen credited for saving the label from certain death.

Even with these records raking in millions, RAL spent millions more on artist advances, lawyer fees, recording costs, video production, new hires, independent promoters, advertising, and marketing programs. RAL's partner, Sony Music, charged back their own promotion costs to the joint venture.

As his debt accumulated, Russell Simmons ramped up his fevered sales pitch to match.

"I got this new record," Simmons enthused to Rick Rubin at another friendly meal at the Beverly Hills Hotel. "It's by this great producer. Lyor's brother. It got so many requests on KMEL, they had to take it off the radio!" Back in his car, Rubin phoned George Drakoulias to repeat Simmons's ridiculous story.[22]

By contrast, Rubin's new label, Def American Recordings, was about to have its best year yet, with new million-selling albums by the Black Crowes and Sir Mix-a-Lot. Rubin took some small satisfaction from Simmons's suffering. He even planned an event to squeeze out a little more: In a year or so, Rubin told friends and associates, he would be changing the name of his company to simply American Recordings, declaring the word "Def" to be dead.

---

[22]Though Keith Naftaly, KMEL's program director at the time, denies that this ever ocurred, another record entrepreneur recounts a similar story about one of his own records. Select's Fred Munao says that in 1984, Philadelphia station WDAS decided to yank UTFO's "Roxanne, Roxanne" off the air because they couldn't deal with all the incoming requests. So it can happen.

It was the ultimate Bud Abbott routine, with Simmons cast as poor Lou Costello, left holding the bag of tomatoes. The punch line to Rubin's joke was simple.

"*Then* what's Russell going to do!?"

As his records cooled, Russell Simmons hired publicists to keep his name hot in the news media. *Manhattan, Inc.*, a business magazine, ran a multi-page feature that drew the inevitable, erroneous comparisons between Simmons and Motown Records founder Berry Gordy.

Def Jam, writer Maura Sheehy wrote, had supplanted Motown as the "largest black-owned business" in the record industry, although with Rubin still a partner and Lyor Cohen in the wings, Def Jam wasn't wholly Black owned. Simmons, Sheehy continued, marketed images of Blackness to mainstream America, just as Gordy had. But unlike Gordy, Simmons eschewed changing his artists' image to make them "safe" for White consumption. Def Jam was a multiracial partnership that sold one unapologetically Black culture, hip-hop, to all American youth.

Though Simmons's vision for hip-hop as pop culture was firm, some of his contemporaries thought that Simmons lacked the commitment to realize his dream. When Sheehy ran the Berry Gordy comparison by Bill Stephney, the former Def Jam president instead likened Simmons to "Spuds MacKenzie," referencing the party animal mascot of Budweiser's latest ad campaign. Indeed, to many people—like Lighty, Rubin, and Stephney—Simmons looked insane: clubbing, starting superfluous businesses like a modeling agency that seemed an outgrowth of his hedonistic lifestyle, all while his core companies burned.

But at least one person understood what Simmons was trying to do.

Carmen Ashhurst's first impressions of Russell Simmons hadn't been much different from Chris Lighty's. At thirty-eight, Ashhurst was older than most of the people in the Def Jam/Rush crew, and definitely the most mature. She had previously been a TV producer and documentary filmmaker in Boston, and had been hired as a television producer by the newly installed Marxist government of Grenada, where she documented the revolution led by prime minister Maurice Bishop. Upon her return to Boston, her comrades in Grenada turned against one another. One friend, Bernard Coard, had Bishop and seven of her other friends lined up against a wall and shot. People whom she cared about and believed in betrayed and murdered people whom she cared about and believed in. The entertainment business, Ashhurst figured, would be a welcome change from all of that.

In the spring of 1988, Ashhurst found a temporary job helping Rush Artist Management publicist Bill Adler implement Rush's upcoming summer package tour. During her first days there, the staff gathered for a conference call, and Simmons—phoning from his apartment just blocks away—wanted to know who this "Carmen" was.

"Bill's new assistant," Lyor Cohen replied.

"So, Bill, are you stickin' her yet?" Simmons asked.

The room fell silent for a moment. "C'mon, Russell." Adler sighed.

What a creep, Ashhurst thought.

Ashhurst's first meeting with Simmons happened the following night, outside Harlem's Apollo Theater.

"So you're the one working with Bill," Simmons said. "I heard I hurt your feelings."

"Yes," Ashhurst said firmly.

"Fuck it," Simmons replied.

Ashhurst's relationship with Simmons changed during the tour. She had been hired to coordinate voter registration events, but Ashhurst gradually noticed the tour accountant—Jake, a lanky, rocker type of White guy with long blond hair, torn jeans, and T-shirt, carrying a briefcase. Inside that case were, invariably, tens of thousands of dollars in cash, Rush's take of the previous night's gate. Now, instead of watching the shows, Ashhurst began sticking around backstage for the all-important settlement process, which pitted the accountant and Rush's promoter—Darryl Brooks of G Street Productions—against the local venues in a nightly effort to determine how many seats had sold and how much the venue owed. For the biggest dates, Lyor Cohen would fly out. Then it was war. Cohen automatically assumed that the locals were trying to fuck him, so Cohen would dispense with formalities like ticket reconciliation and simply ask for whatever the hell he felt he deserved. Ashhurst got her first up-close look at Cohen in action when he sent Brooks into the negotiation room halfway through the show with news that the headline act, Run-DMC, would *not* be going onstage unless he got "X" amount, right now. While he waited for Brooks's return, Cohen got so pumped that he began humping the air. Ashhurst learned what moved Cohen. It wasn't money that turned him on. It wasn't just *winning*, either. It was winning *by the largest possible margin*.

By the time that Simmons joined them on the road, he was surprised to find that Ashhurst had kept track of every significant transaction. Ashhurst surprised herself, too. She became a reliable source of information for Simmons. At the end of the summer, the tour was over, as was her temporary gig. Ashhurst had been offered a publicist job at Motown Records. She asked Simmons to negotiate the gig on her behalf. Instead, Simmons offered her a permanent job as his assistant.

Simmons didn't have an office, so Ashhurst decided to work out of his apartment on Barrow Street in Greenwich Village. The decision gave her a view of Simmons that few others had: as a man of complete focus.

Every day, after the previous night's detritus had been cleared and the sleepover guests hustled out, Ashhurst saw Simmons take a seat on his couch. A bowl of chips in his lap, phone at his ear, Simmons made call after call to radio programmers, MTV bigwigs, Sony executives, Cohen, and the Def Jam staff. He dialed them all from memory. He remembered personal details. When he talked to the radio guys, he recalled the last time he had seen them, where they had hung out, and who they had fucked that night. He'd sit for six hours, without taking a bathroom break. One by one, he worked them all, flattering, cajoling, imploring, arguing, and, much of the time, succeeding. He never gave up.

Simmons worked all the time and with a mantra: "We don't make records. We sell records." And he was always selling something. Even when he was partying. No, *especially* when he was partying. With Russell it was always work.

The new companies that Simmons was starting? Good reason for them. Simmons realized early on that his record and management companies— even when they performed well—were boxed in. He needed to create new growth opportunities, not just for his own artists, but for all of hip-hop. He needed to bust or buy his way out of the box.

His new, syndicated video show, the "New Music Report," and Rush Broadcasting, formed to buy small AM radio stations across the country, were both important moves to exert more control over the distribution and marketing of the music when traditional TV and radio proved less than reliable. Rush Media, his new advertising agency, was a way to create more income streams for himself and hip-hop artists. Simmons may have been doing a million things at once. But his reasons for doing so were the epitome of long-range thinking. He may never have put his plan on paper. But he certainly had a plan. The only thing that Simmons lacked was organization. That was where Carmen Ashhurst came in.

Ashhurst's first order of business was the sloppy accounting situation. Rush Artist Management and Def Jam Recordings were two distinct businesses, but their books were commingled. Ashhurst separated them. At the same time, Def Jam was in the middle of transforming its production deal with Sony into a pressing and distribution arrangement. The sticking point in the negotiations was Def Jam's endemic disorganization. To reassure Sony, Ashhurst divided Def Jam into departments that mirrored Columbia Records' organizational chart—A&R, product management, business affairs, promotion. Simmons, in turn, made her vice president of operations.

Next, Ashhurst put up a whiteboard on Simmons's wall and created headings for each of Simmons's companies—Def Jam, Rush Artist Management, Rush Producers Management, and a new column for Rush Philanthropic—because Simmons had no tax shelter whatsoever. And she suggested an umbrella organization for all of these entities. At first, Simmons called it Russell Rush Associates, but later settled on something more diginified: Rush Communications.

"Carmen," Simmons told her. "Don't you realize how much more you've done for me than any of my assistants?" Ashhurst thought the compliment backhanded. He still saw her as a girl, not an executive.

Ashhurst had become indispensible to Simmons. But as Ashhurst built a structure for Simmons, hiring people for Def Jam and brokering deals, she saw Lyor Cohen seethe.

"Why isn't this going through me?" Cohen would ask.

"It's not going through you because I'm talking directly to Russell," Ashhurst replied.

Cohen's role in Simmons's organization was still nebulous. He ran Rush Artist Management. He had a stake in Rush Associated Labels but not Def Jam. The legalities mattered not to Cohen. He saw himself as Russell's partner in everything.

But Ashhurst understood that Simmons didn't want a new partner. When Rubin was around, the young producer had been lauded as the genius, while Simmons felt reduced to the mere "other half" in the eyes of the industry and media. More than anything, she believed that Simmons wanted to prove that he could do it on his own.

Little more than a year after her arrival Ashhurst decided that her work was done. She had met a man, Lance Watson, and fallen in love. They were going to marry and move to London. When she tendered her resignation, however, Simmons refused to accept it.

"You can't leave!" he said. Simmons offered her more money and a promotion to president of Def Jam Recordings, the position left vacant since Bill Stephney's departure.

Ashhurst took the reins of a struggling, drifting company, its problems multiplied by the proliferation of artist deals through RAL. Simmons required Ashhurst to be at his disposal twenty-four hours a day. If she left work at a normal hour, he often got angry. In April 1991 Ashhurst was nine months pregnant and needed to take a maternity leave. She made arrangements to ensure that things would run smoothly in her absence, temporarily promoting her head of business affairs—a Ivy League lawyer named Dave Harleston—to acting president.

Two months after her son, Garvey, was born Ashhurst returned to Def Jam. But Dave Harleston, the man she had hired, refused to give up her president's chair, telling Ashhurst that if he were demoted, he was leaving.

Ashhurst suspected that Cohen was behind this. He had probably found Harleston to be a more deferential and pliant person with whom to deal.

Ashhurst ran to Russell's new apartment on Fourth and Broadway—the one he had just purchased from pop idol Cher—where Ashhurst was even more shocked to discover that Simmons didn't want Harleston removed, either. She and Simmons had a screaming match. He offered her a new job, president of Rush Communications.

"I already *have* a job!" Ashhurst replied.

Finally, Simmons broke it down. "What would it take for you to let Harleston stay?" he asked.

Ashhurst thought about it. She had never been a music industry person, per se. Her background was in television. Now Simmons was forming a new company to produce TV, in partnership with Stan Lathan—the director of *Beat Street* and dozens of network sitcoms. They were talking about doing a stand-up comedy show together.

If Ashhurst were going to move aside for Simmons and Cohen, she wanted to work on this new venture.

Lyor Cohen thought Carmen Ashhurst capable but weak. If the music business was a war, he thought, one needed a warrior. By 1992, in the midst of Def Jam/RAL's worst year yet, Cohen decided that Def Jam needed him full-time.

Cohen informed Chris Lighty that the two of them would wind down

Rush Artist Management. Rush had been the first company to develop rappers' careers as artists, finding them multiple income streams and multimedia exposure. But Rush was drudgery now, no longer the profitable company it once was. Cohen told Lighty that he could take the best artists for his own management company if the artists themselves were willing.

Lighty formed his new company—Violator Management—around a few key artists: LL Cool J, Busta Rhymes, De La Soul, and A Tribe Called Quest. Lighty also landed a production deal with a rock indie label called Relativity Records. Violator Records would be home to Lighty's new artists—a Bronx MC named Fat Joe, a fifteen-year-old rapper named Chi-Ali, and a production crew called the Beatnuts.

Cohen had never considered Lighty a creative executive. But nothing got Cohen's attention like somebody making a success of themselves without his involvement. When Cohen found out about Lighty's new deal, his prime directive kicked in.

"What the fuck are you doing over at Relativity?!" Cohen bellowed. *Why didn't you bring your artists to Def Jam?*

"Lyor," Lighty replied, "you didn't want to sign them."

"I didn't know what they sounded like."

"What do you mean, 'You didn't know what they sounded like'?" Lighty laughed. "I *gave* you the music!"

Cohen again enticed Lighty to come work for him, this time as the creative chief of Def Jam Recordings. On its face, the move seemed to be a step up. "Baby Chris" would now hold the title of vice president of A&R at the most famous hip-hop label in the world. But the move required more sacrifice on Lighty's part. To extract himself from the Relativity deal, he had to leave all his artists there. And the Def Jam for which he would be working was but a shell of its former self, without any clear A&R direction since the departure of its founder, Rick Rubin.

Lighty would help to change that.

Russell Simmons made a career out of marketing unadulterated Black youth culture to the mainstream. His next move would intensify that process.

Simmons's idea for a stand-up comedy television series arose from his visits to Black comedy clubs in Harlem and L.A.'s Crenshaw district. Like the atmosphere of those comedy clubs, each episode of *Russell Simmons' Def*

Comedy Jam would feature a bevy of Black comedians, playing to a young Black crowd. But Simmons's show would give White America a direct window into that Black world. As such, Simmons said, it would do for comedy what Def Jam Recordings did for music, providing Black entertainers a direct line to a mainstream audience they otherwise wouldn't have and giving mainstream audiences a shot of multicultural adrenaline. Simmons and his television partner, Stan Lathan, successfully pitched the idea to Bridget Potter, senior vice president for original programming at HBO. Potter bought the first four shows for $800,000.

From Rush Communications' new offices in Tribeca, Carmen Ashhurst dispatched her assistant, Bob Sumner, who ran a comedy room in New Jersey called the Peppermint, to find talent for the show. Sumner brought in Black comedians virtually unknown to wider audiences, like Bill Bellamy, who had appeared onstage at Harlem's Apollo Theater; a stand-up from Dallas named Steve Harvey; and a Chicago comedian named Bernie Mac. To host the show, Lathan picked Martin Lawrence, a young performer who had been under a development contract to HBO for several years with little result. Lathan taped the raucous shows in late 1991 at the Academy Theatre on Broadway in Manhattan.

Even before all of the first four shows had aired, HBO ordered more, because *Russell Simmons' Def Comedy Jam* had exploded the channel's Friday-night ratings.

Not every Black comedian wanted in. Chris Rock, who played on NBC's *Saturday Night Live* and had a film acting career, declined to participate because he didn't want to be typecast as a "Black" comedian—meaning that he felt that his appeal was bigger and his comedy broader than what he saw in *Def Comedy Jam*'s more parochial, insular approach.

Nor did everyone who watched the show like what they saw. By the end of the first season *Def Comedy Jam* had turned into a veritable curse-fest, with especially liberal use of the word "nigger." It was just as Russell Simmons planned. White America could now spy on how Black folks talked when they weren't around. But both Ashhurst and Lathan grew uneasy with the concept. At the taping it was hilarious. On TV, playing out for Middle America, it was disconcerting. Bill Cosby publicly called *Def Comedy Jam* a minstrel show. Chris Rock lampooned it on *Saturday Night Live* with his sketch, "Russell Simmons' Def Magic Show Jam" ("I know that you motherfuckers don't think I got a motherfucking rabbit in this hat, right? You niggas want to see a motherfucking rabbit?")

Simmons dismissed the criticism. He was a race man. "Making rich Black kids who have rich Black kids" was his stated goal. Simmons felt the sting of racial bigotry every day—whether it be taxicabs refusing to pick him up in the street or White executives underestimating him in the boardroom. But Simmons didn't spend energy suspecting ulterior motives in the White people around him. After all, Simmons himself used the word "nigger" no matter where he was or whom he was with. To some Black critics, it was evidence of Simmons's vulgarity. But to Simmons himself, it was a measure of his trust in the transformative and unifying power of hip-hop culture, that even racial voyeurism could lead to a new cultural order.

As Simmons widened his social and business circles, what really bothered him was the gulf between his former, narrow idea of success, and the reality of wealth in the larger world. As he sojourned in the Hamptons and traveled to exclusive destinations like St. Barthélemy in the Caribbean, Simmons realized that almost everyone around him had more money than he did. Even with his multimillion-dollar record venture and his hit HBO show, he wasn't truly wealthy. Not even close.

The future of Def Jam wasn't certain. He didn't know how long the HBO show would last. Simmons wanted a business that would create real wealth and lasting security so he wouldn't have to worry about money ever again.

Clothes had been Simmons's first obsession, well before he had ever heard Eddie Cheba on the microphone. Simmons had befriended Mark Regev, the owner of a SoHo boutique where Simmons often bought dresses for his girlfriends and occasional lovers. Just as he had with his music mentor, Rocky Ford, Simmons asked lots of questions about the fashion business. His steady girlfriend, Marita Stavrou, was a professional model, and Simmons attended Fashion Week with her. He had also become friendly with designer Tommy Hilfiger, whose preppy brand had become an unlikely obsession for many hip-hop artists and fans alike.

For a time, even Hilfiger didn't understand his success in the urban youth market, because the hip-hop aesthetic had long been bound up with downscale street clothes like sneakers and jeans. Simmons's act Run-DMC had virtually created that iconography. The first hip-hop-related clothing lines, like Cross Colours and Karl Kani, tapped those street roots.

Simmons knew that street clothes were only half the picture. Hip-hop may have been rooted in the street, but it also reached upward. Classic

American designers like Ralph Lauren and Tommy Hilfiger appealed to the aspirational dimension of the hip-hop generation.

Simmons wanted to combine both halves of the hip-hop experience. He felt that a lot of street clothing lines were cheaply made—at worst, Fruit of the Loom T-shirts with branding slapped onto them. Simmons wanted to make not *hip-hop* clothing, but clothing of a higher quality *for the hip-hop generation.*

He shared his new notion with Carmen Ashhurst. His shirts would be made from Sea Island cotton. The jeans had to have rivets and the stitching on the seams had to be part of the design. The baseball caps would have elastic inside them instead of the cheap plastic clasps, so that they would look good when worn backward. Everything made well, everything slightly oversize, à la mode. Carmen Ashhurst's job was to hire the designers and product managers and find the different vendors to manufacture these items.

In 1992 Russell Simmons's boutique, called Phat Farm, opened on 129 Prince Street in SoHo. The store was upscale, sleek and often mobbed, with customers entertained by a live DJ. The shop was just Simmons's first stop. He told Ashhurst that his ultimate goal was to get his line—with the motto "Classic American Flava"—into department stores across the country, and especially the king of them all, Federated, the owner of Macy's and Bloomingdale's. He set his sights on the annual MAGIC show in Las Vegas in 1993.

Almost as soon as it opened, however, Phat Farm hemorrhaged cash. Both Simmons's and Ashhurst's learning curve was steep. For every item that Phat Farm sold, there were more that didn't. They manufactured seasonal lines that shipped too late for the season. They paid tens of thousands of dollars for designs that didn't work.

Even before the opening of the boutique, Mark Regev had no stomach for Phat Farm's expenses, in the mid-six figures. Regev wanted to shut down the business. Simmons insisted on pumping more capital into it. Ashhurst watched as Regev began squabbling with Simmons's new Phat Farm investor, Lyor Cohen.

"Carmen," Simmons said in an echo of times past, "my Jews are fighting."

As he had with Def Jam, Lyor Cohen won. Simmons bought Regev out, repaying his original investment in the neighborhood of $30,000, and continued to pour his savings into Phat Farm.

Chris Lighty's Violator Records imprint might have been just another mediocre Rush Associated Label had Lighty not met Paul Stewart.

Stewart, a White kid who grew up in the Black middle-class neighborhood of Baldwin Hills, had become one of the key links between Hollywood and the 'hood in the 1990s. He'd written for *The Source*. He had worked for Delicious Vinyl and brought them the West Coast's answer to the Native Tongues, the Pharcyde. He had promoted records for Steve Rifkind, and DJed on the set of *The Fresh Prince of Bel-Air*. As an artist manager, he brought House of Pain and Coolio to Tommy Boy. Stewart was one of the most connected people in the Los Angeles hip-hop world when film director John Singleton tapped him to run his new production deal with Epic, called New Deal Records.

One of Stewart's first errands was to procure the music for Singleton's upcoming movie, *Poetic Justice*, starring Tupac Shakur and Janet Jackson. Stewart and Singleton targeted a track from Snoop Doggy Dogg, the hot new artist on the hottest label in the country, Death Row. Unfortunately, Death Row would commit only to a song by Snoop's protégés, Tha Dogg Pound. But Stewart's long hours in the studio waiting for Dr. Dre's mixdown allowed him to meet Dr. Dre's stepbrother, Warren Griffin. An aspiring producer-rapper whom Death Row CEO Suge Knight had repeatedly snubbed, Griffin thrust a cassette tape into Stewart's hands. Outside in his car, Stewart listened to only one verse of the song before ejecting it. He didn't need to listen to any more to know it was a hit.

The track Griffin produced, "Indo Smoke" by Mista Grimm, became a Top 10 dance track on Billboard, and suddenly made Griffin—professionally known as Warren G—a hot commodity on the open market even as Suge Knight continued to look the other way. Paul Stewart picked Warren G up as a client for the management company he now co-owned with John Singleton.

When Chris Lighty saw the video for "Indo Smoke," he called Stewart immediately; they had known each other since Stewart worked Young MC for Delicious Vinyl, and Lighty road-managed the Jungle Brothers. Lighty, in turn, trumpeted the talents of Warren G to Russell Simmons and Lyor Cohen, who found the prospect of signing a free agent from the Death Row camp—and Dr. Dre's stepbrother to boot—irresistible. Another record like "Indo Smoke" could make Def Jam hot again. When Paul Stewart got a breathless call from Simmons himself, he knew that he had a profitable deal in the offing.

As Warren G's comanager, John Singleton stood to benefit from a possible arrangement with Def Jam. Instead, Singleton was upset that Stewart hadn't steered the rapper to the label he had hired him to run, New Deal. Stewart tried to reason with him: The money from their tiny production deal with Epic would pale in comparison to the cash they would receive from a hit record on Def Jam, whose well-honed promotion team had a much better chance of breaking a new hip-hop artist than any major label. Singleton didn't care. He accused Stewart of disloyalty.

Singleton's intuition was correct. As Def Jam prepared to sign Paul Stewart's client to a six-figure deal through Lighty's Violator Records, they began courting Stewart to run Def Jam's proposed West Coast offices. Stewart took a Friday off and, behind Singleton's back, flew to New York to meet with Simmons and Cohen.

Somehow Singleton found out. When Stewart returned to New Deal Records the following Monday, he was greeted by security guards who ordered him to clean out his desk and promptly escorted him off of the Sony lot.

Singleton wasn't the only person upset about the signing of Warren G to Def Jam. Suge Knight had changed his mind about Dr. Dre's little brother when he heard a song called "Regulate"—Warren G's contribution to the Death Row–produced soundtrack of another Tupac Shakur film, *Above the Rim*. Technically, Knight had to ask Def Jam for permission to have Warren G perform on a Death Row record. So even as Warren G's single began climbing the charts and moving units for Death Row in the hundreds of thousands, Knight could think only of the big money he would now be missing from the sales of Warren G's Def Jam album.

Lighty heard the rumors that the Death Row kingpin was irate about Def Jam muscling in on his territory. When he flew to Los Angeles with Cohen to attend a De La Soul concert, Lighty brought an associate named Lite—the bodyguard and road manager for A Tribe Called Quest. Sure enough, as De La Soul hit the stage, Knight and his entourage made their way toward where Cohen and Lighty were sitting.

"You leave," Lighty told his boss. "I'm going to deal with Suge."

Cohen moved toward the back door, and Lighty and Lite stood to block Knight's way.

"I want to talk to Lyor," Knight said.

"Well, I signed Warren G, so you can talk to me," Lighty replied. There was no way that Lighty was going to let Knight anywhere near Cohen. Knight might try to embarass him, intimidate him, or worse. *Lyor Cohen of the mighty Def Jam get smacked by Death Row out here on the West Coast?* Cohen himself might survive the attack, but his fearsome reputation wouldn't. Lighty had to safeguard Cohen's mystique, for his own good. Otherwise, Lighty would be compelled to react.

"No," Knight bellowed. "I want to talk to Lyor."

"My man doesn't feel that way," Lighty replied.

Lighty motioned to Lite, who showed Knight and his boys that he was indeed holding something very heavy.

"We got two choices," Lighty said. "We can both leave out the door, or one of us can leave in handcuffs." For the moment, Lighty was a Violator once more.

Lighty then spotted behind Suge none other than Eric B—the rapper Rakim's former partner—who had, ironically, joined forces with Death Row to open an East Coast office in Def Jam's "territory."

"Eric," Lighty said. "You should tell him about us. Because *you've* got to come back home."

Suge Knight, Eric B, and friends walked away.

A few days later, Knight figured he would get his revenge on Def Jam by forbidding Death Row artist Nate Dogg—the guest vocalist on "Regulate"—from appearing in Warren G's video. But Knight wasn't expecting a visit from the one Def Jam employee who wasn't intimidated by him nor his fearsome reputation.

On the day of the shoot, Lighty and Lite marched into Interscope's office building on Wilshire Boulevard, down the red-carpeted hallway to Death Row's headquarters, and into Suge Knight's lair.

"C'mon, b. Now I'm in your *office*," Lighty complained. He tried to convince Knight that it was in his own self-interest to let Nate appear.

"You've got 'Regulate' on your soundtrack," Lighty said. "You're going to eat off of this, too."

Lighty's persistence exasperated Knight. "Why you up for this White man?"

Lighty heard this all the time from Black executives and artists. *Why do you fuck with Lyor? Why do you work for that Israeli?* Lighty thought about it, and realized that he had never thought too much about Cohen's race or ethnicity. At first, his relationship with Cohen was about learning the business. But now it was about something more. The guy was practically his father.

"Fuck this 'fuck the White man' shit," Lighty responded. "I don't give a fuck about 'the White man.' Because you're fucking up *my* money right now."

Suge Knight had made certain that he owned himself, and that no one—Black or White—could muscle him. Now, he realized Lighty was just like him.

Knight melted. "You're right. I like you. You came up here and talked straight to me, man-to-man."

Lighty left with a handshake, and Nate Dogg arrived at the video shoot thirty minutes later.

On August 27, 1993, Rick Rubin donned flowing black robes, a white turban, and a somber expression, and rode to Hollywood Memorial Park with his girlfriend, Rosetta Millington. The cemetery's small chapel was packed with press and people from the record business, and Rubin took a seat next to Millington and his old friend George Drakoulias in the front pew. On the dais, surrounded by Black men with berets and machine guns, the Reverend Al Sharpton gave a rousing eulogy to help Rubin and the assembled bid farewell to the dearly departed. A huge flower arrangement next to the casket beside Sharpton read:

RIP DEF

After the service, Rubin and the congregation placed the items they had been asked to bring—records, CDs, T-shirts, and other memorabilia that contained the word "def"—into the casket. The casket was closed and taken outside by pallbearers, among them Bushwick Bill and Bill Stephney, and placed on a horse-drawn carriage. Then, in a New Orleans–style funeral procession that included a "second line" marching band, Rubin was trailed by nearly five hundred mourners, including friends from his past, like Ric Menello, and current collaborators, like Tom Petty and Flea from the Red Hot Chili Peppers. An MTV crew trailed behind Petty.

"I'm sorry, Mr. Petty is too broken up to answer questions now," Menello told them. "He knew the deceased well."

Rubin led the crowd to the burial plot, near the final resting place of Cecil B. DeMille, into which several gravediggers slowly lowered the casket, some of them mumbling about the sacrilege of it all.

Just as Rubin had long threatened to do, he declared the word "def" dead and buried it, literally, six feet under. Def American Recordings' press release said that Rubin's reason for laying the word to rest had to do with its recent appearance in Webster's Dictionary, thereby blunting the word's "cutting edge."

But "def" had years ago passed from the lexicon of hip-hop, and Rubin's rationale had little to do with his concern for staying hip. The jettisoning of the word "def" from "Def American Recordings" could have been a healthy karmic break with the past, the shedding of the last bit of skin from his former life in New York. But part of the inspiration for the public funeral was the Bud Abbott–esque pranking of Rubin's previous partner and current friend, Russell Simmons. Rubin, in fact, had invited Simmons to come out and speak. He didn't. Instead, Bill Stephney read Simmons's brief, good-humored statement: "Now you can be American, but I'll always be proud to be 'Def.'"

The "Death of Def" didn't come at a great time for Simmons. Def Jam Recordings was in a fragile state, piling on the debt month after month. Rubin seemed to miss the fact that his event could conceivably hurt his friend's business—from which, ironically, Rubin had still not legally finalized his departure.

Luckily for Simmons, Rubin did not posess that kind of power. His label's relaunch as American Recordings came in the midst of its first dry period. But Simmons's fortunes were such that even hits couldn't help him out of his black hole. For years Def Jam had been overspending and underperforming. The millions in revenue from their few true sales successes—albums from EPMD, Redman, Onyx—weren't enough to cover the charge-backs from their distributing partner, Sony Music. Even as Sony reaped millions in fees, Sony's accounting put Def Jam $17 million in the hole.

Sony and Def Jam always had a contentious relationship, but by 1994 it had become hostile. Sony's executives had grown exasperated with Def Jam's disorganization. Def Jam chafed under Sony's restrictive budgets, its relative ignorance of hip-hop culture, and its inadequate promotion. Sony had hired away Def Jam employees like Faith Newman, and Simmons suspected that they were trying to lure his label's bigger artists—like LL Cool J and Public Enemy. Sony had launched its own label, Chaos, to handle "edgy" urban and rock projects, under which Def Jam was now subsumed and serviced with less vigor than ever. Columbia chief Donnie Ienner and Lyor Cohen once almost came to blows. Def Jam was dying a slow death at Sony. Simmons and Cohen knew that the only way to survive would be for them to exit.

Despite Rubin's funeral in Hollywood, Simmons's greatest asset was still his brand. Even though his label was cold, *Def Comedy Jam* made Def Jam look hot. And Chris Lighty had just signed Warren G, whose song "Regulate" had become a hit single off of Death Row's soundtrack for *Above the Rim.*

Simmons and Cohen knew that they had a potentially huge album in the can. They didn't want to give it to Sony, so they began to scramble for a way out of their current deal without alerting Sony to Def Jam's new find.

For most major labels, Def Jam's sales didn't merit the expense of doing a deal. Cohen approached Joe Galante, the president of RCA Records. Galante responded with a tersely worded rejection letter that spilled out into Def Jam's general fax machine in view of the entire staff.

Eventually, Def Jam's pitch fell on the ears of Alain Levy, the chairman of Polygram, which had recently purchased the fading Motown Records as a way to gain a bigger foothold in the lucrative market for Black music. The Def Jam brand represented something fresher to Levy, who knew little of the label's fiscal woes. By the time that Polygram and Def Jam entered serious negotiations in 1994, Warren G's "Regulate" had climbed to number two on the Billboard pop chart and sold over two million copies. If Polygram moved fast, Levy would be able to distribute Warren G's album.

By June of 1994, Simmons, Cohen, and Levy reached an agreement. Polygram would distribute Def Jam's product in return for a 50 percent stake in the company, which they would purchase for $33 million. For Russell Simmons and Lyor Cohen, the deal was too good to be true. They could pay off Sony for $17 million and still walk away with over $10 million in cash. But not only that. Under Polygram, they would have something they never had at Sony: control over their own budgets, and the ability to determine their release and promotion schedule.

The deal highlighted an irony: Def Jam, the record company, had been undone in part by Russell Simmons's inattention. But it was one of Simmons's supposed distractions from the record business—an HBO series— that sustained the perception of Def Jam as a cultural force, and ultimately helped clinch the Polygram deal. The lesson was clear. Def Jam—and hip-hop by extension—wasn't just about making records. It was about marketing a lifestyle. Simmons, ironically, had been doing his job all along, although people—both within and without Def Jam—were only beginning to realize how crucial that job actually was.

The Polygram agreement coincided with several other business milestones for Simmons.

Just before the move to Polygram, Simmons officially divorced one partner and married another. Rick Rubin finally signed over his stock in Def Jam so Simmons could make the deal. Simmons then gave Lyor Cohen a substatial stake in Def Jam's share of the new joint venture.[23]

As part of the Def Jam deal, Polygram put money into Phat Farm. To protect his investment, Alain Levy urged Russell Simmons to take on a financial adviser—Ossie Kilkenny, most recently the business manager for Irish rock superstars U2—to try to find some way for Simmons to climb out of the multimillion-dollar hole he had dug for himself. Simmons suffered a huge loss in 1994 when one of Phat Farm's distributors, USA Classics, went bankrupt. Even Cohen was screaming at Simmons to get out of the business. Simmons refused. Levy and other Polygram execs feared that Phat Farm could become a drain on Simmons's faculties and Def Jam's fortunes if left unchecked.

Kilkenny worked with Simmons and Carmen Ashhurst to transform Phat Farm into a true fashion corporation with a board of directors. They hired a search firm to find executive talent from within the established fashion industry. Simmons, however, continued to refuse to sell his product in the downmarket urban stores that catered to Black youth, like V.I.M. and Dr. Jays, opting instead for the cool factor of his own New York store and exclusive boutiques like Fred Segal in West Hollywood. Department stores weren't biting on Simmons's designs. Too upscale for Dr. Jays, too downscale for Macy's, Phat Farm treaded water in a world that didn't seem to understand Simmons's simple idea that hip-hop was growing up.

Lyor Cohen realized that Def Jam's core business had reached a crossroads. It could easily squander its newfound riches and end up in a similar

---

[23]Russell Simmons says that Lyor Cohen's percentage of Def Jam's half of the joint venture was 37.5 percent. Carmen Ashhurst puts it at an even 50 percent. Cohen declined to comment.

situation at Polygram that it had at Sony; or it could become more efficient, lift its intrinsic worth, and perhaps sell the remainder of the company to Polygram at a later date. To do that, Cohen resolved to tighten his organization. Russell's bad hires, whether friends or "flavor bitches"—his term for pretty girls to whom Simmons sometimes gave jobs—all had to go. In their place, Cohen needed to assemble a tireless, tenacious team of people beholden only to him.

Chris Lighty had been Cohen's first soldier, handling A&R. Next came Julie Greenwald. She had started as Cohen's assistant at Rush. It was supposed to be a summer break from "Teach for America," a program that channeled young college graduates into inner-city schools. Greenwald worked in the Calliope Projects of New Orleans, where she had to spend her own money to buy the students' supplies and led her children in "Code Blue" drills as preparation for the occasional burst of gunfire. Working at Rush—even in the early days—was just slightly less chaotic and offered only slightly more pay. Greenwald fell in love with the job and the music, and became Cohen's head of marketing and creative services.

Cohen's new promotion wunderkind, Kevin Liles, also began as an intern. A husky, hyper kid from the streets of Baltimore, Liles had himself once been a rap artist with a local group called Numarx. They had opened for LL Cool J, and recorded a single that went nowhere called "Girl, You Know It's True"—nowhere, that is, until a German producer rerecorded the song with new vocalists and marketed it under the group name Milli Vanilli. Liles had to sue for credit and payment, and the entire episode had been traumatic. He decided instead on a career in radio promotion. Even as an intern, Liles quickly outworked and outran many on the Def Jam staff with his penchant for meticulous paperwork and professional presentations. When fellow promotion people called you an "animal," it was a compliment. Liles was a promotion animal.

He won the admiration of Cohen by being very much like him: a man who vowed to carry any load, great or small, to win the respect of his new boss. When Liles finally graduated to a regional, then a national promotion job, he resolved to get to the office before Cohen, every day, just to show him how committed he was. When Cohen started coming in earlier and leaving later, it became a friendly competition. Like Cohen, Liles was bothered by the lackadaisical attitudes of some Def Jam employees and the chairs that remained unoccupied as the morning wore on. Liles took to walking through the offices with a stack of Post-it notes, tacking them, one by one, on people's closed doors and vacant desks. They read:

What makes you so good that you can come in after me?

Quickly Kevin Liles got everyone in line. From now on, the Def Jam team would start early and end late, every single day. They would write and file tight and timely weekly reports. They would stick to schedules and adhere to due dates. From now on, label employees wouldn't act like miniature stars, rather like hungry apprentices. On Kevin Liles's watch, the company that began in a sloppy dorm room and achieved success despite an almost complete lack of structure would now operate as a well-organized service business. Lyor Cohen echoed the sentiments of his young lieutenant in a pep talk he gave to the staff, comparing the denizens of Def Jam to auto mechanics and its artists to their clients.

"Is Death Row, with their big muscles, going to squeeze under that car? No. Is Bad Boy, with their shiny Versace suits, going to get themselves dirty? No. We're going to be the AAMCO of this. We're going to service the artists, and get them on their way."

In a world with new, potent competitors, Def Jam would succeed by working longer and harder than everyone else and would live by one simple question: "Is it good for the logo?"

Finally Cohen had the team to succeed. When he had one of his ideas, he could run it by his head of marketing, Julie Greenwald, who was strong enough to tell him whether it was any good. He had Kevin Liles, who could take those ideas and turn them into reality with his newly disciplined and motivated staff. And into Rush Communications, Lyor Cohen had slipped another young protégé, a twenty-six-year-old lawyer named Todd Moscowitz, to keep an eye on Phat Farm and handle the business details that Cohen believed Carmen Ashhurst could not.

Lyor called Greenwald his "taste," Liles his "action," and Moscowitz his "brain." No longer would he have to scream in frustration as he felt that old pain in his chest—somewhere above his stomach and below his heart—creeping back with every embarrassing failure. Def Jam started to win again.

With the debuts of Warren G and Method Man, Def Jam came roaring back. Still, nothing symbolized the label's resurgence like the resurrection of Def Jam's first star, LL Cool J.

The revival of LL's music career was spearheaded by Chris Lighty, who inherited the rapper as a Violator Management client when Rush folded. Lighty paired LL with two hot producers, Samuel "Tone" Barnes and Jean-Claude "Poke" Olivier. Collectively known as the Trackmasters, Barnes and Olivier had just produced "Juicy," the first hit record for Bad Boy's Notorious B.I.G. The Trackmasters' formula—using unmistakable samples of successful R&B hits as the basis for rap tracks—gave LL two huge hits: "Hey Lover," an interpolation of Michael Jackson's "Lady in My Life"; and "Doin' It," a reworking of Grace Jones's "My Jamaican Guy."

On LL Cool J's double-platinum album *Mr. Smith*, Lighty also assembled a "posse cut"—wherein LL and several hot young rappers each contributed a verse. "I Shot Ya" included Keith Murray, Prodigy from Mobb Deep, Fat Joe, and the debut of a sultry, slick-tongued seventeen-year-old female rapper named Inga Marchand, who called herself "Foxy Brown." She had found her way to the recording studio and pestered the Trackmasters and Lighty for a shot until they gave it to her. In the studio, Foxy Brown held her own among the male rappers with whom she shared the bill.

Lighty grasped that Foxy Brown—like B.I.G.'s female protégée Lil' Kim—was the answer to a decade-old question in the hip-hop business: How do you make a female rapper sexy and credible at the same time? Sean "Puffy" Combs understood this, too, and began courting Foxy Brown for his Bad Boy label. At first, Lighty had trouble convincing Lyor Cohen that Foxy was a worthy signing.

"Lyor," Lighty pleaded. "We can sign her for a Happy Meal!"

But once Cohen discovered that Combs was after her, the Def Jam CEO sprang into action, even sending Russell Simmons in to help bring in the deal, albeit no longer at fast-food prices.

By the spring of 1996, the buzz on Foxy Brown reached a crescendo, this time with another guest appearance on a record that rocked the streets of New York from the minute it received its first spin on Hot 97. "Ain't No Nigga," owing to its title, had to be extensively edited for airplay. But it was worth the effort. The song featured Foxy trading lines with a young Brooklyn rapper named Shawn "Jay-Z" Carter, who was equally hungry for his big break.

Kevin Liles discovered this one day when Jay-Z and his two partners, Damon Dash and Kareem "Biggs" Burke, entered his office and dropped a brown paper bag on his desk.

Liles stared at the bag. He knew what was inside. Liles suspected that Def

Jam's new A&R man—a brash, ballbusting DJ named Irving Lorenzo—had put Jay-Z and his partners up to this as a goof. Lorenzo had toured with Jay-Z when the rapper was just a hype man for another MC called the Jaz; and he had brokered the meeting between Jay-Z and Liles.

"Guys," Liles said. "We don't need to do none of that." Liles had never taken a bribe; he was too much of a soldier for Cohen and Def Jam.

But Liles liked Jay-Z's record and told the rapper that he would try to help him for free based on that. In fact, Liles liked Jay-Z enough to talk of giving him a record deal. To Liles's shock, the artist wasn't interested.

"I don't rap for a record company," Jay-Z told him. "I own a record company."

The company to which the rap artist referred was called Roc-A-Fella Records. It was a venture that Jay-Z shared with two partners. One of them, Kareem Burke, was largely silent. The other, Damon Dash, was very vocal. And Dash's arrogance yielded a singular benefit for Roc-A-Fella: an audacious vision for the limitlessness of the hip-hop business that surpassed even that of Russell Simmons.

Carolyn Young Dash suffered from asthma all her life. But when the doctors diagnosed her young son, Damon Anthony, with the same condition, she refused to let him have it. She didn't allow him to even speak of the disease. Carolyn believed she had become addicted to her inhaler, and she forbade Damon to use one. Instead, Carolyn Dash made her son drink water—lots of it—until his symptoms disappeared.

For Carolyn Dash it was vindication, and for Damon a lesson. To talk of something, even to think it, was to give it power.

Damon lived alone with his mother in an apartment building near the corner of 109th and First Avenue in East Harlem. Their place wasn't as fancy as those thirteen blocks to the south, across the 96th Street dividing line that marked the northern edge of the tony Upper East Side. Still, it wasn't anywhere near as bad as the burned-out blocks of Central Harlem farther uptown.

To pay the rent, Carolyn Dash toiled as a travel agent during the week. But she craved the finer things. Dash liked pieces by Norma Kamali, the designer who created the wardrobe for *The Wiz*—the film that depicted the downtown fantasy world dreamed of by a young uptown girl who had never ventured south of 125th Street. Carolyn Dash wanted the finest for Damon, too—not only the latest clothes and sneakers, but tuition for private school. So, on the weekends, Carolyn Dash hustled clothes.

When Carolyn went shopping for pieces she could resell for a profit, she often towed along her only son. While his mother rifled through garments, Damon found ways to amuse himself—burrowing into the big, circular racks of clothing and hiding in the open spaces within.

While Damon played, Carolyn didn't. She knew what she wanted. She knew the worth of things. And if she thought for a moment that someone was trying to take advantage of her, that was the moment when she would get loud. Carolyn Dash got loud a lot. As his mother fought, Damon felt the red heat of embarrassment creeping up his back and neck, and looked for another rack in which to hide.

As he got older, Damon Dash began to understand how his mother's mind worked. "No one is smarter than you," she would tell him.

Carolyn regularly sold jeans at the Aqueduct racetrack's flea market, an enterprise made somewhat vexing by the absence of changing rooms. One Sunday, she solved the problem by sewing the end of a long piece of fabric into a tube around a Hula-hoop, and suspending the hoop from the ground. Damon watched as Carolyn pulled in nearly $1,000 for one day's work with her innovation. The next weekend, Damon saw that a few of the other merchants had Hula-hoop dressing rooms, too.

Through the years, Carolyn kept herself and her son looking "fly." Damon—a short, smart, spoiled, light-skinned boy with a soft face—could easily have been the prey of tougher kids in the neighborhood, especially since Damon had inherited his mother's mouth. Damon could break an opponent down in seconds with his cruel wit. He took boxing lessons just in case he needed to back up his words.

By the time he reached his teens, Damon's cocky persona had gotten him kicked out of the prestigious, private Dwight School. Then he got expelled from Isaac Newton Junior High for receiving oral sex from a girl in the school's stairwell. By the time he enrolled in a high school called Manhattan Center, Damon fell in with a crowd of drug dealers who lived in central Harlem. He sold dope, often hanging out until late at night, catching a gypsy cab home, and returning the next morning. To his school friends, he was "Dame from uptown." To his buddies on 142nd and Lenox, he was "Dame from downtown."

Everything Damon Dash had, his mother had given him—his temper, his sense of fashion, his sense of humor, and his sense of entitlement. But

Damon's boisterousness indeed hid one constant fear: He could not stop thinking that his mother would die. Carolyn Dash's own ample powers of manifestation had made Damon's asthma a nonissue and his recent diagnosis of juvenile diabetes seem equally beatable. But she couldn't conjure better health for herself.

One evening in 1986, fifteen-year-old Damon was standing on the block when a strange feeling seized him. He rushed home to find a note from his mother's brother, Uncle Carlton. Carolyn Dash's airways had constricted, choking the air from her lungs before help reached her. She never took another breath.

Returning from Metropolitan Hospital, Damon doubled over with grief. To talk of something, even to think it, was to give it power. And hadn't he thought about this moment every day of his life? Hadn't he, in fearing his mother's death, manifested it?

The day that Damon Dash buried his mother was the day he decided that he shouldn't be scared of anything. *Because,* he concluded, *the thing that you fear is the exact thing that you'll one day have to face.*

Damon still had some family left. His father, a reformed junkie who ran a methadone clinic in Harlem, had rarely been more than a casual presence in his life. Damon had an older half brother, Bobby. And Uncle Carlton Bowen looked after him. But Damon was, in truth, ungovernable.

A standing scholarship offer from a boarding school in Connecticut, South Kent, gave Damon a way to immerse himself in school life without the distraction of the streets. But that, too, ended with his ejection before graduation, at the age of seventeen. Finally, he came to one of New York's schools of last resort, Westside High, where Damon drove his black Nissan Maxima—procured with funds he had earned hustling drugs—into the principal's parking space.

Damon Dash eventually settled for a General Equivalency Diploma.

Dash came of age at the height of the crack epidemic, and he and his crew made a lot of money. Predictably, Dash spent a lot of it on clothes, like the shearling coat from Dapper Dan's with the extra-big hood and pockets deep enough for his guns. But Dash was shaken by the murder of his idol, a young drug dealer named Richard Thomas Porter, the flashy, smiling, gregarious prince of Harlem. If Rich could be touched, little street operators like him couldn't possibly be safe. Dash wasn't prepared to go to prison. His heart wasn't in the game like that. When Dash discovered the truth—that the man who had gunned down Rich was Porter's own partner, Alpo—Dash thought: *Betrayal was worse than murder. If you couldn't count on your family or your partners, you were as good as dead.*

Luckily, he had another enterprise in the works. It wasn't nearly as lucrative as drug dealing, but it made him look drug-dealer rich.

Dash and a group of hustler friends decided to pool their money and throw a party at Harlem's new Cotton Club. It wasn't the original nightspot of renown, which used to be located on their crew's corner, 142nd and Lenox. The new club occupied a small, triangular cement block huddled under a viaduct near the place where 125th Street met the Hudson River—just down the slope from Sugar Hill. The idea was to hire popular club DJ Kid Capri for the entertainment, and pack the club with willing women by offering a bottle of Moët champagne to the first hundred females in line. The night was a great success, even if the expenses exceeded their take of the door. The partners put up the money for more parties, and more people came. Dash's crew called themselves "the Best Out." They printed up a limited run of T-shirts with their name, which became a mark of exclusivity in Harlem and beyond. Dash and friends were approached by people offering hundreds of dollars for just one of the garments.

Dash wanted to turn the Best Out into an empire, start a record label, maybe do more clothes. The problem for Dash was that his crew didn't stick together. One of the partners went behind Dash's back and incorporated under the name "the Best Out." The crew broke up after a few parties, leaving Dash with nothing but a few T-shirts to show for it.

Dash did have one connection to the real music business, however. His cousin Darien Dash's stepfather, Cecil Holmes, had cofounded the classic disco record label Casablanca. As an executive at Columbia Records, he had also signed the boy band New Kids on the Block. After Damon and Darien began collaborating on a project by a rap group called the Future Sound, Holmes arranged for the two to meet his former assistant, Kevin Woodley, who had since taken an A&R job at Atlantic Records. Woodley took the meeting, expressed interest, then strung the Dash cousins along for weeks. Damon Dash spent a lot of time waiting in Atlantic's lobby. That was how he ran into another, junior A&R executive for Atlantic. His name was Rodolfo Franklin, but most in hip-hop knew him as Super DJ Clark Kent— the tall, boisterous sidekick to Profile Records rapper Dana Dane, and now a producer in his own right.

Clark Kent ended up being the person who gave the Future Sound a deal, and Dash his first lesson in the record business. Kent brought Dash in on a scheme: he wanted to sign a group from New Jersey called Original Flavor. He would give the group a $130,000 advance. And since Original Flavor didn't have representation, Kent would recommend them to Dash. As a manager, Dash would be entitled to 15 percent of that advance, or almost $20,000. Kent would set the whole thing up if Dash agreed to give him half of his money.

Dash would later come to understand that the move betrayed his clients, but Dash could never knock Clark Kent's hustle, especially when Kent believed in him enough to keep feeding him business. Dash stuck close, and soon thereafter, Clark Kent introduced him to one of the best rappers Dash had ever heard in his life.

Harlem niggas don't mess with Brooklyn *niggas.* That was Dash's credo. *Harlem cats are hustlers. Brooklyn brothers are straight thugs. Harlem wears suits and nice shoes. Brooklyn wears camouflage, backpacks, and baseball caps. Harlem throws parties. Brooklyn ends them.*

Still there was something about the style of this Brooklyn guy, Jay-Z, that reminded Dash of Harlem. Maybe it was the Nike Airs that Jay wore, the shoes that young New Yorkers called "uptowns" because mostly Harlem people wore them. Jay-Z had an uptown swagger about him. That energy had been in Harlem since colored folk moved up to the nice homes on Sugar Hill, since the eyes of the world turned to Harlem in the 1920s for the latest in American culture. The word was "aspirational," and Jay-Z had it. Actually, he had an equilibrium of thuggery and hustle, Brooklyn and Harlem, street and sophistication. He had hip-hop's yin and yang, art and commerce in equal measure, the perfect blueprint for success.

Dash and Jay became friends. He learned that Jay had grown up, like him, without a father. Jay, like him, started hustling drugs in his early teens. But the lanky Jay-Z had a somewhat darker history. He grew up in the projects. At the age of twelve, he shot his older brother in the shoulder after Jay caught him stealing his jewelry. Unlike Dash, Jay *did* have the steely heart for the game. Fortunately, Jay had other gifts, including an almost eidetic memory for verses. Jay-Z never wrote his rhymes down. He simply recited them, at length, from the hard disk of his mind.

Damon Dash became Jay-Z's manager. By this time, Dash knew enough about the music business to understand that he would not be making real money, nor have real equity, by representing a rapper who had only an artist's share of a typical recording deal. Dash wanted to be neither manager nor middleman. He wanted to be a boss. And it came as no surprise to Dash that Jay-Z felt the same way. So instead of Dash signing to a management or production contract—both inequitable relationships that carried forward the "I win, you lose" ethos of the record business—the two simply became partners. They formed a record company that would also furnish Jay's services as a rapper, a company that Dash named in wry tribute to the richest person in American history, John Davison Rockefeller.

Without real capital, Roc-A-Fella Records would never be a true company and never have any autonomy. So Dash brought in a third partner who had some street money and a low profile, Dash's friend from the Best Out, Kareem "Biggs" Burke. Now Roc-A-Fella was a triumvirate, a holy trinity of cash, hustle, and talent.

Now Damon Dash had a new crew, and a new idea—the circle of success. *Say we've got eleven guys in the crew*, Dash thought. *If all of us are millionaires, and I lose all of my money, the other ten guys are obligated by our code to chip in $100,000 each. And just like that, I'm a millionaire again.* To make it work, the partners would all have to agree to abide by Dash's solemn code—"crew before me." With Roc-A-Fella, Dash vowed that, in the event of a disagreement, no one was allowed to leave the room angry. Dash's notions comprised a kind of utopian risk-management scheme, one that would allow them to live high and bet big.

The first act of business at Roc-A-Fella Records was both backward and brilliant.

Instead of sinking thousands of dollars into manufacturing, distributing, and promoting a single, the Roc-A-Fella partners put $5,000 into shooting an inexpensive video in Brooklyn for a Jay-Z song, produced by Clark Kent, called "I Can't Get Wit That." Dash and Kent were friendly with Ralph McDaniels at *Video Music Box*. The idea was to use that one hot video, played by McDaniels, as leverage to get themselves a better record deal.

It almost worked. Ruben Rodriguez, the former Columbia promotion executive, now had his own label through Elektra, called Pendulum. He had seen the video and invited Dash and Jay-Z to come by his office.

"Rap for me," Rodriguez demanded.

Dash and Jay looked at each other, then at Rodgriguez.

"What the fuck you mean, 'rap'?!" Dash shot back. That this executive felt he could order an artist to perform on command was demeaning. Dash and Jay walked out. But the importance of gaining leverage stayed with them: Use what you own to make yourself look large to gain advantage in any deal.

In 1994, Roc-A-Fella bought some studio time and paid for the manufacturing of Jay-Z's first record, called "In My Lifetime." The label of the 12-inch featured a hand-drawn illustration of a champagne bottle. More than mere symbolism, champagne was the actual currency in which Damon Dash had dealt since his first parties at the Cotton Club. Now he waited in the lobbies and waiting rooms of radio stations with his record in one hand and a bottle of bubbly in the other.

Hot 97 was playing "In My Lifetime" by the time Patrick Moxey discovered Jay-Z's record. Moxey, a former assistant to Lyor Cohen at Rush Artist Management, had promoted the roving Payday parties of the early 1990s, and he now had a Payday Records production deal through Polygram. Dash and his partners took the singles deal to pay for a $16,000 video. Shot on location in Saint Thomas on the estate of one of Burke's friends, the clip for "In My Lifetime" reflected Roc-A-Fella's champagne taste on a beer-bottle budget: stunning ocean views, speedboats, pool parties, and gorgeous models. While Bad Boy and Death Row warred in the streets, Jay-Z rapped from his tropical paradise about worshiping tons of money, instead of guns.

Once the video began receiving airplay, Dash grew angry about the deal with Payday Records. Why did he need a record company at all if they could clearly make their own records and videos and get them played? Dash demanded a release from Moxey and got it.

In 1995 Jay-Z had almost finished recording the songs for his first album, *Reasonable Doubt*, filled with dextrous tales of street deals and Mafia aspirations, when Dash began shopping a new deal. But few would accede to Dash's demand that Roc-A-Fella own all of its masters. New, unproven labels with no sales record simply didn't have that clout. One company, however, was willing.

Freeze Records was founded by Will Socolov a few years after the implosion of his first company, Sleeping Bag Records—home to Mantronix, EPMD, and Nice & Smooth, as well as the first incarnations of KRS-One and Craig Mack. Despite gold and platinum sellers from EPMD, Sleeping Bag overspent and overmanufactured. Socolov ended up having to sell the group to Russell Simmons and Lyor Cohen's RAL just to pay the bills. The company bled to death in 1990.

When Socolov first heard the beat for "Ain't No Nigga," the new song from Jay-Z, he could not help but be reminded of his very first hit with EPMD, "It's My Thing." Both records were based on the same exact classic hip-hop break, "Seven Minutes of Funk" by the Whole Darn Family, so Socolov was predisposed to like the record and agree to Dash's conditions. Socolov had a distribution deal in place with his old friend Bryan Turner at Priority Records. Priority took 20 percent off the top of every Freeze record. Dash offered Socolov 24 percent—meaning 20 for Priority and a 4 point margin for Freeze.

Dash later discovered that his own lawyers had misunderstood the deal: They had given up an additional 24 percent to Freeze, not 4. So he had given up, in total, 44 percent of the retail price to Freeze and Priority combined. Dash learned that he needed to watch both his words and his people a little better. He fired his lawyers, and vowed that this would be the last record he did with Will Socolov and Freeze.

When it came to using leverage, Damon Dash was a novice compared to Lyor Cohen.

"Ain't No Nigga," featuring Foxy Brown, spread across American mix shows in the spring of 1996 even though the female rapper's appearance on the independent release hadn't been cleared with the big label that had just signed her, Def Jam. Cohen used that oversight to get Jay-Z's hot street hit onto his soundtrack album for the Russell Simmons–produced remake of *The Nutty Professor*, starring Eddie Murphy.

Dash, in turn, used his meeting with Cohen to get Def Jam to pay for the song's video.

The first encounter between Cohen and Dash was typically gangster, two hustlers communicating in the language of power. A deal between the two men seemed fated as Roc-A-Fella now had several connections to the world of Def Jam. Irving Lorenzo, whom Jay had given the nickname "Irv Gotti," had an A&R job with Def Jam. Kevin Liles made himself a friend to Roc-A-Fella by promoting their record even before he had reason to do so. And Jay's collaborator, Foxy Brown, had been signed to the label.

But it was Chris Lighty who warmed Cohen up for the coming of Jay-Z, hiring the rapper to ghostwrite most of Foxy's album. When Cohen said he liked the song "Nasty Girl," Lighty told him Jay wrote it. Cohen said he liked "Get Me Home." Lighty told him Jay wrote it. Cohen also liked the new collaboration between Jay and Foxy, "I'll Be." Lighty told him Jay wrote that, too.

In mid-1996, the Roc-A-Fella venture with Freeze and Priority released *Reasonable Doubt*, which moved hundreds of thousands of units as an independent release and was heralded by rap magazines and music critics as a near-perfect slice of hustler hip-hop. By the time Foxy Brown's album debuted a few months later, Roc-A-Fella had sufficient leverage—including another offer from Epic Records—to extract from Cohen a rare and lucrative joint-venture deal: 50 percent owned by Roc-A-Fella, 25 percent by Def Jam, and 25 percent by the parent company, Polygram. The offer included a $1 million advance on profits and another $1 million in overhead.

Dash made it clear to Cohen and the new Def Jam general manager, Kevin Liles, that Roc-A-Fella was to operate as its own center of A&R, and needed to be consulted on all promotional activities. For his part, Jay-Z made it clear he didn't want to be sold short in his own career.

In a meeting with marketing head Julie Greenwald, Jay-Z bristled when the executive referred to him as a "rapper."

"Why are you calling me a rapper?" he asked her. "I'm a star."

Phat Farm was still losing money, and desperately needed a fashion veteran to run the business. Russell Simmons, Carmen Ashhurst, and Todd Moscowitz interviewed over twenty people for the CEO position, and in mid-1996, finally settled on Martin Kace, who came from another clothing brand called Joe Boxer. Moscowitz was nervous about the choice. He didn't like Kace, and worried that the new Phat Farm chief wouldn't listen to Simmons's creative direction.

Kace pressed upon the reluctant Simmons the need to get into the downscale "urban" chains, even though Simmons still clung to his upscale vision. Everything changed, however, when Carmine Petruzello brought Wu-Wear into Macy's. Suddenly, the mainstream shifted toward hip-hop brands like Wu-Wear, FUBU, and Mecca. Phat Farm—founded before all of those companies—started to fare better. Simmons's new girlfriend, Kimora Lee, had taken the name that Ashhurst had trademarked for a future infant clothing offshoot, "Baby Phat," and transformed it into a young women's line.

Carmen Ashhurst, still a feminist after eight years in hip-hop, wasn't amused by the implications of the dimunitive term. But she was set to shift away from Phat Farm anyway. Simmons wanted her out in Hollywood, where he had moved, to help start his movie company. She had packed up her house in Brooklyn, ready to go, when her mother died. Distraught, Ashhurst took two months off of work to grieve and settle her mother's estate.

The last time Ashhurst had taken two months leave from Simmons, she had been replaced. When she returned, she found it had happened again: Simmons had hired a director of production out in Los Angeles without telling her. Her sense of betrayal was mitigated only by the realization that she wouldn't have to move after all. A month after her return to work she took a personal day. Simmons phoned her, livid that she was out of the office.

The call led to an argument the next day at Simmons's apartment in New York. He was still mad about her two months of bereavement leave. She was upset about an incident that had happened a few months back, after she discovered that an accountant working for Phat Farm had been embezzling from the company. Shortly after Ashhurst reported the accountant to the police, she received a whispered phone call from someone who threatened to kill her if she pursued the case. Rush's lawyer called her with news that the police had reason to believe a contract had been taken out on Ashhurst's life. Frightened, Ashhurst called Simmons, but he shrugged it off.

"Carmen, people threaten my life all the time," he said.

Ashhurst put herself up in a hotel for a few days to feel safe, smarting from what she saw as Simmons's callousness about the threat to her. His sensitivity had an on/off switch. Ashhurst remembered the time when Simmons's mother, Evelyn, was dying. She remembered how horrible it was for him, how he went to her bedside every day and night. They were in the midst of renegotiating their contract with Sony, and during one of the meetings, with Def Jam's lawyers on one side and Sony's on the other, she recalled how Simmons literally burst into tears when Sony informed him that his projected sales would not be enough to cover the new multimillion-dollar advance he had requested.

"I need this! I have to have this!" Simmons cried. "My mother is on her deathbed, and she's asking me about this! You can't make me break my mother's heart!"

Everyone at the conference table, including Ashhurst, was stunned. In fact they were so taken aback that the Sony lawyers agreed to work something out with Simmons's representatives. Maybe not the whole amount. But something closer to what Simmons wanted.

Ashhurst rode down the elevator with Simmons in silence, tears still coming down his face. They left the building, stepped into Simmons's white Rolls-Royce, and shut the door. Inside, Simmons turned to her, smiling.

"How'd I do?" he asked.

Ashhurst knew Simmons loved his mother dearly. She never took Simmons's coarseness at face value, anyway. She understood him. Where others saw mania in Simmons's diversification, she saw genius. Where others saw wastefulness on his payroll, she saw a guy who cared for less fortunate friends. She had grown to love Russell, love him enough to make him godfather to her firstborn child. And Simmons knew how to love people, too. But Simmons had the ability to turn his empathy off at will. The same guy who played with her son could also make light of his safety when one of Simmons's employees threatened her life. Maybe that on-off switch was the key to success in business. Simmons had it. Lyor Cohen had it. Ashhurst knew she didn't. And she could no longer live like she did.

Ashhurst offered Simmons her resignation. Simmons accepted and gave her a severance package equal to a year and a half of her salary.

Since moving to Polygram, Def Jam had successfully reinvigorated its roster and its image. Chris Lighty engineered LL Cool J's comeback, his Foxy Brown album went double platinum, and the single Foxy recorded with Jay-Z was certified gold. In 1997, Jay-Z's first album for the Roc-A-Fella/Def Jam joint venture, *In My Lifetime*, snared a platinum plaque.

But Polygram's constant restructuring was hurting Def Jam, as the label—and the pleasure of dealing with Lyor Cohen—was shuffled from one division to another. Simmons and Cohen had a company to sell within the next year, and they needed to get their "multiple" up—a complex equation negotiated with Polygram for any possible buyout. The higher the multiple was, the higher the sale price would be.

The equation itself was managed by Simmons and Cohen's new chief of business affairs, Todd Moscowitz, whom they had recently moved in from Rush Communications. Moscowitz realized that Polygram might have missed the significance of one crucial deal point: The multiple was based not on profits, but on *revenue*. In other words, Def Jam's sale price was tied to how many units they sold, not how much they spent to get there.

Cohen realized that his team, as hard as they already worked, would need incentive to drive the multiple even higher, especially when other companies could poach his best employees at any time. Just before Foxy Brown's debut, for example, RCA Records had made Lighty a lucrative offer, which he had accepted. Lyor Cohen raced to Lighty's home and pleaded with him to stay. Cohen cried. Lighty cried. In the end, Lighty relinquished the RCA offer just as he had with the Relativity deal back in 1992.

Now, as the buyout negotiations approached, Cohen dreaded a replay of that scene. So he proposed an employee retention plan to Simmons: *You and I make the first $50 million. But for every dollar we make over that threshold, we give fifty cents to our best people.* The proposal was too rich for Simmons, so they compromised: half of the first $25 million over the $50 million threshold, meaning a maximum of $12.5 million to split between people like Kevin Liles, Julie Greenwald, and Chris Lighty.

Cohen approached his top staff with the offer: *Promise to stay with us at your current salary, drive sales, and get some of the profits from the buyout. You will all be multimillionaires.*

Liles and Greenwald took the offer. Lighty didn't because Cohen was asking him to focus completely on Def Jam and to give up his management company.

Lighty, for all his loyalty to Cohen, never wanted to be completely beholden to him. It was the reason he kept Violator Management as a separate power base. He didn't want to promise anything that would make Cohen the sole arbiter of his fate. Lighty proposed a different bargain: *When you get bought out of the Def Jam venture, buy me out of my Violator Records venture. Just buy me out, and I'll stick around and work on anything you want me to.*

For Cohen, Lighty's refusal was a slap in the face. It didn't matter that Lighty was sticking around. Cohen felt that Lighty didn't believe him or believe *in* him. So Cohen made the profit-sharing offer to Moscowitz instead.

When the buyout offer came, it was too low to matter in Cohen's scheme anyway. In February of 1998, Polygram offered $50 million for the remaining 40 percent of Def Jam that they didn't own. Simmons and Cohen accepted the offer in principle, until Polygram reduced the offer to $34 million—charging back monies advanced to Simmons for Phat Farm and film production that the larger company claimed were not investments after all, but loans.

The stalemate continued until Def Jam received two strikes of good fortune. The first was the debut of A&R man Irv "Gotti" Lorenzo's signing, a rapper named DMX.

Years earlier, "DMX the Great" garnered one of Matty C's first "Unsigned Hype" columns in *The Source*. His first Def Jam album, *It's Dark and Hell Is Hot*, became a street record of mammoth proportions, its sales fed by years of guest appearances, industry buzz, and advance word of mouth. The album sold hundreds of thousands of copies in first week, and it had reached the one-million mark within a month.

Around the time of DMX's debut, Polygram suddenly sold itself to Universal Music Group, helmed by the rap-friendly Doug Morris. By the middle of 1998, Def Jam had gained more control of its marketing and promotion, just in time for a slew of big albums.

Jay-Z's new single hit the airwaves in the summer. The track, a witty sampling of a well-known Broadway show tune, became the rapper's first pop success. "Hard Knock Life" yielded the Jay-Z album of the same name, his first number one on the Billboard Top 200. It sold almost six million copies, and double that when international sales were counted.

Throughout 1998, the hits continued. Cohen drove the staff mercilessly, telling them at one point that they should be "ashamed to sleep" while the fate of the label was at stake. New albums from old Def Jam stalwarts Redman and Method Man sold over a million copies each. Russell Simmons's protégé Brett Ratner had directed his first big Hollywood film, *Rush Hour*; Def Jam had the soundtrack, and it sold more than a half million copies. So did the debut of the rap supergroup Def Squad, and a new album from Montell Jordan. In November came another gold soundtrack, this time for the film *Belly*, starring Def Jam rapper DMX.

Greenwald began to tire of the crush.

"Why are we doing so many soundtracks, Lyor?" she asked.

"To drive the multiple," Cohen answered.

Cohen would finish the year by asking for the impossible. DMX's album, released in May, was closing in on four million copies sold. The album's fourth single, "Ruff Ryders' Anthem," was still on the charts. But Cohen wanted the rapper to deliver another album by December, with only two months' notice, and charged Irving Lorenzo with the responsibility to make it happen. Surprisingly, the often obstreperous DMX was up to the task. The resistance came from Universal Music Group.

The fourth quarter of the year was typically reserved for superstar albums, few of which came out past Thanksgiving. Every December, the music industry virtually shut down: Radio stations froze their playlists, retail focused on stocking the hits, and record promoters stopped calling. *No one releases an album in December*, they said. *Stores won't take it. You can't do co-op advertising for it. You won't sell a thing.*

But Cohen insisted. He wanted an album out, two weeks before Christmas—for the kids. It seemed like an obvious thing. His counterparts at Universal predicted disaster.

With no single on radio, and just $200,000 in advertising on MTV and BET, DMX's second album, *Flesh of My Flesh, Blood of My Blood*, sold nearly three-quarters of a million copies in its first week out, on its way to the three-million mark. It stayed at number one on the Billboard Top 200 into the New Year.

As 1998 ended, Lyor Cohen and his team looked back. Def Jam, in one year, had done an unprecedented $175 million in billing for its corporate parent.

It meant that the terms of the buyout would change. They were all going to get a lot of money in 1999.

In the middle of Def Jam's madcap year, Russell Simmons and Lyor Cohen elevated the thirty-year-old Kevin Liles to the presidency of Def Jam. Lyor Cohen issued a press release calling Liles "the first president in the label's thirteen-year history"—ignoring the fact that Bill Stephney, Carmen Ashhurst, and David Harleston had each once held that same title.

On one hand, Liles's fairy-tale intern-to-president story line made good inspirational theater. And Liles had, indeed, worked tirelessly, to the detriment of his own health and his marriage. No one could say that Liles didn't deserve the gig.

On the other hand, Cohen never told his other lieutenants about the move beforehand. Julie Greenwald, who had hired Liles, was taken completely by surprise. Todd Moscowitz, who knew the particulars of every Def Jam deal and had once asked for the president's job himself, felt slighted. Eventually, Greenwald and Moscowitz understood that neither of them could be the public face of Def Jam Recordings, especially with another White, Jewish executive in the CEO slot.

Chris Lighty, who agreed that Liles deserved the position, refused to let him get too smug about it.

Lighty said playfully: "The only reason you're president is because I didn't want the job."

Liles's headaches as president of Def Jam began immediately. The chief irritant was Damon Dash, the CEO of Roc-A-Fella Records. Dash began his joint venture demanding assurances that Roc-A-Fella's identity would not be overshadowed by the Def Jam brand. But as Jay-Z became the bestselling act in the Def Jam family of labels, Dash couldn't turn off his fears, and thus saw them coming to fruition at every turn.

Tensions boiled over on Jay-Z's 1999 Hard Knock Life Tour. Although Jay-Z headlined and Roc-A-Fella funded the excursion, the rest of the lineup—DMX, Method Man, and Redman—were Def Jam artists. As the tour progressed, Dash encountered one too many announcements and reviews referencing "Def Jam's Hard Knock Life Tour." Cameras filming the tour for a Dash-produced documentary called *Backstage* captured him fuming as Roc-A-Fella rapper Memphis Bleek enthused over a gift from Kevin Liles: a Def Jam jacket; better, Bleek said, than his Roc-A-Fella jacket because Def Jam embroidered his name on the front. Later, as Dash sat in a dressing room getting his head shaved, he unleashed his fury on Liles as the cameras rolled.

"You're the president of the company, right?" Dash bellowed. "That means you're smart. So don't sit here and play dumb. If everybody on this tour has a Def Jam jacket on, what would be the general perception?"

"They would think it's a Def Jam tour," Liles answered.

"So, knowing this, why wouldn't you be extra sensitive about giving everybody a Def Jam jacket on this tour?!"

Liles tried to get a few words in: "Please don't take an act of love and turn it into—"

"That ain't no love, man; that's promotion," Dash said, suddenly boiling over at being patronized. "YO, WHO DO YOU THINK YOU'RE TALKING TO?! All I need y'all to do is *cut the checks*! We're taking all the chances. . . . We're the ones who put our ass on the line to get this tour. And we still don't get the credit for it."

"Why not?" Liles asked.

"I don't know. Because your fucking fat ass is around all the time."

"Every time you talk, you act like we ain't partners."

"We ain't partners."

"Then what are we?"

"Y'all got twenty-five percent and [Universal] has another twenty-five percent. We're not equal partners. Y'all dont think I know? You got a quarter. You a quarter-water, that's it." Dash's conclusion was an inside insult, referencing cheap flavored waters sold in ghetto corner stores.

The next year, Dash put the heated exchange in the documentary, in a way that seemed to deliberately embarass Kevin Liles, along with a comment from Irving Lorenzo by way of explanation:

"Damon Dash in a nutshell: Roc-A-Fella or 'fuck you.'"

By then, Liles and everyone at Def Jam knew it all too well, and dealt directly with Dash's partner, Jay-Z, whenever they could.

The final sale of Def Jam in 1999 for $135 million made Russell Simmons and Lyor Cohen into very wealthy men. Cohen contracted to stay on for five years as CEO of Def Jam, and Simmons as chairman.

Just a year earlier, rumors abounded that Simmons—long absent from the day-to-day operations of Def Jam—was being retired, or worse, pushed out by Cohen in his supposedly insatiable drive for power and control. It wasn't true, but the whispers forced a mortified Cohen to issue a press statement:

"This confusion demonstrates a complete ignorance of my lifelong friendship and partnership with Russell," he said. "It was Russell's decision years ago to put me in charge of Def Jam Recordings . . . a decision that simultaneously confirmed my own self-confidence and freed him up to carry the Def Jam brand into such previously uncharted waters as televison, movies, and fashion."

Simmons was, in fact, doing just fine. He returned from California, and just like Rick Rubin, he'd taken up a serious yoga practice and become a vegetarian. He'd married Kimora Lee at a wedding in Saint Barts, officiated by his brother Joey—now known as "Reverend Run." The groomsmen were attired completely in matching Phat Farm wear: khaki pants, oxfords, and golf sweaters.

Phat Farm itself had turned a corner. As Todd Moscowitz predicted, Martin Kace clashed with Simmons and had to be replaced. In the wake of Kace's dismissal, Simmons brought in new investors, taking the financial pressure off of himself and Cohen, who also decided to offload many of the company's operations to a colorful but capable character in the fashion business, Ruby Azrak. The new structure was working. FUBU, the ascendant brand since the demise of Wu-Wear, had peaked. Phat Farm sales were passing the $100 million mark.

For Simmons, the sale of one company and the success of another were all the vindication he needed.

The sale of Def Jam had also made Lyor's lieutenants—Kevin Liles, Julie Greenwald, and Todd Moscowitz—into multimillioniares. The amount of the buyout for Chris Lighty's Violator Records was somewhat less.

Lighty's fortunes had dimmed at Def Jam. His most successful artist on Violator, Foxy Brown, had gone from unmanageable to unbearable. In addition to regular temper tantrums, violent incidents, and legal troubles, she fought with her original creative team—Lighty and Jay-Z—turning in a lackluster sophomore album.

Lighty's rap signing, Cru, had landed with the faintest of thuds. Meanwhile, the A&R whiz-kid Irv "Gotti" Lorenzo's hits just kept coming, the latest being a huge, platinum debut from Queens rapper Ja Rule.

When Irv had first arrived, Lighty was happy to have him around. Irv's office was on the Violator side of the floor, and they had been close, literally and figuratively. Lighty saw Lorenzo's victories with DMX as his own, because they brought hot music to the label and raised everyone's profile.

But Lighty soon discovered that Lorenzo didn't feel the same way about him. Lorenzo knew his signings had driven the Def Jam engine in the last few years, and boasted aloud that his ultimate goal was to push Lighty, Liles, and even Lyor out of the way and take over the whole operation. Lorenzo was a loudmouth about everything, and Lighty saw that Irv's arrogant jocularity had morphed into aggresive, acid-tongued disparagement. He was pushing all of Lighty's buttons, and the executive who had once relinquished the brutal code of the street found himself thinking like a Violator again— the Bronx rather than the boardroom version.

If this dude says the wrong thing, Lighty thought, *it could be lights-out at any moment.* He didn't want to debase himself, nor bring scandal to Lyor.

Yet when Lighty complained, it was clear that Cohen wanted to avoid doing anything that might upset Lorenzo. *Really?* Lighty thought. *Weren't you and I, Lyor and Chris, Chris and Lyor, rocking together for ten years? And now this guy gets hot, and those years mean nothing?*

Lighty was sad, but not surprised. Cohen's mercurial nature was exactly why Lighty insisted on keeping Violator autonomous.

Lighty still had a robust management clientele. Now was the time, if ever, to show that he could make it without his mentor. It had been Lyor and Chris. Now it would just be Chris. Lighty determined that he wouldn't return on his knees like the prodigal son, either. This time he would be gone for good.

Side B
Selling

L ighty's first move outside of Def Jam's auspices was improbably auspicious: a joint venture with Michael Ovitz, the founder of Creative Artists Agency and one of the most powerful men in Hollywood.

After a tumultuous tenure running Disney, Ovitz had recently launched the Artists Management Group. His search for a stronger base in young Black talent from the music world led Ovitz to Violator—now the foremost management firm in the rap business. The alliance would give Ovitz first dibs on new talent, and hopefully confer to Lighty, his junior partner Mona Scott, and Violator's clients like Busta Rhymes and Missy Elliott, unprecedented power in Hollywood.

But while Chris Lighty reached for the boardroom, much of the rest of hip-hop fell back toward the street. On the first night of December in 1999, Chris Lighty's client Q-Tip celebrated a new chapter in his life: the release of his first solo album since the breakup of A Tribe Called Quest. Lighty and hundreds of others from the hip-hop business came to Manhattan's Kit Kat Club to revel and catch up with one another.

Jay-Z, however, came seeking one person in particular.

He and Damon Dash arrived wearing matching jackets emblazoned with the logo of their new clothing company, Rocawear. They had just arrived from Irving Plaza, where they held the listening party for their new album, *Vol. 3: Life and Times of S. Carter*, scheduled to hit stores later that month. But all was not well. Someone had bootlegged the album in advance of the release date. It was all over the street. At Irving Plaza, Damon Dash took the stage and shouted, "Fuck the bootleggers!" Jay-Z thought he knew who was responsible. That person would also be at Q-Tip's party tonight.

Lance "Un" Rivera was a friend. He had managed Jay's Brooklyn home-boy the Notorious B.I.G., and there had even been talk of Jay and B.I.G. comprising a rap supergroup called the Commission. Since Biggie's death, Rivera had landed a multimillion-dollar label venture at Sony Music, and had become something of a big deal himself. But Rivera had become competitive with Jay and complained about his career getting so much attention. It seemed gratuitous for someone like Lance Rivera to pirate his old friend's new album. But Jay-Z was convinced that Rivera had done so. In the VIP section of the club, the rapper spotted Rivera and approached his old friend.

"You broke my heart," Jay-Z said, echoing the dramatic scene from *The Godfather II* where Michael Corleone administers the kiss of death to his brother Fredo.

During the pandemonium that followed, Damon Dash stood to the side, pretending to look away. When Jay-Z and his boys walked away, Rivera lay bleeding. Someone had plunged a four-inch knife into Rivera's stomach and back. A "famous East Coast rapper" who asked not to be named later told *Newsweek* that he had seen Jay-Z "push something" into Rivera. Dash returned to the home he shared with his very pregnant girlfriend, Rachel Roy, a former Rocawear intern whom Dash elevated to a design position.

"We just did some boneheaded shit," Dash said as he lay down for the night. "It's all going down tomorrow."

Before the end of the night, the police were looking to arrest Shawn "Jay-Z" Carter for the stabbing of Lance Rivera.

Everything was at stake for Dash and his partner: Jay's career, the record label, and the clothing company. They had founded Rocawear with the help of Russell Simmons, who had introduced them to two businessmen in the rag trade. People called them "the Russians," but Alex Bize and his brother-in-law, Norton Cher, were both Ukranian immigrants; their company, Comet Group, had once manufactured for Wu-Wear. Dash provided the creative direction for Rocawear, while Bize and Cher lent their expertise on how to create a line and get it into stores. For Dash, it was a homecoming of sorts, having grown up watching his mother sell clothes out of their Harlem apartment.

But the night at the Kit Kat Club put it all in jeopardy. The next day, on the advice of his lawyer, Jay-Z turned himself in to the New York Police Department's Midtown South precinct. After posting $50,000 bail, attorney

Murray Richman denied all charges on behalf of the rapper, repudiations echoed in statements issued by Def Jam Recordings.

Jay-Z—recording artist and businessman—wrapped up the most successful year of his career with a violent act that jeopardized everything he and Damon Dash had built.

Twenty-seven days later, another rapper-entrepreneur would lose his own balance in the tug-of-war between the code of the streets and the standards of society.

Sean "Puff Daddy" Combs sold millions of records with Bad Boy Entertainment, and made millions through his joint venture with Arista/BMG. He survived the death of his biggest artist, the Notorious B.I.G., largely by becoming an artist himself. His first solo album sold nearly seven million copies and catapulted him to mainstream stardom. His clothing line, Sean John, grossed $32 million in the two years since its launch; and his restaurants continued to thrive. Combs was said to be worth $53 million.

But Combs's ambition wasn't limited to finance. What he really wanted was entrée into the elite. Combs took his mentor Andre Harrell's fetishing of the Hamptons to the next level. At his house in East Hampton, Combs threw lavish, Gatsbyeqsue "white parties." He attended polo games attired in seersucker suits and straw hats, his son Justin in tow. He befriended real estate mogul Donald Trump and homemaking magnate Martha Stewart. Back in the city, he spent more than a half million dollars on an extravagant birthday party for himself at Cipriani on Wall Street. Combs had even snared himself a celebrity girlfriend: Jennifer Lopez was now a Hollywood icon, with leading roles in multimillion-dollar-grossing films like *Selena*, and *Out of Sight* (for which Miramax hired Steve Rifkind's SRC to create a street marketing campaign).

Combs now banked millions and bedded a starlet, kept lawyers on retainer and dined with moguls. But Combs increasingly responded to his daily challenges and frustrations as if he were a street hustler, or like many of the rap artists he produced, rather than the middle-class kid turned privileged plutocrat that he really was.

In early 1999, Combs was arrested for the brutal beating of an artist manager and Interscope record executive named Steve Stoute. Combs blamed Stoute for failing to remove footage of Combs nailed to a cross in a music video collaboration with Stoute's client, the rapper Nas. Assisted in the deed by two goons, Combs was typically theatrical about it all, brandishing a chair, a telephone, and a champagne bottle in turns, leaving Stoute bloodied. Combs solved his indiscretion with a cash settlement to Stoute, and struck a plea bargain that landed him in a one-day anger-management course.

While Combs may have been financially secure, in the fickle field of hip-hop his insecurity was understandable. His second solo album hadn't done nearly as well as his debut. Two of his major artists had left his label. Combs's detractors—who hated his color-by-numbers approach to music production, his ostentation, and his arrogance—were buzzing that his day was just about done. The perilous days of the war with Death Row were over, but Sean "Puff Daddy" Combs continued to be taunted and tested at every turn.

On December 27, 2000, Combs danced on a table at a Times Square night-club, near his girlfriend Jennifer Lopez and his new rapper who sounded eerily like Biggie, Jamal "Shyne" Barrow. A Brooklyn kid named Scar—real name Matthew Allen—argued with Barrow, and mocked Combs by throwing a wad of cash in his direction. Barrow produced a Ruger pistol and started shooting. Three people were hit.

In the ensuing chaos, Combs and Lopez were hustled out of the night-club and into a waiting Lincoln Navigator by Combs's bodyguard, Anthony Jones, and sped from the scene by Combs's driver, Wardel Fenderson. Not far from the club, the Navigator was pulled over by police, who found an unlicensed gun on the floor of the car.

Combs, Lopez, Jones, and Fenderson were all arrested. Combs and Jones were both charged with gun possession and bribery—as police accused Combs of offering Fenderson money or jewelry to claim that the gun in question was his. Barrow, meanwhile, had been identified by witnesses as the shooter and charged with attempted murder. Lopez, for her part, had been released from police custody without charge, but the public affair with Combs had now become a liability.

Combs, too, had become his own albatross. If convicted, he faced up to fifteen years in prison. A fate all of his riches could not forestall, save by the hiring of a good attorney.

Five months later, on May 24, 2000, nine slugs from a nine-millimeter handgun shot through Curtis Jackson's body as he sat in a car outside his grandmother's house in southeast Queens.

Jackson might have been disregarded as just another young Black victim of street violence in New York, had he not been a rap artist signed to Columbia Records. He wasn't famous, but 50 Cent already had plenty of enemies who might have wished him dead.

Jackson made his name, literally, by borrowing the sobriquet of a notorious Brooklyn stickup kid called "50 Cent"; and figuratively, by releasing a song called "How to Rob (An Industry Nigga)," in which he lyrically targeted four dozen different rappers, R&B singers, and actors. Although many of the figures mentioned understood "How to Rob" as farce, others, like Jay-Z and Big Pun, responded with lyrical return fire.

Jackson dealt drugs from an early age, and had conflicts with other hustlers in the neighborhood. A protégé of local Queens hero Jam Master Jay, 50 Cent felt that he had been snubbed at a local concert by another Queens MC, Ja Rule, now the multiplatinum nucleus of Irv "Gotti" Lorenzo's Murder Inc. Records. While he awaited his Columbia deal—forged by Chris Lighty's superproducer clients the Trackmasters—50 Cent recorded a number of songs dissing Ja Rule and Murder Inc. He released each salvo onto "mix tapes," bootleg cassettes and CDs assembled by top DJs like Whoo Kid and Kay Slay that were tacitly tolerated by the music industry because of their power to break new artists in the streets.

The feud between 50 Cent and Ja Rule boiled over into actual violence between the two rappers at least twice—first when a mutual acquaintance brokered a conversation between them that ended in 50 Cent punching Ja Rule in the face; and next when Ja Rule and the Murder Inc. posse attacked 50 Cent during a recording session at Manhattan's Hit Factory. 50 Cent was also rumored to have incurred the wrath of a well-known Queens drug kingpin named Kenneth "Supreme" McGriff after one of his album cuts, "Ghetto Qu'ran," leaked. The song mentioned McGriff among a host of other underworld figures of southeast Queens lore.

Weeks later, 50 Cent lay in Jamaica Hospital in Queens with wounds in his hands, legs, and face. Although he would later implicate Darryl "Hommo" Baum as the assailant—Baum himself shot dead three weeks after the attack on 50 Cent—his attack turned wary eyes toward McGriff and Murder Inc., especially since McGriff was a friend of Irving Lorenzo.

If 50 Cent's grandmother hadn't stopped an operation on 50 Cent's throat, her grandson might have lost the ability to rap entirely. But 50, despite his shattered jaw and a bullet shard lodged in his tongue, kept his voice.

The executives at Columbia Records didn't care. With seemingly constant violence surrounding their artist, they dropped 50 Cent before his album, *The Power of the Dollar*, could be released. Now bereft of his major-label deal, 50 Cent retreated to his girlfriend's house in the Pocono Mountains of Pennsylvania to heal up, bulk up, and plot his return to hip-hop.

The fiasco with 50 Cent was just another black eye issued by Sony Music in its abusive relationship with hip-hop.

Sony Records chief Tommy Mottola hated that he had let Def Jam go in the mid-1990s just before they had become a hot commodity again. But Sony had never been a great home for hip-hop, save for Nas—brought in by Def Jam alumna Faith Newman. Columbia had a rough partnership with a Philadelphia label called Ruffhouse Records, even though the label yielded huge artists like Cypress Hill, the Fugees (including members Wyclef Jean and Lauryn Hill), and Kris Kross. But Sony never fostered another rap label with the same cultural impact and sales volume as Def Jam.

When Loud Records became a free agent in 1999, Mottola saw his opportunity to bring a credible hip-hop label into the fold. Steve Rifkind and Rich Isaacson's artist roster was small, but highly regarded: Wu-Tang Clan, Mobb Deep, and Big Punisher were all gold- and platinum-selling acts. Rifkind saw, at last, a way to determine his own destiny. Sony made Loud an incredible offer. It had, years back, bought the independent label Relativity and its distribution wing, RED. Instead of piping Loud's product through either Columbia or Epic, Loud would take over Relativity and sell its records through RED. The move would effectively transform Loud into the de facto "third" Sony label and give Loud unprecedented control over its promotion and distribution.

Rifkind and Isaacson moved Loud's small staff into Relativity's offices and presided over the newly merged company. When Isaacson first met the assembled staff of Relativity, his mouth went dry. Almost a hundred people stood before him, comprising a full-service company with departments like A&R, administration, design, production, promotion, marketing, sales, finance, and a business affairs department that had three full-time lawyers. The thirty-two-year-old president of Loud shuddered when he realized that all of these people, many of them older than him, grown-ups with families and children, would now be reporting to him. He had no idea how to run a company of this size, or how to feed it with enough product to keep the engine running.

Then Isaacson heard Chris Lighty was leaving Def Jam. Rifkind and Isaacson liked Lighty. Not only did he manage one of their most successful acts, Mobb Deep, but he had been the person who, years earlier, signed two of the Relativity rap acts they were keeping: Fat Joe and the Beatnuts.

Rifkind and Isaacson met with and struck a deal for Lighty to relaunch his Violator Records at Loud, while continuing to keep Violator Management as his own, separate entity. For the Loud partners, who had always envied Def Jam's success, it was a badge of honor that they could attract an executive of Lighty's caliber. Ultimately, Rifkind and Isaacson hoped that Lighty would bring with him some of that unparalleled Def Jam expertise.

Loud ended up with a double dose. Todd Moscowitz had recently endured a traumatic break of his own with Def Jam patriarch Lyor Cohen. Moscowitz felt that Cohen had promised him an expanded role at Def Jam after the company had sold, but had kept him locked in business affairs. Cohen told Moscowitz that if he wanted to do A&R so badly, he would have to take an entry-level salary. Cohen's affront triggered an icy deterioration between the protégé and mentor, and Lighty prepared a place for Moscowitz at Violator Management. When Steve Rifkind found out that Moscowitz was available, he offered to triple Moscowitz's salary if he came to Loud.

When Moscowitz tendered his resignation, Cohen reacted by calling security to escort his former confidant out into the street.

Cohen phoned Rifkind. "You can have him," he said. "I just kicked him out."

Steve Rifkind and Rich Isaacson had symbolically raided half of Def Jam's brain trust. Lighty and Moscowitz began anew at the expanded Loud Records as executive vice presidents, proving that there was, indeed, life after Lyor.

In Chris Lighty's office at Loud, a rapper played his demo tape for the Violator Records CEO. The beats had barely begun when Lighty received word that his daughter, across the river in New Jersey, was sick.

"Yo," Lighty told him. "I've got to leave. We'll reschedule."

The rapper had every reason to believe that he would never see Lighty again. Everybody else had turned their backs on him. But Lighty lived up to his word, and within a matter of days, 50 Cent was back in his office.

"This shit is incredible," Lighty said.

"You could be Suge and I could be 'Pac," the rapper said. "You could be Puff and I could be Big. We've just got to one-two it like that so people will take me seriously. People are scared of me."

"No, I get it," Lighty responded.

Lighty was fully aware that in bringing 50 Cent to Violator Records, he would be antagonizing the very person he had recently tried to distance himself from—Irving "Gotti" Lorenzo, now the hottest record producer in the business. Success would thus be extra sweet.

But signing 50 Cent through Lighty's Violator imprint at Loud would prove nearly impossible, as the new Loud–Sony venture quickly spun out of control.

Steve Rifkind's problems began just weeks after the deal was signed, when Mottola sent him overseas to meet the heads of Sony's European labels. Rifkind was in Germany when his lawyer called: Sony had just sold RED to a European music company called Edel for $50 million. Mottola had effectively removed the linchpin of Rifkind's plan for independence while Rifkind looked the other way. Now Loud would have no control of their distribution. They would be, in effect, back where they were before.

Rifkind had left RCA because Loud's profit margins weren't nearly big enough for BMG North America chief Strauss Zelnick. Now Rifkind found that Sony demanded no less of him. Mottola and Columbia chief Donnie Ienner began to ratchet up pressure on Rifkind to sell the remainder of his marketing company, SRC, to focus on the job they were paying him to do. But Steve Rifkind had no stomach for running such a large operation. He worked out of Loud's old offices with Lighty. With brother Jon Rifkind piloting Loud's new adventure with Miramax Films, the Rifkinds left the day-to-day operations to an increasingly beleaguered Rich Isaacson.

Lighty and Moscowitz tried to help by remodeling Loud's marketing machine in Def Jam's image. But their first attempts to institute new protocols were met with resistance and outright refusal. At one of the first meetings he attended, Moscowitz quickly identified a number of Loud employees who, to say the least, weren't quite qualified for their positions. But when he broached the subject of personnel changes, he was surprised to find that some of the people he had identified were relatives or friends of the Rifkinds and wouldn't be going anywhere.

The nepotism didn't just bother the two Def Jam transplants. It also troubled longtime Loud employee Matteo Capoluongo, now Loud's A&R chief with an equity stake in the company. The merger with Relativity meant that Loud's once tight roster of hard-core hip-hop had been diluted with acts outside of Capoluongo's purview. But in Capoluongo's reasoning, Rifkind made things worse by doing all kinds of favors for old friends, giving six- and seven-figure deals to artists that Capoluongo would have never touched in his life, like a vocal group called 5 Young Men. Capoluongo cringed at a Biggie tribute concert when members of the group thanked him from the stage, fearing for his own reputation in the industry.

Rifkind couldn't help it; he was three generations deep in music industry favors. Capoluongo viscerally understood the power of *famiglia*, as his great-grandfather had been a judge in Naples, the birthplace of the Mafia. The Capoluongos had to flee Italy to get away from the dark side of nepotism. Now both of Matteo's parents worked for the World Bank, where even a hint of bias or impropriety could get one fired. Capoluongo saw that Rifkind wanted to be a part of that corporate world, but he operated as if he were still in the record promotion business. With lackluster reporting and displays of arrogance and nonchalance, he had driven off SRC's biggest client, Pepsi; by refusing to pay the full amount on a revenue-sharing deal he'd made with Jeff Swierk, the man who had brought in the Pepsi account in the first place, he lost the respect of some of his employees.

The truth was that no one at Loud was suited for the world of global business. Not the largely absent Rifkind, not the overwhelmed Isaacson, and not Capoluongo either, who couldn't yet understand the reason why the Loud roster had to expand. Loud was now part of a multinational public corporation that needed to show its shareholders profits and quarter-over-quarter growth. That institutional imperative had confounded the best music entrepreneurs in the business.

The relationship between Loud and Sony deteriorated amid financial mismanagement. Loud had racked up impressive sales for the year 2000, with gold and platinum albums from Big Pun, Funkmaster Flex, Mobb Deep, Project Pat, Three 6 Mafia, the Wu-Tang Clan, and Xzibit. Despite these impressive numbers, Loud's spending was so out of control that they had no profit to show for it. The Loud partners got double messages from Sony. Mottola told Rifkind that market share mattered more than profits.

"Keep doing what you're doing," he said.

But Mel Ilberman, the chairman of Sony Music International, conveyed his dismay at Loud's spending to Rich Isaacson.

"I don't understand you guys," Ilberman said during a lunch with Isaacson. "I've never seen a company do a hundred million dollars in billing and not make money."

Loud's spendthrift ways were just an inflated version of what they had been doing at RCA/BMG all along: letting their passion for their projects override their business judgment. Rifkind and Isaacson spent $1 million on a Mobb Deep video to promote an album that couldn't possibly sell enough to justify the expense. Where labels like Sony might give up on an album after one failed single, Loud often went four singles deep into projects that had little hope of reviving. Loud was coming dangerously close to tripping the contractual triggers that would legally shift control of their company to their funding partner, Sony Music.

The relationship between Violator and Loud disintegrated, too. Lighty began reciting an emphatic and repeated refrain—*That's not how we did things at Def Jam*. Isaacson began to suspect that Lighty was more interested in helping himself than aiding Loud, and he viewed his partner Moscowitz with mistrust as well.

Though Lighty had lost confidence in the Loud situation, he brought 50 Cent to Steve Rifkind anyway. Rifkind wanted to help, but circumstances had changed. All Loud releases now ran though Columbia Records—the very label that had recently *dropped* 50 Cent. Lighty was going to have to petition Columbia chief Donnie Ienner for his blessing.

Ienner refused. He tried to sell Lighty on the virtues of another rapper, Nature, an associate of Nas. A lively debate ensued. Though Lighty didn't win, Ienner came away from the meeting impressed with the young executive. He offered him a job.

Out of respect, Lighty told Steve Rifkind about Ienner's offer. Rifkind, who didn't know how much longer he would even have his company, told Lighty to go ahead and consider Ienner's proposition. Once again, Lighty brought Moscowitz in on his new opportunity.

It did not go well for either of them. Though Rifkind had consented to the meetings, he hadn't told Isaacson about them. Moscowitz returned to Loud from his parley with Ienner, only to be immediately fired by Rifkind's indignant partner. Moscowitz had little to pack; he had been on the job for only a few months. Lighty, meanwhile, got patched into a Columbia conference call too early, and overheard Ienner and other executives rehearsing their negotiation strategy.

We've got to get Lighty away from the management company, Ienner said.

Violator Management, long his industry insurance policy, saved him again. Lighty quietly walked away from Sony and Loud, with Moscowitz in tow.

As the Loud ship sank, Issacson and Rifkind began to argue. Within months, Sony had wrested control of Loud Records away from its major founders and stakeholders—Steve and Jon Rifkind, and Rich Isaacson. The three executives, who had worked together for almost a decade, went their separate ways.

And Sony Music continued its long tradition of missing the mark in hip-hop.

Chris Lighty turned his back on Sony because he didn't want to relinquish Violator Management as his independent power base. But Lighty had already done that when he took Michael Ovitz as his partner. That relationship had turned toxic, too.

Violator's merger with AMG meant that Lighty received a substantial yearly advance for overhead costs. But Violator Management was having an off year—partly owing to the departure of two key clients, LL Cool J and R&B singer Maxwell, and partly because a few of Violator's mainstay artists, like Busta Rhymes and Missy Elliott, were between albums. As a result, Violator's revenue was far beneath the projections that Lighty had given to Ovitz. And Ovitz was concerned that expenses weren't being pulled back accordingly.

Lighty tried to explain the "on-off" cycles that every one of his artists experienced—an explanation that Ovitz either didn't understand or didn't trust. Ovitz didn't think Lighty knew how to run a business. He wanted to look at Lighty's books. And he wanted to renegotiate the contract in his own favor, to lower the yearly advances.

"You've got a great contract already," Todd Moscowitz advised Lighty. "Don't renegotiate unless you're getting something in return." Lighty agreed.

What had Mr. Hollywood done for him anyway? Aside from his placing Busta Rhymes in a couple of movies, none of Ovitz's promises had transpired. What was more, the mogul's empire was crumbling, and the industry press was full of the news: $100 million lost on his failed television production company; departing clients like Chris Tucker and Katie Couric. Lighty refused to modify the deal. When Ovitz threatened to withhold overhead, in clear breach of their agreement, things got ugly.

Lighty had experienced treachery in business before. He had seen Lyor

Cohen in action. But Cohen was no match for Michael Ovitz. *Cohen didn't want to see you and your kids out in the street,* Lighty thought. *Ovitz was a whole new level of skullduggery.*

Extricating himself and Violator from the Ovitz/AMG deal required a protracted and costly arbitration process and would cost Lighty millions of dollars in legal fees.

On a sunny weekend in July 2000, two rappers and their crews prepared for battle.

Sean Combs gripped a baseball bat, waiting.

Jay-Z watched as his partner Damon Dash, dressed in a blue Rocawear shirt, cocked his arm.

Dash pitched a low and fast underhanded ball to Combs.

Swinging the bat, Combs got a piece of it. The ball skittered along the dirt, easily picked up by Team Rocawear's second baseman. Combs, his white Sean John T-shirt flapping in the wind, ran toward first in a futile race against the ball. He would have been out, too, had Roc's first baseman not erred on the catch. Combs took the base and the crowd cheered.

On the sidelines, Andre Harrell, ousted from Motown Records and now the president of his former protégé's label, Bad Boy, joined with Jay-Z to provide color commentary as another Team Sean John player knocked a high fly ball into the air, caught by the Roc's left fielder. Harrell announced the score: 2–0, Rocawear.

Up to the plate stepped a late addition to Rocawear's summer lineup: a slender, brown-skinned girl in cutoff white shorts and a blue bandanna. The pretty player swung her bat like a tennis racket and hit the ball into a Sean John glove. Out.

"Okay, I at least hit it," R&B singer Aaliyah said as she left the diamond.

Rocawear kept it moving. A few more balls leaped off of their bats, and more runners scored. At the end of the East Hampton afternoon, Rocawear emerged the winner of the First Annual Softball Classic. But off the field and in the marketplace, Sean John led the race.

Sean Combs's fledgling clothing line projected $70 million in sales by the end of the year. Damon Dash and Jay-Z's Rocawear trailed at figures estimated somewhere between $25 to $50 million.

The two fashion lines both stressed quality. But Sean John emphasized innovation while Rocawear stuck to casual basics.

Within months, Sean John would take a huge window at Bloomingdale's flagship New York store, while Rocawear opened a 450-square-foot space in Macy's Herald Square with plans to open over two dozen more across the country.

The sales for "hip-hop labels" like Sean John and Rocawear were up sharply. Bloomingdale's fashion director Kal Ruttenstein told Crain's New York Business that Sean John's fall 2000 line was "one of the strongest" he had seen. "The appeal goes way beyond hip-hop," he said.

Traditional designers like Tommy Hilfiger, Polo Ralph Lauren, and Nautica struggled as Sean John, Rocawear, and Phat Farm moved in to establish a new, hip-hop-inspired order in the fashion world.

But in this new world of fashion, the competition was as friendly as a summer softball game. It was a stark contrast to the music industry–related violence of the two lines' public faces, Sean "Puff Daddy" Combs and Shawn "Jay-Z" Carter. Media coverage of both entrepreneurs' success invariably referenced their legal and criminal woes, and both companies operated under a cloud. Should either of the men end up in prison, they could take their businesses with them.

Throughout his trial, Combs shuttled between the court and his offices, still very much the creative leader of his music and fashion labels. As Jay-Z awaited trial, he channeled his energies into the recording studio, while Dash expanded the Roc-A-Fella artist roster and Rocawear line.

Dash hired former Phat Farm executive Dana Hill as Rocawear's first vice president of marketing. Dash's co-CEO Norton Cher nabbed chief financial officer Ron DeMichael from a rival line, Cynthia Rowley. Rocawear was becoming a legitimate, established business, taking fifteen thousand square feet of space in new Fashion District offices on Seventh Avenue. With Sean John's offices nearby, one trade magazine dubbed the neighborhood the "Gangsta Garment Center."

At Rocawear, Dash continued to guide the company's aesthetic of "clean, casual quality"—his demeanor at turns enthusiastic, brooding, emphatic, or choleric. Dash empowered his employees to execute good ideas but could turn caustic if he didn't like the execution, or if he felt bypassed. But Dash had a new calm in his personal life. His stormy relationship with Rocawear designer Rachel Roy was off again. With his new girlfriend, Dash never fought.

At first, casual observers couldn't tell whether the singer Aaliyah was with Jay-Z or his partner Dash, as she wrapped herself around both of them so comfortably. By the fall, everybody knew she was Dame's girl. Their schedules kept them apart for months at a time, but the distance only intensified his feelings for her. Aaliyah lavished Dash with her sweetness, and sweetened him in the process.

All of Dash's previous relationships had been tumultuous. The police had been called to his home on a number of occasions after screaming fights between Dash and Linda Williams, the mother of his first child. But he didn't have to work to be on his best behavior with Aaliyah. He felt he hadn't really loved a woman since the death of Carolyn Dash.

Sean John Combs, the self-anointed future of fashion, kept himself looking sharp. But on the evening of March 16, 2001, Combs's brown suit was wrinkled, and he trembled visibly as the jury entered the courtroom of Judge Charles Solomon to deliver their verdict.

Within minutes, the jury acquitted Combs on four counts of gun possession and one count of bribery. His bodyguard, Anthony Jones, was acquitted, too. Combs's artist Jamal "Shyne" Barrow was convicted of secondary assault charges, weapons possession, and reckless endangerment. Barrow would receive a prison sentence of ten years. Combs, his former benefactor, walked away a free man.

As Combs celebrated his freedom, Jay-Z awaited his own judgment day. The rap superstar's lawyers still maintained their client's innocence, claiming they possessed video footage from the Kit Kat Club that would exonerate him. While the pretrial dance progressed, Jay-Z dived into the studio again. By August 2001, the new album, called *The Blueprint*, was ready.

Nothing, however, would go as planned.

One evening, just two weeks before his album's release, Jay-Z was jolted by a "911" page from Dash. Within minutes, Jay and much of the Roc-A-Fella and Rocawear family converged on Dash's Tribeca apartment upon the news that Dash's girlfriend, Aaliyah, had perished in a plane crash in the Bahamas.

For five days, Damon Dash barely moved from his bed. And for five days, Jay-Z sat with him. Rachel Roy, his ex-girlfriend and the mother of his daughter, came to help Dash mourn the woman for whom he had left her. The whole crew slept over—on the floor, on the couches—while their CEO wept.

Dash had been with Aaliyah in Miami before she went off to the islands, but he couldn't go with her because he had a court date, and he had promised to see his young son's football game. They had talked about getting married after she promoted her new album and finished shooting the sequel to the film *The Matrix*, in which she was cast. There was never enough time. And now she was gone.

After your mother dies, nothing can be quite as bad, Dash told himself. He figured Aaliyah gave him time to prepare; why else would he have been reading Gary Zukav's *The Seat of the Soul* and other books about transition and death just before she was killed? But the pain was still overwhelming. So Dash set a time limit for his grief. He saw her family. He went to the funeral. And then he forced himself to go back to work. He had a team to lead and an album to promote.

In the postfuneral daze, Dash threw himself into preparations for the coming release of *The Blueprint*. Alas, the album's street date of September 11 would forever be remembered not for the debut of Jay-Z's best album since *Reasonable Doubt*, but for four more plane crashes.

The summer's twin traumatic events shifted everyone's priorities. The following month, Shawn "Jay-Z" Carter's lawyers reached a plea deal with the Rivera case's prosecutors. Carter would plead guilty to third-degree assault and, in return, receive probation rather than prison time.

The rap entrepreneur's emergence from legal limbo also resolved the ambivalence between Jay-Z's thug past and Shawn Carter's corporate future. As a successful artist, Jay-Z had every opportunity to handle his disputes with the pen rather than the sword. From now on, Carter would do that. With all the drama in the world, it was safer and simpler to be a business-man. If there was a beef—as Jay-Z now had with the rapper Nas—it was better left on record, like hip-hop's good old days. Jay-Z left his trial and tribulation with a lighter heart. Damon Dash's personal trauma would make his own coming days darker by comparison.

Sean Combs's personal life had also taken a hit—his relationship with Jennifer Lopez didn't survive the ordeal of the shooting and trial. But Combs was already seeing a renaissance of his professional fortunes. Combs launched a new series on MTV called *Making the Band*. His nascent acting career got a boost with a fortunate casting in *Monster's Ball* opposite Halle Berry, who would go on to receive an Academy Award for her role. For two years in a row, Sean John had been nominated for the "Oscar" of the fashion world, the Council of Fashion Designers of America's Menswear Designer of the Year Award. His clothing line now accounted for $100 million of his companies' yearly revenue of $160 million. *Forbes* now ranked him as number twelve on their "40 Richest People Under 40" list.

Chris Lighty made the rounds with Violator Records' new artist, 50 Cent, with little success.

Tom Whalley at Warner Bros. Records said that 50 Cent reminded him of the artist he had once signed to Interscope, Tupac Shakur. But Whalley didn't get the deal done.

Barry Weiss at Jive Records was too nervous to make the deal because of the violence that seemed to follow 50 Cent.

"I promise you, Barry," Lighty reassured him, "you will be nowhere near the shit if it goes down. I will be the one at ground zero."

One by one, more labels turned Lighty down or waffled, like Atlantic Records. Indeed, an unproven rumor had circulated that someone—perhaps Kenneth "Supreme" McGriff, or Irv "Gotti" Lorenzo—had threatened executives not to do business with 50 Cent. In reality, no one wanted to invest hundreds of thousands of dollars into an artist who could be dead before his album came out.

By the time Lighty had finished "shopping" 50 Cent, he had only one serious offer. The venerable Clive Davis had something in common with 50 Cent. They were both outcasts from Columbia Records. And Davis had recently been ousted from Arista Records, too, in a power struggle with BMG chief Strauss Zelnick. His new label, J Records, was generally thought to be a sop to an old record man way past his prime. Clive Davis's first signing to J Records was yet another Columbia Records refugee: a twenty-year-old piano player from Queens named Alicia Cook—performing under the sobriquet Alicia Keys. Another Lighty client, Busta Rhymes, had also shifted to J.

To Lighty's delight, Clive Davis got 50 Cent immediately.

"He's a star," Davis said, without hesitation.

As gratified as Lighty was, he doubted that J Records would be the right home for 50 Cent. Lighty knew, of course, where 50 Cent really had to be. A record company with a machine he knew and trusted. So Lighty swallowed his pride and called Lyor Cohen.

Cohen was skeptical. He didn't like the thought of two sworn enemies—Ja Rule and 50 Cent—on the same label.

That's what's so perfect about it, Lighty argued. *We can earn from both sides. We can make it the battle of the century. And, at the same time, regulate it so that it doesn't turn into something more serious.* Beef, as theater, was still good business.

"I'm sorry, Chris," Cohen said. "I just can't do that to Irv."

Once again, Lighty's mentor had chosen the new gold and platinum boy over him. The anger welled up inside him.

"Okay, then," Lighty said. "We'll just send you a ransom note for your artist's career."

Since Lyor Cohen ascended to the chairmanship of Island Def Jam in 1999, his labels' share of the American music marketplace had almost doubled, from 5.4 to 9.4 percent. Cohen was now personally responsible for almost a tenth of the music purchased in the United States.

With $500 million in annual sales, Cohen decided to put his enhanced clout to use. The singer Mariah Carey had recently been dropped from rival EMI's Virgin Records. Her disastrous album and movie made EMI's multimillion-dollar deal unrenewable. Carey then suffered a very public nervous breakdown. Cohen made a trip to Carey's apartment to offer his support. His quick compassion earned Cohen the performer's gratitude, and his confident courtship ultimately won her over. Cohen signed Mariah Carey to Island Def Jam for $20 million, his first-ever superstar acquisition.

Cohen felt that he and his team knew how to revive Mariah Carey's career. So, in the early summer of 2002, Cohen convened a quorum of Def Jam executives and artists on the island of Capri in the Mediterranean, where Carey decided to commence recording her next album, *Charm-bracelet.*

Among those present for the festivities was Shawn "Jay-Z" Carter, who made Capri just one stop on a personal jaunt through Europe. He had never taken a real vacation before, as an adult, with his own money. A few things happened to Jay-Z on this trip. In London, he attended Wimbledon and hobnobbed with show-business royalty like Quincy Jones and Bono. And in Saint-Tropez, he fell in love with a young American R&B singer named Beyoncé.

Back in New York, Damon Dash steamed. Jay-Z was off on some trip, with some chick, hanging with people like Lyor and Kevin Liles, while Dash was back home, working. He could only imagine the things that Cohen was saying to his partner right now.

Only recently, Dash uncovered a Cohen scheme to wrest control of Jay-Z from Roc-A-Fella: a proposed early buyout of Roc-A-Fella, after which Cohen would have elevated Jay-Z to the presidency of the newly purchased label, and left Dash and Biggs out on the street.

Dash didn't want to believe that such divide-and-conquer techniques could work on his crew. They were brothers. They had walked through life, and death, together. But something irked Dash about Jay's chummy relationship with Roc-A-Fella's business partners—people like Lyor Cohen and Kevin Liles, Norton Cher and Alex Bize. Dash wanted to scream: *They're the* enemy, *dummy. They'd jerk us if we take our eye off the ball even for a second. They're trying to jerk us even now. And I'm the dude exposing their sneaky shit,* punishing *these guys every day on your behalf.*

As business-minded as Jay-Z could be, he was still an artist. Dash found him difficult, resistant to many ideas at first, whether it be promoting the clothing line or picking a particular single. Dash felt that Jay didn't believe in things until they happened. And Jay was always threatening to quit rapping, ever since *Reasonable Doubt. Talking to the media about retiring is not exactly the best way to build value for your record or clothing labels.*

In Jay's absence, Dash and Kareem "Biggs" Burke looked for ways to expand the Roc-A-Fella empire. Dash dived into film, producing a movie called *Paid in Full* about his childhood hero, Harlem drug kingpin Rich Porter. Meanwhile, Burke found an alcohol manufacturer interested in partnering with them to create a custom brand.

The idea appealed to Dash's strong sense of sovereignty. He had once asked Iceberg jeans for an endorsement deal; their rebuff inspired Dash to create Rocawear, if only for revenge. Now Dash realized that he had been promoting someone else's brand for years, gripping bottles of Cristal champagne and Belvedere vodka in video after video. Why not make and sell his own?

Roc-A-Fella began a joint venture with a British company, William Grant & Sons, Ltd., one of the largest and oldest distilleries in the world, to create Armadale vodka, named after an abandoned castle on the Isle of Skye. The castle itself, built by a wealthy Scottish clan, was more ostentation than fortification. So, too, was Dash and Burke's new product, an eighty-proof "handcrafted, triple-distilled" brand with the stated goal of becoming "the highest-priced vodka on the market."

With their flagship act's uncertain future, Damon Dash worked to fortify Roc-A-Fella's roster with other reliable artists. Dash signed Roc-A-Fella's house producer, Kanye West, to an artist deal of his own. He also brought in a young rapper from Harlem named Cam'Ron.

The signing of Kanye West had been the subject of spirited debate between the three Roc-A-Fella partners. Jay-Z agreed to sign West because it was good business—if only to keep the producer's hot beats in the family. He wasn't altogether convinced, as Dash seemed to be, that West would be a success as an MC. *Maybe*, Jay said.

But the entry of Cam'Ron introduced a dark energy into the Roc partnership. Cam'Ron was from Harlem, and a favorite protégé of Dash's. But Cam'Ron had also once been Lance "Un" Rivera's artist, and was not a favorite of Jay-Z's. Dash pressed ahead anyway. Hostilities were sublimated into passive aggression. Cam'Ron thought that Jay-Z had stolen a Kanye West beat from him, so Cam'Ron took a track that another producer had intended for Jay. Jay-Z contributed a verse to Cam'Ron's song "Oh Boy." Cam'Ron erased it. Jay-Z showed up to support Cam'Ron at the video shoot but refused to appear in the video. Fans and industry people started whispering about a schism at the Roc.

Cam'Ron's two singles "Oh Boy" and "Hey, Ma" became top-five pop hits. Cam'Ron's album, *Come Home with Me*, went platinum. Cam'Ron became the first breakout Roc-A-Fella artist who wasn't Jay-Z. In the video for "Oh Boy," Dash now got to hold his own bottles of premium liquor—and hold his own without Jay, as well.

While Jay-Z enjoyed his vacation, Damon Dash governed the expanding Roc-A-Fella empire. He made decisions without consulting Jay, but this was the natural course of events. Dame let Jay make the records, and Jay let Dame run the business. But Jay-Z's relaxed Mediterranean summer was marred on more than one occasion by disturbing news from home.

At a media listening party, Dash had announced the promotion of Roc-A-Fella artists Cam'Ron and Beanie Sigel to vice presidents at the company. Jay-Z made an equally public denial via phone from Europe.

"That's not taking effect as of yet," he told *The Source*. "I think the talk is a little premature as of right now."

Next Jay-Z found out that Dash was shooting a movie, a fictionalized account of their partnership, with actors playing them both. Jay hadn't even met the guy playing him. It was unsettling.

Then Jay-Z heard that Dash had fired a bunch of folks in the office, including personal assistant Carline Balan, who called Jay, distraught. Jay flew her to Europe and hired her as his own girl Friday.

Jay-Z's friends and colleagues—like Kevin Liles, who accompanied Jay on part of his European tour—could see the artist wrestling with conflicting impulses about Dash. On one hand, when Lyor Cohen offered the buyout in late 2001—the one that would have effectively paid his partners to go away and left Jay-Z in charge of Roc-A-Fella—Jay-Z turned it down out of loyalty to Dash and Burke. On the other hand, Dash's combative style, which had been indispensable when Roc-A-Fella was promoting records and negotiating deals, had become noxious once those ventures became ongoing, workaday relationships. Moreover, the people whom Dash harangued were good people, Jay concluded, people who fought hard for him and his career. Jay happened to like Cohen and Liles, Norton and Alex. Dash saw everyone as the enemy. With Dash's latest moves, Jay began to feel his partner turning his compulsive defiance in his direction. Before Jay-Z returned to the states, the rapper renewed his talk about retirement. His next album—a "black album" with no photography, no artwork—would be his last.

Several months after Jay-Z's homecoming, Damon Dash made another unilateral change at Roc-A-Fella—not widely known, but of fateful import for the future of their partnership—when Dash axed Roc-A-Fella's finance chief, John Meneilly.

Meneilly had come to Roc-A-Fella from Provident Financial Management, a firm that handled the accounts, investments, and businesses of many artists and executives in the entertainment business. Meneilly was something of a rock star himself: He had made partner in his early thirties. Among his clients were pop-music icons like the Dave Matthews Band, and hip-hop executives like Chris Lighty. It had been Lighty who first introduced Meneilly to the music of Jay-Z. When Roc-A-Fella became a Provident client, Meneilly took the account. And when Meneilly left Provident, Roc-A-Fella hired him full-time, where he handled the details for which Damon Dash had neither the time nor the patience. It was Meneilly, for instance, who assembled Roc-A-Fella's 1999 "Hard Knock Life" tour that brought hip-hop back to American arenas.

When he first began working with Roc-A-Fella, John Meneilly dealt exclusively with the mercurial Dash. But Meneilly's cool, even-keeled, intuitive temperament aligned more with that of Jay-Z. Before long, Meneilly had become Jay-Z's de facto manager, and the rapper from the Marcy Projects of Brooklyn came to trust the sharp, silver-templed White guy with the goatee, who harbored a similar ambition for success and an ease with the hip-hop party life. They came to share the same views on some of Dash's deeds, with Meneilly providing Jay-Z quiet confirmation of the artist's better judgment. Meneilly's presence reassured Def Jam's executives, too.

So it came as a shock when Dash circulated a terse memo around Def Jam in late 2002 announcing Meneilly's departure.

Dash justified the dismissal as a fiscal necessity. He wanted money for some new hires and didn't have enough in his budget to do it. When he looked at his payroll and saw that Meneilly had the largest salary, he marched into Meneilly's office and demanded that he take a pay cut. When Meneilly refused, Dash fired him.

Dash held forth additional reasons for the termination. He felt that Meneilly had misled him when he was hired; that Meneilly hadn't revealed that he had already left his former employer, Provident Financial. Dash said that he was uncomfortable with Meneilly representing the label on one hand, and he and Jay as individuals on the other. But the economic and ethical considerations were all just pretext. At base, Dash just didn't trust Meneilly's increasing rapport with Jay.

When Meneilly told Jay-Z what had happened, the artist didn't hesitate to rehire Meneilly as his personal business manager, bypassing Dash.

Just one year earlier, Jay-Z had backed Dash by refusing Cohen's buyout offer. But by now, the notion of loyalty that Jay held for Dash was superceded by the realization that Dash did not have his best interests at heart, nor the ability to look after them in the first place. Dash was great when you needed someone to huff, and puff, and blow the doors down. But now Jay-Z was in the room. He didn't need Dash's bluster anymore. He needed a cool head to make relationships work and get the job done. Increasingly, that person was John Meneilly.

As gossip of an impending Roc-A-Fella split reached a crescendo, Dash dealt with the speculation in a novel way. He released a full-length feature film spoofing every single piece of rumor and innuendo he had heard about himself and Jay—from the talk that they fought over Aaliyah, to the notion that the Rivera stabbing was a publicity stunt, to a back-channel deal between Jay-Z and Lyor Cohen, portrayed in the film by James Toback with little concealment as "Liar Schloen." Dash mocked himself, too—his character an obnoxious, Armadale-and-Rocawear-plugging egotist followed everywhere by a personal videographer.

In the movie he called *Death of a Dynasty*, Dash's narcissism and denial played out upon the big screen for all to see, as if publicly enacting his worst fears could intercept them as they appeared on the horizon.

The meeting at attorney Theo Sedlmayr's offices was tense. On one side sat Chris Lighty and Todd Moscowitz, the principals of Violator Records. On the other, Paul Rosenberg represented the interests of Shady Records, the label he shared with Eminem. Between the two sides was the artist over whom they were negotiating, 50 Cent, and his lawyer, Sedlmayr.

Eminem loved 50 Cent's latest mix tape. *Guess Who's Back* was a mélange of tracks from his unreleased Columbia album and new songs, many of which taunted Ja Rule, Irv "Gotti" Lorenzo, and his label, Murder, Inc. The mix-tape assault—assisted by Lighty—whetted rap fans' appetites for 50 Cent. Eminem had become enraptured by the MC whose slick talk and phoenixlike comeback earned him the mantle of hip-hop's next big thing.

Lighty understood the stakes. 50 Cent, a virtual industry pariah, was now being offered the chance to work with not only the top rapper in the business, Eminem, but by extension, the top producer, Andre "Dr. Dre" Young. To make that happen, both Shady and Dr. Dre's Aftermath, as well as their parent label Interscope, would all have to share a piece. And Rosenberg and Sedlmayr were saying that there weren't enough pieces of the pie to go around to feed Violator, too.

The notion of Violator being pushed out offended Todd Moscowitz. When Lighty found 50 Cent, Moscowitz had been the one urging him to sign the rapper to Violator Records, rather than as just a management client. *A manager makes only 15 percent of an artist's record sales. But a production company can make as much as the artist does.*

Violator *was* the producer, after all. Violator had been the entity that shepherded 50 Cent through his dark period. Violator had subsidized his development. Violator had paid for studio time. Violator had shopped him, turning up the industry heat on an artist's career that was stone-cold.

Now, after Violator had done their job, Rosenberg and Sedlmayr wanted to cut him and Lighty out and bump them back down to management. The thing that angered Moscowitz even more was the collusion between his artist and the executives of another record label. They had all discussed this beforehand, apparently, and come in with a united front.

Moscowitz was Violator's business affairs guy, the person charged with protecting the company's assets. So Moscowitz flatly refused to bow out. Rosenberg wouldn't retreat either, and he and Moscowitz began arguing.

As 50 Cent saw the deal come apart before his eyes, he smoldered. Moscowitz was the guy standing in the way of everything he wanted. After 50 and Moscowitz exchanged some sharp words, 50 lunged at him. Lighty jumped into the tussle and separated the two before any significant blows were landed.

Moscowitz stormed out, leaving Lighty to resolve the impasse.

Lighty understood that Violator would be taking a much smaller cut of any potential record sales if they relinquished their contract. But he had to look at the bigger picture. How many more records could 50 sell if he were standing next to Eminem and Dr. Dre rather than by himself? Millions more, most likely. Given that reasoning, taking a smaller cut might not matter much in the long run.

But the picture got even bigger than that. Record sales were down across the board. In the last three years alone, overall music industry revenues had plummeted by nearly a third. The cause was Internet downloading of pirated music. Few in the industry knew how record companies could sustain a business model based on selling copies of recording artists' work, especially with ever more people sharing files via their computers and getting music for free. With the possible death of the CD, artists would have to rely on other income streams: live shows, merchandise, endorsement deals, and entrepreneurship.

Thus, not being the record company in this case didn't weigh too heavily on Lighty. Record companies rarely had access to those other income streams, anyway. As 50 Cent's manager, however, he would receive 15 percent of every deal he made for his artist, and not just for record sales.

With that understanding, Violator Records relinquished its contract with 50 Cent, allowing the rapper to join the label layer cake of Shady/Aftermath/Interscope. Violator Management kept 50 Cent as a client, and Chris Lighty turned his eyes toward the hip-hop business of the future.

Rohan Oza had risen fast in the Coca-Cola company for his work at Sprite. He understood the power of hip-hop as a youth culture that transcended all racial, ethnic, and class boundaries. Oza had learned much from his mentors Darryl Cobbin, Reginald Jolley, Rob Stone, and even Chris

Lighty, whose artists had been involved with Sprite from the inception of the "Obey Your Thirst" strategy; A Tribe Called Quest appeared in one of the campaign's first TV spots, and Missy Elliott appeared in Sprite's version of "Five Deadly Venoms" featuring all female MCs.

In 2000, Coca-Cola plucked Oza to run their faltering Powerade line. By 2001, *Brandweek* had named Oza one of their top-ten marketers under the age of forty.

Shortly thereafter, Rohan Oza got a phone call from Mike Repole, the president of a small beverage company in Queens called Energy Brands, offering him a job. Oza was happy at Coke, and might never have given the offer a second thought if he hadn't actually tasted Repole's product and liked it.

Oza often used his trips to New York to sample new bottled brands that hadn't yet reached Atlanta, especially those touching the energy drink sector that Powerade inhabited. On Oza's most recent tour of the city's delis and bodegas, he had happened upon a colorful orange drink called Vitaminwater Essential. It looked good on the shelf. It tasted great. He loved the ingredients—low on sugar and high on nutrients and electrolytes. And the label on each bottle contained a brief story about the particular flavor.

Oza told Repole that he drank Vitaminwater whenever he came to New York. All the same, Oza turned him down. He was a rising star at one of the most prestigious companies in the world. Why would he leave when his trajectory there was already so promising?

To Oza's great surprise, the end of the conversation with Repole was the beginning of a restless feeling. He was confronted with a choice between safety and passion: He was paid to represent Powerade. But he was excited about Vitaminwater.

Perhaps it was serendipity that, during this period, Oza happened to visit hip-hop marketer Rob Stone, his old friend and partner from the Sprite days. At his desk, Stone drank from a bottle of Vitaminwater. Oza told Stone about the offer and his refusal. Stone looked at Oza like he was crazy.

"This stuff is going to be huge," Stone said.

Oza called Repole and told him that he was ready to talk. Once Repole had convinced the CEO and founder Darius Bikoff that Oza was worth the money, he offered a title and compensation package for the young executive that included equity—something he didn't have at Coca-Cola. If Energy Brands, which operated under the brand name Glacéau, continued to grow, Oza stood to make a great deal of money.

Oza sought the counsel of Darryl Cobbin—technically his superior at Coca-Cola, but in practice a confidant—and spun an ambitious stratagem.

"Here's the play, DC," Oza told Cobbin. "I go to Vitaminwater. I build it. Coke buys it. And then I come back home."

"I like that," Cobbin replied. "And I think that can happen. But Rohan," Cobbin tacked, gingerly, "what will it take to keep you here? Because I don't want to see you leave."

Cobbin knew that Oza had a great opportunity with Vitaminwater. But he couldn't very well just let one of Coke's best people go.

"I need to be at your level," Oza replied. "You make me a VP, I'll think about staying."

It wasn't going to happen; that much Cobbin knew, even though his bosses had enlisted him to convince Oza to stay. But he went through the motions of asking for the promotion on Oza's behalf. When the inevitable refusal came, Cobbin spoke to his protégé in the common native tongue they shared at Sprite.

"Rohan, man," Cobbin said. "I think you gotta bounce."

Late in the evening on October 30, 2002, Lyor Cohen emerged from his Def Jam office, ashen. He gave orders to his assistant.

"Jam Master Jay has been shot," he told her. "Go find Russell."

Cohen raced from Manhattan to Jam Master Jay's recording studio on Merrick Boulevard in Queens. At 7:30 p.m. that night, a masked intruder entered the building, raised his gun, and shot the thirty-seven-year-old Jason Mizell in the head, killing him instantly. On the sidewalk outside, Lyor Cohen wept. He was joined by a spontaneous gathering of mourners, friends from Cohen's long journey through hip-hop, including Chuck D.

It was Jason who had greeted him with a smile in Los Angeles all those years ago, Jason who encouraged him to call Russell Simmons and move to New York. Jason showed him the road and taught him how to come back with the money. Jason taught him how to dress, speak, and dance. Jason "cosigned" his entry into the hip-hop world. Jason made Lyor Cohen's multimillion-dollar fortune possible, even though Jason himself had struggled for success and money in recent years; Run-DMC was gigging less because of problems between Run and DMC, and issues with D's mysteriously faltering voice. Jason had no piece of the latest phase of his former protégé 50 Cent's career. People said that Jason had even resorted to the drug game, transporting "weight" up and down Interstate 95 to pick up extra cash. Now Jason was dead.

Lyor Cohen didn't attend funerals. In orthodox Judaism, the priestly class—called Kohanim—are supposed to remain pure. A Kohen who is truly observant can't be in a room with a dead body. Such defilement is only permitted if the deceased is a parent, child, sister, or brother.

Cohen considered Jason Mizell his brother.

The casket of Jason Mizell arrived at the Greater Allen Cathedral in Queens by horse-drawn carriage. In the pews, Cohen was joined by Russell Simmons, Chris Lighty, Bill Adler, Bill Stephney, Heidi Smith, Cory Robbins, Ed Lover & Doctor Dre, Queen Latifah, Doug E. Fresh, Ice-T, and literally thousands more—the architects of hip-hop's shining past reunited to grieve hip-hop's tragic present, the real death of "def." On the pulpit, a huge floral arrangement displayed the words, "Love. Respect. LL Cool J, Student."

"You ask: Why murder? Well, Jason was a dramatic DJ. He couldn't just leave without drama, so why not murder?" eulogized Joseph "Run" Simmons, now an ordained minister himself. "I believe that this is Jason's biggest hit ever."

If the words of "Reverend Run" struck some in the audience as glib and disrespectful, the eulogy of Darryl "DMC" McDaniels brought them to their feet.

McDaniels's already weak voice trembled with emotion, as he looked around at the unfamiliar surroundings. This wasn't Jay's place of worship, he said. Jay's church was hip-hop.

"Plain and simple, Jam Master Jay was a b-boy. He was the personification, the embodiment of hip-hop. He had love for the strong, he had love for the weak. He treated all people alike and to him no man was better than the next man. Jam Master Jay hung out with the homies and he also hung out with the nerds. He did everything a so-called hip-hopper was supposed to do. He loved our music."

But hip-hop's love of profit and fame had long since superseded its love for itself.

The murder of Jam Master Jay was the tragic precursor to a very difficult year for Lyor Cohen.

On January 3, 2003, the offices of Def Jam were raided by the FBI as part of a criminal investigation into the affairs of Irving "Gotti" Lorenzo and

Murder, Inc. Years earlier, Lorenzo had teamed with Queens drug kingpin Kenneth "Supreme" McGriff on a movie called *Crime Partners*. The feds suspected not only that Murder, Inc., was laundering money for McGriff through the production, but that McGriff had provided the seed capital for Murder, Inc., itself. Def Jam was not directly implicated in the scandal, but it cast a pall over the business between the two entities as the government began to build a case against Lorenzo and his brother Chris.

For Lyor Cohen, the raid was surreal, and the ensuing investigation incredibly disruptive. He was angry at Lorenzo, whom Cohen had implored time and again to change the name of his company. *It had to be Murder, Inc.*, Lorenzo had said. *We make hits, get it? Number one with a bullet, get it?* Lorenzo had been obsessed with gangster imagery, and now the image had become real.

A few days after the raid—as Chris Lighty, Todd Moscowitz, and their staff wrapped up their workday—a spray of bullets shattered the glass and metal doors of Violator's eleventh-floor offices in Manhattan's Chelsea district. The reception area was vacant at the time of the shooting, and no one in the office was hurt. The gunmen vanished without being seen, but Lighty immediately suspected that his and 50 Cent's nemesis, Irv Gotti, had something to do with it.

The incident was the most serious of a series of threats and altercations that followed 50 Cent—still on the verbal warpath for Murder, Inc.—as he prepared to release his debut album, executive produced by Dr. Dre and Eminem.

One month later, another fusillade of bullets rained on Violator, this time directed at the SUV of client Busta Rhymes, parked outside Chris Lighty's offices.

In the midst of the violence and recriminations, Russell Simmons intervened. Simmons had, since the sale of Def Jam, relaxed into the role of hip-hop's elder statesman. In a sit-down at the Palm Restaurant, Simmons tried to clear the air between Lorenzo and Lighty. It didn't go well. First of all, it was supposed to be a man-to-man sit-down. Lorenzo showed up with over two dozen tough guys. His entourage nearby, Lorenzo calmly protested his innocence, claiming to have no beef with Lighty or Violator. Lighty replied that he had the bullet holes to prove that wasn't so. From his own experience, Lighty knew that Lorenzo lived for drama and confrontation. "If you're going to shoot me," Lighty said, "I walk down the same street at the same time every day."

Lighty had a family now, a half dozen employees, and no time for the street shit he thought he had left behind years ago.

Any assertions of amity by Lorenzo were annulled by his artist Ja Rule's recent mix-tape offering, "Loose Change," where the rapper directly attacked not only 50 Cent but taunted Lighty as well.

"They shootin'!" Ja Rule rapped, paraphrasing a famous song by the rapper Nas. "Aw, Chris, you're shook!"

"Fuck you, Lighty!" Lorenzo screamed in the background. But Murder, Inc's "Loose Change" might as well have been named "Sour Grapes."

On March 8, 2003, "In Da Club," the first single off of 50 Cent's upcoming album, became the number one pop song in America, and stayed there for nine weeks. Produced by Dr. Dre, it also became the most played song on Black radio since Nielsen's Broadcast Data Systems began tracking airplay in 1992.

Three years after being shot, 50 Cent had blasted his own way back into the music business.

Four years after leaving Def Jam, it was Chris Lighty's artist who topped the charts, not Lyor Cohen's favorite son, Irv Gotti.

Murder, Inc. and Irving Lorenzo were the focus of a more personal problem for Cohen, now the target of a multimillion-dollar lawsuit brought by Lorenzo's former employer, Steve Gottlieb of the independent label TVT Records.

Years back, TVT had been the first home for Lorenzo and Ja Rule, then a part of an MC crew called Cash Money Click. Gottlieb shelved the project after one of the members was shot. Lorenzo and Ja Rule moved on to Def Jam. In 2001, after Ja Rule's successful debut, Gottlieb reconsidered what he had on the shelf, and negotiated the release of a revised Cash Money Click album with Lorenzo. But now that Def Jam had exclusive rights to record Ja Rule, Lorenzo and Gottlieb needed Cohen's permission to do the deal.

Cohen approved the deal to placate Lorenzo, who was then in the midst of renegotiating Murder, Inc.'s contract with Def Jam. Paperwork was drawn up. Then, after Lorenzo's and Ja Rule's deals with Def Jam were renewed, Cohen decided he didn't want to do the deal anymore. Gottlieb sued.

In March 2003, after a trial in federal court, Lyor Cohen and Island Def Jam were together convicted of breach of contract, tortious interference, fraudulent concealment, and copyright infringement. Nearly three months later, a civil jury awarded damages to TVT in the amount of $132 million—

of which Cohen was personally responsible for a staggering $52 million, or about $22 million more than his entire net worth.

Overnight, Lyor Cohen became the talk of the music industry. Cohen went from being an asset for the Universal Music Group to a huge potential liability. The trial and ensuing publicity exposed a few of Cohen's less tasteful associations with Murder, Inc.: that he comprised one-half of Murder, Inc.'s board of directors; and that Irv "Gotti" Lorenzo called Cohen "Lansky," short for the famous mob accountant Meyer Lansky. When TVT Records' offices were robbed in July 2003, the media implicated Def Jam and, by extension, Cohen. As the appeals process dragged on, the litigation would embarrass even Russell Simmons, who—in a sworn deposition meant to help determine Cohen's stake in Phat Farm—inadvertently blurted out that he had been lying about the company's numbers to drive up public and investor perception.

Cohen faced personal financial ruin and professional exile. He couldn't sleep. Every night for four months and ten days, Cohen walked out of his Upper East Side townhouse, across Fifth Avenue, and into Central Park. Inside, he found his tree. Cohen hugged it, rehearsing the inevitable speech to his pregnant wife about how they would be losing everything: the house, the cars, and all their assets.

Cohen's demeanor around the office was grim. His loyal lieutenants, Kevin Liles and Julie Greenwald, worried for him. But for those who had experienced the sharp end of Lyor Cohen's sword, however, his fate seemed just.

While the controversies suggested that Def Jam was a nest of criminal business practices, the truth was much less sensational. Irving "Gotti" Lorenzo was more bigmouth than gangster.[24] Russell Simmons was a compulsive promoter, not a racketeer. And Lyor Cohen was still at heart the antagonistic road manager who shook down concert promoters for a few extra bucks.

Luckily for Cohen, a cooler judicial head prevailed. In September, Judge Victor Marrero of the U.S. District Court in Manhattan reduced the $132 million jury award to $53 million, and slashed Cohen's personal liability from $52 million to $3 million. Doug Morris and the Universal Music Group vowed to appeal even the reduced judgment.[25]

---

[24] A federal jury acquitted Irving and Chris Lorenzo of money laundering charges in 2005.
[25] The original verdict against Cohen was thrown out entirely by an appeals court in 2005.

Gradually, the old, familiar pain in Cohen's chest—just above his stomach and just below his heart—began to recede.

By the summer of 2003, 50's debut album, *Get Rich or Die Tryin'*, had sold more than five million copies.

50 Cent was easily on his way to becoming a multimillionaire on these sales alone. But 50 Cent wasn't content to remain a recording artist, and his manager, Chris Lighty, now knew everything he needed to know about how to exploit hip-hop stardom to create multiple income streams.

Like Eminem and Dr. Dre before him, 50 Cent got himself a label venture with Interscope almost immediately. G-Unit—the group composed of 50 Cent and his protégés—would be the first release for G-Unit Records, followed by a succession of solo albums for each member of the crew: Tony Yayo, Lloyd Banks, and Young Buck.

Like Eminem, 50 Cent started a clothing line. But the arrangement that Lighty negotiated with hip-hop-influenced designer Marc Ecko was different from most artist-branded clothing labels—wherein the artist licenses his or her name, or "mark," to a bigger apparel line in return for a royalty. The G-Unit Clothing Company was a joint-venture deal, with Ecko fronting the money, handling the manufacturing and distribution, and splitting the profits fifty-fifty with 50. By the end of the following year, *The New York Times* projected that G-Unit Clothing would gross $50 million—a far cry from the $300 million in sales of the four-year-old Rocawear line, but an auspicious debut nonetheless.

Back at Rush Artist Management, Lighty helped pioneer the use of 900 numbers for his artists. Over a decade later, Lighty negotiated a different kind of phone deal: 50 Cent cellular ringtones to be sold for up to $2.99 per download. Lighty inked other agreements, too: a video game with Interscope's parent company, Vivendi Universal; and a biopic with MTV Films and Paramount Pictures. When Lighty's own agency, CAA, balked at representing a rapper so closely associated with violence, Lighty secured a deal with an eager William Morris.

Lighty and John Meneilly partnered to double-bill their respective superstars on a summer tour of America called "Roc the Mic." 50 Cent and Jay-Z also signed tag-team deals for G-Unit and Rocawear sneaker lines through Reebok's "street" line, RBK, which they promoted on tour.

Lighty's relentless pursuit of the back end surprised his partners. When a buyer for Foot Locker informed Lighty that RBK was pushing its own shoes on the retailer behind 50 Cent's G-Unit sneaker, Lighty placed a call to Reebok USA founder and CEO Paul Fireman.

"We need stock," Lighty said.

"We don't renegotiate deals like this," Fireman replied.

"We do," Lighty continued. "Or we won't be wearing any more G-Unit sneakers."

Fireman returned with enough cash to keep 50 Cent and Lighty happy—about $25 million—but no stock, claiming the board had balked. When Lighty later discovered that Fireman was preparing to sell the company to Adidas, he felt played. But Lighty and 50 Cent had done their share of playing, too. Fireman had recently launched a line of Reebok Fitness Water in partnership with Clearly Canadian. But in an RBK television ad, 50 Cent took a brief swig from a bottle of a competing product.

50 Cent wasn't paid to drink Vitaminwater. He wasn't involved with its parent company, Glacéau, in any way.

Chris Lighty was, however, sending a clear message to an old friend.

Rohan Oza believed himself not a brand manager, but a brand messiah. He believed that passionate proselytizing of his products could transcend costly corporate ad campaigns. Vitaminwater was doing well—more than $100 million in sales, second only to Pepsi's Propel brand in the $245 million "enhanced-water" market. He knew how to take them out.

Taking a page from the hip-hop street-team and word-of-mouth ethos, Oza created a fleet of ten "Glacéau Vitaminwater Tasting Vehicles," staffed by two hundred "hydrologists," to cross the country and spread the gospel of Vitaminwater's growing line. But hydrologists working one-on-one with consumers wouldn't break Vitaminwater out of the gourmet-deli and new-age-health-food market. He needed more than brand messiahs to convert individuals. He needed brand ambassadors to influence millions.

That was when Rohan Oza saw 50 Cent's RBK spot. *Chris Lighty is a smart man*, Oza thought.

He wasn't suprised when Lighty phoned him soon thereafter.

Oza and Lighty spoke for a while about the multimillionaire artist's true love of the product. 50 had grown up around alcoholics, so he didn't drink. He spent hours a day working out and ate healthy. Like Oza—who got bored with imbibing the recommended eight glasses of plain water a day—50 had found Vitaminwater a more pleasurable way to hydrate. Lighty told Oza that he wanted to find a way to work together to make Vitaminwater huge.

On Oza's desk, at that very moment, was a test bottle of a new Vitaminwater flavor, recently formulated by Glacéau's head of product development, Dr. Carol Dollard. Oza knew that Dollard worked very hard to get more vitamins and nutrients into their drinks—much more than the 2 to 3 percent of the recommended daily allowance in other "enhanced" waters. Recently, Oza had asked Dollard for a product that would make it easy to highlight this difference. She had returned with a flavor that contained 50 percent of the RDA of seven different vitamins and minerals. Oza's marketing team responded with a great name for the new variety: Formula 50. The coincidence was uncanny.

What better way to collaborate, Oza suggested, than to have 50 Cent endorse this new product?

But Lighty didn't want an endorsement deal. He didn't want cash.

"We want to invest," Lighty said.

The most ironic thing about Lyor Cohen's continued stewardship of Def Jam was that he eventually became Rick Rubin's partner.

American Recordings had lost its lucrative joint-venture deal with Warner Bros. and then left a lesser one at Sony for Island. When Cohen ascended to the sole chairmanship of Island Def Jam, the founder of Def Jam essentially reported to his former nemesis. Suddenly, Rubin was conciliatory.

"My conflict was never with you; it was with Russell," Rubin told Cohen as a peace offering. Cohen knew it was bullshit. But their age and experience had softened the youthful hubris of the two former adversaries, and Cohen, in fact, was delighted to have Rick Rubin back in the Def Jam family. Russell's Jews weren't fighting anymore. They consummated their new union by pairing Rubin with Jay-Z for a track on his upcoming *Black Album*. The song Rubin produced, "99 Problems," was the first new hip-hop track he had personally helmed since producing LL Cool J's "Going Back to Cali" and "Jack the Ripper."

However, one person in the Def Jam extended family still thought Cohen was a bastard.

As the Def Jam staff prepared for the release of Jay-Z's final album, Damon Dash's protectiveness of the Roc-A-Fella brand and Jay-Z as a Roc-A-Fella artist veered toward paranoia. Dash's outrage boiled over when he stormed into a Def Jam marketing meeting for the *Black Album*. He arrived with the usual cameraman in tow.

"I seen all of y'all yesterday," Dash bellowed, referring to the wake of Kareem "Biggs" Burke's brother. "Why nobody told me about a marketing plan about Jay-Z? This is not your *fucking* artist! Are y'all the ones promoting that me and him got a beef, too? 'Cause we don't. How y'all got a meeting about Jay without me? How y'all make any decisions about Jay without me? Huh, John?"

Dash looked straight at John Meneilly, the former Roc-A-Fella finance chief that he had fired, and the man who was now Jay-Z's independent business manager.

"Damon, how're you gonna have a problem with me?" Meneilly replied.

"I'm asking you because you're here on Jay's behalf. I bet you Jay doesn't know I wasn't invited."

Julie Greenwald entered the meeting to find Dash pacing around the table, yelling, interrupting the Def Jam staff's protestations that they had indeed notified him of the meeting by e-mail.

"Jay's not your artist. It's not for you to call a meeting! He's my artist! None a y'all better than me!"

As Dash continued his rant, Greenwald walked out in protest, followed by Def Jam vice president Randy Acker.

"Get the fuck out!" Dash called after them. "This is treacherous. Go get Lyor! Get out of here, beat it."

Finally, Kevin Liles cleared the room out. Dash responded by calling Liles a coward.

Dash thought he had it all figured out. Def Jam was in trouble. Ja Rule's new album had flopped. As Chris Lighty had once warned, Ja Rule's career had been decimated by the ascendant 50 Cent. Ja Rule looked weak and confused when he went to Minister Louis Farrakhan to broker a truce just before the release of his album—ironically a collage of invective against 50. The latest release of Def Jam's other big artist, DMX, was also a disappointment. Roc-A-Fella's artist Jay-Z was all that Def Jam had for their fourth quarter. And now Def Jam was trying to take Jay yet again.

Damon Dash was, of course, right about everything. Everything, except for one, small detail. No one was trying to take Jay-Z away from him because, in truth, his artist was already gone.

Lyor Cohen's financial reprieve did not bring relief. The TVT lawsuit had soured his relationship with Morris and other Universal executives at a time when his contract was coming up for renegotiation. And the reduction of his penalty came at the same time that he received the devastating news that his daughter, Bea, had been born profoundly deaf. As he looked toward 2004, Cohen prayed for grace.

On the first workday of the new year, Cohen walked into the lobby of Worldwide Plaza and rode the elevator to Island Def Jam's offices on the twenty-eighth floor. Per tradition, he was the first to arrive. But, for whatever reason, Cohen's magnetic entry card wasn't working. The chairman pulled on the glass doors anyway, to no avail.

Cohen would later speak of this moment as an omen, a sign that he was in the wrong place. Cohen needed divine counsel: He had just received a job offer from the new owner of Warner Music Group—the rival of Def Jam's parent, the Universal Music Group. His former boss at Universal, Edgar Bronfman Jr., had assembled a group of investors to purchase Time Warner's troubled music division for $2.6 billion, and Bronfman wanted Cohen to run the entire American operation. If Cohen accepted the job, he would have to leave the only home he had ever known in the music business.

On one hand, Lyor Cohen had assembled a loyal team, who now comprised a finely tuned machine: Def Jam, the best, longest-enduring vehicle for the promotion of hip-hop culture in the world. On the other hand, Cohen was no longer an owner, but an employee of a larger corporation. Although his compensation package at Universal stood at millions, his stake now was more emotional than financial.

Now another corporation had come calling. Not for the value of his artists or his brand, but for his own intrinsic worth as an executive. Not to make him a label head, as he now was, but to elevate him to a position atop one of the world's four major record conglomerates.

"You owe this to hip-hop," his wife told him. Amy was a poet, and she expressed her husband's opportunity in the most lyrical terms. Cohen knew what she meant. Throughout its gradual adoption by corporate interests, hip-hop had ultimately been subject to people who had neither comprehension nor respect for it. Now he had the chance to be the first person from the hip-hop community to ascend to the highest echelon of the music business.

Cohen knew some people who would take exception to his contention that he was "the product of hip-hop." Cohen, after all, arrived on Russell

Simmons's doorstep—White, rangy, graceless, and unintelligible—five years after Kurtis Blow's first record, ten years after DJ Hollywood and Kool Herc's first parties. But Cohen arrived earlier than a lot of other folks had. He had been on the road with Run-DMC long before many of the rappers that he now promoted had learned to read and write. And he had cared for them, for their careers, even if his incentive for doing so was sometimes more about money than love, more about victory than beauty, more about quieting his inner demons than giving artists a voice.

In its earliest stages, when hip-hop needed a promoter, Russell Simmons arrived. When hip-hop needed an auteur, Rick Rubin appeared. And when hip-hop had grown into an industry, it needed a businessman. It was then that Lyor Cohen—half executive, half executioner—found his true calling. As such, Cohen had worked harder on behalf of hip-hop's greatest brand, Def Jam, than its own founders—a point that both Rubin and Simmons now readily, respectfully conceded. The hip-hop business had experienced its share of thugs, gangsters, and tyrants. But their success was transient. What hip-hop needed to survive in the larger world, the world of commerce, were businessmen. And Cohen had never been an entrepreneur. He was quite the opposite: the consummate company man.

In late January 2004, with what he later called "a sense of responsibility," Lyor Cohen accepted the position of chairman and CEO of recorded music, U.S., for the Warner Music Group. Now, hip-hop would have one of its own at the apex of the industry that had once spurned it, someone who had been schooled—not by professors at an Ivy League law school, nor by promoters, programmers, and managers in the world of rock and roll—but by two rappers from Queens and their late, great DJ.

While Lyor Cohen moved from the old world to the new order, Russell Simmons, too, was making a transition. Just one month after Cohen left Def Jam, Simmons sold off his greatest remaining asset, Phat Fashions LLC, to the Kellwood Company, for $140 million in cash—the second-biggest acquisition of a business with roots in hip-hop culture. Simmons remained as chief executive, and his wife, Kimora Lee, although separated from Simmons, stayed on as creative director of the company's most lucrative brand, Baby Phat. Cohen, too, shared the wealth as a smaller but significant partner in Phat Fashions, with a 16 percent stake in the company.

Rush—the company that Simmons started as a party-promoting business in 1977, and Carmen Ashhurst reorganized in 1991 as Rush Communications—had now spawned and sold two companies for a total of over $270 million. Simmons still presided over an empire of both established firms, like the Simmons-Lathan Media Group, with the Def Comedy and Poetry Jam franchises, and a new MTV reality series, *Run's House*, on the way; and baby businesses, like UniRush, a "financial empowerment" service providing prepaid Visa debit cards to communities without access to traditional credit and banking. As he became wealthy, Simmons spent more time and effort mentoring younger executives and growing his community affairs organizations: Rush Philanthropic Arts Foundation; the Hip-Hop Summit Action Network, with former NAACP chief Ben Chavis; and the Foundation for Ethnic Understanding.

Over the decades, many of Simmons's start-ups failed: Rush Modeling Agency, Rush Broadcasting, dRush advertising, *OneWorld* magazine. And despite his success in television, Simmons never got very far in the movie business. But Simmons was, very often, the first to test the waters with hip-hop culture in many industries.

"Here's what other people's business plan is," Simmons told *Business-Week*. "Let Russell bash his head, and then we'll follow."

The results of Simmons's pioneering work were staggering: $1.7 billion in yearly hip-hop domestic record sales; $2 billion in annual clothing sales for hip-hop brands; hip-hop-based films that grossed millions at the box office; and rappers among the wealthiest movie stars.

Bill Stephney, during his Def Jam years, wondered why Simmons was so distracted. But Stephney—who himself had transcended the record business, supervising the music in films by Eddie Murphy, Chris Rock, and Sam Jackson—had come to respect the hustle that was Russell. True, there would never have been a Def Jam without Rick Rubin to name it, to sign the artists and produce them. But if Rick built Def Jam, and if Lyor repaired it, Russell had built something more important. *What the hell was Russell doing?* Building the business of hip-hop.

But hip-hop's biggest winning streak wasn't over yet.

By 2004, 50 Cent was undoubtedly one of the world's biggest pop stars. But it took some amount of convincing on Rohan Oza's part to overcome the trepidation of Glacéau CEO Darius Bikoff and president Mike Repole. 50 Cent, after all, had begun his career on the reputation of being shot nine times. What if their chief spokesperson ended up dead in a rap beef?

But the 50 Cent who showed up for his first meeting with Darius was surprisingly different from the rapper's public image: calm, respectful, and deliberate, without too many flamboyant flourishes. Lighty was the rapper's perfect business complement.

In the weeks and months thereafter, Lighty and Oza hammered out the terms of a deal. 50 Cent would take a stake in the privately owned company, one that would graduate over time and escalate if the company hit certain numbers. The two entities—50 Cent on one hand and Glacéau on the other—signed an agreement of mutual confidentiality. Still, word got around that Lighty had negotiated something close to, but not more than, 10 percent of the value of the company.

During these discussions, Lighty and 50 deliberated the attributes of their new product. Oza presented the pair with several flavor options for Formula 50. For Chris Lighty, the choice was simple. Despite the high-minded science of Glacéau, their product was basically a smarter, more up-scale, more aspirational version of the ultimate ghetto beverage on which Lighty and 50 had grown up: the quarter-waters sold in every bodega, deli, and convenience store from Queens to Compton. The quarter-waters (so named because they once cost 25 cents) were just like the Kool-Aid everybody drank at home. And nobody drank wild flavors like strawberry and kiwi in the 'hood. They drank grape. Formula 50 had to be grape.

Oza hated the comparison to such base beverages, but he had to admire the thought process of his new partners. Lighty and 50's input extended to the marketing and advertising campaign, for which Oza brought in another old accomplice from the Sprite days: Reginald Jolley, who had since left Burrell Communications and started his own agency, called the Ad*itive. Jolley proposed a campaign called "Just 50"—a series of print and outdoor advertisements echoing the minimalist packaging of Vitaminwater and accentuating the "Curtis Jackson" side of 50 Cent, the businessman behind the bluster and bullets. In one ad, 50 Cent took a break from a video shoot—reading a copy of *The Wall Street Journal* while three oil-slicked, bathing-suit-clad women writhed behind him. The copy read: "No groupies. No love. Just 50."

The 50 Cent–Vitaminwater deal was announced in October 2004. Behind the scenes, the relationship between the two parties wasn't always smooth. When Lighty, in one of his first interviews about the deal, spoke of building the brand with the ultimate goal of selling it, Darius Bikoff phoned Lighty, screaming at him for disclosing the strategy. Within a few hours, Bikoff looked up to find a livid Lighty in his office, glowering at him. Lighty had driven from Manhattan to Queens to tell Bikoff one thing.

"Don't curse at me," Lighty said, a heartbeat away from becoming a Violator once more.

Once they understood each other, Bikoff and Lighty, Vitaminwater and 50 Cent built a strong alliance. Soon billboards and bus stops across the country linked the images and joined the fates of two upstarts from Queens—one a scrappy, new-age beverage company; the other a pugnacious, provocative rapper with an eye for opportunity and a history of hitching himself to winners.

If all press is good press, then Damon Dash had a very good day on January 14, 2004, when two stories about him appeared in the *New York Post*.

The first article reported that a "leggy former model" named Kirstie Thompson had filed a $15 million lawsuit against Dash, accusing him of raping her during a bizarre fifteen-second encounter in Brazil on New Year's Day the previous year. Dash's publicist denied the accusation, pointing out that he hadn't been charged with anything. It wasn't Dash's first such allegation. He had been accused of raping a fourteen-year-old girl at a summer camp when he was sixteen.[26]

The second article quoted anonymous sources claiming that Jay-Z was parting ways with Dash and forming his own record company, in part because the rap star thought that Dash was "trying to become too much of a star himself." Dash denied this story, too.

With publicists supplying plenty of press access, Dash was very purposefully trying to shine. He was preparing to sustain his Roc-A-Fella empire in a world without Jay—who didn't communicate with him anymore, didn't come to the Rocawear office, and remained cagey about his own postretirement plans with Dash and Biggs.

Dash jetted off to London to promote his Rocawear campaign and recording sessions with former Spice Girl Victoria "Posh" Beckham. At every turn, Dash bragged about his business acumen—"I'm the Jay-Z of business.

---

[26]Neither accusation ever made it to court, nor was Damon Dash convicted of a sexual crime.

I'm the Tiger Woods." In every moment, he flaunted his wealth, whether it be his recent lease of a multimillion-dollar London mansion—paid for by Rocawear—or simply the seemingly endless supply of new jeans, T-shirts, and sneakers that he wore once and tossed. The British press blessed Dash with ink. One moment, he was berating his employees for show. In others, he waxed philosophical: "I am most proud of my kids, and least proud of my temper."

The list of businesses that Dash ran was impressive, and growing. In addition to Rocawear, Roc-A-Fella Records, Roc-A-Fella Films, Dash Films, Armadale vodka, and a marketing company called Native/DBG, Dash added two more clothing lines: State Property, a label for his artist Beanie Sigel, and a fashion venture with New York scenester Charlotte Ronson. Next, he announced the launch of *America* magazine, an upscale "urban" publication, the brainchild of former *Source* magazine editor Smokey Fontaine; and a luxury timepiece company called Tiret New York, a joint venture with watch designer Daniel Lazar.

At first, Dash's rabid expansionism seemed to be paying off. He had put a million dollars into a Lee Daniels art film called *The Woodsman* starring Kevin Bacon, that was nominated for a Grand Jury Prize at the Sundance Film Festival, and picked up by Newmarket Films. And Kanye West's debut, *The College Dropout*, made West the second multiplatinum artist in the history of Roc-A-Fella, and a likely successor to flagship artist Jay-Z. Armadale vodka's annual sales were reported at $2 million; Roc-A-Fella Records' sales at $65 million; and Rocawear's wholesale gross somewhere between $200 and $300 million.

Then, in July 2004, Dash and Burke licensed the rights to Stride Rite's sneaker brand PRO-Keds. It marked the first time that a hip-hop entrepreneur gained control of a mainstream brand.

The PRO-Keds and Armadale deals had the potential to change the archetype for how hip-hop did business. In the early days, artists took the products they liked and put them into their songs and videos, as when Run-DMC rapped about Adidas. On occasion, brands might acknowledge the free publicity by kicking in some product or an endorsement deal. But many companies either didn't know about, didn't care about, or didn't want the attentions of the hip-hop audience, as when Fila once rejected the overtures of Ann Carli at Jive Records, and Timberland refused to give samples to *The Source*. As the years progressed and executives got wise, brands began hiring hip-hop artists to give their products a patina of "cool," as when Sprite tapped rappers KRS-One or Nas for their TV spots. And sometimes, hip-hop brands themselves went mainstream, as did Def Jam Recordings, Wu-Wear, Rocawear, and Sean John. But Roc-A-Fella's purchase of Armadale and PRO-Keds flipped the traditional order of things. *No longer will we market your brands and consumer products*, Damon Dash was saying. *We'll build our own. Or buy our own. Or buy yours from you.*

Russell Simmons could lay rightful claim to being the first hip-hop entrepreneur to diversify beyond music into TV, clothing, film, marketing, and more. Other entrepreneurs, like Master P and Sean Combs, followed suit. But Damon Dash's outsize sense of entitlement and Harlemesque aspirations—*Roc-A-Fella, or fuck you*—drew hip-hop's horizontal expansion to its extreme conclusion. Hip-hop could be everything to its audience. Not just the music they listened to, but the movies and TV they saw, what they wore, what they ate and drank, even the money they spent. And hip-hop could do more than partner with corporate America. It could simply buy them out entirely.

"The Roc will use hip-hop to take over the world," Dash often said.

In other words, *Rockefeller, or fuck you.*

Damon Dash's visions of empire might have been achieved had it not been for the countless acts of sabotage committed by Damon Dash. Indeed, many of his ventures seemed to sour almost as soon as they were announced. Just two months after Dash's London jaunt, he publicly split with "Posh" Beckham. He called her management team "corny," and Simon Fuller, her manager, he renamed "Simon Fullershit." Not more than a year after forming Native/DBG, his partner, David Gensler, left and took five people with him. "Differences in management styles and vision" was the official reason given. At the nascent *America* magazine, editor in chief Smokey Fontaine found that the quarterly disbursements of cash that Dash promised simply never came; Fontaine carried on as best as he could without them.

Despite his inability to keep up with the demands of his established businesses and new acquisitions, Dash continued his ostentatious lifestyle—jetting to Spain with DJ Clark Kent for a party in Ibiza, and then flying back to New York hours later; more clothes, more homes, more companies, including a clothing line for his onetime and current girlfriend, Rachel Roy. He continued to rule with bile and caprice at his businesses, firing eleven people from Rocawear in November 2004, including Roy Edmondson, the marketing executive Dash hired away from Levi Strauss to replace David Gensler.[27]

Edmondson joined Rocawear because he was convinced the company could be a $2 to $3 billion brand. When he and Dash toured the European trade shows—from Edmondson's native Britain to Holland and Germany—people were diving for the Rocawear booth. The only problem was that Europeans wanted a tighter fit than the baggy African-American style. Edmondson begged Dash to make some smaller sizes.

"If you can just allow yourself to sell a 32- and 34-waist jean, you'll double your business overnight," Edmondson told him.

Dash refused. Edmondson even modeled clothes for him so Dash could see how ridiculous Rocawear looked on a European like him.

To Edmondson, Dash's narrow tactics seemed incompatible with his wide vision. Dash wanted Rocawear to be Gucci; he wanted to shoot a $2.5 million spread for *GQ* with photographer Mario Testino. Edmondson went to Alex Bize, because when Edmondson was hired, Bize had taken him aside, telling him explicitly to "watch my money."

When Dash found out what Edmondson had done, he accused Edmondson of disrespect. The next day, he sent Ron DeMichael into Edmondson's office to fire him.

"I'm sorry." DeMichael sighed.

Edmondson called the Rocawear culture "unpredictable." Others called Dash "irrational."

All the while, Jay-Z seemed to be doing things that conflicted with his current partners' interests. The *New York Post* reported that the rapper was launching his own brand of vodka with Grey Goose, and they continued their Dame-Jay deathwatch, with more unnamed sources alleging that Jay-Z had "lost his patience" with Dash.

Finally, even Damon Dash stopped denying what seemed manifest.

"It's kind of obvious by his new demeanor that he's not as involved with us anymore," Dash told *The Washington Post*. "If he chooses to be an independent entity, that's fine. I choose to stay with the Roc."

Dash was about to find out that he really didn't have that choice at all.

---

[27]Dash characterized the firings in an industry trade magazine interview as "regrettable." He explained: "I have 12 companies, so it was like one person per company. The dollars weren't making sense."

Dash and Jay-Z had talked about going their separate ways, at least as it concerned Jay's music career. The Roc-A-Fella joint-venture contract was up, and Island Def Jam would be exercising its option to purchase the Roc-A-Fella partners' 50 percent. Dash, Burke, and Jay-Z would split the proceeds three ways. The understanding was that Dash and Burke would stay together to run Roc-A-Fella, and Jay would do his own thing. Initially, rumors flew that Jay-Z would jump to Warner to start his "S. Carter" label, rejoining Lyor Cohen and the former Def Jam crew in their new digs. But Cohen's replacement at Island Def Jam, L. A. Reid, had offered Jay-Z a powerful incentive to stay: the presidency of Def Jam itself—as Kevin Liles had left to become executive vice president of the Warner Music Group under Lyor Cohen, joining an exodus of other Def Jam alumni, including Julie Greenwald.

Jay-Z accepted the job and was effectively out of the partnership. That much was certain. They just needed to finalize the Roc-A-Fella sale. But then Dash heard something he could scarcely believe from L. A. Reid.

Jay wants the name, Reid said. *He wants the Roc-A-Fella name and he doesn't want you to be able to use it anymore.*

"What?!" Dash said, screwing his face into a skeptical look.

That can't be coming from Jay. Jay wouldn't say that. That's got to be coming from Meneilly.

And so the two estranged Roc-A-Fella partners arranged a sit-down at Da Silvano, an Italian restaurant on Sixth Avenue. Sixteen years and ten city blocks away from the restaurant where Rick Rubin and Russell Simmons ended their partnership, two latter-day hip-hop entrepreneurs convened at another Greenwich Village eatery to discuss their own divorce.

Is it true? Dash asked Jay-Z.

It's just business, Jay-Z answered.

Dash was dumbfounded. Jay-Z, as the new Def Jam president, could indeed control the label, its catalog, and the use of the Roc-A-Fella name.

But you're *the one who doesn't want to do Roc-A-Fella anymore,* Dash said. *Me and Biggs still do.*

Jay-Z replied that there was one condition under which he would relinquish control of the Roc-A-Fella name: Dash and Burke would have to agree to give him full ownership of the master to *Reasonable Doubt,* Jay-Z's classic first album made before the start of the Def Jam/Roc-A-Fella joint venture.

Reasonable Doubt was about as good a catalog record as any in hip-hop. Every year, it kept selling. The album had fed them through cold periods.

No. Dash replied. *No way.*

Jay-Z looked at Dash. *Then it is what it is.*

Dash shifted in his seat. He was dressed in all black, everything: black suit, black shirt, black tie, attired to attend the New York debut of *The Woodsman* just after dinner.

Well. Dash sighed. *At least can you come through to the premiere?*

Nah, Jay-Z replied. *You all dressed up.*

Damon Dash had spent the better part of two years clinging to his romanticized ideal of Roc-A-Fella, born out of the betrayals he witnessed in his Harlem youth. *The circle of success. Crew before me.*

Even when Jay was contrary or resistant, Dash didn't dare think that there was anything that could break their bond.

Even when Jay was breaking those bonds, Dash wouldn't let himself admit it.

And even after he admitted it, Dash made himself believe that there would be, at the very least, goodwill among brothers.

But now Dash looked across the table at Jay and he didn't see a brother. He got that Jay didn't want to be partners anymore. The money part, he understood. But Dash still couldn't understand one thing: Why didn't Jay-Z want to be his friend?

On the ides of December 2004, Damon Dash walked out of Da Silvano, onto the street, and off to his premiere, solo.

A few days later, the Universal Music Group announced the buyout of Roc-A-Fella: just shy of $10 million, split three ways between Damon Dash, Kareem "Biggs" Burke, and Shawn "Jay-Z" Carter.

Jay-Z was now the president of Def Jam—the chair most recently occupied by Kevin Liles. No one, of course, expected Jay-Z to be sitting behind a desk every day. No one expected him to be a promotion animal. Doug Morris and L. A. Reid thought that he might be a great artist magnet and, perhaps, a good creative executive. But Jay-Z's ascension was momentous nonetheless. He wasn't the first former rapper to take over a record label— Heavy D had taken the presidency of Uptown Records when Andre Harrell left to head Motown. But Jay-Z was a former artist of Def Jam's family of labels, running Def Jam, the most powerful and lasting hip-hop brand.

Jay-Z's decision had more than historical significance. It was a clever business move. In essence, it was the fulfillment of the plan that Dash long suspected Lyor Cohen of trying to execute. Jay-Z couldn't outvote his two partners. But if he allowed himself to be bought out and then took the reins of Def Jam, he could basically wrest control of the company from them. The best part of the new deal with Def Jam was that his own masters would eventually revert to him.

As a consolation prize, Dash was given his own label in the Def Jam system—the Damon Dash Music Group—and he kept the Roc-A-Fella artists who chose to come with him. Only two did.

Beanie Sigel was in prison by the time Dash released his album *The B. Coming*. Ol' Dirty Bastard, who had jumped from Elektra, had just died of a drug overdose. "As far as auspicious beginnings go, it is not a great one," critic Lola Ogunnaike wrote in *The New York Times*.

The albums bombed. Dash complained loudly to a Def Jam staff that now effectively reported to his former partner. Within a few months, Dash and Def Jam ended their arrangement.

In 2005, Dash's other ventures—professional and personal—didn't fare well, either. When Dash defaulted on payments to Charlotte Ronson, she simply took her brand and walked away. His PRO-Keds deal suffered from distribution issues and a structure that required Dash to make minimum payments regardless of his sales volume. Armadale suffered because its chief marketing strategy had been mentions in Jay-Z's lyrics and placement in the rapper's new 40/40 nightclub. And by the end of the year, *America* magazine would be history.

In a loud argument over a photo spread of Rocawear competitor Sean Combs—and over the money that Dash was supposed to supply but didn't— Dash punched his partner Smokey Fontaine in the chest and sent him tumbling over a couch. Hearing the commotion, Dash's bodyguard rushed in, gun drawn. Dash wouldn't allow Fontaine to leave until they had "squashed this shit." It was a perverse version of Dash's old code of "crew before me"—in which no one was allowed to leave the room angry; except, in this case, Dash enforced his rule through intimidation. After Dash finished venting, he let Fontaine leave.

"You're gonna be all mad at me now, right?" Dash asked. "You're gonna press charges?"

"Naw, man," Fontaine said as he walked away.

Fontaine did indeed contemplate suing, but decided against it after Dash threatened to fight it all the way. Fontaine wondered if he could continue to run *America* when his relationship to Dash was so impossible. So Fontaine sought the advice of John Meneilly, who had always been supportive of him and the magazine. Meneilly was the *expert* at dealing with Dame.

"Let me tell you," Meneilly said. "Ice him. Just don't talk to him. If he calls you, don't take his calls. You have an LLC; why ever deal with him? Deal with him in court. Force him to sue you."

But with no money coming from Dash to pay the staff, Smokey Fontaine decided that it was easier to close the magazine and start again elsewhere.

The media coverage of Dash turned skeptical. In May 2005, a fashion trade magazine reported Damon Dash's imminent exit from his most successful company, Rocawear, which he had built largely without input from Jay-Z, and of which he still owned 25 percent. Both Dash and co-owner Alex Bize denied the rumors. But the rumors, again, were true.

Why are we meeting here? Dash asked.

So nobody can hear you screaming, they replied.

Jay-Z, Bize, and Norton Cher had asked Dash to join them not in Rocawear's offices, but in a hotel suite. For the first time in the company's history, Jay-Z had thrown his 25 percent of the company in with Bize and Cher to override a decision that Dash had made. Dash wanted to spend $3 million for yet another proposed Mario Testino ad campaign to be shot with Kevin Bacon and Naomi Campbell, this time in the South of France. His partners told him it was too much money, and he would have to cancel. Instead, they would do another, less expensive photo shoot featuring Jay-Z, shot by Mark Seliger.

The new Testino shoot was, in reality, the final provocation that Bize and Cher needed to wrest control of Rocawear from Dash, because now Jay-Z saw that Dash's mania was crippling the company. Dash's spending was out of control. His lifestyle was looting the corporate coffers. His new fashion ventures—not only State Property, but Team Roc and the Damon Dash Collection—were bleeding money and diverting resources, as Dash had a significant number of employees working on these baby brands. His last Rocawear photo shoot—also with Bacon and Campbell—featured no Rocawear clothes at all, but instead placement for many of Dash's other products, like Armadale, Tiret, and the Dash Collection. Another Dash boondoggle was out of the question.

The new dynamic among the four Rocawear partners—three against one—presaged the inevitable buyout and departure of Damon Dash, and transformed the company almost immediately. Dash's cronies were purged. Rocawear ceased paying the $35,000-per-month rent on Dash's London pad. Many of Rocawear's beleaguered employees no longer cringed under Dash's often moody reign. But others, even some of the seasoned fashion-industry professionals, missed Dash's presence around the company that he built. While it was true that Rocawear sold its clothes around Jay-Z's image, without Damon Dash there would have been no company at all. Dash, in his best moments, had been creative, supportive, and fun to be around.

One month after denying his impending exit, Dash began lashing out in the press against Rocawear, distancing himself from the line and the new ad campaign—even appearing at MAGIC in Las Vegas at the far end of the Rocawear booth, telling a trade reporter, "I'm only here to push PRO-Keds, Team Roc, and State Property."

In late September 2005 it was official. The company announced that Dash had been bought out of Rocawear for $22.5 million in cash and other considerations that included his State Property and PRO-Keds brands, bringing the total value of the buyout to a reported $30 million.

Several observers noted that the cashout seemed low, considering Rocawear's stated gross sales, reported inconsistently at somewhere between $350 to $450 million. But the actual figure was even lower than that. For the company he built and guided, Dash received just $7 million cash and a $5 million promissory note. It may have meant that Rocawear was drastically overstating its earnings in the same way that Phat Farm had, or perhaps Dash was being debited for the expenses he foisted on the company.

Jay-Z announced he would be taking a more active role in running Rocawear. The situation was particularly galling for Dash, because he had always struggled to get Jay more involved. *Imagine,* he thought, *how much more money we would have made if he had done this sooner.*

Dash publicly disparaged the new direction of Rocawear. He accused his former partners of using cheaper fabrics and narrowing his original vision for a mainstream company. They were making Rocawear "ghetto," as far as Dash was concerned. "Corny," Dash called it, the ultimate Harlem insult. This wasn't the way you operated if you were building a brand. This was the way you operated if you were after a quick buck.

After all, Dash thought, *there's more to business than making money.*

As Def Jam's new president, Jay-Z oversaw successful new albums by Kanye West and Ghostface Killah, and shepherded the debuts of rapper Young Jeezy and a new teenage singer named Rihanna. He even lured his onetime rival Nas to the label. But at the end of 2006, the president of Def Jam contributed to the annual fourth-quarter push in a way that no other Def Jam executive ever had: He recorded an album himself.

Kingdom Come contained fourteen new tracks, including three produced by Dr. Dre. In one of those tracks, "Lost One," Jay-Z seemed to be challenging Dash's remaining claim on his career. *If you're running around telling everyone that you "made me,"* Jay goaded Dash, *then make* another *me.*

Jay-Z's retirement thus proved itself merely a sabbatical, a crucial break during which he could get his business affairs in order: control of his recording career, control of his label, and control of his clothing company. Within months, everyone would see how important that control really was.

Chris Lighty was in London, on tour with 50 Cent, Snoop Dogg, and Sean "Puffy" Combs—who had over the course of the last decade changed his brand name from "Puff Daddy" to "P. Diddy," and now just "Diddy."

Lighty and Combs were riding together from Heathrow to the hotel in the back of a Maybach when Combs got the news over the phone. Jay-Z, Alex Bize, and Norton Cher had just sold the rights to the Rocawear trademark to a public company, Iconix Brand Group. Bize and Cher would depart, and Jay-Z, John Meneilly, and his team would stay on to run the Roc Apparel Group, which would continue to create and manufacture the Rocawear brand and foster new ones.

Lighty could not stop repeating the number he heard, as he stared at Combs in disbelief.

"Two hundred million? Two hundred million?"

Actually, at $219 million, the sale of the Rocawear mark was the biggest deal in hip-hop history. Combs—whose own Sean John line had finally won the coveted Council of Fashion Designers menswear award in 2004, taking its place among previous winners like Calvin Klein and Ralph Lauren—responded in the only way he knew how.

"I need a *billion* for mine," he huffed.

But of those two men, it would be Lighty who reached that symbolic mark first. Just two months later, in May 2007, the Coca-Cola Company purchased Glacéau for $4.1 billion. It was just as Rohan Oza had once predicted to Darryl Cobbin, although for an amount that even Oza could scarcely imagine.

In the media, initial reports put 50 Cent's cashout at $400 million, calculated by dividing the purchase amount by 50 Cent's reputed 10 percent share.

But in reality, 50 Cent's take was much less. Another stakeholder needed to be paid off first—the diversified Indian conglomerate Tata had invested $677 million for 30 percent of Glacéau in 2006, and got $1.2 billion when Coca-Cola bought them out.

When all the other costs had been deducted, 50 Cent was thought to have walked away with a figure somewhere between $60 million and $100 million, putting his net worth at nearly a half billion dollars.

On his next album, 50 Cent could barely contain his own incredulity at the power of the dollar. "I took quarter-water, sold it in bottles for two bucks," he rapped. "Coca-Cola came and bought it for billions. What the fuck?"

But Lighty silently pocketed his 15 percent and kept it moving.

On the evening of March 12, 2007, a few days after the sale of Rocawear, the thirty-seven-year-old rapper mounted the stage at Manhattan's Waldorf-Astoria Hotel.

Wearing a suit and sneakers, Shawn "Jay-Z" Carter faced hundreds of influential and powerful people from the music business, past and present: Mo Ostin, who built Warner Bros. Records by signing Jimi Hendrix, Prince, and Madonna; and Lyor Cohen, Warner Music Group's current CEO. Onstage, Carter followed no greater legends than Aretha Franklin and Keith Richards of the Rolling Stones.

Now Carter was one of them, not only as a recording artist who had sold more than twenty-three million albums over the course of his eleven-year career, but as a record company president, a fashion mogul, a restaurateur, and, more recently, part owner of the New Jersey Nets basketball team.

As if to make that point, Carter reached into his pocket and produced a BlackBerry, from which he read a speech that would, for the first time, induct a hip-hop group into the Rock and Roll Hall of Fame.

"Grandmaster Flash and the Furious Five," Carter said, "became hip-hop's first supergroup."

Carter proclaimed Flash as one-third of hip-hop's holy trinity—three DJs from the Bronx who had given birth to the genre in the 1970s: Kool Herc, Flash, and Afrika Bambaataa.

"What Les Paul and Chuck Berry did for the guitar, Flash did for the turntables," Carter explained to the mostly White and middle-aged crowd at the Rock Hall event.

"Thirty years later," Carter continued, "Rappers have become rock stars, movie stars, leaders, educators, philanthropists . . . even CEOs." The luminaries in the audience laughed at Carter's nod to himself. Both Jay-Z and hip-hop had come a long way.

"But none of this would be possible," Carter concluded, "without the work of the men I have the honor of inducting into the Rock and Roll Hall of Fame tonight."

Grandmaster Flash & the Furious Five walked in from the wings, each pausing to embrace Carter. At the podium, Flash humbly affirmed the spiritual connection between hip-hop and rock and roll. Next, Scorpio, one of the Flash's five original MCs, practically begged Carter and Kevin Liles—Carter's predecessor at Def Jam, and now Cohen's right hand at Warner—to give the aging group a record deal. When it was Melle Mel's turn at the mic, the craggy, irascible forty-five-year-old MC dispensed with the niceties, accusing "the industry people out there" of turning hip-hop into a "culture of violence," instead of the "culture of music" it once was.

Melle Mel may well have been addressing the three people in the room who most fit that description: Lyor Cohen, Kevin Liles, and Carter himself, who between them were responsible for a third of the rap hits on the charts at that moment.

Mel decried the vapidity of the music promoted by these executives, much as a corner café owner might rail against the coming of a corporate chain store. But without the likes of Cohen and Carter, it is doubtful that hip-hop would have survived long enough for its forebears to be honored by the Rock Hall on that night. After all, the two people who produced the very first rap records weren't even present at the gala. Bobby Robinson, eighty-nine, sat in his apartment, blocks from the Harlem storefront where he founded Enjoy Records, which released Flash's first single, "Superrappin'." The seventy-one-year-old Sylvia Robinson—who produced the first rap hit, "Rapper's Delight," and Grandmaster Flash & the Furious Five's signature song, "The Message"—lay in a New Jersey hospital bed, sick with pneumonia. Both of those entrepreneurs had gotten to hip-hop first. But neither was able to convert their advantage into lasting commercial success. Nor, for that matter, were Grandmaster Flash and Melle Mel.

Like the early figures of rock and roll, the first people in the hip-hop business failed for a variety of reasons, like naïveté and greed, but foremost among them was a lack of perspective. The artists, entrepreneurs, and executives who succeeded had one thing in common: the vision of hip-hop as a culture without boundaries. The successful people who lasted long enough to see hip-hop truly fulfill that global vision possessed something else altogether.

Hip-hop, like all pop culture, had been created by an extraordinary partnership between two kinds of individuals: artists and businesspeople. But the source of hip-hop's singular, spectacular rise was that hip-hop bred individuals who can be both. People like Sean "P. Diddy" Combs. People like Curtis "50 Cent" Jackson. And people like Shawn "Jay-Z" Carter, who gained his perch atop the rap world—instead of Melle Mel and Flash and the Robinsons, instead of any number of artists, entrepreneurs, or executives who had arrived, flowered, and then faded—because he was endowed with the two essentials for success in the entertainment business: the soul of a poet, and the instincts of a killer.

"Baby Chris and Chris Lighty are two different people," Grandmaster Flash had once told Lighty. "Baby Chris was a criminal. Chris Lighty is a businessman."

Lighty's mother, a devout Jehovah's Witness, had once told him, "If you want to succeed, you have to be ten times better than the White kid next to you."

So every morning, before he dressed, Lighty consulted his daily schedule. He chose his outfit consciously. If he was just going into the office, he might wear jeans and a button-down shirt. But if he had a meeting, say, with corporations like Johnson & Johnson or an agency like DDB Worldwide, he'd select one of his many suits, maybe a Giorgio Armani.

Of his company, Violator, Lighty had said: "We are able to articulate 125th Street to the corporate boardroom, while at the same time protect the integrity and nuances of the streets."

Lighty took his job seriously. He answered his e-mails promptly. He made sure his voice mail was never full. His clients, his partners, and hip-hop itself deserved nothing less.

Nearly two decades had passed since Lyor Cohen forced Lighty to choose his path. And even though Lighty had felt spurned at times by his former benefactor, Lighty never forgot how, with that ultimatum—*do you want to be that guy or this guy?*—Cohen saved his life. Now they were all working together again: Cohen, Lighty, Simmons, Liles, Greenwald, Moscowitz. The former Def Jam crew now ran at least a quarter of the American music business.

Lighty's first crew, the Violators, had followed him on the straight path. They were now grown men with good city jobs and pensions. Chris Ali had just received his master's degree from the College of New Rochelle and had been hired, ironically, as a guidance counselor.

Lighty himself had come from the indignity of life in the projects to the honor of planning his first mentor Red Alert's fiftieth birthday party, complete with flyers done up to look like the old uptown parties from back in the day.

"Why are you telling everyone my age?" Red had complained.

"You gotta embrace it," Lighty responded. "It's great that you can be fifty in hip-hop. You *look* fifty. You ain't fooling nobody."

Lighty considered their good fortune. After all, so many of them hadn't made it.

The late DJ Scott La Rock's partner, KRS-One, gave a raucous live performance in Prospect Park on a sultry August night in Brooklyn, 2007. Twenty years earlier, a hip-hop show in Brooklyn might have been marred by fights and, perhaps, gunfire. But Brooklyn had changed. In 2007, a KRS-One concert was family friendly; and the artist who had been the epitome of new school in the late 1980s was now decidedly old-school.

In the audience with his wife and young sons was James Bernard.

It had been Bernard, along with Reginald C. Dennis, who had worked behind the scenes at the Rock and Roll Hall of Fame to nominate Grandmaster Flash as the first hip-hop inductee. Bernard and Dennis couldn't get a table at the induction ceremony, so they had to sneak in.

Bernard had returned to a career of union organizing and education consulting. But it surprised him that people from all walks of life—especially big-time professional business folks—fawned over Bernard's hip-hop credentials more than his Ivy League pedigree.

It was truly surreal how far everyone had come. *Grandmaster Flash is in the Rock Hall. Jay-Z is president of Def Jam and owns a basketball team. Lyor Cohen runs the Warner Music Group, and Rick Rubin is the chief creative officer of Columbia Records. Four of the top-selling rap artists of* *all time—Tupac, Eminem, Jay-Z, and the Beastie Boys—have collectively sold over a hundred million records, each alone surpassing the sales of legends like the Beach Boys, Johnny Cash, Stevie Wonder, and Bob Marley. Rappers who couldn't get videos into regular rotation on MTV are now Hollywood icons: Ice Cube was a gangster rapper; now he's a matinee teddy bear. Queen Latifah was a Native Tongue; now she's an Academy Award nominee and a jazz singer. Ice-T, the composer of "Cop Killer," has been making his living for nearly a decade playing a cop on TV. And Will Smith makes $20 million a picture. Corporations now readily employ that hip-hop invention, the "street team." Hip-hop slang issues from the mouths of television anchors and politicians, and words like "dis" and "props" and even "bling" have taken their place in the American lexicon. Hip-hop is spoken in almost every major language across the globe. All of the current candidates for president in France have their own rap theme songs. In West Africa and the Caribbean, children wear Tupac T-shirts and people place portraits of the slain rapper in their homes and at their businesses. In Japan, breakdancers congregate in Tokyo's famous Yoyogi Park. In Israel and Palestine, a feud between pro-Zionist rapper Subliminal and Palestinian rapper Tamar bears an eerie Middle Eastern echo of the feud between the Notorious B.I.G. and Tupac.*

Truly surreal, Bernard thought. Even his old friend from Harvard Law, Barack Obama, had just announced his candidacy for president of the United States.

"I hope that I'm inspiring someone tonight to go after their dreams," KRS-One said from the stage.

"You can't see it, because it's dark, but right back here, in 1980, I was homeless. I was sleeping right here," the rapper said, "me and a couple of other guys.

"We used to visualize.

"I used to say, 'Yo, one day, we gon' rock this park.'

"You know, it's so crazy. . . .

"Because I'm in my dreams *right now.*"

EPILOGUE

HARLEM,
NOVEMBER 4, 2008

125th Street begins its journey at the East River. From there it slices straight across the Harlem plain, banks right through the gorge separating Morningside Heights from Hamilton Heights, and stops dead at the mighty Hudson.

More than two hundred years have passed since Alexander Hamilton settled in the hills here, the master of American capital. Four score have transpired since this thoroughfare ranked as America's cultural capital. Twenty years ago the man-made canyon of 125th had decayed into a windswept, drug-ridden relic of its glorious past. But on this chilly night in early November 2008 the crowds have returned once more to Harlem's Main Street.

Many of the old theaters and nightclubs from the 1920s have disappeared, but thousands now crowd outside the one that remains: Apollo, still gleaming with its iconic neon logo and new liquid-crystal marquee. The clothing stores for the hustlers and strivers of the 1970s and 1980s—A. J. Lester's and Dapper Dan's—are gone too, along with the heroin and crack that fueled much of the economy here. So are the bodegas with bulletproof Plexiglas, the sidewalks outside them, once littered with broken bottles and discarded tobacco from packages of Phillies Blunts, swept clean. In their place, corporate America has finally arrived: the Starbucks halfway between Sylvia's Restaurant and the Lenox Lounge, where Miles and Coltrane used to play; the H&M clothing store down the block from the Hotel Teresa where Malcolm X kept his headquarters; the Old Navy across from the Apollo. Once, 125th Street was one of the rare places where a Black man could open his own business. But a few months ago, the real estate specula-tors pushed out the first colored man to do so, ninety-one-year-old Bobby Robinson—the proprietor of Bobby's Happy House and Enjoy Records. Other neighborhood businesses have fallen as new condominiums for the rich rise.

In the twenty-first century, it's success that's killing Harlem.

African-American entrepreneurs, no longer confined to America's ghet-tos, can now set up shop anywhere they please. But they're on 125th Street in spirit, their faces and products adorning the billboards that overlook this crowded canyon tonight: Sean John, Rocawear, Phat Farm. Even the nieces of Russell Simmons have their own marquee now, Angela and Vanessa, the daughters of Run, hawking their clothing line, Pastry.

This is the Harlem that hip-hop built. The young who've come here to-night can scarcely remember a time when the faces of Jay-Z and Sean Combs didn't peer down at them from the skies as modern demigods. They have no reference for the time before hip-hop: when rappers couldn't get their re-cords played on radio or shown on TV; when Black artists of any genre were asked, literally, to make their music sound and make themselves look Whiter; when Black actors and actresses didn't star in summer blockbuster films; when Black women who actually looked like Black women didn't grace the covers of magazines; when young Black men and women didn't own multimillion-dollar companies based on selling their own culture to the nation and the world.

From the time the Sugar Hill Gang hit the American airwaves, the cul-ture of America has been steadily "browning." The benefits accorded to all, as Wonder Mike once rapped with prescience: the Black, White, red, brown, and yellow. From hip-hop, but even more so its diverse fan base, a vision of America's new Manifest Destiny: multiracial, multicultural, and willing to revel in differences rather than suppress them. That vision is manifest on 125th Street tonight.

Hip-hop was not the sole cause of this cultural transformation. The door was opened in the 1980s by Bill Cosby, Michael Jackson, Prince, Michael Jordan, Oprah Winfrey—the icons of Black crossover. But the young White Americans who are here in Harlem tonight grew up on hip-hop. They jumped with House of Pain and Kris Kross. They cried at the deaths of Tupac and Biggie. They rode with Dr. Dre and Snoop. They partied with Puffy and Jay-Z, danced with Jennifer Lopez and Beyoncé—symbolic of the rise of a new, multiracial beauty aesthetic, the cultural dividend of "Baby Got Back" and other peans to the Black and brown female form. The movies they saw and the TV shows they watched starred the icons of rap—Queen Latifah and Ice-T, Ice Cube and Will Smith. And they are here tonight because they believe that a Black man can save the world. Young White Americans have already voted overwhelmingly for the Black presidential candidate, Senator Barack Obama of Illinois.

Ironically, most of today's young hip-hop fans came of age after the decline of overtly political hip-hop. Twenty years have passed since Public Enemy's sonic manifesto, *It Takes a Nation of Millions to Hold Us Back*. Political calls to action were drowned out long ago by more insistent urgings of weed, guns, girls, and champagne. But Russell Simmons, hip-hop's sophomoric sage, has it right: *Hip-hop succeeded not by being correct. It succeeded by being.* In its materialistic ubiquity, hip-hop won. While hip-hop's critics bemoaned the text, they forgot the power of the subtext: Twenty years ago, no rappers in the top twenty. This year, they are ten of the top twenty. In 2003, for the first time in history, every artist in the Billboard Top 10 was Black; most of their fans were White. This isn't crossover anymore. It is takeover. America has officially been remixed.

Instead of political artists, hip-hop's businessmen and journalists now lead the practical political charge. Simmons, once decidedly apolitical, now runs the Hip-Hop Summit Action Network with former NAACP chair Ben Chavis. Two former contributors to *The Source*, Billy Wimsatt and Bakari Kitwana, helped found the League of Young Voters and the National Hip-Hop Political Convention, respectively. And in the weeks before the election, Kevin Liles led a barnstorming, multicity tour of the swing states with Simmons, Jay-Z, Sean Combs, Beyoncé, and Mary J. Blige, drawing crowds and registering voters by the thousands.

If hip-hop is becoming a political force without being political, its candidate is hip-hop without being hip-hop. Barack Obama, at forty-seven years old, isn't a rap junkie, but his own multiracial, multicultural mélange seems to embody hip-hop's vision of America.

Obama, like hip-hop, has his skeptics. Can a politician like Obama really be an agent of change? Once in power, won't he become beholden to power, and a part of the structure? When people or things become successful, they become debased. Just like with hip-hop, as ensconced as any other pop music genre now. Its leaders, its entrepreneurs, its executives—from Jay-Z to Russell Simmons—have sold their greatest assets. Billions have been made. Little wealth has been shared. Hip-hop's cultural legacy may be long, but its economic coattails for the Black community seem short. Despite Black cultural dominance, there still is no great Black-owned major record company, no film studio. The winning paradigm—for hip-hop in particular and Black America in general—seems to be the joint venture. Indeed, just six months ago, Jay-Z left Def Jam and announced a new $150 million partnership with Live Nation, a tour-promoting, venue-owning behemoth. Jay-Z's new company, Roc Nation, will split with Live Nation the proceeds for almost every aspect of the artist's career—deemphasizing record sales, which have declined industry-wide by a third since the beginning of the decade, for more profitable enterprises like touring, merchandising, endorsement deals, and entrepreneurship. Perhaps hip-hop's lasting legacy won't be the creation of an independent power base, but the penetration of the power structure; not a declaration of independence, but a viral revolution. For hip-hop and for Barack Obama, time will reveal.

The crowds in front of the Adam Clayton Powell State Office Building stare at the Jumbotron. At precisely 11:00 p.m., when the networks announce that Barack Obama has been elected the forty-fourth president of the United States, a loud cheer fills the plaza and the intersection beyond it. Friends and family grab one another, shouting and weeping. American flags come out—who knew Harlem had so many flags in hiding? *Guess what, America, we love you. . . .*

Down in Times Square, where the son of "Pretty Melvin" Combs raises his fist on a billboard ten stories above the multitudes, there's another party going on. But up in Harlem, the people celebrate the uptown way.

Across from the massive television screen, a DJ drops the needle on "Ain't No Stoppin' Us Now," by McFadden & Whitehead—the same record to which DJ Hollywood sang, rapped, and danced his routines thirty years ago.

As the evening progresses, the music regresses. A New Orleans–style second line trails behind a pickup jazz band that meanders down the street and comes to a stop in front of the Lenox Lounge, the crowd shouting, "Obama!" in rhythm. In the street, hand-clapping teenagers "get lite"— dance steps so new that they haven't yet made it to the mainstream. By midnight, the drum circles form all along 125th Street.

Throughout the morning, the shouts and beats echo from the East River to the Hudson. You can hear the drums all the way up on Alexander Hamilton's old estate on Sugar Hill, the sounds of the sons and daughters of Africa, shareholders at last in the joint venture of the New World.

ACKNOWLEDGMENTS

The creation of *The Big Payback* was not a solitary accomplishment. I am humbled by the support of the following people:

I doubt I could have completed this work without the encouragement, endorsement, and advice of Bill Adler. Back in 1987 when I was a college student, Bill launched my career in hip-hop journalism by furnishing me a backstage pass to interview the headliners of the Def Jam Tour. Ever since then, Bill Adler has given me, and many of my peers, the gift of his mentorship, and a dose of his fierce musical and moral sense. He was my consigliere for the duration of my research and writing, selfless with his time and gracious in sharing his famed Adler Archive. To him, and to his family—Sara, Ruth and Sam—I send gratitude and love.

In 1989 Bill Stephney read my college thesis on racism in the music business and offered me a job. His act of validation, an assurance that my voice mattered, sustains me to this day. Though I never ended up working for Bill, he introduced me to his mentor, Rick Rubin, who employed me for seven years and to whom I owe similar thanks for his support. Special thanks to Tanya Cepeda Stephney for her enthusiasm and keen eye.

David Dunton, my agent, believed in the concept for this book from its inception as a one-page proposal. His commitment sold this book, and his steady hand and tough love kept me delivering. I'm also indebted to Sophia Chang, who lent her valuable and generous assistance throughout my project and—along with Laurie Liss and Hank Shocklee—put me on the road to becoming a published author.

I created the proposal for this book under the stern, loving guidance of Samuel G. Freedman, the best writing coach I've ever had. His guidance, and that of my fellow classmates in Freedman's seminar, Book Writing, at the Columbia Graduate School of Journalism, made this work possible. On my honor roll are the members of the Writers Bloc who labored over my earliest pages: Daniel Weiss, Jody Rosen Knower, and Lauren Weber. Lauren gets extra credit for introducing me to my wife.

How fitting that a book about hip-hop's triumph over the naysayers would meet initial resistance from many publishers. But Mark Chait, my editor, did not have to be sold. In my eyes, he resembles the heroes of this book who understood both hip-hop's historical import and its commercial potential. Mark graciously gave me time, insight, and a wide berth to write. For his valor, Mark deserves his own big payback. So, too, do the champions of this book at New American Library/Penguin, including Kara Welsh, Talia Platz, Frank Walgren, Craig Burke, and Heather Connor. Special thanks to my copyeditor, Tiffany Yates.

The Big Payback was funded in part by a Pulitzer fellowship and a Lynton Book Writing prize, both awarded by the faculty of the Columbia Graduate School of Journalism. Many thanks to Dean Nicholas Lemann, David Klatell, and Lynnell Hancock; Sree Sreenivasan, Melanie Huff, and Julie Hartenstein; to professors June Cross, Richard C. Wald, Bruce Porter, Nancy Sharkey, Mel McRay, David Blum, and Tony Dec; and to my mentor, Michael Scherer. Special thanks are due to Kim Nauer, and to all my RW1 comrades, including Phil Wabha, Christy Nicholson, Lia Araujo, Sarah Feightner, Austin Fido, Erin Fuchs, Jessica Heasley, Anne Machalinski, Alli McConnon, Kristina Parker, Renee Rosen, Brooke Sopelsa, Jesse Torrisi, Alexander Waterfield, Leinz Vales, Lawrence Strauss; and Robert Wagner, the Handsome American.

The Big Payback began in 1999 as a proposed magazine article called "Last Night a DJ Saved My Business," about the first generation of white, ethnic entrepreneurs whose disco-and-dance record labels were saved by rap music. More than anyone, Reginald C. Dennis encouraged my idea, and he has had my back ever since. I am eternally grateful to the founders of *The Source*, Jonathan Shecter and Dave Mays, James Bernard and Ed Young, for inviting me to be a part of the birth of their magazine. Shout out to my *Source* colleagues: Matty Capoluongo, Rob "Reef" Tewlow, dream hampton, Kierna Mayo, Chris Wilder, Disco, and the whole crew.

This book rests upon the foundation laid by the writers and authors who created the canon of hip-hop history, among them David Toop (*Rap Attack*), Nelson George (*The Death of Rhythm & Blues* and *Hip Hop America*), Stacy Gueraseva (*Def Jam, Inc.*), Michael Gonzales and Havelock Nelson (*Bring the Noise*), Bill Adler (*Tougher Than Leather*), Ronin Ro (*Have Gun Will Travel*), Alan Light (*The Vibe History of Hip-Hop* and *The Skills to Pay the Bills*), Brian Cross (*It's Not About a Salary*), Jim Fricke and Charlie Ahearn (*Yes Yes Y'all*), Cheo Hodari Coker (*Unbelievable*), Ethan Brown (*Queens Reigns Supreme*). Stan Cornyn's *Exploding* was also helpful, as was RZA's *The Tao of Wu* and *Ego Trip's Book of Rap Lists*. I am indebted to the serious scholarship and oral histories of the Web sites WestCoastPioneers.com, Gregory "G-Bone" Everett's Ultrawave online almanac, and JayQuan's thafoundation.com. For their friendship and support I would like to thank Brian Coleman, who wrote hip-hop's finest musical history, *Check the Technique*; and Jeff Chang, author of the great book that set the bar for us all, *Can't Stop Won't Stop*.

Respect goes out to my colleagues in the fraternity/sorority of hip-hop journalism, including Cheo H. Coker, Harry Allen, John Leland, Nelson George, Bonz Malone, Sheena Lester, Michael Gonzales, Havelock Nelson, Serena Kim, Soren Baker, Bakari Kitwana, Hua Hsu, Raquel Cepeda, Jason King, Minya Oh, John Caramanica, Billy Wimsatt, Chairman Mao, Elliott Wilson, Adario Strange. Special shout to Jay Smooth for keeping us all honest. Warm regards to my comrades in ACT: Elizabeth Mendez-Berry, Joe Schloss, MiRi Park, Martha Cooper. I'm indebted to Sacha Jenkins for allowing me access to the Ego Trip archives. Thanks also to the editors for whom I've worked: Andre Torres, Leah Furman, Daisy Hernández, Josh duLac, Peter Kaufman, Richard Leiby, Andrea Kowalski, Erica Rodefer.

Many thanks to my mentors in the entertainment business: Cory Robbins, who gave me my first rap industry job; Rick Rubin, who believed in me; Forest Whitaker and Mio Vukovic; Tom Silverman, a friend and teacher; Jim Biederman, and Jesse Collins. Praise is due to Russell Simmons, whose nonstop hustle allowed us all to eat.

I don't know what I would have done without the resourcefulness and toil of my research assistant, the great Lisa Payton. Likewise, I want to thank Kelly Jackson, Adisa Banjoko, Sarika Chopra, Cedric Thornton and Cortney Charnas, who all came to my aid in key moments.

The following people were instrumental in my research—whether helping me strategize, sharing their contacts, tracking people down, pulling favors, providing access, schooling me, or giving me feedback: Adrian Miller, Alonzo Brown, Andy Tavel, Billy Jam, Charles Stettler, Doug Young, Emil Wilbekin, Fab 5 Freddy, Freddy Fresh, Gerard Babitts, James Lopez, Johann Kugelberg, John Mietus, Esq., Lanise and Denise Benjamin, Lauren Wirtzer, Marisol Segal, Michael "Emz" Greene, and Karen Rait and Roy Trakin.

Even a book with as large a scope as *The Big Payback* has its limits. My gratitude and heartfelt apologies go out to the very important people who generously shared their incredible stories with me—stories that I wasn't able to include in the final edit: Ed Eckstine, Aaron Fuchs, Eric Brooks, Ern Llamado, Faith Newman-Orbach, Gary Harris, David Gossett, Helena Echegoyan, Larkin Arnold, MC Serch, Kevvy Kev Montague, Amanda Scheer-Demme, and DJ Muggs.

I am eternally grateful for the kindness and openness of each and every person who allowed me to interview them for this book. Those that haven't already been thanked in the preceding paragraphs are Adam Dubin, Al Teller, Alan Light, Alex Mejia, Ali Shaheed Muhammed, Andre Brown, Andre Harrell, Andy Borowitz, Angelo Anastasio, Ann Carli, Anne-Marie Reggie, Anthony "DJ Hollywood" Holloway, Anthony Samad, Atron Gregory, Barry Mayo, Ben Fong-Torres, Ben Soco-lov, Beni B, Benny Medina, Bert Padell, Bill Curtis, Bob Merlis, Bobbito Garcia, Bobby Robinson, Brett Wright, Brian Samson, Bruce Reiner, Bryan Turner, Bryna Naftaly, Cameron Paul, Carmen Ashhurst, Carmine Petruzello, Carol Smith, Carolyn Baker, Carsten Willer, Cedric Walker, Chris Ali, Chris Joyce, Chris Lasalle, Chris Lighty, Chuck D, Cynamin Jones, Damon Dash, Dana Hill, Daniel Glass, Danny Schechter, Danyel Smith, Darryl Cobbin, Darryl Thompson, Dasez, Dave Lighty, Dave Morales, David "Davey D" Cook, David Paul, Diane Harris, Dino Delvaille, Dionne Warwick, Don Macmillan, Donna Jones, Doug Herzog, Duk-Ki Yu, Ed Chalpin, Eddie O'Loughlin, Frank Lozano, Frank Owen, Fred Munao, Gale Sparrow, Gary Davis, Gary J. Casson, Geoff Weiss, Gerald Levin, Gerry Thomas, Gil Rogin, Glenn White, Grandmaster Caz, Greg Mack, Greg Sandow, H. Edward Young, Hammer, Hank Shocklee, Harold Austin, Hosh Gureli, Howard Shecter, Howard Thompson, Howie Klein, J. B. Moore, Jac Benson, Jack Allen, James "Ed Lover" Roberts, Jamie Roberts, Jenette Kahn, Jeff Pollack, Jeff Sledge, Jeff Swierk, Jeff Tweedy, Jeff Wyatt, Jen Demme, Jerry Heller, Jesse Maidbrey, Jocelyn Cooper, Joel Salkowitz, Jon Coleman, Jon Rifkind, Jonathan Van Meter, Jorge Hinojosa, Josefa Salinas, Joseph "Reverend Run" Simmons, Judy Ellis, Jules Rifkind, Julia Chance, Julie Greenwald, Julio G, Keith Naftaly, Kevin Liles, Kevin Mitchell, Kevin Powell, Kevon Glickman, Khalid Shah, Kim Hughes, King Tech, Kool DJ Red Alert, Kool Moe Dee, Kurtis Blow, Large Professor, Len Fichtelberg, Lenny Waronker, Leyla Turkkan, Lionel Ridenour, Lisa Cortes, Liz Nealon, Liz Swados, Lonzo Williams, Lynda West, Lyor Cohen, Manny Bella, Manny Velazquez, Mark Goldstein, Mark Siegel, Martha Diaz, Master P, Meg Cox, Michael "Serch" Berrin, Michael Aczon, Michael Fuchs, Michael Holman, Michael McDonald, Michael Ostin, Michael Ross, Michelle Mercer Bazemore, Mike Espindle, Mike Parker, Mimi Valdes, Mitchell "Divine" Diggs, Mitchell Krasnow, Mo Ostin, Monica Lynch, Monte Lipman, Morey Alexander, Mr. Magic, Murray Elias, Nancy Heller, Nick and Eric Vidal, Nick deKrechewo, O. J. Wedlaw, Oli "Power" Grant, Paris, Patrick Moxey, Paul Stewart, Paul Winley, Peter Dougherty, Peter Lubin, Peter Thea, Pierre Bouvard, Quincy Jones, Ralph McDaniels, Ranadeb Choudhury, Reggie Griffin, Reginald Jolley, Renay Palome Dodge, Ric Menello, Ricardo Frazer, Rich Isaacson, Rick Cummings, Rick Joseph, Rob Stone, Robin Wolaner, Rocco Macri, Rohan Oza, Ron Bienstock, Ron DeLord, Ron Demichael, Ron Rose, Ronald Skoler, Roy Edmondson, Ruza Blue, Sal Abbatiello, Scarface, Schott "Free" Jacobs, Scott Poulson-Bryant, Sean Ross, Sophie Bramly, Steve Greenberg, Steve Knutson, Steve Plotnicki, Steve Ralbovsky, Steve Rifkind, Steve Smith, Steve Yano, Steven Baker, Sue Drew, Sway, T La Rock, Ted Field, Teymour Butrous-Ghali, Tim Mandelbaum, Tobin Costen, Todd Moscowitz, Tommy Quon, Tony Gonzalez, Tony Gray, Tony

Quarterone, Tracey Miller, Tyrone Williams, Violet Brown, Vito Bruno, Walter Zelnick, Ward White, Wendy Credle, Wendy Day, Will Socolov.

The following people went out of their way to help me communicate with their clients or employers: Adair Curtis, Alexander Robb, Allison Bergstrand, Anna Willard, Billy Moore, Diondrea Tribbet, Donna Torrence, Fred Hanba, Heidi Ellen Robinson Fitzgerald, Jackie Davis, Jana Fleishman, Janine at Wu Music, Jared Malamed, Jody Miller, Kate Snedeker, Katharine Chang, Lauren Thompson, Laurie Dobbins, Lindsay Chase, Marie Maullon, Michelle Rice, Miles Carroll, Rachel Carr, Rachel Noerdlinger, Rasheem Barker, Rema Zarwi, Rex Polkinghorne, Shirea Carroll, Tamika Layton, Tamika McCormack, Whiteboy at Fever Records.

Thanks to the photographers who were kind enough to license their work for this book: Bobby Grossman, Dana Lixenberg, Christine Smith, David Salidor, Janette Beckman, Chi Modu and Steve Proctor, Pat Johnson, and the legendary Ricky Powell.

These good folks came through with help in a pinch: Bob Kranes, Carmelita Sanchez, Dana Perry, Dee Brown, Eric Mar, Geoff Weiss, Jane Turkewitz, Joy Bailey, Kate Miller, Teresa Wiltz, Tony Abner, Tracey Cooper.

I appreciate the hard and quick work of EMG Music Clearance: Evan Greenspan, Lloyd Cook, and Mary Montes De Oca.

Much appreciation to the bosses whose trust and understanding enabled me to write and work for them simultaneously: Ryan Dadd, Steven Murray, Michelle Kerrigan, Smokey Fontaine, and Tom Newman. Thanks to my former colleagues and their families, including: Adrian Jank, Alexis Yates, Alicia Dadd, Brian Smith, Cliff Tomczyk, Dalmar James, Danny Ornelas, Donal Neligan, E. J. DeCoske, Jamey Wishner, Janet Hagan, Jim and Deb Fennell, Mark "Boogie" Bugayong, Matt Carrano, Michael Pico, Mike Beck, Rashaun Hall, Roger McAulay, Sara Murray, Stacia Bedford, Steve Yanosey, Warren Wolfson. And a special shout to my current crew: Ashton Lattimore, Big Ced Thornton, Bill Johnson, Casey Gane-McCalla, Danielle "D Cheezy" Cheesman, Dave Hall, Deborah Bennett, Iliana Rabun-Wood, Jeanene James, Jerry Barrow, Nazneen Patel, Shamika Sanders, and the rest of the staff at Interactive One.

Much respect to industry legends like Alison Pember, Big Boy, Carlito Rodriguez, Chris Landry, David Belgrave, Eric Lobato, Fuzzy, Ill Will Fulton, Jamieson Grillo, Jennifer Norwood, Joe Quixx, Kutmasta Kurt, Orlando Aguillen, Raaka, Rachel Crick, Rhettmatic, Scoop and Shanda, Scott Gordon, Sean Carasov, Tyesh Harris, and countless others.

The following artists provided the soundtrack for the creation of *The Big Payback*: Kerri Chandler, Phonte Coleman, Nicolay, DJ Brainchild, Coltrane, Miles, Sir Duke, Monk, Shuggie, 4Hero, Dwele, Onra, Jill, Erykah, Roberson, Primo, Timbo, and Ski. RIP: Tony D and Dilla.

Special thanks to the dear friends and family who gave me shelter and a base of operations on my travels to California: Avi Hoffer, Aviva Bernat, Morris Taft, Andy and Renee Charnas.

Much appreciation to Liz Siegel at Brad's for keeping the coffee coming, and to Johan Thomas for the company.

I am honored by the enduring friendship of the MCs and producers with whom I collaborated for many years: Derek Barbosa (pka Chino XL), Thomas St. John (pka Kwest Tha Madd Lad), Kerri Chandler, Robert Humbert (pka Bobbie Fine), Craig Bullock (pka DJ Homicide), Kirk Robinson (pka Milk D).

My wife and I have been sustained by the love and support of our friends. Their acts of kindness, whether great or small, all meant something: Aina Abiodun, Aina Hunter, Alex Chasin, Andy Carlson, Angie Chait, Bash Doran, Ben Whine, Cey Adams, Chris Black, Christian Du Lac and Miranda Pinckert, Craig LeMoult, Craig Taborn, David and Jane Weissman, David Neff, David Ressell, Derek Bermel, Dohra Ahmad and Orin Herskowitz, Elizabeth Kendall, Eric Karten and Karen Moncrieff, Faith and Gideon Orbach, Florine Jones and family, Greg Gilderman, Joe Gould, John Barrier, John Twombly, Jonathan and Trixie Ferguson Gray, Joseph and Tasha Willis, Kyumin Lee, Liz Whyte, Luxie Aquino, Marcelle Hopkins, Margo Jefferson, Maria Castro Mensen, Mark Brodie and Amy Benedict, Mary Harvey, Megan Shaw and Joel Virgel, Michael Ferraro, Mike Nixon, Mykell and Sheeri Mitchell, Nina Gregory and Kemper Bates, Patricia Barbeito, Patricia Ybarra, Rebecca Castillo, Stacy Parker Aab and Ed LeMelle, Susana Ferreira, Temple and Cyndi Williams, Thembisa Mshaka and Anthony Morris, Tim Ratanapreukskul and Jon Smith, Toni Ann Johnson, Wendy D. Mayhan. Mega bass to the Fifth Compound, Antonio Neves and Laila Al-Arian and the Al-Arian Family. Love to the Lopez family (James, Andrea, Victoria, Hannah, and Rea and Edy Machette), the Bernard family (James, Margarita, Jefferson, Hayden, and Myla), and the Mietus family (John, Andrea, Juliana, Madeline, Sophia, and Leah).

Respect to my teachers: Santokh and Suraj Khalsa, Gurmukh and Gurushabd Khalsa, Kartar and Deva Khalsa, Hari Kaur and David Frank, Jim Curtan, and Yogi Bhajan.

My family has been beyond supportive and forbearing in this years-long endeavor. I cherish my mother, Dr. Jane Charnas; my father Robert Charnas; my stepmother Joan Charnas; my stepfather Lee Sartoph; my parents-in-law: Kenneth and Toni Walters; my sisters and brothers: Hillary, Cortney, and Perry Charnas; Avram, Jeff, Anna, Ronald, and Brandi Sartoph; Jamie Kaye Walters and Vince Keenan; my aunts and uncles: Andy and Renee Charnas, Barbara and David Feldman, Vivian Sobchack, Tom and Deb Tomko (and family), George and Barbara Jay (and family); Gary Cole and Stephanie Springs, Ruth and Evelyn Malina; my nieces and nephews: Karina Garcia, Nicholas and David Sartoph; my cousins: Noah, Carol,

Gavin, and Steven Mitchell, Jen and Eric Williams, Rebecca and Scott Grant, Mick Coburn and Elizabeth Charnas, Sarah Mitchell, Mischa and Monty Cole, Jon Charnas, Maggie Malina, Chris and Nicole Sobchack, Steve and Suzy McKee Charnas, and the *other* Dan Charnas; all the Kerns, Malinas, Levinsons, Sartophs, Finsmiths, Keenans, and Charnases. And friends who are family: Lodine Joseph, Verina Samuel, Margie Seides. Extra-special salute to "Mom," aka Helen Cole.

This book is dedicated to the memory of my grandparents: Benjamin and Edythe Charnas, Joseph and Irene Finsmith.

On the day that I first met Wendy S. Walters, she forewarned me, "I don't know much about hip-hop, but that doesn't mean I don't respect it." Now that she is my wife and has read almost every page of this book, she knows more than she ever dreamed she would. Her incisive comments and line edits elevated the quality of my writing. More than anyone, her patience, love, and sacrifice have enabled me to complete this project. Wendy has never known me without this book in my life. I am, at last, happy to put away history and join her in the present.

As for our son, Isaac, who was born while this book was being delivered, our future belongs to him.

ENDNOTES

For details about sources and research, please visit
www.endnotes.bigpaybackbook.com.

INDEX

Photo by Rue Sakayama

DAN CHARNAS began his career as one of the first writers for *The Source*, and was part of a generation of young writers who helped create hip-hop journalism. He scouted talent and promoted records for the seminal rap label Profile and was Vice President of A&R for Rick Rubin's Def American Recordings. His writing has appeared in the *Washington Post*, the *Chicago Tribune*, and the *Village Voice*. Charnas holds a master's degree from the Columbia Graduate School of Journalism, and was awarded a Pulitzer Prize Fellowship. This is his first book.

www.dancharnas.com
www.bigpaybackbook.com